READINGS ON DRUGS
AND SOCIETY

READINGS ON DRUGS AND SOCIETY

The Criminal Connection

MARGARET S. KELLEY

University of Oklahoma

Boston ■ New York ■ San Francisco
Mexico City ■ Montreal ■ Toronto ■ London ■ Madrid ■ Munich
Paris ■ Hong Kong ■ Singapore ■ Tokyo ■ Cape Town ■ Sydney

Series Editor: *Jennifer Jacobson*
Series Editorial Assistant: *Elizabeth DiMenno*
Senior Marketing Manager: *Kelly May*
Production Editor: *Patrick Cash-Peterson*
Editorial Production Service: *Nesbitt Graphics, Inc.*
Composition Buyer: *Linda Cox*
Manufacturing Buyer: *Megan Cochran*
Electronic Composition: *Nesbitt Graphics, Inc.*
Cover Administrator: *Kristina Mose-Libon*

Copyright © 2006 Pearson Education, Inc.

For related titles and support materials, visit our online catalog at
www.ablongman.com.

Between the time website information is gathered and then published, it is not unusual for
some sites to have closed. Also, the transcription of URLs can result in typographical errors.
The publisher would appreciate notification where these errors occur so that they may be
corrected in subsequent editions.

Library of Congress Cataloging-in-Publication Data

Readings on drugs and society: the criminal connection / [edited by] Margaret S. Kelley. —
    1st ed.
        p. cm.
    Includes bibliographical references.
    ISBN 0-205-43972-1
      1. Drug abuse and crime—United States. 2. Criminals—Drug use—United States. 3.
Juvenile delinquents—Drug use—United States. 4. Drug control—United States. I. Kelley,
Margaret S.

HV5825.R38 2006
362.29—dc22   2005053529

Printed in the United States of America

10 9 8 7 6 5 4 3 2 1   09 08 07 06 05

For my parents

CONTENTS

It is not uncommon to hear the remark that "drug use causes crime." Indeed, much of criminal justice policy with respect to drugs appears to be based on this premise, with harsh penalties for possession or sales of illicit drugs. Yet academics still debate the scope and contours of the relationship between drugs and crime. This reader makes it abundantly clear that the connections between drugs and crime are complex and multidimensional, and that we are still lacking research in fundamental areas (i.e., drug markets, women's roles). The book explores questions about which drugs are criminogenic under which circumstances, and in which eras. It also includes the important policy dimension, which has a complex interaction with drugs and crime.

It's truly refreshing to find such a superb collection of articles that really educates readers about the drug–crime nexus. *Readings on Drugs and Society* begins with outstanding theoretical and research-based papers on the nexus by longtime contributors to the literature. Many articles address the importance of class, age, and race when examining the drugs–crime relationship. There is a nice mix of articles including theoretical, quantitative research, statistically sophisticated, and ethnographic studies. A section examines the drugs and crime relationship among women, particularly focusing on the prostitution connection and the role of women in drug sales. Articles help to highlight the high levels of victimization, especially among women and youth, but among many heavily drug involved offenders. In meaningful ways, the collection helps to establish that drug involved offenders are both predators and victims.

One of the book's major strengths is its exploration of the relationship between specific drugs and crime. For example, alcohol isn't illegal to adults except in some situations, which stands in stark contrast to drugs like heroin and crack cocaine that are uniformly illegal and carry stiff penalties. Yet, as Parker and Auerhahn make abundantly clear, alcohol is the drug that is statistically most associated with crime. National surveys of the incarcerated population of state prisons have shown repeatedly over time, that alcohol is implicated in more crimes than all illicit drugs combined; yet it's heroin and cocaine that grab the public's and policymaker's perceptions of the greatest drug threats. Perhaps they are, but under what conditions? The chapter by Killias and colleagues on the Swiss implementation of heroin

prescription to those especially recalcitrant to methadone or other traditional treatment shows a drop in both self-reported crime and offenses known to the police at the 6-month follow-up. Bourgois provides further details about research on Swiss heroin prescription, arguing they have definitively proved the superiority of heroin over methadone maintenance, while his research demonstrates how U.S. methadone clinics exercise power over clients in shaping their dependency. Obviously, the relationship between drugs and crime is conditioned by availability, which is affected by policy. The most basic lesson from methadone maintenance in the U.S. is that if drugs of reasonable quality are relatively available, the drugs–crime nexus is greatly reduced. It's primarily the over-inflated costs of illicit drugs on the black market that drives the drugs–crime relationship.

It's remarkable to realize that illicit drug use in one society may not be defined as illicit in another, which means that laws and policies help to define criminal behavior and subsequent criminal justice responses. This is also apparent by examining U.S. history with respect to the drug laws, as only a hundred years ago, drugs were available to virtually all in society. They were affordable, and "morphine addicts" were viewed as having a vice—not as loathsome characters willing to do virtually anything to get their drug of choice. Further, most morphine addicts were middle class women. This gives rise to questions about how the drugs–crime relationship has evolved over the century, and pushes the reader to think about the conditions that could give rise to changing the shape of the relationship.

Any exploration of the drugs–crime nexus must include youth, since few initiate drug use or criminal careers beyond young adulthood. The article by Kandel and colleagues importantly uses longitudinal research following youth from adolescence into adulthood to examine the continuation of drug use and crime, and their interrelationship over time. White and colleagues combine four waves of data from a longitudinal study of teenagers to examine the types of crime youth commit when under the influence of alcohol and marijuana. Violent offenses were more likely to be committed under the influence of alcohol or drugs than property offenses, but alcohol was more strongly associated with violence than marijuana. There is a particularly interesting article on "street youth" who congregate in large Canadian cities, a phenomenon that is not restricted to the United States' closest neighbor culturally, but too much of Europe and South America. These youth are particularly at risk for drug use, as well as criminal offending and victimization. This also begs the question of what conditions in society give rise to such a phenomenon?

As several chapters in the book help to illustrate, the United States has taken a particularly punitive approach to dealing with illicit drug use. Over the past few decades, other types of crime have also been treated more harshly by the criminal justice system, but drug arrests and the proportion of the population incarcerated for drug-related offenses has grown at a much faster pace. However, there is evidence that the tide may be turning. The United States is increasingly embracing drug treatment approaches in the criminal justice system with Treatment Alternatives to Street Crime (TASC) programs for more than a quarter century, and with drug courts the normative approach for substantial proportions of drug offenders nationwide. Although the numbers in prison and jail receiving treatment are still small, the number of treatment slots has grown tremendously in recent years. Restorative justice is a relatively new concept, but Braithwaite introduces us to its promise.

Harm reduction, a paradigm that has gained a strong foothold in Canada, Australia, and Europe, (as evident by the Swiss heroin maintenance program) is explored in the United States in terms of treatment, and needle exchange. The principle of harm reduction is that drug policies should not cause further harm; but the question is always, "for whom?" Does society have the right to coerce individuals into treatment? How about incarcerated individuals? The articles contained herein, and most research over the past decade examining treatment outcomes, show reductions in subsequent drug use and criminal behavior (regardless of coercion). More controversial are needle exchange programs, but the articles by Kelley and colleagues and Marx and colleagues demonstrate they are reducing harm, and there was no evidence of increased drug use nor crime. These issues are being grappled with in the United States, although most countries that embrace harm reduction support needle exchange and treatment, although oftentimes not coerced treatment. Most of those countries, as well, have socialized medicine, welfare, much greater availability of methadone maintenance and treatment, and greater outreach to drug users in general—which may protect against the drugs–crime relationship for individuals. These countries are also less punitive than the United States, and most have decriminalized marijuana.

Overall, get ready for a really good read. This book raises important considerations on the relationship between drugs and crime, from classic race, class, and gender issues, to important policy dimensions. It helps to illuminate the many relationship(s) between drug(s) and crime(s), and gives satisfying insights, while creating new questions.

—Lana Harrison, University of Delaware

The organizing principle of *Readings on Drugs and Society: The Criminal Connection* is the attempt to understand the links between illicit drug use and crime. Drugs and crime are most clearly linked in that the use of many drugs is a crime in and of itself. That is, users are often criminals. Illicit drug use is also associated with many other types of crime, however. These two important social issues, drugs and crime, are highly relevant given the changing nature of the drug war in the United States and fluctuations in crime rates, both locally and nationally. Drugs and crime are two active fields of research that are moving the state of our knowledge forward very quickly. New and interesting research is constantly being produced, and this book is designed to outline the current trends. The overlapping worlds of drugs and crime, mostly unknown to the general population, are often extreme and unpleasant, yet the individuals involved are certainly worthy of our continued research and efforts to improve policy.

This collection of readings is distinctive in a number of ways. Most books that address general drugs and society issues do not focus on crime. Therefore, this work is an important contribution to the field for both its general approach to drugs and its inclusion of the central theme of crime. The book brings together leading contemporary research intended to clarify the relationship between drugs and crime, with a focus on street crime. The selections in this book all confront the relationship between drugs and crime within current U.S. policy. Some challenge the policy directly, whereas others simply describe and explain the relationship between drugs and crime. Authors in most selections conclude with policy implications that arise from their research.

This book uses a multimethod approach by including both qualitative and quantitative research. The readings have been selected for their research content and scholarly focus. Overall, they present a wide range of theories and methodological approaches to understanding the nature of the relationship between drugs and crime. Issues of race, class, and gender are also highlighted in chapter introductions where relevant. Although approached primarily from a sociological perspective, the information in this interdisciplinary book will inform a wide audience, including students of many social science and medical fields, as well as members of the general public who have an interest in social policy.

The Introduction provides a brief overview of current perspectives on drugs and crime by examining the extent of drug use, sources of data on drugs and crime, theories of drugs and crime, and the social correlates of illegal drug use and crime. The U.S. drug war and harm reduction efforts are also discussed. Each chapter introduction identifies important themes from all of the articles. In Chapter One, the drugs–crime connection is examined in depth with articles that highlight theory. Chapter Two provides representative readings on primary drugs of abuse, including alcohol. Two topics often overlooked in books like this are covered in detail: women (Chapter Three) and adolescent drug use (Chapter Four). Chapters Five and Six cover the two main responses to illicit drug use, the criminal justice approach and the treatment approach. In Chapter Six, two articles deal specifically with harm reduction, an international approach to drugs that focuses on reducing the personal and social harm associated with use. Finally, Chapter Seven contains additional examples of interesting and current topics in research on drugs and crime. For all chapters, Research Navigator permits comprehensive coverage by referrals to research in additional substantive areas, such as international trafficking, organized crime, drug cartels, money laundering, and drug use among the elderly.

Drug use has been around for a very long time. The misuse of drugs and their relationship to criminal behavior are two aspects of drugs that require close attention. This book provides a forum for scrutiny that enables us to locate new approaches and solutions to old problems. It is an attempt to demystify drug use, break down stereotypes about drug users and criminals, and allow readers to enter a world perhaps quite different from their own. The harm-reduction lens is one way of viewing these complex relationships, and it emerges as a theme throughout the book.

KEY FEATURES

Although some readings are long, with few exceptions all are presented in their original form so as to provide the reader with all the available information required to evaluate the content. Internet-based research is an important tool in such a dynamic field. Links to Research Navigator guide readers to related readings from academic journals and the *New York Times*. Research Navigator includes extensive help on the research process and access to four exclusive research databases (the EBSCO Academic Journal and

Abstract Database, *New York Times* Search by Subject Archive, "Best of the Web" Link Library, and *Financial Times* Article Archive and Company Financials). Discussion questions for each chapter focus on theory, method, and policy, encouraging critical thinking about the subject material. Visit www.researchnavigator.com for more information on this resource. Access to Research Navigator is provided at no additional charge with *Readings on Drugs and Society: The Criminal Connection*. By assigning two readings per week, all the readings can be covered in the course of a 14-week semester (including one week for an exam).

SUPPLEMENTARY MATERIALS

The instructor's manual begins with a cross-reference guide on using the reader in conjunction with *Drugs, Society, and Criminal Justice* by Charles F. Levinthal (Allyn & Bacon © 2006). Next, a number of suggested films are included for each chapter. Some films are mainstream, others are more independent. All are recommended because they illustrate central issues in the quest to understand the relationship between drugs and crime. Finally, a comprehensive test bank contains key terms and multiple-choice, true/false, and essay questions for each reading, along with page numbers from the text where the answers are located.

ACKNOWLEDGMENTS

The graduate and undergraduate students in several of my seminars at the University of Oklahoma contributed to the design of this book through their heated discussions on key topics. Juanita Ortiz worked hard at securing copyright permissions and assisting with overall production efforts. Reviewers offered excellent advice about the book's organization and content. They include Barry Spunt, John Jay College; Robert O. Keel, University of Missouri—St. Louis; David Orrick, Norwich University; Raymond L. Sparks, California State University—Bakersfield; and Ann Lucas, San Jose State University. Jennifer Ellis commented on sections and helped write the instructor's manual. Her assistance this summer was invaluable. I am also indebted to Jennifer Jacobson at Allyn and Bacon for getting me started and providing guidance and encouragement. Finally, I could not have finished this project without the love and support of my partners in crime, Robert Warrior and Frances Hope Warrior.

READINGS ON DRUGS AND SOCIETY

UNDERSTANDING DRUGS AND CRIME

The American public is very concerned about the social problem of drugs. But it can be difficult to understand the difference between drug abuse and the occasional use of illegal drugs, much less the use of such drugs in relation to other criminal behavior. The problem use of legal drugs such as tobacco, alcohol, and prescription medications is much greater than the use of illegal drugs. Legal drugs are also more dangerous. For example, alcohol and tobacco annually kill many more Americans and people around the world than all the illegal drugs combined (National Drug Research Institute, 2003). Research suggests that most people who use illicit drugs use them in moderation. The public is also very concerned about crime, even though crime rates have been falling for the past two decades according to the two most commonly used measures of crime, the National Crime Victimization Survey and the Uniform Crime Reports (UCR). However, drugs and crime are closely linked both in public perception and in research findings.

The basic premise here is that people have always used drugs and they most likely always will. With that premise, it follows that we should work to reduce the personal and social harm that drug use might cause. One social harm is the connection of drugs with criminal behavior. Given that drug use is likely to persist, what can we learn about patterns of use and the relationship between these patterns and crime? Americans are worried about drugs because of the pervasive belief that drug use causes crime and violence, yet existing evidence about the relationship between drugs and crime is complex. The incidence and prevalence of drug use vary widely by region and other factors. There has been a decline in the use of illegal drugs in the general population with an increase among young people until the past couple of years. Overall, teens and young adults have the highest rates of drug offenses. Teenagers are increasingly turning to marijuana as their drug of choice, but their rates of drug use appear to have stabilized for the time being, with some sources reporting slight declines. Many of the selections in this book examine prevalence and address the complexity of the relationship between drugs and crime.

But what exactly do we mean when we talk about licit and illicit drugs? What is addiction? What types of crime are we referencing? One way to look at drug use and addiction is as a continuum, with complete abstinence at one end and physical addiction to a chemical at the other (Doweiko, 2002). A large amount of variation exists in between these end points, with many people using drugs regularly without physical addiction. According to another source, a general definition for "drug" is "any substance, natural or artificial, other than food, that by its chemical nature alters structure or function in the living organism" (Ray and Ksir, 2002, p. 5). Although many people would exclude alcohol and nicotine because they are legal, they meet this criterion of pharmacology. The three main categories of drugs, based on what they are and what they do, according to several sources, are depressants, stimulants, and hallucinogens. Marijuana and ecstasy often get separate categories because of their unique effects on the body. Marijuana, for example, can be a depressant, a stimulant, and a hallucinogen. The effect of any drug will vary with the social context of its use and amount ingested, method of ingestion, purity of drug, and frequency of use (Goode, 2005; Thio, 2004). A longer list of drug categories that reflects the standard categories used in research is provided in Duane McBride and Clyde McCoy's selection (Reading 1).

Addiction can mean different things when applied to many kinds of social behavior, including heavy use of drugs, food, and sex. There are different types of addiction, such as physical and psychological. A general definition describes addiction as the physical or psychological inability to stop using a substance. There are many social contexts in which this might occur, and addiction alternatively may be labeled drug abuse or drug misuse. Not all scholars agree on the meanings and definitions of "drug" and "addiction", as is evidenced by the selections in Chapters 1 and 2.

THE CRIMINALIZATION OF DRUGS

Of course, the use of many drugs is itself a crime. The seriousness of the crime depends in part on where the drug falls within the federal schedule of drugs as determined by the Comprehensive Drug Abuse Prevention and Control Act of 1970 (also called the Controlled Substances Act). This act categorizes drugs based on a number of factors, including likelihood of abuse and medicinal use. Schedule I drugs, such as heroin and marijuana, are purported to have higher abuse potential and are not allowed for medical use. Schedule V drugs are unlikely to be abused and are therefore minimally controlled. There is debate about the accuracy of the classification because it is used primarily for criminal justice enforcement.

Different drugs have different pharmacological properties that are often hypothesized to be predictive of crime. These effects vary widely, as do their potential effect on criminal behavior. Heroin is the most commonly used example of the relationship between withdrawal symptoms and subsequent criminal behavior. It is during withdrawal that drug-seeking crimes are more likely to occur. On the other hand, it is during intoxication that violence is most likely to occur for abusers of alcohol (Parker and Auerhahn, 1998).

The most common crimes committed by drug users are copping (buying heroin from a drug dealer for an associate to make enough money or drugs to keep themselves from suffering withdrawal) and dealing drugs (Kelley, 1999). Several articles in this book focus on drug sales. Alcohol is most clearly linked with violent crimes, which is also examined by selections in this book. Other economically motivated crimes, such as burglary, have been the subject of much scrutiny, along with crimes of violence. Selections in Chapter 2 are good examples of the variety of crimes examined by drug and alcohol researchers because they are associated with specific types of drugs. Chapter 7 has an important article about the victimization of drug users, recognizing that drug users are victims as well as perpetrators of crime (Reading 23). The selections in this volume are primarily concerned with street crimes,

such as those listed as Index crimes by the UCR (murder and nonnegligent manslaughter, forcible rape, robbery, aggravated assault, burglary, larceny-theft, and motor vehicle theft).

DATA ON DRUGS AND CRIME

Research has consistently shown a strong correlation between crime and violence with the use of alcohol and drugs, as many selections in this volume confirm. One of the main sources of data is self-report, in which researchers ask people to tell the truth about their drug use and criminal behaviors. For the most part, we can trust these types of data to provide a partial picture of individual drug use (Goode, 2005; White, Tice, Loeber, and Stouthamer-Loeber, 2002). In a similar sociological example about gathering data of a very personal nature, beginning in the 1960s, Richard Gelles and Murray Straus conducted controversial research with families about the extent of child abuse (Gelles and Straus, 1988; Straus and Gelles, 1980). Gelles and Straus did not expect to find that people of all types were willing to share great detail about intimate abuse. As for reporting specifics about illicit drug use, research has shown that people are better at details (daily reporting) than with big generalizations about their patterns of use because they will exaggerate their drug use rather than underreport it. Techniques have been developed to deal with such problems, including using the bounding of interviews or providing detailed time frames to assist respondents in clarifying days and times of use. One example is the use of a timeline or life-history calendar (Hser, Huang, Chou, Teraya, and Anglin, 2003). Self-report data can be either quantitative (survey based) or qualitative (interview based).

One quantitative form of self-report data is large household surveys, such as the National Survey on Drug Use and Health (formerly known as the National Household Survey on Drug Abuse) (Office of Applied Studies, 2004), which is used by several authors in this volume. This survey is sponsored by the National Institute on Drug Abuse (NIDA). An advantage of this data set is that it is nationally representative; the data, however, tend to underestimate both drug use and crime because both are relatively rare in the general population. Nonetheless, they provide important general population prevalence estimates, which deviant samples (for example, those comprised entirely of incarcerated individuals) cannot. Three other national projects that are sources of information about drugs and crime include the High School Senior survey (sponsored by NIDA), the Monitoring the Future survey (sponsored by the Institute on Survey Research at the University of Michigan), and the Drug Abuse Treatment Outcome Study (sponsored by several collaborating agencies and used by David Farabee and colleagues in this volume).

Another major source of data is collected in collaboration with the criminal justice system (prisons, jails, police contacts, etc.). The Drug Use Forecasting program was initiated in 1988 by the National Institute of Justice (NIJ). It involved testing for drugs in the urine of individuals arrested for crimes in twenty-three cities. The program was renamed the Arrestee Drug Abuse Monitoring (ADAM) program in 2000 after being restructured to improve sampling and data collection, and it was expanded to about 40 cities. Although ADAM gathered important data for researchers and policy makers, it was also an incredibly expensive project. The NIJ cut funding for ADAM in 2004. Efforts are under way to reestablish some form of ADAM, but it is unclear if or when that will happen. Testing positive in ADAM data collection does not mean that the drug caused the crime. For example, some drugs stay in the body longer than others and may have had no connection to the crime. Several articles in this volume use ADAM data. Other sources of criminal justice data are the Drug Abuse Warning Network (sponsored by NIDA) and the UCR (sponsored by NIJ and used by Eric Baumer and colleagues in this volume).

Our data on drug use have been plagued by a number of problems. For example, for smaller projects, many researchers use nonrandom techniques. Some of these data sets are qualitative in nature and are an excellent source of rich description of the context of drug use and crime. This type of research is often situated in overwhelmingly poor and mostly minority neighborhoods. Not only are they not random, but these samples also tend to be small. Both of these factors limit the generalizability of the findings. These techniques, however, are better than prison-only population methods, which constituted the bulk of the available data until the past two decades. Other problems include the low prevalence in household surveys as noted previously. That is, absolute drug use is rather small, and when sampling households you find fewer users than when sampling deviant populations. Finally, there are concerns about the validity of self-report data, but on the whole these data are trusted to provide

reliable estimates of certain types of drug and criminal behaviors. The readings in this book use many different data sets, including some of those mentioned here. Additional information on concerns about methods and sampling can be found in many of the individual selections.

THEORIES OF DRUGS AND CRIME: A SYNTHESIS

Even though many people do not drink and most people do not use illegal drugs, those who do are more likely to commit crimes. We rely on theory to help us explain this pattern. According to numerous sources, theories explaining drug use have been sorely lacking (Farabee, Joshi, and Anglin, 2001; MacCoun, Kilmer, and Reuter, 2003; McBride and McCoy, 1993). Philip Bean describes models of drug use as falling into one of three categories: moral, disease, or behavioral (Bean, 2002). Proponents of the moral model see individuals with a dependence as suffering from moral weakness and who need to be punished or put through moral training to be cured. According to the disease model, individuals suffer from dependence because of physiological or psychobiological reasons that require medical treatment. Finally, from the behavioral model perspective, dependence can be changed using cognitive or behavioral techniques. Sociologically, changes would be seen in theories focusing on coping or self-medication, structure or strain, and status or economic gain. According to Bean, these models of drug use are not well integrated with mainstream sociological theories.

Other authors categorize theories of drug use as biological, psychological, and sociological (Goode, 2005; Thio, 2004). Sociological explanations focus on the social context of use. Erich Goode provides probably the best overview of theories of drug use with special attention to sociological theories, including anomie/strain, social control, self-control, social learning and subculture theory, selective interaction/socialization, social disorganization, and conflict theory (Goode, 2005). Some of the articles in this book are explicitly framed by one of the above types of theories, whereas others are more descriptive in nature.

Evaluating theories on addiction is important if we are suggesting that addiction and crime originate from the same sources or cause each other. The selections in Chapter 1 identify current theories of drug use and crime. To summarize the theories, there are two main approaches to understanding the relationship between drugs and crime: either drug use causes crime or crime causes drug use. According to the first approach, sometimes called the drug enslavement theory (Bean, 2002; Goode, 2005), "drug users are forced into a life of crime because they cannot afford to pay for their prohibitively expensive drug habit unless they rob or steal" (Thio, 2004, p. 279). Enslavement suggests that something about the drug changes the users' personalities, making them behave in unusual ways. There are two adaptations of the drug enslavement approach. The first, the pharmacological model, posits that the pharmacological effects of certain drugs can induce violence and criminal acts. The second adaptation, the economic model, suggests that the prohibitive price of some drugs causes those addicted to them to turn to criminal activities as a source of income. The end result of both adaptations, according to Bean, is that the fault for committing crimes lies elsewhere, such as in unequal access to participation in the capitalist economy or in the pharmacology of the drug.

The second approach to understanding the relationship between drugs and crime posits that crime causes drug use. That is, something about the involvement in criminal activity provides a context conducive to drug use. This approach has also been called the subcultural model (McBride and McCoy, 1993), the general deviance syndrome model (Thio, 2004), and the predisposition model (Goode, 2005). From this approach, it is hypothesized that something is responsible for both drug use and crime while also recognizing that most who are involved with drugs were involved with crime first. A modification of this approach has been called the intensification model, which recognizes the overlapping causes without hypothesizing which comes first (Goode, 2005). This final modification seems especially relevant given that research has consistently shown that involvement in drug use does increase criminal activity, as selections in this book confirm.

There is also a third approach to understanding the relationship between drugs and crime which posits that the criminalization of drugs causes crime. It centers on the argument that the criminal justice response to certain drugs has exacerbated, if not created, a drugs–crime connection. Sometimes called criminogenic, or radical, theory (McBride and McCoy, 1993), this approach provides an important reminder that what is defined as criminal is relative to time and place and can change given different circumstances. For example, heroin use was not illegal until the Harrison Narcotic Act in 1914. Intended to regulate the transfer and taxing of narcotics, the act had many unintended consequences. By some accounts, the passing of the act and the implementation of the act itself created a new class of criminals, or at least recognized that criminals used narcotics (Goode, 2005; Inciardi, 2002).

SOCIAL CORRELATES OF DRUGS AND CRIME

The major social correlates of crime and drug use include gender, age, race, and class, and these factors aid in explaining patterns and trends. Overall, men use drugs at higher rates than women, and young people more than older people. Patterns by race and class are not as clear, however. Some of these patterns are addressed in Chapters 3 and 4. Our understanding of these patterns has been hampered by data problems. For example, early data collection was often limited to male samples and provided little information about the experiences of female drug users or women as criminals. Although many studies now include both males and females. Some continue to focus on male experiences. Readings in Chapter 3 deal with issues that are specific to female drug users. Definitional problems have also hampered our understanding. For example, social class is a variable that can be defined in many different ways, yielding different results.

The relationship between drugs and crime is complex and depends on the kind of drug, the kind of crime, and many mediating and moderating factors. Overall, few people use illicit drugs, and certainly not all of them commit crimes. In relative numbers, few people fit into the categories we are examining. Yet the absolute numbers indicate that we should pay attention to understanding the relationship between drugs and crime. Given the ever-changing landscape of illicit drug use, we are not always up to date about the relationship a specific drug has to criminal behavior. For example, there is little research that investigates methamphetamine and club drugs as they influence criminal behaviors. What research that exists often focuses on drug-related offenses, such as drug sales. One selection in Chapter 7 (Reading 25) departs from this pattern by focusing on drug trafficking and the effects of trafficking on consumption patterns. Another, Reading 26, examines why individuals choose to engage in criminal behavior related to drug use by asking about their motives for distributing drugs. Many of the selections in this book explore the social correlates of drugs and crime in detail, using both quantitative and qualitative data to unravel the link between drugs and crime.

U.S. DRUG POLICY

The Drug War

Federal, state, and local governments in the United States have taken a rigid approach to the problem of drugs, one that is quite different from that of other countries (Braithwaite, 2001; Killias, 1998; Killias, Aebi, and Ribeaud, 2000). Probably the most important factor affecting the relationship between drugs and crime is the formal abstinence policy of the U.S. government embedded in the "war on drugs." Proponents of the "zero-tolerance" abstinence policy advocate no drug use *at all*. Although there was a political and legal campaign against drugs during most of the twentieth century, President Richard Nixon added fuel to the efforts in the late 1960s by calling it a drug *war*. President Ronald Reagan refocused attention on the campaign in the 1980s with the media blitz about the "crack epidemic" (Kandall, 1996). Critics of the war on drugs argue that current punitive policies have not stopped the flow of illegal drugs (Zimring and Hawkins, 1992) and have effectively lumped together many different illicit drugs that warrant unique responses (Wagner, 1997). The war has been called the United States' longest and most destructive (Duke and Gross, 1993), punishing individuals for consuming disfavored drugs at the expense of prevention and treatment. Opponents further claim that the current abstinence policies condemn millions of Americans to lives of concealment and deceit (Lenson, 1995), while many legal drugs, such as tobacco and alcohol, cause more disability and death (Meier, 1994). Many drug policy researchers have called for an end to the war on drugs and for redirecting energies to prevention and treatment (Besteman, 1991; Inciardi, 1993; Rosenbaum and Doblin, 1991; Szasz, 1988; Trebach, 1989). Current U.S. policy, however, focuses efforts on punishment of drug users, which leads to increased penalties and higher rates of incarceration for offenders. In fact, less than 4% of substance abuse spending by U.S. states is used to fund prevention, treatment, and research (National Center on Addiction and Substance Abuse, 2001). Although this figure might sound grim, promising innovative approaches are being tested. Chapter 5 includes selections that deal with the criminal justice response to drug use and some of its shortcomings.

Harm Reduction

An international response to failed drug policies, and in the United States to the drug war, has been the development of a new perspective known as harm reduction (Brettle, 1990; Des Jarlais, 1995; Des Jarlais, Friedman, and Ward, 1993; Duke and Gross, 1993; Kelley, Murphy, and Lune, 2001; Nadelmann, 1988; Newcombe, 1992; Newmeyer and Rosenbaum, 1998; Odets, 1994; O'Hare, Newcombe, Matthews, Buning, and Drucker, 1992; Roche, Evans, and Stanton, 1997; Stevenson, 1994; Strang, 1992; van Ameijden, van den Hoek, van Haastrecht, and Coutinho, 1992). This perspective recognizes that there always have been and always will be individuals who use drugs (Weil, 1972) and advocates for drug policy that seeks to reduce all aspects of drug-related harm for those engaging in drug use. Harm reduction is not synonymous with the legalization of drugs (Moore, 1989; Nadelmann, 1989; Wilson, 1990), although elements of decriminalization are central (Bayer, 1993; Bayer and Oppenheimer, 1993; Kornblum, 1993; McVay, 1991; Warner, 1993).

Early harm-reduction language for both drug and alcohol treatment models touted "moderation" versus "restraint" (abstinence) or "loss of control" (addiction) (Casswell, 1994; Marlatt and Gordon, 1985; Single, 1994). This language continues to frame harm-reduction approaches to treatment. Methadone is one of the earliest methods of harm reduction in drug treatment policy. In adequate doses, it eliminates physical symptoms of heroin withdrawal and provides injection drug users (IDUs) "an opportunity to control or eliminate their need to inject heroin" (Rosenbaum et al., 1995, p. 206). Methadone clients have shown interest in reducing drug-related harm (Kelley et al., 2001; MacGowan, Fichtner, Swanson, Collier, Kroliczak, and Cole, 1997), even working to develop advocacy groups (Clarke, 1998). After initial government support for methadone in the 1960s, however, enrollment in methadone treatment programs decreased in the 1980s due to lack of funding that coincided with Reagan's attention to the drug war (Stimmel, 1993).

Methadone is usually dispensed only in clinical settings and rarely by private physicians. Critics of methadone programs condemn them on the grounds that methadone recipients sometimes do not take the methadone but instead manage to take it out of the clinic and sell it or give it away. Even though the danger associated with diversion has proven to be minimal, and considering that most of what is diverted is purchased by other drug users on the street, fear of contributing to drug trafficking keeps the government from expanding what has been recognized by many in the medical community as the key treatment for opiate addiction. The vast majority of heroin addicts cannot gain access to methadone treatment because there are simply not enough treatment slots to meet the demand. Estimates suggest that fewer than 15% of IDUs are in treatment at any given time (DeCarlo and Gibson, 2003). While in office, former New York City mayor Rudolph W. Giuliani, as part of a welfare-to-work plan, called for abolishment of all methadone programs within the city because they were thought to prevent some welfare clients from overcoming addiction and returning to work. This position sparked harsh criticism and intense debate about the merits of methadone treatment in New York City and nationwide (Fisher, 1998; Lewis, 1998; Peyser, 1998; Satel, 1998; Swarns, 1998; Topousis, 1998; Wren, 1998). Contributing to methadone's poor public image is the tendency for clients to hide their methadone status. As a result, "successes are not always visible, while failures are well publicized" (Stimmel, 1993, p. 165). Methadone is examined in great detail in Reading 21 when Phillippe Bourgois details the complexity of living as a methadone client.

Syringe exchange programs exemplify current harm-reduction efforts. By exchanging used syringes for new ones, these programs eliminate the risk for IDUs of using a contaminated needle (assuming they use a new one for each injection), while also removing used syringes from circulation. Chapter 6 introduces key concepts of harm reduction, examines the effects of its application, and reviews key issues regarding treatment for drug users in the United States. Several articles in this book examine the role of needle exchange in reducing risky behaviors, and one focuses explicitly on its relation to crime (in Chapter 7). Harm reduction focuses on prevention and treatment rather than punishment of drug offenders.

Drugs and crime are linked. Although research has historically suffered from sampling and other problems, efforts are constantly improving and our knowledge base is expanding. Theories, while also suffering from conceptual problems, have been constantly revised and improved. All these efforts help identify and isolate the social correlates of drugs and crime. New approaches to the "drug problem" highlight harm-reduction elements. These new approaches are beginning to spark debate, research, and revision of existing cultural perceptions and policies. This volume represents some of the best examples of rigorous and interdisciplinary research addressing the links between drugs and crime.

INTRODUCTION: DISCUSSION QUESTIONS

1. What are the key terms relevant to drug abuse?

2. How do we get data on drug use? What are some of the problems with these data?

3. What are the three primary approaches to understanding the drugs–crime relationship?

4. What have been the consequences of the United States' "war on drugs"?

5. What is harm reduction and how does it affect drug use?

THE DRUGS–CRIME CONNECTION

As outlined in the Introduction, there has been a lot of speculation about the nature of the relationship between drugs and crime. The three selections in this chapter clarify this relationship. The purposes of Duane McBride and Clyde McCoy's piece are to examine the historical underpinnings of current perceptions about the drugs–crime relationship and to suggest an organizational paradigm for interpreting the literature. There is overlap between drug behaviors and criminal behaviors, but McBride and McCoy note the relationship appears to be "recursive" and that drug use is certainly not a direct and simple cause of crime. The authors provide a solid overview of perspectives on the relationships and posit that current and developing approaches need to take into account the different types of drugs, types of crime, and the recursive nature of the overlap. Much contemporary theorizing about the drugs–crime relationship is based on Paul Goldstein's useful theoretical framework linking drugs and violence (Goldstein, 1985). This approach and other theoretical perspectives are reviewed in the McBride and McCoy article. The authors remind us that some common themes emerge from these perspectives.

David Farabee and colleagues use quantitative statistical methods to examine the drug–crime relationship. Using the Drug Abuse Treatment Outcome Study data, they also find that the relationship is complex and depends on a number of factors, including how drug use and crime are defined. Many social correlates are important in explaining the relationship, including age at onset (of drug use and criminal behavior), drug of choice, and treatment. The authors include the use of alcohol to clarify the relationship further. They offer several possible sociological explanations for their findings.

The piece by Robert MacCoun and colleagues provides another strong overview of existing research on the drugs–crime connection in addition to suggestions for future research. The authors note that perhaps too much attention has been paid to the Goldstein framework. Although this framework is promising, they propose that we need to continue testing it while also pursuing other plausible explanations for the relationship between drugs and crime. Because so much of the existing research points to the link between drug markets and violence, the authors categorize types of markets and provide an analysis of the level of crime likely to be associated with each. They find that several factors (age of participants, value of drugs, law enforcement, and indirect consequences of drug use) affect the type and level of violence associated with drug markets. Some of the issues raised in this piece are addressed in other readings in this volume.

These readings summarize the literature on the drugs–crime link to date. There are a number of common themes. First, the authors all note the limitations of existing approaches to understanding the complex relationship between drugs and crime. Although being overly concerned with causality (which comes first, drug use or crime), studies often overlook any important mediators and moderators of the relationship between drugs and crime, including cultural variations. Two of the three selections discuss the career concept of drug use and criminality. This concept connotes the tendency for some individuals to embark on a career of drugs and crime, comparable to the process of following a legitimate, conforming career. Most individuals who use drugs, however, eventually drop out of the deviant career path. Second, all the articles distinguish between violent and nonviolent criminal behavior (seriousness of offense); highlighting that patterns are very different by offense type. Third, all recognize that drug involvement is a crime and that there are higher rates of criminal involvement during addiction periods. Finally, all three articles recognize that both quantitative and qualitative data are helpful in clarifying the relationship between drugs and crime.

One important policy implication that arises from this chapter is that different strategies are necessary to reduce crime and drug use for different individuals. These readings challenge current drug use policy and suggest elements that can be improved. They also raise important issues for further research.

The Drugs–Crime Relationship: An Analytical Framework

DUANE C. McBRIDE

CLYDE B. McCOY

ABSTRACT

The relationship between drug use and criminal behavior has been of primary interest to researchers and practitioners for most of [the twentieth] century. As such, it is the purpose of this article to examine the historical underpinnings of current perceptions and to suggest an organizational paradigm for interpreting current drugs–crime literature. An overview of the literature and issues suggests that there is strong empirical evidence of the statistical overlap between drug using and criminal behavior. Further, drug use is seen as increasing and sustaining criminal behavior. However, a wide body of research suggests that drug use and crime have a complex recursive nature to their relationship, and that drug use, in spite of a long history of public perceptions, cannot be viewed as a direct and simple cause of crime. A review of subcultural, role, and ecological theory suggests that drug use and crime may emerge from the same etiological variables and become an integral part of a street-drug using lifestyle and subculture. Radical theory argues that the drugs–crime relationship is created by social policy that makes drugs illegal. It is argued that this perspective fails to recognize the complexity of the drugs–crime relationship. The existing research suggests the need for increasing treatment availability and increasing economic opportunities within the framework of a careful review of drug policy and enforcement.

The relationship between drug using and criminal behavior has been a primary concern of researchers, policymakers and the general public for most of [the twentieth] century (see McBride and McCoy, 1982). Both the scientific and popular media have tended to view the existence of the drugs–crime relationship as the basis of the public concern about drug use, as well as of national and international drug policy and the current infrastructure of drug law enforcement, treatment, and research. Although in the public mind, the relationship between drugs and crime is often seen as fairly straightforward—with drug use being viewed as directly causing criminal behavior—critical research analysis has indicated that the relationship is conceptually and empirically quite complex. Given this, it is the purpose of this article to suggest an organizational paradigm for examining the literature on the drugs–crime relationship, to use that paradigm to review relevant literature and to examine the policy implications of recent research on the drugs–crime relationship.

AN ORGANIZATIONAL PARADIGM

Although the phrase "drugs–crime relationship" is commonly used, it often masks the variety of substances that are included under the concept of *drugs*, and the specific types of violations of the criminal law that is encompassed by the term *crime*. In addition, the phrase does not elucidate issues of the etiology of the relationship. It might be helpful if an analysis of the relationship between drug using and criminal behavior were organized within the following framework:

1. The historical underpinnings of current perspectives
2. Types of drugs and types of criminal behavior
3. The statistical relationship: the extent and type of criminal behavior among various types of drug users and the extent and type of drug use among various types of criminals
4. The etiological nature of the relationship, including such issues as causality and interaction
5. Theoretical interpretations of the relationship
6. The policy implications of research conclusions

HISTORICAL UNDERPINNINGS OF CURRENT PERSPECTIVES

The 19th-Century National Drug Culture

During the late 19th century, American society had a fairly laissez faire attitude toward what were called "patent medicines." These medicines, often containing opium, were touted as cure-alls for whatever ailed a person, from general aches and pains to sexual dysfunctions. They were available through a variety of means, including private physicians, the Sears catalog, and the traveling medicine show. The claims of one patent medicine, Hamlin's Wizard Oil, well illustrate the exaggerated assertions. The advertisement for the Hamlin product claimed that "there is no sore it will not heal, no pain it will not subdue." The oil was "Pleasant to take and magical in its effects" (Inciardi, 1992, p. 4). The makers and distributors of patent medicines were effective entrepreneurs organizing themselves as the Proprietary Medicine Manufactures Association in 1881. For over two decades they successfully prevented any attempt to limit their enterprise. They effectively marketed their products in most of the mass and professional media and catalogs of the era. The development of the hypodermic needle in the middle of the 19th century and advances in chemistry resulted in the development of more potent drugs that could be delivered in the most efficacious manner. As David Musto (1973) observed, "Opiates and cocaine became popular—if unrecognized— items in the everyday life of Americans" (p. 3). Although exact figures on the consumption of opium during this time period are not a available, the U.S.

Public Health Service estimated that between 1859 and 1899, 7,000 tons of crude opium and 800 tons of smoking opium were imported in the United States (Kolb and Du Mez, 1924).

The turn of the twentieth century seemed to initiate a broad-based social reform movement in a wide variety of areas of American culture. The developing American Medical Association (AMA) began questioning the effectiveness claims of the patent medicines. As a result of the failure to scientifically verify the claims, the AMA removed advertisements for patent medicines from their journals. By this means, the professional physicians began to disassociate themselves from the medicine show. Perhaps as a results of these professional critiques of patent medicines, journalists also began to focus on the industry. One of the most noted series of articles was in the national weekly magazine *Collier's*. For about a 4-month period during 1905 and 1906, a *Collier's* reporter, Samuel Adams, chronicled the fraudulent claims of the patent medicine sellers, the toxic ingredients they contained (often high dosages of opium and cocaine), and the consequences of their use. Adams claimed that the use of these medicines made criminals of young men and harlots of young women (see Young, 1967, p. 31).

Although the *Collier's* articles on the patent medicine industry did cause a great deal of discussion in the popular press, it was the impact of Upton Sinclair's *The Jungle* on legal policy that most affected the patent medicine industry. As a result of the documented filthy conditions in the American meat-packing industry, Congress passed the Pure Food and Drug Act in 1906. Although this act did not outlaw patent medicines, it did require that the ingredients and their proportions be listed on each bottle. This, coupled with persistent media focus on the horrors of opium and other drug use, appeared to prepare the public and the Congress for further restrictions on the industry. Within the next few years, many states severely restricted the distribution of narcotics through physicians and pharmacists or over the counter (see Musto, 1973, p. 18). The distribution was further restricted by the Harrison Act of 1914. In spite of what is popularly thought, this act did not make the manufacture, distribution, or use of opium, cocaine, or marijuana illegal. What it did was require that individuals and companies that manufactured or distributed these substances register with the Treasury Department and pay special taxes. The Treasury Department's interpretation of the Harrison Act and Subsequent Supreme Court decisions served to make a wide variety of narcotics and other drugs illegal to manufacture, distribute, or even prescribe.

Perceptions of Drugs and Crime in the Early 20th Century

Some critics have argued that the Harrison Act turned law-abiding users of patent medicines into criminals (King, 1974). Although this is probably an oversimplification, the Harrison Act did culminate and strongly support a popular social reform movement that increasingly defined drug use as criminal and often the cause of violent, bizarre behavior.

The medical literature of the early 20th century, by contrast, viewed the opiate user as lethargic and less likely to engage in violent crime. Whatever criminal behavior resulted from drug user was seen as occurring to obtain money to buy drugs. Shoplifting and other forms of petty theft were seen as the primary types of criminal behavior. Many observers noted that debauchery, laziness, and prostitution were the primary deviant behavioral consequences of opiate use—not violent predatory crime (see Kolb, 1925; Lichtenstein, 1914; Terry and Pellens, 1928). Overall, the medical and psychiatric literature of the early 20th century viewed opiate use as debilitating and a cause of petty property crimes or prostitution, but not as a cause of violet crime.

Some medical practitioners did consider cocaine to be different from opiates in its behavioral consequences (Kolb, 1925). Kolb's observation was that cocaine tended to make individuals more paranoid and that consequently, a cocaine user might strike out violently at an imagined pursuer. Although cocaine was used in many patent medicines and was included in the Harrison Act, the official government position seemed to conclude that cocaine use, although potentially a cause of crime, was relatively small and therefore of insignificant consequence (U.S. Treasury Department, 1939).

Although the medical literature did not see opiate use as a prime cause of violent street crime or crime in general, there were many popular lecturers who did. Perhaps the most prolific and popular anti-narcotic lecturer was Richmond P. Hobson. He founded a number of anti-narcotics-use organizations and both published and lectured extensively on the violent crimogenic nature of narcotics use. Throughout the 1920s, Mr. Hobson argued that most property and violent crimes were committed by heroin and other types of drug addicts. He further argued that the continuity of civilization itself depended on the elimination of narcotics use (Hobson, 1928). With his frequent radio broadcasts, he played a significant role in creating a national perception of the direct link between all types of drug use and all types of crime.

Somewhat surprisingly, the primary drugs–crime connection portrayed in popular and government media involved marijuana use. On July 6, 1927, the *New York Times* reported that a family in Mexico City had become hopelessly insane by eating marijuana leaves. The epitome of the marijuana-causes-crime perspective was probably the Hollywood production of the film *Reefer Madness*. This film was strongly influenced by the Commissioner of the Treasury Department's Bureau of Narcotics, Harry J. Anslinger. *Reefer Madness* portrayed marijuana as the great destroyer of American youth. Marijuana, it was shown in the film, not only caused young people to become sexually promiscuous but also violently criminal and prone to suicide. Marijuana was viewed as the most dangerous substance in America and one that, unless stopped, would lead to the violent downfall of Western civilization. It was not only in the movies that marijuana was portrayed as causing violence. Anslinger and his colleagues at the Bureau of Narcotics published a number of books focusing on the direct violent criminal behavior caused by narcotics, particularly by marijuana use, and on the involvement of criminal gangs in the distribution of illegal drugs (Anslinger and Oursler, 1961; Anslinger and Tompkins, 1953). In all of his work, Anslinger listed cannabis as a narcotic and always described its consequences as the most violent and dangerous. For example, in the *The Murders*, he claimed that "All varieties (of Cannabis) may lead to acts of violence, extremes, madness, homicide" (p. 304). In this book, Anslinger provided many examples of the criminal horrors committed by those who had smoked even one reefer. The most gruesome illustration was the case of a 17-month-old White female raped and murdered by a cotton picker who had smoked one marijuana cigarette (Anslinger and Tompkins, 1953, p. 24). The popular book entitled *Dope* argued that "when you have once chosen marijuana, you have selected murder and torture and hideous cruelty to your bosom friends" (Black, 1928, p. 28). Popular periodicals such as *American Magazine* also told in lurid detail about ax-murdering marijuana-intoxicated youths on rampages (Sloman, 1979, p. 63).

A crucial implicit and often explicit aspect of the portrayal of the relationship between drugs and crime was the strong antiforeign feelings and racism of the 1920s and 1930s. Many of the horror stories that focused on the violence and degradation of narcotics users centered on African Americans, Mexicans, and Chinese. All of the illegal drugs were portrayed as foreign imports brought in by dark- or yellow-skinned outsiders wanting to corrupt White youth, seduce

White women, and/or overthrow Northern European ascendancy. The drugs–crime relationship was thus an important aspect of a popular racial and national isolationist perspective (see Inciardi, 1992; Musto, 1973).

During the 1930s and 1940s, and even into the 1950s, the American government and the popular media seemed to work closely in continuing to create the image of the "dope fiend" as a violent, out-of-control sexual predator who accounted for a large proportion of America's heinous crimes. By the late 1950s, this image had been strongly challenged by a wide variety of academic and other critics. However, these formative images of the bizarre, violent dope fiend continue to provide at least a background schemata that affects cultural perceptions of the drugs–crime relationship.

THE INTERSECTION OF TYPOLOGIES

Although the historical and current discussions of the drugs–crime relationship often assume a particular intersection between specific types of drugs and specific types of crime, that intersection is generally not explicit or examined in a logical, sequential manner. As McGlothlin (1979) noted, if the drugs–crime relationship is to be examined logically, it is important to use typologies of both types of behaviors and proceed to review how each type of drug use relates to each type of crime. Drug abuse and crime are complex issues that include a multitude of specific behaviors.

Types of Drugs

At the turn of the century almost all drugs were called narcotics—including opium, marijuana, and cocaine. However, as is apparent, each of these substances has a very different chemical structure and a different psychopharmacological effect. Thus each potentially has a very different relationship to various types of criminal behavior. During the 1960s and 1970s, the term *drug abuse* primarily seemed to mean heroin use and, to a lesser extent, LSD use. Today, the term probably conjures up images of cocaine use. Regardless of what specific drug the term may be most associated with, an analysis of the drugs–crime relationship must conceptually use the major specific categories of drugs.

Generally, it has been recognized that the various types of illegal drugs have different possible relationships to criminal behavior, based on their chemical structure, subculture of use, cost, or differential patterns of control. Over the last decade, major national surveys on illegal drug use have tended to develop a list of drug types that are routinely included in questionnaires (for example, see Clayton et al., 1988; Johnston, O'Malley, and Bachman, 1993; Liska, 1990). These are

1. Narcotic analgesics: including heroin, Demoral, Percodan, and Dilaudid
2. Stimulants: including cocaine in all of its forms and amphetamines
3. Hallucinogens: for example, LSD, PCP, and MDA
4. Inhalants: including gasoline, paint thinner, glue, other volatile hydrocarbons and amyl/butyl nitrites
5. Sedatives: for example, barbiturates and methaqualone
6. Major and minor tranquilizers
7. Marijuana (although the effects of this drug combine some aspects of sedatives, tranquilizers, and hallucinogens, it is usually placed in its own seperate classification)
8. Steroids and other types of hormonal substances designed to build muscle or increase aggressiveness.

In some research projects, these categories might need to be expanded to include more specific drugs within each category. However, these are the general categories used in drug research.

Types of Crime

Types of criminal behavior also need to be constructed in drugs–crime research and conceptual understandings. For the last two decades, researchers have explicitly argued that drugs–crime research needs to work within common parameter definitions of categories of criminal behavior (see Inciardi and McBride, 1976). Traditionally, criminologists have had a major focus on the construction of criminal behavior typologies. The aim has been to construct mutually exclusive homogeneous categories (see Hood and Sparks, 1970). Typically, typological constructions in criminology have been based on legal categories, such as the Uniform Crime Reports (UCR) (1993), the public's perception of the severity ranking of specific criminal behaviors (Rossi, Waite, Bose, and Berk, 1974), the social psychology and behavioral characteristics of offenders (Duncan, Ohlin, Reis, and Stanton, 1953), or combinations of all of the preceding (Clinard and Quinney, 1967). Recent criminology and criminal justice texts have tended to use the categorization of the UCR, which includes a sense of public and official views of seriousness plus elements of social psychological characteristics (see Inciardi, 1993). The following categories of crimes are commonly used in criminal justice research:

1. Crime against persons: including homicide, manslaughter, rape of all types, aggravated assault, assault and battery, and child molestation
2. Armed robbery
3. Property crimes: including breaking and entering, larceny, auto theft, arson, forgery, counterfelting, passing worthless checks, buying, concealing, and receiving stolen property, vandalism
4. Income-producing victimless crimes: including prostitution, commercialized vice, and gambling
5. Violation of drug laws: including the possession or sale of dangerous drugs or the implements for their use
6. Other offenses: for example, disorderly conduct, vagrancy, loitering, and resisting arrest.

Sequentially examining each of the specific intersections between each type of drug and each type of crime could help build a systematic body of knowledge about the totality of the drugs–crime relationship.

THE STATISTICAL OVERLAP

Historically, and currently, one of the major arguments for the existence of a drugs–crime relationship is the high level of drug use among populations of criminals and the frequent involvement in criminal activities of street-drug users. Anslinger and Tomkins (1953), as a part of their argument that drug use was a component of a criminal culture, claimed that a large proportion of federal prisoners were users of illegal drugs. During the late 1960s and early 1970s, many epidemiologists, and certainly the popular culture, believed that the United States was undergoing a drug epidemic. The evidence for the epidemic was large increases in drug overdosages, drug-related arrests and drug treatment admissions (see O'Donnell, Voss, Clayton, Slatin, and Room, 1976). One of the major perceived consequences of increased drug use was the

perception of an associated increase in street crime. This apparent epidemic stimulated the development or reinvigoration of a vast drug treatment, enforcement, and research endeavor culminating in the establishment of the National Institute on Drug abuse (NIDA) in 1975. In 1971, during an address to Congress on June 17, President Richard M. Nixon called the drug epidemic a national emergency. The Federal Strategy Report of 1975 noted that the crime associated with drug use was a major reason for the national attention focused on drug abuse in the era.

Drug Use in Populations of Criminals

One of the tasks of the newly created NIDA and the National Institute of Justice was a series of studies and symposiums on the drugs–crime relationship (see Gandossy, Williams, Coben, and Harwood, 1980; Inciardi and McBride, 1976). As these study groups documented, many research projects conducted in a variety of urban areas during the early 1970s found that somewhere between 15% and 40% of arrestees and prisoners were users of illegal drugs—mostly marijuana and heroin (see Eckerman, Bates, Rachal, and Poole, 1971; Ford, Hauser, and Jackson, 1975; McBride, 1976). These findings were seen, at the time, as dramatic evidence of the existence of the drug–crime connection and the need to integrate the criminal justice system with the drug treatment system. One of the outcomes of these types of studies was the establishment of the Treatment Alternatives to Street Crime (TASC) program, which attempted to identify drug users in populations of offenders, assess their treatment needs, and refer them to appropriate treatment facilities (see Inciardi and McBride, 1991).

Recent research has shown an even more extensive use of drugs in a variety of criminally involved populations. In a study of nonincarcerated delinquents in Miami, Florida, Inciardi, Horowitz, and Pottieger (1993) found that some three fourths of male and female delinquents used cocaine at least weekly. Further, the Drug Use Forecasting (DUF) program collects and analyzes urine from arrestees in 24 major cities across the United States. In most, over 60% of the male and female arrestees are positive for illegal drugs. The lowest rates for males were in Omaha and San Antonio, where only 48% were positive for an illegal drug. The lowest rate for females was 47% in New Orleans. The highest for females was 81% in Manhattan, and the highest rate for males was 80% in Philadelphia. In almost all of the cities in the study, cocaine was the most common drug found through urinalysis followed by marijuana and opiates (see DUF, 1993; Wish, 1987).

Surveys of incarcerated populations show a similarly high rate of illegal drug use just prior to incarceration. In 1990, for example, the Bureau of Justice Statistics found that over 40% of the state prison inmates reported the daily use of illegal drugs in the month prior to the offense that resulted in their incarceration. A comparison of these data to that of criminally involved populations in the 1970s shows a much higher rate of illegal drug use in the current criminal justice population and a dramatic shift from heroin and marijuana to primarily cocaine and marijuana. These data also suggest a virtual saturation of the criminal justice system by illegal drug users who mostly consume cocaine in some form.

There is also a body of research that indicates a high level of drug use among incarcerated individuals. In a study of Delaware prison inmates, Inciardi, Lockwood, and Quinlan (1993) found that 60% of the respondents reported the use of drugs, mostly marijuana, while in prison. However, urinalysis found only about a 1% positivity rate. A random sample of urine collected in Wisconsin discovered a rate of 25% positive, mostly marijuana (Vigdal and Stadler, 1989). There is also some ethnographic evidence that drugs are integrated in the prison culture as a part of control, management, and reward systems (see Hawkins and Alpert, 1989; Inciardi, Horowitz, and Pottieger, 1993). Although there is no evidence that drug use is rampant in jails and prisons, the high use rates in the population prior to incarceration as well as the level of continuing use while in prison have stimulated the development of drug treatment services in prisons throughout the United States (Hayes and Schimmel, 1993).

Criminal Behavior in Populations of Drug Users

Examinations of drug-using populations for the last few decades have found similarly high rates of criminal behavior. Surveys of populations of illegal drug users in the late 1960s and early 1970s generally found that a large majority had extensive criminal histories (see Defleur, Ball, and Snarr, 1969; Voss and Stephens, 1973). Recent local and national research has confirmed these early findings. In a population of over 400 street-injection-drug users in Miami, Florida, for example, McBride and Inciardi (1990) found that over 80% had been in jail in the last 5 years and about 45% had been incarcerated within the last 6 months. An analysis of over 25,000 street-injection-

drug users from 63 cities found that some two thirds were in jail in the last 5 years, with over one third currently on probation or parole or awaiting trial (Inciardi, McBride, Platt, and Baxter, 1993). Consistently, examinations of populations of nonincarcerated drug users clearly show a high level of current involvement with criminal behavior and with the criminal justice system.

The Statistical Overlap in the General Population

General-population surveys also show the overlap between drug using and criminal behaviors. In 1991, the National Household Survey of drug use conducted by the NIDA included questions on criminal behavior. Analysis of that data showed a correlation between drug use and engaging in criminal, particularly violent, behavior. Less than 5% of those who drank alcohol only or who consumed no substance engaged in a violent or property crime during the last year. About 25% of those who had used marijuana and cocaine in addition to alcohol admitted to the commission of a violent and/or property crime in the last year (Harrison and Gfroerer, 1992).

Analyses of data from the National Youth Survey also show a strong correlation between serious drug use and serious delinquent behavior. The National Youth Survey is a longitudinal study initiated in the late 1970s and was designed to survey a variety of behaviors, including substance use and crime (see Huizinga, 1978, for a description of the survey and its methodology). In an analysis of these data, Johnson, Wish, Schmeidler, and Huizinga (1993) found that only 3% of nondelinquents used cocaine, whereas 23% of those with multiple delinquency index crimes were current cocaine users. Examining the data from the perspective of drug-using behavior, they found that only 2% of those who used alcohol only had multiple index offenses compared to 28% of the cocaine users. Overall, these researchers found a correlation of .53 between the delinquency and drug use scales.

Although the complexity and causal nature of the drugs–crime relationship is open to considerable debate, there is little contention about the statistical correlation between drug use and crime. For a number of decades, the existence of the empirical relationship has been documented by researchers as well as by criminal justice practitioners and drug treatment professionals. The size of the relationship between using drugs and criminal behavior is a daily reality in criminal justice systems and drug treatment programs throughout the United States. This reality has stimulated a wide variety of critical thinking and research projects designed to sort out the nature of the drugs–crime relationship and policies that could be used to reduce the extent of the relationship.

THE ETIOLOGICAL NATURE OF THE DRUGS–CRIME RELATIONSHIP

Which Came First?

This issue of behavioral and causal priority in the drugs–crime relationship has been a primary research focus of numerous investigators. Researchers have consistently found that individuals who frequently use illegal drugs such as cocaine, heroin, or marijuana have engaged in criminal behavior prior to or concurrent with the initiation of any stable illegal drug use pattern (see Anglin and Speckart, 1988; Huizinga, Menard, and Elliot, 1989; Inciardi, Lockwood, and Quinlan, 1993; O'Donnell et al., 1976; Stephens and McBride, 1976). Rather than innocents seduced or propelled into criminal activity by their drug use, existing data and research indicate that drug abuse and criminal activity are a part of a broader set of integrated deviant behaviors involving crime, drug use, and, often, high-risk sex. Although a variety of empirical data indicate that drug use does not appear to initiate a criminal career, a large volume of research clearly indicates that frequency of drug use has a strong impact on the extent, direction, and duration of that career.

The Impact of Drug Use on Frequency of Criminal Behavior

A wide body of research indicates that although criminal behavior may be initiated prior to or concomitant with the genesis of illegal drug use, once illegal drug use is initiated it has a dramatic effect on the amount of criminal activity (Anglin and Hser, 1987; Anglin and Speckart, 1988; Ball, Rosen, Flueck, and Nurco, 1981; Chambers, Cuskey, and Moffett, 1970; Chaiken and Chaiken, 1990; Stephens and McBride, 1976). Particularly the work of Ball and his colleagues (1981), using longitudinal data, and Anglin and his colleagues (Anglin and Hser, 1987; Anglin and Speckart, 1988), using a life history method, clearly indicate the effect of narcotics use on rates of criminal behavior. These researchers found sharp decreases in criminal activity during periods of abstinence from heroin and large increases in criminal activity during periods of increased heroin use (see Anglin and Speckart, 1988; Ball et al., 1981; Ball, Shaffer, and Nurco, 1983).

The expense of cocaine and heroin use and the fact that most frequent users of these drugs are unemployed result in a high level of criminal activity in user populations. Inciardi, McBride, McCoy, and Chitwood (1994) describe what they call an amazing amount of criminal activity involving over 100,000 criminal acts (excluding drug law violations) committed by some 700 cocaine users in the 90 days prior to being interviewed. Johnson and his colleagues (1985) reported that over 40% of the total income of a population of street-drug users was generated from illegal activity. Using a variety of methodologies, including life histories, surveys, and longitudinal data, the existing research literature suggests that the frequent use of illegal drugs is clearly a part of the motivation for an increase in criminal activities that are designed to obtain funds for drugs or as a part of other activities designed to access, possess, and use drugs. In addition, the available data suggest that, rather than a simple linear relationship between drugs and crime, both may emerge at a similar time period and that the two behaviors may have a recursive element to their relationship. That is, drug use may be involved in increasing criminal behavior, but the initiation of criminal behavior may also result in subcultural participation and individual-risk decision making that involves taking high-risk drugs (see Clayton and Tuchfeld, 1982).

The Impact of Drug Use on Sustained Criminal Behavior

There is some evidence that frequent hard-drug use may be involved with a sustained criminal career. Longitudinal research indicates that most delinquents cease their illegal activity by late adolescence or early adulthood (e.g., see Kandel, Simcha-Fagan, and Davies, 1986). Traditionally, getting a steady job, getting married, and having children was viewed as a sign of maturation and as increasing an individual's stakes in conformity and therefore decreasing rates of illegal behavior. The UCR indicates a sharp drop in arrest rates for populations over 25 years of age. A wide variety of research data indicates that frequent drug use may severely interfere with that maturation process and consequent reduction in crime. National (Elliott and Huizinga, 1985) and local studies (Dembo et al., 1987) have indicated that chronic serious delinquent offenders are more likely to become involved with hard-drug use, which, in turn, relates to continued participation in a criminal subculture and high rates of criminal behavior. Life history research (Faupel and Klockars, 1987) also documents the recursive relationship of using drugs and criminal behavior.

The recursive nature of the drugs–crime relationship appears to act to reinforce continued drug use and crime. Ethnographers have described this as "taking care of business" (Hanson, Beschner, Walters, and Bovelle, 1985). Essentially, the argument is that the subcultural values that emerge in street-drug-using cultures encompass crime as a means to obtain drugs and as a cultural value itself in opposition to the straight world of legitimate low-paying jobs. Using drugs and criminal behavior become well integrated within the cultural/social role of the street-drug user (see Stephens, 1991). From this perspective, drug use does not directly cause crime, but, rather, is an integral part of the street-drug subculture. To focus only on drug-using behavior as a primary means to reduce crime misses the intertwined complexity of the drugs–crime relationship.

Drug Use and Type of Crime

Probably as a result of images created by decades of government and media messages about the violent dope fiend, the public has been concerned about the types of crime in which drug users engage. The particular concern has been that the use of many types of drugs causes extreme violence. As noted earlier in this article, many years ago, Kolb (1925) argued against the prevailing popular view of the crazed dope fiend. From a psychopharmacological perspective, he contended that the biochemical effect of opiate use was to make a user lethargic and less likely to engage in violent crime at least while under the influence of the drug. This original perspective continued to find empirical support for decades. For example, Finestone (1957) claimed that heroin users were much more likely to engage in petty property crime to support their use than in noneconomically productive violent crime. In fact, he observed that as street groups initiated and increased heroin use, the rate of violent crime decreased and their rate of property crime increased. These types of research findings continued through most of the next two decades. Basically, heroin users were found to be overrepresented among property criminals and underrepresented among those charged with crimes of violence (see Inciardi and Chambers, 1972; Kozel and DuPont, 1977; McBride, 1976).

In the late 1970s, researchers began to report an increase in violence in the street-heroin-using subculture, particularly among younger cohorts of users (Stephens and Ellis, 1975; Zahn and Bencivengo, 1974). During the 1980s, epidemiological data indicated a rapid increase in cocaine use. As has been noted, DUF (1993) data indicate a virtual saturation of cocaine use in arrested populations. This rapid rise in cocaine use and in rates of violent behavior has stimulated a variety of speculation and research about the impact of cocaine on criminal behavior and on the world of the street-drug user. For most of the last decade, researchers have been reporting that increased cocaine use was related to violent confrontational crime for men and women (Datesman, 1981; Goldstein, 1989; Simonds and Kashani, 1980; Spunt, Goldstein, Bellucci, and Miller, 1990). Research has also indicated that cocaine use may be related not only to being a violent offender but also to being a victim of violent crime. McBride, Burgman-Habermehl, Alpert, and Chitwood (1986), in an analysis of homicides in Miami, Florida, found that after alcohol, cocaine was the most common drug found in the bodies of homicide victims. Almost 10% of homicide victims had cocaine in their bodies at the time of death. This was more than 8 times the rate of any other illegal drug. Goldstein, Bellucci, Spunt, and Miller (1993), in a study in New York City, found that increased cocaine was associated with being a victim of violent crime for women.

Paul Goldstein (1989) has proposed a very useable framework for interpreting the relationship between drugs and violence that seems particularly appropriate to interpreting the relationship between cocaine and violence. He calls this paradigm "a tripartite scheme." Goldstein sees this scheme as involving psychopharmacological, economically compulsive, and systemic aspects. Essentially, a part of the violent behavior of cocaine users may relate to the psychopharmacological consequences of cocaine use. This effect includes a strong stimulant impact, long periods without sleep, and increased paranoia. All of these effects could result in an increased willingness on the part of those using cocaine (and other stimulants, such as amphetamines) to engage in aggressive behavior or to put themselves into situations where aggressive behavior is more likely to occur. The economic demands involve the cost of heavy cocaine or crack use that may result in violent predatory behavior designed to obtain the most money. The systemic aspect of the model involves violent subcultural behavior patterns that are integral to being a street-drug user and those violent behavior patterns that are a part of the street distribution of cocaine. Other researchers (McBride and Swartz, 1990) have suggested that the drugs–violence and cocaine–violence relationship is also occurring within the framework of a rapid increase of heavy armaments in general society. That is, our whole society has undergone an increase in the availability and distribution of powerful automatic weapons. This general availability of weapons has also become a part of the street-drug-using culture. Rather than drug use being a direct cause of violence, it might be important to recognize that the drug culture has adapted the weaponry of the general culture and has used it for its own purposes. Regardless of the exact nature of the relationship, the existing data suggest that, increasingly, drug use, particularly cocaine use, has become integrated with a high level of international, national, and local street violence. The extent of cocaine use among felony offenders and the perceived relationship between cocaine and violence has played a major role in the reinvigoration of the debate about national drug policy and the issue of the decriminalization of drug use.

SOME THEORETICAL PERSPECTIVES ON THE DRUGS–CRIME RELATIONSHIP

From every conceivable methodological perspective, data consistently show that there is a strong correlation between drug use and criminal behavior and that increases in drug use are related to increases in crime. However, the theoretical analysis of the relationship has not been as extensive. Some perspectives argue that the interpretation of the empirical relationship might be very different from what the data initially suggest.

Subcultural, Role Theory, and Ecological Perspectives

Ethnographic and role theory analyses have tended to view the crime and drug relationship as associated with subcultural roles that include what general society would call extreme deviant behavior (Hanson et al., 1985; Stephens, 1991). High frequencies of drug use, high rates of crime, and extensive high-risk sexual behavior are seen from this perspective as "taking care of business" or an integral part of the social role of the street-drug user. This type of conceptual analysis suggests that the drugs–crime relationship may not be directly linear in cause, but, rather, drug use and crime exist as a part of an intertwined mutually reinforcing subculturally contexted set of behaviors.

Ecological theoretical analysis has suggested that the drugs–crime relationship appears to be related because both types of behavior are caused by similar environmental conditions, such as poverty and lack of social control and economic opportunity. In that sense, some observers have concluded that drug use is spuriously related to crime. That is, there is the appearance of a statistical causal relationship, but that relationship may be an artifact of common etiology (Fagan, Weis, and Cheng, 1990; McBride and McCoy, 1981). Drugs and crime occur together because they share a similar set of causal variables and they are a part of the same subcultural value and role system. From these ecological and subcultural theoretical perspectives, the drugs–crime relationship is not so much affected by attempts to stop or reduce drug use but, rather, by attempts to address the common underlying initiating and sustaining causes of both behaviors.

A Radical Interpretation of the Drugs–Crime Relationship

Another major theoretical critique of the apparent drugs–crime relationship comes from radical theory. This perspective maintains that the drugs–crime relationship is an artifact of legal policy since 1914. From this viewpoint, the existence of a drugs–crime relationship simply resulted from laws that effectively criminalized a variety of drug-using behaviors. As the result of the Harrison Act and subsequent law, American society created a criminal subculture where none existed; drove up the cost of drugs, thereby providing an economic motivation for drug-related crime; and left the distribution of drugs to organized criminal networks. These, in turn, grew immensely wealthy and powerful through the distribution of the much-in-demand and now-expensive illegal drugs. The current violence, corruption, and civil rights issues associated with drug use and drug law enforcement are seen, from this perspective, as the inevitable result of the social construction of deviance. Radical theorists argue that the drugs–crime relationship can best be disentangled by decriminalizing drugs and treating drug abuse and addiction as mental and public health problems that are best addressed through psychological counseling and social work case management. The drug policy of the Netherlands is often advocated as an example of an enlightened, less criminogenic strategy (see Lindesmith, 1965; Nadelmann, 1989; Trebach and Inciardi, 1993).

There is considerable evidence that much of the crime committed by drug users involves only violations of drug laws involving possession and distribution of illegal drugs. For example, Inciardi et al.

(1994) found that during the 90 days prior to being interviewed, their sample of some 700 cocaine users had committed over 1.7 million criminal acts with well over 95% of them involving violations of drug laws. Further evidence exists in examinations of the current operation of drug courts. Originally, these courts were designed to focus on the increasing number of drug-involved cases coming before the court. However, these courts may be increasing the focus on drug users who are involved only in drug law violations and not implicated in other types of crime and thereby furthering the appearance of a relationship between drug use and crime, particularly among African Americans in the inner city (Klofas, 1993).

The radical perspective does provide a valuable insight into how society may create by law that which it is attempting to avoid by law, and there may be some applicability to the interpretation of the drugs–crime relationship. The perspective is, however, often built on the notion that somehow the relationship between drug use and crime would virtually disappear if drugs were just decriminalized, that there would be no or minimal increase in drug use, and that any increase would have virtually no impact on violence or crime. Such a view would seem to ignore psychopharmacological aspects of the relationship, the fact that criminal behavior generally precedes drug use, and the findings that both behaviors arise from similar etiological variables and act in a mutually reinforcing manner.

In a recent analysis of the drug–crime relationship in Amsterdam by Grapendaal, Leuw, and Nelen (1992), it was shown that 53% of a sample of 148 polydrug users engaged in acquisitive crime during an average month, and those 79 individuals netted almost $66,000 per month from their property crimes to buy drugs. Further, it was found that property crime accounted for 24% of total income in the sample. This was the second highest percentage of total income after welfare payments. During 1991, the city of Zurich, Switzerland, experimented with the decriminalization of drugs and experienced an increase in property and violent crimes. Public pressure forced a reversal of Swiss policy (see the *New York Times*, February 11, 1992, A10). Although, as Grapendaal and his colleagues (1992) noted, the extent of drug-related crime in the Netherlands may not be as extensive as in New York or other American cities, there is a significant relationship even in a highly tolerant city. These researchers also noted that the policy of tolerance has created a permanent underclass whose crime may only be lessened by a generous welfare system but not eliminated. Just as the perspective arguing that drug use seduced innocent youth into a life of crime has been shown to be simplistic, so the perspective that drug laws throw otherwise peaceful citizens into a life of criminal violence that can be eliminated if drugs are just decriminalized may also be more simplistic than is warranted by the facts (for perspectives against decriminalization see Inciardi and McBride, 1989; Wilson, 1993).

POLICY IMPLICATIONS OF THE DRUGS–CRIME DATA

Although the drugs–crime data and conceptual understandings may be complex and even contradictory, there appear to be three major common implications from current knowledge.

1. There is a strong need for treatment services for drug-using, criminally involved populations. This would include both those who are incarcerated as well as those on probation or in a diversion program. Regardless of the complexity of the data, there is a clear indication that levels of drug use relate to levels of criminal activity. Reducing drug demand through treatment has a strong possibility for reducing levels of crime. Increasing treatment resources at all levels of the criminal justice system to eliminate waiting lists, as well as increasing recruitment outreach in criminal populations, has a significant potential to reduce the level of crime in a community.

2. The ecological and subcultural perspectives remind our society that the drugs–crime relationship is at least in part the result of a history of differential social, political, and economic opportunity. The development of oppositional subcultures in which drug use and crime are an integrated part will be addressed only by major efforts to provide educational and economic development opportunities. Social and economic progress in communities with high rates of drug use and crime must be a local and national priority.

3. The radical perspective reminds us that in any application of drug policy, civil rights must be protected, that there are severe limits to the effectiveness of law enforcement, and enforcement practices can increase the appearance of the drugs–crime relationship well beyond the framework of psychopharmacology, economic demand, and subcultural roles. Drug laws and policy should focus on demand reduction at least equal to supply reduction. Drug law enforcement must never be an excuse for a retreat on hard-won legal and civil rights, and drug law and policy must rest on a strong public support base.

REFERENCES

Anglin, M. D., and Hser, Y. (1987). Addicted women and crime. *Criminology, 25,* 359–397.

Anglin, M. D., and Speckart, F. (1988). Narcotics use and crime: A multi sample, multi method analysis. *Criminology, 26,* 197–233.

Anslinger, H. J., and Ourlser, W. (1961). *The murderers.* New York: Farrar, Straus and Cudahy.

Anslinger, H. J., and Tompkins, W. F. (1953). *The traffic in narcotics.* New York: Funk and Wagnalls.

Ball, J. C., Rosen, L., Flueck, J. A., and Nurco, D. N. (1981). The criminality of heroin addicts: When addicted and when off opiates. In J. A. Inciardi (Ed.), *The drugs–crime connection* (pp. 39–65). Beverly Hills, CA: Sage.

Ball, J. C., Shaffer, J. W., and Nurco, D. N. (1983). The day-to-day criminality of heroin addicts in Baltimore: A study in the continuity of offense rates. *Drugs and Alcohol Dependence, 12,* 119–142.

Black, W. (1928). *Dope: the story of the living dead.* New York: Star and Co.

Bureau of Justice Statistics. (1990). *Drugs and crime facts, 1989.* Washington, DC: Author.

Chaiken, J. M., and Chaiken, M. R. (1990). Drugs and predatory crime. In M. Tonry and J. Q. Wilson (Eds.), *Drugs and crime* (pp. 203–239). Chicago: University of Chicago Press.

Chambers, C. D., Cuskey, W. R., and Moffett, A. D. (1970). Demographic factors associated with opiate addiction among Mexican Americans. *Public Health Reports, 85,* 523–531.

Clayton, R. R., and Tuchfeld, B. S. (1982). The drug–crime debate: Obstacles to understanding the relationship. *Journal of Drug Issues, 12,* 153–166.

Clayton, R. R., Voss, H. L., Loscuito, L., Martin, S. S., Skinner, W. F., Robbins, C., and Santos, R. L. (1988). *National household survey on drug abuse: Main findings, 1985.* Washington, DC: U.S. Department of Health and Human Services.

Clinard, M. B., and Quinney, R. (1967). Criminal behavior systems. New York: Rinchart and Winston.

Datesman, S. (1981). Women, crime, and drugs. In J. A. Inciardi (Ed.), The drugs/crime connection (pp. 85–104). Beverly Hills, CA: Sage.

Defleur, L. B., Ball, J. C., and Snarr, R. W. (1969). The long-term social correlates of opiate abuse. *Social Problems, 17,* 225–234.

Dembo, R., Washburn, M., Wish, E. D., Yeung, H., Getreu, A., Berry, E., and Blount, W. R. (1987). Heavy marijuana use and crime among youths entering a juvenile detention center. *Journal of Psychoactive Drugs, 19,* 47–56.

Drug use forecasting. (1993, May). Washington, DC: National Institute of Justice.

Duncan, O. D., Ohlin, L. E., Reis A. J., and Stanton, H. E. (1953). Formal devises for making selection decisions. *American Journal of Sociology, 58,* 537–584.

Eckerman, W. C., Bates, J. J. D., Rachal, J. V., and Poole, W. K. (1971). *Drug usage and arrest charges.* Washington, DC: Drug Enforcement Administration.

Elliott, D. S., and Huizinga, D. (1985). The relationship between delinquent behavior and ADM problems. *Proceedings of the Prevention Research Conference on Juvenile Offenders with Serious Drug, Alcohol and Mental Health Problems.* Washington, DC: Alcohol, Drug Abuse and Mental Health Administration, Office of Juvenile Justice and Delinquency.

Fagan, J., Weis, J. G., and Cheng, Y. T. (1990). Delinquency and substance use among inner-city students. *Journal of Drug Issues, 20,* 351–402.

Faupel, C. E., and Klockars, C. B. (1987). Drugs–crime connections: Elaborations from the life histories of hardcore heroin addicts. *Social Problems, 34,* 54–68.

Federal strategy for drug abuse and drug traffic prevention. (1975). Washington, DC: U.S. Government Printing Office.

Finestone, H. (1957). Narcotics and criminality. *Law and Contemporary Problems, 9,* 69–85.

Ford, A., Hanser, H., and Jackson, E. (1975). Use of drugs among persons admitted to a county jail. *Public Health Reports, 90,* 504–508.

Gandossy, R. P., Williams, J. R., Cohen, J., and Harwood, H. J. (1980). *Drugs and crime: A survey and analysis of the literature* (National Institute of Justice). Washington, DC: U.S. Government Printing Office.

Goldstein, P. J. (1989). Drugs and violent crime. In N. A. Wiener and M. E. Wolfgang (Eds.), *Pathways to criminal violence* (pp. 16–48). Newbury Park, CA: Sage.

Goldstein, P. J., Bellucci, P. A., Spunt, B. J., and Miller, T. (1993). Volume of cocaine use and violence: A comparison between men and women. In R. Dembo (Ed.), *Drugs and crime* (pp. 141–177). New York: University Press of America.

Grapendaal, M., Leuw, E., and Nelen, H. (1992, Summer). Drugs and crime in an accommodating social context: The situation in Amsterdam. *Contemporary Drug Problems,* pp. 303–326.

Hanson, B., Beschner, G., Walters, J. M., and Bovelle, E. (1985). *Life with heroin: Voices from the inner city.* Lexington, MA. Lexington Books.

Harrison, L., and Gfroerer, J. (1992). The intersection of drug use and criminal behavior: Results from the national household survey on drug abuse, *Crime and Delinquency, 38,* 422–443.

Hawkins, R., and Alpert, G. P. (1989). *American prison systems: Punishment and justice.* Englewood Cliffs, NJ: Prentice-Hall.

Hayes, T. J., and Schimmel, D. J. (1993). Residential drug abuse treatment in the Federal Bureau of Prisons. *Journal of Drug Issues, 28,* 61–73.

Hobson, R. P. (1928). The struggle of mankind against its deadliest foe. *Narcotic Education, 1,* 51–54.

Hood, R., and Sparks, R. (1970). *Key Issues in criminology.* New York: McGraw-Hill.

Huizinga, D. H. (1978). *Sample design of the National Youth Survey.* Boulder, CO: Behavioral Research Institute.

Huizinga, D. H., Menard, S., and Elliot, D. S. (1989). Delinquency and drug use: Temporal and developmental patterns. *Justice Quarterly, 6,* 419–455.

Inciardi, J. A. (1992). *The war on drugs II.* Palo Alto, CA: Mayfield.

Inciardi, J. A. (1993). *Criminal Justice.* Fort Worth, TX: Harcourt Brace Jovanovich.

Inciardi, J. A., and Chambers, C. D. (1972). Unreported criminal involvement of narcotic addicts. *Journal of Drug Issues, 2,* 57–64.

Inciardi, J. A., Horowitz, R., and Pottieger, A. E. (1993). *Street kids, street drugs, street crime.* Belmont, CA: Wadsworth.

Inciardi, J. A., Lockwood, D., and Quinlan, J. A. (1993). Drug use in prison: Patterns, processes, and implications for treatment. *Journal of Drug Issues, 23,* 119–129.

Inciardi, J. A., and McBride, D. C. (1976). Considerations in the definition of criminality for the assessment of the relationship between drug use and crime. In Research Triangle Institute (Ed.), *Crime and drugs* (pp. 123–137). Springfield, VA: National Technical Information Service.

Inciardi, J. A., and McBride, D. C. (1989). Legalization: A high risk alternative in the war on drugs. *American Behavioral Scientist, 32,* 259–289.

Inciardi, J. A., and McBride, D. C. (1991). *Treatment alternatives to street crime (TASC): History, experiences, and issues.* Rockville, MD: National Institute on Drug Abuse.

Inciardi, J. A., McBride, D. C., Platt, J. J., and Baxter, S. (1993). Injecting drug users, incarceration, and HIV: Some legal and social service delivery issues. In *The national AIDS demonstration research program.* Westport, CT: Greenwood.

Inciardi, J. A., McBride, D. C., McCoy, H. V., and Chitwood, D. D. (1994). Recent research on the crack cocaine crime connection. *Studies on crime and crime prevention, 3,* 63–82.

Johnson, B. D., Goldstein, P. J., Proble, E., Schmeidler, J., Lipton, D. S., and Miller, T. (1985) *Taking care of business: the economics of crime by heroin abusers.* Lexington, MA: Lexington Books.

Johnson, B. D., Wish, E. D., Schmeidler, J., and Huizinga, D. (1993). Concentration of delinquent offending: Serious drug involvement and high delinquency rates. In R. Dembo (Ed.), *Drugs and crime* (pp. 1–25). Lanham, MD: University Press of America.

Johnston, L. D., O'Malley, P. M., and Bachman, J. G. (1993). *Drug use among high school seniors, college students and young adults, 1975–1990* (NIH Publication No. 93-3597). Washington, DC: U.S. Department of Health and Human Services.

Kandel, D. B., Simcha-Fagan, O., and Davies, M. (1986). Risk factors for delinquency and illicit drug use from adolescence to young adulthood. *Journal of Drug Issues, 16,* 67–90.

Klofas, J. M. (1993). Drugs and justice: The impact of drugs on criminal justice in a metropolitan community. *Crime and Delinquency, 39,* 204–224.

Kolb, L. (1925, January). Drug addiction in its relation to crime. *Journal of Mental Hygiene,* pp. 74–89.

Kolb, L., and Du Mez, A. G. (1924, May 23). The prevalence and trend of drug addiction in the United States and factors influencing it. *Public Health Reports.*

Kozel, N. J., and DuPont, R. L. (1977). *Criminal charges and drug use patterns of arrestees in the District of Columbia.* Washington, DC: U.S. Government Printing Office.

King, R. (1974). The American system: Legal sanctions to repress drug abuse. In J. A. Inciardi and C. D. Chambers (Eds.), *Drugs and the criminal justice system* (pp. 17–37). Beverly Hills, CA: Sage.

Lichtenstein, P. M. (1914, November 14). Narcotic addiction. *New York Medical Journal,* pp. 962–966.

Lindesmith, A. R. (1965). *The addict and the law.* Bloomington, IN: Indiana University Press.

Liska, K. (1990). *Drugs and the human body.* New York: Macmillan.

McBride, D. C. (1976). The relationship between type of drug use and arrest charge in an arrested population. In Research Triangle Institute (Ed.), *Drug use and crime* (pp. 409–418). Springfield, VA: National Technical Information Service.

McBride, D. C., Burgman-Habermehl, C., Alpert, J., and Chitwood, D. D. (1986). Drugs and homicide. *Bulletin of the New York Academy of Medicine, 62,* 497–508.

McBride, D. C., and Inciardi, J. A. (1990). AIDS and the IV drug user in the criminal justice system. *Journal of Drug Issues, 20,* 267–280.

McBride, D. C., and McCoy, C. B. (1981). Crime and drug using behavior. An areal analysis. *Criminology, 19,* 281–302.

McBride, D. C., and McCoy, C. B. (1982). Crime and drugs: The issues and literature. *Journal of Drug Issues, 12,* 137–151.

McBride, D. C., and Swartz, J. (1990). Drugs and violence in the age of crack cocaine. In R. A. Weisheit (Ed.), *Drugs, crime and the criminal justice system* (American Academy of Criminal Justice Series, pp. 141–169). Cincinnati, OH: Anderson.

McGlothlin, W. (1979). Drugs and crime. In R. L. DuPont, A. Goldstein, and J. A. O'Donnell (Eds.), *Handbook on drug abuse* (pp. 357–364). Washington, DC: National Institute on Drug Abuse, Office of Drug Abuse Policy.

Musto, D. F. (1973). *The American disease.* New Haven, CT: Yale University Press.

Nadelmann, E. A. (1989, September). Drug prohibition in the United States, costs, consequences, and alternatives. *Science,* pp. 939–947.

O'Donnell, J. A., Voss, H. L., Clayton, R. R., Slatin, G. T., and Room, R. G. W. (1976). *Young men and drugs—A national survey* (National Institute on Drug Abuse Research Monograph 5). Washington, DC: U.S. Government Printing Office.

Rossi, P. H., Waite, E., Bose, C. E., and Berk, R. E. (1974). The seriousness of crimes: Normative structure and individual differences. *American Sociological Review, 31,* 324–337.

Simonds, J. F., and Kashani, J. (1980). Specific drug use and violence in delinquent boys. *American Journal of Drug and Alcohol Abuse, 7,* 305–322.

Sloman, L. (1979). *Reefer madness: A history of marijuana in America.* Indianapolis: Bobbs-Merrill.

Spunt, B. J., Goldstein, P. J., Bellucci, P. A., and Miller, T. (1990). Race/ethnic and gender differences in the drugs–violence relationship. *Journal of Psychoactive Drugs, 22,* 293–303.

Stephens, R. C. (1991). *The street addict role.* New York: State University of New York Press.

Stephens, R. C., and Ellis, R. D. (1975). Narcotic addicts and crime: An analysis of recent trends. *Criminology, 12,* 474–488.

Stephens, R. C., and McBride, D. C. (1976). Becoming a street addict. *Human Organization, 35,* 87–93.

Terry, C. E., and Pellens, M. (1928). *The opium problem.* New York: Bureau of Social Hygiene.

Trebach, A. S., and Inciardi, J. A. (1993). *Legalize it? Debating American drug policy.* Washington, DC: American University Press.

U.S. Department of Justice, Federal Bureau of Investigation. (1993). *Uniform crime reports.* Washington, DC: U.S. Government Printing Office.

U.S. Treasury Department, Bureau of Narcotics. (1939). *Traffic in opium and other dangerous drugs.* Washington, DC: U.S. Government Printing Office.

Vigdal, G. L., and Stadler, D. W. (1989, June). Controlling inmate drug use: Cut consumption by reducing demand. *Corrections Today,* pp. 96–97.

Voss, H. L., and Stephens, R. C. (1973). Criminal history of narcotic addicts. *Drug Forum, 2,* 191–202.

Young, J. H. (1967). *The medical messiahs: A social history of health quackery in twentieth-century America.* Princeton, NJ: Princeton University Press.

Wilson, J. Q. (1993). Against the legalization of drugs. In R. Goldberg (Ed.), *Taking sides* (p. 25). Guildford, CT: Dushkin.

Wish, E. D. (1987). *Drug use forecasting: New York 1984–1986.* Washington, DC: U.S. Department of Justice.

Zahn, M. A., and Bencivengo, M. (1974). Violent death: A comparison between drug users and non drug users. *Addictive Diseases, 1,* 293–298.

Addiction Careers and Criminal Specialization

DAVID FARABEE

VANDANA JOSHI

M. DOUGLAS ANGLIN

ABSTRACT

For many drug users, the initiation of drug use and the subsequent transition to an addiction career is accompanied by criminal activities. However, the use of general crime and drug use categories often obscures important features of their relationship. In the present study, data from the national Drug Abuse Treatment Outcome Studies sample of 7,189 clients in substance abuse treatment were analyzed to explore the relationships between several addiction career variables and the likelihood of lifetime participation in predatory, victimless, and nonspecialized criminal behaviors. The order of initiation of addiction and criminal careers was significantly related to participation in certain types of crimes, with those beginning criminal careers after beginning their addiction careers being more likely to engage exclusively in victimless than in predatory crimes. Likewise, dependence on cocaine, heroin, or both, relative to alcohol, was associated with greater criminal diversity but a reduced likelihood of participating specifically in predatory crimes.

Although there is a considerable amount of research concerning the drug–crime relationship, many studies emphasize the prevalence of these behaviors during a specific time period (typically centered around incarceration or treatment) rather than their long-term patterns of interaction (Fishbein and Reuland, 1994; National Institute of Justice, 1997; Rajkumar and French, 1997). These time-specific approaches are likely to produce biased results because rates of both criminal activity and drug use tend to be atypically high during the months immediately preceding treatment and/or incarceration (Anglin and McGlothlin, 1984). [1]

Over the past 15 years, criminologists have devoted increasing attention to longitudinal, individual-level patterns of criminality (Holden, 1986). Two important observations have emerged from this line

[1]This work was supported by the National Institute on Drug Abuse (NIDA) (Grant U01-DA10378) as part of a cooperative agreement on the Drug Abuse Treatment Outcome Study (DATOS). The project includes a coordinating DATOS research center (Robert L. Hubbard, principal investigator at the National Development and Research Institutes) and two collaborating research centers (M. Douglas Anglin, principal investigator at the University of California, Los Angeles, and D. Dwayne Simpson, principal investigator at Texas Christian University) that conduct treatment evaluation studies in connection with NIDA (Bennett W. Fletcher, principal investigator at NIDA). Barry S. Brown chairs the DATOS Steering Committee and oversees the internal review process for publications. Dr. Anglin is also supported by NIDA research scientist development awards (K02-DA00146). The interpretations and conclusions in this article do not necessarily represent the positions of the other DATOS research centers, NIDA, or the Department of Health and Human Services.

of research: Early onset of criminal activity is one of the strongest predictors of criminal severity, and frequent criminality is positively correlated with high levels of drug and alcohol use (Blumstein and Cohen, 1987). However, although there is substantial evidence that the onset of, or an increase in, drug use often serves to intensify rates of criminal activity (Ball, Rosen, Flueck, and Nurco, 1981), criminal activity often persists beyond the addiction career (Nurco, Hanlon, Kinlock, and Duszynski, 1988).[1] Thus, the nature of interacting addiction and criminal careers is complex and merits further study.

The general drug-crime association is relatively well established. High levels of lifetime drug use are reported among incarcerated populations (Center on Addiction and Substance Abuse, 1998). Similarly, cocaine users and narcotic users are far more likely than non–drug users to report involvement in criminal activity (Anglin and Speckart, 1988; Nurco et al., 1988). Further exploration of their criminal activity reveals considerable diversity in the criminal patterns of drug-abusing offenders. For example, a majority of drug abusers report drug sales as their primary illegal activity, but a substantial minority also report engaging in nondrug crimes such as burglary or robbery (Ball, Schaffer, and Nurco, 1983). More specifically, in a study of criminally active youths in Miami, participation in the crack trade (relative to drug sales in general) was shown to have a particularly criminogenic effect (Inciardi and Pottieger, 1991). Conversely, there is evidence that increased criminal involvement may serve to intensify drug use, either by further enhancing commitment to an illicit lifestyle or by providing additional money to support higher levels of use (Hser, Chou, and Anglin, 1990).

According to Hagan and Palloni's (1988) "life course" perspective of criminal involvement, knowledge of the order in which delinquent acts are committed is crucial in understanding the ultimate life course and impact of criminal trajectories. Indeed, drug-involved offenders show substantial variation in the trajectories of their criminal activity, with early onset and high severity of drug use being associated with both greater intensity and higher levels of persistence (Nurco, Kinlock, and Balter, 1993).

But, a clearer delineation of the relationship between drug use and crime requires descriptions of not only their overall co-occurrence but also the specific drug use and criminal patterns that define their relationship. Combined, the aggregated facets of addiction and criminal career profiles can provide important clues regarding the extent to which the two activities relate to, and potentially augment, each other.

The goal of the present study, therefore, was to further specify the relationship between addiction and criminal careers using empirically and theoretically justified categories of criminal and drug use behaviors. The rationales for these measures are discussed below.

Measurement of Criminal Activity

To accurately measure criminal behavior, a number of important features must be taken into consideration. As mentioned above, rates of criminal behavior tend to be atypically high during the period immediately preceding incarceration or drug abuse treatment (Anglin and McGlothlin, 1984). Consequently, estimates of an in-treatment or incarcerated offender's criminal career based on past-year criminal behaviors are likely to be inflated. Such an approach also excludes basic information about the etiology of the offender's criminal career, such as the age of initiation and more typical rates of criminal activity (Blumstein and Cohen, 1987) averaged over the life course. Lifetime crime patterns, however, allow for the exploration of both the genesis of criminal careers and their intensity and diversity over the long term.

A more accurate measurement of criminal behavior also requires that a distinction be made between participation in a particular type of crime and the frequency with which these crimes are committed. Because not all drug users are involved in nondrug criminal activity, criminal participation (as opposed to frequency) should be the dependent measure of interest if the goal is to identify factors involved in the transition from drug use to other forms of criminality. The alternative strategy of predicting criminal involvement as a continuum, with noncriminals coded 0, addresses a qualitatively different issue, given that the factors predicting participation are often quite different from those that predict frequency (Blumstein and Cohen, 1987). Although both measures are of interest, they represent different phenomena and should be examined separately.

A final measurement consideration relates to the nature of the crimes committed. Although few criminals specialize in a narrow category of crime (Simon, 1997), there is a tendency for long-term offenders (particularly White offenders) to engage in more specialized and more serious crimes as they grow older (Blumstein, Cohen, Das, and Moitra, 1988). Furthermore, there does appear to be a distinction between victimless and predatory offenders.

Based on a review of the criminological literature, a number of characteristics have been identified that reliably distinguish victimless and predatory offenders (Ellis, 1988). Relative to victimless offenders, predatory offenders are more likely to be poor, urban, African American, and male, and to have been raised in single-parent households. Hence, although most criminals do not limit their criminal repertoires to a specific type of crime, there is some empirical justification for grouping them into broader categories of victimless, predatory, and nonspecialized (i.e., both victimless and predatory) criminal behaviors. There is also an intuitive justification for these categories with regard to the different types and levels of societal costs they present.

Measurement of Substance Use

Just as our understanding of criminal behavior is often obscured by oversimplified categories, so is the concept of problematic drug use. Drugs vary substantially in their pharmacological properties, addiction potentials, and costs. Thus, although it is important to note that 50% to 80% of arrestees in major U.S. cities test positive for illicit drugs (National Institute of Justice, 1997), the variations within the "drug" category are often underplayed, and their specific associations with other forms of criminal behavior are lost in the generalization. In their analysis of the 1991 National Household Survey on Drug Abuse, Harrison and Gfroerer (1992) found that respondents reporting past-year alcohol, cannabis, and cocaine use were nearly twice as likely to have committed violent or property crimes during that period than were respondents reporting only alcohol and cannabis use. Likewise, in a comparison of heroin users and crack users, Inciardi and Pottieger (1994) found that crack users had committed their first crimes at younger ages and were much more likely to be involved in the drug trade. In addition, whereas male heroin users were more likely than female heroin users to have ever been incarcerated, there were no significant gender differences among crack users. Thus, collapsing across drug categories provides a convenient, but often inaccurate, measure of substance use as it relates to other forms of criminality.

The second drug-use measurement consideration concerns severity. When specifying the drug–crime relationship, it is important to distinguish between casual and problematic use, particularly with regard to lifetime drug-use careers. The American Psychiatric Association's (1994) *Diagnostic and Statistical Manual of Mental Disorders (4th Edition) (DSM-IV)* defines dependence as the presence of cognitive, behavioral (compulsive use), and physiological (including tolerance and withdrawal) symptoms indicating continued use of a psychoactive drug despite negative consequences. Substance dependence, therefore, clearly holds different implications for criminal behavior than occasional use or even abuse. For example, in a study of male and female prison inmates, the severity of drug-related problems was the single best predictor of past-year violent and property crime rates, particularly for female inmates (McClellan, Farabee, and Crouch, 1997).

In the current study, we sought to build on these conceptual advancements in the fields of drug abuse and criminological research. In doing so, we hoped to describe more accurately the subgroups of drug-involved offenders and to uncover the variations within the general drug–crime relationship.

To this end, the present study was undertaken to explore the lifetime patterns of addiction and criminal behaviors of a nationwide sample of clients entering community-based substance abuse treatment. The first phase of analysis is devoted to describing various aspects of respondents' criminal careers (e.g., age committed first illegal act, age at first arrest, number of illegal acts committed, types of illegal acts committed) and addiction careers (e.g., age first used any illicit drug, age of first regular use, number of drugs used). In the second phase, respondents reporting lifetime participation rates in predatory,[2] victimless, and nonspecialized criminal behaviors are profiled using multinomial logistic regression. In the third phase, ordinary least squares regression is used to model overall diversity in the types of lifetime crimes committed and the frequencies of victimless and predatory crimes. Lastly, four sets of regressions are conducted to compare predictors of any participation versus the frequencies of participation in predatory and victimless crimes.

METHOD

Overview of Drug Abuse Treatment Outcome Study Data Collection

The Drug Abuse Treatment Outcome Study (DATOS) is a comprehensive, multisite, prospective study of drug treatment effectiveness. A total of 10,010 DATOS clients were interviewed at entry to treatment in a sample of 96 programs in 11 cities in the United States from 1991 to 1993. Cities and programs were purposively chosen for participation; these programs were typical of stable drug treatment programs in large and medium-size U.S. cities. Clients were selected from four drug treatment modalities that were seen as reflecting the current treatment system: 3,122 clients from 14 short-term inpatient programs, 2,774 clients from 21 long-term residential programs, 1,540 clients from 29 outpatient methadone treatment programs, and 2,574 clients from 32 outpatient drug-free programs.

The initial interviews for DATOS data used in this analysis were conducted by a staff of 107 professional interviewers who were hired, trained, and supervised by a staff of survey supervisors based at the Research Triangle Institute.

Sample

Two-thirds (66%) of the DATOS sample was male. The mean age was 32.6 years ($SD = 7.6$). Almost half of the participants (47%) were African American, 38% were White, 13% were Hispanic, and the remaining 3% were either Asian or classified as "other." About 77% had ever committed an illegal activity and ever been arrested, and 44% entered DATOS treatment under criminal justice supervision.

Measures

The DATOS questionnaire was a careful compilation of standardized measures used in the field of drug abuse treatment (see Flynn, Craddock, Hubbard, Anderson, and Etheridge, 1997). The final composition of the measures was reviewed and recommended by a panel of experts representing each domain covered in the interview. Although more objective accounts of long-term drug use and criminal patterns would be preferable, no such data exist that would provide the level of detail required for the analyses presented here.

The analyses addressing the variations within the drug–crime relationship were limited to participants who reported ever having engaged in any illicit activity. These included aggravated assault, burglary, theft, robbery, dealing in stolen property, pimping or prostitution, or selling illegal drugs. This reduced the final analysis sample from 10,010 to 7,189.[3]

The measurement and classification of criminal acts were based on a conceptual scheme that distinguished between predatory, victimless, and nonspecialized (i.e., both predatory and victimless) lifetime criminal patterns. Although prior research has supported this distinction among offenders (Ellis, 1988), a varimax-rotated factor analysis was conducted to empirically confirm the underlying structure of the seven lifetime criminal acts mentioned above.

Factor analysis of self-reported lifetime involvement in the seven types of criminal behaviors listed resulted in a two-factor solution. The first factor primarily comprised predatory criminal behaviors such as burglary, theft, and assault. The second factor was dominated by drug sales and pimping or prostitution (also referred to as consensual crimes because the victim is a willing participant in the offense; see Hunt, 1990).

The major domains of interest for the present study are summarized below:

Demographics. Demographics included standard variables such as sex (male = 1), ethnicity, age, and marital status (ever married = 1).

Addiction Career

Mean Age Began Regular Use of Any Drugs. The age of first regular drug use, rather than any use or greater than weekly use, was chosen as the age of initiation of one's addiction career to distinguish between experimental use, which is by no means uncommon in the general population (Wills, McNamara, Vaccaro, and Hirky, 1996), and the onset of regular—albeit not necessarily problematic— drug use. This was measured as first regular use (i.e., at least once a week) of any illicit drug, including marijuana, cocaine, heroin, narcotics, sedatives, amphetamines, hallucinogens, and inhalants. Ages of onset ranged from 7 to 54 years, with fewer than 2% of the clients reporting an age of first weekly use greater than 31 years.

Drug Dependence. Clients were classified based on the DSM-III-R lifetime dependence criterion specifying combinations for drug dependence on cocaine only, heroin only, cocaine and heroin, and alcohol only. The remaining combinations were classified in the "other" category.[4]

Drugs Before Crime. Clients who reported an age of first use of any drug prior to the age of first illegal activity were coded 1. Because very few cases reported the same age for first use of any drug and first illegal activity, they were also coded 1; otherwise, they were coded 0.

Treatment Utilization

Age at First Drug Treatment.   This was measured in continuous years and ranged from 7 to 74, with fewer than 5% of the clients reporting an age at first drug treatment greater than 42 years.

Number of Treatment Episodes.   This variable measured the number of times individuals had entered drug treatment prior to entering DATOS treatment and ranged from 0 to 75, with fewer than 2% reporting 13 or more prior drug treatments.

Total Weeks in Treatment.   This variable measured the number of weeks individuals had stayed in drug treatment prior to DATOS and ranged from 0 to 1,003.

Years of Treatment Career.   This was calculated based on the client's current age minus the age at which he or she entered the first drug treatment (excluding DATOS) and ranged from 0 to 40 years.

Criminal Career

Entered DATOS Treatment Under Criminal Justice Supervision.   Clients were coded 1 for being under criminal justice supervision if they were in jail, on probation, on parole, or if their cases were pending at the time of DATOS treatment entry; otherwise, they were coded 0.

Ever Arrested.   Clients were coded 1 if they had ever been arrested and 0 otherwise.

Crime Type.   Because the present study primarily sought to identify factors associated with drug abusers' participation (rather than level of involvement) in other forms of criminality, we created a lifetime criminal participation variable based on the factor structure of criminal acts. Specifically, DATOS clients were classified as having committed only predatory crimes, only victimless crimes, or nonspecialized (i.e., both predatory and victimless) crimes during their lifetimes.

Age First Illegal Act.   The ages at which clients first committed any of the above-mentioned seven illegal acts were measured in continuous years. They ranged from 7 to 53 years, with fewer than 2% of the clients reporting an age of first illegal act greater than 38 years.

Age First Arrest.   The ages at which the clients reported their first arrests ranged from 7 to 55 years.

Annualized Crime Rate.   Annualized crime rates were calculated based on the sum of lifetime frequency estimates for each of the seven crime types divided by the difference in the client's current age and his or her age of first criminal act. The DATOS clients had an average crime rate of 1.4 crimes per year. As is typically the case with criminal activity, there was substantial variation in these rates (ranging from 0.001 to 39 crimes per year), with a median annual crime rate of only 0.30. However, the distribution was also positively skewed, with the top 10% of the sample averaging between 5 and 39 crimes per year.

Analytic Approach

The first of the series of analyses below were conducted to describe the criminal and addiction careers of DATOS clients at the univariate and bivariate levels. One-way analyses of variance and *t* tests were used to test for significance between group means; chi-square tests were used for nominal variables. Once these basic relationships were established, multinomial logistic regression was used to model multiple-outcome processes (i.e., participation in predatory, victimless, or nonspecialized criminal activities).

Multiple-outcome processes can be modeled in two ways, using either a "two-step" or "competing risks" model estimated through a multinomial logistic regression. In a two-step model, one can first model the occurrence of an event, in this case, any criminal activity. In the second step, one would model which event (specific crime category) occurred, conditional on whether any event (crime) had occurred. However, the two-step model is inappropriate when the two steps are intertwined. If the two processes or multiple outcomes cannot be separated because the determinants of moving from one category to another are likely to vary with changes in the types of moves made, then the competing risks model is more appropriate (Allison, 1984). The determinants of the different crime categories were expected to vary depending on which crime was committed; hence, a competing risks model using multinomial logistic regression was chosen. The logistic procedure also requires fewer assumptions of the data than multiple discriminant analysis (Hosmer and Lemeshow, 1989).

Finally, two sets of multiple regressions were conducted. The first model predicts the number of different types of crimes committed as a function of the same addiction career variables employed in the multinomial models. The second set, which consists of four regressions, was conducted to determine the consistency of these same predictors in predicting participation in and frequencies of predatory and victimless criminal acts.

RESULTS

Criminal Careers of DATOS Clients

At its simplest level, the structure of a criminal career can be partitioned into three factors: age at initiation, mean number of crimes committed per year, and age at termination (Blumstein and Cohen, 1987). Although criminal career termination dates could not be reliably ascertained from these data, the first two variables were available for those who had ever committed any illegal act. In addition, the DATOS baseline interview collected relatively detailed information regarding the types of crimes committed and their frequencies.

Limiting the sample to those reporting ever having committed the illegal acts defined above ($N = 7,189$), DATOS clients began their criminal careers at an average age of 19.8. Age of first criminal act was significantly lower for male clients ($M = 19.2$, $SD = 6.7$) than for female clients ($M = 21.7$, $SD = 7.2$; $t[4,066] = 14.6$, $p < .001$), and male clients reported significantly higher annualized crime rates ($M = 1.9$, $SD = 3.9$) than female clients ($M = 1.4$, $SD = 3.3$; $t[4,235] = -3.6$, $p < .001$). The late age of onset and the relatively low mean annualized crime frequencies are likely due to the fact that the participants in the present study were drawn from a national sample of clients in community-based drug treatment rather than directly from the criminal justice population. Furthermore, three types of criminal activity (driving under the influence, forgery, and gambling) were excluded from these analyses because of the difficulty in classifying them according to the predatory-victimless scheme that forms the basis of this study. Lastly, this rate may be lower because the estimates of average lifetime crime frequencies include periods of regular drug use as well as periods of lesser use.

Classification of DATOS clients according to their participation in any of the factor-based crime categories indicates that the largest category of clients (56.3%) had engaged in "nonspecialized criminal patterns" (i.e., both victimless and predatory), and about 43.7% reported some degree of criminal specialization, with 25.5% having engaged only in predatory crimes and 18.2% reporting that they had engaged exclusively in victimless crimes.

For the present study, the initiation of an addiction career was defined as the age of first weekly use of any illicit drug. On average, DATOS clients began their addiction careers shortly before their 18th birthdays ($M = 16.9$ years, $SD = 4.9$), with male clients beginning at a significantly younger age ($M = 16.6$, $SD = 4.6$) than female clients ($M = 17.8$, $SD = 5.4$; $t[5,749] = 11.8$, $p < .001$). In spite of some slight variations, the primary substances of dependence were similar for both sexes, with 62.4% meeting the *DSM-III-R* dependence criteria for cocaine only, 13.9% for heroin only, 10.7% for heroin and cocaine, and 6.4% for alcohol. The remaining 6.6% either did not meet the criteria for dependence or were dependent on other substances.

Not counting the current treatment episode, DATOS clients had received substance abuse treatment an average of 2.2 times, with female clients reporting a slightly higher number of prior treatment episodes ($M = 2.4$, $SD = 4.3$; $t[9,932] = 2.1$, $p < .05$) than male clients ($M = 2.0$, $SD = 4.0$) and a greater number of total weeks in treatment ($M = 36.2$, $SD = 94.7$; $t[6,622] = 2.0$, $p < .05$) than male clients ($M = 29.3$, $SD = 84.4$).

Given our emphasis on the interaction of criminal and addiction careers, a variable of particular interest was the order of initiation of regular drug use and other forms of criminal activity. Overall, 86.9% of the DATOS clients who had engaged in both regular drug use and crime began with the former. Female clients (89.2%) were significantly more likely than male clients (85.9%) to have begun regular drug use prior to engaging in other forms of criminal behavior, $\chi^2(1, N = 6,965) = 18.2$, $p < .001$.

Although the sample characteristics for demographics, addiction variables, and criminal career variables vary significantly by dependence category, a few bivariate and univariate contrasts are worth noting. With regard to the addiction career variables, clients who were dependent on both heroin and cocaine began using drugs regularly at a significantly younger age than those in the other dependence categories (see also Anglin, Hser, and Grella, 1997). Among male clients, those who were heroin dependent were more likely than those in any of the other dependence groups to have begun their criminal careers after they had begun weekly illicit drug use. Regardless of gender, dependence on both cocaine and heroin was also associated with the likelihood of ever having committed an illegal act and ever having been arrested.

For both male and female clients, dependence on cocaine, heroin, or both was associated with an increased likelihood of being classified in the nonspecialized crime category. Those who were alcohol dependent only were more likely to be classified in the noncriminal category than in any of the other three crime categories.

Addiction Patterns and Participation in the Factor-Based Crime Categories

Because the five dependence categories differed substantially in demographic composition as well as in their criminal and addiction profiles, the next stage of analysis relied on multivariate procedures to isolate the specific associations between addiction career variables and the likelihood of participating in one of the factor-based crime categories.

Table 1 shows log odds and odds ratios for three multinomial logistic regression models predicting the likelihood of participating in predatory versus victimless crimes, predatory versus nonspecialized crimes, and nonspecialized versus victimless crimes. It is interesting to note that across all three of the models, gender was the only consistent demographic predictor. The other demographic controls made only modest contributions to our ability to accurately classify DATOS clients by crime category. In contrast, the addiction career variables proved quite powerful in distinguishing crime categories across all three models.

The first model in Table 1 compares DATOS clients who had participated exclusively in predatory versus victimless crimes. Relative to victimless offenders, predatory offenders tended to be older, male, to have begun using drugs regularly at a younger age, and to have initiated their criminal careers prior to initiating their addiction careers. Predatory offenders also reported having more prior episodes of substance abuse treatment and were less likely to be dependent on cocaine only, heroin only, cocaine and heroin combined, or other illicit drugs as compared with alcohol. Put differently, dependence on alcohol only (the reference group for the substance-dependent variables) was the only dependence category positively associated with exclusive participation in predatory versus victimless crimes.

The second model compares predatory offenders with those engaging in both predatory and victimless (nonspecialized) crimes. As in the first model, predatory offenders were more likely than nonspecialized offenders to be male. Predatory offenders also tended to have begun regular illicit drug use later in

TABLE 1   Multinomial Logistic Results Predicting Participation in Predatory, Victimless, and Nonspecialized Crimes (n = 6,588)

| | CRIME CATEGORY | | | | | |
| | PREDATORY VERSUS VICTIMLESS | | PREDATORY VERSUS NONSPECIALIZED | | NONSPECIALIZED VERSUS VICTIMLESS | |
VARIABLE	Log Odds	Odds Ratio	Log Odds	Odds Ratio	Log Odds	Odds Ratio
Age	0.02	1.02**	−0.01	0.99	0.03	1.03***
Male (reference = female)	0.73	2.08**	0.19	1.21**	0.53	1.70***
Ethnicity (reference = White)						
African American	0.14	1.15	0.00	1.00	0.14	1.15
Hispanic	−0.28	0.76*	−0.07	0.93	−0.21	0.81
Other	0.20	1.22	−0.17	0.84	0.37	1.45
Ever married	0.03	1.03	0.07	1.07	−0.03	0.97
High school degree	−0.09	0.91	−0.06	0.94	−0.02	0.98
Age began regular drug use	−0.02	0.98**	0.02	1.02**	−0.04	0.96***
Drugs before crime	−1.44	0.24**	−0.48	0.62***	−0.96	0.38***
Number of drug treatments	0.05	1.05**	−0.02	0.98**	0.07	1.07***
Drug dependence						
Cocaine	−0.33	0.72*	−0.69	0.50***	0.36	1.43*
Cocaine and heroin	−0.55	0.58**	−0.93	0.39***	0.38	1.46*
Heroin	−0.48	0.62**	−0.85	0.43***	0.37	1.45*
Other drug	−0.48	0.62*	−0.37	0.69***	−0.12	0.89
Age of first illegal activity	0.01	1.01	0.10	1.11***	−0.09	0.91***

−2log likelihood = −5877.45, $p < .001$

*$p < .05$. **$p < .01$. ***$p < .001$.

life and to have had fewer prior episodes of substance abuse treatment. Consistent with the first model, predatory offenders were less likely than nonspecialized offenders to have initiated their addiction careers prior to their criminal careers. Moreover, dependence on alcohol was associated with a greater probability of predatory versus nonspecialized crime participation relative to illicit drug dependence.

The third model predicts the likelihood of participating in nonspecialized crime versus only victimless crimes. As shown in Table 1, nonspecialized offenders tended to be older and were more likely to be male than victimless offenders. Nonspecialized offenders initiated regular illicit drug use at younger ages and were less likely than victimless offenders to have begun their addiction careers prior to their criminal careers. The likelihood of participating in nonspecialized crimes versus only victimless crimes was positively associated with dependence on cocaine only, heroin only, and cocaine and heroin combined, relative to dependence on only alcohol. Nonspecialized offenders also began their criminal careers at younger ages than victimless offenders.

Addiction Patterns and Criminal Diversity

Because the models in Table 1 suggest that substance dependence is more closely associated with nonspecialized crime than with specialized crime, an ordinary least squares regression was conducted to predict the number of different types of crimes committed as a function of the same addiction career variables employed in the multinomial models. The dependent measure for this model was the number of types of crimes in which DATOS clients reported participating during their lifetimes (as above, the sample was limited to those reporting any lifetime criminal involvement). The types of crimes consisted of aggravated assault, burglary, theft, robbery, dealing in or fencing stolen property, pimping or prostitution, and selling illegal drugs.

As shown in Table 2, the diversity of criminal involvement was significantly associated with a number of demographic and addiction career variables, with the overall model accounting for 23% of the variance. Increased criminal diversity was positively associated with age, being male, and being White. With regard to the addiction career predictors, increased criminal diversity was strongly and positively associated with dependence on either cocaine only or cocaine and heroin combined, relative to dependence on only alcohol. Engaging in regular drug use prior to

initiating one's criminal career was associated with less criminal diversity, as was beginning regular drug use at a later age. In other words, although dependence on cocaine only and cocaine and heroin combined were associated with participating in a broader array of crimes relative to alcohol dependence, the primacy of an addiction career over a criminal career was associated with reduced criminal diversity.

The final set of regressions contrasted predictors of any participation versus frequency of participation in the criminal acts making up the predatory and victimless crime categories. Unlike the multinomial logistic regressions, presented in Table 1, these categories were not mutually exclusive. In other words, rather than attempting to predict membership in either the predatory, victimless, or nonspecialized categories, these final models predicted participation (dichotomous) and frequency of participation (continuous) in predatory and victimless crimes for the entire sample of criminally involved DATOS clients.

The log odds ratios predicting any participation and the standardized coefficients predicting frequency of participation are presented in Table 3. Because the logistic and least squares models provide different types of estimates, the most appropriate comparisons between these models must be based on the statistical significance and direction of the relationships of the predictor variables and their respective dependent measures. Consistent with the criminal careers perspective, the predictors of participation and frequency of participation in the two crime categories are not always the same. For example, although the drug dependence measures are not significant predictors of any participation in predatory crimes, they are positively associated with the frequency of participation.

For victimless crimes, however, the results are mixed: Cocaine dependence was positively related to both participation and frequency, but dependence on cocaine and heroin combined attained significance only for the frequency of participation. Likewise, engaging in regular drug use prior to initiating a criminal career was negatively related to participation in predatory crimes and positively related to participation in victimless crimes, but this variable was not a significant predictor of the frequency of participation in either crime category. Other predictors, however, did show a consistent relationship across the models. For instance, being male was negatively related to both participation and frequency of participation in victimless crimes.

TABLE 2   Ordinary Least Squares Regression Predicting Number of the Seven Types of Illegal Activities Ever Committed (n = 5,805)

VARIABLE	UNSTANDARDIZED COEFFICIENT	STANDARDIZED COEFFICIENT
Age	0.03	0.12***
Male (reference = female)	0.27	0.08***
Ethnicity (reference = White)		
African American	0.11	0.03*
Hispanic	0.00	0.00
Other	0.33	0.03***
Ever married	–0.02	0.00
High school degree	–0.03	–0.01
Age began weekly use of any drug	–0.03	–0.10***
Used drug before crime	–0.16	–0.03*
Number of drug treatments	0.04	0.09***
Drug dependence		
Cocaine	0.48	0.14***
Cocaine and heroin	0.72	0.13***
Heroin	0.39	0.08***
Other drug	0.17	0.02
Age of first illegal activity	–0.10	–0.40***
Intercept	3.6***	
R^2	0.23	

*$p < .05$. **$p < .01$. ***$p < .001$.

SUMMARY

The primary goals of this study were (a) to describe the addiction and criminal careers of a national sample of substance abusers in community-based treatment and (b) to explore the relationships between several addiction career variables and the likelihood of lifetime participation in predatory, victimless, and nonspecialized criminal behaviors.

Of the 71.8% of DATOS clients who reported ever having committed an illegal act, the average age of initiation of a criminal career was 19.8 years. Overall, male clients tended to initiate their criminal careers earlier and to commit crimes at higher frequencies than female clients. The most common offender in the sample participated in both predatory and victimless crimes, but a plurality of the DATOS clients participated exclusively in one or the other.

On average, DATOS clients began their addiction careers before they initiated their criminal careers (86.9%), which exceeds other estimates in the literature most likely because ours was a treatment-based sample. Given that our drug–crime sample consisted of substance abusers who had also committed at least one illegal act, it is not surprising that drug use played an earlier (and perhaps more dominant) role in this study than has been reported in studies of offenders who also use illicit drugs. Among the general population, other forms of deviance or criminality typically precede the onset of illicit drug use (Apospori, Vega, Zimmerman, Warheit, and Gil, 1995).

Our series of multinomial logistic regressions showed a number of interesting distinctions in the addiction patterns of those participating in predatory, victimless, and nonspecialized crimes. Relative to victimless offenders, predatory offenders tended to begin their addiction careers at earlier ages but after they had already initiated their criminal careers. Predatory offenders, relative to either victimless or nonspecialized offenders, were also more likely to be dependent on alcohol only than on cocaine, heroin, or other illicit substances. This may be more aptly attributed to the strong association between alcohol and predatory crime rather than to a weak drug–crime relationship. This would certainly be the case for violent crime, which is much more closely associated with the use of alcohol than with the use of illicit drugs (Bureau of Justice Statistics, 1998). However, this effect must also be interpreted with regard to the construction of the crime categories. Because the predatory and victimless crime categories are mutually exclusive, the modest association between the illicit drug dependence categories and predatory (only) crimes may be due in part to the fact that illicit

TABLE 3 Comparison of Predictors for Any Participation (N = 7,189) and Frequency of Participation in Predatory[a] and Victimless[b] Crimes

VARIABLE	PARTICIPATION IN CRIME		FREQUENCY OF CRIME	
	Predatory Odds Ratio	Victimless Odds Ratio	Predatory β	Victimless β
Age	1.02***	0.99	.11***	.03
Male (reference = female)	1.96***	0.74***	−.02	−.05**
Ethnicity (reference = White)				
Black	1.04	1.02	−.09***	−.11***
Hispanic	0.77	0.98	−.03***	−.06***
Other	1.42	1.41*	.00	−.01
Ever married	0.94	0.94	.02	−.02
High school degree	0.95	1.12*	.05***	.02*
Age began weekly use of any drug	0.97***	1.01	−.05***	−.04**
Used drugs Before crime	0.47***	1.27***	−.01	.02
Number of drug treatments	1.05***	1.01	.07***	.00
Drug dependence				
Cocaine	1.05	1.32**	.09**	.08**
Cocaine and heroin	0.83	1.24	.13***	.06***
Heroin	0.87	1.27	.16***	.10**
Other drug	0.75	1.04	.00	.02
Age of first illegal activity	0.96***	0.97***	−.35***	−.16***
−2log likelihood	6421.82***	8331.15***		
R^2			.20	.06

a. n = 5,295.

b. n = 4,712.

*$p < .05$. **$p < .01$. ***$p < .001$.

drug dependence was associated with both predatory and victimless crimes. Our findings also suggest that offenders who segued into criminal careers via their addiction careers were more likely to participate in victimless than in predatory crimes. In contrast, substance-abusing offenders for whom criminal activity preceded regular drug use were at greater risk for participating exclusively in predatory crimes.

In contrast to victimless offenders, nonspecialized offenders were less likely to begin their addiction careers prior to their criminal careers and more likely to be dependent on illicit substances than on alcohol. The robustness of this finding across both models comparing either predatory-only or victimless-only offenders against nonspecialized offenders suggests a tendency for offenders who are dependent on cocaine, heroin, or both to show less criminal specialization. This assumption was supported in the final

least squares regression model, in which dependence on cocaine only and on cocaine and heroin combined (relative to alcohol dependence) was positively associated with the number of types of crimes committed.

A final interesting feature across the three multinomial logistic models was the minimal amount of variation accounted for by demographic and background variables. Addiction measures proved far superior in distinguishing between predatory, victimless, and nonspecialized offenders. This was particularly true of the dependence and order of initiation variables. Although the severity of illicit drug use problems was associated with an increased likelihood of participating in nonspecialized crime, the initiation of the criminal career before initiation of the addiction career was associated with an increased likelihood of engaging in predatory crimes and a decreased likelihood of engaging in victimless crimes.

DISCUSSION

The primary limitation of the present study is that the data are based on self-reports. Although more objective accounts of these sensitive behaviors would be preferable, no such data exist. Arrest records have been acknowledged to capture only a fraction of actual criminal activity (Huizinga and Elliott, 1986). Likewise, biological indicators of substance use (e.g., urinalysis, hair assays), unless collected longitudinally, cannot adequately measure long-term patterns of use, abuse, or dependence. The fact that these data were collected from a treatment sample, however, may be advantageous given that drug users who have received prior substance abuse treatment are more likely to disclose sensitive information such as drug use than untreated drug users (Amsel, Mandell, Mathias, Mason, and Lockerman, 1976; Farabee and Fredlund, 1996). Moreover, because the DATOS clients are not a statistically representative sample of the drug-using population at large, caution should be taken when generalizing these findings. Still, in spite of these limitations, we maintain that the large sample size and diverse content areas covered in DATOS provide a valuable opportunity for confirmatory analyses and preplanned hypothesis testing (Flynn et al., 1997).

The variation in addiction career parameters predicting classification in predatory, victimless, and nonspecialized offense categories underscores the need to move beyond simple generalizations regarding the drug–crime relationship. In fact, our data indicate that some forms of illicit drug dependence, when compared with alcohol dependence alone, are associated with reduced likelihood of participating exclusively in predatory crimes.

On the other hand, dependence on cocaine only or cocaine and heroin combined was significantly and positively related to the diversity of lifetime criminal patterns. Although our data did not allow us to empirically test the possible causes of this relationship, there are at least two plausible candidates. First, because illicit drugs cost substantially more than alcohol, supporting one's addiction to the former requires more income, whether licit or illicit. Thus, given that less than half of the DATOS sample reported full-time employment during the year prior to entering treatment (Craddock, Rounds-Bryant, Flynn, and Hubbard, 1997), the need for supplemental income sources is clear. The second possibility relates to the culture in which regular, illicit drug use is embedded. Illegal activities are rarely compartmentalized (Simon, 1997). As a result, engagement in one form of illegal activity often leads to engagement in other forms. Therefore, in addition to its direct links to income-generating crimes, illicit drug use may foster participation in a broader array of criminal activities through its attendant subcultural norms. Indeed, there is some evidence that addicts who are not criminally involved report much weaker subcultural affiliations than active criminal addicts (Byqvist and Olsson, 1998).

Likewise, the order in which addiction and criminal careers were initiated was significantly related to the types of crimes committed. Most notably, those who began committing crimes after initiating regular drug use were much less likely to engage in predatory (relative to victimless) crimes than those for whom criminality preceded regular drug use. That this relationship exists in spite of the fact that age of first illegal activity was not significant for the predatory–victimless comparison suggests that the route leading to one's criminal career may be more important than the age at which it begins. For the comparisons between predatory and nonspecialized crimes and nonspecialized and victimless crimes, however, age of first illegal activity did retain statistical significance.

Finally, the last set of logistic and least squares regression models predicting participation and frequency of predatory and victimless acts provides some support for the criminal careers perspective. That is, the predictors of any criminal participation were not always the same as the predictors of frequency of participation. Of particular interest was the relationship between drug dependence and predatory crime. Whereas the drug dependence measures were not predictive of ever engaging in a predatory criminal act (relative to alcohol dependence), these measures were significantly associated with the number of predatory crimes ever committed. In contrast, cocaine dependence was positively associated with both participation and frequency of participation in victimless crimes. Taken together, these findings provide further support for conceptualizing illicit drug dependence as an intensifying, rather than causal, factor in the commission of predatory crimes. However, for victimless crimes, our data suggest that regular illicit drug use and dependence may serve as both causal and intensifying factors.

Public discourse concerning the drug-crime nexus is often driven by atypical events and anecdotal accounts. Unfortunately, the result of this type of information is an overly simplistic view of both substance use and criminality. The present study contributes to a growing body of research suggesting the importance of the type, severity, and order of initiation of regular substance use in predicting criminal participation and diversity.

NOTES

1. It should be noted that the participants in the studies of Ball, Schaffer, and Nurco (1983) and Nurco, Hanlon, Kinlock, and Duszynski (1988) were primarily heroin abusers. However, multiple drug use, including alcohol, was also common among these participants. Thus, it is difficult to associate the use of individual substances with specific patterns of criminal behavior.

2. The term *predatory* as used in the present study is not limited to violent crimes; rather, it refers to crimes in which the "victim" is not a consenting participant, as contrasted with drug sales or prostitution.

3. Three hundred forty-seven participants did not complete crime data tear-off sheets and therefore were not included in the crime sample.

4. The "other" category includes those clients dependent on other substances as well as those not dependent on cocaine, heroin, or alcohol.

REFERENCES

Allison, P. (1984). *Event history analysis: Regression for longitudinal event data.* Thousand Oaks, CA: Sage.

American Psychiatric Association. (1994). *Diagnostic and statistical manual of mental disorders* (4th ed.). Washington, DC: Author.

Amsel, Z., Mandell, W., Mathias, L., Mason, C., and Lockerman, I. (1976). Reliability and validity of self-reported illegal activities and drug use collected from narcotics addicts. *International Journal of the Addictions, 11,* 325–336.

Anglin, M. D., Hser, Y. I., and Grella, C. E. (1997). Drug addiction and treatment careers among clients in the Drug Abuse Treatment Outcome Study (DATOS). *Psychology of Addictive Behaviors, 11*(4), 308–323.

Anglin, M. D., and McGlothlin, W. H. (1984). Outcome of narcotic addict treatment in California. In F. M. Tims and J. P. Ludford (Eds.), *Drug abuse treatment evaluation: Strategies, progress, and prospects* [NIDA Research Monograph No. 51], (pp. 106–128). Washington, DC: U.S. Government Press.

Anglin, M. D., and Speckart, G. (1988). Narcotics use and crime: A multisample, multimethod analysis. *Criminology, 26*(2), 197–233.

Apospori, E. A., Vega, W. A., Zimmerman, R. S., Warheit, G. J., and Gil, A. (1995). A longitudinal study of the conditional effects of deviant behavior on drug use among three racial/ethnic groups of adolescents. In H. B. Kaplan (Ed.) *Drugs, crime, and other deviant adaptations: Longitudinal studies* (pp. 211–230). New York: Plenum.

Ball, J. C., Rosen, L., Flueck, J. A., and Nurco, D. (1981). The criminality of heroin addicts: When addicted and when off opiates. In J. A. Inciardi (Ed.), *Drugs-crime connection* (pp. 39–65). Beverly Hills, CA: Sage.

Ball, J. C., Schaffer, J. W., and Nurco, D. (1983). The day-to-day criminality of heroin addicts in Baltimore—A study in the continuity of offense rates. *Drug and Alcohol Dependence, 12,* 119–142.

Blumstein, A., and Cohen, J. (1987). Characterizing criminal careers. *Science 237,* 985–991.

Blumstein, A., Cohen, J., Das, S., and Moitra, D. (1988). Specialization and seriousness during adult criminal careers. *Journal of Quantitative Criminology, 4,* 303–345.

Bureau of Justice Statistics. (1998). *Alcohol and crime.* Washington, DC: U.S. Department of Justice.

Byqvist, S., & Olsson, B. (1998). Male drug abuse, criminality and subcultural affiliation in a career perspective. *Journal of Psychoactive Drugs, 30*(1), 53–68.

Center on Addiction and Substance Abuse. (1998). *Behind bars: Substance abuse and America's prison population.* New York: Columbia University.

Craddock, S. G., Rounds-Bryant, J. L., Flynn, P. M., and Hubbard, R. L. (1997). Characteristics and pretreatment behaviors of clients entering drug abuse treatment: 1969 to 1993. *American Journal of Alcohol and Drug Abuse, 23*(1), 43–59.

Ellis, L. (1988). The predatory-victimless crime distinction, and seven universal demographic correlates of predatory criminal behavior. *Personality and Individual Differences, 9,* 525–548.

Farabee, D., and Fredlund, E. (1996). Self-reported drug use among recently admitted jail inmates: Estimating prevalence and treatment needs. *Substance Use and Misuse, 31*(4), 423–435.

Fishbein, D. H., and Reuland, M. (1994). Psychological correlates of frequency and type of drug use among jail inmates. *Addictive Behaviors, 19*(6), 583–598.

Flynn, P. M., Craddock, S. G., Hubbard, R. L., Anderson, J., and Etheridge, R. M. (1997). Methodological overview and research design for the Drug Abuse Treatment Outcome Study (DATOS). *Psychology of Addictive Behaviors, 11*(4), 230–243.

Hagan, J., and Palloni, A. (1988). Crimes as social events in the life course: Reconceiving a criminal controversy. *Criminology, 26,* 87–100.

Harrison, L., and Gfroerer, J. (1992). The intersection of drug use and criminal behavior. Results from the National Household Survey on Drug Abuse. *Crime and Delinquency, 38,* 422–443.

Holden, C. (1986). Growing focus on criminal careers. *Science, 233,* 1377–1378.

Hosmer, D. W., and Lemeshow, S. (1989). *Applied logistic regression.* New York: Wiley.

Hser, Y. I., Chou, C. P., and Anglin, M. D. (1990). The criminality of female narcotics addicts: A causal modeling approach. *Journal of Quantitative Criminology, 6,* 207–228.

Huizinga, D., and Elliott, D. S. (1986). Reassessing the reliability and validity of self-report delinquency measures. *Journal of Quantitative Criminology, 2*(4), 293–327.

Hunt, D. E. (1990). Drugs and consensual crimes: Drug dealing and prostitution. In M. Tonry and J. Wilson (Eds.), *Drugs and crime* (pp. 159–202). Chicago: University of Chicago Press.

Inciardi, J. A., and Pottieger, A. E. (1991). Kids, crack, and crime. *Journal of Drug Issues*, *21*(2), 257–270.

Inciardi, J. A., and Pottieger, A. E. (1994). Crack-cocaine use and street crime. *Journal of Drug Issues*, *24*, 273–292.

McClellan, D., Farabee, D., and Crouch, B. M. (1997). Early victimization, drug use, and criminality: A comparison of male and female prisoners. *Criminal Justice and Behavior*, *24*(4), 455–476.

National Institute of Justice. (1997). *1996 drug use forecasting: Annual report on adult and juvenile arrestees*. Washington, DC: Author.

Nurco, D. N., Hanlon, T. E., Kinlock, T. W., and Duszynski, K. R. (1988). Differential criminal patterns of narcotic addicts over an addiction career. *Criminology*, *26*, 407–423.

Nurco, D. N., Kinlock, T. W., and Balter, M. B. (1993). The severity of preaddiction criminal behavior among urban, male narcotic addicts and two non-addicted control groups. *Journal of Research in Crime and Delinquency*, *30*(3), 293–316.

Rajkumar, A. S., and French, M. (1997). Drug abuse, crime costs, and the economic benefits of treatment. *Journal of Quantitative Criminology*, *13*(3), 291–323.

Simon, L.M.J. (1997). Do criminal offenders specialize in crime types? *Applied and Preventive Psychology*, *6*, 35–53.

Wills, T. A., McNamara, G., Vaccaro, D., and Hirky, A. E. (1996). Escalated substance use: A longitudinal grouping analysis from early to middle adolescence. *Journal of Abnormal Psychology*, *105*, 166–180.

Research on Drugs–Crime Linkages: The Next Generation

ROBERT MACCOUN

BEAU KILMER

PETER REUTER

INTRODUCTION

The association between drugs and crime in the public mind is so strong that a recent psychology experiment showed the word "drug" tightly linked to such words as "choke," "knife," "fight," and "wound" in participants' associative memory networks (Bushman, 1996). Although it is routine in academia to deride public ignorance of all things criminological, in this case the public is hardly deluded. Consider the following facts:[1]

- Across 35 cities in 1998, between 40 and 80 percent of male arrestees in the Arrestee Drug Abuse Monitoring (ADAM) Program tested positive for at least one drug at arrest (Arrestee Drug Abuse Monitoring Program, 1999).
- Nearly one-quarter (22 percent) of Federal prison inmates and one-third (33 percent) of State prison inmates—nearly 40 percent of State inmates convicted of robbery, burglary, or motor vehicle theft—reported being under the influence of drugs at the time of their offense (Bureau of Justice Statistics, 1997a, 1997b).
- Among State and Federal prison inmates, 27 percent of those serving sentences for robbery and 30–32 percent of those serving sentences for burglary said they committed their offense to buy drugs (Bureau of Justice Statistics, 1991a, 1991b).
- In the 70 percent of cases in which the victim formed an opinion, 31 percent believed the offender was under the influence of drugs or alcohol (National Crime Victimization Survey, 2000).
- A recent estimate of the economic costs of drug abuse reported that 60 percent were associated with crime and criminal justice (Harwood, Fountain, and Livermore, 1998).

Considerable complexities and nuances underlie these associations. Although many of these subtleties were anticipated by astute observers in the 1970s (see Gandossy et al., 1980), the past decade has seen a solid scholarly consensus form around the following principles (see Fagan, 1990; Parker and Auerhahn, 1998; White and Gorman, 2000):

1. Many different data sources establish a raw correlation between drug use and other criminal offenses. But correlation does not equal causation: In principle, drug use might cause (promote, encourage) crime; criminality might cause (promote, encourage) drug use; and/or both might be caused (promoted, encouraged) by some set of "third variables"—environmental, situational, dispositional, and/or biological. In fact, all three pathways have empirical support in at least some settings and populations.
2. These causal influences are probabilistic, not deterministic. Most drug users are not otherwise criminally active, and the vast majority of drug-using incidents neither cause nor accompany

Research on Drugs-Crime Linkages: The Next Generation. September 2003. In *Toward a Drugs and Crime Research Agenda for the 21st Century* (NCJ 194616) (pages 65–95). National Institute of Justice. This and other NIJ publications can be found at and downloaded from the NIJ Web site (http://www.ojp.usdog.gov.nij.)

other forms of criminality. Nevertheless, drugs clearly play an important causal role in violent and property crime.

3. These causal influences are contingent, not unconditional. There is little evidence that drug use per se directly causes people to become aggressive in some direct and unconditional manner or that criminality per se causes someone to use drugs. The drugs–crime link varies across individuals, over time within an individual's development, across situations, and possibly over time periods (as a function of the dynamics of drug epidemics and, possibly, drug control policies).

4. That drug use can causally influence criminality does not necessarily implicate the psychopharmacological properties of the drug. Intoxication, the need or desire to raise money to buy drugs, and the nature of illicit markets are distinct mechanisms by which drugs can cause crime. Thus, drug prohibition cannot be only a *response* to drug-related crime, but it may also be a *causal antecedent* to some drug-related crime.

5. Alcohol is a drug, and it stimulates or augments a great deal of criminal behavior, almost certainly more than the street drugs combined.

We expect that understanding the considerable heterogeneity of effects across users, substances, cities, neighborhoods, and situations—and the interactions among these factors—will be the central focus of drugs–crime research during the remainder of this decade. This paper reviews the existing literature, focusing particular attention on Goldstein's (1985) taxonomy, the temporal dynamics of drug markets, and the consequences of prohibition. These highlight some of the questions that should drive this research.

DRUGS–CRIME LINKAGES: EXPANDING THE GOLDSTEIN TAXONOMY

Goldstein's Framework

Paul Goldstein's (1985) conceptual essay offered a tripartite classification of drugs–violence connections:

- **Psychopharmacological:** Violence due to the direct acute effects of a psychoactive drug on the user.
- **Economic-compulsive:** Violence committed instrumentally to generate money to purchase expensive drugs.

- **Systemic:** Violence associated with the marketing of illicit drugs, such as turf battles, contract disputes, and so on.

Goldstein and his colleagues (Brownstein et al., 1992; Goldstein et al., 1989; Goldstein, Brownstein, and Ryan, 1992) applied this scheme empirically to homicides in New York State (1984) and New York City (1988). They found that drugs and alcohol were important causes for a large share of all homicides in both samples. For 1988, near the height of the crack epidemic, they classified 53 percent of 414 homicides as drug or alcohol related; there was also a substantial percentage whose drug-relatedness could not be determined. Of those homicides that could be determined to be drug or alcohol related, 14 percent were psychopharmacological (68 percent alcohol, 16 percent crack), 4 percent were economic-compulsive, and 74 percent were systemic (61 percent crack, 27 percent powder cocaine). By contrast, in 1984, before the crack surge, only 42 percent of homicides were drug or alcohol related; 59 percent of those were psychopharmacological (79 percent alcohol), 3 percent were economic-compulsive, and 21 percent were systemic. The difference between the findings of the two years might reflect differences in geography to some extent (New York State versus New York City), but it also reminds us that these numbers are not eternal verities; they result from complex and historically dependent market dynamics.

Subsequent Applications

The generalizability of Goldstein et al.'s (1989) original findings was limited by their location (New York) and timing (the height of the crack explosion; see U.S. Sentencing Commission, 1995, 106).[2] Many studies have tried to determine whether crimes were drug related, but few have assessed whether the offender's drug need, drug use, or role in the drug market was directly responsible for the crime. Although most of the studies that used this framework were conducted by Goldstein and his colleagues in New York (Parker and Auerhahn, 1998), there are others worthy of attention, especially given their unique approaches. General findings include the following:

1. Non-NDRI (National Development and Research Institutes, Inc.) studies of New York City in the mid- to late 1980s found that crack sellers are more violent than other drug sellers and that their violence is not confined to the drug-selling context (U.S. Sentencing Commission, 1995, citing Fagan and Chin, 1990).

2. Studies of juvenile delinquents in Miami in the mid- to late 1980s found that they were much more likely to commit a drug-related economic-compulsive crime than a psychopharmacological or systemic crime (Inciardi, 1990).[3]

3. The per capita drug-related homicide rate remained fairly stable in Chicago from 1973 to 1984 and fluctuated from 1985 to 1995 (data are from the Chicago Homicide Dataset; Block, Block, and Illinois Criminal Justice Information Authority, 1998). Despite the fluctuations, the 1995 homicide rate was strikingly similar to the 1985 rate for all drug-related motives except for homicides that resulted from a drug transaction; the latter increased tenfold from 1985 to 1995.

4. Results from Lattimore et al.'s (1997) homicide study of eight cities, which included surveys of local officials and ADAM/UCR (Uniform Crime Reports) analyses for 1985–94, suggest that drugs other than cocaine and crack were not associated with homicide trends "in any discernible way." They also found that the drug market structure was less associated with violence than was expected.

The Lattimore et al. study questioned the role of crack and systemic crime because the crack markets were described as highly competitive in cities where the homicide rate was declining, increasing, or remaining the same (1997, p. 89). It is not clear, however, that the same conclusions could be drawn if disaggregated homicide rates (by circumstance) were considered. (Additional discussion and methodological descriptions of these studies are reported in Appendix A.)

Limitations of Existing Research on the Goldstein Framework

The Goldstein tripartite framework has been a boon to drug research reviewers—it is invaluable as an organizing scheme—but still, we are struck by the relative rarity of actual empirical applications. Existing applications overrepresent New York, and they overrepresent the crack epidemic at its height relative to earlier and later periods. In fairness, the taxonomy was not proposed until 1985, but it could be applied retrospectively to earlier homicide case files. In our view, such comparisons would be invaluable. There has been little consistency in the methods used to implement the scheme (e.g., Goldstein's trained coders versus Inciardi's survey approach). Little has been learned from that methodological diversity because, to our knowledge, no two methods have ever

been applied to the same sample of cases for comparative purposes. Indeed, if one imagines a three-dimensional matrix of major cities by time periods by methods, almost every cell is empty and there are almost no vectors with more than one cell occupied. This spotty record makes it hard to identify either temporal trends or the influence of local variations on drug popularity, drug market structures, or policies and enforcement practices. Finally, the scheme has been applied mostly to homicide and less often to other, more prevalent violent crimes.[4]

Parker and Auerhahn (1998) complain that Goldstein's categories are not mutually exclusive. This critique presumes a classical set-theoretic approach that, in our opinion, is neither feasible nor scientifically useful for drugs-violence research. Mutually exclusive categories are not necessary for scientific classification (Meehl, 1995), and they are usually impossible to achieve using sparse and noisy archival data (Ragin, 2000). But we agree with Parker and Auerhahn's (1998) contention that "the Goldstein tripartite framework . . . is not treated as a set of testable propositions but rather as a set of assumptions about the nature of drug- and alcohol-related violence."

In our view, an understanding of the taxometric properties of drug-related violence ought to emerge inductively from more fine-grained coding of the underlying features of these events—whether various drugs were found as evidence, the results of toxicology on the offender and the victim, various features of witness reports, prior record information, and so on. Because each property or attribute would be coded separately, there would be no effort to force events into a single classification. Psychometric analysis could be used to test the hypothesized latent structure.[5] Such analyses pose enormous logistical difficulties, but the payoffs for advancing our understanding of drug violence would surely justify the effort.

In the remainder of this section, we will examine other ways in which Goldstein's taxonomic scheme might be expanded and refined.

Psychopharmacological Violence

The prevailing view about psychopharmacological (as opposed to economic-compulsive or systemic) violence is that it is rare and attributable mostly to alcohol rather than illicit drugs (Fagan, 1990; Parker and Auerhahn, 1998; White and Gorman, 2000). According to Fagan (1990, p. 243):

> [I]ntoxication does not consistently lead to aggressive behavior . . . only limited evidence that consumption of alcohol, cocaine, heroin, or other

substances is a direct, pharmacologically based cause of crime.

According to Parker and Auerhahn (1998, p. 306):

> Our review of the literature finds a great deal of evidence that the social environment is a much more powerful contributor to the outcome of violent behavior than are pharmacological factors associated with any of the substances reviewed here.[6]

The Goldstein et al. (1989) analysis provides some support for these claims; only 14 percent of the drug-related homicides appeared to be psychopharmacological, and these largely involved alcohol either alone or in combination with other drugs. But one in seven is hardly a trivial fraction, and those results reflect the peak of the crack market wars, when systemic homicides were occurring in unprecedented numbers, inflating the denominator.

Moderators. Examining the literature cited in many recent review essays, it is difficult to avoid the suspicion that some authors hold neuropharmacological factors to a stricter standard of proof than the sociological factors under study. If the psychopharmacological claim is that marijuana, heroin, or cocaine ingestion directly promotes violent behavior absent any situational provocation or stressors, then that claim is probably false. But evidence for Drug × Situation and Drug × Psychology interaction effects hardly exonerates drug use as a causal factor. It may be that no drug is sufficient to produce aggression in isolation from psychological and situational moderators. But it seems clear that some drugs—certainly alcohol—can amplify the psychological and situational facilitators of aggression. Relevant moderators (see Bushman, 1997; Fagan, 1990; Ito, Miller, and Pollock, 1996) include:

- Situational stressors and frustrators (see Ito, Miller, and Pollock, 1996).
- Expectancy effects: personal and cultural beliefs about the effect of the drug on behavior, and local norms about tolerable versus unacceptable conduct when under the influence (e.g., Critchlow, 1986; Stacy, Widaman, and Marlatt, 1990).
- Disinhibition (e.g., Parker and Auerhahn, 1998; but see Fagan, 1990).
- Impaired cognitive functioning, including reduced executive functioning (self-control and decisionmaking ability; Fishbein, 2000; Giancola, 2000), reduced attention to situational cues

(Steele and Josephs, 1990), and reduced self-attention (Ito, Miller, and Pollock, 1996).
- Social threats to self-identity or self-esteem (Baumeister, Smart, and Boden, 1996) that seem particularly relevant in "cultures of honor" (see Anderson, 1994; Bourgois, 1996; Cohen et al., 1996).

Moreover, the absence of evidence does not equal evidence of absence; the laboratory literature on drugs and aggression is simply too spotty at present to permit any firm conclusions. Almost the entire experimental literature on moderators of the drugs-aggression relationship has examined alcohol rather than illicit drugs.

Comorbidity: Drugs in Association With Mental Illness or Alcoholism.   A second potential class of moderators of the drugs–aggression link involve comorbid conditions—substance abuse in tandem with schizophrenia or other psychoses, personality disorders, or alcoholism. Numerous studies have identified a high prevalence of illicit substance abuse among individuals diagnosed with psychiatric disorders (e.g., Compton et al., 2000; Kessler et al., 1996; Mueser et al., 2000).[7] The causal nexus of these comorbid conditions is unclear. The MacArthur Violence Risk Assessment Study (Steadman et al., 1998), a prospective followup study of clients admitted to acute psychiatric inpatient facilities, found that substance abuse increased the probability of violent behavior, but this was true for both psychiatric patients and matched community controls. Neither drug dependence nor psychiatric illness predicted subsequent violent crime in a 6-year followup of released jail detainees (Teplin, Abram, and McClelland, 1994).

Drug Use and Victimization[8]

Increased victimization provides another mechanism by which drugs can become linked with violence. Although this category can be subsumed under Goldstein's psychopharmacological category, treating it as a fourth category might have merit because the causal mechanisms differ and it has been largely neglected by researchers. There are a number of reasons to expect that drug users ought to be particularly vulnerable to criminal victimization, especially when intoxicated. First, intoxicated people often appear (and sometimes are) more vulnerable than other targets for such offenses as robbery, rape, or hate crimes. Second, intoxicated people are often obnoxious, annoying, and/or offensive in their appearance, conduct, and speech. Third, intoxication makes people's conduct unpredictable and ambiguous—intoxication impairs the perception of signals, but it also impairs the transmission of clear signals to others. Finally, in an active illicit drug market, drug sellers are sometimes both intoxicated and flush with cash.

Fagan (1990) notes that the vulnerability of drug users to victimization has been long recognized. For example, Wolfgang (1958) studied "victim-precipitated homicides" by assessing the incidence of intoxication among victims. And Fagan (1990) reviews evidence from animal studies showing that "substances that induce changes in an opponent's behavior might result in increased aggression by a drug-free attacker . . ." (p. 251).

Although Goldstein (1985) acknowledged that the victimization of drug users constituted a distinct drugs–violence linkage, he did not include it as a separate category in his classification scheme. Since then, the victimization of drug users has received little attention in the drugs and crime literature. This is not surprising given how difficult it is to assess the relationship. First, as Goldstein (1985) argues, it is difficult to obtain this information because victims do not want to talk to the police while intoxicated and often do not remember the details of the offense; thus, it may go unreported. Second, the victimization surveys that ask about substance use usually include it as a predictor but do not ask whether it contributed to a specific event. Third, many of these surveys only ask about (or report) general drug use, not about specific drugs or the circumstances of their use. Finally, the label "victim" is often problematic when the participants are codisputants; indeed, the "victim" may have initiated the provocation. In our view, these concerns are valid, but they do not undermine the importance of victimization as a research topic.

The ubiquity of alcohol has made it the subject of victimization work for 50 years, and there is general agreement about its role in victimizations, especially sexual assaults. The research on drugs is not as robust, but there are some important findings that should be addressed in future works on drugs and crime. The following sections provide insight about this relationship by examining existing victimization studies of the general population, women, and hard drug users.

The General Population. The Nation's largest victimization survey, the National Criminal Victimization Survey (NCVS), does not ask about victim drug use, but it is used in conjunction with other data to provide insight about drugs and crime. Using NCVS, Markowitz's (2000) multivariate analysis of almost 450,000 observations found that marijuana decriminalization (a proxy for lower marijuana prices) will result in a higher incidence of robbery and assault while higher cocaine prices will decrease these crimes.[9] Neither measure was significantly related to rape or sexual assault. When victims' perceptions of offender drug and alcohol use during assaults were used as the dependent variable, the significance of marijuana decriminalization and cocaine prices was ambiguous (significance depends on model specification). For perceived use during robberies, neither was significant. Although Markowitz suggests the perception variable is questionable because of underreporting, these findings raise questions about the causal relationship and the role of drug use by victims, especially marijuana.

Based on an instrument similar to NCVS, Fisher et al.'s (1998) survey of 3,472 randomly selected college students found that regularly taking recreational drugs predicted an increased likelihood of a violent victimization but not of a theft victimization. For the general population, Cottler et al.'s (1992) survey of a probability sample of 2,663 household residents found that those who had used cocaine or heroin more than five times in their lives were more than three times as likely to have experienced a physical attack than nonusers. Those who used marijuana more than five times (no use of other drugs) and those who used pills or hallucinogens more than five times were no more likely to have experienced a physical attack than nonusers. This is one of the few studies that presents its results by drug and raises questions about the situations in which hard drug users put themselves.

Women. Much of the victimization research focuses on women because many of the studies are about sexual assault. Fisher, Cullen, and Turner (2000) randomly selected 4,446 college women to participate in their National College Women Victimization Study. That study did not find that marijuana use was a significant predictor of sexual victimization and stalking.[10] These findings are consistent with Markowitz's claim that the price of cocaine and marijuana are not significant predictors of sexual victimization.

Beyond using prices and self-reports, some researchers have drug-tested rape victims to assess their drug use. Hindmarch and Brinkmann (1999) found that 41 percent of the 1,033 participants tested negative for alcohol and other drugs, 37 percent tested positive for alcohol, 19 percent tested positive for cannabinoids, and 0.6 percent tested positive for flunitrazepam (Rohypnol); however, the lack of information about participant characteristics and site locations would prevent researchers from creating the necessary control groups.

Drug Users. Tardiff et al. (1994) found that 31 percent of one sample of homicide victims tested positive for cocaine metabolites. This rate did not vary for firearm deaths versus nonfirearm deaths. McElrath, Chitwood, and Comerford (1997) surveyed 308 intravenous drug users who were receiving methadone and/or inpatient drug treatment about their victimization and drug use in the previous 6 months. Those reporting heroin use were significantly less likely to be victims of violent and property crimes. McElrath et al. argue that heroin users sometimes have "running partners" who may also look out for each other, thus decreasing victimization. Crack cocaine users were four times as likely to be victims of property crime than nonusers, leading the authors to suggest, "it is possible that the drug-seeking behavior associated with crack-cocaine places users in contact with a larger pool of motivated offenders."

Drug-user-on-drug-user crime was also addressed in Inciardi's delinquency study (1990). Respondents were asked about not only drug-related offenses they committed but also drug-related victimizations; 4.6 percent reported being victims of psychopharmacological-related crimes, 39.9 percent reported being victims of drug robberies, and 9.0 percent reported being victims of systemic violence.

Although every youth in the survey used at least one drug daily, it is not clear whether the victimizations occurred while the victim was under the influence.

Crime victim surveys and offender surveys require respondents to make attributions about the causes of offenders' behavior. Such causal attributions are susceptible to numerous well-documented biases (e.g., Nisbett and Ross, 1980), but to date there has been little methodological work validating these survey responses.

Economic-Compulsive Violence

Arrested and incarcerated offenders report that they committed their offenses to raise money to purchase drugs. Of course, this might be a convenient rationalization or excuse for antisocial behavior. Should we believe them?

At least for heroin addiction, the answer is probably yes. Studies of heroin "careers" show that the frequency of criminal activity tends to covary with periods of intense use (see Fagan, 1990, for review),

and addicts significantly reduce their criminal involvement during periods of methadone maintenance (see review in Rettig and Yarmolinsky, 1995). But in studies applying the Goldstein taxonomy (see above), economic-compulsive criminality has been relatively rare. White and Gorman (2000) argue, "[B]ecause there is more money in crack distribution than in previous illegal drug markets, drug dealing may have obviated the need to commit property crimes and income-generating violent crimes" (p. 189). Indeed, in our survey of drug sellers in Washington, D.C., in the late 1980s (Reuter, MacCoun, and Murphy, 1990), more than 40 percent reported keeping some drugs for their own consumption—39 percent of crack sellers and 69 percent of heroin sellers. However, the claim about the high returns for crack selling is probably no longer correct. Bourgois (1996) reports that proceeds from crack sales by experienced users who could not maintain legitimate jobs were less than minimum wage.[11]

But the argument that drug selling has replaced other income-generating crime might reflect limitations of recent work. First, as we have noted, most studies applying the Goldstein framework were conducted at the peak of the crack epidemic, when the sheer prevalence of street drug sales was probably at an all-time high (see Saner, MacCoun, and Reuter, 1995). Second, most studies have largely examined crimes with violent outcomes rather than robberies or burglaries in which no homicide occurred. One exception is the Caulkins et al. (1997) study, which attributed a substantial fraction of robberies and burglaries to economic-compulsive crime, and a sizeable fraction of those economic-compulsive crimes to cocaine.

The ADAM Program provides some opportunities for studying these issues (e.g., Arrestee Drug Abuse Monitoring Program, 1999). The ADAM/DUF (Drug Use Forecasting) instrument was modified in 1995 to include a question asking whether the arrestee needed drugs or alcohol at the time of the offense.[12] Appendix B summarizes data for the period 1995 to 1999 for this survey item. As one would expect, these attributions are more common for income-generating offenses (14 percent) than for non-income-generating offenses (10 percent)—a reliable but quite modest difference.

Our understanding and interpretation of economic-compulsive crime ought to evolve as the scientific understanding of drug dependence evolves. Recent decades have seen great progress in the understanding of such phenomena as tolerance, withdrawal, reinforcement, and drug craving (see *Science*, 1997).

Leshner (1997, pp. 45–46) notes that many assume the following:

> [T]he more dramatic the physical withdrawal symptoms, the more serious or dangerous the drug must be. This thinking is outdated . . . many of the most addicting and dangerous drugs do not produce severe physical symptoms upon withdrawal. . . . What does matter tremendously is whether or not a drug causes what we now know to be the essence of addiction: compulsive drug seeking and use, even in the face of negative health and social consequences.

There are also intriguing new findings from behavioral economics research on the price elasticity of demand for cocaine and opiates—the percentage decline in demand for a 1-percent increase in price. The conventional wisdom is that addicts are relatively insensitive to price, at least in the short run, because they are enslaved to their drug and must find ways to obtain it to avoid withdrawal symptoms. If addicts were relatively insensitive to price, one would expect price increases to produce increased economic-compulsive crime. But recent studies (reviewed in Caulkins and Reuter, 1996) suggest considerable price sensitivity, with elasticities for cocaine ranging from –0.7 to –2.0. A possible explanation for the high elasticity among heavy users is that they spend most of their earnings on the drug and may respond to the increased difficulty of maintaining desired consumption levels (i.e., avoiding withdrawal) by seeking treatment.

Systemic Violence

The third of Goldstein's categories is systemic violence. This has been narrowly interpreted as referring to struggles for competitive advantage. We suggest here that drug markets generate violence in a variety of ways and that market violence varies systematically over time and place.

A Brief History of the Markets.   There was an epidemic of initiation into heroin use in the 1970s; after that, heroin initiation rates remained low until the late 1990s. The number of heroin addicts (a function of the number of initiates and the length of their addiction careers) remained fairly stable at about 750,000 from 1981 to 1997.[13] During that period, most heroin purchases were made by an aging cohort of experienced users.

Powder cocaine and crack had a similar dynamic, only with different parameters. Powder cocaine initiation rates were high from about 1975 to 1988; the number of dependent users has been quite stable since about 1988. The crack epidemic came later, from about 1982 to 1990 (depending on the city; see Blumstein and Cork, 1996). Estimates of the number of dependent users of either crack or powder cocaine range from 600,000 to 3,600,000 (see Rhodes et al., 2000).

Many retailers are now also frequent users (Arrestee Drug Abuse Monitoring Program, 1999). Selling seems to be opportunistic for many users; sudden access to an unusually large source of cash may lead a regular buyer to become a seller for a day. Thus, at the low end of the market, it may be difficult to distinguish systemic from psychopharmacological violence.

Enforcement against these markets, as measured by years of jail time per ton of drugs, probably declined through the early 1980s but then intensified from 1985 onward. In 1990, the Colombian government aggressively attacked the principal exporters of cocaine from Colombia. There are a number of indications that this led to a temporary tightening of the cocaine market; otherwise, prices have declined throughout the period, while consumption has been declining modestly since 1988.

Conceptual Issues.   The markets for illegal drugs operate without the usual protections against fraud and violence offered by the civil tort system. The state, instead of attempting to facilitate transactions, aims to disrupt them. Contracts cannot be enforced through written documents and the legal system; agreements are made hurriedly, sometimes in ambiguous code, and orally.[14] Territories cannot be allocated through bidding for desirable locations because there is no enforceable ownership of property for these purposes.

Yet the illegality itself is insufficient to generate high levels of violence in the market. Prostitution, although frequently unsightly and sometimes a nuisance, does not generate much by way of additional violence. Bookmaking, notwithstanding the drama of the film "The Sting," was also a generally peaceful affair; bookies were more likely to die in bed than on the job. Even for some drugs, the markets generate little violence; marijuana in general does not spark much injury as the result of competitive or transactional disputes.[15]

Some drug markets, however, are clearly violent; many participants are at risk of being killed or seriously wounded by others in the same business, either as buyers or sellers, and there are unintended shootings of innocent bystanders. The crack market is thought to be particularly prone to market-related violence.

Why are these drug markets, particularly for crack, so violent? We suggest that four factors contribute:

1. *The youth of participants.* Rates for violent crime peak early, at about ages 18–22. The young are particularly likely to lack foresight and thus engage in violence to settle disputes. The crack market was the first mass drug market in which most of the sellers were young.
2. *The value of the drugs themselves.* The cocaine that fills a plastic sandwich bag is worth thousands of dollars. The return to sudden, situational violence could be very high.
3. *The intensity of law enforcement.* Transactions are conducted under considerable uncertainty as a consequence of increased law enforcement. Intensified enforcement increases the incentives for violence by raising the adverse consequences of identifying someone as a potential informant.
4. *The indirect consequence of drug use.* Users are more violent and aggressive, and this encourages dealers to prefer selling out of doors or in highly protected settings. It also promotes unreliable behavior among user/dealers and thus more retaliation by their suppliers.

It is probably the combination of these factors, rather than any one of them, that accounts for the extraordinary violence associated with crack markets in the late 1980s. That violence seems to have fallen substantially in the late 1990s, perhaps reflecting the aging of participants in crack markets (Golub and Johnson, 1997), although violence itself, as well as enforcement, may also have selected out the most violent participants; Taylor, Caulkins, and Reuter (2000) present a model in which violence declines with more intense enforcement as a consequence of selective incarceration.

Competitive and Internal Violence. Attention has been given to violence generated by competition between sellers. Less attention has been given to violence within selling organizations, although the older literature on organized crime and illegal markets reported a great deal on this (e.g., Block, 1980).

Criminal organizations are hindered internally by lack of access to the civil courts. Employment contracts cannot be enforced except privately. Managerial succession is complicated by the specificity of reputation within the organization; a promising midlevel manager cannot readily provide evidence of performance to another potential employer so higher level managers get weaker market signals and may withhold deserved promotions or merit increases. This gives incentives to lower level agents to use violence for upward mobility.

Symmetrical with successional violence is disciplinary violence. Managers have reason to fear subordinates who can provide evidence against them; the longer lasting the relationship, the greater the potential for harm from informing. Thus, managers may use violence as a tool to reduce risks of informing. They have more incentive for doing so than do high-level dealers in transactions with low-level dealers because the information about these acts will spread more rapidly and extensively.[16] There are numerous stories of this kind of violence in Colombian drug-dealing organizations.

Thus, the violence in atomistic markets has different sources than that in markets serviced by larger selling organizations. Which generates greater violence from a given set of participants cannot be determined theoretically, but some of the decline in market-related violence may reflect changes in organizational structure.

Other Market Characteristics and Violence. Table 1 presents a simple classification of markets according to whether buyers and sellers come from the neighborhood or elsewhere. We believe that this

TABLE 1 Types of Illicit Drug Markets

	CUSTOMERS	
DEALERS	*Mostly Residents*	*Mostly Outsiders*
Mostly residents	Local market	Export market
Mostly outsiders	Import market	Public market

taxonomy, originally identified for purposes of analyzing vulnerability to enforcement (Reuter and MacCoun, 1992), may also be useful in the study of violence. Markets characterized by mostly resident dealers and customers are labeled *local markets*. *Export markets* are ones in which residents of the neighborhood sell drugs to nonresidents. Markets in which mostly nonresident dealers sell to local residents are characterized here as *import markets*. Finally, markets in which both sellers and customers are mostly nonresidents are labeled here as *public markets* because they tend to occur at such large public locations as parks, train or bus stations, or schoolyards.

Each class of market differs in the potential for violence. Local markets, precisely because they involve buyers and sellers who know each other, do not lend themselves to territorial competition. At the other extreme are public markets, in which buyers and sellers cannot readily find each other except at specific locations; the incentives for territoriality are consequently greater.

Transactional violence may also vary in these dimensions. Local markets discourage cheating of buyers as a consequence of the ongoing connections between buyers and sellers; a local customer is more likely to spread information effectively to other potential customers than one who has little connection to other buyers. It is not clear whether much of the transactional violence comes from buyers, as opposed to associates and rival sellers.

If this is correct, then the maturation of cocaine and heroin markets will tend to reduce market-related violence by reducing the size of all but local markets. Moreover, as a result of the dissemination of beepers and cell phones, an increasing share of cocaine transactions may be occurring in locations (apartments, restaurants, offices) that are agreed on by the buyer and seller for their mutual convenience. Johnson, Golub, and Dunlap (2000, p. 191, table 6.1) report that in New York City in the 1990s, the "seller style" included phone and delivery services as well as freelancers. Poor and socially isolated cocaine users still frequently conduct transactions in exposed locations, chosen precisely because they facilitate the coming together of buyers and sellers. So probably do many heroin addicts, given their generally impoverished state. The ability to choose locations on the basis of specific situational need not only reduces territorially motivated violence but also reduces the vulnerability of buyers to robbery and other victimization because fewer of them need to congregate at specific locations, which thus become less attractive to predators.

The Temporal Dynamics of Drug Markets

In the past several years, numerous authors have examined the emergence and decline of crack markets as a key factor in the steep rise in American violence from 1985 to 1990, and the even steeper drop since 1993 (see Blumstein and Wallman, 2000). In our view, the case for crack's role in the crime rise is quite compelling; its role in the post-1993 decrease is more subtle and by no means an open-and-shut case.

Many discussions of the crime drop fail to distinguish between a decline in the crack market and a decline in the linkage between crack and crime—but a decline in the crack–crime link is part of the crime drop outcome to be explained. It is true that DUF (and now ADAM) data show declines in positive cocaine tests among arrestees in many cities (e.g., Arrestee Drug Abuse Monitoring Program, 1999). And the reduced violence attributable to crack selling has made crack markets less visible. But nationwide, hardcore cocaine use remained surprisingly stable during the 1990s (Rhodes et al., 2000). Indeed, from 1990 to 1998, there were rising cocaine mentions in emergency rooms (Substance Abuse and Mental Health Services Administration, 2001) and rising cocaine seizures. Nevertheless, recent multicity comparisons (Baumer et al., 1998; Lattimore et al., 1997) indicate reliable positive correlations between various indices of crack use and homicide and other offense rates.

Various experts have suggested that the changing dynamics of drug markets may matter as much or more as any decline in total market activity (e.g., Ousey and Lee, 2000). Below, we consider a few more complex accounts of the link between crack market dynamics and violence.

NDRI'S Conduct Norm Account. Johnson and his colleagues at NDRI (Lipton and Johnson, 1998) have produced a valuable interdisciplinary, multimethod program of research on street drug markets in New York, spanning several decades. They recently offered an account of the decline in drug-related violence based on the notion of "conduct norms" (Johnson, Golub, and Dunlap, 2000), arguing that New York street drug markets have passed through three phases. (They vacillate between "period" and "cohort" versions of the story.) The "heroin injection era" peaked during 1960–73; the "cocaine/crack era" peaked during 1984–89; and the "marijuana/blunts era" started around 1990. Associated with each era are distinct birth cohorts with distinctive behavioral patterns. "HeroinGen" drug users (born 1945–54) were active in drug sales and property crime, but gun use was relatively rare. "CrackGen" drug users (born 1955–69) frequently participated in robbery and used guns for protection and reputation. Finally, "BluntGen" drug users (born 1970–79) are less likely than early cohorts to engage in violence.

Drawing on their rich ethnographic database, Johnson and colleagues (2000) argue that these behavior changes reflect two successive transformations of conduct norms for appropriate behavior in the drug-using community. For example, in CrackGen's "Subculture of Assault," a shared norm counseled: "Be aggressive and threatening to avoid robbery. . . . Carry weapons for protection. . . . Threaten or assault those who attempt to sell crack in your territory. Maintain your reputation as dangerous, tough, and 'crazy,' regardless of the physical harm inflicted or suffered" (p. 181). But for the BluntGen, the norm states: "Don't use crack. Crackheads are s—! . . . Addicts are the scum of the earth. Stay safe, stay alive. Don't mix cocaine or heroin with my marijuana. Shun and exclude heroin and crack users from peer groups" (p. 185).

This norm account is fascinating and quite plausible. From a policy perspective, it would be tremendously useful to find a way to preserve and promote the BluntGen's more pacifist stance (though not, of course, their consumption of blunts). Still, the evidence is causally ambiguous. Are these conduct norms actually *causes* of the decline in violence during the 1990s, are they *descriptions* of it, or are they *consequences* of it?

There is little doubt that conduct norms exist and are important in shaping deviant behavior. Cialdini, Kallgren, and Reno (1991) make a useful distinction between *injunctive norms* (what others think I should do) and *descriptive norms* (what others are actually doing). There is ample evidence that purely descriptive norms—changes in the local prevalence of a behavior—can have a self-reinforcing action. But attitudes and norms are shaped by behavior as well as shaping it; research on cognitive dissonance theory and self-perception theory suggests that such conformity-based behavioral changes will tend to produce corresponding (but retrospective) changes in relevant attitudes (see Eagly and Chaiken, 1993). Controlled social psychology experiments show that norm diffusion effects occur and that they can be strong, but these experiments also show that apparent norm effects are sometimes spurious (e.g., Kerr et al., 1987).

Clearly, research on drug-using norms cannot move to the laboratory—although one can imagine informative scenario-based experiments embedded in field interviews. But it would be enormously useful to make additional use of the NDRI data (and related data sources, such as the Office of National Drug Control Policy's *Pulse Check*), linking the timing of the ethnographic material more precisely to month-to-month quantitative archival data on drug selling (or its proxies) and violent crimes. Furthermore, archives of ethnographic data collected in different cities during the past decade might be reanalyzed to search for cross-city norm differences that might correlate with cross-city differences in violent crime. Ideally, one might develop methods for identifying "leading indicators" of emerging trends in drug using, drug selling, and drug-related violence.

Blumstein and Cork's Drug-Gun Diffusion Account. In a series of articles (see Blumstein, 2000a; Blumstein and Cork, 1996; Cork, 1999), Alfred Blumstein and his collaborator Daniel Cork hypothesize a causal chain linking the late 1980s crack epidemic to rising violence nationwide. According to Blumstein, the 1980s growth in illicit drug markets, together with stringent enforcement crackdowns, led to the recruitment of juvenile drug sellers. The intense market competition together with the recruitment and rewarding of particularly aggressive youths created a need for sellers (as well as nonseller youths in market neighborhoods) to be armed. This increased demand fueled an expansion in the illicit gun market and a diffusion of guns. The linkage between drug selling and gun possession is well established (see Decker, Pennell, and Caldwell 1997; Sheley, 1994; Tardiff et al., 1994).[17] Cork (1999) found support for the temporal sequence of the Blumstein account using a sophisticated diffusion modeling analysis of time-series data from multiple cities.

The Blumstein model is a compelling account of the rise of violent crime, but more work is needed to establish its explanatory power as an account of the subsequent decline in violence. The model is not inconsistent with that decline—a decline in the crack market should have reduced the need to be armed—but future research will have to assess whether declines in the prevalence of drug selling (as opposed to changes in other features of the markets) have produced reductions in the likelihood of gun possession and gun violence.

The Maturation of Addicts and of Illicit Drug Markets. Because of reduced initiation rates, it appears that the hardcore cocaine-using population consists mostly of an aging cohort who started using in the late 1980s, in much the same way that heroin addicts disproportionately belong to cohorts who initiated use in the 1970s. If this is correct, drug-related criminality should continue to decline, absent new waves of initiation, as addicts "mature out" of violent crime or die from drug-related illnesses or natural causes.

Many observers were struck by the violence of 1980s crack markets relative to earlier heroin and marijuana markets. Many have speculated that such markets "mature" over time as (a) dealer territories are firmly established, (b) casual users drop out of the market, and (c) hardcore users establish reliable dealer connections. All these factors suggest a shift from open-air public markets toward more clandestine arrangements that seem less prone to violence.[18] But at present, this is largely speculative; there is anecdotal and ethnographic evidence for such changes but little systematic longitudinal research that establishes a clear trajectory over time.

The Consequences of Prohibition and its Enforcement

Drug Involvement as Crime.   The convention in articles on drugs–crime linkages is to state that for the purposes of the essay, the fact that drug use (and sometimes drug selling) per se is a crime is not relevant to the analysis. But the illicit status of street drugs is vitally important to the analysis in several ways. First, drug prohibition is arguably necessary for Goldstein's category of systemic (market-related) violence (MacCoun and Reuter, 2001).[19] We simply do not observe routine violence among alcohol or tobacco vendors. Second, Goldstein's economic-compulsive violence, although not caused by prohibition, is surely exacerbated by it because drug prohibition almost certainly raises the price of heroin or cocaine far above what would be their retail market prices (MacCoun and Reuter, 2001). Finally, there are reasons to believe that the illicit status of drugs might have subtle criminogenic effects through several different mechanisms, including forbidden fruit effects, labeling or stigmatization effects, and "stigma swamping."[20] Here we highlight two such mechanisms.

Incapacitation and Replacement Effects.   Several authors (e.g., Blumstein, 2000b; Freeman, 1996; Kleiman, 1997) have suggested that the incarceration of drug sellers is likely to produce a weaker incapacitation effect than would occur for other offense categories, such as property and sex offenses. Indeed, some have speculated that a *replacement* process might even produce a net increase in the prevalence of drug selling. In a highly competitive illicit market, the incarceration of a drug seller creates lucrative drug-selling opportunities (customers and sales territory) for others. According to Blumstein (2000b):

The pathological rapist's crimes almost certainly are not replaced on the street, and so one can expect his full array of crimes to be incapacitated. . . . A burglar's crimes may be replaced if he is serving a fence, who would recruit a replacement; alternatively, if he is simply operating on his own, the crimes are not likely to be replaced. And the participant in organized vice activity such as drug dealing would be likely to have his transactions replaced by whatever organizational structure is serving the market demand. That replacement could be achieved by some combination of recruiting new sellers or by increasing the rate of activity of sellers already active in the market.

Freeman (1996) offers a formal economic model that interprets this replacement effect in terms of the elasticity of supply of dealers with respect to drug market wages. The supply of dealers should reflect this sensitivity to wages as well as changes in earnings opportunities in the licit market (i.e., shift in the supply curve) and the demand for drugs (i.e., shifts in the demand curve).

At present, there is surprisingly little evidence either for or against the replacement hypothesis. One indirect argument for its plausibility is that the explosive growth in the incarceration of drug sellers during the past decade was not accompanied by increases in street cocaine prices, as one might expect if the supply of street dealers was tightening (Blumstein, 2000b; see also DiNardo, 1993). Indeed, street prices have dropped substantially (Rhodes et al., 2000). Another indirect argument is the sheer prevalence of drug market participation in some communities during the late 1980s, when drug sellers were being incarcerated at record levels. For example, Saner et al. (1995) estimated that in Washington, D.C., during 1985–91, nearly one-third of African-American male residents from the 1964–67 birth cohorts were charged with drug selling.

Statistical analyses of archival data might test the replacement hypothesis by looking for evidence of increases in the initiation to drug selling as a function of the arrest and incarceration of dealers. Ethnographic studies might examine whether recruitment activities increase following police crackdowns and whether existing street dealers increase their activity. But isolating replacement effects will be tricky; note that general deterrence and replacement effects, if they exist, will offset each other, which may make it hard to find *any* effect of sanctions on subsequent dealing.

Can Enforcement Amplify Violence?   Several authors (Eck and McGuire, 2000; MacCoun and Reuter, 2001, Chapter 6; Reuter, 1989; Riley, 1998) have argued that under certain conditions, aggressive drug enforcement might actually increase drug-related violence. Rasmussen, Benson, and their associates have examined whether more intense drug enforcement increases violent crime; much of this work is summarized in Rasmussen and Benson (1994). The mechanisms involved are quite varied. For example, enforcement might lead to more violence in competition. Benson and colleagues (1992) found that the violent crime rate in a community increased with more drug arrests in a neighboring community. This, they argue, is a displacement effect; dealers move from the targeted community to the neighboring one and struggle over the establishment of territories. Another mechanism works through the limited capacity of the correctional system; increased prison space for drug offenders reduces the penalties for other crimes, including violent crimes, and thus induces higher victimization. Benson and Rasmussen (1991) argue that, even assuming that prison is effective only through incapacitation and not deterrence, the observed rise in the resources devoted to drug enforcement in Florida in the 1980s might have increased other crime by 10 percent.

Supply Reduction Versus Violence Reduction. An important dialogue with respect to drug users involves the prospects and tensions of integrating use reduction strategies with harm reduction strategies (MacCoun, 1998; MacCoun and Reuter, 2001). We see an analogous issue with respect to the policing of drug markets (MacCoun and Reuter, 1994). Police tactics designed to reduce the supply of drugs (and of drug suppliers) may or may not be the most effective means of reducing the total social harm caused by street drug selling. Some tactics might directly reduce drug-related violence.

One example involves efforts to drive dealers indoors (see Kennedy's 1993 analysis of Tampa's QUAD program). Of course, crack houses are not without their harms. In an ethnographic study of the crack market in Detroit, Mieczkowski (1990, p. 90) concludes that "tavern-style crack houses may encourage and make possible hypersexuality among participants and thus increase the STD and HIV rates. The use of barter as a supplement to a cash economy in the crack trade represents further complications in creating social policies in reaction to this behavior." Still, indoor markets are likely to be less violent. But the effects are multiple and hard to balance. On one hand, indoor markets are less susceptible to police surveillance or sting operations. On the other hand, driving dealers indoors might increase users' search costs (Moore, 1990) and thus reduce demand. Consumers in export markets would bear a

disproportionate share of these search costs because the locals often know the local dealers and could easily locate them. This might lead to new local markets in the areas from which the export consumers are coming and the associated neighborhood violence that Benson et al. (1992) examined. Further research on these issues is needed.

Heroin Maintenance.   If the drugs–crime link is mediated by the high price and conditions of sale of a drug, and if a relatively small number of frequent users are responsible for much of the crime, then perhaps allowing access to that drug legally for those least able to quit might reduce associated crime. There is increasing information and interest in exploring just this possibility for heroin (see MacCoun and Reuter, 2001).

In January 1994, Swiss authorities opened a number of government-administered heroin maintenance clinics.[21] Registered addicts can inject heroin at a government clinic under the care of a nurse up to three times a day, 7 days a week. Patients have to be over 18, have injected heroin for 2 years, and have failed at least two treatment episodes. By the end of the initial research trials of this program, more than 800 patients had received heroin on a regular basis without any leakage into the illicit market. No overdoses were reported among participants while they stayed in the program. A large majority of participants had maintained the regime of daily attendance at the clinic; 69 percent were in treatment 18 months after admission. This was a high rate relative to those found in methadone programs. About half of the "dropouts" switched to other forms of treatment; some chose methadone and others chose abstinence-based therapies. The crime rate among all patients dropped during the course of treatment, use of nonprescribed heroin dipped sharply, and unemployment fell from 44 to 20 percent.

Critics, such as an independent review panel of the World Health Organization, reasonably asked whether the claimed success was a result of the heroin or the many additional services provided to trial participants. And the evaluation relied primarily on the patients' own reports, with few objective measures. Nevertheless, despite the methodological weaknesses, the results of the Swiss trials provide evidence of the feasibility and potential effectiveness of this approach. In late 1997, the Swiss government approved a large-scale expansion of the program. A similar program is under development in the Netherlands and in Hamburg, Germany.

The proposal to study heroin maintenance on a trial basis in the United States is politically controversial and would be logistically difficult. Moreover, the normative and moral issues are clearly complex (MacCoun and Reuter, 2001, chapter 15). But we should not reflexively dismiss, without serious analysis, an intervention that could in theory (and with some fragmentary evidence) help reduce the criminality of existing heroin users and perhaps shrink the heroin street market, thereby creating new barriers to heroin initiation. If nothing else, serious discussion of such a program, and perhaps even formal modeling of alternative hypotheses about its likely effects, might significantly advance our thinking about drug market dynamics and the possibilities for effective intervention.

Summing Up: Directions for Future Research

Here we summarize our suggestions for profitable future research, in the order in which we discussed them:

- Methodological attention to the measurement of Goldstein's taxonomy of drugs–violence links and to the validation of self-reports of victim and offender causal attributions for the role of drugs in criminal offenses.
- Greater attention to the role of drug use in criminal victimization.
- Retrospective historical analysis of long-term trends in drug use, drug arrests, and drug-related crime, including recoding of ethnographic databases, application of the Goldstein coding scheme to homicide case files, age/period/cohort analyses, and econometric time-series analyses.
- Determination of the causal relationships underlying comorbid drug abuse and mental illness conditions.

- Extension and replication of the rich experimental literature on situational moderators of alcohol-related aggression, as applied to other drugs.
- Econometric analysis of the effects of drug price changes on drug-related criminality.
- Assessment of the effects of the availability of licit work and licit wage levels on criminality.
- Additional multicity analyses (and cross-neighborhood analyses within cities) with an emphasis on understanding heterogeneity in drugs–crime relationships: Spatial analyses, analyses of variation in the demand for different drugs, gang versus nongang involvement, ethnic and other demographic groupings, indoor versus outdoor markets, import versus export versus local versus public markets, etc.
- Estimation of incapacitation versus replacement effects resulting from the incarceration of drug sellers.
- Simulation modeling and eventual pilot tests of the efficacy of heroin maintenance.

One other topic that was not even hinted at in our analysis and has been almost totally neglected in the empirical research literature also should receive attention: the likelihood of causal linkages between illicit drug use and such white-collar crimes as corruption, fraud, and embezzlement.[22]

This is a long list of topics. That in itself is a reminder of how little has been done to implement and build on Goldstein's insightful taxonomy. Advances will require an acceptance of the fact that drugs may differ widely in the extent and form of their criminogenic effects. That substantially complicates an already difficult enterprise but is likely to be the source of considerable policy insight.

NOTES

1. Except where noted, these statistics were reported in *Drug-Related Crime* (Office of National Drug Control Policy, 2000).
2. In fact, Goldstein et al.'s (1989) findings might not fully represent New York City since they did not look at the entire population or a random sample of homicides. Rather, they chose one zone in each of four different boroughs, with the goal of sampling precincts that represented a cross-section of New York City.
3. These findings challenge the recent generalization by White and Gorman (2000, p. 189) that "the economic motivation explanation has not been supported among adolescents."

4. Our understanding is that the new NIBRS (National Incident-Based Reporting System) database perpetuates this. Officers only have to report the circumstances of the offense (which includes drug dealing) for aggravated assaults/homicide (considered one category in the victim-level file).
5. Approaches might include confirmatory factor analysis, cluster analysis, Q-sort, or Ragin's (2000) fuzzy-set approach. We are less interested in defending a particular method than in pointing out the surprising lack of attention to these measurement and conceptualization issues in the field.

6. Fagan (1990, p. 255) and White and Gorman (2000, p. 185) argue that, if anything, marijuana and opiates serve to suppress aggression. Actually, Bushman's (1990) meta-analysis found more aggression among marijuana smokers than placebo controls in laboratory experiments. But this effect is partly due to the fact that the placebo controls showed significantly less aggression than nondrug controls, indicating that participants also believed marijuana would induce passivity.

7. Note that other psychiatric disorders are less common among substance abusers than substance abuse is among the mentally ill (Miller, 1993).

8. Beau Kilmer's work on this section was supported by NIDA grant R01DA12724.

9. The assumption that decriminalization (as opposed to legalization) is an indicator of lower price is questionable. In theory, it might increase demand by reducing the nonmoney costs, which should increase price. However, evaluations of decriminalization in 11 U.S. States, South Australia, the Australian Capital Territory, and the Netherlands fail to show any effects on demand (MacCoun and Reuter, 2001).

10. The authors report the statistically significant variables, not the entire model. The entire model is listed is Fisher, Cullen, and Turner (forthcoming) and includes a variable for "Frequency of smoking pot or hashish." Because the significant predictors for stalking are the same in the published and unpublished pieces, we assume the same model was used. Because this is likely to be the model used to predict sexual victimization in the published piece, we report that marijuana use does not predict sexual victimization.

11. Even if true, high returns from crack selling do not lessen the criminogenic consequences of the market; the issue is what share of revenues are generated by legitimate earnings or welfare and other transfer payments received by buyers.

12. The question yields four binary variables about whether the arrestee was in need of drugs/alcohol (NEEDNO), alcohol (NEEDALC), cocaine (NEEDCOCR), and marijuana (NEEDMAR) during the crime and one text variable (NEEDOTHR) where the coder is asked to specify if the arrestee mentioned another drug. Curiously, the 1995 (part 2) and 1999 ADAM codebooks do not report any binary variable for heroin—widely believed to be the major source of economic-compulsive crime. Of the 44,000 ADAM arrestees in 1999, we estimate (using the open-ended field responses) that about 1,100 reported they needed heroin, 1,800 needed alcohol, 2,150 needed cocaine/crack, and 700 needed marijuana. Of those reporting that they needed heroin, about 35 percent committed income-generating crimes.

13. ONDCP reports, based on Rhodes et al. (1995, 2000), that the prevalence of frequent use fell by one-third between 1988 and 1993 and then returned to its 1988 level by 1998. It is difficult to identify supporting evidence for such a dramatic fluctuation in the figures.

14. The bookmaking business has certainly generated written records; but that is more central to the business itself, which involves the extension of credit and usually numerous near-simultaneous transactions between any one buyer and seller.

15. In the District of Columbia in the mid- to late 1990s, it was reported that some street gangs were in violent disputes over the marijuana market (Pierre, 1996; Lattimore et al., 1997).

16. Smith and Varese (2001) model the use of coercive violence in markets for Mafia extortion; the model can be applied to intraorganizational violence as well.

17. Decker, Pennell, and Caldwell (1997) did not find that drug users (rather than sellers) were more likely to be carrying a gun than other arrestees.

18. Alfred Blumstein appeared to endorse this account in his public comments at the 2000 Annual Meeting of the American Society of Criminology.

19. Necessary, but not sufficient; see Zimring and Hawkins, 1997; Ousey and Lee, 2000.

20. The term "stigma swamping" was suggested to us by Jon Caulkins as an apt label for a phenomenon about which many have speculated (e.g., Jacobsen and Hanneman, 1992; McGraw, 1985; Petersilia, 1990)—the notion that the stigma associated with arrest and even incarceration is reduced by the sheer prevalence of those sanctions. The term "stigma swamping" is an informal control counterpart to Kleiman's (1993) formal control version, "enforcement swamping."

21. The earlier British experience with prescription heroin is more notorious but less informative; see MacCoun and Reuter, 2001, chapter 12.

22. We thank Terence Dunworth for making this observation.`

REFERENCES

Anderson, E. (1994). Code of the streets: How the inner city environment fosters a need for respect and a self-image based on violence. *Atlantic Monthly, 273*, 80–94.

Arrestee Drug Abuse Monitoring Program (1999). *1998 annual report on drug use among adult and juvenile arrestees* (Research Report, NCJ 175656). Washington, DC: U.S. Department of Justice, National Institute of Justice.

Baumeister, R. F., Smart, L., and Boden, J. M. (1996). Relation of threatened egotism to violence and aggression: The dark side of high self-esteem. *Psychological Review, 103*, 5–33.

Baumer, E., Lauritsen, J. L., Rosenfeld, R., and Wright, R. (1998). The influence of crack cocaine on robbery, burglary, and homicide rates: A cross-city longitudinal analysis. *Journal of Research on Crime and Delinquency, 35*, 316–340.

Benson, B. L., Kim, I., Rasmussen, D. W., and Zuehlke, T. W. (1992). Is property crime caused by drug use or by drug enforcement policy? *Applied Economics, 24*, 679–692.

Benson, B. L., and Rasmussen, D. W. (1991). The relationship between illicit drug enforcement and property crimes. *Contemporary Policy Issues, 9*, 106–115.

Block, A. (1980) *East side–west side*. Cardiff: University of Wales Press.

Block, C., Block, R., and Illinois Criminal Justice Information Authority. (1998). *Homicides in Chicago, 1965–1995*. Ann

Arbor: Intra-university Consortium for Political and Science Research.

Blumstein, A. (2000a). Disaggregating the violence trends. In A. Blumstein and J. Wallman (eds.), *The crime drop in America* (pp. 13–44). New York: Cambridge University Press.

Blumstein, A. (2000b). The replacement of drug offenders to diminish the effects of incarceration. Unpublished manuscript, Carnegie Mellon University.

Blumstein, A., and Cork, D. (1996). Linking gun availability to youth gun violence. *Law and Contemporary Problems, 59,* 5–24.

Blumstein, A., and Wallman, J. (eds.) (2000). *The crime drop in America.* New York: Cambridge University Press.

Bourgois, P. (1996). In search of masculinity: Violence, respect and sexuality among Puerto Rican crack dealers in East Harlem. *British Journal of Criminology, 36,* 412–427.

Brownstein, H., Baxi, H., Goldstein, P., and Ryan, P. (1992). The relationship of drugs, drug trafficking, and drug traffickers to homicide. *Journal of Crime and Justice, 15,* 25–44.

Bureau of Justice Statistics (1997a). *Survey of inmates in Federal correctional facilities.* Washington, DC: U.S. Department of Justice, Bureau of Justice Statistics and Federal Bureau of Prisons.

Bureau of Justice Statistics (1997b). *Survey of inmates in State correctional facilities.* Washington, DC: U.S. Department of Justice, Bureau of Justice Statistics.

Bureau of Justice Statistics (1991a). *Survey of inmates in Federal correctional facilities.* Washington, DC: U.S. Department of Justice, Bureau of Justice Statistics and Federal Bureau of Prisons.

Bureau of Justice Statistics (1991b). *Survey of inmates in State correctional facilities.* Washington, DC: U.S. Department of Justice, Bureau of Justice Statistics.

Bushman, B. J. (1990). Human aggression while under the influence of alcohol and other drugs: An integrative research review. *Psychological Science, 2,* 148–152.

Bushman, B. J. (1996). Individual differences in the extent and development of aggressive cognitive-associative networks. *Personality and Social Psychology Bulletin, 22,* 811–819.

Bushman, B. J. (1997). Effects of alcohol on human aggression: Validity of proposed explanations. In M. Galanter (ed.), *Recent developments in alcoholism, Vol. 13: Alcohol and violence: Epidemiology, neurobiology, psychology, family issues* (pp. 227–243). New York: Plenum Press.

Caulkins, J., and Reuter, P. (1996). Editorial: The meaning and utility of drug prices. *Addiction, 91,* 1261–1264.

Caulkins, J., Rydell, C., Schwabe, W., and Chiesa, J. (1997). *Mandatory minimum drug sentences: Throwing away the key or the taxpayers' money?* Santa Monica: RAND Drug Policy Research Center.

Chin, K. L., and Fagan, J. (1992). The impact of crack on criminal careers: Crime and drug involvement following initiation into cocaine smoking. Unpublished manuscript on file with Rutgers University School of Criminal Justice.

Cialdini, R. B., Kallgren, C. A., and Reno, R. R. (1991). A focus theory of normative conduct: A theoretical refinement and reevaluation of the role of norms in human behavior. In M. Zanna (ed.), *Advances in experimental social psychology* (vol. 24, pp. 201–234). New York: Academic Press.

Cohen, D., Nisbett, R. E., Bowdle, B. F., and Schwarz, N. (1996). Insult, aggression, and the Southern culture of honor: An "experimental ethnography." *Journal of Personality and Social Psychology, 70,* 945–960.

Compton, W. M., Cottler, L. B., Phelps, D. L., Abdallah, A. B., and Spitznagel, E. L. (2000). Psychiatric disorders among drug dependent subjects: Are they primary or secondary? *American Journal on Addictions, 9,* 126–134.

Cork, D. (1999). Examining space-time interaction in city-level homicide data: Crack markets and the diffusion of guns among youth. *Journal of Quantitative Criminology, 15,* 379–406.

Cottler, L. B., Compton, W. M., Mager, D., Spitznagel, E., and Janca, A. (1992). Posttraumatic stress disorder among substance users from the general population. *American Journal of Psychiatry, 149,* 664–670.

Critchlow, B. (1986). The powers of John Barleycorn: Beliefs about the effects of alcohol on social behavior. *American Psychologist, 41,* 751–764.

Decker, S. H., Pennell, S., and Caldwell, A. (1997). *Illegal firearms: Access and use by arrestees* (Research in Brief, NCJ 163496). Washington, DC: U.S. Department of Justice, National Institute of Justice.

DiNardo, H. (1993). Law enforcement, the price of cocaine, and cocaine use. *Mathematical and Computer Modeling, 17,* 53–64.

Eagly, A. H., and Chaiken, S. (1993). *The psychology of attitudes.* Fort Worth, TX: Harcourt Brace Jovanovich.

Eck, J., and McGuire, E. (2000). Have changes in policing reduced violent crime? An assessment of the evidence. In A. Blumstein and J. Wallman (eds.), *The crime drop in America* (pp. 207–265). New York: Cambridge University Press.

Fagan, J. (1990). Intoxication and aggression. In M. Tonry and J. Q. Wilson (eds.), *Drugs and crime,* vol. 13 of *Crime and justice: A review of research* (pp. 241–320). Chicago: University of Chicago Press.

Fagan, J., and Chin, K. (1990). Violence as regulation and social control in the distribution of crack. In M. De La Rosa, E. Lambert, and B. Gropper (eds.), *Drugs and violence: Causes, correlates, and consequences* (Research Monograph 103, pp. 8–43). Rockville, MD: U.S. Department of Health and Human Services, National Institute on Drug Abuse.

Fishbein, D. (2000). Neuropsychological function, drug abuse, and violence: A conceptual framework. *Criminal Justice and Behavior, 27,* 139–159.

Fisher, B., Cullen, F., and Turner, M. (2000). *The sexual victimization of college women* (Research Report, NCJ 182369). Washington, DC: U.S. Department of Justice, National Institute of Justice.

Fisher, B., Cullen, F. and Turner, M. (forthcoming). Being pursued: Stalking victimization in a national study of college women. *Criminology and Public Policy.*

Fisher, B., Sloan, J., and Chunmeng, L. (1998). Crime in the ivory tower: The level and sources of student victimization. *Criminology, 36,* 671–710.

Freeman, R. B. (1996). Why do so many young American men commit crimes and what might we do about it? *Journal of Economic Perspectives, 10,* 25–42.

Gandossy, R., Williams, J., Cohen, J., and Harwood, H. (1980). *Drugs and crime: A survey and analysis of the literature* (NCJ 159074). Washington, DC: U.S. Department of Justice, National Institute of Justice.

Giancola, P. R. (2000). Executive functioning: A conceptual framework for alcohol-related aggression. *Experimental and Clinical Psychopharmacology, 8,* 576–597.

Goldstein, P. (1985). The drug/violence nexus: A tripartite conceptual framework. *Journal of Drug Issues, 14,* 493–506.

Goldstein, P., Brownstein, H. H., and Ryan, P. J. (1992). Drug-related homicide in New York: 1984 and 1988. *Crime and Delinquency, 38,* 459–476.

Goldstein, P., Brownstein, H. H., Ryan, P. J., and Bellucci, P. A. (1989). Crack and homicide in New York City, 1988: A conceptually based event analysis. *Contemporary Drug Problems, 16,* 651–687.

Golub, A., and Johnson, B. D. (1997). *Crack's decline: Some surprises across U.S. cities* (Research in Brief, NCJ 165707). Washington, DC: U.S. Department of Justice, National Institute of Justice.

Harwood, H., Fountain, D., and Livermore, G. (1998). *The economic costs of alcohol and drug abuse in the United States— 1992.* Bethesda, MD: U.S. Department of Health and Human Services, National Institute on Drug Abuse.

Hindmarch, I., and Brinkmann, R. (1999). Trends in the use of alcohol and other drugs in cases of sexual assault. *Human Psychopharmacology: Clinical and Experimental, 14,* 225–231.

Inciardi, J. A. (1990). The crack-violence connection within a population of hard core adolescent offenders. In M. De La Rosa, E. Lambert, and B. Gropper (eds.), *Drugs and violence: Causes, correlates, and consequences* (Research Monograph 103, pp. 92–111). Rockville, MD: U.S. Department of Health and Human Services, National Institute on Drug Abuse.

Inciardi, J. A., and Pottieger, A. E. (1994). Crack-cocaine use and street crime. *Journal of Drug Issues, 24,* 273–292.

Inciardi, J. A., and Pottieger, A. E. (1991). Kids, crack, and crime. *Journal of Drug Issues, 21,* 257–270.

Ito, T. A., Miller, N., and Pollock, V. E. (1996). Alcohol and aggression: A meta-analysis on the moderating effects of inhibitory cues, triggering events, and self-focused attention. *Psychological Bulletin, 120,* 60–82.

Jacobsen, C., and Hanneman, R. A. (1992). Illegal drugs: Past, present and possible futures. *Journal of Drug Issues, 22,* 105–120.

Johnson, B., Golub, A., and Dunlap, E. (2000). The rise and decline of hard drugs, drug markets, and violence in inner-city New York. In A. Blumstein and J. Wallman (eds.), *The crime drop in America* (pp. 164–206). New York: Cambridge University Press.

Kennedy, D. (1993, March). *Closing the market: Controlling the drug trade in Tampa, Florida* (Program Focus, NCJ 139963). Washington, DC: U.S. Department of Justice, National Institute of Justice.

Kerr, N. L., MacCoun, R. J., Hansen, C. H., and Hymes, J. A. (1987). Gaining and losing social support: Momentum in decision making groups. *Journal of Experimental Social Psychology, 23,* 119–145.

Kessler, R. C., Nelson, C. B., McGonagle, K. A., Edlund, M. J., Frank, R. G., and Leaf, P. J. (1996). The epidemiology of co-occurring addictive and mental disorders: Implications for prevention and service utilization. *American Journal of Orthopsychiatry, 66,* 17–31.

Kleiman, M. A. R. (1993). Enforcement swamping: A positive-feedback mechanism in rates of illicit activity. *Mathematical and Computer Modeling, 17,* 65–75.

Kleiman, M. A. R. (1997). The problem of replacement and the logic of drug law enforcement. *Drug Policy Analysis Bulletin, 3,* 8–10 [Online]. Available: www.fas.org/drugs/issue3.htm

Klein, M., Maxson, C., and Cunningham, L. (1991). "'Crack,' street gangs, and violence." *Criminology, 29,* 623–650.

Lattimore, P. K., Trudeau, J., Riley, K. J., Leiter, J., and Edwards, S. (1997). *Homicide in eight U.S. cities: Trends, context, and policy implications* (Research Report, NCJ 167262). Washington, DC: U.S. Department of Justice, National Institute of Justice.

Leshner, A. I. (1997). Addiction is a brain disease, and it matters. *Science, 278,* 45–47.

Lipton, D., and Johnson, D. (1998). Smack, crack, and score: Two decades of NIDA-funded drugs and crime research at NDRI 1974–1994. *Substance Use and Misuse, 33,* 1779–1815.

MacCoun, R. (1998). Toward a psychology of harm reduction. *American Psychologist, 53,* 1199–1208.

MacCoun, R. J., and Reuter, P. (1994, March 7). *Harm reduction as a response to drug selling and violence.* Paper presented at the Fifth International Conference on the Reduction of Drug-Related Harm, Toronto.

MacCoun, R. J., and Reuter, P. (2001). *Drug war heresies: Learning from other vices, times, and places.* New York: Cambridge University Press.

Markowitz, S. (2000). *An economic analysis of alcohol, drugs, and crime in the National Criminal Victimization Survey.* National Bureau of Economic Research Working Paper 7982. Cambridge, MA: National Bureau of Economic Research.

McElrath, K., Chitwood, D., and Comerford, M. (1997). Crime victimization among injection drug users. *Journal of Drug Issues, 27,* 771–783.

McGraw, K. M. (1985). Subjective probabilities and moral judgments. *Journal of Experimental Social Psychology, 21,* 501–518.

Meehl, P. E. (1995). Bootstraps taxometrics: Solving the classification problem in psychopathology. *American Psychologist, 50,* 266–275.

Mieczkowski, T. (1990). The operational styles of crack houses in Detroit. In M. De La Rosa, E. Lambert, and B. Gropper (eds.), *Drugs and violence: Causes, correlates, and consequences* (pp. 60–91). Rockville, MD: U.S. Department of Health and Human Services, National Institute on Drug Abuse.

Miller, N. S. (1993). Comorbidity of psychiatric and alcoholic/drug disorders: Interactions and independent status. *Journal of Addictive Diseases, 12,* 5–16.

Moore, M. H. (1990). Supply reduction and drug law enforcement. In M. Tonry and J. Q. Wilson (eds.), *Drugs and crime,* vol. 13 of *Crime and justice: A review of research* (pp. 109–157). Chicago: University of Chicago Press.

Mueser, K. T., Yarnold, P. R., Rosenberg, S. D., Swett, C., Miles, K. M., and Hill, D. (2000). Substance use disorder in hospitalized severely mentally ill psychiatric patients: Prevalence, correlates, and subgroups. *Schizophrenia Bulletin, 26,* 179–192.

National Crime Victimization Survey (2000). *Criminal victimization in the United States, 1998 statistical tables* (NCJ 181585). Washington, DC: U.S. Department of Justice, Bureau of Justice Statistics.

Nisbett, R., and Ross, L. (1980). *Human inference: Strategies and shortcomings of social judgment.* Englewood Cliffs, NJ: Prentice-Hall.

Office of National Drug Control Policy. (1995). *National drug control strategy.* Washington, DC: The White House.

Office of National Drug Control Policy. (2000, March). *Drug-related crime: ONDCP drug policy information Fact Sheet* (NCJ 181056). Washington, DC: The White House.

Ousey, G. C., and Lee, M. R. (2000). Examining the conditional nature of the illicit drug market-homicide relationship: A partial test of the theory of contingent causation. Paper presented at the 2000 meeting of the American Society of Criminology, San Francisco.

Parker, R., and Auerhahn, K. (1998). Alcohol, drugs, and violence. *Annual Review of Sociology, 24,* 291–311.

Petersilia, J. (1990). When probation becomes more dreaded than prison. *Federal Probation, 54,* 23–27.

Pierre, R. E. (1996, September 24). Marijuana's violent side. *Washington Post,* A1.

Ragin, C. C. (2000). *Fuzzy-set social science.* Chicago: University of Chicago Press.

Rasmussen, D. W., and Benson, B. L. (1994). *The economic anatomy of a drug war: Criminal justice in the commons.* Lanham, MD: Rowman and Littlefield.

Rettig, R. A., and Yarmolinsky, A. (eds.) (1995). *Federal regulation of methadone treatment.* Committee on Federal Regulation of Methadone Treatment, Institute of Medicine, National Academy of Sciences. Washington, DC: National Academy Press.

Reuter, P. (1989, March 26). An economist looks at the carnage. *Washington Post.*

Reuter, P., and MacCoun, R. (1992). Street drug markets in inner-city neighborhoods: Matching policy to reality. In J. B. Steinberg, D. W. Lyon, and M. E. Vaiana (eds.), *Urban America: Policy choices for Los Angeles and the Nation* (pp. 227–251). Santa Monica, CA: RAND.

Reuter, P., MacCoun, R., and Murphy, P. (1990). *Money from crime.* Santa Monica, CA: RAND.

Rhodes, W., Scheiman, P., Pittayathikhun, T., Collins, L., and Tsarfaty, V. (1995). *What America's users spend on illegal drugs, 1988–1993.* Washington, DC: Office of National Drug Control Policy.

Rhodes, W., Layne, M., Johnston, P., and Hozik, L. (2000). *What America's users spend on illegal drugs: 1988–1998.* Washington, DC: Office of National Drug Control Policy.

Riley, K. J. (1998). Homicide and drugs: A tale of six cities. *Homicide Studies, 2,* 176–205.

Saner, H., MacCoun, R., and Reuter, P. (1995). On the ubiquity of drug selling among youthful offenders in Washington, DC, 1985–1991: Age, period, or cohort effect? *Journal of Quantitative Criminology, 11,* 337–362.

Science (1997, October 3). Frontiers in Neuroscience: The science of substance abuse. 278, special section.

Sheley, J. F. (1994). Drug activity and firearms possession and use by juveniles. *Journal of Drug Issues, 24,* 363–382.

Smith, A., and Varese, F. (2001, August 1). Payment, protection and punishment: The role of information and reputation in the Mafia. *Rationality and Society, 13,* 349–393.

Spunt, B., Goldstein, P., Bellucci, P., and Miller, T. (1990). Race/ethnicity and gender differences in the drugs–violence relationship. *Journal of Psychoactive Drugs, 22,* 293–303.

Spunt, B., Brownstein, H., Goldstein, P., Fendrich, M., and Liberty, H. (1995). Drug use by homicide offenders. *Journal of Psychoactive Drugs, 27,* 125–134.

Stacy, A. W., Widaman, K. F., and Marlatt, G. A. (1990). Expectancy models of alcohol use. *Journal of Personality and Social Psychology, 58,* 918–928.

Steadman, H. J., Mulvey, E. P., Monahan, J., Robbins, P. C., Appelbaum, P. S., Grisso, T., Roth, L. H., and Silver, E. (1998). Violence by people discharged from acute psychiatric inpatient facilities and by others in the same neighborhoods. *Archives of General Psychiatry, 55,* 393–401.

Steele, C. M., and Josephs, R. A. (1990). Alcohol myopia: Its prized and dangerous effects. *American Psychologist, 45,* 921–933.

Substance Abuse and Mental Health Services Administration. (2001). *Mid-year 2000 preliminary emergency department data from the Drug Abuse Warning Network.* Rockville, MD: U.S. Department of Health and Human Services, Substance Abuse and Mental Health Services Administration.

Tardiff, K., Marzuk, P. M., Leon, A. C., Hirsch, C. S., Stajic, M., Portera, L., and Hartwell, N. (1994). Homicide in New York City: Cocaine use and firearms. *JAMA: The Journal of the American Medical Association, 272,* 43–46.

Taylor, L., Caulkins, J., and Reuter, P. (2000). *Some simple economics of illegal drug markets and violence.* Unpublished manuscript, Carnegie Mellon University.

Teplin, L. A., Abram, K. M., and McClelland, G. M. (1994). Does psychiatric disorder predict violent crime among released jail detainees? A six-year longitudinal study. *American Psychologist, 49,* 335–342.

U.S. Sentencing Commission (1995, February). *Cocaine and Federal sentencing policy.* Special Report to Congress. Washington, DC: U.S. Sentencing Commission [Online]. Available: www.ussc.gov/crack/EXEC.HTM

White, H. R., and Gorman, D. M. (2000). Dynamics of the drug-crime relationship. In *Crime and justice 2000, vol. 1: The nature of crime: Continuity and change* (NCJ 182408, pp. 151–218). Washington, DC: U.S. Department of Justice, National Institute of Justice.

Wolfgang, M. E. (1958). *Patterns in criminal homicide.* Philadelphia: University of Pennsylvania Press.

Zimring, F. E., and Hawkins, G. (1997). *Crime is not the problem: Lethal violence in America.* New York: Oxford University Press.

OTHER APPLICATIONS OF GOLDSTEIN'S FRAMEWORK

NEW YORK

Even excluding the works of Goldstein and his colleagues, much of the work using the tripartite framework focuses on New York during the mid- to late 1980s. The U.S. Sentencing Commission (1995) used Goldstein's framework to compare the incidence of violence related to the use of powder cocaine and crack. Using expert testimony and existing literature, and largely focusing on the studies done in New York,[1] the Commission concluded that crack was a greater source of systemic violence than powder cocaine, that economic-compulsive violence was relatively rare among cocaine users, and that "neither powder nor crack cocaine excite or agitate users to commit criminal acts and that the stereotype of a drug-crazed addict committing heinous crimes is not true for either form of cocaine" (p. x).

MIAMI

Inciardi's (1990) survey of 611 serious juvenile delinquents in Miami and Dade County assessed offender self-reports of drug-related systemic, economic-compulsive, and psychopharmacological crime. In the 12 months prior to the interviews, which occurred from 1985 to 1989, about 5 percent of the sample reported being a psychopharmacological victim, 59 percent reported having committed robberies ("the majority of which were committed to purchase drugs," p. 100), and 8 percent reported being the perpetrators of systemic crimes. Inciardi also administered a supplementary crack survey to 254 of these delinquents from October 1986 to November 1987. This survey and other data analyses by Inciardi led him to conclude that the Miami crack market was much less violent and less (juvenile) gang-related than portrayed in the media and may be "kindler[sic] and

gentler" than other large cities. He also reported that the worst years for murders in Miami were during its cocaine wars in the early 1980s. Inciardi found that "those more proximal of the crack distribution market were more involved in violent crime" (p. 104). This study has at least two advantages over Goldstein et al. (1989): Crimes other than homicide were considered, and respondents were asked about drug-related victimization. But the drug associated with these crimes was not listed as it was in the Goldstein et al. study.

CHICAGO

One source that was developed to assess homicide fluctuations and motivations is the Chicago Homicide Dataset (CHD). Detailed information on every homicide in the records of the Chicago Police Department is available for 1965–95 (Block, Block, and Illinois Criminal Justice Information Authority, 1998). CHD does not include data on specific drugs, but its motive classification fits nicely with the tripartite framework. The four types of drug-related motives for homicide are selling or drug business (this includes any homicides during or because of a transaction);[2] an argument over possession, use, quality, or cost of drugs; getting money for drugs or acquiring drugs for personal use; and other drug involvement (e.g., baby dies of malnutrition because the parents were high; offender was drug crazed).[3]

The per capita drug-related homicide rate remained fairly stable from 1973 to 1984 (around 0.4 homicides per 100,000 Cook County residents), with "arguments" at a slightly higher rate from 1974 to 1977. Homicide rates related to all of the motives fluctuated from 1984 to 1995, but it is interesting that the aggregate rate for every motive except "business/transaction" was virtually the same for 1984–85 and 1995 (still close to 0.4). The advent of crack likely explains why homicide rates related to all of the motives increased from 1985 to 1989, but it is of special interest that the "business/transaction" motive skyrocketed during those years. Clearly, more might be learned by examining the specific drugs associated with "business/transaction" homicides in Chicago over this time period.

EIGHT-CITY STUDY

To learn why city homicide rates did not change uniformly in the early 1990s, Lattimore and colleagues (1997) comprehensively examined homicide in eight cities for 1985–94: Atlanta, Detroit, Indianapolis, Miami, New Orleans, Richmond, Tampa, and Washington, D.C. In addition to comparing ADAM results with UCR data for these cities, Lattimore et al. interviewed key policymakers, law enforcement and criminal justice officials, and community leaders in the cities. These interviews revealed that crack was most likely associated with community violence and homicide, while the market violence associated with marijuana was a growing concern in Washington, D.C., and Richmond. Methamphetamines, LSD, PCP, and heroin were not associated with homicide rates and were rarely mentioned by local authorities. It is important to note that Lattimore et al. found that in many cases the perceptions about local drug trends differed substantially from drug trends as measured by DUF/ADAM.

Lattimore and colleagues question the relationship between crack and market violence because the crack markets were described as highly competitive in cities in which the homicide rate was declining, increasing, or remaining the same (1997, p. 89). But it is not clear that the same conclusions could be drawn if disaggregated homicide rates (by circumstance) were considered. The authors not only looked at how competitive the market was, they also considered the stability of prices, transactions, and participants. Their argument that links between drugs and homicide "appear to fall mainly on the use side" (p. 92) relies on their findings about participants:

> The general structure of participation in crack markets and the nature, duration, and consequences of

the "crack high" may account for the relationship between the cocaine prevalence rates among arrestees and homicide rates. Crack users reported the large number of "buys," extensive networks of potential suppliers, and less reliance on a primary supplier, suggesting that transactions were likely to occur in an opportunistic manner. The high from crack lasts as little as 10 minutes; thus, when the high wears off, the crack user may still be in the market and motivated to buy more of the drug— and to commit a crime to obtain the money to do so. (p. 141)

This is essentially an argument about economic-compulsive violence, which other crack-specific studies have dismissed (see U.S. Sentencing Commission, 1995). While this difference may be geographic (the other studies were primarily done in New York City), it may also be the artifact of a bivariate analysis of two datasets (UCR and ADAM) that did not always cover the same populations.

NATIONAL ESTIMATES

Others used nationwide data to learn more about the drugs–crime nexus. Caulkins and colleagues (1997) used the tripartite framework to assess the impact that mandatory minimum sentences have on cocaine consumption and subsequent crime. Relying on estimates from Goldstein and his colleagues (Goldstein, Brownstein, and Ryan, 1992; Spunt et al., 1990; Spunt et al., 1995), the National Criminal Victimization Survey, inmate surveys, and murder data for large urban counties, Caulkins et al. determined the number of systemic, economic-compulsive, and psychopharmacological crimes that were drug related. Their next step was to determine how much of this crime was related to cocaine. Based on information from Rhodes et al. (1995), the ADAM Program, the Office of National Drug Control Policy (1995), and Goldstein (Goldstein et al., 1989; Goldstein, Brownstein, and Ryan, 1992; Spunt et al. 1995), Caulkins et al. (1997) suggest that cocaine accounts for about 75 percent of drug-related economic-compulsive crime, 50 percent of illicit psychopharmacological homicides, and 75 percent of systemic homicides.

NOTES

1. New York: Chin and Fagan, 1992; Fagan and Chin, 1990; Goldstein et al., 1989. Miami: Inciardi, 1990; Inciardi and Pottieger, 1991; Inciardi and Pottieger, 1994. Los Angeles: Klein et al., 1991. Detroit: Mieczkowski, 1990. The Commission also cited an unpublished DEA report and a review article by Fagan (1990). The former found "that seven crack-related homicides were 'multi-dimensional,' with systemic being one of the dimensions," but it is not clear where these homicides occurred and what the other dimensions were.

2. The codebook reads: "Use code 1 when BUSINESS is the motive for the incident (e.g., both victim and offender involved in dealing, victim killed as a bystander of a drug business hit, victim killed because he interfered with the business, victim killed during a drug transaction or because of a drug transaction)."

3. Cases where there was no positive evidence or no information are not included. Of the 23,817 homicides occurring between 1964 and 1995, 22,282 either had no information about drug motive or were not drug related. Unfortunately, the non-drug-related homicides cannot be separated from the no-information group.

ARRESTEES NEEDING DRUGS AND/OR ALCOHOL AT THE TIME OF THE OFFENSE, 1995–99

City	INCOME-GENERATING OFFENSES		NON-INCOME-GENERATING OFFENSES	
	Total	%Needing Drugs and/or Alcohol	Total	% Needing Drugs and/or Alcohol
Albuquerque	249	40	1,308	19
Anchorage	105	16	723	9
Atlanta	1,526	17	2,833	9
Birmingham	1,216	17	3,646	12
Chicago	1,825	26	4,183	17
Cleveland	1,569	16	4,191	12
Dallas	1,934	12	3,432	8
Denver	1,195	8	5,842	6
Des Moines	182	20	744	10
Detroit	903	9	2,876	8
Ft. Lauderdale	1,209	19	4,032	13
Houston	1,257	6	4,252	5
Indianapolis	2,447	15	5,248	8
Laredo	185	13	531	5
Las Vegas	355	26	1,638	14
Los Angeles	4,022	10	6,951	7
Miami	1,395	15	2,182	11
Minneapolis	179	21	953	10
New Orleans	2,072	16	4,020	10
New York	3,162	16	6,247	16
Oklahoma City	394	14	1,298	9
Omaha	678	13	3,249	5
Philadelphia	2,201	21	1,645	17
Phoenix	1,828	15	5,929	7
Portland	1,550	11	5,032	10
Sacramento	389	14	1,307	9
Salt Lake City	333	17	1,044	13
San Antonio	2,060	8	5,570	4
San Diego	2,407	8	3,982	7
San Jose	1,549	8	4,441	6
Seattle	301	21	1,090	13
Spokane	261	20	1,063	12
St. Louis	1,160	17	2,592	12
Tucson	308	14	1,965	9
Washington, DC	1,529	10	3,200	8
Total	**43,935**	**14% (r = 6,141)**	**109,239**	**10% (n = 10,431)**

Notes: Percentages rounded to nearest whole percentage point. Observations with missing data for any of these variables were deleted. Sixty-four observations from 1998 and 374 observations from 1999 were not considered because of a unique charge-coding strategy. Income-generating offenses include burglary, burglary tools, prostitution, embezzlement, larceny/theft, pickpocketing/jostling, robbery, stolen property, stolen vehicle, and drug sales.

Source: 1995–99 data from the Arrestee Drug Abuse Monitoring Program.

CHAPTER 1: DISCUSSION QUESTIONS

1. What are the major social scientific theories about the relationship between drugs and crime?

2. Why have theories of drug use and of the drugs–crime connection seemingly developed outside of mainstream deviance research?

3. What is the Goldstein model? What are three possibilities for explaining the link between drugs and violence?

4. What was the link between the Harrison Act and crime by addicts? How does the Harrison Act continue to influence drug policy? What other legislation frames current policies?

5. What do Farabee and colleagues propose as explanations for the relationship between cocaine and lifetime criminal patterns?

6. What are the limitations of each selection?

7. What are the policy implications of each selection?

CHAPTER 1: ADDITIONAL RESOURCES IN RESEARCH NAVIGATOR AND IN THE *NEW YORK TIMES*

Broadhead, R. S. (2001). Hustlers in drug-related AIDS prevention: Ethnographers, outreach workers, injection drug users. *Addiction Research and Theory, 9,* 545–556.

Buchanan, J., and Young, L. (2000). The war on drugs—a war on drug users? *Drugs: Education, Prevention, and Policy, 7,* 409–422.

Butterfield, F. (2004, January 28). Justice Department ends testing of criminals for drug use. *New York Times.*

Foster, J. (2000). Social exclusion, crime, and drugs. *Drugs: Education, Prevention, and Policy, 7,* 317–330.

Glaberson, W. (2003, December 10). Brooklyn man guilty in murder case linked to drug gang. *New York Times.*

Helm, H. W., Jr., Boward, M. D., McBride, D. C., and Del Rio, R. I. (2002). Depression, drug use and gender differences among students at a religious university. *North American Journal of Psychology, 4,* 183–197.

Jensen, E. L., Gerber, J., and Mosher, C. (2004). Social consequences of the war on drugs: The legacy of failed policy. *Criminal Justice Policy Review, 15,* 100–121.

Kaplan, H. B., Tolle, G. C., Jr., and Yoshida, T. (2001). Substance use-induced diminution of violence: A countervailing effect in longitudinal perspective. *Criminology, 39,* 205–224.

Lichtblau, E. (2003, February 5). White House report stings drug agency on abilities. *New York Times.*

Lillibridge, J., Cox, M., and Cross, W. (2002). Uncovering the secret: Giving voice to the experiences of nurses who misuse substances. *Journal of Advanced Nursing, 39,* 219–229.

McCoy, H. V., Messiah, S. E., and Yu, Z. (2001). Perpetrators, victims, and observers of violence: Chronic and nonchronic drug users. *Journal of Interpersonal Violence, 16,* 890–909.

Newman, A. (2004, February 10). Police tie drugs and gangs to killing in Coney Island. *New York Times.*

Phongpaichit, P., and Baker, C. (2003, May 24). Slaughter in the name of a drug war. *New York Times.*

SPECIFIC DRUGS AND CRIME

This chapter contains articles that deal with specific types of drugs—alcohol, marijuana, heroin, crack cocaine, and ecstasy—and their relationships to criminal behavior. In the first selection, Robert Nash Parker and Kathleen Auerhahn investigate the intersection of alcohol, drugs, and violence. They claim that there is no convincing evidence that illicit drug use is associated with increased violence. In almost all cases, however, alcohol is associated with violence of all types. Noting that existing research fails to sufficiently explain these findings, they proceed to review promising theoretical approaches. While the authors take an unusual and firm approach to perspectives on causality, this reading is important both for its presentation of existing research and the authors' contributions to theory.

Andrew Golub and Bruce Johnson present convincing evidence that young people are increasingly turning to marijuana as their drug of choice. They examine several national data sets for trends in marijuana use. Consistent with findings reported elsewhere, the authors present a conceptual model of epidemic drug use in the United States. The main focus of their analysis relies on ADAM data, providing some important connections between drug use and arrests.

Martin Killias, Marcelo Aebi, and Denis Ribeaud report on a controversial program that prescribes heroin to addicts in Switzerland. Findings from this international research project have sparked a great deal of debate. Here they examine the possibility that reduction in criminal behavior is a function of police behavior rather than a real change in addict behavior.

Eric Baumer and colleagues examine trends associated with robbery, burglary, and homicide in relation to the crack epidemic. Although robbery and burglary have historically tracked with each other, they diverged in the late 1980s. Baumer and colleagues' findings about the role of crack in this divergence are especially useful.

Blake Urbach, K. Michael Reynolds, and George Yacoubian also use quantitative methods to examine race and ecstasy involvement. Using official arrest data, they compare data for white respondents with data for other respondents and find that there are significantly higher arrests rates for whites. Drug use and involvement preferences vary by social groupings, with ecstasy use being primarily a white phenomenon. This finding lays the groundwork for future research to examine the social context of ecstasy involvement.

Even though the readings are quite different in focus, several themes can be identified. First, the most common crime committed by illicit drug users is copping or dealing drugs, which is reflected in several of the readings. Economically motivated crimes are the next most commonly committed by drug users. Second, not everyone agrees on the definitions of use and abuse. For example, Parker and Auerhahn claim that there is no convincing evidence that illicit drug use is related to crimes of violence. Definitional problems often lead to differences in measurement of key variables, which can then lead to large differences in findings. Third, sampling concerns are evident in all the studies. Although it is impossible to generate the perfect sample for this type of research, it is also important to recognize limitations. Fourth, much research in this area does not sufficiently frame findings within existing theoretical schools of thought, nor do researchers offer new approaches. Despite measurement, sampling, and theory deficiencies, however, all the research supports the contention that drugs and crime (at least crimes of violence) are closely related.

Alcohol, Drugs, and Violence

ROBERT NASH PARKER

KATHLEEN AUERHAHN

ABSTRACT

A review of the scientific literature on the relationship between alcohol and violence and that between drugs and violence is presented. A review and analysis of three major theoretical approaches to understanding these relationships are also presented. A number of conclusions are reached on the basis of these efforts. First, despite a number of published statements to the contrary, we find no significant evidence suggesting that drug use is associated with violence. Second, there is substantial evidence to suggest that alcohol use is significantly associated with violence of all kinds. Third, recent theoretical efforts reviewed here have, despite shortcomings, led to significant new understanding of how and why alcohol and drugs are related to violence. Fourth, these theoretical models and a growing number of empirical studies demonstrate the importance of social context for understanding violence and the ways in which alcohol and drugs are related to violence. Fifth, the shortcomings of these theoretical models and the lack of definitive empirical tests of these perspectives point to the major directions where future research on the relationship between alcohol and violence, and between drugs and violence, is needed.

INTRODUCTION

That the United States leads the industrialized nations in rates of interpersonal violence is a well-documented fact (National Research Council 1993). Examples of this can be seen in the extraordinarily high rates of violent crimes such as homicide, robbery, and rape in the United States (National Research Council 1993, Parker and Rebhun, 1995); an additional and disturbing fact that has come to light in recent years is the increasing rate of youth violence, particularly lethal violence (Blumstein, 1995; Alaniz et al., 1998).

During the last decade, interest has grown in the relationship between alcohol, drugs, and violence. In addition to the mostly misguided attention in mass media and in political circles to the relationship between illegal drugs and violence, a number of empirical studies have attempted to disentangle the associations between alcohol, drugs, and violence. Several studies have attempted to organize this knowledge into a comprehensive theoretical framework. This chapter synthesizes this body of work to assess the state of the art in thinking about the relationships between psychoactive substances and violent behavior.

Defining and understanding the complex relationships among alcohol, drugs, and violence require that we examine issues of pharmacology, settings, and larger social contexts to understand the mechanisms that associate substance use and violence in individuals. In addition to this, we must also consider not only the ways in which individuals are nested within larger social contexts, but also the ways in which these contexts themselves may create conditions in which violent behavior takes place, for example, the ways in which availability of substances, while itself conditioned to some degree by larger social forces, contributes to the spatial distribution of crime and violence.

We do not attempt to review the growing literature on the biological aspects of violence. Despite increased interest in this area of research, no credible scientific evidence currently exists that demonstrates any significant link between biological characteristics and violence (National Research Council 1993). Future research may reveal complex interactions among biological, pharmacological, psychological, and contextual aspects of alcohol- and drug-related violence, but no conclusive evidence exists to support this idea at present.

Reprinted, with permission, from the Annual Review of Sociology, Volume 24, © 1998 by Annual Reviews
www.annualreviews.org, pages 291–311.

In addition to trying to understand the ways in which alcohol and drug use may contribute to violent behavior, it is also important to consider the ways that alcohol and other drugs relate to human behavior in general. Some advances have been made in the study of psychological expectancies concerning alcohol's effect on behavior (Brown, 1993; Grube et al., 1994), the relationship between alcohol and cognitive functioning (Pihl et al., 1993), the impact of alcohol on aggressive behavior (Leonard and Taylor, 1983), and the dynamic developmental effects of early exposure to alcohol and violence among young people (White et al., 1993) and among women who have been victimized as children and as adults (Miller and Downs, 1993; Widom and Ames, 1994; Roesler and Dafle, 1993).

Similar work has attempted to understand the links between illicit drugs and behavior, although due to the attention focused on the illegality of these substances, this body of work tends to be most concerned with illegal behaviors that might be associated with drugs. Examples from this literature include examinations of the links between drug use and delinquent behavior among juveniles (Watts and Wright, 1990; Fagan, 1993; Fagan et al., 1990); relationships between substance use and domestic violence (Bennett, 1995; Bennett et al., 1994; Roberts, 1987; Blount et al., 1994); the ways in which the use and distribution of illicit drugs are related to all types of crime, particularly nonviolent property offenses (Ball et al., 1982; Ball, 1991; Baumer, 1994; Greenberg, 1976; Johnson et al., 1994; Klein and Maxson, 1985; McCoy et al., 1995; Meiczkowski, 1994; Feucht and Kyle, 1996); and the impact of drug use on the ability to maintain interpersonal relationships (Joe, 1996; Fishbein, 1996; Lerner and Burns, 1978).

A fairly common problem specific to theoretical and empirical investigations of the relationship between drugs and violence is the tendency—largely ideological—to lump all illicit drugs together, as if all drugs might be expected to have the same relationship to violent behavior. Different drugs certainly do have different pharmacological effects, which may or may not influence the user's tendency toward violence; this should be treated as a prominent empirical question, rather than as an afterthought usually addressed only when results are disaggregated by drug type. Another problem specific to the analysis of the impacts of illicit drugs on behavior that hinders our understanding of the relationship between drugs and violence in real-world (as opposed to laboratory) settings was cogently pointed out by one researcher—that the degree of both impurity and deception in the illicit drug market

"makes any direct inferences between drug-taking and behavior seem almost ludicrous" (Greenberg, 1976, p. 119; see also Johnson, 1978). Evidence of the greater likelihood of polydrug use among more violent research subjects also confuses any causal inferences that can be made with respect to particular drugs (e.g., Spunt et al., 1995, Inciardi and Pottieger, 1994).

DRUGS, ALCOHOL, AND VIOLENCE AT THE INDIVIDUAL LEVEL

A rather fragmented research literature attempts to identify links between alcohol, drugs, and violence at the individual or pharmacological level. This work is discussed briefly below, mainly as a prelude to theoretical models developed in light of these empirical findings.

Evidence of an individual level association between alcohol and violence is widespread. For example, Collins (1981) reviewed a number of studies in which alcohol and violence were associated among individuals. Experimental studies have also shown a consistent relationship at the individual level between alcohol use and aggressive behavior, especially in the presence of social cues that would normally elicit an aggressive response; the consumption of alcohol increases the aggressiveness of this response (Taylor, 1983; Gantner and Taylor, 1992; Pihl et al., 1993). Roizen (1993, pp. 4–5) reports that in nearly 40 studies of violent offenders, and an equal number of studies of victims of violence, alcohol involvement was found in about 50% of the events and people examined. Although most individual-level studies assume that alcohol has a potentially causal role, an argument supported by the experimental studies cited here, some have argued variously that the relationship is spurious (Collins, 1989), that both are caused by third factors (Jessor and Jessor, 1977), or that aggression and violence precede alcohol and drug abuse (White et al., 1987).

In general, little evidence suggests that illicit drugs are uniquely associated with the occurrence of violent crime. While respondents of the 1991 National Criminal Victimization Survey perceived more than one fourth of violent criminal assailants to be under the influence of alcohol, less than 10% of these assailants were reported by victims to be under the influence of illicit drugs. Of these, more than half were reported to be under the influence of both alcohol and drugs (Bureau of Justice Statistics, 1992a). These percentages are supported by urinalysis data for persons arrested for violent offenses, which yield the finding that in 1990, only 5.6% of violent offenders were under the influence of illicit drugs at the time of their offense (Bureau of Justice Statistics, 1992b).

Studies of the drug and alcohol involvement of homicide offenders and victims also support the notion that alcohol is, overwhelmingly, the substance most frequently implicated in this particular form of violence (Abel, 1987; Spunt et al., 1994, 1995; Wieczorek et al., 1990; Yarvis, 1994; Fendrich et al., 1995; Goldstein et al., 1992). Interview studies with homicide offenders as well as toxicology studies of homicide victims consistently report that approximately half of all homicide offenders are intoxicated on drugs or alcohol at the time of the crime; similar percentages of homicide victims test positive for substance use as well (Abel, 1987; Langevin et al., 1982; Ray and Simons, 1987; Fendrich et al., 1995; Spunt et al., 1994, 1995; Wieczorek et al., 1990; Kratcoski, 1990; Welte and Abel, 1989; Garriott, 1993; Tardiff et al., 1995). Some evidence suggests that alcohol is the substance most frequently implicated in other violent events as well (Buss et al., 1995, Bureau of Justice Statistics 1992a).[1]

A shortcoming common to much of the work that has attempted to disentangle the individual-level relationships between drugs, alcohol, and violence is that many researchers fail to make a theoretical and/or empirical distinction between different types of drugs. For this reason, a short review of the literature concerning the links between violence and specific types of illicit drugs is presented below in the hope that some general conclusions can be drawn about the nature and magnitude of the relationship between illicit drugs and violence.

Heroin

Evidence to support a link between heroin and violence is virtually nonexistent. While there is some evidence that heroin users participate in economically motivated property crimes (see Kaplan, 1983, pp. 51–58 for a thoughtful and critical discussion of this issue), the work of Ball and his colleagues (Ball et al., 1982; Ball, 1991) fails to uncover persuasive evidence for a link between heroin use and violent crime. Although no specific measures for violent crime are reported in the analysis of self-reported criminality (validated by official records) from a sample of 243 heroin addicts in Baltimore, only 3% of the sample reported committing, on a daily basis, any crime other than theft; the figures for the weekly and "infrequent" commission of crimes other than theft are 3% and 9%, respectively (Ball et al., 1982). A later, more comprehensive analysis undertaken to determine whether or not "common forces attributable to heroin addiction are of primary etiological importance with respect to crime" (Ball, 1991, p. 413) compares addict samples from three major Eastern cities. Echoing the results of the 1982 study, involvement in violent crime was negligible, accounting for between 1.5% and 5.6% of all addict criminality across cities (Ball, 1991, p. 419).

Amphetamines

Considerable investigation has been made into a possible pharmacological link between amphetamines and violence. Some evidence indicates that in rare cases, either sustained periods of heavy use or extremely high acute doses can induce what has variously been called "toxic psychosis" or "amphetamine-induced psychosis," a reaction that is virtually indistinguishable from schizophrenia (Ellinwood, 1971; Fukushima, 1994). Aside from these extremely rare cases, some evidence may speak to a link between violent behavior and amphetamine use in ethnographic samples (Joe, 1996) and in case-study research (Ellinwood, 1971). One researcher notes, however, that this link may result from situational influences: "several . . . subjects seem to have lost intellectual awareness because they lived alone and had little chance to cross-check their delusional thinking. A long-term solitary lifestyle

---

[1]Difficulties inherent in trying to assess the involvement of alcohol relative to other drugs in violent events are largely the result of the way in which the research agenda surrounding the relationship between drugs, alcohol, and violence has been constructed. The majority of data collection efforts seem to be focused either on one particular substance (e.g., cocaine) and its relationship to or involvement in violent episodes or on comparisons between alcohol and illicit drugs in general, thereby hindering comparisons not only between alcohol and other drugs, but between different illicit drugs as well. A recent example is the National Institute of Justice report entitled *Drugs, Alcohol, and Domestic Violence in Memphis* (1997), which details research conducted to determine the role of substance use in incidents of domestic violence. At no point in the report are alcohol and drug use separated into distinct phenomena, making it impossible to determine what substances may be associated with domestic violence.

seems particularly significant in fostering this effect" (Ellinwood, 1971, p. 1173).

The importance of context and situation for the association between amphetamine use and violent behavior is supported by animal studies as well; Miczek and Tidey (1989) report that the social relationship between experimental animals significantly influences the level and type of violent behavior that they manifest when on amphetamines (Miczek and Tidey, 1989, p. 75). Additionally, the baseline rate of violent or aggressive behavior prior to amphetamine administration was an important predictor of violent behavior after drug administration. The authors conclude from this review of animal studies that:

> Among the most important determinants of amphetamine effects on aggressive and defensive responses are the stimulus situation, species, prior experience with these types of behavior, and . . . dosage and chronicity of drug exposure. (Miczek and Tidey, 1989, p. 71)

Cocaine

Some evidence suggests that cocaine use and violent behavior may be associated (Miller et al., 1991; Budd, 1989; Inciardi and Pottieger, 1994); one of the most widely reported pharmacological effects of cocaine in users is feelings of paranoia (Goode, 1993; Miller et al., 1991). At least one group of researchers suggest that cocaine-associated violence "may in part be a defensive reaction to irrational fear" (Miller et al., 1991, p. 1084).

The route of administration may influence the likelihood of violent behavior in users, with methods delivering the most intense and immediate effects being most closely associated with some forms of violent behavior. Users who smoked the drug in the form of "crack" were most likely to engage in violence proximate to cocaine use, followed by users taking the drug intravenously. Users who "snorted" the drug were found to be least likely to engage in violence (Giannini et al., 1993).[2] However, these researchers also reported that forms of violence "requiring sustained activity" (defined by the authors to include such acts as rape and robbery) were not associated with route of administration of cocaine. Because of this, the authors conclude that "circumstance and situation may be as important as route of administration" (Giannini et al., 1993, p. 69).

The greater influence of social rather than pharmacological factors on the cocaine–violence relationship has also been reported elsewhere. Goldstein et al. (1991) found that the relationship of violence to volume of cocaine use varied according to gender, with only male "big users" of cocaine contributing disproportionately to the distribution of violent events reported by the sample as a whole (Goldstein et al., 1991, p. 354). Additional evidence for the importance of context can be found in ethnographic research, which reports that a great deal of violent behavior experienced by crack-using women arises as a result of their involvement in prostitution, which is related circumstantially, although not pharmacologically, to their drug use (Mieczkowski, 1994; Johnson et al., 1994).

An issue of research design has emerged in the extensive literature surrounding cocaine use and violence. Chitwood and Morningstar (1985) report systematic differences between samples of cocaine users in and out of treatment programs, with samples from those in treatment characterized by greater cocaine use in both frequency and volume. This difference has been reported elsewhere (e.g., Miller et al., 1991); Inciardi and Pottieger (1994) also report that a comparison of cocaine users in treatment to users not in treatment reveals that treatment users were substantially more likely to be polydrug users and to engage in violence. These findings are important in that the type of sample used may, at least in the case of cocaine, greatly influence the findings about a drug–violence association.

Phencyclidine

Phencyclidine (PCP) is widely believed to be associated with violence; this conclusion is based almost exclusively on case study research, often of individuals with psychiatric disturbances (e.g., Lerner and Burns, 1978; McCarron et al., 1981). Ketamine, a drug pharmacologically quite similar to PCP, has enjoyed increasing popularity in recent years (Dotson et al., 1995). PCP and Ketamine are classified as "dissociative anaesthetics" because they diminish awareness not only of pain but also of the environment in

---

[2]Miller et al. (1991) failed to find any such relationship between route of administration and violence; however, the authors point out that this lack of finding may be explained by the use of a treatment sample of users who were likely using cocaine in such high dosage and frequency as to blur any distinction between acute toxicity effects specific to route of administration (Miller et al., 1991, p. 1084).

general. Delusions, paranoia, and (in rare cases) psychosis are among the most commonly reported effects of these drugs by users and clinicians (Marwah and Pitts, 1986; Lerner and Burns, 1978; McCarron, 1986; Dotson et al., 1995). However, one researcher concludes that "emotionally stable people under the influence of PCP probably will not act in a way very different from their normal behavior" (Siegel, 1978, p. 285).

Official crime statistics fail to show conclusive evidence for a unique link between PCP use and violent crime; arrestees who were not under the influence of illicit drugs (according to urinalysis) were more likely to be charged with assault than were persons testing positive for PCP (Wish, 1986). Among PCP-positive arrestees, the conditional distribution of offenses is influenced toward a greater likelihood of robbery charges, but Wish (1986) notes that this may be an artifact of demographic coincidence; PCP users tend to be younger than the average user of illicit drugs and thus coincide with the age group that dominates robbery arrests (Wish, 1986; Maguire et al., 1993).

Summary

This review of the evidence concerning the relationship between the use of various illicit drugs and violence makes it clear that support for such linkages is absent. At best, we can characterize the available results as inconclusive. The strongest evidence is for a link between cocaine use and violence; however, the conclusions of researchers whose findings support this idea universally highlight a social rather than a pharmacological basis for this link. At present, no compelling evidence exists to support an association between violence and amphetamines, Phencyclidine/Ketamine, or heroin. While there is some evidence that some of these drugs may induce psychosis, this reaction is exceedingly rare; virtually all research on this phenomenon consists of case studies, making it impossible to even estimate the frequency of such reactions in the population.

The most extensive research literature concerning drugs and violence is that of investigations of the relationship between cocaine use and violence. A search through *Sociological Abstracts* reveals that this literature has grown concurrently with concern about, if not use of, cocaine (see White House Office of National Drug Control Policy, 1997, for use statistics). Between 1970 and 1980, only four articles with "cocaine" or "crack" in the title are indexed, while

between 1980 and 1990 there are approximately 75; in the 1990s, this figure is at nearly 200 before the decade's end. However, even in the face of this profusion of research interest, we are still unable to say with any certainty that cocaine use and violent behavior are related. In part this may be attributable to the limitations inherent in ideologically driven research (e.g., Inciardi and Pottieger, 1994); it may also indicate that such a link really does not exist, and that any amount of looking will continue to fail to uncover it. At this point in the state of our knowledge, it is clear that we must look beyond the level of the individual user in order to adequately understand and characterize the relationship (if any) between illicit drugs and violence.

THEORETICAL APPROACHES

We have identified four recent attempts to specify and/or explain the linkages among drugs, alcohol, and violence that are worthy of discussion, either for the fact of their prominence in the research literature or for the promise of greater understanding that they afford. Three of these four approaches have associated with them at least some empirical tests of the theories; these are discussed along with the explication of the theories. Each is discussed in turn, with attention then passing to the commonalities between these theories, to determine whether a useful synthesis can be made.

Fagan's Approach: Intoxication, Aggression, and the Functionality of Violence

Jeffrey Fagan has produced several attempts to formulate a comprehensive theory of the relationship between the use of psychoactive substances, violence, and aggression (Fagan, 1990, 1993; Fagan et al., 1990). In addition, he has also been part of a joint effort to further our understanding of youth violence in general (Fagan and Wilkinson, 1998); this work is discussed here briefly vis-à-vis its complementarity with Fagan's formulations of the relationship of alcohol, drugs, and violence.

Above all, Fagan and his colleagues argue for the use of hierarchical or "nested contexts" models if we are to gain any understanding of the etiology of violence in general and of the relationships between substance use and violence (Fagan, 1993, 1990). In his most recent work Fagan has argued for a "situated transactions" framework as the most promising way to understand youth violence (Luckenbill, 1977).

In assessing the relationships between alcohol, drugs, and violence, Fagan (1990) has reviewed research and theoretical arguments from biological and physiological research, psychopharmacological studies, psychological and psychiatric approaches, and social and cultural perspectives in an attempt to present a comprehensive model of this relationship. He argues that the most important areas of consensus from these different perspectives are that intoxication has a significant impact on cognitive abilities and functioning, and that the nature of this impact varies according to the substance used but is, in the last instance, moderated by the context in which behavior takes place. For example, social and cultural meanings of how people function under the influence of alcohol, understandings about the impact of intoxication on judgment, the ability to perceive social cues, and the ability to focus on long- as well as short-term outcomes and desires are all extremely important factors in determining the outcome of a social situation in which drugs or alcohol are present and whether that situation will result in violence. The nature of the setting in which interaction takes place and the absence or presence of formal and informal means of social control are also important factors whereby intoxication influences aggression. Fagan also posits that intoxicated individuals tend to have limited response sets in situations of social interaction (1990, pp. 299–300); Fagan and Wilkinson (1998) extend this view to a general analysis of the etiology of youth violence.

To date, no empirical tests of this model exist. Fagan's approach leads to a very general theoretical model that would require substantial revision to permit empirical testing. For example, the outcome measure, aggression, is hardly the same thing as violence, although there is certainly some relationship between these concepts. Further theoretical explanation is needed to establish the transition from aggression to violence, as well as the linkages between the antecedents of aggression and aggression itself.

Fagan and Wilkinson propose a general model of youth violence that is relevant to this discussion. They propose that youth violence is "a functional, purposive behavior that serves definable goals within specific social contexts" (Fagan and Wilkinson, 1998, p. 2). Fagan and Wilkinson argue that one of the most important benefits that accrue to youth from the use of violence is the attainment of status, something to which youths have limited access. The social world in which adolescents operate places an increasingly high premium on status and reputation; broader contextual influences such as technology (in the form of

weapons) are important in "raising the stakes" of potentially violent situations, which may change the meanings attributed to different behaviors (Fagan and Wilkinson 1998). Another factor that may influence the meanings attributed to the actions of others is the consumption of drugs or alcohol, due to the behavioral expectancies that may be associated with them. These potentially violence-producing combinations in meaning-assignment may be particularly significant when considered in the context of the cognitive limitations of the developmental stage of adolescence (Leigh, 1987). Dating violence may be a particularly relevant phenomenon to examine within this framework, given the highly charged adolescent expectancies surrounding alcohol consumption and sexuality (George et al., 1988; Corcoran and Thomas, 1991) as well as the heightened importance of sexuality to status attainment at this developmental stage (Fagan and Wilkinson, 1998).

Selective Disinhibition: Parker's Approach

Parker (1993) and Parker and Rebhun (1995) attempt to specifically link alcohol and violence in an overall conceptual model, utilizing rates of homicide as the indicator of violent behavior. Parker and Rebhun (1995) advance a sociological approach to the relationship between alcohol and violence that is much different from earlier, biologically based formulations of this relationship (see Room and Collins, 1983, for a review of that literature and the widespread criticisms applied to this notion). In these earlier conceptualizations, alcohol was conceived as a biochemical agent that had a universal effect on social behavior, despite substantial evidence from cross-cultural studies that alcohol has a differential impact on behavior depending on the social and cultural contexts in which it is consumed (see Marshall, 1979, for a number of examples of this point).

Noting this limitation of previous formulations, Parker and Rebhun (1995) advance a social disinhibition approach, which tries to explain why normatively proscribed behavior is "disinhibited" in relatively few cases. Alcohol selectively disinhibits violence depending on contextual factors specific to the situation, the actors involved and their relationships to one another, and the impact of bystanders. In U.S. society, norms about the appropriateness of violence in solving interpersonal disputes argue both for and against such behavior (Parker, 1993). The theory proposes that individuals are constrained from engaging in certain behaviors in a social situation by the norms that they have internalized; however, people do violate norms and may have conflicting sets of norms to draw on in some situations. It is possible that norms that have the least institutional support are more likely to be disinhibited in a situation, all else being equal (Parker, 1993, p. 118).

To explain how choices are made between these conflicting normative structures, Parker and Rebhun (1995, pp. 34–35) introduce the tandem concepts of active and passive constraint. In potentially violent situations, it takes active constraint—a proactive and conscious decision not to use violence to "solve" the dispute—to preclude violence. In some of these cases, alcohol may disinhibit norms that usually prevent or constrain individuals from engaging in violent behavior. Thus, the selective nature of alcohol-related homicide is dependent upon the interaction of an impaired rationality and the nature of the social situation. The nature of the social situation, or the context in which behavior takes place, is of paramount importance in determining the outcome of a potentially violent situation. This is indicated by the fact that most alcohol-involved interpersonal disputes do not result in violence and homicide, but a few of these situations do (Parker and Rebhun, 1995; see also Wilbanks, 1984).

Parker and Rebhun (1995) further refined and specified their theoretical model of the ways in which alcohol consumption and homicide rates might be related at the aggregate level by incorporating into the model control variables suggested by previous literature on the etiology of homicide, such as subcultural theories (e.g., Wolfgang and Ferracuti, 1976), social bonds theory (e.g., Hirschi, 1969; Krohn, 1991), deterrence theory, routine activities (Cohen and Felson, 1979), and taking a cue from strain and social disorganization theories (e.g., Merton, 1949; also Wilson, 1987), controls for economic inequality and poverty rates.

A test of this particular specification of the theory was reported by Parker (1995). Cross-sectional analysis of state-level data was undertaken for five different types of homicide, differentiated by circumstances of crime and/or victim-offender relationship (e.g., robbery homicide, family homicide). Alcohol consumption was a significant predictor of family intimate and primary nonintimate homicide, or those homicides involving the closest interpersonal relationships. These results suggest that norms prohibiting violence in resolving interpersonal disputes in close or intimate relationships may be weaker than such norms prescribed in other interactions; alcohol consumption would appear to contribute to the "selective disinhibition" of an already weak normative

apparatus. Parker (1995, p. 27) also reported that the impact of poverty on robbery and other felony homicides was stronger in states with above average rates of alcohol consumption; the deterrent effect of capital punishment on homicide rates was strongest in states that had below average rates of alcohol consumption, providing further support for the importance of the interplay between alcohol consumption and contextual and social situational factors in the disinhibition of active constraint.

Parker and Rebhun (1995) also report the results of two tests of this approach that utilize longitudinal research designs. The first, using city-level data, yielded evidence that increases in alcohol availability help to explain why homicide nearly tripled in these cities between 1960 and 1980. This study also found some evidence for mediating effects of poverty, routine activities, and a lack of social bonds on the relationship between homicide and alcohol availability at the city level.

In an examination of the general hypothesis that alcohol has a causal impact on homicide, Parker and Rebhun (1995, pp. 102–117) conducted a dynamic test of the impact of increases in the minimum drinking age on youth homicide at the state level. Using data from 1976 through 1983, Parker and Rebhun (1995) estimated a pooled cross-section and time series model in which two general types of homicide, primary and nonprimary (based on the prior relationship between victim and offender), in three age categories (15–18, 19–20, and 21–24) were analyzed. In the presence of a number of important predictors, the rate of beer consumption was found to be a significant predictor of homicide rates in five of the six age-homicide type combinations, and increases in the minimum drinking age had a negative and significant impact on primary homicides in all age categories.

Violence Across Time and Space: The Cultural Consequences of Availability

In another theoretical formulation that attempts to explain the links between alcohol availability and violence, Maria Luisa Alaniz, Robert Nash Parker, and others (1998, 1999) propose some mechanisms by which the spatial distribution of alcohol outlets and the targeted advertising of alcohol to particular communities—in both the spatial and demographic sense—may mediate this relationship.

The work of Alaniz et al., (1998, 1999) focuses on the relationship of youth violence to alcohol availability. Given the recent increases in youth violence, including the increasing proportional contribution to overall rates of lethal violence (Blumstein, 1995), this appears to be a very fruitful line of research to pursue, if one of the ultimate goals of such research is the prevention and reduction of the incidence of violence. Additionally, these authors propose that due to the differences in cultural and legal status for alcohol and drugs (even taking into account the illegality of alcohol to minors), the relationship between illicit drugs and violence is more likely to stem from properties of the illicit distribution system (see Goldstein, 1985), while the relationship between alcohol and violence would be expected to be more related to ingestion of the substance, whether due to the effects of pharmacology, cultural expectancies surrounding alcohol's use, or both (Parker, 1995; Alaniz et al., 1998).

The authors propose two pathways by which alcohol availability may be related to youth violence. The first of these is largely grounded in Parker and Rebhun's (1995) selective disinhibition approach, in specifying the ways in which norms proscribing violence may be overcome (disinhibited) given the particular characteristics of a social situation, including the presence of alcohol. The second considers the distribution of alcohol outlets in physical space and the ways in which this distribution may produce "great attractors" (Alaniz et al., 1998, p. 14), areas where social controls of all kind are diminished, if not completely absent; such areas have also been conceptualized as "hot spots" (Sherman et al., 1989; Roncek and Maier, 1991) and "deviance service centers" (Clairmont and Magill, 1974). Alaniz et al. theorize that in this kind of "anything-goes" atmosphere (1998, p. 15), active constraint may be more likely to become disabled. Add to this the kinds of circumstances in which youths usually drink; due to the illegal status of alcohol for minors, youths must usually consume alcohol in "semi-private" spaces, such as cars or deserted public parks, "thus [further] limiting the effectiveness of most external forms of social control" (Alaniz et al., 1998, p. 13).

Alaniz et al. (1999) also highlight the role of advertising in helping to articulate the link between outlet density and youth violence that is particularly relevant in minority communities, which bear a disproportionate share of all types of violence, including youth violence. This aspect of the theory is further explicated by Alaniz and Wilkes (1995), who undertook a semiotic analysis of alcohol advertising targeted at Latino com-

munities. The authors argue that such attempts to target minority communities are very effective because, for minority groups in the United States,

> . . . the state exhibits indifference or hostility to claims of citizenship; the market openly embraces the same people . . . components of Latino cultural armature are appropriated by advertisers, reinvented, and returned . . . [;] this form of reinvention constructs a symbolic system that builds alcohol consumption into an idealized lifeworld of its constituents. (Alaniz and Wilkes, 1995, p. 433)

While this process of transforming cultural symbols into the commodity form is relevant for all sorts of products and services, it is especially relevant in the case of alcohol, given the highly charged nature of cultural expectancies surrounding its use (Brown et al. 1987). In support of this thesis, Alaniz et al. (1999) found that the density of alcohol advertising using sexist and demeaning images of minority women was associated, at the neighborhood level, with rates of sexual violence against females aged 12–18.

The importance of context and the cultural effects of advertising on youths is demonstrated particularly well by the findings of researchers who initially set out to study links between illicit drugs and delinquency among Latino youth populations; these researchers found that tobacco use was significantly related to violent delinquency, while the use of alcohol and illicit drugs was not found to be so related. The authors explain this finding thus:

> Youngsters who use tobacco act out tobacco-associated identities available in the media and popular culture. They express a range of symbols about themselves that suggest being independent, adult, adventuresome, and tough. These values are also associated with drug use and violent delinquency. (Watts and Wright, 1990, p. 152)[3]

Goldstein's Tripartite Framework

In 1985, Paul J. Goldstein made an explicit attempt to develop a theoretical framework to describe and explain the relationship between drugs and violence. Goldstein developed a typology of three ways in which drug use and drug trafficking may be causally related to violence.

---

[3]It should be pointed out that the majority of the variance in violent delinquency is explained by prior incarceration; however, tobacco use also emerges as a significant, albeit weaker, predictor of violent delinquency, thus highlighting the importance of social context in the links between substance use and violent behavior.

"Psychopharmacological violence" is violence that stems from properties of the drug itself. In Goldstein's framework, this can be violence associated with drug ingestion by the victim, the perpetrator, or both. "Economic compulsive violence" is violence associated with the high costs of illicit drug use. This type of violence does not stem directly from the physiological effects of drugs but is motivated by the need or desire to obtain drugs. Based on the capacity to induce physical dependency, the drugs one would expect to be most often associated with economic compulsive violence would be opiates (particularly heroin) and cocaine, due to the capacity of these to produce strong physical and psychological dependencies in users. "Systemic violence" is defined by Goldstein as that type of violence associated with "traditionally aggressive patterns of interaction within the system of drug distribution and use" (Goldstein, 1985, p. 497). Goldstein maintains that the risks of violence are greater to those involved in distribution than to those who are only users (Goldstein et al., 1989).

In the years since Goldstein's original formulation, a fairly large number of empirical studies have been undertaken using this framework. Nearly all of them have been produced by researchers associated with Narcotic and Drug Research, Inc. as part of one of two major research initiatives; these are the Drug Relationships in Murder (DREIM) and the Drug Related Involvement in Violent Episodes/Female Drug Related Involvement in Violent Episodes (DRIVE/FEMDRIVE) projects.

The DREIM project involved extensive interviews with 268 homicide offenders incarcerated in New York State correctional facilities. One of the purposes of this project was to gain a more extensive understanding than that afforded by official police records of the role that drugs and alcohol play in homicide.

The DREIM project data indicated that the substance most likely to be used by homicide offenders on a regular basis as well as during the 24 hours directly preceding the crime was, overwhelmingly, alcohol. Marijuana and cocaine were the second and third most frequently implicated drugs in the lives of homicide offenders as well as in the offense itself (Spunt et al., 1994, 1995).

Other empirical investigations that rely on the Goldstein framework have attempted to classify the relationship between drugs and all types of violence, under the auspices of the DRIVE/FEMDRIVE research initiative. The data collection for this project consisted of interviews with 152 male and 133 female subjects concerning both drug and alcohol use and also their participation in violent events, over an eight week period. In one analysis, Spunt et al. (1990) reported that violent events are drug-related if any of the participants report drug use proximate to the incident; similarly, if there is no link to drug distribution or robbery, these "drug-related events" are classified as psychopharmacological. These researchers fail to identify any mechanism by which these psychopharmacological effects of drugs manifest themselves in violent behavior. For example, they conclude that 'heroin and methadone were the [illicit] drugs most likely to be associated with psychopharmacological violence" (Spunt et al., 1990, p. 299), despite the fact that virtually no evidence exists to support individual-level associations between opiate use and violence (Kaplan 1983; Ball et al., 1982; Ball, 1991).

Goldstein et al. (1989) reported the results of research that was concerned primarily with the effect of the "crack epidemic" on homicide. Utilizing data from official police reports of homicides supplemented by an observational instrument designed by Goldstein and his research team, the authors concluded that slightly over half of the 414 New York City homicides sampled were drug-related. Evidence from official records indicated that 65% of these drug-related homicides involved crack cocaine as the primary substance, while another 22% were related to other forms of cocaine; combined, nearly 90% of drug-related homicides in the sample involved cocaine. Of these, the overwhelming majority (74.3% of all drug-related homicides) were classified as "systemic" by the researchers. Interestingly, all homicides in which alcohol was the primary substance involved were classified as psychopharmacological.

Another example of the use of the Goldstein typology is the analysis of nine female homicide offenders, reported by Brownstein et al. (1994). This analysis provides further evidence that alcohol is the substance most commonly associated with homicide. The authors also conclude from these data that the use of alcohol or drugs by either perpetrator or victim proximate to the homicide makes the homicide primarily drug- or alcohol-related (Brownstein et al., 1994, p. 110) despite the fact that the authors report, in some cases, long histories of spousal abuse on the part of the homicide victim, which another researcher might consider at least as important a causal factor as the fact of drug or alcohol consumption in leading up to the homicide.

A central problem that characterizes all the work that utilizes the Goldstein tripartite framework is that it is not treated as a set of testable propositions but rather as a set of assumptions about the nature of drug- and alcohol-related violence. Because of this, studies guided by this set of assumptions do not address the task of explaining mechanisms by which violent events might be related to the presence or use of drugs or alcohol; additionally, all of these studies fail to provide a detailed explanation of the way in which study events come to be classified into one type or another. Another problem with Goldstein's classificatory scheme is that the categories are not mutually exclusive. For example, many of the situations coded by researchers as events of systemic violence are economic in nature. Robbery of a drug dealer would seem to be an economically motivated crime but is classified as systemic in this framework, based on drug trafficking involvement of the victim and/or perpetrator. In short, the Goldstein framework seems biased toward support of the systemic model of drug-effected violence, which also limits the utility of the framework for explaining the relationship between alcohol—the substance most frequently implicated in violent events of all kinds—and violence. Additionally, the rigidity and inherently descriptive nature of the classification scheme fails to take into account the possibility of interactions between social context, individuals, and pharmacology.

CONCLUSIONS

Several clear conclusions can be drawn from this extensive review of the literature concerning drugs, alcohol, and violence. One is the overwhelming importance of context in any relationship that may exist between substance use and violent behavior. Our review of the literature finds a great deal of evidence that the social environment is a much more powerful contributor to the outcome of violent behavior than are pharmacological factors associated with any of the substances reviewed here.

The other consistent finding that we can report from this review of the empirical evidence is that when violent behavior is associated with a substance, that substance is, overwhelmingly, alcohol. Study after study indicates that, even in samples containing relatively high baseline rates of illicit drug use, violent events are overwhelmingly more likely to be associated with the consumption of alcohol than with any other substance. In fact, a review of the literature concerning rates of co-occurrence of violent crimes with the use of illicit substance fails to provide any support whatsoever for a link. The 1991 Criminal Victimization Survey indicates that less than 5% of violent

assailants were perceived by their victims to be under the influence of illicit drugs; the corresponding figure for alcohol is more than four times that.

The consensus among the authors of previous reviews of research on alcohol, drugs, and violence (Roizen, 1993; Collins, 1981; Pernanen, 1991) was that evidence existed for an association especially between alcohol and violence, but that the research base would not support any stronger conclusions. These and other reviews would invariably end with a call for more and better research to address the issue of whether evidence about a causal relationship between alcohol, drugs, and violence could be found. What was missing from those reviews, however, was a full recognition of the importance of theoretical development in the search for evidence about causality. Until the last ten years, such efforts were largely absent; a number of the studies cited here would replicate associational findings and end with this same lament about the absence of causal evidence. However, recent developments, especially the work of Goldstein and colleagues, Fagan, and Parker and colleagues, have led to an increased conceptual and theoretical base from which questions of causality can be better assessed. None of these approaches has succeeded in fully theorizing the potential relationships among alcohol, drugs, and violence, and none of these perspectives has provided definitive empirical tests of these theoretical models. Indeed, all of these approaches need more theoretical development as well as better data and methodological approaches to advance the state of knowledge about these relationships. However, at least it is reasonable to claim that research on alcohol, drugs, and violence demonstrates some promising theoretical approaches and some useful empirical studies based on those approaches. Much work is yet to be done, but the prospects for greater understanding of how and why alcohol and drugs contribute to violence have never been brighter.

ACKNOWLEDGMENTS

We would like to acknowledge the support of the University of California, Riverside; Raymond Orbach, Chancellor; David Warren, Vice Chancellor; Carlos Velez-Ibanez, Dean of the College of Humanities, Arts and Social Sciences; Linda Brewster Stearns, Chair, Sociology Department; as well as the State of California, for their support of the Presley Center for Crime and Justice Studies, which supported the authors during the completion of this article.

LITERATURE CITED

Abel, E. L. (1987). Drugs and homicide in Erie County, New York. *Int. J. Addictions* 22(2), 195–200.

Alaniz, M. L., Parker, R. N., Gallegos, A., and Cartmill, R. S. (1998). Immigrants and violence: The importance of context. *Hispanic J. Behav. Sci.*, 20(2): In press.

Alaniz, M. L., Parker, R. N., Gallegos, A., and Cartmill, R. S. (1999). Ethnic targeting and the objectification of women: Alcohol advertising and violence against young Latinas. In R. N. Parker (Ed.), *Currents in Criminology*.

Alaniz, M. L., and Wilkes, C. (1995). Reinterpreting Latino culture in the commodity form: The case of alcohol advertising in the Mexican American community. *Hispanic J. Behav. Sci.*, 17(4):430–451.

Ball, J. C., Rosen, L., Flueck, J. A., and Nurco, D. N. (1982). Lifetime criminality of heroin addicts in the United States. *J. Drug Issues*, 12, 225–239.

Ball, J. C. (1991). The similarity of crime rates among male heroin addicts in New York City, Philadelphia, Baltimore. *J. Drug Issues*, 21, 413–427.

Baumer, E. (1994). Poverty, crack, crime: A cross-city analysis. *J. Res. Crime Delinq.*, 31, 311–327.

Bennett, L. W. (1995). Substance abuse and the domestic assault of women. *Soc. Work*, 40, 760–771.

Bennett, L. W., Tolman, R. M., Rogalski, C. J., and Srinivasaraghavan, J. (1994). Domestic abuse by male alcohol and drug addicts. *Violence Victims*, 9, 359–368.

Blount, W. R., Silverman, I. J., Sellers, C. S., and Seese, R. A. (1994). Alcohol and drug use among abused women who kill, abused women who don't, and their abusers. *J. Drug Issues*, 24(2), 165–177.

Blumstein, A. (1995). Youth violence, guns, the illicit drug industry. *J. Crim. Law Criminol.*, 86(1), 10–36.

Brown, S. A. (1993). Drug effect expectancies and addictive behavior change. *Exp. Clin. Psychopharmacol.*, 1(Oct.), 55–67.

Brown, S. A., Christiansen, B. A., and Goldman, M. S. (1987). The alcohol expectancy questionnaire: An instrument for the assessment of adolescent and adult alcohol expectancies. *J. Stud. Alcohol*, 48(5), 483–491.

Brownstein, H. H., Spunt, B. L., Crimmins, S., Goldstein, P. L., and Langley, S. (1994). Changing patterns of lethal violence by women: A research note. *Women Crim. Justice*, 5, 99–118.

Budd, R. D. 1989. Cocaine abuse and violent death. *Am. J. Drug Alcohol Abuse*, 15, 375–382.

Bureau of Justice Statistics. (1992a). *Drugs and Crime Facts. 1992*. Washington, DC: USGPO.

Bureau of Justice Statistics. (1992b). *Drugs, Crime, the Justice System*. Washington, DC: USGPO.

Buss, T. F., Abdu, R., and Walker, J. R. (1995). Alcohol, drugs, and urban violence in a small city trauma center. *J. Substance Abuse Treat.*, 12, 75–83.

Chitwood, D. D., and Morningstar, P. C. (1985). Factors which differentiate cocaine users in treatment from nontreatment users. *Int. J. Addictions*, 20, 449–459.

Clairmont, D. H., and Magill, D. 1974. *Africville: The Life and Death of a Canadian Black Community*. Toronto: McClelland and Stewart.

Cohen, L. E., and Felson, M. (1979). Social change and crime rate trends: A routine activities approach. *Am. Sociol. Rev.*, 44, 588–607.

Collins, J. J., Jr. (1981). Alcohol use and criminal behavior: An empirical, theoretical, and methodological overview. In J. J. Collins Jr. (Ed.), *Drinking and Crime: Perspectives on the Relationship between Alcohol Consumption and Criminal Behavior*, pp. 288–316. New York: Guilford.

Collins, J. J., Jr. (1989). Alcohol and interpersonal violence: Less than meets the eye. In N. A. Weiner and M. E. Wolfgang (Eds.), *Pathways to Criminal Violence*, pp. 49–67. Newbury Park, CA: Sage.

Corcoran, K. J., and Thomas, L. R. (1991). The influence of observed alcohol consumption on perceptions of initiation of sexual activity in a college dating situation. *J. Appl. Soc. Psychol.*, 21(6): 500–507.

Dotson, J. W., Ackerman, D. L., and West, L. J. (1995). Ketamine abuse. *J. Drug Issues*, 25, 751–757.

Ellinwood, E. H., Jr. (1971). Assault and homicide associated with amphetamine abuse. *Am. J. Psychiatry*, 127, 1170–1175.

Fagan, J. (1993). Interactions among drugs, alcohol, and violence. *Health Affairs*, 12(4), 65–79.

Fagan, J. (1990). Intoxication and aggression in drugs and crime. In M. Tonry and J. Q. Wilson (Eds.), *Crime and Justice: A Review of Research*, 13, 241–320. Chicago: Univ. Chicago Press.

Fagan, J., and Wilkinson, D. L. (1998). The functions of adolescent violence. In D. S. Elliott, K. R. Wilson, and B. Hamburg (Eds.), *Violence in American Schools*, Cambridge Univ. Press.

Fagan, J., Weis, J. G., and Cheng, Y. (1990). Delinquency and substance use among inner-city students. *J. Drug Issues*, 20(3), 351–402.

Fendrich, M., Mackesy-Amiti, M. E., Goldstein, P., Spunt, B., and Brownstein, H. (1995). Substance involvement among juvenile murderers: Comparisons with older offenders based on interviews with prison inmates. *Int. J. Addictions*, 30(11), 1363–1382.

Feucht, T. E., and Kyle, G. M. (1996). *Methamphetamine Use Among Adult Arrestees: Findings from the Drug Use Forecasting (DUF) Program*. Washington, DC: Natl. Inst. Justice.

Fishbein, D. H. (1996). Female PCP-using jail detainees: Proneness to violence and gender differences. *Addictive Behav.*, 21(2), 1:55–172.

Fukushima, A. (1994). Criminal responsibility in amphetamine psychosis. *Jpn. J. Psychiatr. Neurol.*, 48(Suppl.): 1–4

Gantner, A. B., and Taylor, S. P. (1992). Human physical aggression as a function of alcohol and threat of harm. *Aggressive Behav.*, 18(1), 29–36.

Garriott, J. C. (1993). Drug use among homicide victims: Changing patterns. *Am. J. Forensic Med. Pathol.*, 14(3), 234–237.

George, W. H., Gournic, S. L., and McAfee, M. P. (1988). Perceptions of postdrinking female sexuality: Effects of gender, beverage choice, and drink payment. *J. Appl. Soc. Psychol.*, 18(15), 1295–1317.

Giannini, A. L., Miller, N. S., Loiselle, R. H., and Turner CE. (1993). Cocaine-associated violence and relationship to route of administration. *J. Substance Abuse Treatment*, 10, 67–69.

Goldstein, P. J. (1985). The drugs/violence nexus: a tripartite conceptual framework. *J. Drug Issues*, 15, 493–506.

Goldstein, P., Brownstein, H. H., Ryan, P. J., and Belluci, P. A. (1989). Crack and homicide in New York City 1988: A conceptually based event analysis. *Contemp. Drug Problems*, Winter, 651–687.

Goldstein, P., Brownstein, H. H., and Ryan, P. J. (1992). Drug-related homicide in New York: 1984 and 1988. *Crime Delinq.*, *38*(4), 459–476.

Goldstein, P. J., Bellucci, P. A., Spunt, B. J., and Miller, T. (1991). Volume of cocaine use and violence: A comparison between men and women. *J. Drug Issues*, *21*, 345–367.

Goode, E. (1993). *Drugs in American Society*. New York: McGraw-Hill, 4th ed.

Greenberg, S. W. (1976). The relationship between crime and amphetamine abuse: An empirical review of the literature. *Contemp. Drug Probl.*, *5*, 101–130.

Grube, J., Ames, G. M., and Delaney, W. (1994). Alcohol expectancies and workplace drinking. *J. Appl. Soc. Psychol.*, *24*(7), 646–660.

Hirschi, T. (1969). *Causes of Delinquency*. Berkeley: Univ. Calif. Press.

Inciardi, J. A., and Pottieger, A. E. (1994). Crack-cocaine use and street crime. *J. Drug Issues*, *24*, 273–292.

Jessor, R., and Jessor, S. L. (1977). *Problem Behavior and Psychosocial Development: A Longitudinal Study of Youth*. New York: Academic.

Joe, K. A. (1996). The lives and times of Asian-Pacific American women drug users: An ethnographic study of their methamphetamine use. *J. Drug Issues*, *26*, 199–218.

Johnson, B. D., Natarajan, M., Dunlap, E., and Elmoghazy, E. (1994). Crack abusers and noncrack abusers: Profiles of drug use, drug sales, nondrug criminality. *J. Drug Issues*, *24*, 117–141.

Johnson, K. M. (1978). Neurochemical Pharmacology of Phencyclidine. In R. C. Petersen and R. C. Stillman (Eds.), *Phencyclidine (PCP) Abuse: An Appraisal, NIDI Research Monograph No. 21*, pp. 44–52. Rockville, MD: Dep. Health Human Serv.

Kaplan, J. (1983). *The Hardest Drug: Heroin and Public Policy*. Chicago: Univ. Chicago Press.

Klein, M. W., and Maxson, C. L. (1985). "Rock" sales in central Los Angeles. *Sociol. Soc. Res.*, *69*, 561–565.

Kratcoski, P. C. (1990). Circumstances surrounding homicides by older offenders. *Criminal Justice Behav.*, *17*(4), 420–430.

Krohn, M. D. (1991). Control and deterrence theories. In J. Sheley (Ed.), *Criminology: A Contemporary Handbook*, pp. 295–314. Belmont, CA: Wadsworth.

Langevin, R., Paitich, D., Orchard, B., Handy, L., and Russon, A. (1982). The role of alcohol, drugs, suicide attempts, situational strains in homicide committed by offenders seen for psychiatric assessment. *Acta Psychiatr. Scand.*, *66*(3), 229–242.

Leigh, B. C. (1987). *Drinking and unsafe sex: Background and issues*. NIMH/NIDA Workshop, Women and AIDS: Promoting Healthy Behaviors. Washington, DC.

Leonard, K. E., and Taylor, S. P. (1983). Exposure to pornography, permissive and nonpermissive cues, and male aggression toward females. *Motivation Emotion*, 7(3), 291–299.

Lerner, S. E., and Burns, R. S. (1978). Phencyclidine use among youth: History, epidemiology, and acute and chronic intoxication. See Johnson, 1978, pp. 66–118.

Luckenbill, D. F. (1977). Criminal homicide as a situated transaction. *Social Probl.*, *25*, 176–186.

Maguire, K., Pastore, A. L., and Flanagan, T. J. (Eds.). (1993). *Sourcebook of Criminal Justice Statistics 1992*. U.S. Dep. Justice, Bur. Justice Statist. Washington, DC: USGPO.

Marshall, M. (Ed.). (1979). *Beliefs, Behaviors, Alcoholic Beverages: A Cross-Cultural Survey*. Ann Arbor: Univ. Mich. Press.

Marwah, J., and Pitts, D. K. (1986). Psychopharmacology of phencyclidine. In D. H. Clout (Ed.), *Phencyclidine: An Update, NIDA Res. Monogr. No. 64*, pp. 127–135. Rockville, MD: Dep. Health Human Serv.

McCoy, H. V., Inciardi, J. A., Metsch, L. R., and Pottieger, A. E. (1995). Women, crack, crime: Gender comparisons of criminal activity among crack cocaine users. *Contemp. Drug Probl.*, *22*, 435–451.

McCarron, M. (1986). *Phencyclidine intoxication*. In D. H. Clout (Ed.), *Phencyclidine: An Update, NIDA Res. Monogr. No. 64*, pp. 209–217. Rockville, MD: Dep. Health Human Serv.

Merton, R. K. (1949). *Social Theory and Social Structure*. Glencoe, IL: Free.

Miczek, K. A., and Tidey, J. W. (1989). Amphetamines: aggressive and social behavior. In K. Asghar and E. Souza (Eds.), *Pharmacology and Toxicology of Amphetamine and Related Designer Drugs*, pp. 68–100. Washington, DC: USGPO.

Mieczkowski, T. (1994). The experiences of women who sell crack: Some descriptive data from the Detroit Crack Ethnography Project. *J. Drug Issues*, *24*, 227–248.

Miller, B. A., and Downs, W. R. (1993). The impact of family violence on the use of alcohol by women: Research indicates that women with alcohol problems have experienced high rates of violence during their childhoods and as adults. *Alcohol Health Res. World*, *17*(2), 137–142.

Miller, N. S., Gold, M. S., and Mahler, J. C. (1991). Violent behaviors associated with cocaine use—possible pharmacological mechanisms. *Int. J. Addictions*, *21*, 1077–1088.

National Institute of Justice. (1997). *Drugs, Alcohol, and Domestic Violence in Memphis: Research Preview*. Natl. Criminal Justice Ref. Serv.

Parker, R. N. (1995). Bringing "booze" back in: The relationship between alcohol and homicide. *J. Res. Crime Delinquency*, *32*(1), 3–38.

Parker, R. N. (1993). Alcohol and theories of homicide. In F. Adler and W. Laufer (Eds.), *Advances in Criminological Theory*, *4*, 113–142. New Brunswick, NJ: Transaction.

Parker, R. N., with Rebhun, L. A. (1995). *Alcohol and Homicide: A Deadly Combination of Two American Traditions*. Albany: State Univ. NY Press.

Pernanen, K. (1991). *Alcohol in Human Violence*. New York: Guilford.

Pihl, R. O., Peterson, J. B., and Lau, M. A. (1993). A biosocial model of the alcohol-aggression relationship. *J. Stud. Alcohol*, *11*(Sept), 128–139 (Suppl.).

Ray, M. C., and Simons, R. L. (1987). Convicted murderers accounts of their crimes: A study of homicide in small communities. *Symbolic Interact.*, *10*(1), 57–70.

Reiss, A. J., Jr. and Roth, J. A. (Eds.). (1993). *Understanding and Preventing Violence*. Washington, DC: Natl. Acad. Press.

Roberts, A. R. (1987). Psychosocial characteristics of batterers: A study of 234 men charged with domestic violence offenses. *J. Family Violence 2*, 81–93.

Roesler, T. A., and Dafler, C. E. (1993). Chemical dissociation in adults sexually victimized as children: alcohol and drug use in adult survivors. *J. Substance Abuse Treatment*, *10*, 537–543.

Roizen, J. (1993). *Issues in the Epidemiology of Alcohol and Violence in Alcohol and Interpersonal Violence: Fostering Multidisciplinary Perspectives, Natl. Inst. on Alcohol Abuse and Alcoholism Res. Monogr. No. 24.* S. E. Martin (Ed.). Washington, DC: Natl. Inst. Health.

Roncek, D. W., and Maier, P. A. (1991). Bars, blocks, crimes revisited: Linking the theory of routine activities to the empiricism of "hot spots." *Criminology, 29,* 725–754.

Room, R., and Collins, G. (Eds.). (1983). *Alcohol and Disinhibition: Nature and Meaning of the Link.* Washington, DC: Natl. Inst. Alcohol Abuse and Alcoholism, Res. Monogr. No. 2

Sherman, L. W., Gartin, P. R., and Buerger, M. E. (1989). Hot spots of predatory crime: Routine activities and the criminology of place. *Criminology* Vols. 27–56.

Siegel, R. K. (1978). Phencyclidine, criminal behavior, the defence of diminished capacity. In R. C. Petersen and R. C. Stillman (Eds.), *Phencyclidine (PCP) Abuse: An Appraisal,* pp. 272–288. Rockville, MD: Dep. Health Human Serv.

Spunt, B., Brownstein, H., Goldstein, P., Fendrich, M., and Liberty, H. J. (1995). Drug use by homicide offenders. *J. Psychoactive Drugs, 27*(2), 125–134.

Spunt, B., Goldstein, P., Brownstein, H. H., Fendrich, M., and Langley, S. (1994). Alcohol and homicide: Interviews with prison inmates. *J. Drug Issues, 24*(1), 143–163.

Spunt, B. J., Goldstein, P. J., Belluci, P. A., and Miller, T. (1990). Race, ethnicity and gender differences in the drugs-violence relationship. *J. Psychoactive Drugs, 22,* 293–303.

Stets, J. E. (1990). Verbal and physical aggression in marriage. *J. Marriage Family, 43,* 721–732.

Tardiff, K., Marzuk, P. M., Leon, A. C., Hirsch, C. S., Stajik, M., et al. (1995). Cocaine, opiates, ethanol in homicides in New York City: 1990 and 1991. *J. Forensic Sci., 40*(3), 387–390.

Taylor, S. P. (1983). Alcohol and human physical aggression. In E. Gottheil, K. A. Druley, T. E. Skoloda, and H. M. Waxman (Eds.), *Alcohol, Drug Abuse, and Aggression.* Springfield, IL: Thomas.

Watts, W. D., and Wright, L. S. (1990). The drug use–violent delinquency link among adolescent Mexican-Americans. In M. De La Rosa, E. Y. Lambert, and B. Gropper (Eds.), *Drugs and Violence: Causes, Correlates, Consequences, NIDA Res. Monogr. No. 103,* pp. 136–159. Washington, DC: USGPO.

Welte, J. W., and Abel, E. L. (1989). Homicide: Drinking by the victim. *J. Stud. Alcohol, 50*(3), 197–201.

White, H. R., Hansell, S., and Brick, J. (1993). Alcohol use and aggression among youth. *Alcohol Health Res. World, 17*(2), 144–150.

White, H. R., Pandina, R. J., and LaGrange, R. L. (1987). Longitudinal predictors of serious substance abuse and delinquency. *Criminology, 25*(3), 715–740.

White House Office of National Drug Control Policy. (1997). *Fact Sheet: Drug Use Trends. National Criminal Justice Reference Service.* Available online at http://www.ncjrs.org.

Widom, C. S., and Ames, M. A. (1994). Criminal consequences of childhood sexual victimization. *Child Abuse Neglect, 18*(4), 303–318.

Wieczorek, W., Welte, J., and Abel, E. (1990). Alcohol, drugs, murder: A study of convicted homicide offenders. *J. Criminal Justice, 18,* 217–272.

Wilbanks, W. (1984). *Murder in Miami.* Lantham, MD: Univ. Press Am.

Wilson, W. J. (1987). *The Truly Disadvantaged: The Inner City, the Underclass, and Public Policy.* Chicago: Univ. Chicago Press.

Wish, E. D. (1986). PCP and crime: Just another illicit drug? In D. H. Clout (Ed.), *Phencyclidine: An Update. NIDA Res. Monogr. No. 64,* pp. 174–189. Rockville, MD: Dep. Health Human Serv.

Wolfgang, M. E., and Ferracuti, F. (1976). *The Subculture of Violence: Towards an Integrated Theory in Criminology.* London: Tavistock.

Yarvis, R. M. (1994). Patterns of substance abuse and intoxication among murderers. *Bull. Am. Acad. Psychiatry Law, 22*(1), 133–144.

The Rise of Marijuana as the Drug of Choice Among Youthful Adult Arrestees

ANDREW GOLUB

BRUCE D. JOHNSON

ABSTRACT

Discussed in this brief are trends in marijuana use detected through urinalysis among booked adult arrestees at 23 locations across the Nation served by the Arrestee Drug Abuse Monitoring (ADAM) program from 1987 through 1999 as well as trends within the mainstream population based on self-reports of past month marijuana use recorded by the National Household Survey on Drug Abuse (NHSDA) and Monitoring the Future (MTF) programs.

An epidemiological perspective is taken to place in context the increased use of marijuana among arrestees and the general population. The course of the recent marijuana upsurge is compared with that observed for previous crack and heroin epidemics in which four phases with distinct variations in prevalence and age of users occurred. The analysis also compares time trends in marijuana use across age groups, populations and geographic locations.

Key findings include:

- *Increases in marijuana use during the study period were limited primarily to youths. Starting around 1991, most ADAM locations experienced a rapid increase in recent use among youthful adult arrestees (ages 18–20) from an average low of 25 percent in 1991 to 57 percent in 1996, as detected by urinalysis. The MTF and NHSDA surveys also recorded rapid but more modest increases in youthful marijuana use within the mainstream population starting in 1992 (1 year later than among ADAM arrestees). Around 1996, the rates of marijuana use among arrestee and mainstream populations reached a plateau.*
- *With exceptions at a few ADAM locations, the pattern of growth in marijuana use among youthful adult arrestees was similar to that observed previously for heroin and crack: full rapid expansion, and plateau. Use of both heroin and crack is now in decline.*
- *Marijuana appears to be the drug of choice for arrestees born since 1970, who seem much less likely to progress to crack or heroin injection than their predecessors.*

The target audience includes local law enforcement and public health officials, drug-crime researchers, administrators of juvenile justice agencies and youth departments, and local criminal justice policymakers.

Various surveys have identified a rapid increase in marijuana use during the 1990s, especially among youths. This raises a variety of questions about the future of the Nation's drug problems. On one hand, the gateway theory posits that youthful use of alcohol and/or tobacco and marijuana tends to precede use of other illicit drugs like crack and heroin (see "The Gateway Theory"). The recent increase in youthful marijuana use has fueled speculation that a new epidemic of hard drug abuse may be imminent[1] and that the burden of drug abuse will be dramatically increasing in the near future.[2] On the other hand, the start of this new epidemic coincides with the decline of the crack epidemic. This suggests that youthful subcultures may have shifted from the destructive nature of crack abuse to the use of less dangerous drugs.

The recent upsurge in marijuana use is referred to as the New Marijuana Epidemic to distinguish it from widespread use of marijuana prevailing in the

The Rise of Marijuana as the Drug of Choice Among Youthful Adult Arrestees. June 2001. National Institute of Justice, Research in Brief (NCJ 187490). This and other NIJ publications can be found at and downloaded from the NIJ Web site (http://www.ojp.usdog.gov/nij).

1960s and 1970s.[3] This Research in Brief examines trends in marijuana use detected through urinalysis to track the progress of the recent epidemic among arrestees at 23 locations across the Nation served by the Arrestee Drug Abuse Monitoring (ADAM) program—formerly the Drug Use Forecasting (DUF) program—from 1987 through 1999.

In addition, this report identifies nationwide drug use trends within the mainstream population on the basis of self-reports of past-month use, a measure roughly parallel to the length of time in which marijuana can be detected by urinalysis. Those trends were derived from data collected by the National Household Survey on Drug Abuse (NHSDA) and Monitoring the Future (MTF) programs. (See "The Study's Data Sources.")

Overall, study findings suggest the following:

- **Recent increases in youthful marijuana use followed a natural pattern similar to previous drug epidemics.** Use of a particular drug sometimes follows a wave of popularity: starting from a lull, expanding rapidly, leveling to a plateau, and subsequently fading away. Prior research with ADAM/DUF data suggests that the popularity of heroin injection (which mostly peaked in the 1960s and early 1970s) and crack (which mostly peaked in the late 1980s) followed this pattern. The current analysis suggests that the recent wave of marijuana use has followed a similar pattern so far, although unlike the previous epidemics, the increases in use were primarily limited to youths.
- **Local differences are important.** There were exceptions at a few ADAM locations to every one of the major regularities in the New Marijuana Epidemic. Some locations did not observe an epidemic. At other locations, the epidemic either was not limited to youthful adult arrestees (ages 18–20), expanded more slowly, expanded for a longer period, or was less prevalent at its peak.
- **In the 1990s, marijuana replaced crack cocaine as the drug of choice among youthful adult arrestees.** Arrestees born since 1970 have been increasingly likely to be detected as recent marijuana users. Unlike their predecessors, however, few of them had progressed to crack or heroin by 1998. This provides some evidence to suggest that viewing marijuana as a gateway drug may be inappropriate for this new generation. Ethnographic evidence from New York City suggests that use of marijuana by youths may be associated with strong cultural

and subcultural norms that militate against use of more dangerous drugs.
- **The New Marijuana Epidemic had plateaued by 1996 at most affected locations and by 1999 at all affected locations.** From 1996 to 1999, most ADAM locations as well as the MTF and NHSDA surveys identified stable, high levels of recent marijuana use among youths.
- **The New Marijuana Epidemic had a larger impact on youthful adult arrestees than on youths in the general population.** The epidemic in youthful marijuana use recorded by the MTF and NHSDA programs started 1 year later, increased more slowly, and was less prevalent at its peak than the epidemic among youths who tended to get in trouble with the law as recorded by the ADAM program.

A CONCEPTUAL MODEL OF THE NEW MARIJUANA EPIDEMIC

Much research suggests that drug epidemics tend to follow a predictable course. This analysis employs a conceptual model that distinguishes the characteristics of four phases: incubation, expansion, plateau, and decline. This model was originally developed to explain the course of the Crack Epidemic.[4] It has since been used to study the Heroin Injection Epidemic and has been adapted for the study of the recent increase in marijuana use.[5] This study found that the dynamics of recent increases in marijuana use followed a pattern similar to that of the Crack and Heroin Injection Epidemics, suggesting that all three epidemics were the result of a comparable diffusion phenomenon.

Theoretically, the passing of each phase of the New Marijuana Epidemic should result in a distinguishable pattern for the prevalence of marijuana use detected by the ADAM program, particularly among youthful adult arrestees and, to a lesser extent, among the overall population of adult arrestees (ages 18 and older).[6]

Incubation Phase

Historical evidence suggests that a drug epidemic typically grows out of a specific social context; the Heroin Injection Epidemic grew out of the jazz era[7] and the Crack Epidemic started among inner-city drug dealers.[8] In both cases, there was an initial incubation phase during which the new drug-use practice was developed and nurtured among a relatively small, cohesive group of adult users. Marijuana use has been widespread since the 1960s; however, the prevalence of its use had been declining since 1979.[9] During the incubation phase, the ADAM program would be expected to detect relatively low levels of marijuana use by adult arrestees, including those in the youthful category.

Ethnographic research in New York City suggests that the reemergence of interest in marijuana use was pioneered as part of the youthful, inner-city, predominately black hip-hop movement.[10] These youths celebrated marijuana use in their music and on T-shirts. In New York City, they also preferred to smoke their marijuana in a blunt (an inexpensive cigar whose contents are replaced with marijuana). The extent to which the New Marijuana Epidemic outside of New York City is associated with blunt smoking is not clear. Unfortunately, major national surveys, such as MTF, NHSDA, and ADAM, do not distinguish among ways of consuming marijuana. A number of focus groups across the Nation on cigar use[11] and reports by leading drug abuse experts[12] provide limited (but far from conclusive) support for the idea that blunt smoking may be a national phenomenon.

Expansion Phase

Eventually, marijuana use spread rapidly as part of a newly emerging subculture indigenous to youths. In contrast, the Crack and Heroin Injection Epidemics spread first among adults and only afterward to youths. This dynamic suggests that the ADAM program would be expected to detect rapidly increasing marijuana use among youthful adult arrestees during an expansion phase. The rate of use among all adult arrestees would be expected to increase more slowly and for a longer period as members of the New Marijuana Generation aged and came to constitute a larger portion of the ADAM sample and as the renewed interest in marijuana diffused to older arrestees.

Plateau Phase

Subsequent to its expansion, the New Marijuana Epidemic could be expected to enter a plateau phase at each ADAM location. During this period, youths coming of age and getting involved with illegal drugs would use the current drug of choice, marijuana. During this phase, the ADAM program would be expected to detect stable and high levels of marijuana use among youthful adult arrestees and slowly increasing rates of use overall.

Decline Phase

In the 1990s, both the Heroin Injection and Crack Epidemics were experiencing their decline phases. These drugs have been much less popular among

---

THE GATEWAY THEORY

Much research has identified that most American youths tend to progress through as many as four stages of substance use: nonuse, alcohol/tobacco, marijuana, and other drugs including cocaine and heroin.[a] Individuals who do not use substances associated with one stage rarely use those associated with later stages, but not all users at one stage progress to the next.[b] Because of their intermediary role, alcohol, tobacco, and marijuana have come to be regarded as "gateway drugs." Today, policies pertaining to substance use prevention seek to forestall or delay youthful use of gateway drugs to reduce the likelihood of subsequent abuse of drugs like heroin and crack.

In contrast, several analyses suggest the gateway sequence may not be as relevant to the inner-city populations that disproportionately generate youths who get in trouble with both drug abuse and the law.[c] Moreover, the gateway sequence may no longer characterize the experiences of mainstream youths. Calculations based on National Household Survey on Drug Abuse data suggest that youths coming of age in the 1990s were much less likely to progress from marijuana to cocaine powder, crack, or heroin than were youths born previously.[d]

These recent studies suggest that youthful substance use progression reflects cultural or subcultural norms among youths about which substances are acceptable and that these norms vary over time and across locations. Thus, it seems essential to monitor not just which substances youths are using but what that substance use represents to them.

[a]Kandel, Denise B,, "Stages in Adolescent involvement in Drug Use," *Science, 190*(1975), 912–914.

[b]Ibid. For a review of replications, see Kandel, Denise B., ed., *Stages and Pathways of Involvement in Drug Use: Examining the Gateway Hypothesis*, New York: Cambridge, forthcoming.

[c]Golub, Andrew, and Bruce D. Johnson, "Substance Use Progression and Hard Drug Abuse in Inner-City New York," in *Stages and Pathways of Involvement in Drug Use: Examining the Gateway Hypothesis*, ed. Denise B. Kandel. New York: Cambridge, forthcoming.

[d]Golub, Andrew, and Bruce D. Johnson, "Variation in Youthful Risk of Progression From Alcohol and Tobacco to Marijuana and Hard Drugs Across Generations," *American Journal of Public Health, 91*(2)(2001), 225–232.

youths coming of age in the 1990s than among their predecessors. However, heroin injection and crack smoking are still quite widespread because many older users have persisted in their habits. By analogy, when the New Marijuana Epidemic enters a decline phase, the ADAM program would be expected to detect a rapid decrease in marijuana use among youthful adult arrestees but a slower, more drawn-out decline among all adult arrestees.

RESULTS

If data had conformed to the conceptual model described above, the expansion phase of marijuana use should be readily distinguished by steady increases in each year (perhaps as large as 5 percentage points or more per year), the plateau phase distinguished by high rates of use in each year (perhaps varying by no more than 2 percentage points from year to year), and

THE STUDY'S DATA SOURCES

The authors collected data from three major programs: Arrestee Drug Abuse Monitoring (ADAM), National Household Survey on Drug Abuse (NHSDA), and Monitoring the Future (MTF). The absolute magnitude in the prevalence of recent marijuana use was expected to differ among the foregoing data sources because of differences in sample populations (across ADAM locations and across NHSDA and MTF surveys), differences in survey procedures, and the use of urine tests for ADAM in contrast to self-reports for NHSDA and MTF.

ARRESTEE DRUG ABUSE MONITORING PROGRAM

In 1987, the National Institute of Justice (NIJ) established the Drug Use Forecasting (DUF) program to measure trends in illicit drug use among booked arrestees in most large cities (or counties) with a total population of at least 1 million, as well as in many smaller cities for geographical diversity. In 1997, DUF evolved into the ADAM program, which plans to expand to 75 locations over the next few years.[a] The program collects urine samples (along with self-reported information) from about 300 adult arrestees each quarter at each location. Female arrestees are oversampled at many locations and constitute about 30 percent of the total. Some locations also recruit samples of juvenile arrestees. This study examined trends at the 23 locations using information obtained from more than 300,000 arrestees between 1987 and 1999. ADAM samples typically are not representative of the general population in communities where data collection occurs. Given the drug-crime nexus, ADAM data provide excellent information about drug use among many of the most serious drug abusers at each location. This information is of particular interest to criminal justice and other agencies. Analyses of ADAM data may be of even broader interest to the extent that drug use among arrestees tends to parallel or perhaps even lead trends in the general population.

At inception, the DUF program sought to monitor substance use among serious offenders: individuals charged with a felony offense were oversampled; individuals charged with a citation offense were excluded from DUF samples at most locations; and individuals charged with drug offenses were not allowed to exceed 20 percent of the sample.[b] As part of the transition to ADAM, NIJ phased in sampling strategies so that ADAM samples would be representative of arrestees passing through the central booking facility at each location. Starting in 1998, the prevalence of arrestees for drug offenses and citations increased substantially. Several locations experienced increases in detected marijuana use in 1999 inconsistent with the trend in previous years, including, most notably, Atlanta, Birmingham, Houston, Miami, Phoenix, San Diego, and San Jose. Continuation of the upward trend in Los Angeles and Portland also may have been due to the change in sampling strategy.

Throughout the life of the DUF and ADAM programs, urine testing and many core questions have remained constant, allowing for analysis of trends over time. Urine test results provide particularly valid indications of recent marijuana use. Marijuana metabolites tend to remain in the body. Marijuana consumption can be detected by the EMIT (Enzyme Multiplied Immunoassay Testing) urinalysis screen used by ADAM up to 7 days after last use for infrequent users and 30 days or longer for chronic users. In contrast, the drug detection period for opiates (such as heroin) and cocaine is only 2 to 3 days. In 1996, the cutoff level for determining recent marijuana use was lowered from 100 to 50 nanograms.[c] More than 34,000 samples from 1995 were tested at both cutoff levels. Overall, the prevalence of detected marijuana use increased 5 to 7 percentage points when the lower cutoff level was used. The difference was most pronounced among very young arrestees (under age 15) and older arrestees (over age 30), two groups that tend to use marijuana less frequently.

NATIONAL HOUSEHOLD SURVEY ON DRUG ABUSE PROGRAM

NHSDA was established in 1971 to measure the prevalence and correlates of illegal drug use and monitor trends over time in the noninstitutionalized population of the United States.[d] The survey tends to undersample many of the most serious drug abusers, who are prone to incarceration, residence in other institutions, and unstable living arrangements. Eligible participants are visited and interviewed in their homes. Through 1998, respondents were given a separate sheet to record their confidential answers to questions about drug use to help ensure disclosure of sensitive information. The survey was conducted in 1971 and 1972 and then every 2 or 3 years until 1990, when it became an annual survey. Analyses presented in this report are based on more than 200,000 responses available in public use data files for surveys conducted in 1979, 1982, 1985, 1988, and 1990–97 and in a published report for 1998.[e] NHSDA employs a complex sampling design and oversamples Hispanics, blacks, and youths ages 12 to 17. The authors used sample weights in all calculations to obtain unbiased estimates.

MONITORING THE FUTURE PROGRAM

Each spring since 1975, the University of Michigan's Institute for Social Research has conducted a survey to estimate the prevalence of drug use among high school seniors in the United States and to monitor trends over time.[f] The survey tends to undersample many of the most serious drug users, who are disproportionately likely to drop out of school or be absent on the day of the survey. Students at selected schools complete confidential questionnaires at their own pace during a normal class period. Analyses presented in this report are based on more than 350,000 responses obtained in the 1976–97 period and contained in a published report for 1998–99.[g] The MTF program employs a complex sampling design. The

authors used sample weights in all analyses to obtain unbiased estimates of substance use.

[a]National Institute of Justice, *1998 Annual Report on Drug Use Among Adult and Juvenile Arrestees*, Washington, DC: U.S. Department of Justice, National Institute of Justice, 1999, NCJ 175656.

[b]National Institute of Justice, *1999 Annual Report on Drug Use Among Adult and Juvenile Arrestees*, Washington, DC: U.S. Department of Justice, National Institute of Justice, 2000, NCJ 181426.

[c]National Institute of Justice, *Drug Use Forecasting: Annual Report on Adult and Juvenile Arrestees, 1996*, Washington, DC: U.S. Department of Justice, National Institute of Justice, 1997, NCJ 176800.

[d]Substance Abuse and Mental Health Services Administration, *National Household Survey on Drug Abuse Series: H-10 Summary of Findings from the 1998 National Household Survey on Drug Abuse*, Rockville, MD: Office of Applied Studies, 1999, U.S. Department of Health and Human Services Publication No (SMA) 99-3295.

[e]Ibid.

[f]Johnson, Lloyd D., Patrick M. O'Malley, and Jerald G. Bachman, *National Survey Results on Drug Use from the Monitoring the Future Study, 1975–1998*, vol. 1, Bethesda, MD: National Institutes of Health, National Institute on Drug Abuse, 1999, NIH Publication No. 99–4660.

[g]Johnston, Lloyd D., Patrick M. O'Malley, and Jerald G. Bachman, *Drug Trends in 1999 Are Mixed*, press release, Ann Arbor, MI: University of Michigan News and Information Services, 1999. Available online at www.monitoringthefuture.org/pressreleases/99drugpr.html.

the decline phase distinguished by steady decreases in youthful marijuana use comparable in size to the increases observed during the expansion phase. The rate of increase and subsequent decrease would depend on the speed at which marijuana use spread within the target population represented by each survey sample.

The findings from the NHSDA and MTF surveys in Exhibit 1 fit this overall pattern quite well, although the rate of increase during the apparent expansion phase was modest. Nationwide, overall marijuana use had steadily declined from 13 percent in 1979 to a low of 4 percent in 1992. Marijuana use among high school seniors declined from a peak of 37 percent in 1978 to a low of 12 percent in 1992 (an average decline of 1.8 percentage points per year). NHSDA recorded a remarkably similar decline in use among youthful household members (ages 18–20) for this period. Then from 1992 to 1996, the rate among high school seniors steadily increased to 22 percent (an average increase of 2.5 percentage points per year); the rate among youthful household members rose more modestly to 17 percent. Relatively stable

rates were subsequently recorded through 1999 for high school seniors and through 1998 for household members, which suggests that the epidemic in the general population may have reached a plateau around 1996.

The trend data on individual ADAM locations were often somewhat ambiguous. The increases in youthful marijuana use detected during the expansion phase were sometimes unsteady and the year-to-year variations during the plateau phase were sometimes greater than 5 percentage points. There are numerous possible reasons for year-to-year variations, including changes in policing priorities and random chance (samples for individual ADAM locations are much smaller than MTF and NHSDA samples). Sometimes this variation confounded the study's efforts to precisely pinpoint the timing of the phases of the New Marijuana Epidemic. In response, small variations from one year to the next were often disregarded by the authors as potentially attributable to the limited precision of the ADAM estimates. Such ambiguous trends are clearly identified in this report and the basis for an interpretation is provided. The most credence

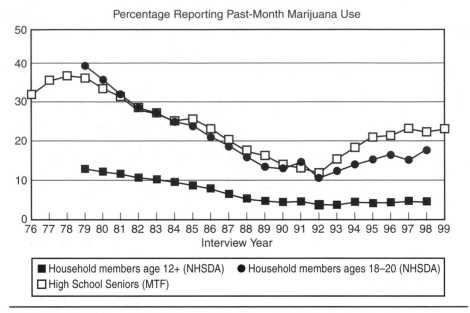

*NHSDA: National Household Survey on Drug Abuse; MTF: Monitoring the Future

EXHIBIT 1   Variation in Past-Month Marijuana Use Within the U.S. General Population, NHSDA and MTF Surveys.*

was placed on strong trends consistently affecting marijuana use across multiple years.

Exhibit 2 depicts the status in 1999 of the New Marijuana Epidemic at each ADAM location across the Nation. By 1999, the marijuana epidemic among arrestees had clearly reached the plateau phase at ADAM locations in the Northeast, Midwest, and Southwest. Miami and San Diego did not appear to have observed epidemics. The epidemic had shown signs of possibly having plateaued at almost all of the other Southeast and West Coast ADAM locations. The similarity in findings across ADAM locations suggests that the New Marijuana Epidemic was national in scope. Based on this finding, an ADAM program average was calculated to facilitate presentation of the general characteristics of the phenomenon by simply averaging findings across locations. This program average does not necessarily represent the average across arrestees nationwide. Furthermore, it is not necessarily a good idea to focus on this type of an average when determining the rate of detected use of such other drugs as cocaine/crack, amphetamines, and heroin because prevalence rates vary more widely across locations. Indeed, even marijuana use was affected by important local differences, which are depicted in Exhibit 2.

Exhibit 3 shows that, on average, the variation in recent marijuana use detected among youthful ADAM arrestees conformed to the conceptual model for the New Marijuana Epidemic and that year-to-year distortions of the overall pattern were quite modest. From 1988 to 1990, detected marijuana use among all adult arrestees declined, on average, from 35 percent to 19 percent and declined among youthful adult arrestees from 44 percent to 24 percent. Subsequently, the rate among youthful adult arrestees increased steadily from 25 percent in 1991 to 57 percent in 1996 (an average of 6.4 percentage points per year), suggesting that the expansion phase, on average, occurred among arrestees from 1991 to 1996.

This doubling of marijuana use among youthful ADAM arrestees provides some of the strongest evidence to suggest that a New Marijuana Epidemic has occurred, primarily among youths and especially among youths who tend to get in trouble with the law. This increase preceded the ADAM program's 1996 change in the standard for determining marijuana use and, therefore, could not have been caused by that methodological improvement. From 1996 to 1999, the rate of use among youthful adult arrestees held steady at around 60 percent and the rate among all

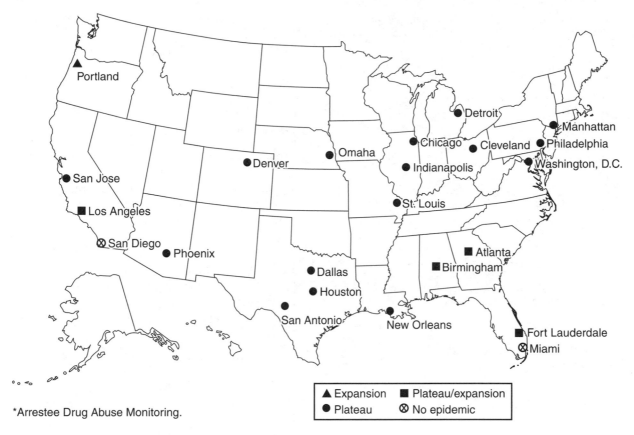

*Arrestee Drug Abuse Monitoring.

EXHIBIT 2　Status of the New Marijuana Epidemic Among ADAM* Arrestees, 1999.

adult arrestees held constant at around 37 percent. The modest increase of use among youthful adult arrestees to 62 percent in 1999 may have resulted from changes in the ADAM sampling procedure. Thus, the plateau phase among arrestees appears to have set in by 1996 and lasted, on average, at least through 1999.

All three major national surveys (NHSDA, MTF, and ADAM) recorded a similar overall pattern in youthful marijuana use: a decline in the 1980s reaching a low in the early 1990s, followed by a rise in the mid-1990s and stabilization in the late 1990s. These findings, along, with the ethnographic information cited previously, strongly suggest that a new nationwide epidemic in marijuana use passed through its expansion phase by 1996 and was in its plateau phase through 1999.

There were several important differences across surveys. The increase in marijuana use started among youthful adult arrestees (ADAM) about 1 year before it started within the general population (NHSDA and MTF). In addition, the peak rate of reported past-month use among high school seniors occurring during the plateau phase (about 22 percent) was far below the previous peak (37 percent) recorded in the late 1970s. It was also far below the peak rate of detected marijuana use among youthful adult arrestees in the same period (about 57 percent) as well as their rate of reported past-month use (about 60 percent).[13] This suggests that the New Marijuana Epidemic started among those individuals who tended to get in trouble with the law and spread more widely within this group than among youths in the general population. Conceivably, the prevalence of marijuana use in the general population could undergo another expansion if use diffused to other youthful subpopulations. Further research is clearly needed to identify which groups of mainstream youth have been most affected so far.

The following sections examine geographic variation among ADAM arrestees across the program's locations in the following regions: Northeast,

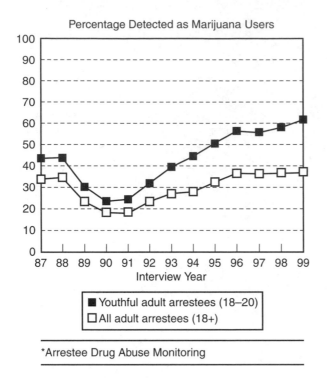

Percentage Detected as Marijuana Users

■ Youthful adult arrestees (18–20)
□ All adult arrestees (18+)

*Arrestee Drug Abuse Monitoring

EXHIBIT 3 Variation in Recent Marijuana Use Detected Among U.S. Arrestee Population, ADAM* Program Average.

Midwest, Southeast, Southwest, and West Coast. From 1996 to 1999, the majority of ADAM locations detected rates of marijuana use among adult and youthful adult arrestees close to the ADAM program average shown in Exhibit 3. However, five Midwest locations (Chicago, Detroit, Indianapolis, Omaha, and St. Louis) had substantially higher rates, while five Southwest and West Coast locations (Houston, Los Angeles, Phoenix, San Antonio, and San Jose) had substantially lower rates.

THE NEW MARIJUANA EPIDEMIC AMONG ADAM ARRESTEES IN THE NORTHEAST

Manhattan—Plateau Since 1996

Marijuana use in Manhattan had dropped from 27 percent overall (i.e., among all adult arrestees) in 1987 to 16 percent in 1991. From 1991 to 1993, the popularity of marijuana started to rise among youthful adult arrestees (hereinafter referred to as "youthful arrestees"). Assessing the start date of the increase in the rate of use is difficult because the upward trend was quite slow at first and a 1-year dip in youthful marijuana use occurred in 1993. Subsequently, the

popularity of marijuana among youthful arrestees increased to a peak of 61 percent in 1996. From 1996 to 1999, the rate of marijuana use among youthful arrestees held steady at about 60 percent, with the overall rate holding at about 30 percent.

Philadelphia—Plateau Since 1995

Marijuana use among all adult arrestees in Philadelphia dropped precipitously from 30 percent in 1988 to 16 percent in 1990. From 1990 to 1993, marijuana use among youthful arrestees expanded rapidly and the rate among all adult arrestees returned to its former level. In 1993, the rate among youthful arrestees appeared to have entered a plateau at about 52 percent, but it subsequently inched up to 59 percent in 1995. The rate among youthful arrestees remained around 60 percent from 1995 through 1999, and the overall rate held steady around 35 percent.

Washington, D.C.—Plateau Since 1996

In 1990, only 7 percent of all Washington, D.C., adult arrestees were detected as recent marijuana users. The rate increased rapidly among youthful arrestees and then among older arrestees. By 1996, about 60 percent of youthful arrestees and 35 percent of all arrestees were detected as recent marijuana users. These rates remained relatively stable from 1996 through 1998. (This location did not collect a full sample in 1999.)

THE NEW MARIJUANA EPIDEMIC AMONG ADAM ARRESTEES IN THE MIDWEST

Chicago—Plateau Since 1996

Marijuana use among all adult arrestees in Chicago dropped from 48 percent in 1988 to 23 percent in 1991. In 1993, however, the overall rate bounced up to about 40 percent, where it approximately remained through 1999. The rate of recent marijuana use detected among youthful arrestees rose dramatically from 27 percent in 1992 to 75 percent in 1996, where it approximately remained through 1999.

Cleveland—Plateau Since 1998

Marijuana use among all adult arrestees in Cleveland dropped from 26 percent in 1988 to 11 percent in 1991. Subsequently, the rate among youthful arrestees began a steady rise from 14 percent in 1991 to 72 percent by 1998. The overall rate reached just below 40 percent in 1997, where it remained through 1999. The rate of marijuana use detected among youthful arrestees in 1999 dipped slightly, suggesting that the epidemic in Cleveland had entered a plateau in 1998.

Detroit—Plateau Since 1995

Marijuana use among all adult arrestees in Detroit dropped from 32 percent in 1988 to 13 percent by 1990. Subsequently, the rate among youthful arrestees increased steadily from 25 percent in 1990 to 73 percent in 1995. The rate of marijuana use detected among youthful arrestees fluctuated in a broad range from 62 percent to 75 percent from 1995 through 1999. The rate of recent marijuana use detected among all adult arrestees inched upward from 38 percent in 1995 to 46 percent in 1999.

Indianapolis—Plateau Since 1996

Marijuana use among all adult arrestees in Indianapolis dropped steadily from 41 percent in 1988 to 23 percent in 1991. Subsequently, the rate among youthful arrestees increased steadily from a low of 27 percent in 1991 to 70 percent in 1996 and remained around that level through 1999. Overall, the rate of recent marijuana use ranged from 39 to 45 percent from 1995 through 1999.

Omaha—Plateau Since 1996

Marijuana use among all adult arrestees in Omaha dropped from 45 percent in 1988 to 21 percent in 1990. Subsequently, that rate rose steadily to 39 percent in 1992 and to 49 percent by 1996. The rate among youthful arrestees rose from 25 percent in 1990 and then held steady around 55 percent from 1993 through 1995. In 1996, the rate of marijuana use detected among youthful arrestees jumped to 71 percent, where it approximately remained through 1999. This change was probably not attributable to a change in the ADAM cutoff standard for determining recent marijuana use. (The prevalence of marijuana use among Omaha's youthful arrestees in 1995 increased only slightly from 53 percent under the previous 100 nanogram cutoff to 56 percent under the new 50 nanogram standard.)

St. Louis—Plateau Since 1996

Marijuana use among youthful arrestees in St. Louis rose steadily from a low of 15 percent in 1990 to 72 percent in 1996, where it approximately remained

through 1998. The rate of overall use increased from a low of 14 percent in 1991 to a steady 45 percent by 1996, where it remained through 1998. (This ADAM location did not collect a sample in 1999.)

THE NEW MARIJUANA EPIDEMIC AMONG ADAM ARRESTEES IN THE SOUTHEAST

Atlanta—Plateau/Possibly Expansion

In 1990, the prevalence of recent marijuana use detected among youthful (6 percent) and all adult (3 percent) arrestees in Atlanta was the lowest of any ADAM location. The rate among all adult arrestees increased to 33 percent by 1996. The epidemic did not appear centered on youthful arrestees only; rather, the rate of recent marijuana use detected increased among all adult arrestees as early as 1991. The rate among youthful arrestees, however, did increase the most, reaching 69 percent in 1996. From 1996 to 1998, the rate among youthful arrestees drifted slightly downward to 62 percent. The rate of use among all adult arrestees also decreased, from 33 percent in 1997 to 25 percent in 1998. Both rates bounced back to new peaks in 1999, suggesting the New Marijuana Epidemic in Atlanta could still have been in its expansion phase. On the other hand, the relatively steady rate observed from 1996 to 1998 suggests that the epidemic might have plateaued by 1996 and that the 1999 jump was an anomalous fluctuation.

Birmingham—Plateau/Possible Expansion

Marijuana use among all adult arrestees in Birmingham dropped precipitously from 33 percent in 1988 to 12 percent by 1990. Subsequently, the rate among youthful arrestees increased dramatically from 15 percent in 1990 to 64 percent in 1996. The overall rate reached 40 percent in 1996. In 1998, the rate among youthful arrestees declined modestly to 57 percent and then jumped to 69 percent in 1999. This suggests that the expansion phase may have continued through 1999. On the other hand, the lack of any increase in the rate of use from 1996 to 1998 suggests that the epidemic may have plateaued by 1996 and that the 1999 jump was an anomalous fluctuation.

Fort Lauderdale—Plateau/Possible Expansion

Marijuana use among all adult arrestees in Fort Lauderdale dropped from 42 percent in 1988 to 20 percent in 1990. The rate of detected marijuana use among youthful arrestees started a very slow but steady increase from a low of 28 percent in 1990 to 63 percent in 1998. The overall rate increased even more slowly, from 20 percent in 1990 to 38 percent in 1998. The modest dip in the rate in 1999 suggests that the epidemic might have reached a plateau in 1998. On the other hand, the relatively slow expansion and a history of 2 previous years in which the expansion appeared to have halted (1992–93 and 1996–97) suggest that the expansion may not have plateaued by 1999.

Miami—No Epidemic

From 1988 through 1999, marijuana use among all adult arrestees in Miami fluctuated around 30 percent. The rate among youthful arrestees fluctuated within a wider range—between 31 and 66 percent. The dramatic 1-year jump in marijuana use among youthful arrestees, from 45 percent in 1998 to 66 percent in 1999, may have been caused by changes to the ADAM sampling procedures. The data suggest no sustained trend in marijuana use has occurred among arrestees. Miami experienced neither a sustained decline in marijuana use among arrestees nor the epidemic-like growth in use among youthful arrestees observed at other ADAM locations.

THE NEW MARIJUANA EPIDEMIC AMONG ADAM ARRESTEES IN THE SOUTHWEST

Dallas—Plateau Since 1996

Marijuana use among all adult arrestees in Dallas had dropped steadily from 32 percent in 1988 to 17 percent in 1991. The rate of detected marijuana use among youthful arrestees subsequently increased from 22 percent in 1991 to 57 percent in 1996. The overall rate increased to 38 percent. Both rates remained stable from 1996 through 1999.

Denver—Plateau Since 1994

In Denver, the rate of detected marijuana use among youthful arrestees rose rapidly from 26 percent in 1991 to 60 percent in 1994, dropped modestly to 54 percent in 1995, and inched up to 62 percent by 1999. The overall rate rose more slowly, from 23 percent in 1991 to 41 percent by 1999.

Houston—Plateau Since 1995

The rate of detected marijuana use among all adult arrestees in Houston dropped precipitously from 43 percent in 1988 to 14 percent by 1991. The rate among youthful arrestees bounced back from a low of 19 percent in 1992 to 43 percent in 1995. In 1996 and 1997, the rate among youthful arrestees dipped to about 31 percent and then returned to 49 percent by 1999. This increase in marijuana use among youthful arrestees—well above the previously established plateau level in 1995—may have been attributable to changes in ADAM sampling procedures. By 1999, the rate of detected marijuana use overall had returned to 31 percent, still far below the rate observed in the late 1980s and below the ADAM program average.

New Orleans—Plateau Since 1995

Marijuana use among all adult arrestees in New Orleans dropped precipitously from 46 percent in 1987 to 14 percent by 1991. Marijuana use among youthful arrestees subsequently increased from 17 percent (1991) to 54 percent (1995) and then fluctuated in the 50 percent to 60 percent range. The overall rate of detected marijuana use inched up to 35 percent by 1999, still well below the rate observed in the late 1980s.

Phoenix—Plateau Since 1998

The rate of detected marijuana use among all adult arrestees in Phoenix dropped steadily from 42 percent in 1987 to 19 percent in 1991. Subsequently, the rate among youthful arrestees entered a slow but steady expansion, increasing from 22 percent in 1991 to 40 percent in 1995. At that time, the marijuana epidemic appeared to have entered a plateau. However, youthful marijuana use jumped to 54 percent in 1998, where it remained in 1999. This increase suggests that the marijuana epidemic may have diffused in the 1997–98 period to another portion of youths who tend to get arrested. This change could have also been caused by changes in police priorities or ADAM sampling procedures.

San Antonio—Plateau Since 1996

Marijuana use among all adult arrestees in San Antonio decreased from 34 percent in 1988 to 18 percent by 1991. The rate among youthful arrestees then slowly increased from 20 percent in 1991 to 45 percent in 1996, where it remained through 1999. Overall marijuana use had increased to 32 percent by 1996 and fluctuated around this rate through 1999.

THE NEW MARIJUANA EPIDEMIC AMONG ADAM ARRESTEES ON THE WEST COAST

Los Angeles—Plateau/Possible Expansion

It is difficult to determine the timing of a New Marijuana Epidemic in Los Angeles because the rate of increase in detected marijuana use among youthful arrestees was very slow in the early 1990s and because it took a dip in 1994, which suggests the rate had plateaued. However, the increase in detected marijuana use among youthful arrestees from 22 percent in 1991 to 49 percent in 1996 strongly suggests that a marijuana epidemic took place. In 1997, the rate among youthful arrestees declined modestly to 46 percent and inched up to 54 percent by 1999. This continued increase suggests that the epidemic may not yet have plateaued by 1999. However, it is possible that the modest increase in youthful marijuana use from 49 percent (1998) to 54 percent (1999) was caused by changes in ADAM sampling procedures. If this was the case, the marijuana epidemic among youthful arrestees in Los Angeles may have plateaued as early as 1996. The overall rate of marijuana use inched up from 16 percent in 1991 to a high of 30 percent in 1999.

Portland (Oregon)—Expansion 1992–99

Marijuana use among all adult arrestees in Portland decreased from 47 percent in 1988 to 25 percent in 1992. The rate of detected marijuana use among youthful arrestees subsequently expanded from 28 percent in 1992 to 57 percent in 1999. The overall rate increased only modestly to a peak of 33 percent in 1998.

San Diego—No Epidemic

Marijuana use among San Diego's youthful arrestees remained steady and relatively high from 1987 through 1999, ranging from 37 to 55 percent. Marijuana use among all adult arrestees exhibited a modest drop from 44 percent in 1988 to 29 percent in 1991. The rate then fluctuated around 34 percent through 1999. The rate of detected marijuana use among youthful arrestees exhibited a modest 1-year increase from 37 percent in 1991 to 47 percent in 1992. The rate among youthful

arrestees subsequently fluctuated in the mid-40-percent range. The modest dip and recovery in youthful marijuana use from 1989 to 1992 seem much too small to constitute a new drug epidemic, although their timing is consistent with that of the New Marijuana Epidemic at other ADAM locations. Another steady but short increase in youthful marijuana use occurred from 1997 to 1999, when the rate among youthful arrestees inched up from 44 to 55 percent. Again, the short period and rather modest increase suggest that this change was not part of a longer, sustained epidemic.

San Jose—Plateau Since 1995

Overall, marijuana use among San Jose arrestees was relatively stable at about 24 percent from 1989 through 1998. The rate among youthful arrestees increased from 21 percent in 1992 to 43 percent in 1995, where it roughly remained through 1998. The sharp increase to 56 percent in 1999 may be an anomalous 1-year fluctuation.

CONCLUSION

This study identified that the increase in marijuana use among ADAM arrestees in the 1990s generally conformed to the conceptual model described earlier for the diffusion of a drug epidemic. Marijuana appears to have become the drug of choice among youths coming of age in the 1990s who tend to get in trouble with the law in the same way that crack had been the drug of choice previously. Analyses with two additional datasets on general population samples (the NHSDA and MTF surveys) further confirmed the existence and timing of this New Marijuana Epidemic. Continued monitoring of drug use among arrestees is essential to determine how long prevailing conditions will persist. Some of the key issues include the following:

- How long will marijuana remain the drug of choice among youths coming of age who tend to get in trouble with the law?
- Will marijuana-using members of the New Marijuana Generation continue to avoid use of other illicit drugs?
- To what extent will marijuana-using members of the New Marijuana Generation desist from such use as they grow older?

There are numerous ways to attempt to control drug abuse, including prevention, treatment, interdiction, and law enforcement. In response to recent trends, drug abuse control policies might logically shift much of their focus to marijuana. However, this is not as simple as just targeting marijuana use and users instead of crack or heroin users. For one, the nature of marijuana abuse is quite different, as noted by Grinspoon and Bakalar, who report that proportionately fewer marijuana smokers become dependent than users of alcohol, tobacco, heroin, or cocaine.[14] They suggest that psychotherapy may be the most appropriate treatment for a troubled youth who uses marijuana frequently, such as one who manifests alienation, emotional withdrawal, overreaction to minor frustration, and antisocial behavior. They emphasize that the treatment is not for marijuana use itself but for an underlying problem that has marijuana abuse as one of its symptoms. They also suggest that the health risks of marijuana use are much less profound than those of cocaine or heroin use.

A standing argument for controlling marijuana use, based on the gateway theory, is that it can lead to use of more dangerous drugs. As determined in this study, however, the drug of choice for persons born in the 1970s and coming of age in the 1990s has been marijuana. These youths have been much less prone to progress to other drugs than their predecessors. This suggests that the gateway theory may be less relevant to their substance use experiences, which would be good news. It would also be good news if the marijuana use were associated with a rejection of crack and heroin due to their potentially devastating consequences.[15]

This rejection of other drugs may not be as characteristic of the broader population. From 1992 to 1997, the proportion of high school seniors reporting lifetime use of LSD increased from 8.6 percent to 13.6 percent, its highest recorded level since the start of the MTF program in 1975.[16] Use of hallucinogens in England and the United States has been frequently associated with the rave or dance party scene, typically involving white youths from middle- and upper-class suburban enclaves.[17] However, that is a different story about a different population of youths.

It would appear that more has changed than the prevailing drug of choice among arrestees. Ethnographic studies in inner-city communities suggest that there has been a dramatic shift in the subculture of drug use and that interpersonal interactions have become more congenial and less violent.[18] In this way, drug-using members of the New Marijuana Generation are damaging themselves less physically and socially than the preceding generations of crack smokers and heroin injectors. They are also causing much less harm to the broader population.

In this regard, the potential for integrating persons from distressed inner-city communities into mainstream culture seems more promising than in the 1970s and 1980s. Perhaps this is the time to deemphasize "tough" drug enforcement policies in favor of indirect drug abuse control through the reduction of the economic, educational, and social barriers faced by many inner-city youths in establishing a healthy and productive mainstream lifestyle. Providing youths struggling in distressed inner-city households with a greater stake in society may help create a more productive labor force and ensure further declines in drug abuse and its attendant criminality. If inner-city youths born in the 1970s who get in trouble with the law could be transformed into fully employable workers, their marijuana use might also decline as they assume conventional adult roles, just as marijuana use tends to recede among members of the general population.[19]

THREE GENERATIONS OF DRUG USE AMONG ARRESTEES

In a previous study,[a] the authors used ADAM data for Manhattan to identify three generations of arrestees with distinct drug use patterns the Heroin Injection Generation (born 1945–54), Cocaine/Crack Generation (born 1955–69), and Marijuana/Blunts Generation (born 1970 and later). These findings show variation across birth cohorts in reported lifetime (ever) heroin injection,[b] lifetime (ever) crack use, and detected marijuana use.[c] The authors performed a comparable analysis for each ADAM location and produced similar findings at each with only two exceptions.[d] In Phoenix, it appears that among arrestees, the Crack Epidemic had not ended by 1998. San Antonio appears to have never experienced a serious epidemic of crack use.

Findings based on all available ADAM data from 1989 to 1998 in Washington D.C., were typical. The prevalence of lifetime heroin injection peaked with persons born around 1950 and exhibited a sustained decline starting somewhere around the 1954 birth cohort reaching near zero among birth cohorts of the 1970s. The prevalence of lifetime crack cocaine use peaked among persons born around 1960 and started to decline around the 1964 birth cohort, Recent marijuana use exhibited a dramatic and continuous increase with successive birth cohorts starting around 1970. Arrestees born since 1970, but especially after 1974, were likely to be detected as recent marijuana users and very unlikely to report lifetime heroin injection or crack use.

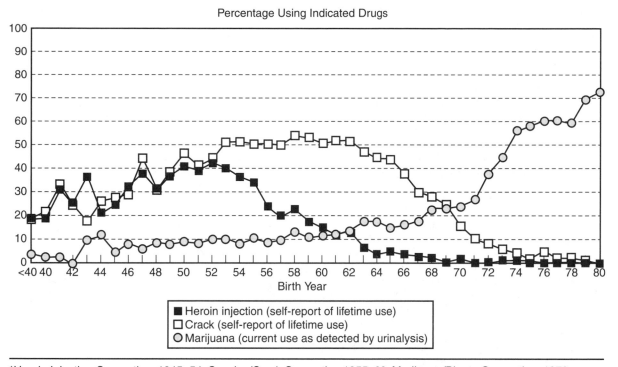

*Heroin Injection Generation: 1945–54; Cocaine/Crack Generation 1955–69; Marijuana/Blunts Generation; 1970+.

EXHIBIT 4 Three Generations* of Drug Users Among Washington, D.C., Arrestees in the ADAM Program.

[a]Golub, Andrew, and Bruce D. Johnson, Cohort Changes in Illegal Drug Use Among Arrestees in Manhattan. From the Heroin Injection Generation to the Blunts Generation. *Substance Use and Misuse*, *34*(13)(1999), 1733–1763.

[b]Lifetime heroin injection was approximately determined from persons who reported both lifetime heroin use and lifetime injection of illicit drugs. This calculation was necessary because the ADAM questionnaire did not ask explicitly about heroin injection in all years of the survey. At some locations, many individuals reported injection drug use but not heroin use (they may have been injecting cocaine or amphetamines) and others reported heroin use but no injection drug use (many were presumably sniffers).

[c]Variations in substance use across birth years can be caused by age, period, or cohort effects. The authors confirmed that heroin injection crack smoking, and marijuana use among ADAM-Manhattan arrestees were the result of period effects in three separate age-period-cohort analyses for detected use of opiates, cocaine, and marijuana (see Golub, Andrew, and Bruce D. Johnson, "Cohort Changes in Illegal Drug Use Among Arrestees in Manhattan From the Heroin Injection Generation to the Blunts. Generation," *Substance Use and Misuse*). Similar confirmation was performed for each of the remaining ADAM sites for detected use of marijuana (see Golub, Andrew, and Bruce D. Johnson, "Monitoring the Marijuana Upsurge With DUF/ADAM Arrestees," final report submitted to the U.S. Department of Justice, National Institute of Justice, Washington, DC, 2000) and for detected use of cocaine (see Golub, Andrew, and Bruce D. Johnson, *Crack's Decline Some Surprises Across U.S. Cities*, Research in Brief, Washington, DC: U.S. Department of Justice, National Institute of Justice, July 1997, NCJ 165707).

[d]Golub, Andrew, and Bruce D. Johnson, "Monitoring the Marijuana Upsurge With DUF/ADAM Arrestees."

NOTES

1. Office of National Drug Control Policy, *The National Drug Control Strategy: 1997*, Washington, DC: Office of National Drug Control Policy, 1997:23, NCJ 163915.
2. Gfroerer, Joseph C., and Joan F. Epstein, "Marijuana Initiates and Their Impact on Future Drug Abuse Treatment Need," *Drug and Alcohol Dependence*, *54*(3) (1999), 229–237.
3. Research in a wide variety of fields has documented that new innovations often spread within a population following a pattern similar to a disease epidemic (see Rogers,

Everett M., *Diffusion of Innovations*, 4th ed., New York: Free Press, 1995). The term "epidemic" is employed in this report as a synonym for "diffusion of innovation" and refers to the rapid and broad spreading of a practice (such as smoking marijuana) within a population or subpopulation (such as among 16- to 25-year-olds).

4. Golub, Andrew, and Bruce D. Johnson, "A Recent Decline in Cocaine Use Among Youthful Arrestees in Manhattan (1987–1993)," *American Journal of Public Health*, *84*(8)(1994), 1250–1254; Golub, Andrew, and Bruce D. Johnson, *Crack's Decline: Some Surprises Across U.S. Cities*, Research in Brief, Washington, DC: U.S. Department of Justice, National Institute of Justice, July 1997, NCJ 165707.

5. Golub, Andrew, and Bruce D. Johnson, "Cohort Changes in Illegal Drug Use Among Arrestees in Manhattan: From the Heroin Injection Generation to the Blunts Generation," *Substance Use and Misuse*, *34*(13)(1999), 1733–1763; Johnson, Bruce D., and Andrew Golub, Generational Trends in Heroin Use and Injection Among Arrestees in New York City," in *One Hundred Years of Heroin*, ed David Musto, Westport, CT: Greenwood, forthcoming.

6. In a more detailed report, the authors provide analyses of marijuana use trends over time within five mutually exclusive age categories. See Golub, Andrew, and Bruce D. Johnson, "Monitoring the Marijuana Upsurge With DUF/ADAM Arrestees," final report submitted to the U.S. Department of Justice, National Institute of Justice, Washington, DC, 2000.

7. Johnson, Bruce D., and Andrew Golub, "Generational Trends in Heroin Use and Injection Among Arrestees in New York City."

8. Johnson, Bruce D., Andrew Golub, and Jeffrey Fagan, "Careers in Crack, Drug Use, Drug Distribution and Nondrug Criminality," *Crime and Delinquency*, *41*(3)(1995), 275–295; Hamid, Ansley, "The Developmental Cycle of a Drug Epidemic: The Cocaine Smoking Epidemic of 1981–1991," *Journal of Psychoactive Drugs*, *24*(1992), 337–348.

9. Johnston, Lloyd D., Patrick M. O'Malley, and Jerald G. Bachman, *National Survey Results on Drug Use from the Monitoring the Future Study, 1975–1998*, vol. 1, Bethesda, MD: National Institutes of Health, National Institute on Drug Abuse, 1999, NIH Publication No. 99–4660; Substance Abuse and Mental Health Services Administration, *National Household Survey on Drug Abuse Series: H-10. Summary of Findings from the 1998 National Household Survey on Drug Abuse*, Rockville, MD: Office of Applied Studies, 1999, Department of Health and Human Services Publication No. (SMA) 99–3295.

10. Furst, R. Terry, Bruce D. Johnson, Eloise Dunlap, and Richard Curtis, "The Stigmatized Image of the 'Crack Head': A Sociocultural Exploration of a Barrier to Cocaine Smoking Among a Cohort of Youth in New York City," *Deviant Behavior*, *20*(2)(1999), 153–181; Golub, Andrew, and Bruce D. Johnson, "Cohort Changes in Illegal Drug Use Among Arrestees in Manhattan: From the Heroin Injection Generation to the Blunts Generation," *Substance Use and Misuse*, *34*(13)(1999), 1733–1763;

Sifaneck, Stephen J., and C. Small, "Blunts and Forties: The Drugs of Choice for the New Generation," New York: National Development and Research Institutes, Inc., 1997, working manuscript; Sifaneck, Stephen J., and Charles D. Kaplan, "New Rituals of Cannabis Preparation and Self-Regulation in Two Cultural Settings and Their Implications for Secondary Prevention," New York: National Development and Research Institutes, Inc., 1996, working manuscript.

11. Department of Health and Human Services, *Youth Use of Cigars: Patterns of Use and Perceptions of Risk*, Washington, DC: Department of Health and Human Services, 1999, publication number OEI–06098–00030.

12. Community Epidemiology Work Group, *Identifying and Monitoring Emerging Drug Use Problems: A Retrospective Analysis of Drug Abuse Data/Information*, Bethesda, MD: National Institute on Drug Abuse, 1999. Available online at www.nida.nih.gov/cweg/retro.html.

13. The rate of self-reported past-month use among youthful adult arrestees was calculated separately to support this comparison. Across all sites and interview years, most youthful adult arrestees (80 percent) detected as recent marijuana users via urinalysis also reported past-month use. The nondisclosers were more than offset by individuals who tested negative for recent marijuana use but still reported use in the past month.

14. Grinspoon, Lester, and James B. Bakalar, "Marijuana," in *Substance Abuse: A Comprehensive Textbook*, ed. J.H. Lowinson, P. Ruiz, R.B. Millman, and J.G. Langrod, 3d ed., Baltimore: Williams and Wilkins, 1997:199–206.

15. Furst, R. Terry, Bruce D. Johnson, Eloise Dunlap, and Richard Curtis, "The Stigmatized Image of the 'Crack Head': A Sociocultural Exploration of a Barrier to Cocaine Smoking Among a Cohort of Youth in New York City"; Golub, Andrew, and Bruce D. Johnson, "Cohort Changes in Illegal Drug Use Among Arrestees in Manhattan: From the Heroin Injection Generation to the Blunts Generation."

16. Johnston, Lloyd D., Patrick M. O'Malley, and Jerald G. Bachman, *National Survey Results on Drug Use from the Monitoring the Future Study, 1975–1998*.

17. Parker, Howard, Judith Aldridge, and Fiona Measham, *Illegal Leisure: The Normalization of Adolescent Recreational Drug Use (Adolescence and Society)*, London: Routledge, 1998; Hunt, Dana, *Rise of Hallucinogen Use*, Research in Brief, Washington, DC: U.S. Department of Justice, National Institute of Justice, 1997, NCJ 166607.

18. Johnson, Bruce D., Andrew Golub, and Eloise Dunlap, "The Rise and Decline of Hard Drugs, Drug Markets, and Violence in New York City," in *The Crime Drop in America*, ed. Alfred Blumstein and Joel Wallman, New York: Cambridge, 2000:164–206.

19. Bachman, Jerald G., Katherine N. Wadsworth, Patrick M. O'Malley, Lloyd D. Johnston, and John E. Schulenberg, *Smoking, Drinking, and Drug Use in Young Adulthood: The Impacts of New Freedoms and New Responsibilities*, Mahwah, NJ: Erlbaum, 1997.

Effects of Heroin Prescription on Police Contacts Among Drug-Addicts

MARTIN KILLIAS

MARCELO AEBI

DENIS RIBEAUD

ABSTRACT

Switzerland's programme of opiate prescription to drug-addicts has been thoroughly evaluated in many ways. The results published so far on the final findings, covering the programme's first year of operation, have focused on self-reported delinquent acts and victimisation reported during interviews. This article addresses these two issues. How did police-recorded crime develop over time, taking the offence type into account? Have these trends been affected by changing police control over the addicts participating in the programme? In other words, has an eventual drop been produced by less strict crime reporting (or recording) practice for programme participants, rather than by lower crime rates among this group? The analysis reported here confirms the results based on self-reported delinquency and victimisation data. According to police files, the drop in serious property offences was indeed comparable. As it turned out, this drop was not due to the reduced probability of the police recording offences committed by participants after their admission to the heroin prescription programme.

BACKGROUND

Switzerland's programme of opiate prescription to drug-addicts has been thoroughly evaluated in many ways (Uchtenhagen, 1997). One of the aspects evaluated was the programme's impact on criminal involvement among drug-addicts. The methodology of this criminological evaluation has been published before, as

well as preliminary results (Killias and Uchtenhagen, 1996; Killias and Rabasa, 1997). The results published so far on the final findings, covering the programme's first year of operation, have focused on self-reported delinquent acts and victimisation reported during interviews (Killias and Rabasa, 1998a, 1998b). They showed, overall, a strong decline in criminal activities in general, and in property crimes and drug-related offences in particular. Table 1 summarises these findings. The drop in victimisation was less marked, but followed generally the same trend (Killias and Rabasa, 1997).

So far, the published data has included only summary indications on trends of crime recorded by the police. Overall, there was a drop of approximately 60%, less than according to the self-report measures. This leaves two questions:

1. How did police-recorded crime develop over time, *taking the offence type into account*?
2. Have these trends been affected by *changing police control* over the addicts participating in the programme? In other words, has an eventual drop been produced by less strict crime reporting (or recording) practice for programme participants, rather than by lower crime rates among this group?

This article tries to address these two issues. They may be particularly important since, not surprisingly, certain observers challenged the validity of measures of self-reported delinquency in the present context.

European Journal on Criminal Policy and Research 6: 433–438, 1998. © 1998 Kluwer Academic Publishers.
Printed in the Netherlands with kind permission from Springer Science and Business Media.

POLICE-RECORDED OFFENCES

The Sample

In order to assess the effect of heroin prescription on criminal involvement among programme participants, we considered all those subjects who were interviewed at least three times, that is at admission to the programme and then every six months. The reference period for all three measurement points was six months. This group comprised 319 persons. Those participating in the programme operating at Basle were excluded, since no local police data could be collected for this group. Thus, the sample considered here consists of 253 individuals, of whom 72% are males. The average age is 30.

Comparisons with police data for these individuals are only possible for the first two periods (six months before and six months after admission to the programme). Indeed, only a few had been in treatment for at least 12 months when police data was collected.

Trends in Recorded Crime

Table 2 gives the incidence rates of police contacts during the two periods under consideration, during the last six months before admission, and during the first six months under treatment. The overall drop in contacts recorded by the police was, according to the details given here, 76%. For offences which seem to be particularly relevant for the public's safety, burgulary and robbery for example, the drop is quite consistent with the trends in self-report data (see Table 1). For drug trafficking, the incidence rates dropped by 61%; use of drugs other than heroin dropped by about the same proportion. Although illegal heroin use, as recorded by the police, dropped by 83%, the general drop in illegal drug use underlines the conclusions of the medical evaluation which found that, contrary to expectation, heroin prescription tended to reduce also use of other (that is not prescribed) drugs (Uchtenhagen, 1997). The use of cocaine and other drugs may, to some extent at least, have been opportunistic rather than the expression of an intrinsic need, a second choice whenever heroin was unavailable, or not available at reasonable rates.

According to the data in Table 2, the drop in police-recorded offences seems to be greater than what the overall results, published so far, would seem to suggest (Killias and Rabasa, 1998a, 1998b). The reason for this is that the results published so far have been based on periods of 12 and 18 months, while in this article we are considering periods of 6 months.

Changes in Police Control of Deviant Behaviour?

Although the trends, as reported in Table 2, seem to be very consistent with the drop in self-reported delinquency, the point could be raised whether the lower incidence rates of police-recorded offences may not reflect changed strategies of police control, rather than reduced criminal activity among programme participants. The lower rates after admission to the programme could, theoretically at least, indeed be due to having less chance of addicts to make a police contact after an offence, once they have entered the programme.

TABLE 1

Drop in prevalence and incidence rates of self-reported *criminality*, after one year of treatment in the programme, compared to the time before admission (reference period of six months, $n = 319$). Unless otherwise indicated, all changes are significant at the 0.05 level at least.

OFFENCE TYPE	PREVALENCE RATES	INCIDENCE RATES
Serious property offences[a]	–94%	–98%
Other property offences[b]	–55%	–88%
Selling "soft" drugs	–50%	–70%
Selling "hard" drugs	–82%	–91%
Assault[c]	NS	NS

[a]Burglary, mugging, robbery, pick-pocketing.

[b]Theft, shoplifting, receiving or selling stolen property.

[c]With or without weapon.

TABLE 2
Incidence rates of police contacts, by offence type, before admission and after six months of treatment ($n = 253$).[a]

OFFENCE TYPE	BEFORE	AFTER	p^*
Violent and sex offences	0.020	0.012	NS
Shoplifting	0.123	0.043	0.010
Burglary	0.059	0.008	0.009
Robbery/mugging	0.012	0.004	NS
Trespassing	0.028	0	0.052
Theft of vehicles	0.047	0.032	NS
Other theft and property offences[b]	0.111	0.032	0.020
Other criminal code offences[c]	0.024	0.008	0.045
Traffic offences	0.051	0.016	NS
Use/possession of cannabis	0.130	0.047	0.036
Use/possession of heroin	0.715	0.123	< 0.001
Use/possession of cocaine/ecstacy	0.257	0.071	<0.001
Use possession of several substances	0.142	0	NS
Trafficking/smuggling of any drug	0.091	0.036	0.023
Violations of other laws[d]	0.020	0	0.025
Overall incidence rate	1.830	0.431	<0.001

[a]Incidence rates allow—by multiplying the rate by the number of individuals—to calculate the number of contacts recorded (that is 463 contacts were recorded by the police for the period before admission and 109 for the period after admission).

[b]Including receiving stolen property and forgery.

[c]Including fare dodging.

[d]Including searches.

In order to assess this in detail, we would need the offence-level data on self-reported police contacts. This information was indeed requested during the interviews and prevalence (that is at an individual level) data are available. If there had been any relevant change in police reaction to crimes committed by programme participants, the prevalence data given in Table 3 should, however, have reflected it. Thus, Table 3 indicates, for the two reference periods under consideration, how many programme participants reported police contacts in connection with offences committed, and for how many it was indeed possible to locate a recorded offence (as a suspect) in the police files.

Two interesting trends appear in Table 3:

1. Many respondents admitted to having had police contacts, whereas no corresponding record could be located in police files. This may be true particularly for drug offences where many respondents may have indeed been searched by the police, but where, apparently, no formal proceedings were taken. This tendency to ignore (that is not recording) offences seems to apply particularly where pushing cannabis is concerned, and more so before than after admission to the programme. This may reflect increased police control of the drug scene in general, rather than a change in policy towards the participants in the programme in particular.

2. For other offences, the absolute numbers of offenders are, particularly after admission to the programme, often too small to yield reliable rates. But overall, the rates of recorded offences do not seem to change consistently, or strongly, in any direction. Therefore, we may conclude that the changes in police-recorded offences, as indicated in Table 2, reflect real changes in behaviour, and not merely a reduced probability of being prosecuted by the police.

TABLE 3
Prevalence rates of self-reported and recorded police contacts among programme participants, by offence type, before admission and after 6 months of treatment ($n = 253$).

Offence Type	BEFORE		AFTER	
	Reported	Recorded	Reported	Recorded
Shoplifting	8.3	6.7	3.2	4.0
Theft and serious property offences[a]	7.1	5.5	1.2	1.2
Trafficking cannabis	4.3	0.4	1.2	0.8
Trafficking hard drugs	13.8	6.3	2.4	2.4
Any offence in this table	26.1	17.0	6.3	7.9

[a]Burglary, mugging, robbery, pick-pocketing, other thefts, receiving stolen property.

CONCLUSIONS

The analysis reported here confirms the results based on self-reported delinquency and victimisation data. According to police files, the drop in serious property offences was indeed comparable. As it turned out, this drop was not due to the reduced probability of the police recording offences committed by participants after their admission to the heroin prescription programme.

REFERENCES

Killias, M., and Rabasa, J. (1997). *Rapport final sur les effets de la prescription de stupéfiants sur la délinquance des toxicomanes.* Lausanne: Institut de Police Scientifique et de Criminologie de l'Université de Lausanne.

Killias, M., and Rabasa, J. (1998a). Auswirkungen der Heroin-Verschreibung auf die Delinquenz Drogenabhängiger: Ergebnisse der Versuche in der Schweiz. *Monatsschrift für Kriminologie und Strafrechtsreform, 81*(1), 1–16.

Killias, M., and Rabasa, J. (1998b). Does heroin prescription reduce crime? Results from the evaluation of the Swiss heroin prescription projects. *Studies on Crime and Crime Prevention, 7*(1), pp. 127–133.

Killias, M., and Uchtenhagen, A. (1996). Does medical heroin prescription reduce delinquency among drug-addicts? On the evaluation of the Swiss heroin prescription projects and its methodology. *Studies on Crime and Crime Prevention, 5*(2), 245–256.

Uchtenhagen, A. (1997). *Versuche für eine ärztliche Verschreibung von Betäubungsmitteln. Syntheseberich.* Zurich: Institut für Suchtforschung (University of Zurich).

The Influence of Crack Cocaine on Robbery, Burglary, and Homicide Rates: A Cross-City, Longitudinal Analysis

ERIC BAUMER

JANET L. LAURITSEN

RICHARD ROSENFELD

RICHARD WRIGHT

ABSTRACT

After tracking one another closely for decades, the U.S. robbery rate increased and the burglary rate declined in the late 1980s. The authors investigate the impact of crack on this divergence using a two-stage hierarchical linear model that decomposes between- and within-city variation in crime rates for 142 cities. Given its prominence in discussions of crack and criminal violence, homicide offending is also examined. Net of other influences, cities with higher levels of crack use experienced larger increases in robbery and decreases in burglary. Cities with greater levels of crack had higher homicide rates but did not show more rapid increases in these rates than other cities. The results suggest that the emergence and proliferation of crack shifted the balance of urban offending opportunities and rewards from burglary to robbery.

An abundance of anecdotal evidence links crack cocaine to an upsurge in violent crime during the 1980s (e.g., Anderson, 1990; "The Bloodiest Year Yet?" 1990; "Cops under Fire," 1990; Hinds, 1990; Treaster, 1992). Crack first appeared in the early 1980s in Miami and New York City, but it quickly spread to other cities across the United States (Adler, 1995, pp. 63–75; Inciardi, 1992, pp. 108–113). Increases in violence appeared to follow closely on the heels of crack's appearance on the streets. Yet, although considerable scholarly speculation exists regarding the connection between crack and increasing rates of urban violence, that connection has not been well documented in the research literature. Compared with the attention devoted to the increase in violent crime, the equally substantial *decline* in rates of property crime—and the possibility that the decrease in property crime is also related to the rise of crack—has gone almost unnoticed.

We suggest that the emergence and proliferation of crack cocaine is responsible, at least in part, for both the increase in violent crime and the decrease in property crime observed during the last decade. Following insights from recent ethnographic research on offending patterns, our analysis focuses specifically on the offenses of robbery and burglary. After tracking one another closely for decades, U.S. robbery and burglary rates began to diverge in the late 1980s. This divergence is associated with the epidemic growth in the demand for crack, which fundamentally changed the context of illicit drug use and marketing in America's inner cities (see, e.g., Johnson, 1991). That change, we hypothesize, altered the opportunities and rewards associated with different types of criminal offending. The perceived rewards of robbery increased relative to the rewards of burglary for offenders, regardless of whether they were crack users

The research on which this article is based was funded in part by the Harry Frank Guggenheim Foundation and the National Institute of Justice (Grant 94-IJ-CX-0030 and 3-8050-MO-IJ). The opinions expressed do not necessarily reflect those of the funding agencies.

themselves, contributing to a dramatic increase in urban robbery rates in the middle and late 1980s and a corresponding decline in rates of burglary.

If our argument is correct, higher levels of crack use in cities should be associated with escalating robbery rates and declining burglary rates, net of other influences. We discuss the qualitative research on changes in the patterns and context of offending in inner-city communities where crack use and marketing are heavily concentrated. After documenting the hypothesized changes in robbery and burglary rates, we then use a two-level hierarchical linear model to examine the impact of crack use on robbery and burglary trends across 142 U.S. cities for the period 1984 through 1992. Because of its prominence in popular and scholarly commentary on the crack-violence connection, we also include city homicide rates in this analysis. We assess the effects of crack cocaine on the three crime types controlling for other known correlates of violent and property crime in urban areas.

CRACK AND THE CONTEXT OF URBAN CRIME

Findings from qualitative research suggest multiple and distinct influences of crack use on robbery, burglary, and homicide. Unlike homicide, robbery and burglary are offenses motivated primarily by pressing economic need (see Shover, 1996; Wright and Decker, 1994). Crack cocaine is a stimulant that produces a "high" that typically lasts less than 10 minutes (Ratner, 1993). This high often is followed by an intense desire for more crack. Because it perpetuates a desire that can never be satisfied—or, alternatively, requires incessant satisfaction—crack use is a cash-intensive activity that can quickly exhaust a user's financial resources (see, e.g., Inciardi, 1993; Johnson, 1991). Thus, regular crack users frequently find themselves in situations where they need more crack immediately but have no legitimate means of quickly obtaining the funds needed to purchase it. Desperate to generate cash by any means necessary, many users are willing to consider illegitimate solutions to their immediate needs; any "proximate and performable" crime will do (Lofland, 1969, p. 61).

Illegitimate opportunities for quick money, however, are severely limited during the late night and early morning hours when crack use tends to be most prevalent (French, 1993; Weisburd and Green, 1994). Certainly, opportunities for residential burglary are restricted during these hours, because most dwellings are occupied and outlets for stolen goods are largely unavailable. Likewise, few crack users possess the technical know-how needed to overcome the sophisticated security devices protecting unoccupied commercial premises during the night (Wright and Decker, 1994). Robbery, on the other hand, usually nets cash directly and is easily perpetrated during the hours of darkness when the streets are less crowded (Wright and Decker, 1997). Hence, crack users are likely to find robbery to be a more attractive crime than burglary.

More important, in neighborhoods characterized by the widespread use of crack cocaine, addicts already have flooded the informal economy with guns, jewelry, and consumer electronic goods. As a result, the price commanded by hot merchandise has tumbled; there is little money to be made through burglary in these neighborhoods (Wright and Decker, 1994). In this sense, crack has changed the context of many high-crime neighborhoods by driving down the street value of goods and thereby dramatically enhancing the attractiveness of cash. Such changes have altered the balance of offending opportunities and rewards not only for crack users in need of additional cocaine but also for property offenders operating in these areas. These are the principal mechanisms, we propose, that underlie the increase in robbery and decrease in burglary during the crack epidemic of the late 1980s.

THE DIVERGENCE IN ROBBERY AND BURGLARY TRENDS

Robbery rates in most large American cities rose substantially from the mid-1980s through the early 1990s. Between 1985 and 1992, robbery rates for U.S. cities with 250,000 or more residents increased by 22.8 percent. Burglary rates in these cities declined by 16.7 percent during the same period (Federal Bureau of Investigation, 1986, p. 147; 1993, p. 96). Figure 1 displays robbery and burglary rates for the nation between 1973 and 1992 based on Uniform Crime Reporting (UCR) data on the number of robberies and burglaries known to the police per 100,000 population (Maguire and Pastore, 1995, p. 304). The pattern of change over time is nearly the same for both crime types until the mid-1980s. Both rise and fall together to a peak around 1980 and then decline during the early 1980s. The common trends in the two crime types diverge sharply after 1987, and they

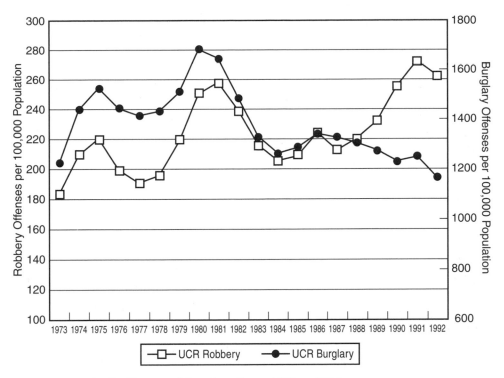

FIGURE 1   UCR Robbery and Burglary Rates 1973 to 1992.

do not appear to be artifacts of changes over time in the reporting of these crimes to the police.[1]

Although these national trends suggest that something may have occurred in the mid-1980s to alter the covariation between robbery and burglary trends, the plausibility of our hypothesis is more directly illustrated by examining trend data from two cities that vary in levels of crack cocaine use. We compare these crime trends for two cities believed to be quite different in drug context: Oakland, California, and Rockford, Illinois. The burglary and robbery trends for Rockford, where crack use is estimated to be relatively low, parallel each other throughout the 1980s. The trend data for Oakland, where crack is much more prevalent, show a divergence in trends comparable to the average national patterns.[2] The analyses presented in this article expand the logic of this comparison by systematically examining crime trends across 142 U.S. cities.

The potential relationship between crack and violent crime has received some attention in recent literature on homicide. Blumstein (1995) attributes the rise in youth firearm homicides over the last decade to an escalating arms race in inner-city neighborhoods where illicit drug markets are concentrated. He argues that the increase in demand for crack in the

late 1980s led dealers to recruit and arm growing numbers of inner-city youths as street-level drug sellers. The firearm violence initially associated with the illegal drug trade, however, quickly took on a life of its own, as other young people armed themselves in response to an increasingly threatening urban environment. Rates of gun assault and homicide increased accordingly (see also Sheley and Wright, 1995).

Although his discussion is restricted primarily to the relationships among illicit drug markets, youth firearm possession, and homicide, Blumstein briefly considered the possible connection between escalating crack use and the divergence of robbery and burglary offending patterns in the late 1980s (Blumstein, 1995, pp. 12–13). Baumer (1994) systematically addresses this issue in a cross-sectional analysis of the relationship between arrestee crack use in 1990 and rates of robbery, burglary, and homicide in large U.S. cities. He reports a sizable and significant relationship, net of other influences, between arrestee crack use and rates of robbery, a somewhat smaller and nonsignificant association with homicide, and no appreciable relationship with burglary. Although the above analyses also are suggestive of our hypothesis, this research has not addressed the question of whether city-level differences in crack involvement can account for differences across cities in robbery, burglary, or homicide *trends*. That is the research issue to which our analysis of urban crime rates is directed.

ANALYTIC STRATEGY

We examine city-level trends in robbery, burglary, and homicide rates using a two-level hierarchical model in which within-city changes in these crimes between 1984 and 1992 are examined in conjunction with between-city differences in trends. The analyses build on the work of Bursik and Grasmick (1992), who applied hierarchical linear modeling techniques to the study of longitudinal crime profiles for Chicago neighborhoods. Hierarchical linear modeling (HLM) is chosen over other pooled cross-section time-series models because of its flexibility in decomposing between- and within-city variation in crime rates (Bursik and Grasmick, 1992) and because the method provides estimates that are readily understood by persons familiar with standard OLS regression techniques. These models permit us to estimate whether between-city differences in levels of crack involvement are related to the various crime trends for each city. We briefly describe the logic of hierarchical modeling below (for a more detailed discussion, see Bryk and Raudenbush, 1992; Raudenbush and Chan, 1992).

In the two-level hierarchical model used here, the first level represents changes in crime rates within each city over time, whereas the second level reflects differences between cities in these trends. The first step in the procedure is to estimate a level 1 model, which provides the longitudinal profile parameters for the crime trends for each city in the study. The parameters of these trajectories (the intercept, slope, and acceleration of the trend lines) describe crime rates over time for each city. The level 1 model for the crime rate of a particular city in a given year can be represented as a function of a systematic trajectory associated with time, plus random error:

$$Y_{it} = \pi_{0i} + \pi_{1i}(Time_{it}) + \pi_{2i}(Time^2)_{it} + e_{it}, \qquad (1)$$

where Y_{it} is the observed crime rate for city i (for $i = 1$, ..., n cities) at time t (for $t = -4, ..., 4$); (π_{0i}), (π_{1i}), and (π_{2i}) are the intercept, slope, and acceleration parameters, respectively, for the trend lines, and e_{it} is the random within-city error for city i at time t (see also Bursik and Grasmick, 1992). Annual data for 142 cities are available for the years 1984 through 1992, a period that captures both the divergence in robbery and burglary rates and the crack epidemic in urban

areas. Given our coding of time, π_{0i} is the intercept of city i when $t = 0$ (i.e., 1988, the midpoint of the nine-year period). Because we are interested in the trends for three types of crime, we estimate profile parameters for 426 different trajectories (3 crime types × 142 cities). Ordinary least squares regression procedures provide the estimates for these parameters.

The parameters obtained from the level 1 model are then used as outcome variables in a level 2 model, which investigates variation in the crime trends across cities. The level 2 analyses are premised on finding (in the level 1 results) that significant variation exists in the trend parameters across cities. For the crimes of robbery, burglary, and homicide, this is a reasonable expectation. Previous research has shown that crime trends vary across neighborhoods and census tracts (Bursik and Grasmick, 1992; Schuerman and Kobrin, 1986). If significant variation is found in the slope and acceleration parameters of robbery, burglary, and homicide rates for the cities included in this study, a level 2 model can be specified to assess the role of urban characteristics that may help to explain this variation.

A starting point for estimating the amount of variation in within-city changes in crime rates is to specify a level 2 model containing no covariates for between-city differences. The corresponding equations for this model can be represented as follows:

$$\pi_{0i} = \beta_{00} + \mu_{0i}$$
$$\pi_{1i} = \beta_{10} + \mu_{1i} \qquad (2)$$
$$\pi_{2i} = \beta_{20} + \mu_{2i},$$

where β_{00} is the grand mean crime rate across cities (when Time = 0), β_{10} is the grand mean rate of change in crime rates, β_{20} is the nonlinear acceleration rate for the crime trend, μ_{0i} is the random effect of city i on crime rate, μ_{1i} is the random effect of city i on the rate of change in crime rates, and μ_{2i} is the random effect of city i on the acceleration parameter in crime rates.

Combining the level 1 and level 2 equations shown above nets the following equation:

$$Y_{it} = \beta_{00} + \beta_{10}(Time_{it}) + \beta_{20}(Time^2_{it}) + e_{it}. \qquad (3)$$

Ordinary least squares regression is inappropriate for estimating this equation because the errors are correlated over time within each city and are heteroscedastic due to their dependence on time. HLM software estimates these parameters using maximum likelihood procedures (see Bryk and Raudenbush, 1992; Raudenbush and Chan, 1992, p. 396). Together, the parameters in equation (3) describe the average trend across cities for each of the three crime types. Following estimation of the above model, the analyses turn to assessing the influence of crack involvement and other covariates on these parameters.

As indicated earlier, we hypothesize that city-level differences in levels of crack involvement help explain variations in robbery and burglary rate trends. More specifically, we expect that increases in robbery rates and declines in burglary rates will be greater in cities where crack use is high. Prior research leads us to expect that changes in homicide rates will more closely resemble the changes in robbery rates than those for burglary rates. To examine these hypotheses, a new level 2 model is specified in which X_i represents our measure of levels of crack use for each city:

$$\pi_{0i} = \beta_{00} + \beta_{01}X_i + \mu_{0i}$$
$$\pi_{1i} = \beta_{10} + \beta_{11}X_i + \mu_{1i} \qquad (4)$$
$$\pi_{2i} = \beta_{20} + \beta_{21}X_i + \mu_{2i}$$

The level 1 model remains as noted in equation (1), and the new combined equation becomes:

$$Y_{it} = \beta_{00} + \beta_{01}(\text{Crack}) + (\beta_{10} + \beta_{11}(\text{Crack}))\text{Time}_{it} +$$
$$(\beta_{20} + \beta_{21}(\text{Crack}))\text{Time}_{it}^2 + e_{it} \qquad (5)$$

In this equation, β_{01} represents the influence of between-city differences in crack involvement on the intercept of a given crime trend, where β_{11} and β_{21} capture the influence of crack on the slope and acceleration parameters of these trends. Once this model is estimated for each of the three crime types, additional covariates will be added to the level 2 model to control for factors that might produce a spurious relationship between our crack measure and the crime trend parameters.

Our decision to treat city-level differences in crack involvement as a level 2 variable rather than a level 1 measure was based on two concerns. First, our hypothesis specifically predicts that differences in levels of crack across cities in the late 1980s are related to differences in crime trends across cities. The ethnographic literature suggests that in places where crack use and markets are more prevalent, we should observe a greater preference for cash-intensive crimes like robbery and a corresponding reduced preference for burglary. As discussed earlier, high levels of crack involvement may alter the context of offender decision-making in a relatively enduring manner, which justifies the use of a between-city indicator to capture such differences (e.g., Anderson, 1990; Currie, 1993; Finnegan, 1990). Thus, our focus is on how urban differences in levels of crack involvement influence variations in these crime trends.

Second, we have greater confidence in our crack measure for differentiating crime levels and trends between cities than for use as a time-varying measure for examining within-city changes over time. High reliability of our proxy measure (discussed below) has been shown in cross-sectional studies of cities, but the reliability of this variable for use as a time-varying measure is not known. By treating crack involvement as a measure of differences in urban contexts, we minimize the impact of measurement error in this variable.

DATA AND MEASURES

Data for these analyses include UCR crime rates, an indicator of levels of crack involvement, and measures of resource deprivation, population composition, and family structure for 142 U.S. cities. Robbery, burglary, and homicide data for the 142 cities were obtained from Federal Bureau of Investigation (FBI) summarized annual tapes and represent offenses reported to the police in each of these jurisdictions between 1984 and 1992. We use yearly population estimates provided by the FBI to construct rates per 100,000 for each of these crimes. The limitations of the UCR crime data are well known, the most important of which is that they are restricted to offenses known to the police (Biderman and Lynch, 1991; Gove, Hughes, and Geerken, 1985; O'Brien, 1985). Comparisons between UCR offense data and data from victimization surveys indicate that a large fraction of robberies and burglaries are not reported to the police. Nevertheless, year-to-year changes in the UCR and the National Crime Victimization Survey (NCVS) indicators for these crime types are highly similar (Biderman and Lynch, 1991; Blumstein, Cohen, and Rosenfeld, 1991). As described earlier, the divergence in robbery and burglary rates during the latter part of the 1980s—the empirical issue of central concern in our analysis—is apparent in both the UCR and NCVS crime indicators.

We use UCR drug arrest rates as a proxy for city-level differences in crack involvement. Doing so poses important validation issues. Arrest rates, of course, are far from perfect indicators of underlying patterns of offending. The use of arrest data to measure illicit drug use would seem to be particularly problematic. Drug enforcement policy is driven by a variety of social and political factors, which are not necessarily associated with variation in drug use per se (Currie, 1993). Moreover, drug arrest data provide a gross indication, at best, of drug offending within specific drug types. The UCR's classification of drug arrests by drug type combines cocaine with heroin and other opiates; nor are powder and crack cocaine distinguished in the arrest data. Different types and forms of illicit drugs may have quite distinct and changing patterns of distribution and use from one city to another and over time.

These considerations place a strong burden on researchers to justify the use of drug arrest rates as a measure of crack use for this time period. We address this issue with data on cocaine and crack use from two distinct sources, the Drug Use Forecasting Program (DUF) and the Drug Abuse Warning Network (DAWN). The DUF program operates in more than 20 cities and measures the use of a range of illicit drugs by booked arrestees. Recent drug use is measured by urine tests as well as by self-reports of arrestees (for a description of the DUF sample and protocol, see National Institute of Justice, 1995, p. 10). The DAWN data are based on drug mentions and episodes in reports from emergency rooms and medical examiners' offices in more than two dozen cities across the country (for descriptions, see Substance Abuse and Mental Health Services Administration, 1994, pp. 38–40; 1995, pp. 1–3). Prior research has shown that each of these data sources has high internal reliability and that they yield estimates of illicit drug use that are strongly correlated across cities (Rosenfeld, 1995; Rosenfeld and Decker, 1993). Furthermore, these estimates covary strongly with variations in drug arrest rates for cities. Specifically, cities with high levels of cocaine use, as measured by the DUF urine test results and the DAWN medical reports, also tend to display high drug arrest rates. The strongest relationships are between the DUF and DAWN cocaine measures and the arrest rate for sale-manufacture of cocaine or opiates. Weaker and nonsignificant relationships were found between this arrest measure and the DUF and DAWN indicators for marijuana and opiates. These results suggest that the arrest measure discriminates well between drug types and is a good proxy for underlying patterns of cocaine use across cities.[3]

These findings leave open the question of whether the drug arrest measure reflects variation in the use of crack cocaine specifically, because neither the DUF urine data nor the DAWN reports separate crack from other forms of cocaine. However, the DUF protocol does ask arrestees whether they have used crack or some other form of cocaine during the three days preceding the interview. In most of the DUF cities, and especially in those where the urine tests detect high levels of cocaine use, a large proportion of arrestees report using crack compared with other forms of cocaine within the previous three days, roughly the window for which the urine test is calibrated. In some cases, the differences are substantial.

For example, Atlanta arrestees are almost three times as likely to report using crack than cocaine in some other form; the ratio is five to one in Ft. Lauderdale and more than ten to one in Detroit. In addition, the fraction of arrestees who test positive for cocaine is more highly correlated with self-reported crack use than with self-reported use of cocaine in other forms.[4] For these reasons, it seems reasonable to assume that the observed association between the DUF urine data and the drug arrest rate reflects between-city variation in levels of crack involvement.

To capture the fact that crack emerged in most U.S. cities at somewhat different points in the mid- to late-1980s, our measure of crack involvement uses the highest drug arrest rate for each city between 1986 and 1989, the time period during which crack arrived in most U.S. cities. This measurement strategy minimizes the amount of between-city error due to variations in the timing of the arrival of crack cocaine. In sum, although this measure does not allow us to model the length of time between crack's arrival in a given city and subsequent changes in crime, it does allow a reasonable comparison of the robbery, burglary, and homicide trends of cities with high levels of crack in the late 1980s to those with lower levels.

To isolate the influence of crack on variation in levels and trends in city robbery, burglary, and homicide rates, we control for measures found in prior research to be related to between-city differences in crime rates as well as to changes in crime rates over time (e.g., Land, McCall, and Cohen, 1990; Liska and Bellair, 1995; Sampson and Lauritsen, 1994). Prior research has shown that crime rates tend to be higher in cities with larger populations, larger proportions of Blacks and young persons, and higher levels of family instability and resource deprivation. Research also has shown that changes in these structural conditions are associated with changes in crime rates over time (Bursik and Grasmick, 1992; Cantor and Land, 1985; Liska and Bellair, 1995). Thus, we consider measures of each of these dimensions in the present research.

Census data from 1980 and 1990 are used to examine the influence of both general structural conditions and changes in these conditions on levels of and trends in robbery, burglary, and homicide rates (Bureau of the Census, 1980, 1990). In addition, we assess the effects of regional location on crime rates by identifying each city as either a southern, western, northeastern, or north central city as defined by the Census Bureau (see, e.g., McCall, Land, and Cohen, 1992). Summary statistics for each of the measures considered in the analyses are presented in the appendix. The 142 cities in our sample are highly representative of the largest 200 U.S. cities in population size and composition, age structure, economic conditions, and crime rates.

As expected, strong bivariate correlations exist among many of the variables available for the study. To correct for the potential confounding influence of multicollinearity, we performed principal components analyses on these measures (cf. Land et al., 1990; McCall et al., 1992). Eight distinguishable factors emerged from the principal components analysis: (1) resource deprivation (composed of percentage of persons below the poverty line, percentage unemployed, percentage of households headed by a female with children under the age of 18, and percentage of persons receiving public assistance), (2) changes in resource deprivation, (3) percentage of the population aged 15 to 29, (4) population size, (5) percentage of buildings that are vacant, (6) divorce rates, (7) change in unemployment rates and percentage of buildings that are vacant (i.e., business flight), and (8) population change. These results are, by and large, consistent with previous macrolevel research. Together with percentage Black and change in percentage Black, these factors are considered as control variables in the multivariate level 2 models.

RESULTS

Overall Trends

We begin our analyses by estimating the average crime trajectories for the 142-city sample. Determining the best fitting trajectory involves a process of estimating the simplest linear model and comparing the results to more complex nonlinear specifications. For robbery and burglary trends, a quadratic specification was found to be necessary, whereas for homicide trends, a linear model was preferred (table not shown). As one might expect from the national data, robbery rates were found to be increasing at an accelerating rate from 1984 through 1992. Burglary rates, on the other hand, increased slightly for the first part of the time series but began to decline at an increasing rate during the second half of the period. Finally, the mean homicide rate for the 142 cities also rose steadily between 1984 and 1992, showing no increase or decrease in the rate of change over time.[5]

The variance components indicate the amount of variation attributable to each of the estimated parameters. The variance in π_{0i} is τ_{00} (e.g., robbery = 101,293.08), which represents the amount of between-city variation in crime rates (when $t = 0$, or

1988); τ_{11} is the level of between-city variation in the linear trend in crime rates; τ_{22} is the amount of between-city variation in the rate of acceleration for the crime trends; and σ^2 represents the residual within-city variation in robbery rates over time. Most of the total variance in city crime rates over time is attributable to differences between cities rather than to changes over time within cities. The chi-square tests for the variance components show that there is significant variation in the trend components for the 142 cities. For instance, robbery and homicide rates increased between 1984 and 1992 in most cities in our study; however, the rate of increase in these crimes varied considerably across cities, and in some cities, robbery and homicide rates declined during the period. Burglary trends also display significant across-city variation. Most of the cities experienced declines in burglary rates; however, the rate of decline in burglary was much smaller in some cities, and burglary rates increased in others.

The Influence of Crack on Crime Rate Trends

The level 2 analyses determine whether increases in robbery rates and decreases in burglary rates were greater in cities where crack involvement was higher. These analyses estimate the combined equation (5) described earlier (table not shown). The results for robbery show that cities with higher levels of crack involvement had significantly higher levels of robbery ($\beta_{01} = .371$) and more rapid increases in robbery rates over time ($\beta_{11} = .014$). Burglary rates were somewhat higher in cities where crack use was high ($\beta_{01} = .320$); however, contrary to the pattern observed for robbery, the relationship between crack use and burglary rate trends is negative ($\beta_{11} = -.025$). In other words, declines in burglary were significantly greater in cities with higher levels of crack use. The magnitude of this coefficient also reveals that, although significant, the differences in burglary trends between high and low crack cities are somewhat small. Finally, the results for homicide closely parallel those observed for robbery. Cities in which levels of crack use were higher experienced significantly higher homicide rates ($\beta_{01} = .009$) and more rapid increases in homicide ($\beta_{11} = .0004$) over this time period than cities with lower levels of crack use. Thus, the findings suggest that regardless of initial levels of robbery, burglary, or homicide, cities with greater levels of crack use in the late-1980s experienced the greatest increases in robbery and homicide rates, and somewhat faster decreases in burglary rates.

Multivariate Results

The results so far are consistent with our hypothesis. However, because levels of crack involvement and trends in various crime rates share common social-structural causes, we incorporate the variables discussed earlier and shown in previous research to be related to between- or within-city differences in crime rates. Following Bryk and Raudenbush (1992), we use a "step-up" strategy in developing our level 2 model. This strategy allows us to examine the influences of a variety of measures both on crime levels and trends by introducing variables into the level 2 equations in a stepwise manner. The factors described earlier were each considered as level 2 indicators in these analyses. Only those factors that were found to have statistically significant influences on the intercept, slope, or acceleration parameters of a given

crime trend are retained in the models. The final models for each crime type are shown in Table 1.

The factors that influence the intercepts of each of the crime trajectories are found in the top panel of the table (i.e., β_{01} through β_{07}). Because the intercepts represent between-city levels of crime (when Time = 0), these findings are generally consistent with previous cross-sectional analyses. For example, robbery, burglary, and homicide rates were significantly greater in cities with higher levels of resource deprivation and divorce. However, after controlling for the effects that these characteristics have on urban crime rates, between-city differences in levels of crack involvement continue to have significant and positive effects on overall rates of robbery and homicide (see β_{01}). In other words, crack involvement appears to be an independent predictor of levels of robbery and homicide, and its relationship to these crimes is not simply a func-

TABLE 1   Hierarchical Linear Model Results for the Influence of Crack Use on City-Level Robbery, Burglary, and Homicide Rates, Controlling for Covariates of Crime, 1984 through 1992 (N = 142)

FIXED EFFECTS PREDICTOR	ROBBERY			BURGLARY			HOMICIDE		
	Coefficient	SE	t Ratio	Coefficient	SE	t Ratio	Coefficient	SE	t Ratio
For base rate, π_{0i}									
Intercept, β_{00}	205.06	30.29	6.77*	2100.29	60.75	34.57*	5.75	.77	7.48*
Crack, β_{01}	.211	.035	5.99*	—[a]	—	—	.003	.001	4.05*
Deprivation, β_{02}	100.07	19.08	5.24*	223.47	43.25	5.17*	3.24	.49	6.67*
Divorce, β_{03}	41.91	14.36	2.92*	235.86	42.03	5.61*	1.96	.36	5.44*
Percentage Black, β_{04}	5.65	1.18	4.77*	—	—	—	.29	.03	8.92*
Population size, β_{05}	55.10	14.19	3.88*	—	—	—	1.78	.35	5.06*
Percentage vacant, β_{06}	—	—	—	—	—	—	.88	.38	2.30*
Southern city, β_{07}	—	—	—	—	—	—	3.59	.85	4.24*
For linear change, π_{1i}									
Intercept, β_{10}	1.65	2.41	.69	−29.90	12.04	−2.48*	−.22	.10	−2.21*
Crack, β_{11}	.007	.003	2.36*	−.027	.014	−1.96*	—	—	—
Divorce, β_{12}	—	—	—	−13.22	6.65	−1.99*	—	—	—
Percentage Black, β_{13}	.71	.10	7.28*	1.89	.48	3.94*	.043	.004	10.21*
Western city, β_{14}	—	—	—	−41.89	17.06	−2.46*	—	—	—
Percentage young, β_{15}	—	—	—	—	—	—	.13	.06	2.11*
For quadratic effect, π_{2i}									
Intercept, β_{20}	−.09	.70	−.13	−16.06	2.47	−6.49*	—	—	—
Crack, β_{21}	.002	.001	2.49*	.008	.003	2.77*	—	—	—

VARIANCE COMPONENTS PARAMETER	ROBBERY		BURGLARY		HOMICIDE	
	Estimate	Chi-Square	Estimate	Chi-Square	Estimate	Chi-Square
Var $(\pi_{0i}) = \tau_{00}$	38,780.13	4,475.73*	509,074.95	4,900.64*	21.57	2,485.92*
Var $(\pi_{1i}) = \tau_{11}$	255.75	583.32*	4,138.82	717.73*	.51	520.12*
Var $(\pi_{2i}) = \tau_{22}$	20.51	324.43*	402.02	436.57*	—	—
Var $(e_{it}) = \sigma^2$	4,798.49		58,620.23		11.20	

[a]Indicates variables omitted from final round estimations due to nonsignificant effects.

*p < .05.

tion of shared causal factors (see also Baumer, 1994). On the other hand, levels of crack are not significantly related to between-city differences in burglary levels after controlling for resource deprivation and divorce.

We next consider whether the significant impact of crack involvement on trends in robbery, burglary, and homicide rates persists once other substantive influences are controlled for. The coefficient β_{11} reveals that the direction and significance of the relationships between crack and robbery and burglary trends are unaffected by controls for a variety of social conditions. Regardless of factors such as a city's population composition or level of resource deprivation, increases in robbery rates and decreases in burglary rates were greater in cities with higher levels of crack involvement in the late 1980s. In addition, the crack measure was found to be the only significant predictor of whether cities would experience accelerating robbery rates or decelerating burglary trends.

Urban homicide trends appear to be related to levels of crack involvement in a different way. Once percentage Black and percentage of the population aged 15 to 24 are controlled for, the level of crack in a city had no significant, direct influence on increases or decreases in homicide rates. Although cities with higher levels of crack use did have higher levels of homicide, subsequent changes in overall homicide rates appear to have been no greater in cities with higher levels of crack use.

To summarize this set of complex relationships between crack use and robbery and burglary trends under different social-structural conditions, we present the average annual rates of change (in 1988) for these two crime types in Tables 2 and 3. The estimated rates of change shown here incorporate those variables that

were found to have statistically significant influences on changes in robbery and burglary rates. The estimated rates of change are derived from the coefficients shown in Table 1, when time = 0 (i.e., at the midpoint of the time period under consideration). Table 2 compares the annual rate of change in robbery for cities with high versus low levels of crack involvement according to whether the percentage Black in the city is high, average, or low. The rate of increase in robbery was highest (39.62 per 100,000 in 1988) in cities with high levels of crack use and a high percentage of Black residents. This rate of increase is more than double that found in cities with average levels of crack use and percentage Black residents (17.41 per 100,000), and more than 14 times greater than cities with low levels of crack use and percentage Black residents (2.80 per 100,000).

Table 3 shows the annual rate of change in city-level burglary rates along high and low dimensions of the variables identified in Table 1 as significant predictors of burglary rate trends. Declines in burglary were greatest in western cities, particularly those with high levels of crack involvement, high divorce rates, and low percentages of Black residents (−119.05 per 100,000). Burglary rates declined the least in nonwestern cities and, in fact, were found to have increased over time in certain types of cities (e.g., low crack involvement, low divorce, and high percentage of Black residents). Taken together, these findings support the hypothesis that the emergence and proliferation of crack cocaine in the mid- to late-1980s created an urban context in which robbery rates were more likely to escalate and burglary rates were more likely to fall. In this sense, crack cocaine may be said to be responsible for the temporal divergence in robbery and burglary trends.

TABLE 2   Summary Results of the Influence of High versus Low Levels of Crack Use on Average Annual Rate of Change in Robbery

AVERAGE ANNUAL RATE OF CHANGE IN ROBBERY RATES (AT TIME = 0, 1988)

City Characteristics	LEVEL OF CRACK USE	
	High	Low
High percentage Black	39.62	31.19
Average percentage Black	22.77	14.35
Low percentage Black	11.46	2.80
Average percentage Black, crack use	17.41	

Note: High values for city characteristics represent mean values for upper quartile of sample, low values represent mean values for lower quartile of sample, and average values are based on the sample means. Rates of change in robbery rates are the annual change in the number of robberies per 100,000 population when time = 0 (1988).

TABLE 3   Summary Results of the Influence of High versus Low Levels of Crack Use on Average Annual Rate of Change in Burglary

AVERAGE ANNUAL RATE OF CHANGE IN BURGLARY RATES (AT TIME = 0, 1988)

City Characteristics	LEVEL OF CRACK USE	
	High	Low
Western city		
High divorce		
High percentage Black	−43.96	−11.51
Low percentage Black	−119.05	−86.58
Low divorce		
High percentage Black	−10.75	21.73
Low percentage Black	−85.82	−53.34
Average divorce, percentage Blank, crack use	−52.30	
Nonwestern city		
High divorce		
High percentage Black	−2.09	30.38
Low percentage Black	−77.16	−44.69
Low divorce		
High percentage Black	31.14	63.62
Low percentage Black	−43.93	−11.45
Average divorce, percentage Black, crack use	−10.41	

Note: High values for city characteristics represent mean values for upper quartile of sample, low values represent mean values for lower quartile of sample, and average values are based on the sample means. Rates of change in burglary rates are the annual change in the number of burglaries per 100,000 population when time = 0 (1988).

CONCLUSION

We investigated the hypothesis that the emergence and proliferation of crack cocaine was responsible, at least in part, for observed increases in robbery rates and declines in burglary rates during the late 1980s. We evaluated the influence of crack involvement on within- and between-city differences in robbery, burglary, and homicide trends for 142 U.S. cities from 1984 through 1992. Consistent with our hypothesis, the results indicate that cities with high rates of crack involvement were significantly more likely to have experienced increases in robbery rates. In general, cities with high levels of crack use also experienced significantly greater declines in burglary rates. Declines in burglary were not universal, but in those cities where burglary rates increased, the increases were considerably smaller in the presence of high levels of crack involvement. Taken as a whole, then, the robbery and burglary findings support our contention that crack involvement was significantly associated with the divergence in robbery and burglary rates that began about 1987.

In the presence of controls, our results for homicide differ from those found for robbery. No significant effects of crack involvement on homicide *trends* were found after controlling for the race and age composition of urban populations. The results for homicide may have more closely resembled those for robbery within specific subtypes of homicide, such as drug-related homicides, felony homicides, firearm homicides, and murders committed by teenagers and young adults. These are the types of events that constitute the increases in homicide rates and that figure centrally in the explanation of the increase in criminal violence offered by Blumstein (1995). We would encourage further research on homicide trends that examines the connection between crack use and city homicide rates disaggregated by age, race, and event circumstance.

Our results depend heavily on the validity of drug arrest rates as an indicator of differences across cities in levels of crack involvement. We presented evidence of a substantial association between drug arrest rates and public health and criminal justice indicators of cocaine and crack use. It is possible that this arrest-based proxy measure of crack involvement reflects other systematic differences across cities that produce divergent trends in robbery and burglary rates. If that is the case, however, we are at a loss to know what these differences might be. For example, it is difficult to imagine how the patterns of findings here could be accounted for by differences across cities in enforcement policies. We invite other researchers to offer alternative hypotheses and measures that can account for the results of this research.

We also encourage researchers to look to field studies of offenders for a better understanding of the behavioral mechanisms and day-to-day contexts of rewards and opportunities that drive changes in crime rates. The results of this research replicate at the aggregate level the findings of street-based research with active criminals. Our hypothesis was stimulated by ethnographic interviews and observations suggesting that the influx of crack cocaine was changing the context of urban crime, thereby leading some offenders to abandon burglary in favor of robbery.

If these findings are correct, they may help to explain the recent decline in violent crime, including robbery rates, observed in many U.S. cities. The early and pronounced decline in crime rates reported for New York City, widely attributed to enforcement measures, is also consistent with New York being among the first cities where crack appeared and, in turn, plateaued. As the crack epidemic abates, the pressure to engage in violent property offending to obtain quick cash for crack should be expected to ease.[6] However, the ethnographic evidence suggests that a high level of crack involvement can have an enduring impact on the structure and functioning of many inner-city communities, including their illicit economies (e.g., Anderson, 1990; Currie, 1993; Finnegan, 1990). It remains uncertain, therefore, whether robbery and burglary will resume their common pattern of change that was broken by the dramatic growth in the use of crack during the last decade.

NOTES

1. The same general pattern emerges from surveys of crime victims that include offenses not reported to or founded by the police. Data from the National Crime Victimization Survey also reveal that robbery and burglary victimization rates decline similarly during the first half of the 1980s and then diverge in the second half of the decade, with robbery rates increasing and burglary rates decreasing through the early 1990s (Bureau of Justice Statistics, 1994).

2. These cases are drawn from the data used in subsequent analyses. Our estimate of each city's level of crack involvement is discussed in detail below.

3. Pearson's correlation (r) between the arrest rate for sale-manufacture of cocaine or opiates (hereafter termed the "drug arrest rate") and the fraction of Drug Use Forecasting Program (DUF) arrestees with a positive urine test for cocaine is .77. The correlations between the arrest measure and emergency room cocaine mentions per 100 drug episodes and medical examiner cocaine mentions per 100 drug deaths are .72 and .67, respectively. The correlations are based on pairwise compar-

isons of cities for which 1990 to 1992 three-year averages of the drug arrest rates and at least one of the other drug indicators could be computed (a minimum of 10 cities and a maximum of 15). All correlations are significant at $p < .05$. A listwise analysis of the eight cities for which all of the indicators were available produced nearly identical results (see Rosenfeld, 1995, Table 3).

4. Finally, the urine test results indicate appreciably higher levels of cocaine use than marijuana or heroin use by arrestees in most of the DUF cities. These findings are based on the authors' analysis of DUF data for 1990. Results are available on request.

5. Because inclusion of the quadratic term does not provide a better fitting line for the average homicide trajectory across these 142 cities, this term is eliminated from subsequent analyses.

6. On the ebbing of the crack epidemic, see Golub, Hakeem, and Johnson (1996). See Krauss (1996), Lacayo (1996), and Pooley (1996) for evidence and commentary on recent declines in urban crime rates.

REFERENCES

Adler, W. M. (1995). *Land of Opportunity: One Family's Quest for the American Dream in the Age of Crack*. New York: Atlantic Monthly Press.

Anderson, E. (1990). *Streetwise*. Chicago: University of Chicago Press.

Baumer, E. (1994). Poverty, crack and crime: A cross-city analysis. *Journal of Research in Crime and Delinquency, 31*, 311–27.

Biderman, A. D., and Lynch, J. P. (1991). *Understanding Crime Incidence Statistics: Why the UCR Diverges from the NCS*. New York: Springer-Verlag.

The bloodiest year yet? (1990). *Newsweek*, July 16, p. 24.

Blumstein, A. (1995). Youth violence, guns and the illicit-drug industry. *Journal of Criminal Law and Criminology, 86*, 10–36.

Blumstein, A., Cohen, J., and Rosenfeld, R. (1991). Trend and deviation in crime rates: A comparison of UCR and NCS data for burglary and robbery. *Criminology, 29*, 237–263.

Bryk, A. S., and Raudenbush, S. W. (1992). *Hierarchical Linear Models: Applications and Data Analysis Methods*. Newbury Park, CA: Sage.

Bureau of the Census. (1980). STF-1 and STF-3 Census summary tapes. Washington, DC: Author.

Bureau of the Census. (1990). STF-1 and STF-3 Census summary tapes. Washington, DC: Author.

Bureau of Justice Statistics. (1994). *Criminal Victimization in the United States: 1973–92 Trends*. Washington, DC: U.S. Department of Justice.

Bursik, R. J., Jr., and Grasmick, H. G. (1992). Longitudinal neighborhood profiles in delinquency: The decomposition of change. *Journal of Quantitative Criminology, 8*, 247–263.

Cantor, D., and Land, K. C. (1985). Unemployment and crime rates in the post-World War II United States. A theoretical and empirical analysis. *American Sociological Review, 50*, 317–323.

Cops under fire. (1990). *U.S. New and World Report*, December 3, pp. 32–44.

Currie, B. (1993). *Reckoning: Drugs, the Cities, and the American Future*. New York: Hill and Wang.

Federal Bureau of Investigation. (1986). *Crime in the United States, 1985*. Washington, DC: U.S. Government Printing Office.

Federal Bureau of Investigation. (1993). *Crime in the United States, 1992*. Washington, DC: U.S. Government Printing Office.

Finnegan, W. (1990). Out There, Part 1. *New Yorker*, September 10, pp. 51–86.

French, J. (1993). Pipe Dreams: Crack and the Life in Philadelphia and Newark. In M. Ratner (Ed.), *Crack Pipe as Pimp: An Ethnographic Investigation of Sex-for-Crack Exchanges*. New York: Lexington.

Golub, A. L., Hakeem, F., and Johnson, B. D. (1996). Monitoring the decline in the crack epidemic with data from the drug use forecasting program. Paper presented at the Drug Use Forecasting Site Directors' Meeting, June, Washington, DC.

Gove, W. R., Hughes, M. and Geerken, M. (1985). Are Uniform Crime Reports a valid indicator of the Index Crimes? An affirmative answer with minor qualifications. *Criminology, 23*, 451–501.

Hinds, M. deC. (1990). Number of killings soars in big cities across U.S. *New York Times*, July 18, pp. A1, A10.

Inciardi, J. A. (1992). *The War on Drugs II: The Continuing Epic of Heroin, Cocaine, Crack, Crime, AIDS, and Public Policy*. Mountain View, CA: Mayfield.

Inciardi, J. A. (1993). "Kingrats, chicken heads, slow necks, freaks, and blood suckers: A glimpse at the Miami sex-for-crack market. In M. Ratner (Ed.), *Crack Pipe as Pimp: An Ethnographic Investigation of Sex-for-Crack Exchanges*, pp. 37–67. New York: Lexington.

Johnson, B. (1991). The crack era in New York City. *Addiction and Recovery*, May/June, pp. 24–27.

Krauss, C. (1996). Now, how low can crime go? *New York Times*, January 28, sec. 4, p. 5.

Lacayo, R. (1996). Law and Order. *Time*, January 15, pp. 48–54.

Land, K. C., McCall, P., and Cohen, L. E. (1990). Structural covariates of homicide rates: Are there any invariances across time and social space? *American Journal of Sociology, 95*, 922–963.

Liska, A., and Bellair, P. (1995). Violent crime rates and racial composition: Conversion over time. *American Journal of Sociology, 101*, 578–599.

Lofland, J. (1969). *Deviance and Identity*. Englewood Cliffs, NJ: Prentice Hall.

Maguire, K., and Pastore, A. L. (1995). *Sourcebook of Criminal Justice Statistics—1994*. Washington, DC: U.S. Government Printing Office.

McCall, P., Land, K. C., and Cohen, L. E. (1992). Violent criminal behavior: Is there a general and continuing influence of the South? *Social Science Research, 21*, 286–310.

National Institute of Justice. (1995). *Drug Use Forecasting: 1994 Annual Report on Adult and Juvenile Arrestees*. Washington, DC: U.S. Department of Justice.

O'Brien, R. M. (1985). *Crime and Victimization Data*. Beverly Hills, CA: Sage.

Pooley, E. (1996). One good apple. *Time*, January 15, pp. 54–56.

Ratner, M. (1993). Sex, drugs and public policy: Studying and understanding the sex-for-crack phenomenon. In M. Ratner (Ed.), *Crack Pipe as Pimp: An Ethnographic Investigation of Sex-for-Crack Exchanges*. New York: Lexington Books.

Raudenbush, S. W., and Chan, W. S. (1992). Growth curve analysis in accelerated longitudinal designs. *Journal of Research in Crime and Delinquency, 29*, 387–411.

Rosenfeld, R. (1995). Multiple indicators of drug abuse in American cities. Paper presented at the meeting of the American Society of Criminology, November, Boston, MA.

Rosenfeld, R., and Decker, S. H. (1993). Discrepant values, correlated measures: Cross-city comparisons of self reports and urine tests of cocaine use among arrestees. *Journal of Criminal Justice, 21*, 223–230.

Sampson, R. J., and Lauritsen, J. L. (1994). Violent victimization and offending: Individual-, situational-, and community-level risk factors. In A. J. Reiss, Jr. and J. Roth (Eds.), *Understanding and Preventing Violence: Social Influences on Violence*, vol. 3, Committee on Law and Justice, National Research Council. Washington, DC: National Academy Press.

Schuerman, L. A., and Kobrin, S. (1986). Community careers in crime. In A. J. Reiss, Jr. and M. Tonry (Eds.), *Communities and Crime*. Chicago: University of Chicago Press.

Sheley, J. F., and Wright, J. D. (1995). *In the Line of Fire: Youth, Guns, and Violence in Urban America*. New York: Aldine de Gruyter.

Shover, N. (1996). *Great Pretenders: Pursuits and Careers of Persistent Thieves*. Boulder, CO: Westview.

Substance Abuse and Mental Health Services Administration. (1994). *Preliminary Estimates from the Drug Abuse Warning Network: 1993 Estimates of Drug-Related Emergency Department Episodes*. Washington, DC: U.S. Department of Health and Human Services.

Substance Abuse and Mental Health Services Administration. (1995). *Annual Medical Examiner Data 1993. Data from the Drug Abuse Warning Network*. Washington, DC: U.S. Department of Health and Human Services.

Treaster, J. B. (1992). 20 years of war on drugs, and no victory yet. *New York Times*, June 14, sec. E, p. 7.

Weisburd, D., and Green, L. (1994). Defining the street-level drug market. In D. MacKenzie and C. Uchida (Eds.), *Drugs and Crime: Evaluating Public Policy Initiative*, Thousand Oaks, CA: Sage.

Wright, R., and Decker, S. (1994). *Burglars on the Job: Streetlife and Residential Break-Ins*. Boston. Northeastern University Press.

Wright, R., and Decker, S. (1997). *Armed Robbers in Action: Stickups and Street Culture*. Boston: Northeastern University Press.

8

Exploring the Relationship Between Race and Ecstasy Involvement Among a Sample of Arrestees

BLAKE J. URBACH

K. MICHAEL REYNOLDS

GEORGE S. YACOUBIAN JR.

ABSTRACT

Previous research has indicated that whites are disproportionately involved in the use of 3,4-methylenedioxymethamphetamine (MDMA or "ecstasy"). To date, however, no studies have explored the relationship between race and ecstasy possession and sale among adult criminal populations. To address this limitation, official arrest data were utilized from a sample of 1,216 arrestees charged with drug offenses between 1995 and 1999 in Orange County, Florida. Arrestees were divided into those whose primary charge was related to ecstasy possession (n = 331), those who primary offense was related to ecstasy sale (n = 180), and those whose primary charge was unrelated to ecstasy (n = 705). Chi-square statistics and logistic regression were utilized to examine the relationships between race and the possession and sale of ecstasy. Arrestees charged with ecstasy possession and sale were significantly more likely to be white than their non-ecstasy-charged counterparts (95% and 93% vs. 46%, p < 0.001). Moreover, white arrestees were more than 20 times as likely to be arrested for an MDMA-related offense than non-white arrestees, holding all other variables constant. Policy implications are assessed in light of the current findings.

INTRODUCTION

A patent was issued in 1914 to the E. Merck Pharmaceutical Company in Darmstadt, Germany, to produce 3,4-methylenedioxymethamphetamine (MDMA or "ecstasy") as an appetite suppressant for soldiers in the First World War (Seymour, 1986; Shulgin, 1990; Beck and Rosenbaum, 1994). With the exception of several isolated animal studies during the 1950s, the compound was ignored until the late 1970s and early 1980s, at which point it gained popularity as both an adjunct to psychotherapy (Grinspoon and Bakalar, 1986; Greer and Tolbert, 1990, 1998) and as a recreational drug (Peroutka, 1987). For psychotherapy, MDMA increased self-esteem and self-insight and enhanced empathy, communication, and interpersonal relations (Grinspoon and Bakalar, 1986; Greer and Tolbert, 1990, 1998). MDMA became popular recreationally because it increased self-confidence, lowered defenses and inhibitions, and induced feelings of empathy and love (Beck and Rosenbaum, 1994).

Preceding MDMA on the streets was a drug virtually identical in chemical composition—3,4-methylenedioxyamphetamine (MDA). MDA emerged in California's drug subculture during the 1960s and quickly gained a reputation for producing a sensual euphoria (Beck and Rosebaum, 1994). These qualities were particularly appealing to therapists and recreational users, who were also attracted to its legal status. Beginning in 1976, therapists began using MDMA for purposes similar to those for MDA. They found Adam (the therapists' nickname for MDMA) to be even more beneficial than MDA as a therapeutic agent, particularly in facilitating communication, acceptance, and reduction of fear. Despite this success, therapists were reluctant to publish their findings for fear they would lead to MDMA's criminalization. It was not until the late 1970s that Shulgin and Nichols (1978) published the first pharmacological study of MDMA in humans. They noted that MDMA led to an ". . . easily controlled state of consciousness, with emotional and sensual overtones . . . and that these properties established the unique character of MDMA" (Shulgin and Nichols, 1978, p. 34).

Journal of Ethnicity in Substance Abuse, Vol. 1(4) 2002. © 2002 by The Haworth Press, Inc. All rights reserved.

The therapeutic value of MDMA remained unknown to the public until the early 1990s when distribution patterns changed and its popularity as a recreational drug expanded. The recreational market for MDMA underwent a slow expansion in the early 1980s. The increasing financial stake of some distributors was reflected in the renaming of MDMA as "ecstasy." By the mid-1980s, MDMA was no longer used exclusively in therapeutic circles. It was this transformation that started MDMA on its path toward criminalization.

The first administrative acknowledgment of MDMA was a request from the World Health Organization (WHO) to the Food and Drug Administration (FDA) for specific information about MDMA (Randolph, 1984). Immediately thereafter, the Drug Enforcement Administration (DEA) filed a request for specific comments about MDMA, with the hope that it would eventually be classified as Schedule I under the Controlled Substances Act (Mullen, 1984). Although the DEA first learned of MDMA in the early 1970s, it was ignored for close to a decade. In July 1985, however, reports of potential neurotoxicity in laboratory animals (Ricaurte, Bryan, Strauss, Seiden, and Schuster, 1985) led the DEA to propose MDMA's criminalization. This proposal was met with strong opposition from therapists who continued to assert that MDMA's ability to enhance communication, increase empathy, and reduce fear made it extremely valuable for therapy (Grinspoon and Bakalar, 1986).

Federal hearings were held during the summer and fall of 1985 to determine the final scheduling of MDMA (Holsten and Schieser, 1986). The DEA had several options. Schedule I substances are reserved for drugs that are deemed to have high abuse potential, no accepted medical value, *and* no accepted safety for use under medical supervision (Lawn, 1985). Schedules II-V are used for drugs that have some accepted medical uses and safety and have varying potential for abuse. During the course of these hearings, excessive marketing and distribution of ecstasy in bars and nightclubs, in addition to the findings of Ricaurte et al. (1985), led the DEA to invoke emergency scheduling powers granted by the Comprehensive Control Act (CCA) of 1984. The CCA allowed the attorney general to place any substance posing "an imminent hazard to public safety" into Schedule I for a period of one year (plus an additional six months if necessary) while the final scheduling process was underway (Lawn, 1985). On July 1, 1985, MDMA was temporarily placed in Schedule I (Lawn, 1985).

During the one-year suspension, hearings were convened to decide what permanent measures should be taken against MDMA. The DEA and the FDA believed that it belonged in Schedule I. Defenders of MDMA's medical use testified on behalf of its therapeutic value at the federal hearings. Researchers feared that a Schedule I classification would destroy any hope of evaluating MDMA's therapeutic potential. Psychiatrists also sought to distance MDMA from psychedelic drugs like lysergic acid diethylamide (LSD). Grinspoon (1985, p. 3) noted, for example, that "MDMA appears to have some of the advantages of LSD-like drugs without most of the corresponding disadvantages."

From the beginning of the hearings, the administrative judge expressed serious doubt regarding the lawful placement of MDMA into any of the available schedules (Holsten and Schieser, 1986). Ultimately, the judge recommended that MDMA be placed into the less restrictive Schedule III. He concluded that MDMA did not appear to possess a high potential for abuse and that it did have a currently accepted medical use, as well as accepted safety of use under medical supervision (Lawn, 1988). The DEA rejected the court's ruling and permanently placed MDMA in Schedule I on March 23, 1988 (Lawn, 1988). A final appeal to the DEA was rejected during the spring of 1988.

In July 1992, federal government meetings reopened the door for investigating MDMA's potential as a therapeutic adjunct. In October 1992, the FDA approved the first human study of MDMA. While today MDMA remains a Schedule I substance in the United States—illegal to manufacture, use, buy, and sell—clinical studies exploring the potential neurotoxic effects of MDMA have been undertaken in the United States (Ricaurte, McCann, Szabo, and Scheffel, 2000; McCann, Ridenour, Shaman, and Ricaurte, 1994).

To summarize, MDMA emerged during the mid-1970s as a therapeutic agent used by psychologists and psychiatrists. During this period of legal distribution, the recreational use of MDMA increased. Although the use of MDMA was relatively controlled through the early 1980s, increased production and concern over its potential neurotoxic effects ultimately led to its classification by the DEA as a Schedule I substance in 1985. While its proponents still insist that it has therapeutic value, recent studies have begun to identify negative long-term neurotoxic effects.

Relationship Between Race and Ecstasy Use

Previous research has identified drug-*using* preferences within certain ethnic groups (Kandel, Single, and Kessler, 1976; Wallace and Bachman, 1991; Chilcoat and Schutz, 1995; Warheit and Vega, 1996; Amey and Albrecht, 1998; Oetting, Deffenbacher,

Taylor, Luther, Beauvais, and Edwards, 2000; Hoffman, Welte, and Barnes, 2001). Kandel et al. (1976), for example, identified that white students were more likely than black and Hispanic students to report lifetime use of alcohol, marijuana, LSD, and tranquilizers, while black and Hispanic students were more likely to report lifetime use of cocaine and heroin. Chilcoat et al. (1995), using data from the National Household Survey on Drug Abuse (NHSDA), found that blacks aged 30–34 had higher odds of lifetime crack cocaine use than a comparable group of white respondents. Amey et al. (1998) found that Latino household members were significantly more likely than their black and white counterparts to report lifetime use of marijuana. Finally, Oetting et al. (2000) identified that American Indians and Hispanics were more likely than whites, blacks, and Asians to report 30-day methamphetamine use.

While anecdotal reports have suggested that the use of ecstasy is primarily a white phenomenon, the relationship between race and ecstasy use is noticeably absent in scholarly social science literature. In addition to Monitoring the Future (MTF) findings (Johnston, O'Malley, and Bachman, 2001), which indicated that white high school seniors were almost six times as likely to report past-year ecstasy use than their black counterparts, only four studies have addressed empirically the relationship between race and ecstasy (Yacoubian, 2002; Yacoubian and Urbach, 2004; Yacoubian, 2002; Yacoubian, Arria, Fost, and Wish, 2002). Yacoubian et al., 2002 surveyed 209 juvenile offenders through Maryland's Offender Population Urinalysis Screening (OPUS) Program between July and August 2000 and determined that 12-month ecstasy users were significantly more likely to be white (82% vs. 22%, $p < 0.001$) than their non-using counterparts. Yacoubian, 2002 analyzed data collected from 3,376 10th graders surveyed through the 1999 MTF project and determined that past-year ecstasy users were significantly more likely to be white (97% vs. 84%, $p < 0.001$) than respondents who reported no lifetime ecstasy use. Most recently, Yacoubian and Urbach (2004) examined the temporal relationship between race and the use of ecstasy with data collected from 120,446 respondents surveyed through the National Household Survey on Drug Abuse (NHSDA) between 1990 and 1998. Consistent, statistically significant relationships between race and ecstasy use were discerned throughout the 1990s (Yacoubian and Urbach, 2004).

While these studies indicate that whites are disproportionately involved in the *use* of ecstasy, no research has examined correlates of ecstasy possession and/or sale among adult criminal populations. If the possession and sale of ecstasy is primarily a white phenomenon, there are clear implications for law enforcement and drug prevention initiatives. To explore the relationship between race and ecstasy possession and sale, official arrest data were utilized from a sample of 1,216 arrestees charged with drug offenses in Orange County, Florida, between 1995 and 1999. One primary hypothesis is proffered—white arrestees are significantly more likely to be charged with an ecstasy-related offense than their non-white counterparts. With this preliminary hypothesis, research methods are described below.

METHODS

To assist in combating drug addiction among the adult arrestee population, the Orange County Drug Study (OCDS) was developed in 2000 to explore the prevalence of illicit drug use and identify drug use trends in Orange County, Florida. Official arrest data were collected from several law enforcement agencies in Orange County between 1995 and 1999. Only those arrestees whose primary charge was a drug-related offense (possession and/or sale) were eligible for inclusion (N = 75,898).

The data available to the OCDS were limited. Information was available on gender, race, age, primary charge, zip code of residence, and zip code of arrest. For the purposes of the current analysis, arrestees were divided into three subgroups: those whose primary charge was related to ecstasy possession, those whose primary offense was related to ecstasy sale, and those whose primary charge was unrelated to ecstasy. Because such a large percentage of arrestees were charged with non-ecstasy-related offenses (N = 75,387), a 1% random sample of this subgroup was selected for analysis. Analyses were thus conducted on arrestees whose primary charge was related to ecstasy possession (n = 331), those whose primary offense was related to ecstasy sale (n = 180), and those whose primary charge was unrelated to ecstasy (n = 705).

DATA ANALYSIS AND FINDINGS

Data analysis was accomplished in three phases. First, descriptive statistics were generated for all arrestees in the sample. Second, chi-square statistics were used to detect significant associations between race and ecstasy possession and sale. Third, logistic regression was utilized to identify predictors of ecstasy possession/sale among the sample of arrestees.

TABLE 1   Logistic Regression on Primary Criminal Offense (N = 1,216)

| | MULTIPLE LOGISTIC REGRESSION MODEL | |
	OR	CL
Male	1.77	1.19–2.63
White	20.28	13.37–30.76
Age	.88	.86–.90

Demographic Characteristics

A majority of the arrestees in the sample were male (85%) and white (66%). A majority of the arrestees were under 30 years of age. Twenty-seven percent of the sample was arrested for MDMA possession, 15% for MDMA sale, while 58% were arrested for a non-MDMA offense.

Correlates of MDMA Possession and Sale

Arrestees charged with ecstasy possession (n = 331) and sale (n = 180) were significantly more likely (95% and 93% vs. 46%, $p < 0.001$) to be white than their non-ecstasy-charged counterparts (n = 705). In addition, arrestees charged with ecstasy possession and sale were significantly more likely to be under 30 years of age than the non-MDMA arrestees (90% and 91% vs. 55%, $p < 0.001$).

Logistic Regression

To supplement these descriptive findings, logistic regression was utilized to explore the extent to which race predicted ecstasy involvement (possession or sale). Because the arrestees charged with MDMA possession and sale were virtually identical demographically, they were pooled to form one "MDMA-related offense" group of arrestees. Thus, the dependent variable in the current model was a primary offense related to the possession or sale of ecstasy. The three independent variables were gender, race, and age (measured continuously). The variable measuring race was recoded into two categories–"white" and "non-white." The reference categories used in the current model were "female" and "non-white."

Logistic regression coefficients are used to estimate the odds ratios (OR) for each of the independent variables in the model (Long, 1997). That is, the coefficients provide the estimated change in the OR per unit change in the explanatory variables, assuming all other predictors are held constant. The confidence interval (CI) is comparable to a test of significance. The strongest predictors will have a tight CI away from 1.00 (Long, 1997).

The results of the logistic regression model are shown in Table 1. As shown, if an arrestee was male, the OR of being arrested for an ecstasy-related offense was almost double that of a female arrestee, holding race and age constant. If an arrestee was white, the OR of being arrested for an ecstasy-related offense was more than 20 times higher than a non-white arrestee, holding gender and age constant. These results indicate that, among this sample of arrestees, race was the strongest predictor of being arrested for ecstasy-related offense.

DISCUSSION

The use of ecstasy is unquestionably injurious to the human body. While initial effects include feelings of peacefulness, acceptance, and empathy, MDMA users can encounter problems similar to those experienced by amphetamine and cocaine users (Hayner and McKinney, 1986; Peroutka, Newman, and Harris, 1988). Psychological effects, which can linger for weeks after ingestion, include anxiety, depression, insomnia, memory loss, and paranoia (Bolla, McCann, and Ricaurte, 1999; Morgan, 2000; Parrott, Sisk, and Turner, 2000). Physical effects include blurred vision, involuntary teeth clenching, muscle tension, nausea, and sweating (Peroutka et al., 1988; Solowij, Hall, and Lee, 1992). While the long-term neurotoxic effects of ecstasy use are just now being investigated, initial evidence suggests that serotonin depletion is a major complication of MDMA ingestion (Ricaurte, McCann, Szabo, and Scheffel, 2000). In rare cases, ecstasy-related deaths have also been reported in both rave (Karch, 1992; Henry, 1992) and non-rave (Henry, Jeffreys, and Dawling, 1992) settings.

To date, five scholarly works have indicated that ecstasy users are significantly more likely to be white (Yacoubian, 2002; Yacoubian and Urbach, 2002; Yacoubian, 2002; Yacoubian et al., 2004; Johnston et al., 2001). None of these studies, however, examined the relationship between race and ecstasy possession and sale among adult criminal populations. To address this limitation, official arrest data were utilized from a sample of 1,216 arrestees charged with drug offenses between 1995 and 1999 in Orange County, Florida. Our findings illustrated that arrestees charged with ecstasy possession or sale were significantly more likely to be white than their non-ecstasy-charged counterparts. Moreover, logistic regression analyses indicated that white arrestees were more than 20 times as likely to be arrested for an MDMA-related offense than non-white arrestees, holding all other variables constant.

There are two methodological limitations to the current study. First, the variables available to the OCDS were relatively limited. Only official demographic data were accessible. Second, the analysis was conducted exclusively with drug and alcohol offenders—those offenders whose *primary charge* was related to alcohol or other drugs. Clearly, however, offenders whose primary charge was related to another type of offense (e.g., violent or property) could have had a secondary charge related to alcohol or other drugs. There is no way to know, therefore, the extent to which our findings are generalizable to other types of offenders. This is an empirical question that can only be addressed with future research. These caveats aside, the current findings are valuable and should be used as a springboard to undertake additional ecstasy-related research with adult criminal populations. Future research should consider administering a survey to all adult arrestees to collect ecstasy-specific data that cannot be obtained through official records, including, for example, information on ecstasy markets and patterns of ecstasy distribution.

As discussed earlier, a body of research has identified drug-*using* preferences among ethnic groups (Kandel et al., 1976; Wallace and Bachman, 1991; Chilcoat and Schutz, 1995; Warheit and Vega, 1996). The relationship between race and a preference for certain drugs, however, extends beyond *use*. A minimal body of literature has also indicated a relationship between race and a preference for the *sale* of specific drugs. Dembo, Williams, and Schmeidler (1994), for example, used data from a longitudinal study of juvenile detainees and determined that blacks were more involved in cocaine selling than whites (Dembo et al., 1994). Most recently, the Central Florida High Intensity Drug Trafficking Area (HIDTA) reported that while methamphetamine use was not prevalent in black neighborhoods, " . . . the amount of blacks distributing the drug has increased . . ." (HIDTA, 1999; p. 32). The findings in the current study support this notion that members of a certain race (whites) may be more inclined to sell a specific drug (ecstasy) than their non-white counterparts.

The results of this study, when amalgamated with the literature on ecstasy use (Yacoubian, 2002; Yacoubian and Urbach, 2002; Yacoubian, 2002; Yacoubian et al., 2004; Johnston et al., 2001), suggest that ecstasy *involvement* (use, possession, and sale) may be primarily a white phenomenon. There are two major policy implications for these findings. First, if individuals involved with ecstasy are primarily white, prevention and treatment programs should target white populations. Given finite resources, schools comprised primarily of white students, for example, would benefit from ecstasy education programs considerably more than schools whose racial composition is mixed or predominantly non-white. Second, interdiction efforts aimed at reducing ecstasy distribution should be concentrated in areas where the majority of potential offenders are white. Such efforts would target the race most inclined to ecstasy's distribution. Until future research detects a shift in the relationship between race and ecstasy participation, it is highly recommended that policy efforts be targeted to the subpopulation most inclined to its involvement.

REFERENCES

Amey, C. H., and Albrecht, S. L. (1998). Race and ethnic differences in adolescent drug use: The impact of family structure and the quantity and quality of parental interaction. *Journal of Drug Issues, 28*(2), 283–299.

Beck, J., and Rosenbaum, M. (1994). *In Pursuit of Ecstasy*. New York, NY: State University of New York Press.

Bolla, K. I., McCann, U. D., and Ricaurte, G. A. (1999). Memory impairment in abstinent MDMA ("ecstasy") users, *Neurology, 51*, 1532–1537.

Chilcoat, H. D., and Schutz, C. G. (1995). Racial/ethnic and age differences in crack use within neighborhoods. *Addiction Research, 3*(2), 103–111.

Dembo, R., Williams, L., and Schmeidler, J. (1994). Cocaine selling among urban black and white adolescent males. *International Journal of the Addictions, 29*(14), 1813–1834.

Greer, G. R., and Tolbert, R. (1998). A method of conducting therapeutic sessions with MDMA. *Journal of Psychoactive Drugs, 30*(4), 371–379.

Greer, G. R., and Tolbert, R. (1990). The therapeutic use of MDMA. In S. J. Peroutka (Ed.), *Ecstasy: The Clinical, Pharmacological and Neurotoxic Effects of the Drug MDMA* (pp. 21–35). Norwell, MA: Kluwar Academic Publishers.

Grinspoon, L. (1985). *Written Testimony Submitted on Behalf of Dr. Grinspoon and Greer, Professors Bakalar and Roberts* (Drug Enforcement Administration Law Hearings, Docket No. 84–48). Washington, DC: U.S. Department of Justice.

Grinspoon, L., and Bakalar, J. B. (1986). Can drugs be used to enhance the psychotherapeutic process? *American Journal of Psychotherapy, 40*(3), 393–403.

Hayner, G. N., and McKinney, H. E. (1986). MDMA: The dark side of ecstasy. *Journal of Psychoactive Drugs, 18,* 341–347.

Henry, J. A. (1992). Ecstasy and the dance of death, *British Medical Journal, 305,* 5–6.

Henry, J. A., Jeffreys, K. J., and Dawling, S. (1992). Toxicity and deaths from 3,4-methylenedioxymethamphetamine ("ecstasy"). *Lancet, 340,* 284–287.

Hoffman, J. H., Welte, J. W., and Barnes, G. M. (2001). Co-occurrence of alcohol and cigarette use among adolescents. *Addictive Behaviors, 26,* 63–78.

Holsten, D. W., and Schieser, D. W. (1986). Controls over the manufacture of MDMA. *Journal of Psychoactive Drugs, 18*(4), 371–372.

Johnston, L. D., O'Malley, P. M., and Bachman, J. G. (2001). *National Survey Results on Drug use from the Monitoring the Future Study, 2000* (Volume I). Rockville, MD: U.S. Department of Health and Human Services.

Kandel, D. B., Single, E., and Kessler, R. (1976). The epidemiology of drug use among New York state high school students: Distribution, trends, and changes in rates of use. *American Journal of Public Health, 66,* 43–53.

Karch, S. (1992). "Ecstasy": The dance of health. *Forensic Drug Abuse Advisor, 4*(7), 49–50.

Lawn, J. C. (1988). Schedules of controlled substances: Scheduling of 3,4-methylenedioxymethamphetamine (MDMA) into Schedule I of the Controlled Substances Act. *Federal Register, 51*(198), 36552–36560.

Lawn, J. C. (1985). Schedules of controlled substances: Temporary placement of 3,4-methylenedioxymethamphetamine (MDMA) into Schedule I. *Federal Register, 50*(105), 23118–23120.

Long, J. S. (1997). *Regression Models for Categorical and Limited Dependent Variables.* California: Sage Publicatons.

McCann, U. D., Ridenour, A., Shaman, Y., and Ricaurte, G. A. (1994). Serotonin neurotoxicity after 3,4-methylenedioxymethamphetamine (MDMA, "ecstasy"): A controlled study. *Neuropsychopharmacology, 10*(2), 129–138.

Morgan, M. J. (2000). Ecstasy (MDMA): A review of its possible persistent psychological effects. *Psychopharmacology, 152*(3), 230–248.

Mullen, F. M. (1984). Schedules of controlled substances: Proposed placement of 3,4-methylenedioxymethamphetamine into Schedule I. *Federal Register, 49*(146); 30210–30211.

Oetting, E. R., Deffenbacher, J. L., Taylor, M. J., Luther, N., Beauvais, F., and Edwards, R. W. (2000). Methamphetamine use by high school seniors: Recent trends, gender and ethnicity differences, and use of other drugs. *Journal of Child and Adolescent Substance Abuse, 10*(1), 33–51.

Parrott, A. C., Sisk, E., and Turner, J. J. D. (2000). Psychobiological problems in heavy "ecstasy" (MDMA) polydrug users. *Drug and Alcohol Dependence, 60,* 105–110.

Peroutka, S. J. (1987). Incidence of recreational use of 3,4-methylenedioxymethamphetamine (MDMA, "ecstasy") on an undergraduate campus. *New England Journal of Medicine, 317*(24), 1542–1543.

Peroutka, S. J., Newman, H., and Harris, H. (1988). Subjective effects of 3,4-methylenedioxymethamphetamine in recreational users. *Neuropsychopharmacology, 1,* 273–277.

Randolph, W. F. (1984). International drug scheduling: Convention on psychotropic substances, stimulant and/or hallucinogenic drugs. *Federal Register, 49*(140), 29273–29274.

Ricaurte, G. A., McCann, U. D., Szabo, Z., and Scheffel, U. (2000). Toxicodynamics and long-term toxicity of the recreational drug, 3,4-methylenedioxymethamphetamine (MDMA, "ecstasy"). *Toxicology Letters, 112–113,* 143–146.

Ricaurte, G. A., Bryan, G., Strauss, L., Seiden, L., and Schuster, C. (1985). Hallucinogenic amphetamine selectively destroys brain serotonin nerve terminals. *Science, 229,* 986–988.

Seymour, R. B. (1986). *MDMA.* San Francisco, CA: Haight-Asbury Publications.

Shulgin, A. (1990). History of MDMA. In S. J. Peroutka (Ed.), *Ecstasy: The Clinical, Pharmacological and Neurotoxic Effects of the Drug MDMA* (pp. 1–20). Norwell, MA: Kluwar-Academic Publishers.

Shulgin, A. (1985). What is MDMA? *PharmChem Newsletter, 14*(3), 3–5, 10–11.

Shulgin, A., and Nichols, D. (1978). Characterization of three new psychotomimetics. In R. J. Stillman and R. E. Willette (Eds.), *The Psychopharmacology of Hallucinogens.* New York: Pergamon Press.

Solowij, N., Hall, W., and Lee, N. (1992). Recreational MDMA use in Sydney: A profile of 'ecstasy' users and their experiences with the drug. *British Journal of Addictions, 87,* 1161–1172.

Wallace, J. M., and Bachman, J. G. (1991). Explaining racial/ethnic differences in adolescent drug use: The impact of background and lifestyle. *Social Problems, 38*(3), 333–357.

Warheit, G. J., and Vega, W. A. (1996). A comparative analysis of cigarette, alcohol and illicit drug use among an ethnically diverse sample of Hispanic, African-American, and non-Hispanic white adolescents. *Journal of Drug Issues, 26*(4), 901–922.

Yacoubian, G. (2002). Assessing the temporal relationship between race and ecstasy use among high school seniors. *Journal of Drug Education, 32*(3), 213–226.

Yacoubian, G. (2002). Correlates of ecstasy use among 10th graders surveyed through Monitoring the Future. *Journal of Psychoactive Drugs, 34*(2), 225–230.

Yacoubian, G., Arria, A., Fost, E., and Wish, E. D. (2002). Estimating the prevalence of ecstasy use among juvenile offenders. *Journal of Psychoactive Drugs, 34*(2), 209–214.

Yacoubian, G., and Urbach, B. J. (2004). Exploring the temporal relationship between race and the use of ecstasy: Findings from the National Household Survey on Drug Abuse. *Journal of Ethnicity in Substance Abuse, 3*(3), 67–77.

CHAPTER 2: DISCUSSION QUESTIONS

1. According to Parker and Auerhahn, what are the problems associated with the practice of lumping all drugs together when studying drug use?

2. According to Parker and Auerhahn, what are the four theoretical approaches to explaining the linkages between drugs and crime? Compare these approaches. Which is the strongest? Why do the authors highlight the importance of context for understanding the drugs–crime relationship?

3. What are the four phases of the conceptual model of epidemics as proposed by Golub and Johnson?

4. What is the gateway theory of drug addiction? Is it a strong theory? What are some criticisms?

5. What are the implications for harm reduction that can be drawn from the Golub and Johnson selection?

6. What sample was used for the Killias and colleagues project? What are some limitations of this sample?

7. What are the two interesting trends that Killias and colleagues draw from information in Table 3?

8. How is treatment of heroin addicts different in Switzerland than in the United States?

9. What factors influenced the findings of Baumer and colleagues? How do the trends for robbery, burglary, and homicide differ in relation to crack?

10. Do you think robbery and burglary rates will converge again? Why or why not? What role did crack play in the divergence of robbery and burglary rates?

11. What is MDMA? What events led to the criminalization of MDMA? What are the physical effects of MDMA? Could these effects be related to criminal activity?

12. What are the limitations of each selection?

13. What are the policy implications of each selection?

CHAPTER 2: ADDITIONAL RESOURCES IN RESEARCH NAVIGATOR AND IN THE *NEW YORK TIMES*

Archibold, R. C. (2004, October 12). Edwards calls for drug crackdown in rural areas. *New York Times.*

Associated Press. (2004, April 22). Leave medical marijuana group alone, judge tells government. *New York Times.*

Benoit, E., Randolph, D., Dunlap, E., and Johnson, B. (2003). Code switching and inverse imitation among marijuana-using crack sellers. *British Journal of Criminology, 43,* 506–525.

Bourgois, P. (2003). Crack and the political economy of social suffering. *Addiction Research and Theory, 11,* 31–37.

Butterfield, F. (2002, December 29). Freed from prison, but still paying a penalty. *New York Times.*

Butterfield, F. (2004, January 4). Across the rural midwest, drug casts a grim shadow. *New York Times.*

Butterfield, F. (2004, January 28). Justice Department ends testing of criminals for drug use. *New York Times.*

Dewan, S. K. (2003, April 6). A drug feared in the '70's is tied to suspect in killings. *New York Times.*

Duterte, M., Hemphill, K., Murphy, T., and Murphy, S. (2001). Tragic beauties: Heroin images and heroin users. *Contemporary Drug Problems, 30,* 595–617.

Fountain, J. W. (2003, April 28). A west side story: From crime king to mentor. *New York Times.*

Huang, B., White, H.-R., Kosterman, R., Catalano, R. F., and Hawkins, J. D. (2001). Developmental associations between alcohol and interpersonal aggression during adolescence. *Journal of Research in Crime and Delinquency,* 2001, *8*(1), 64–83.

Kandel, D. B. (2003). Does marijuana use cause the use of other drugs? *Journal of the American Medical Association, 289,* 482–483.

McElrath, K., and McEvoy, K. (2001). Heroin as evil: Ecstasy users' perceptions about heroin. *Drugs: Education, Prevention and Policy, 8,* 177–189.

McNeil, D. G., Jr. (2003, September 6). Report of ecstasy drug's great risks is retracted. *New York Times.*

O'Neil, J. (2004, January 20). Testing: Drug eases heroin withdrawal. *New York Times.*

Romero, S., and Liptak, A. (2003, April 2). Texas court acts to clear 38, almost all black, in drug case. *New York Times.*

Sanneh, K. (2004, April 18). The woozy, syrupy sound of codeine rap. *New York Times.*

Seal, K. H., Kral, A. H., Gee, L., Moore, L. D., Bluthenthal, R. N., Lorvick, J., Edlin, B. R. (2001). Predictors and prevention of nonfatal overdose among street-recruited injection heroin users in the San Francisco Bay Area, 1998-1999. *American Journal of Public Health, 91,* 1842–1846.

Sullivan, J. (2004, January 11). It's not the heroin, it's the needle. *New York Times.*

Sullum, J. (2003, May 30). When holding a party is a crime. *New York Times.*

Williams, M. L., Bowen, A. M., Elwood, W. N., McCoy, C. C., McCoy, H. V., Freeman, R. C., Weatherby, N. L., and Pierce, T. (2000). Determinants of condom use among African Americans who smoke crack cocaine. *Culture Health and Sexuality, 2,* 15–32.

WOMEN AND DRUGS

Research in drugs and crime has often overlooked women as subjects and actors. Unfortunately, this led to the creation and perpetuation of false notions about the experiences of female drug users. Beginning in the 1960s, several prominent female researchers began to rectify this situation by designing research projects focused specifically on women (for example, see Rosenbaum, 1981). Since then a lot has been learned about women and deviant behavior, but many questions remain.

Intended to address the gaps in the literature, the three selections in this chapter highlight the core experiences of drug-using women as they move in and out of criminal behavior. Lisa Maher and Kathleen Daly investigate the position of women in the drug economy and conclude that not much has changed in the past few decades. Using ethnographic methods, they find that women are still relegated to the lowest positions or not allowed to participate at all. Catherine Ingram Fogel and Michael Belyea confront the experiences of women in prison as they negotiate violence, drugs, and HIV. Finally, Sheila Royo Maxwell and Christopher Maxwell, using quantitative methods, apply a criminal careers approach to look at the intersection of drug use and criminal behaviors for sex workers. They differentiate between onset of a prostitution career and frequency of prostitution and examine predictors of both.

In all three pieces several themes are evident. First, women for the most part are not in positions of power in the drug economy. When they do participate it is most likely to be as sex workers, although not all female drug users are prostitutes. Maxwell and Maxwell found that when women in their sample were allowed to participate in the drug economy as sellers, they were less likely to engage in prostitution. Second, past and present violence is a common experience among female drug users. In fact, Fogel and Belyea found that 25% of their respondents were afraid of their current partner. Third, women's participation in the drug economy and criminal behaviors put women at increased risk of contracting HIV. This risk is related to a number of factors, including the increased likelihood of having an injection-drug-using sex partner. Furthermore, this risk is even higher for women in prison and is compounded by them perceiving themselves as not at risk. Finally, all three articles confront the complex issues involved when women use drugs.

9

Women in the Street-Level Drug Economy: Continuity or Change?*

LISA MAHER

KATHLEEN DALY

ABSTRACT

Images of women in the contemporary drug economy are highly mixed. Most scholars emphasize change in women's roles, some emphasize continuity, and others suggest that both change and continuity are evident. At issue is whether an increased share of women were involved in selling and higher-level distribution roles in the crack cocaine markets of the late 1980s and early 1990s, compared to the heroin markets of the 1960s and 1970s. We present the results of an ethnographic study of women drug users conducted during 1989–92 in a New York City neighborhood. Contrary to those who suggest that crack cocaine markets have provided "new opportunities" for women, we find that such opportunities were realized by men. At the same time, the conditions of street-level sex work, which has traditionally provided women drug users with a relatively stable source of income, have deteriorated.

Images of women in the contemporary drug economy are highly mixed. Most scholars emphasize change in women's roles in U.S. drug markets of 1960–1985, organized primarily around heroin, compared to women's roles in more recent drug markets with the advent of crack cocaine (e.g., Baskin et al., 1993; Bourgois, 1989; Dunlap and Johnson, 1992; Inciardi et al., 1993; Mieczkowski, 1994; C. Taylor, 1993). Some emphasize continuity from previous decades (Adler, 1985; Koester and Schwartz, 1993; Maher and Curtis, 1992). Others suggest that both change and continuity are evident, with women inhabiting "two social worlds" (Fagan, 1994, p. 212): one of increased participation in, and the other of continued restriction by, male-dominated street and drug networks.

One should expect, on the one hand, to see variation in women's positions in the drug economy. Research on drug markets in New York City (Bourgois, 1995; Curtis and Sviridoff, 1994; Hamid, 1990, 1992; Johnson et al., 1985, 1992; Williams, 1989), Miami (Inciardi et al., 1993), Washington, D.C. (Reuter et al., 1990), Detroit (Mieczkowski, 1986, 1990; C. Taylor, 1990), Chicago (Padilla, 1992), Milwaukee (Hagedron, 1994), Los Angeles, and the West Coast (Adler, 1985; Morgan and Joe, 1994; Skolnick, 1989; Waldorf et al., 1991) reveals differences in the racial and ethnic composition of participants and who controls markets, the kinds of drugs sold, how markets are organized, and participants' responses to law enforcement. Such differences are likely to affect women's positions and specific roles.

*The research on which this article is based was supported by the award of a Dissertation Fellowship from the Harry Frank Guggenheim Foundation. We are indebted to the women who participated in the study, to Richard Curtis and Ansley Hamid for their many contributions to the research, and to the reviewers for helpful comments on earlier drafts of this manuscript.

Maher, Lisa and Kathleen Daly. 1996. Women in the Street-Level Drug Economy: Continuity or Change? *Criminology*, *11*(1):21–28. Reprinted with permission.

At the same time, the varied characterizations of women's roles reflect differences in the theoretical assumptions and methodological approaches taken by scholars. For example, women's increasing presence in the drug economies of the late 1980s and early 1990s is said to reflect (1) emancipation from their traditional household responsibilities (Bourgois, 1989; Bourgois and Dunlap, 1993), (2) an extension of their traditional household responsibilities (Wilson, 1993), and (3) the existence of "new opportunities" in street-level drug markets (Mieczkowski, 1994), especially with increased rates of incarceration of minority group men (Baskin et al., 1993). These explanations reveal different assumptions about changes (or not) in the gendered structure of drug markets and about the links (or not) between women's participation in crime and their domestic responsibilities.

Data sources and methods also affect the quality and content of the inferences drawn. Some have analyzed Uniform Crime Report (UCR) arrest data (e.g., Wilson, 1993), others have interviewed women arrested on drug charges or through snowball samples (e.g., Baskin et al., 1993; Fagan, 1994; Inciardi et al., 1993; C. Taylor, 1993), and a handful have conducted ethnographies of particular neighborhoods (e.g., Bourgois, 1989; Maher and Curtis, 1992). While interview-based studies may offer an empirical advantage over the inferences that can be drawn from UCR arrest data, the one-time interview may not elicit complete or reliable information about the changing contexts of women's income generation in the informal economy.

This article presents the results of an ethnographic study of women drug users conducted during 1989–1992 in a New York City neighborhood. We assess whether women's involvement in U.S. drug markets of the mid-1980s onward reflects change, continuity, or a combination of change and continuity from patterns in previous decades. We find that contrary to the conclusions of Baskin et al. (1993), Fagan (1994), Inciardi et al. (1993), Mieczkowski (1994), and C. Taylor (1993), crack cocaine markets have not necessarily provided "new opportunities" for women, nor should such markets be viewed as "equal opportunity employers" (Bourgois, 1989; Wilson, 1993). Our study suggests that recent drug markets continue to be monopolized by men and to offer few opportunities for stable income generation for women. While women's *presence* on the street and in

low-level auxiliary roles may have increased, we find that their *participation* as substantive labor in the drug-selling marketplace has not.

WOMEN IN THE DRUG ECONOMY

Drug Markets of the 1960s to the Mid-1980s

Prior to the advent of crack cocaine in the mid-1980s, research on women in the drug economy used one or more of four elements to explain women's restricted roles in selling and distributing drugs:[1] intimate relationships with men, the availability of alternative options for income generation, restrictions on discretionary time, and institutionalized sexism in the underworld.

Female heroin users were often characterized as needing a man to support their consumption (e.g., File, 1976; File et al., 1974; Hser et al., 1987; Smithberg and Westermeyer, 1985; Sutter, 1966). They were also described as being "led" into crime by individual men (Covington, 1985; Pettiway, 1987), although this may apply more to white than minority group women (Anglin and Hser, 1987; Pettiway, 1987). The typical pattern was of low-status roles in which participation was short-lived, sporadic, and mediated by intimate relationships with men (Adler, 1985; Rosenbaum, 1981). Alternative sources of income generation, such as prostitution and shoplifting, may have been preferable to female drug users, especially heroin users (File, 1976; Goldstein, 1979; Hunt, 1990; Inciardi and Pottieger, 1986; James, 1976; Rosenbaum, 1981). Some suggest, in addition, that women's household and childcare responsibilities may have limited their full participation in the drug economy (e.g., Rosenbaum, 1981; A. Taylor, 1993; see also Wilson, 1993).

Women's peripheral roles in male-dominated drug selling networks (Auld et al., 1986; Goldstein, 1979; Rosenbaum, 1981) can also be explained by "institutionalized sexism" in the "underworld" (Steffensmeier, 1983; Steffensmeier and Terry, 1986; see also Box, 1983). Steffensmeier (1983, pp. 1013–1015) argues that male lawbreakers prefer to "work, associate, and do business with other men" (homosocial reproduction); they view women as lacking the physical and mental attributes considered essential to working in an uncertain and violent context (sex-typing and task environment of crime). In the drug economy, in particular, women are thought to be unsuitable for

---

[1]*Selling* refers to the direct exchange of drugs for cash; *distributing* refers to low-level distribution roles that do not involve direct sales but provide assistance to sellers.

higher-level distribution roles because of an inability to manage male workers through threatened violence (Waterston, 1993, p. 114).

Crack Cocaine Markets of the Mid-1980s Onward

Women have been depicted as more active participants in selling and distributing drugs in the crack cocaine economy of the late 1980s compared to previous drug eras. While some find that women's roles continue to be mediated by relationships with men (Koester and Schwartz, 1993; Murphy et al., 1991) and that women remain at the bottom of the drug market hierarchy (Maher and Curtis, 1992), others suggest that there has been decisive change. Specifically, it is argued that "drug business" crimes (that is, street-level drug sales) generate a higher share of women's income than in the past, with a concomitant decrease in prostitution-generated income (Inciardi et al., 1993). More generally, it is argued that the crack-propelled expansion of drug markets has provided "new opportunities" for women.

The "new opportunities" argument is made by the majority of those in the field (see, e.g., Baskin et al., 1993; Bourgois, 1989; Bourgois and Dunlap, 1993; Fagan, 1994; Inciardi et al., 1993; Mieczkowski, 1994). It takes two forms: a general claim that women's emancipation in the wider society is evident in "all aspects of inner-city street life" (Bourgois, 1989, pp. 643–644) and a more restricted claim that the weakening of male-dominated street networks and market processes has made it possible for women to enter the drug economy. For example, in his study of New York City women, Fagan (1994, p. 210) concludes that

> while women were consigned secondary, gender-specific roles in . . . [drug] businesses in the past, the size and seemingly frantic activity of the current drug markets has made possible for women new ways to participate in street networks. Their involvement in drug selling at high income levels defies the gendered norms and roles of the past, where drug dealing was an incidental income source often mediated by domestic partnerships . . . the expansion of drug markets in the cocaine economy has provided new ways for women to escape their limited roles, statuses and incomes in previous eras.

While two-thirds of the women in Fagan's (1994) sample did not sell drugs and while most who sold drugs acted alone (p. 197), Fagan was struck by "the emergence of women sellers earning high incomes and avoiding prostitution" (p. 211). He concluded that "two social worlds" of continuity and change characterized women's participation in drug markets. One difficulty in assessing this claim is that no estimate is given of the proportion of women who were earning high incomes from drug business, avoiding prostitution, and "def[ying] the gendered norms and roles of the past."

Fagan's research offers a good comparison to our study. He draws from interviews with 311 women, the majority of whom were drug users or sellers, in two New York City neighborhoods (Washington Heights and Central Harlem in northern Manhattan). The interviews were conducted during the late 1980s; the sample included women with police arrest records, in residential treatment programs, and those who had not been arrested. The women in our sample lived just a few miles away in Bushwick, a Brooklyn neighborhood. Very few of the Bushwick women were active dealers, and virtually all supported themselves by prostitution. Whereas Fagan sees two worlds of continuity and change, we see just one of continuity. Before describing that social world, we sketch the study site and the methods used in gathering the data.

RESEARCH SITE AND METHODS

Research Site

Bushwick, the principal study site, has been described as hosting "the most notorious drug bazaar in Brooklyn and one of the toughest in New York City" (*New York Times*, October 1, 1992, p. A1). Historically home to large numbers of European Jews, by the 1960s Bushwick was dominated by working-class Italians. Since the late 1960s, the area has become the home of low-income Latino populations, predominantly Puerto Ricans, although Dominicans and Columbians have begun to move in. In 1960 the population was 89% white, 6% black, and 5% Hispanic. By 1990 it was 5% white, 25% black, and 65% Hispanic (Bureau of the Census, 1990). In 1990 Bushwick was Brooklyn's poorest neighborhood with a median household income of $16,287; unemployment was twice the citywide rate; and more than half of all families and two-thirds of all children lived under the official poverty line (Bureau of the Census, 1990).

Between 1988 and 1992 drug distribution in Bushwick was intensely competitive; there were constant confrontations over "turf" as organizations strove to establish control over markets. Like many drug markets in New York City (see, e.g., Curtis and

Sviridoff, 1994; Waterston, 1993), Bushwick was highly structured and ethnically segmented. The market, largely closed to outsiders, was dominated by Dominicans with networks organized by kin and pseudo-kin relations.[2]

Fieldwork Methods

Preliminary fieldwork began in the fall of 1989 when the senior author established a field presence in several Brooklyn neighborhoods (Williamsburg, East Flatbush, and Bushwick). By fall 1990 observations and interviews were intensified in Bushwick because it hosted the busiest street-level drug market in Brooklyn and had an active prostitution stroll. As fieldwork progressed, it became apparent that the initial plan of conducting interviews with a large number of women crack users was not, by itself, going to yield a complete picture. For example, few women initially admitted that they performed oral sex for less than $20, and none admitted to participating in sex-for-crack trades.

By the end of December 1991, interviews had been conducted with 211 active women crack users in Williamsburg, East Flatbush, and Bushwick. These were tape recorded and ranged from 20 minutes to 3 hours; they took place in a variety of settings, including private or semiprivate locations (e.g., apartments, shooting galleries, abandoned buildings, cars) and public locales (e.g., restaurants, parks, subways, and public toilets).[3] From January to March 1992, a preliminary data sort was made of the interview and observational material. From that process, 45 women were identified for whom there were repeated observations and interview material. Contact with these women was intimate and extensive; the number of tape-recorded interviews for each woman ranged from 3 to 15. Unless otherwise noted, the research findings reported here are based on this smaller group of 45 Bushwick women.

Profile of the Bushwick Women

The Bushwick women consisted of 20 Latinas (18 Puerto Ricans and 2 Dominicans), 16 African-Americans, and 9 European-Americans; their ages ranged from 19 to 41 years, with a mean of 28 years. At the time of the first interview, all the women used smokable cocaine (or crack), although only 31% used it exclusively; most (69%) had used heroin or powder cocaine prior to using crack. The women's average drug use history was 10.5 years (using the mean as the measure); heroin and powder cocaine initiates had a mean of about 12 years and the smokable cocaine initiates, about 6 years.

Most women (84%) were born in the New York City area, and more than half were born in Brooklyn. About one-quarter were raised in households with both parents present, and over one-third (38%) grew up in a household in which they were subjected to physical abuse. Most (84%) had not completed high school, and 55% had no experience of formal-sector work. A high proportion were homeless (91%), alternating between the street and short-term accommodations in shelters, apartments of friends, and homes of elderly men (see also Maher et al., 1996). Most women were mothers (80%); the 36 mothers had given birth to 96 children, whose ages ranged from newborns to 26 years. Few of the mothers (9%) had their children living with them during the study period. Fourteen women (31%) had tested positive for HIV, and an additional five women believed that they were HIV positive; but most women said they did not know their serostatus. By the end of the study period, two women had stopped using illicit drugs, and five had died: two from HIV-related illnesses and three from homicide.

These 45 women represent the range of ages, racial-ethnic backgrounds, life experiences, and histories of crack-using women among the larger group of Brooklyn women interviewed. We are cognizant, however, of the limits of using ethnographic research in one area to generalize to other areas. For example, there is a somewhat higher proportion of Latinas (44%) in our sample than in Fagan's (1994, p. 225) sample in Central Harlem (23%) and Washington Heights (33%). A higher share of the Bushwick women had not completed high school, had no experience in the formal labor force, and were homeless.

---

[2]At one level, language served as a marker of identity; "outsiders" were those who were not "Spanish," with country of origin often less salient than an ability to speak Spanish or "Spanglish." However, the distribution of opportunities for income generation also involved finely calibrated notions of ethnicity.

[3]Each woman was given $10 or the equivalent (e.g., cash, food, clothing, cigarettes, makeup, subway tokens, or a combination) for the initial tape-recorded interview. However, field observations and many of the repeat interviews were conducted on the basis of relations of reciprocity that did not involve direct or immediate benefit to those interviewed. While this research focused on women's lives, interviews and observations were also undertaken with the women's female kin, male partners, and children.

Structure of New York City Crack Markets

Street-level crack markets have frequently been characterized as unregulated markets of freelancers engaged in individual entrepreneurial activity (Hunt, 1990; Reuter et al., 1990). Some evidence suggests, however, that once demand has been established, the freelance model may be superseded by a more structured system of distribution. When the crack epidemic was at its peak in New York City during the late 1980s, Bushwick (like other neighborhoods) hosted highly structured street-level drug markets with pooled interdependence, vertical differentiation, and a formal, multi-tiered system of organization and control with defined employer-employee relationships (Curtis and Maher, in press; Johnson et al., 1990, 1992). This model is similar to the "runner system" used in heroin distribution (see Mieczkowski, 1986).

In selling crack cocaine, drug business "owners" employ several "crew bosses," "lieutenants," or "managers," who work shifts to ensure an efficient organization of street-level distribution. Managers (as they were known in Brooklyn) act as conduits between owners and lower-level employees. They are responsible for organizing and delivering supplies and collecting revenues. Managers exercise considerable autonomy in the hiring, firing, and payment of workers; they are responsible for labor force discipline and the resolution of workplace grievances and disputes. Next down the hierarchy are the street-level sellers, who perform retailing tasks having little discretion. Sellers are located in a fixed space or "spot" and are assisted by those below them in the hierarchy: lower-level operatives acting as "runners," "look-outs," "steerers," "touts," "holders," and "enforcers." Runners "continuously supply the sellers," look-outs "warn of impending dangers," steerers and touts "advertise and solicit customers," holders "handle drugs or money but not both," and enforcers "maintain order and intervene in case of trouble" (Johnson et al., 1992, pp. 61–64).

In New York City in the early 1990s, it was estimated that 150,000 people were involved in selling or helping to sell crack cocaine on any given day (Williams, 1992:10). Crack sales and distribution became a major source of income for the city's drug users (Hamid, 1990, 1991; Johnson et al., 1994). How, then, did the Bushwick women fit into this drug market structure? We examine women's involvement in a range of drug business activities.

Selling and Distributing Drugs

During the entire three years of fieldwork, including the interviews with the larger group of over 200 women, we did not discover any woman who was a business owner, and just one worked as a manager. The highly structured nature of the market in Bushwick, coupled with its kin-based organization, militated against personal or intimate sexual relationships between female drug users and higher-level male operatives. To the limited extent that they participated in drug selling, women were overwhelmingly concentrated at the lowest levels. They were almost always used as temporary workers when men were arrested or refused to work, or when it was "hot" because of police presence. Table 1 shows how the 45 women were involved in Bushwick's drug economy.

Of the 19 women (42%) who had some involvement, the most common role was that of informal steerer or tout. This meant that they recommended a particular brand of heroin to newcomers to the neighborhood in return for "change," usually a dollar or so. These newcomers were usually white men, who may have felt more comfortable approaching women with requests for such information. In turn, the women's perceptions of "white boyz" enabled them to use the situation to their advantage. Although they only used crack, Yolanda, a 38-year-old Latina, and Boy, a 26-year-old African-American woman, engaged in this practice of "tipping" heroin consumers.

> They come up to me. Before they come and buy dope and anything, they ask me what dope is good. I ain't done no dope, but I'm a professional player . . . . They would come to me, they would pay me, they would come "What's good out here?" I would tell them, "Where's a dollar," and that's how I use to make my money. Everyday somebody would come, "Here's a dollar, here's two dollars." (Yolanda) [What other kinds of things?] Bumming up change. [There ain't many people down here with change.] Just the white guys. They give you more faster than your own kind. [You go cop for them?] No, just for change. You tell them what's good on [the] dope side. Tell them anything, I don't do dope, but I'll tell them anything. Yeah, it's kicking live man. They buy it. Boom! I got my dollar, bye. (Boy)

Within the local drug economy, the availability of labor strongly determines women's participation in street-level distribution roles. Labor supply fluctuates with extramarket forces, such as product availability and police intervention. One consequence of police activity in Bushwick during the study period was a recurring, if temporary, shortage of male workers. Such labor market gaps promoted instability: The replacement of "trusted" sellers (i.e., Latinos) with

TABLE 1   Bushwick Women's Roles in the Drug Economy, 1989–92

	N	%
No Role	26	58
Had Some Role	19	42
	45	100

Of the 19 women with roles in the drug economy during the three-year study period, the following shows what they did. Because most women (N = 13) had more than one role, the total sums to greater than 19.

Selling and Distributing Roles	
Owner	0
Manager	0
Regular Seller	0
Irregular Seller	7
Runner	0
Look-out	0
Steerer or Tout	9
Holder	0
Enforcer	0
Selling/Renting Paraphernalia	
Works Sellers	4
Stem Renters	6
Running a Gallery	3
Copping Drugs for Others	14
Other Drug Business Hustles	
Street Doc	1

Note: While we have tried to be precise, we should note that it can be difficult to characterize women's roles—not only because drug markets are fluid and shifting but also because some women had varied mixes of roles over time.

"untrustworthy" drug users (i.e., women and non-Latinos) eroded the social and kinship ties that had previously served to reduce violence in drug-related disputes (see also Curtis and Sviridoff, 1994).

Early in the fieldwork period (during 1989 and early 1990), both men and women perceived that more women were being offered opportunities to work as street-level sellers than in the past. Such opportunities, it turned out, were often part of a calculated risk-minimization strategy on the part of owners and managers. As Princess, a 32-year-old African-American woman observed, some owners thought that women were less likely to be noticed, searched, or arrested by police:

> Nine times out of ten when the po-leece roll up it's gonna [be] men. And they're not allowed to search a woman, but they have some that will. But if they don't do it, they'll call for a female officer. By the time she gets there, (laughs) if you know how to move around, you better get it off you, unless you jus' want to go to jail. [So you think it works out better for the owners to have women working for them?] Yeah, to use women all the time.

As the fieldwork progressed and the neighborhood became more intensively policed, this view became less tenable. Latisha, a 32-year-old African-American woman, reported that the police became more aggressive in searching women:

> [You see some women dealing a little bit you know.] Yeah, but they starting to go. Now these cop around here starting to unzip girls' pants and go in their panties. It was, it's not like it was before. You could stick the drugs in your panties 'cause you're a female. Now that's garbage.

Thus, when initially faced with a shortage of regular male labor and large numbers of women seeking low-level selling positions, some managers appear to have adopted the opportunistic use of women to avoid detection and disruption of their businesses. How frequent this practice was is uncertain; we do know that it was short-lived (see also Curtis and Sviridoff, 1994, p. 164).

In previous years (the late 1970s and early 1980s), several Bushwick women had sold drugs in their roles as wives or girlfriends of distributors, but this was no longer the case. During the three-year study period only 12 women (27%) were involved in selling and distributing roles. Of this group of 12, only 7 were able to secure low-level selling positions on an irregular basis. Connie, a 25-year-old Latina, was typical of this small group, and in the following quotation she describes her unstable position within the organization she worked for:

> I'm currently working for White Top [crack]. They have a five bundle limit. It might take me an hour or two to sell that, or sometimes as quick as half an hour. I got to ask if I can work. They say yes or no.

Typically the managers said no to women's requests to work. Unlike many male street-level sellers who worked on a regular basis for this organization and were given "shifts" (generally lasting eight hours), Connie had to work off-hours (during daylight hours), which were often riskier and less financially rewarding. Temporary workers were usually given a "bundle limit" (one bundle contains 24 vials), which ensured that they could work only for short periods of time. As Cherrie, a 22-year-old Latina, said,

> The last time I sold it was Blue Tops [crack]. That was a week ago. [What, they asked you or you asked them to work?] Oh, they ask me, I say I want to work. [How come they asked you?] I don't know. They didn't have nobody to work because it was too hot out there. They was too full of cops.

Similarly, although Princess was well-known to the owners and managers of White Top crack, had worked for them many times in the past year, and had "proved" herself by having never once "stepped off" with either drugs or money, she was only given sporadic employment. She reported,

> Sometime you can't [sell]. Sometime you can. That's why it's good to save money also. So when you don't get work. [How come they wouldn't give you work on some days?] Because of some favor that someone might've done or y'know, jus' . . . [It's not like they're trying to punish you?] No, but they will do that y'know. Somebody go and tell them something, "Oh, this one's doin' this to the bags or this one's doin' this to the bottles." OK, well they check the bags and they don' see nothin' wrong, but they came to look at it so they're pissed off so they'll take it away from you, y'know.

Violence and Relationships. In addition to being vulnerable to arrest and street robbery, street-level sellers who use drugs constantly grapple with the urge to consume the product and to abscond with the drugs and/or the money. Retaliation by employers toward users who "mess up the money" (Johnson et al., 1985, p. 174) was widely perceived to be swift and certain. Rachel, a 35-year-old European-American woman, said,

> Those Dominicans, if you step off with one piece of it, you're gonna get hurt. They don't play. They are sick people.

The prospect of violent retaliation may deter women from selling drugs. Boy, a 26-year-old African-American woman, put it this way:

> I don' like their [the managers'] attitude, like if you come up short, dey take it out on you . . . I don' sell no crack or dope for dese n*****s. Because dey is crazy. Say for instance you short ten dollars, n*****s come across you wit bats and shit. It's not worth it, you could lose your life. If dey say you are short, you could lose you life. Even if you were not short and dey say you is short, whatever dey say is gonna go, so you are f***ed all the way around.

However, considerable uncertainty surrounds the likelihood that physical punishment will be meted out. This uncertainty can be seen in the comments by Princess, who had a long but sporadic history of street-level sales before and after the advent of crack:

> It's not worth it. Number one, it's not enough. Come on, run away, and then *maybe* then these people want to heavily beat the shit out of you. And then they *may* hit you in the wrong place with the bat and *maybe* kill you (emphasis added).

Such disciplinary practices resemble a complex interplay between "patronage" and "mercy," which features in relations of dependence (Hay, 1975). The unpredictability of punishment may work as a more effective form of control than actual punishment itself. In Bushwick, the actuality of violent retaliation for sellers who "messed up" was further mediated by gender and ethnicity. In this Latino- (mainly Dominican) controlled market, the common perception was that men, and black men especially, were more likely than Latinas to be punished for "stepping off." Rachel described what happened after an African-American man had been badly beaten:

> [What happened to him. I mean he stepped off with a package, right?] Yeah, but everybody has at one time or another. But it's also because he's a black

and not a Puerto Rican, and he can't, you know, smooze his way back in like, you know, Mildred steps off with every other package, and so does, you know, Yolanda, they all do. But they're Spanish. And they're girls. So, you know, they can smooze their way back in. You know, a guy who's black and ugly, you know, so they don't want to hear about it.

Relationships in the drug economy are fueled by contradictory expectations. On the one hand, attributes such as trust and reliability are frequently espoused as important to drug-selling organizations. On the other hand, ethnographic informants often refer to the lack of trust and solidarity among organization members. This lack of trust is evident in the constant "scams" sellers and managers pull on each other and the ever-present threat of violence in owner-manager-seller relations.

Strategies of Protection and "Being Bad." Women who work the streets to sell or buy drugs are subject to constant harassment and are regularly victimized. The Bushwick women employed several strategies to protect themselves. One of the most important was the adoption of a "badass" (Katz, 1988), "crazy," or "gangsta bitch" stance or attitude, of which having a "bad mouth" was an integral part. As Latisha was fond of saying, "My heart pumps no Kool Aid. I don't even drink the shit." Or as Boy put it,

> Ac' petite, dey treat you petite. I mean you ac' soft, like when you dress dainty and shit ta come over here an' sit onna f***in' corner. Onna corner an' smoke an you dressed to da teeth, you know, you soft. Right then and there you the center of the crowd, y'know what I'm sayin'? Now put a dainty one and put me, she looks soft. Dey look at me like "don't f**** wid dat bitch, she looks hard." Don' mess wit me caus I look hard y'know . . . Dey don't f*** wit me out here. Dey think I'm crazy.

Acting bad and "being bad" are not the same. Although many Bushwick women presented themselves as "bad" or "crazy," this projection was a street persona and a necessary survival strategy (see also Spalter-Roth, 1988). Despite the external manifestation of aggression, a posture and rhetoric of toughness, and the preemptive use of aggression (Campbell, 1993), women were widely perceived (by men and women alike) as less likely to have the attributes associated with successful managers and street-level sellers.

These included the requisite "street cred" and a "rep" for having "heart" or "juice"—masculine qualities associated with toughness and the capacity for violence (Bourgois, 1989; Steffensmeier, 1983; Waterston, 1993). Women's abilities to "talk tough" or "act bad" were apparently not enough to inspire employer confidence. Prospective drug business employers wanted those capable of actually "being bad" (Bourgois, 1989, p. 632). Because female drug users were perceived as unreliable, untrustworthy, and unable to deploy violence and terror effectively, would-be female sellers were at a disadvantage.

Selling Drug Paraphernalia

In Bushwick the sale of drug paraphernalia such as crack stems and pipes was controlled by the bodegas, or corner stores, whereas syringes or "works" were the province of the street. Men dominated both markets although women were sometimes employed as part-time "works" sellers. Men who regularly sold "sealed" (i.e., new) works had suppliers (typically men who worked in local hospitals) from who they purchased units called "ten packs" (10 syringes). The benefits of selling syringes were twofold: The penalties were less severe than those for selling drugs, and the rate of return was higher compared to the street-level sale of heroin or crack.[4]

The women who sold works were less likely than their male counterparts to have procured them "commercially." More often they "happened across" a supply of works through a family member or social contact who was a diabetic. Women were also more likely to sell works for others or to sell "used works." Rosa, a 31-year-old Latina, described in detail the dangerous practice of collecting used works strewn around the neighborhood. While she often stored them and later exchanged them for new works from the volunteer needle exchange (which was illegal at the time), Rosa would sometimes select the works she deemed in good condition, "clean" them with bleach and water, and resell them.

Although crack stems and pipes were available from neighborhood bodegas at minimal cost, some smokers chose not to carry stems. These users, almost exclusively men, were from outside the neighborhood. Their reluctance to carry drug paraphernalia provided the women with an additional source of income, usually in the form of a "hit," in exchange for the use of their stem. Sometimes these men were

---

[4]Street-level drug sellers typically made $1 on a $10 bag of heroin and 50 cents on a $5 vial of crack. Syringe sellers made at least $1.50 per unit, depending on the purchase price and the sale price.

"dates," but more often they were "men on a mission" in the neighborhood or the "working men" who came to the area on Friday and Saturday nights to get high. As Boy put it,

> I be there on the block an' I got my stem and my lighter. I see them cop and I be askin' "yo, you need a stem, you need a light?" People say "yeah man," so they give me a piece.

An additional benefit for those women who rented their stems was the build up of crack residues in the stems. Many users savored this resin, which they allowed to accumulate before periodically digging it out with "scrapers" fashioned from the metal ribs of discarded umbrellas.

Some women also sold condoms, another form of drug-related paraphernalia in Bushwick. Although condoms were sold at bodegas, usually for $1 each, many of the women obtained free condoms from outreach health workers. Sometimes they sold them at a reduced price (usually 25 cents) to other sex workers, "white boyz," and young men from the neighborhood. Ironically, these same women would then have to purchase condoms at the bodegas when they had "smoked up" all their condoms.

Running Shooting Galleries

A wide range of physical locations were used for drug consumption in Bushwick. Although these sites were referred to generically as "galleries" by drug users and others in the neighborhood, they differed from the traditional heroin shooting gallery in several respects.[5] Bushwick's "galleries" were dominated by men because they had the economic resources or physical prowess to maintain control. Control was also achieved by exploiting women drug users with housing leases. Such women were particularly vulnerable, as the following quotation from Carol, a 40-year-old African-American woman, shows:

> I had my own apartment, myself and my daughter. I started selling crack. From my house. [For who?] Some Jamaican. [How did you get hooked up with that?] Through my boyfriend. They wanted to sell from my apartment. They were supposed to pay me something like $150 a week rent, and then something off the profits. They used to, you know, f*** up the money, like not give me the money. Eventually I went through a whole lot of different dealers. Eventually I stopped payin' my rent because I wanted to get a transfer out of there to get away from everything 'cause soon as one group of crack dealers would get out, another group would come along. [So how long did that go on for?] About four years. Then I lost my apartment, and I sat out in the street.

The few women who were able to maintain successful galleries operated with or under the control of a man or group of men. Cherrie's short-lived effort to set up a gallery in an abandoned burned-out building on "Crack Row" is illustrative. Within two weeks of establishing the gallery (the principal patrons of which were women), Cherrie was forced out of business by the police. The two weeks were marked by constant harassment, confiscation of drugs and property, damage to an already fragile physical plant, physical assaults, and the repeated forced dispersal of gallery occupants. Within a month, two men had established a new gallery on the same site, which, more than a year later, was thriving.

Such differential policing toward male- and female-operated galleries is explicable in light of the larger picture of law enforcement in low-income urban communities, where the primary function is not so much to enforce the law but rather to regulate illegal activities (Whyte, 1943, p. 138). Field observations suggest that the reason the police did not interfere as much with activities in the men's gallery was that they assumed that men were better able than women to control the gallery and to minimize problems of violence and disorder.

Other factors contributed to women's disadvantage in operating galleries, crack houses, and other consumption sites. Male drug users were better placed economically than the women in the sample, most of whom were homeless and without a means of legitimate economic support. When women did have an apartment or physical site, this made them a vulnerable target either for exploitation by male users or dealers (as in Carol's case) or for harassment by the police (as in Cherrie's). Even when a woman claimed to be in control of a physical location, field observations confirmed that she was not. Thus, in Bushwick, the presence of a man was a prerequisite to the successful operation of drug-consumption sites. The

---

[5] While consumption settings in Bushwick more closely resembled heroin shooting galleries (see, e.g., Des Jarlais et al., 1986; Murphy and Waldorf, 1991) than crack houses (see, e.g., Inciardi et al., 1993; Williams, 1992), many sites combined elements of both and most provided for polydrug (heroin and crack) consumption (for further details see Maher, in press).

only choice for those women in a position to operate galleries or crack houses was between the "devils they knew" and those they did not.

Copping Drugs

Many Bushwick women supplemented their income by "copping" drugs for others. They almost always copped for men, typically white men. At times these men were dates, but often they were users who feared being caught and wanted someone else to take that risk. As Rachel explained,

> I charge them, just what they want to buy they have to pay me. If they want twenty dollars they have to give me twenty dollars worth on the top because I'm risking my free time. I could get busted copping. They have to pay me the same way, if not, they can go cop. Most of them can't because they don't know the people.

Those who cop drugs for others perform an important service for the drug market because as Biernacki (1979, p. 539) suggests in connection with heroin, "they help to minimize the possibility of infiltration by undercover agents and decrease the chance of a dealer's arrest." In Bushwick the copping role attracted few men; it was regarded by both men and women as a low-status peripheral hustle. Most women saw the female-dominated nature of the job to be part of the parallel sex market in the neighborhood. Outsiders could readily approach women to buy drugs under the guise of buying sex. As Rosa recounted,

> You would [be] surprise. They'd be ahm, be people very important, white people like lawyer, doctors that comes and get off, you'd be surprised. Iss like I got two lawyer, they give me money to go, to go and cop. And they stay down over there parking . . . . [How do you meet them?] Well down the stroll one time they stop and say you know, "You look like a nice girl though, you know, you wanna make some money fast?" I say, how? So they say you know, "Look out for me." First time they give me like you know, twenty dollars, you know. They see I came back, next time they give me thirty. Like that you know. I have been copping for them like over six months already.

Sometimes this function was performed in conjunction with sex work, as Latisha's comment illustrates,

He's a cop. He's takin' a chance. He is petrified. Will not get out his car . . . But he never gets less than nine bags [of powder cocaine]. [And he sends you to get it?] And he wants a blow job, right, okay. You know what he's givin' you, a half a bag of blue (blue bag cocaine). That's for you goin' to cop, and for the blow job. That's [worth] two dollars and fifty . . . I can go to jail [for him]. I'm a piece of shit.

Women also felt that, given the reputation of the neighborhood as very "thirsty" (that is, as having a "thirst" or craving for crack), male outsiders were more likely to trust women, especially white women, to purchase drugs on their behalf. Often this trust was misplaced. The combination of naïve, inexperienced "white boyz" and experienced "street smart" women produced opportunities for additional income by, for example, simply taking the "cop" money. This was a calculated risk and sometimes things went wrong. A safer practice was to inflate the purchase price of the drugs and to pocket the difference. Rosa explained this particular scam,

> He think it a ten dollar bag, but issa five dollar. But at least I don't be rippin' him off there completely. [But you're taking the risk for him.] Exactly. Sometime he give me a hunert dollars, so I making fifty, right? But sometime he don't get paid, he got no second money, eh. I cop then when I come back the car, he say, "Dear I cannot give you nothin' today," you know. But I still like I say, I gettin' something from him because he think it a ten dollar bag.

Similar scams involved the woman's returning to the client with neither drugs nor money, claiming that she had been ripped off or, less often, shortchanging the client by tapping the vials (removing some crack) or adulterating the drugs (cutting powder cocaine or heroin with other substances). These scams reveal the diversity of women's roles as copping agents and their ingenuity in making the most of limited opportunities.[6]

Other Drug Business Hustles

The practice of injecting intravenous drug users (IDUs) who are unable to inject themselves, because they are inexperienced or have deep or collapsed veins, has been documented by others (e.g., Johnson et al., 1985; Murphy and Waldorf, 1991). Those performing this role are sometimes referred to as "street

[6]By their own accounts, women took greater risks in order to generate income than they had in the past. More generally, the incidence of risky behavior increased as conditions in the neighborhood and the adjacent street-level sex market deteriorated (Maher and Curtis, 1992; see also Curtis et al., 1995).

docs" (Murphy and Waldorf, 1991, pp. 16–17). In Bushwick, men typically specialized in this practice. For example, Sam, a Latino injector in his late thirties, lived in one of the makeshift huts or "condos" on a busy street near the main heroin copping area. Those who were in a hurry to consume or who had nowhere else to go would use Sam's place to "get off." Sam had a reputation as a good "hitter" and injected several women in the sample on a regular basis. He provided this service for a few dollars or, more often, a "taste" of whatever substance was being injected.

Only one woman in the sample, Latisha, capitalized on her reputation as a good "hitter" by playing the street doc role. Latisha had a regular arrangement with a young street thug named Crime, notorious for victimizing the women, who had only recently commenced intravenous heroin use and was unable to "hit" himself. While women IDUs were likely to have the requisite level of skill, they were less likely than men to be able to capitalize on it because they did not control an established consumption setting.

DISCUSSION

A major dimension of drug economies, both past and present, is the "human qualities" believed necessary for the performance of various roles. Opportunities for income generation are defined, in part, by who has the necessary qualities or traits and who does not. These traits, whether grounded in cultural perceptions of biology and physiology (e.g., strength and capacity for violence), mental states (e.g., courage and aggressiveness), or kinship (e.g., loyalty and trustworthiness), are primarily differentiated along the lines of gender and race-ethnicity. In this study, we found that women were though to be not as "strong" as men and that men, particularly black men and Latinos, were thought to be more "bad" and capable of "being bad." The gendered displays of violence that men incorporate into their work routines not only cement their solidarity as men, but also reinscribe these traits as masculine (Messerschmidt, 1993). As a consequence, men are able to justify the exclusion of women from more lucrative "men's work" in the informal economy. All the elements of underworld sexism identified by Steffensmeier (1983)—homosocial reproduction, sex-typing, and the qualities required in a violent task environment—featured prominently in Bushwick's street-level drug economy.

The significance of gender-based capacities and the symbolism used to convey them was evident in the women's use of instrumental aggression. Boy's discussion of how to "dress for success" on the streets reveals that power dressing is "dressing like a man" or "dressing down." It is anything but "dressing dainty." Both on the street and in the boardroom, it appears that a combination of clothing and attitude makes the woman (Kanter, 1981, citing Henning, 1970). In the drug business, conveying the message "don't mess with me" is integral to maintaining a reputation for "craziness," which the women perceived as affording them some measure of protection.

The Bushwick women's experiences within a highly gender-stratified labor market provide a counter to the romantic notion of the informal drug economy as an "equal opportunity employer" (Bourgois, 1989, p. 630). Their experiences contradict the conventional wisdom, shaped by studies of the labor market experiences of minority group men (e.g., Anderson, 1990; Bourgois, 1989, 1995; Hagedorn, 1994; Padilla, 1992; C. Taylor, 1990; Williams, 1989), that the drug economy acts as a compensatory mechanism, offering paid employment that is not available in the formal labor force. While in theory the built-in supervision and task differentiation of the business model, which characterized drug distribution in Bushwick, should have provided opportunities to both men and women (Johnson et al., 1992), our findings suggest that sellers were overwhelmingly men. Thus, the "new opportunities" said to have emerged with the crack-propelled expansion of drug markets from the mid-1980s onward were not "empty slots" waiting to be filled by those with the requisite skill. Rather, they were slots requiring certain masculine qualities and capacities.

CONTINUITY OR CHANGE?

Those scholars who emphasize change in women's roles in the drug economy with the advent of crack cocaine are correct to point out the *possibilities* that an expanded drug economy might have offered women. Where they err, we think, is in claiming that such "new opportunities" were in fact made available to a significant proportion of women. Granted, there were temporary opportunities for women to participate in street-level drug distribution, but they were irregular and short-lived and did not alter male employers' perceptions of women as unreliable, untrustworthy, and incapable of demonstrating an effective capacity for violence.

The only consistently available option for women's income generation was sex work. However, the conditions of street-level sex work have been adversely affected by shifts in social and economic relations produced by widespread crack consumption in low-income neighborhoods like Bushwick. The market became flooded with novice sex workers, the going rates for sexual transactions decreased, and "deviant" sexual expectations by dates increased, as did the levels of violence and victimization (Maher and Curtis, 1992). Ironically, the sting in the tail of the recent crack-fueled expansion of street-level drug markets has been a substantial reduction in the earning capacities of street-level sex workers.

Of the four elements that have been used to explain women's restricted involvement in drug economies of the past, we see evidence of change in two: a diminishing of women's access to drug-selling roles through boyfriends or husbands, especially when drug markets are highly structured and kin based, and decreased economic returns for street-level sex work. Because few Bushwick women had stable households or cared for children, we cannot comment on changes (if any) in discretionary time. Underworld institutionalized sexism was the most powerful element shaping the Bushwick women's experiences in the drug economy; it inhibited their access to drug business work roles and effectively foreclosed their ability to participate as higher-level distributors. For that most crucial element, we find no change from previous decades.

How can we reconcile our findings with those of researchers who say that the crack cocaine economy has facilitated "new opportunities" for women or "new ways for women to escape their limited roles, statuses and incomes [compared to] previous eras" (Fagan, 1994, p. 210)? One answer is that study samples differ: Compared to Fagan's sample, for example, our sample of Bushwick women contained a somewhat higher share of Latinas, whose economic circumstances were more marginal than those of the women in Central Harlem and Washington Heights. It is also possible that Latino-controlled drug markets are more restrictive of women's participation than, say, those controlled by African-Americans. Those who have studied drug use and dealing in Puerto Rican (Glick, 1990) and Chicano (Moore, 1990) communities suggest that "deviant women" may be less tolerated and more ostracized than their male counterparts. For Bushwick, it would be difficult to disentangle the joint influences of a male-dominated and Dominican-controlled drug market on women's participation. While seven women (16%) engaged in street-level sales during the study period, all women—whether Latina, African-American, or European-American—were denied access to higher levels of the drug business.

We lack research on how racial-ethnic relations structure women's participation in drug markets. Fagan's (1994, pp. 200–202) comparison of Central Harlem and Washington Heights indicates that a lower proportion of women in Central Harlem (28%) than in Washington Heights (44%) reported being involved in drug selling; similar proportions (about 16%) were involved in group selling, however. While Fagan noted that drug markets in Washington Heights were Latino-controlled, he did not discuss the organization or ethnic composition of drug markets in Central Harlem. His study would appear to challenge any clear links between "Latino culture"—or the Latina share of women studied—and greater restrictions on women's roles compared to other racial-ethnic groups.

While disparate images of women in the drug economy may result from differences in study samples (including racial-ethnic variation in drug market organization, neighborhood-level variation, and when the study was conducted), a researcher's methods and theories are also crucial. For methods, virtually all U.S. studies of women drug users have employed one-time interviews. The ethnographic approach used in this study reveals that in the absence of a temporal frame and observational data, interviews may provide an incomplete and inaccurate picture. For example, in initial interviews with the larger group of Brookyn women, we found that when women were asked about sources of income, it was more socially desirable for them to say that it came from drug selling or other kinds of crime than from crack-related prostitution (Maher, in press). The one-time interview also misses the changing and fluid nature of relations in the informal economy. For example, for a short period there was a perception in Bushwick that "new opportunities" existed for women to sell crack. That perception faded as it became clear that managers and owners were "using" women to evade the constraints imposed on them by law enforcement and police search practices. Ethnographic approaches can offer a more dynamic contexualized picture of women's lawbreaking. While such approaches are relatively numerous in the study of adolescent and adult men in the United States (e.g., Anderson, 1990; Bourgois, 1989; Sullivan, 1989; Sullivan, 1989), they are rarely utilized in the study of women and girls.

For theory, women lawbreakers are rarely studied as members of social networks or as participants in collective or group-based activity (see also Steffensmeier and Terry, 1986). Nor have women been viewed as economic actors in illegal markets governed by occupational norms and workplace cultures (Maher, 1996).

Those making a general claim about "women's emancipation" in the current drug economy ignore the obdurateness of a gender-stratified labor market and associated beliefs and practices that maintain it. Those making the more restricted claim that male-dominated street networks and market processes have weakened, thus allowing entry points for women, need to offer proof for that claim. We would expect to see variation in women's roles, and we would not say that Bushwick represents the general case. However, assertions of women's changing and improved position in the drug economy have not been well proved. Nor are they grounded in theories of how work, including illegal work, is conditioned by relations of gender, race-ethnicity, and sexuality (see, e.g., Daly, 1993; Game and Pringle, 1983; Kanter, 1977; Messerschmidt, 1993; Simpson and Elis, 1995).

Our findings suggest that the advent of crack cocaine and the concomitant expansion of the drug economy cannot be viewed as emancipatory for women drug users. To the extent that "new opportunities" in drug distribution and sales were realized in Bushwick and the wider Brooklyn sample, they were realized by men. Women were confined to an increasingly harsh economic periphery. Not only did the promised opportunities fail to materialize, but the expanding crack market served to deteriorate the conditions of street-level sex work, a labor market which has historically provided a relatively stable source of income for women drug users.

REFERENCES

Adler, P. A. (1985). *Wheeling and Dealing: An Ethnography of an Upper-Level Drug Dealing and Smuggling Community.* New York: Columbia University Press.

Anderson, E. (1990). *Streetwise: Race, Class and Change in an Urban Community.* Chicago: University of Chicago Press.

Anglin, M. D., and Hser, Y.-I. (1987). Addicted women and crime. *Criminology, 25,* 359–397.

Auld, J., Dorn, N., and South, N. (1986). Irregular work, irregular pleasures: Heroin in the 1980s. In R. Matthews and J. Young (Eds.), *Confronting Crime.* London: Sage.

Baskin, D., Sommers, I., and Fagan, J. (1993). The political economy of violent female street crime. *Fordham Urban Law Journal, 20,* 401–407.

Biernacki, P. (1979). Junkie work, "hustles," and social status among heroin addicts. *Journal of Drug Issues, 9,* 535–549.

Bourgois, P. (1989). In search of Horatio Alger: Culture and ideology in the crack economy. *Contemporary Drug Problems, 16,* 619–649.

Bourgois, P. (1995). *In Search of Respect: Selling Crack in El Barrio.* New York: Cambridge University Press.

Bourgois, P., and Dunlap, E. (1993). Exorcising sex-for-crack: An ethnographic perspective from Harlem. In M. S. Ratner (Eds.), *Crack Pipe as Pimp: An Ethnographic Investigation of Sex-for-Crack Exchanges.* New York: Lexington Books.

Box, S. (1983). *Power, Crime and Mystification.* London: Tavistock.

Bureau of the Census. (1990). *Brooklyn in Touch.* Washington, DC: U.S. Government Printing Office.

Campbell, A. (1993) *Out of Control: Men, Women, and Aggression.* London: Pandora.

Covington, J. (1985). Gender differences in criminality among heroin users. *Journal of Research in Crime and Delinquency, 22,* 329–354.

Curtis, R., and Maher, L. (in press). Highly structured crack markets in the southside of Williamsburg, Brooklyn. In J. Fagan (Ed.), *The Ecology of Crime and Drug Use in Inner Cities.* New York: Social Science Research Council.

Curtis, R., and Sviridoff, M. (1994). The social organization of street-level drug markets and its impact on the displacement effect. In R. P. McNamara (Ed.), *Crime Displacement: The Other Side of Prevention.* East Rockaway, NY: Cummings and Hathaway.

Curtis, R., Friedman, S. R., Neaigus, A., Jose, B., Goldstein, M., and Ildefonso, G. (1995). Street-level drug markets: Network structure and HIV risk. *Social Networks, 17,* 229–249.

Daly, K. (1993). Class-race-gender: Sloganeering in search of meaning. *Social Justice, 20,* 56–71.

Des Jarlais, D. C., Friedman, S. R., and Strug, D. (1986). AIDS and needle sharing within the IV drug use subculture. In D. A. Feldman and T. M. Johnson (Eds.), *The Social Dimensions of AIDS: Methods and Theory.* New York: Praeger.

Dunlap, E., and Johnson, B. D. (1992). Who they are and what they do: Female crack dealers in New York City. Paper presented at the Annual Meeting of the American Society of Criminology, New Orleans, November.

Fagan, J. (1994). Women and drugs revisited: Female participation in the cocaine economy. *Journal of Drug Issues, 24,* 179–225.

File, K. N. (1976). Sex roles and street roles. *International Journal of the Addictions, 11,* 263–268.

File, K. N., McCahill, T. W., and Savitz, L. D. (1974). Narcotics involvement and female criminality. *Addictive Diseases: An International Journal, 1,* 177–188.

Game, A., and Pringle, R. (1983). *Gender at Work.* Sydney: George Allen and Unwin.

Goldstein, P. J. (1979). *Prostitution and Drugs.* Lexington, MA: Lexington Books.

Glick, R. (1990). Survival, income, and status: Drug dealing in the Chicago Puerto Rican community. In R. Glick and J. Moore (Eds.), *Drugs in Hispanic Communities.* New Brunswick, NJ: Rutgers University Press.

Hagedorn, J. M. (1994). Homeboys, dope fiends, legits, and new jacks. *Criminology, 32,* 197–219.

Hamid, A. (1990). The political economy of crack-related violence. *Contemporary Drug Problems, 17,* 31–78.

Hamid, A. (1991). From ganja to crack: Caribbean participation in the underground economy in Brooklyn, 1976–1986. Part 2, Establishment of the cocaine (and crack) economy. *International Journal of the Addictions, 26,* 729–738.

Hamid, A. (1992). The developmental cycle of a drug epidemic: The cocaine smoking epidemic of 1981–1991. *Journal of Psychoactive Drugs, 24,* 337–348.

Hay, D. (1975). Property, authority, and the criminal law. In D. Hay, P. Linebaugh, J. G. Rule, E. P. Thompson, and C. Winslow (Eds.), *Albion's Fatal Tree.* London: Allen Lane.

Hennig, M. (1970). Career Development for Women Executives. Ph.D. dissertation, Harvard University, Cambridge, MA.

Hser, Y.-I., Anglin, M. D., and Booth, M. W. (1987). Sex differences in addict careers, Part 3, Addiction. *American Journal of Drug and Alcohol Abuse, 13,* 231–251.

Hunt, D. (1990). Drugs and consensual crimes: Drug dealing and prostitution. In M. Tonry and J. Q. Wilson (Eds.), *Drugs and Crime, Crime and Justice, Vol. 13.* Chicago: University of Chicago Press.

Inciardi, J. A., and Pottieger, A. E. (1986). Drug use and crime among two cohorts of women narcotics users: An empirical assessment. *Journal of Drug Issues, 16,* 91–106.

Inciardi, J. A., Lockwood, D., and Pottieger, A. E. (1993). *Women and Crack Cocaine.* New York: Macmillan.

James, J. (1976). Prostitution and addiction: An interdisciplinary approach. *Addictive Diseases: An International Journal, 2,* 601–618.

Johnson, B. D., Goldstein, P. J., Preble, E., Schmeidler, J., Lipton, D. S., Spunt, B., and Miller, T. (1985). *Taking Care of Business: The Economics of Crime by Heroin Abusers.* Lexington, MA: Lexington Books.

Johnson, B. D., Williams, T., Die, K., and Sanabria, H. (1990). Drug abuse and the inner city: Impact on hard drug users and the community. In M. Tonry and J. Q. Wilson (Eds.), *Drugs and Crime. Crime and Justice, Vol. 13.* Chicago: University of Chicago Press.

Johnson, B. D., Hamid, A., and Sanabria, H. (1992). Emerging models of crack distribution. In T. M. Mieczkowski (Ed.), *Drugs and Crime: A Reader.* Boston: Allyn and Bacon.

Johnson, B. D., Natarajan, M., Dunlap, E., and Elmoghazy, E. (1994). Crack abusers and noncrack abusers: Profiles of drug use, drug sales, and nondrug criminality. *Journal of Drug Issues, 24,* 117–141.

Kanter, R. M. (1977). *Men and Women of the Corporation.* New York: Basic Books.

Kanter, R. M. (1981). Women and the structure of organizations: Explorations in theory and behavior. In O. Grusky and G. A. Miller (Eds.), *The Sociology of Organizations: Basic Studies,* 2d ed. New York: The Free Press.

Katz, J. (1988). *Seductions of Crime: Moral and Sensual Attractions of Doing Evil.* New York: Basic Books.

Koester, S., and Schwartz, J. (1993). Crack, gangs, sex, and powerlessness: A view from Denver. In M. S. Ratner (Ed.), *Crack Pipe as Pimp: An Ethnographic Investigation of Sex-for-Crack Exchanges.* New York: Lexington Books.

Maher, L. (in press). *Making It at the Margins: Gender, Race and Work in a Street-Level Drug Economy.* Oxford: Oxford University Press.

Maher, L. (1996). Hidden in the light: Discrimination and occupational norms among crack using street-level sex-workers. *Journal of Drug Issues, 26(1),* 145–175.

Maher, L., and Curtis, R. (1992). Women on the edge of crime: Crack cocaine and the changing contexts of street-level sex work in New York City. *Crime, Law, and Social Change, 18,* 221–258.

Maher, L., Dunlap, E., Johnson, B. D., and Hamid, A. (1996). Gender, power and alternative living arrangements in the inner-city crack culture. *Journal of Research in Crime and Delinquency, 33,* 181–205.

Messerschmidt, J. D. (1993). *Masculinities and Crime.* Lanham, MD: Rowman and Littlefield.

Mieczkowski, T. (1986). Geeking up and throwing down: Heroin street life in Detroit. *Criminology, 24,* 645–666.

Mieczkowski, T. (1990). Crack dealing on the street: An exploration of the YBI hypothesis and the Detroit crack trade. Paper presented at the Annual Meeting of the American Society of Criminology, Baltimore, November.

Mieczkowski, T. (1994). The experiences of women who sell crack: Some descriptive data from the Detroit crack ethnography project. *Journal of Drug Issues, 24,* 227–248.

Moore, J. W. (1990). Mexican American women addicts: The influence of family background. In R. Glick and J. Moore (Eds.), *Drugs in Hispanic Communities* New Brunswick, NJ: Rutgers University Press.

Morgan, P., and Joe, K. (1994). Uncharted terrains: Contexts of experience among women in the illicit drug economy. Paper presented at the Women and Drugs National Conference, Sydney, November.

Murphy, S., and Waldorf, D. (1991). Kickin' down to the street doc: Shooting galleries in the San Francisco Bay area. *Contemporary Drug Problems, 18,* 9–29.

Murphy, S., Waldorf, D., and Reinarman, C. (1991). Drifting into dealing: Becoming a cocaine seller. *Qualitative Sociology, 13,* 321–343.

Padilla, F. M. (1992). *The Gang as an American Enterprise.* New Brunswick, NJ: Rutgers University Press.

Pettiway, L. E. (1987). Participation in crime partnerships by female drug users: The effects of domestic arrangements, drug use, and criminal involvement. *Criminology, 25,* 741–766.

Reuter, P., MacCoun, R., and Murphy, P. (1990). *Money from Crime: A Study of the Economics of Drug Dealing in Washington, D.C.* Santa Monica, CA: Rand Corporation.

Rosenbaum, M. (1981). *Women on Heroin.* New Brunswick, NJ: Rutgers University Press.

Simpson, S. S., and Elis, L. (1995). Doing gender. Sorting out the caste and crime conundrum. *Criminology, 33,* 47–81.

Skolnick, J. H. (1989). The Social Structure of Street Drug Dealing. Report to the State of California Bureau of Criminal Statistics and Special Services. Sacramento: State of California Executive Office.

Smithberg, N., and Westermeyer, J. (1985). White dragon pearl syndrome: A female pattern of drug dependence. *American Journal of Drug and Alcohol Abuse, 11,* 199–207.

Spalter-Roth, R. M. (1988). The sexual political economy of street vending in Washington, D.C. In G. Clark (Ed.), *Traders Versus the State: Anthropological Approaches to Unofficial Economies.* Boulder, CO: Westview Press.

Steffensmeier, D. (1983). Organization properties and sex-segregation in the underworld: Building a sociological theory of sex differences in crime. *Social Forces, 61,* 1010–1032.

Steffensmeier, D. J., and Terry, R. M. (1986). Institutional sexism in the underworld: A view from the inside. *Sociological Inquiry, 56,* 304–323.

Sullivan, M. L. (1989). *Getting Paid: Youth Crime and Work in the Inner City.* Ithaca, NY: Cornell University Press.

Sutter, A. G. (1966). The world of the righteous dope fiend. *Issues in Criminology, 2,* 177–222.

Taylor, A. (1993). *Women Drug Users: An Ethnography of a Female Injecting Community.* Oxford: Clarendon Press.

Taylor, C. S. (1990). *Dangerous Society.* East Lansing: Michigan State University Press.

Taylor, C. S. (1993). *Girls, Gangs, Women and Drugs.* East Lansing: Michigan State University Press.

Waldorf, D., Reinarman, C., and Murphy, S. (1991). *Cocaine Changes: The Experience of Using and Quitting.* Philadelphia, PA: Temple University Press.

Waterston, A. (1993). *Street Addicts in the Political Economy.* Philadelphia, PA: Temple University Press.

Whyte, W. F. (1943). *Street Corner Society.* Chicago: University of Chicago Press.

Williams, T. (1989). *The Cocaine Kids.* Reading, MA: Addison-Wesley.

Williams, T. (1992). *Crackhouse: Notes from the End of the Line.* New York: Addison-Wesley.

Wilson, N. K. (1993). Stealing and dealing: The drug war and gendered criminal opportunity. In C. C. Culliver (Ed.), *Female Criminality: The State of the Art.* New York: Garland Publishing.

10

The Lives of Incarcerated Women: Violence, Substance Abuse, and at Risk for HIV

CATHERINE INGRAM FOGEL

MICHAEL BELYEA

ABSTRACT

High rates of human immunodeficiency virus (HIV) infection and sexually transmitted diseases (STDs) are seen in women prisoners. These high rates may be related to the nature of their lives, which may include violence, substance abuse, promiscuity, prostitution, and exchange of sex for drugs—all of which increase their risk for acquiring HIV. The purpose of this study was to examine the HIV-related risk behaviors and protective practices of women prisoners in a rural southern state and factors related to these behaviors. The sample included 57 women incarcerated in a medium-to-maximum security prison. Key findings included high rates of substance abuse, extensive past and current violent experiences including sexual abuse, high percentage of multiple partners, and low use of condoms. Additionally, women in this sample did not perceive themselves to be at risk for HIV infection. Practical suggestions for reducing the HIV risks of incarcerated women are offered.

More than 63,000 women are currently in state and federal prisons, and women are the fastest growing segment of incarcerated persons today (Gilliard and Beck, 1996). Although women are a relatively small fraction of the prison and jail population nationally (6% and 9%, respectively), since 1980 the female prison population has increased by more than 300% (National Women's Law Center, 1995). High rates of human immunodeficiency virus (HIV) infection and sexually transmitted diseases (STDs) are seen in women prisoners (Hammett, Harrold, Gross, and Epstein, 1994; Holmes et al., 1993). These high rates may be related to the nature of their lives, which may include violence, substance abuse, promiscuity, prostitution, and exchange of sex for drugs—all of which increase their risk for acquiring HIV. A few studies have described certain drug- and sex-related risky behaviors of women incarcerated in urban areas—the traditional center of high levels of HIV infection (Bond and Semann, 1996; Magura, Kang, Shapiro, and O'Day, 1993; Schilling et al., 1994; Stevens et al., 1995). No studies have documented substance abuse, violence, and risky sexual behaviors among women prisoners in rural areas or the South, where levels of HIV infection are growing and STD rates are highest. The purpose of this study was to examine the HIV-related risk behaviors and protective practices of women prisoners in a rural, southern state and factors related to these behaviors.

BACKGROUND

STDs are common in prison and jail populations (Fogel, 1991; Fogel and Belyea, 1996; Holmes et al., 1993), and HIV seropositive rates among incarcerated women range from 3% to 35%. Rates are higher among incarcerated women with histories of intravenous drug use (DeGroot, Hammett, and Scheib, 1996; Hankins et al., 1994). HIV seroprevalence rates are often higher in female inmates (especially those younger than age 25) than in male inmates (Hammett et al., 1994). Indeed, acquired immune deficiency syndrome (AIDS) is now the leading cause of death among female prisoners (El-Bassel et al., 1995).

Female inmates are often poorly educated, economically disadvantaged, and members of ethnic minorities. Typically, they are between the ages of 25 and 34 years and are single. In 1991, nearly one in three women was serving a sentence for a drug-related offense, and one in four women reported committing the crime leading to their current incarceration in order to pay for drugs. Furthermore, almost half of all women prisoners report being under the influence of drugs or alcohol at the time of their offenses (Snell, 1994). Drug and/or alcohol addiction is common among incarcerated women. More than 50% of all women prisoners report using drugs in the month prior to their arrest (Snell, 1994). The most commonly used drug was cocaine or crack, followed by alcohol and heroin.

Violence is a common experience for incarcerated women often beginning early in life from someone close to them (Human Rights Watch, 1996). More than 40% of women in state prisons have been physically or sexually abused at least once in their lives (Snell and Martin, 1992). Stevens and colleagues (1995) found that women prisoners who had been sexually abused were 2.5 times more likely to engage in HIV-risk behaviors than were incarcerated women without histories of sexual abuse.

Few studies have examined histories of unprotected sexual intercourse among women who are incarcerated. However, they appear to use condoms infrequently (El-Bassel et al., 1995; Schilling et al., 1994), and when they do use condoms, the use is more frequent with casual or commercial (sex for pay) partners than with regular partners (El-Bassel et al., 1995; Schilling et al., 1994). Though information is limited about the number of sexual partners of women prior to their incarceration, many have reported multiple partners (El-Bassel et al., 1995; Magura et al., 1993). Furthermore, these partners were likely to be injection drug users and to engage in HIV risk behaviors.

METHODOLOGY

A descriptive survey design was used to examine and quantify STD/HIV knowledge, attitudes, perceived risk, risky sexual behaviors, substance abuse, violence experiences, and sexual protective practices of incarcerated women.

Setting

The study was conducted at a major correctional facility for women located in a southern state. The institution, a maximum-security prison, is one of the largest for women in the United States. At the time of the study (1997), it was the incarceration site for the majority of the state's female inmates, although many of this group do not require maximum-security precautions. When the study was conducted, it housed more than 1,100 women.

Sample

The sample included 57 newly incarcerated women who were interviewed within 4 weeks of initial imprisonment. Inclusion criteria were ability to provide oral and written consent and previous/anticipated heterosexual behavior. Prison admission logs were reviewed to compile a list of women who had been incarcerated within the previous 4 weeks. Every third name on these lists was approached to participate in the study. No potential participant refused to participate. Typically, respondents in this study were poorly educated, young women of color who were single heads of household. The majority (61%) identified themselves as women of color, with 56% describing themselves as African American and 37% as White. Although the age of the respondents ranged from 18 to 46 years, women were typically in their late 20s to early 30s ($M = 31.9$ years, $SD = 6.9$). The mean educational level of the sample was 10.7 years ($SD = 1.8$, range 6 to 14). Two thirds of the women had not completed high school and 10% reported less than an eighth-grade education. Although only 12% were currently married, 70% of the respondents stated they had a primary sexual partner. At the time of their arrest, the majority (65%) of respondents reported working in unskilled, manual, or service jobs such as a factory worker, nurse's aid, or waitress. More than one quarter were unemployed.

At the time of their arrest, most respondents (95%) were sexually active with men and slightly more than 10% reported bisexual activity. The majority (86%) engaged in vaginal intercourse and almost half (46%) reported oral-genital sexual activity. Only one woman stated she had had anal intercourse.

Procedure

The Institutional Review Boards of the university with which the authors were affiliated and the state Department of Corrections approved the study. The study was described to potential participants, they were asked to participate, and, if they agreed, were read the consent form and given the opportunity to ask questions. They were assured that failure to participate in the study would not affect their health care or status at the facility.

The participants were interviewed within the first month of their incarceration by the first author or trained research assistant. Because of the low literacy of this population, the structured interview and standard questionnaires were read to all respondents to maximize comprehension and reliability. To ensure confidentiality for the inmates and to maximize reliability and thoroughness of responses, all interviews were conducted in a private room with the door closed. At no time were correction officers, other prison personnel, or other inmates present.

Measurement

Instruments included measures to assess knowledge of HIV/STDs, perceived risk, sexual risk behaviors and protective practices, violence experiences, use/abuse of substances, and attitudes toward condoms.

Knowledge of STD/HIV was assessed by true/false statements drawn from items used to measure knowledge of AIDS (Kinnick et al., 1989; O'Leary, Goodhart, Jemmott, and Boccher-Lattimore, 1992). Items used to measure perceived risk were developed using recommendations from Ajzen and Fishbein (1980).

Several tools were used to assess respondents' risk behaviors and protective practices. The Dilorio Safe Sex Behavior Questionnaire (SSBQ) (Dilorio, Parsons, Lehr, Adame, and Carlone, 1993) measures women's experiences with protective practices. This 27-item questionnaire, scored on a 4-point Likert-type scale (1 = *never*, 4 = *always*), includes items such as "I insist on condom intercourse when I have sexual intercourse," and "I use cocaine or other drugs prior to or during sexual intercourse." The instrument has a reported total scale reliability of 0.92. Construct validity has been established by correlating the SSBQ with measures of general assertiveness and general risk taking (Dilorio et al., 1993). Women also were asked about specific sexual activities and behaviors (e.g., unprotected vaginal intercourse, anal intercourse, oral-genital intercourse)

with different types of partners (e.g., primary, casual), for many time periods (e.g., at time of incarceration, prior week, month, 3 months, 1 year). In addition, women were asked to report their use of alcohol and drugs in the 30 days, 6 months, 1 year, and 5 years prior to incarceration.

Attitudes toward protective practices in general were assessed using the Barriers to Sexual Protective Practices Scale (BSPPS). Using health belief model (HBM) definitions, Gilelen and colleagues (1994) developed this scale to assess low-income, predominantly minority women's perceived barriers to protective sexual practices. The scale includes items such as "Protecting yourself against AIDS would be hard given your lifestyle," and "If you tried to protect yourself from AIDS, it would be a hassle." Respondents use a 5-point Likert-type scale to indicate the strength of agreement with each item (1 = *strongly agree* to 5 = *strongly disagree*). Cronbach's alpha for this scale was 0.68. The authors state that the scale appears to have substantial face validity in relation to the intended meaning of the HBM construct. In addition, items such as "My partner told me he was HIV negative," and "I was afraid he would think I didn't trust him" were added to tap other attitudes our previous pilot work with women prisoners had suggested were relevant.

Attitudes toward condoms were assessed by the Attitudes Toward Condoms Scale (ATCS) (Jemmott and Jemmott, 1991) and by items developed by the researcher based on a previous qualitative study of women prisoners' high-risk practices. The ATCS asks respondents to indicate on a 7-point scale (1 = *disagree strongly* to 7 = *agree strongly*) the extent to which they agree with statements such as "Condoms cost too much money," "It's too much trouble to carry a condom around," and "Sex doesn't feel as good when you use a condom." No psychometric properties were reported for this scale. An example of items added from our previous work is the statement, "It is not safe to carry condoms when tricking."

Respondents' violence history and current experiences of violence were measured by items adapted from questions used to screen women seeking health care for abuse and recommended to screen women for violence in their lives (McFarlane, Parker, Soeken, and Bullock, 1992). Specific questions about physical, emotional, and sexual abuse were asked. In addition, composite variables to measure presence/absence of abuse and to quantify the extent of violence experienced (0 = *no abuse* to 4 = *experienced violence of all types*) were constructed.

In addition to the structured interview items and standard questionnaires, women were encouraged to comment on the questions and to provide additional information if they wished.

Data Analysis

Frequency distributions and univariate descriptive statistics were computed for all variables. Chi-square tests, *t* tests and bivariate correlations were used to explore relationships between variables. Significance level was set at the customary 0.05.

FINDINGS

Violence Experiences

Almost all women (90%) had experienced some form of violence from partners. The number of physical abuse incidences in the preceding year ranged from 0 to 50 with a median of 1. During their lifetime, 70% of the women reported having been physically abused by a partner or someone important to them, and 49% reported being forced to have sex with a partner, which could have included being raped. Of the respondents, 25% stated that they were afraid of their current partner. In addition, nine women volunteered that they had been abused by parents and other family members and five disclosed that they had been raped.

Substance Abuse

Women in this sample reported high levels of substance abuse. In the 3 months prior to incarceration, three quarters of respondents reported drinking on a regular basis. Furthermore, more than 20% drank up to 4 days a week and almost one third (32%) drank nearly every day. Almost 45% had more than four drinks every time they drank. Most (86%) women reported using some form of drugs in the 3 months before imprisonment. Most commonly, the women used crack (61%) and marijuana (54%); furthermore, 25% reported injecting drugs, usually heroin. Almost 20% abused prescription drugs such as percocet and other pain relief medications. More than 70% of the women reported using drugs before sex or had sex while "high," but three women said that getting high protected them because they lost their interest in sex with drug use.

Risky Sexual Behaviors

Women reported a variety of risky sexual behaviors prior to coming to prison. Although two thirds of the women reported 1 partner at the time of their incarceration, more than 10% had 3 or more current partners. Although almost half reported only 1 partner in the month preceding imprisonment, the number of partners ranged up to 30. During the year prior to imprisonment, women had a median of 2 partners (range 0 to 50). Almost two thirds (65%) had 3 or more partners, and 21% reported 10 or more partners in the year prior to imprisonment. One woman stated that she had had so many sexual partners that "I can't count them." When asked about sexual activity with their primary partner in the month prior to incarceration, 72% reported unprotected vaginal sex every time. Additionally, almost half of the women reported oral-genital sexual activity without protection. The one woman who had reported anal sexual activity did not use a condom. More than half (53%) reported having sex with secondary or casual partners in the month prior to lock-up, and the majority (71%) of these encounters were unprotected. Almost all of the women (97%) reported having had sex with an intravenous drug user at some time.

Knowledge of Protective Practices

For women to enact protective practices, they must first label their behavior as risky. Prerequisites to labeling one's behavior as risky are accurate STD/HIV knowledge and a personal perception of risk. Although all women in the study prison were required to attend an educational session on HIV at admission to prison, these women showed a lack of knowledge of HIV/STDs. The majority knew that unprotected sexual activity increased the likelihood of contracting HIV (81%) and that having more sexual partners increased risk (88%); yet almost a third (30%) believed that there was no need for protection if one of the partners had an STD, and more than one third did not know or were unsure if latex condoms were best for preventing sexually transmitted diseases. More than two thirds (70%) did not know that using condoms with spermicides decreased a woman's chances of contracting HIV. Somewhat less than half (42%) believed that animal skin condoms afforded the best protection against STDs.

Perception of Risk

The majority of women perceived themselves to have little or no risk for contacting HIV (57%) or an STD (56%) after their release from prison. A few stated that they did not plan to be sexually active (7%, *n* = 4) or would become monogamous (5%, *n* = 3) after their release. Two women volunteered that they were HIV-positive and thus were not worried about contracting any other diseases. Nevertheless, most women said that contracting AIDS or an STD would be very serious for them.

Barriers to Protective Practices

Three quarters of the women did not believe using sexual protective practices would decrease the quality of their sexual experiences and only a few said their lifestyle (e.g., drug use, prostitution) prevented the use of protective practices (16%), or that they felt protecting oneself was a hassle (12%). Some women made comments about condoms, saying that "sex ain't so bad, feels no different" or they hated using condoms because of the latex odor.

Women who reported sexual activity without condoms were asked about reasons why this occurred (see Table 1). The most common reasons reported were an agreement to mutual monogamy (91%), previous unprotected sexual activity (87%), and being in love (85%). Women also assumed that their partner(s) did not want to use condoms (78%), that not using a condom would please their partner (75%), or that their partner would ask if they wanted to use a condom (63%). Several women volunteered that they had never discussed condom use with partners. Almost two thirds stated that alcohol/drug use was the reason for not using a condom. Some women reported being afraid that their partners would not trust them (30%), would leave them (21%), would hurt them (16%), or would force them to have sex without a condom (18%). Some women stated that when they had been with the same partner for several years they saw no need for condoms; three women specifically noted that they had another method of birth control. Similar comments were made by low-income community women and women prisoners participating in focus groups exploring their risky behaviors and protective practices (Fogel, 1999). Three women stated that they had never used condoms and one commented that it was "the man's responsibility."

TABLE 1 Reasons Why Women Did Not Use Condoms

REASON	PERCENTAGE	NUMBER/TOTAL RESPONDENTS[a]
Agree to mutual monogamy	91.3	42/46
Previous unprotected sex	87.2	41/47
Was in love	85.1	40/47
Both had same HIV status	79.1	34/43
Partner refused to use one	78.0	32/41
Feels better without condom	77.8	35/45
Thought it would please partner	75.0	33/44
Thought once without was okay	68.2	30/44
Turned on/did not want to stop	63.4	26/41
Assumed partner would ask	63.0	29/46
Partner agreed not to come	62.5	25/40
Using alcohol/drugs	61.4	27/44
No condoms available	56.4	22/39
Afraid partner would think she did not trust him	53.0	24/45
Assumed partner would not ejaculate	47.5	19/40
Partner said he was HIV negative	45.5	20/45
Afraid partner would refuse to have sex if insisted on condom	44.7	17/36
Afraid partner would not trust her	29.5	13/44
Afraid partner would leave	20.9	9/43
Afraid to bring up topic	19.6	9/46
Embarrassed to discuss condoms	19.6	9/46
Condoms cause loss of erection	19.5	9/41
Afraid partner would force her	18.2	8/44
Afraid partner would hit/hurt her	16.3	7/43
Tired of having safe sex	13.3	6/45

[a]Number of respondents varies with response; total sample size was 57.

Factors Influencing Risky Behaviors

To determine if there were significant differences in experiences of violence, substance abuse, and risky sexual behaviors among women prisoners, additional analyses were performed. These analyses revealed some significant differences. Women who reported being abused were more often substance abusers (Fisher's Exact Test, $p = 0.031$), and had sex without a condom with secondary partners (Fisher's Exact Test, $p = 0.024$). Furthermore, women who reported a history of abuse had significantly more current ($t = 2.83$, $p = 0.01$) and past ($t = 2.33$, $p = 0.02$) sexual partners. Women who reported a history of sexual abuse also reported significantly more current ($t = 2.23$, $p = 0.03$) and past ($t = 1.99$, $p = 0.05$) sexual partners. In addition, women who were substance abusers reported significantly more current ($t = 3.34$, $p = 0.02$) and past sexual partners ($t = 4.18$, $p = 0.0001$).

DISCUSSION

Women are the fastest growing prison population in the United States and are disproportionately affected by the HIV epidemic. Findings from this study demonstrate that women incarcerated in one southern state from predominately rural areas are at high risk for HIV infection. The sociodemographic characteristics of the study sample closely mirror those of women in prisons and jails throughout the United States. For example, age (study median age of 32 vs. national median age of 30) and educational level (two thirds of our sample had not completed high school compared with 50% nationally) were quite similar (U.S. Department of Justice, 1992). The racial composition of study sample differed somewhat from the racial composition of U.S. women's prisons in that the sample had more African American women (54% vs. 43% nationally) and far fewer Latinos (2% vs. 38% nationally); the proportion of White women was similar (36% in study sample vs. 38% nationally).

The types of risky sexual behaviors and substance abuse reported by the respondents in this study are consistent with other studies of incarcerated women (Bond and Semann, 1996; Magura et al., 1993; Schilling et al., 1994; Stevens et al., 1995). For example, in their study of incarcerated women in New York City, Schilling and associates (1994) reported that their sample had a history of crack cocaine use in the 30 days prior to incarceration almost identical to that reported by our respondents (61.5% vs. 61.4%). Similarly, Magura and colleagues (1993) reported that

more than half of their participants never used condoms during vaginal sex, a percentage similar to that reported by the study sample. In contrast, the percentage of injection drug use reported by women in this study was lower than that reported in other studies (25% vs. 41% by Schilling et al., and 35% by Bond and Semann). In our study, 49% reported a history of sexual abuse, a finding similar to that of Bond and Semann (50%) and higher than the 33% reported in a study of women in jails nationwide. Similarly, the 70% physical abuse reported by respondents in this study is remarkably similar to the 72% reported by Bond and Semann in their sample of women in an urban jail.

Slightly more than one third of the women in this study considered themselves to be at high risk for getting AIDS or STDs. Although this percentage is high when compared with general population studies (Prohaska, Albrecht, Levy, Sugrue, and Kim, 1990) and higher than adult injection drug users who were arrested (Henson, Longshore, Kowalewski, Anglin, and Annon, 1998), when the reported rates of sexual and drug use risks are considered, this self-assessment appears inaccurate and overly optimistic. Clearly, incarcerated women need assistance in labeling their behaviors as risky to make a commitment to enact protective practices.

This study had methodological limitations. First, it was conducted at only one correctional facility, thus limiting the extent of generalizability of results to women prisoners in general. Second, self-report data may reflect a bias toward social desirability, particularly in the reports on sexual behavior rather than drug use (Kleyn, Schwebke, and Holmes, 1993; Schilling et al., 1994). This could result in the magnitude of sexual risk behaviors being greater than what was reported. It should be noted that women were willing to report high-risk activities, even those that were illegal suggesting that they were comfortable discussing sexual- and drug-related behaviors and they had nothing to gain by lying to the researchers. Other limitations were the use of a convenience sample and small sample size.

CLINICAL IMPLICATIONS

Despite the high risk of HIV/AIDS among incarcerated women and the likelihood that once released they will continue to be at risk and may in turn become reservoirs of infection for others (Institute of Medicine, 1997), the majority of prisons provide only minimal prevention programs consisting of group information sessions and/or videos (El-Bassel et al.,

1995; Stevens, 1993). Furthermore, many are at a teachable moment as they wish to change behavior and improve themselves prior to release (Fogel, 1990). This situation offers nurses, in general, and correctional health nurses, specifically, great challenges and opportunities to provide sorely-needed interventions to reduce HIV-related risk behaviors of incarcerated women. It is essential that these interventions be targeted to the special characteristics and needs of female inmates, and that they address the contexts in which they live. The extensive preincarceration substance abuse history of women in prison and its link to HIV infection necessitates that drug treatment and harm reduction be a component of any interventions offered to women prisoners. Women can be helped to identify drug-related risk behaviors and the need for drug abstinence or reduction, initiate preliminary drug treatment effort and be linked to community-based treatment opportunities for use upon release while still in prison.

Past and current experiences with violence, particularly sexual abuse, increase the likelihood of risky sexual behaviors and erode women's sense of self-efficacy to exercise control over sexual behaviors (Richie and Johnsen, 1996; Zeigler et al., 1991). Fear of retribution, including physical harm and loss of economic support, hampers women's efforts to enact sex- and drug-related protective practices (Fullilove, Fullilove, Haynes, and Gross, 1990; Mays and Cochran, 1988; Singer, 1995; Worth, 1989). Women in this study reported extensive abuse histories that must be considered when designing risk reduction interventions. Merely teaching women facts about STDs and HIV, how to use condoms, and correctly clean drug paraphernalia are inadequate when women are afraid they will be hurt or abused. Rather, women need an opportunity to develop successful sexual communication skills and to learn how to negotiate safer sex practices with partners.

Women who have lived with violence and abuse may also report symptoms of anxiety and depression (Trimpey, 1989). Depression, with its characteristic feelings of hopelessness, despair, and powerlessness, can interfere with a woman's ability to assume responsibility for changing behaviors that place her at risk (Weissman and Brown, 1995). Several studies have documented high rates of depression among incarcerated women (Fogel, 1991, 1993; Jordan, Schlenger, Fairbank, and Caddell, 1996; Singer, Bussey, Song, and Lunghofer, 1995). Incarcerated women also report feeling out of control, helpless, and powerless (Fogel, 1991, 1993; Fogel and Belyea, 1996). Thus, risk reduction interventions for incarcerated women must also address depression and hopelessness.

Women who have been incarcerated and who are often impoverished and drug using may have survival concerns that influence their ability to practice sex- and drug-related protection. The need to secure shelter, food, clothing, safety for self and children, and money may override any concerns about preventive health promotion and thus prevent women from changing risky sex behaviors (Nyamathi and Lewis, 1991; Stevens, 1993).

The sex- and drug-related risk factors and complex contexts in which women who have been incarcerated live require both immediate and long-term efforts. Successful interventions must begin in prison and extend beyond the correctional facility. Links to appropriate social agencies, support groups, and case management should be an integral component of prerelease planning and HIV risk-reduction interventions.

Efforts to reduce the spread of HIV among incarcerated women are limited by the small number of prevention programs targeting women prisoners. Yet, jails and prisons provide an excellent opportunity for risk-reduction interventions to populations at great risk for infection. This opportunity requires strong commitments of financial and human resources. Nursing is challenged to provide women prisoners with the education, counseling, and support they need to reduce their HIV risk.

REFERENCES

Aizen, I., and Fishbein, M. (1980). *Understanding attitudes and predicting social behavior.* Englewood Cliffs, NJ: Prentice Hall.

Bond, L., and Semann, S. (1996). At risk for HIV infection: Incarcerated women in a county jail in Philadelphia. *Women and Health, 24*(4), 27–45.

DeGroot, A. S., Hammett, T. M., and Scheib, R. G. (1996). Barriers to care of HIV-infected inmates: A public health concern. *The AIDS Reader, 6*(3), 78–87.

Dilorio, C., Parsons, M., Lehr, S., Adame, D., and Carlone, J. (1993). Measurement of safe sex behavior in adolescents and young adults. *Nursing Research, 41*, 203–208.

El-Bassel, N., Ivanoff, A., Schilling, R. F., Gilbert, L., Borne, D., and Chen, D-R. (1995). Preventing HIV/AIDS in drug-abusing incarcerated women through skill building and social support enhancement: Preliminary outcomes. *Social Work Research, 19*(3), 131–141.

Fogel, C. I. (1990). Evaluation of weight reduction interventions with incarcerated women. Unpublished raw data.

Fogel, C. I. (1991). Health problems and needs of incarcerated women. *Journal of Prison and Jail Health, 10*(1), 43–75.

Fogel, C. I. (1993). Hard time: The stressful nature of incarcerations. *Issues in Mental Health Nursing, 14,* 367–377.

Fogel, C. I. (1999, February). *Exploring incarcerated women's risky sexual behaviors and sexual protective practices.* Southern Nursing Research Society, Charleston, S.C.

Fogel, C. I., and Belyea, M. J. (1996). *Pregnant prisoners and their progeny.* American Nurses Foundation Final Report. Kansas City, MO.

Fullilove, M. T., Fullilove, R. E., Haynes, K., and Gross, S. (1990). Black women and AIDS prevention: A view towards understanding the gender rules. *Journal Sex Research, 27,* 47–64.

Gilliard, D. K., and Beck, A. J. (1996). Prison and jail inmates, 1995. *Bureau of Justice Statistics Bulletin,* pp. 1–30.

Hammett, T. M., Harrold, L., Gross, M., and Epstein, J. (1994, January). *1992 update: HIV/AIDS in correctional facilities.* Washington, DC: Department of Justice.

Hankins, C. A., Gendron, S., Handley, M. A., Richard, C., Lai Tung, M. T., and O'Shaughnessy, M. (1994). HIV infection among women in prison: An assessment of risk factors using a nonnomial methodology. *American Journal of Public Health, 84*(10), 1637–1640.

Henson, K. D., Longshore, D., Kowalewski, M. R., Anglin, M. D., and Annon, K. (1998). Perceived AIDS risk among adult arrestee injection drug users in Los Angeles county. *AIDS Education and Prevention, 10*(5), 447–464.

Holmes, M., Safyer, S., Bickell, N. A., Vermund, S. V., Hanff, P. A., and Phillips, R. S. (1993). Chlamydial cervical infection in jailed women. *American Journal of Public Health, 83*(4), 551–555.

Human Rights Watch. (1996). *All too familiar: Sexual abuse of women in U.S. prisons. Women's rights project.* New York: Author.

Institute of Medicine. (1997). *The hidden epidemic confronting sexually transmitted diseases.* Washington, DC: National Academy Press.

Jemmott, L. S., and Jemmott, J. B. (1991). Increasing condom-use intentions among sexually active black adolescent women. *Nursing Research, 40*(5), 273–279.

Jordan, B. K., Schlenger, W. E., Fairbank, J. A., and Caddell, J. M. (1996). Prevalence of psychiatric disorders among incarcerated women. *Archives of General Psychiatry, 53,* 513–519.

Kinnick, B. C., et al. (1989). An assessment of AIDS-related knowledge, attitudes, and behaviors among selected college and university students. *AIDS and Public Policy Journal, 4,* 112–119.

Kleyn, J., Schwebke, J., and Holmes, K. K. (1993). The validity of injecting drug users' self-reports about sexually transmitted diseases: A comparison of survey and serological data. *Addiction, 88,* 673–680.

Magura, S., Kang, S-Y., Shapiro, J., and O'Day, J. (1993). HIV risk among women injecting drug users who are in jail. *Addiction, 88,* 1351–1360.

Mays, V. M., and Cochran, S. D. (1988). Issues in the perception of AIDS risk and risk reduction activities by Black and Hispanic/Latina women. *American Psychiatry,* November, 949–957.

National Women's Law Center. (January, 1995). *Women in prison fact sheet.* Washington, DC.

Nyamathi, A. M., and Lewis, C. E. (1991). Coping of African-American women at risk for AIDS. *Women's Health International, 1*(2), 53–62.

O'Leary, A., Goodhart, F., Jemmott, L., and Boccher-Lattimore, D. (1992). Predictors of safer sex on the college campus: A social cognitive theory analysis. *Journal of the Association of College Health, 40,* 254–263.

Richie, B. E., and Johnsen, C. (1996). Abuse histories among newly incarcerated women in a New York jail. *Journal of American Medical Women's Association, 51*(3), 111–117.

Prohaska, T., Albrecht, G., Levy, J., Sugrue, N., and Kim, J. H. (1990). Determinants of self-perceived risk for AIDS. *Journal of Health and Social Behavior, 31,* 384–394.

Schilling, R., El-Bassel, N., Ivanoff, A., Gilbert, L., Su, K-H., and Safyer, S. M. (1994). Sexual risk behavior of incarcerated drug-using women, 1992. *Public Health Reports, 109*(4), 539–545.

Singer, M. I., Bussey, J., Song, L-Y., and Lunghofer, L. (1995). The psychosocial issues of women serving time in jail. *Social Work, 40*(1), 103–112.

Singer, N. (1995). Understanding sexual risk behavior from drug users' accounts of their life experiences. *Qualitative Health Research, 5*(2), 237–249.

Snell, T. (1994). Women in prison. *Bureau of Justice Bulletin* (Report No. NCJ-145321). Washington, DC: Department of Justice.

Snell, T. L., and Martin, D. C. (1992, March). *Women in prison: Survey of state prison inmates, 1991.* Bureau of Justice Statistics Special Report. Washington, DC: Department of Justice.

Stevens, J., Zierlier, S., Cram, V., Dean, D., Mayer, K., and DeGroot, A. (1995). Risks for HIV infection in incarcerated women. *Journal of Women's Health, 4*(5), 569–577.

Stevens, S. (1993). HIV prevention in a jail setting: Educational strategies. *The Prison Journal, 3,* 379–390.

Trimpey, M. L. (1989). Self-esteem and anxiety: Key issues in an abused women's support group. *Issues in Mental Health Nursing, 10,* 297–308.

Weissman, G., and Brown, V. (1995). Drug-using women and HIV. In A. O'Leary and L. S. Jemmott (Eds.), *Women at risk: Issues in the primary prevention of AIDS* (pp. 175–193). New York: Plenum.

Worth, D. (1989). Sexual decision-making and AIDS: Why condom promotion among vulnerable women is likely to fail. *Studies in Family Planning, 20,* 297–307.

Zeigler, S., Feingold, L., Laufer, D., Velentgas, P., Kantrowits-Gordon, I., and Mayer, K. (1991). Adult survivors of childhood sexual abuse and subsequent risk of HIV infection. *American Journal of Public Health, 81*(5), 572–575.

11

Examining the "Criminal Careers" of Prostitutes Within the Nexus of Drug Use, Drug Selling, and Other Illicit Activities*

SHEILA ROYO MAXWELL

CHRISTOPHER D. MAXWELL

ABSTRACT

This paper examines the co-occurrence of prostitution, drug use, drug selling, and involvement in non-drug crimes among women who have used serious drugs (e.g., crack, heroin). Existing perspectives on the drug use-prostitution nexus are re-examined using three dimensions of the criminal career paradigm: prevalence, lambda, and age of onset. Results show that approximately one-half of the women who reported regular drug use never prostituted, and that, except for use of crack cocaine, use of other drugs was unrelated to the prevalence, frequency, or age of onset into prostitution. The results also show that committing property crime was associated with an increased prevalence and early onset into prostitution, while selling drugs coincided with a decreased prevalence and delayed onset into prostitution.

Since the mid-1980s, criminological explanations of individual offending patterns have been dominated by two competing, though not completely distinct, paradigms; these are the general propensity paradigm and the developmental or typological paradigm. The general propensity paradigm stipulates that variations in offending, ranging from no participation to the most frequent and severe, are explainable by one or a limited number of time-invariant causal attributes (Cohen and Vila, 1996). Alternatively, the developmental models argue that more than one type of offender exists and that each type and stage of an offenders' career have somewhat unique causal structures (Blumstein et al., 1988). This model is most closely tied to the criminal career research paradigm advocated by the National Academy of Science's (NAS's) Panel on *Criminal Career and "Career Criminals"* (Blumstein et al., 1986). In the Panel's view, an individual's offending pattern is a longitudinal and sequential process that can be partitioned into such key parameters as age of onset, prevalence of criminal activities, the annual frequency of offenses or lambda, the length of participation, and the rate of termination or desistance.

Several research studies have tested the viability of either the general propensity or the criminal career paradigm in explaining individual offending patterns (see Dean et al., 1996; Farrington, 1989; Nagin and Farrington, 1992), but after almost 15 years of research, it is still not clear which of the two models is the dominant paradigm. The debate, in part, centers on the question of whether the empirical correlates of an individual's offending pattern are variant or invariant across criminal career dimensions and over the life course (Smith et al., 1991).

*The authors thank Merry Morash, many colleagues, Robert Bursik, and the four anonymous reviewers for insightful comments on previous versions of the paper.

Maxwell, Sheila Royo and Christopher D. Maxwell. 2000. Examining the "Criminal Careers" of Prostitutes Within the Nexus of Drug Use, Drug Selling, and Other Illicit Activities. *Criminology*, *38*(3):787–809. Reprinted with permission.

Studies that have examined individual offending patterns have generally used two types of research designs: the prospective design or the retrospective longitudinal design. The prospective design, which uses population-based samples, tracks individuals over time and relies on self-reports of criminal activities or criminal history checks for information; the retrospective longitudinal design uses samples of offenders with at least one officially recorded criminal offense. The prospective design has many advantages over the retrospective design in that it allows the gathering of substantial information on respondents over time, which consequently enables modeling of criminal activities by both officially and unofficially known offenders (e.g., Nagin and Farrington, 1992). However, this design generally limits modeling more than one or two criminal career dimensions because the samples generally have low base rates of offending and little variation in types of offenses (e.g., Smith and Brame, 1994). Thus, except in a few studies (e.g., Feld and Straus, 1989), much of the research using the prospective design has not examined specific types of offenses.

The retrospective longitudinal design, on the other hand, relies on samples of high-rate offenders followed over time through criminal history checks or self-reports from incarcerated offenders. These samples often provide a sufficient number of offenders who have committed a variety of offenses over a short period of time as well as information on the specific dates of these offenses. This sampling allows more detailed analyses that illustrate important distinctions among types of criminal careers. For example, this type of analysis can indicate how a person's onset into a particular type of crime is related to other offending patterns as well as potential causal mechanisms (see Dean et al., 1996). However, this design is also limited because it typically comprises individuals who have been apprehended by the criminal justice system at least once. Unlike the studies using prospective designs, therefore, these studies do not say anything about unofficially known offenders. These studies also have little information about subjects beyond what they can retrospectively report or what was found in their criminal history files.

In an effort to address some of these methodological shortcomings, this paper examines the criminal "career" of prostitutes, and it addresses both issues of low base rates of offending (in prospective designs) and the absence of unofficially known offenders (in retrospective designs) in studying prostitution "careers." Specifically, the analysis is based on a sample of women who were potentially high-rate offenders and who have retrospectively self-reported recent and serious drug use and other criminal activities, but who were not, predominantly, in criminal justice custody at the time of the interview. This sampling parameter has provided a good opportunity to model simultaneously several dimensions of a criminal career among those who have and have not participated in the criterion measure (e.g., prostitution).

Using earlier research as foundation, this paper examines the relationship among prostitution and several of its hypothesized correlates, namely, the frequency of drug use, drug selling, and nondrug crimes. To measure the dimensions of a prostitution "career," three key criminal career parameters are examined: the prevalence of prostitution, the age of onset to prostitution, and the frequency or lambda of prostitution. Using these three criminal career parameters enables a more comprehensive assessment of the careers of prostitutes than has been provided by prior research. The paper also adds to the criminal career literature by focusing on an offense that is typically unique to women but without the limitation of relying solely on an incarcerated sample.

PROSTITUTION AND DRUG USE

Since the 1970s, studies have found widespread and serious drug use among prostitutes (see Darrow, 1988; Des Jarlais and Friedman, 1987; Goldstein, 1979) and prostitution among drug users (see Inciardi, 1986; Inciardi et al., 1993). Among these, Des Jarlais and Friedman (1987) reported that among a sample of street-level prostitutes they interviewed, a large proportion were also serious drug users. Darrow (1988) similarly found that more than 50% of the 1,456 prostitutes he interviewed in eight cities had used cocaine or heroin the year before the interview. However, studies examining the relationships among prostitution, drug use, and non-drug crimes have been limited in at least three respects. Many studies have relied on small samples of women (see James, 1976; Sterk and Elifson, 1990); some have used exclusively ethnographic techniques (see Maher and Curtis, 1992), and some have sampled on the dependent measure (i.e., prostitution). Furthermore, the associations found were typically bivariate correlations, and few studies have specifically examined the relative timing between drug use and prostitution when other illicit activities were considered (see James, 1976). In the following section, we have reviewed the most common explanations for the observed drug use–prostitution relationship. From these explanations, we derived several research questions.

Enslavement Theory

In 1979, Goldstein developed his Enslavement Theory of prostitution when he found that among lower class prostitutes, addiction to heroin often preceded prostitution and that prostitution became the means by which women met the economic necessities that succeeded addiction. Other researchers have reported similar findings, noting that among women who have used drugs but have not prostituted, addiction to illicit drugs eventually resulted in prostitution (McKeganey and Barnard, 1992). This explanation was used during the explosion of crack cocaine in the mid-1980s, when news articles and ethnographic studies (Inciardi, 1986; Maher and Curtis, 1992; Ouellet et al., 1993) documented what seemed to be the intense and addictive effects of crack on its users. Ethnographic studies of crack-house environments portrayed a dimension of enslavement resulting from the use of crack cocaine that was not previously observed among women who had used other serious drugs, such as heroin (Goldstein et al., 1992; Inciardi, 1986). For example, Inciardi et al. (1993) as well as others (Ouellet et al., 1993) documented the willingness by both women and men to do almost anything for a hit, including exchanging sex for a hit in depraved and vicious conditions and becoming active providers of sex in crack houses in exchange for a regular supply of crack (Inciardi et al., 1993; Ouellet et al., 1993; Ratner, 1993). What was not clear from this research, however, was how widespread this experience was among women who used crack or how the effect of crack cocaine on prostitution was mediated by such factors as drug selling, age, or involvement in other deviant behaviors.

A Common Etiology of Prostitution, Drug Use, and Other Crimes

In contrast to the argument that drug use increases the likelihood of prostitution, other researchers contend that prostitution and drug use are co-occurring behaviors with a common etiology, similar to Gottfredson and Hirschi's (1990) *A General Theory of Crime*. Like Gottfredson and Hirschi's approach to all crime, these researchers argue that drug use and prostitution belong to a larger set of deviant behaviors and street networks that include such activities as larceny, burglary, or robbery, and that all of these behaviors have a common etiology (Davis, 1985; Miller, 1986). Supporting this position, some researchers have shown that deviance and delinquency are the first steps on the pathway to drug use and the first stages in illicit careers that may include prostitution (Davis, 1985). Some researchers have also argued that women prostitute with little forethought, that prostitution is only one among several options available to women to generate income in the street hustle scene, and that women do not necessarily "select" prostitution as their means of financial support over other forms of income-generating illicit activities (Benjamin and Masters, 1964).

Structural-Economic Perspectives

Besides the enslavement and the general deviance explanations, structural-economic theories have also been used to explain prostitution. These theories suggest that women become involved in prostitution because of economic and structural barriers that prevent them from earning sufficient capital in both the licit and illicit economies (Benjamin and Masters, 1964; Fagan, 1994; Maher and Curtis, 1992). In the licit economy, the need for unskilled labor that had been the hallmark of urban employment began to decline substantially during the 1960s, which Wilson (1987) claimed left large proportions of inner-city residents, particularly minority women, competing with a larger population of semiskilled, but displaced, men for unskilled positions. This, in turn, led many women with little or no human capital to switch to the illicit job market, including prostitution, for income (Fagan, 1992).

In illicit economies in the 1980s, the expansion of street-level drug markets in low-income neighborhoods seemingly provided both women and men with the opportunity to augment their limited economic opportunities through drug selling (Maher and Curtis, 1992; Sommers et al., 1996). However, some researchers have argued that, contrary to this assumption, the drug-selling environment was also gendered, and that lucrative positions for women were meager and almost nonexistent (Maher and Daly, 1996; Sommers et al., 1996). These researchers have argued that the entry of women into the drug-selling business is difficult and "managerial" positions are almost nonexistent (Maher and Daly, 1996; Sommers et al., 1996). Women's positions in the local drug-selling environment, if any, were seldom more than temporary replacements for arrested men and provided few opportunities for long-term financial gain and advancement (Goldstein et al., 1992; Maher and Daly, 1996). The few women who make it in the drug-selling hierarchy must know the market, have established connections to procure drugs to sell, know the users, and be able to deal with an environment fraught with violence and potential legal sanctions (Fagan, 1994). Therefore, these women may have particular behavioral or social characteristics that are different from women who do not make it in this illicit market (Maher and Curtis, 1992).

RESEARCH QUESTIONS

Using the multiple perspectives outlined above, two sets of questions are examined in the succeeding sections. The first set examines the participation rate and the annual frequency (lambda) of prostitution as a function of women's demographic characteristics, their patterns of drug use, nondrug criminality, and drug-selling activities. Consistent with the enslavement theory, it is hypothesized that women increase their risk of prostitution with increased drug use, particularly, heroin and crack cocaine. Among active prostitutes, increased incidents of drug use should also increase their annual frequency of prostitution. Consistent with the structural-economic theory, it also expected that women with more human capital (i.e., those who are involved in income-producing licit activities or illicit activities, such as drug selling and property crimes) will less likely engage in prostitution and, even if they do, will engage less frequently.[1]

The second set of questions examines whether age of onset into prostitution is associated with age of onset into drug use and nondrug-related crimes. Consistent with the enslavement theory, we expect that onset into drug use and prostitution are closely timed events and that the age at which women initiate into prostitution is strongly associated with the age they begin to use drugs. On the other hand, if drug use, nondrug crimes, and prostitution are co-occurring events (perhaps all related to a similar etiology), the age that women initiate into drug crimes, nondrug crimes, and prostitution should not be statistically distinguishable.

METHODS

Sample

This paper uses data collected by the *Careers in Crack Project* that was conducted in 1988–1989 during the height of the crack epidemic in New York City. The purpose of this project was to examine the impact of crack cocaine on the careers of drug users and abusers and its impact on drug selling and nondrug criminality (Johnson et al., 1995). The recruitment process was thoroughly documented by Lewis et al. (1992), and details on the interview schedules and protocols were documented by Dunlap et al. (1990). Because of the undefined parameters of crack-cocaine users, the original researchers employed an extensive survey-based data collection method to locate, recruit, and interview a sample of hard-core drug users. To locate the sample, theoretically relevant "social contexts" were used as parameters to determine where a large number of crack users and other-drug users were likely to be found. The social contexts were (1) street drug users from the northern Manhattan areas of Harlem and Washington Heights, where high concentrations of arrests for crack use and sales were documented, (2) arrestees charged with crack/cocaine use or selling, (3) drug users and sellers who were under criminal justice supervision and institutionalized in jails or prisons, and (4) residential drug treatment clients. In each "social context," subjects included crack users or sellers, cocaine HCL users or sellers who were not involved in crack, heroin users or sellers, and polydrug users. The selection of interviewees was based on snowball sampling procedures because of the ill-defined nature of the target group, and quotas were set to recruit sufficient numbers within subpopulations of theoretical interest (e.g., ages 18–20, females, noncrack drug users). Sampling was also varied by time and space to ensure variances among the participants (Lewis et al., 1992). The final sample comprises 1,006 interviewees; however, this study only uses the 311 female respondents.

Interview Procedures

To collect accurate information about each respondent's involvement with drugs and other illicit activities as well as income generated from illicit activities, the researchers designed the interview protocol using the life history approach (Dunlap et al., 1990). This technique had been employed successfully in other studies with offender-based populations (Frazier, 1978; Horney et al., 1995) and had been shown to have strong validity with opiate addicts (Ball et al., 1981; Stephens, 1972). This approach obtains specific

---

[1]Human capital represents individual attributes that make one a valuable and desired commodity in the labor market and often includes measures like age, educational attainment, job skills and experience, and race (Fagan, 1992).

counts of illicit behaviors within small time periods by having the interviewees use time reference points to assist them in their recall of drug use and criminal activities (Dunlap et al., 1990). Several questions were then asked about each type of behavior as a means to check the internal consistency of the responses (Lewis et al., 1992; Johnson et al., 1995). The interviews were conducted in many settings, consistent with the sampling parameters outlined above, and occurred in places where smoking was allowed, urine specimens could be easily obtained, people other than the interviewer could not overhear the conversation or identify the subjects interviewed, and the subject and interviewer could be comfortable and safe for about two hours. Interviews were conducted in either English or Spanish and lasted from one to two hours, depending on the life histories of the respondents. The interviewing staff consisted of "straight" interviewers (those without a drug abuse history) and fully trained ex-addicts who had been off drugs for about three or more years. The ex-addict interviewers provided advantages in their knowledge of street life, their ability to develop rapport with the subjects because of their own experiences with drugs, and their ability to detect inaccurate information on top of consistency checks. Furthermore, interview items were read aloud and cards with response sets were shown to respondents with the choices read aloud, so that literacy problems were minimized.

Interview stipends of $25 were provided along with two subway tokens and a pack of cigarettes. Five additional dollars were also provided to subjects willing to provide a urine sample, and an additional small amount was given if the subject provided referrals to potential interviewees (refer to Dunlap et al., 1990, for more information on the sampling and interview procedure).

Self-Report of Illicit Activity Measures

The study's design was strongly influenced by the NAS's criminal careers report (see Blumstein et al., 1986) and, therefore, includes many measures that can be used to model key dimensions of the criminal career paradigm (Johnson et al., 1995; Lewis et al., 1992). The interview schedule included four domains

of information: initiation into substance use or selling; lifetime and recent annual involvement with both drug and nondrug crimes; the social processes of substance use or selling; and income sources and expenditures from legitimate and illegal activities. A calendar was also used to record time spent in treatment programs, incarceration, and stays in other institutions.

For initiation patterns, respondents were asked at what age and in what year they first engaged in drug use, selling, nondrug criminal behavior, and the time from first drug use to regular use. Fifteen types of drugs, such as crack, powdered cocaine, heroin, illicit methadone, marijuana, "uppers," and "downers" were included in the list of illicit substances. Additionally, respondents were asked the ages at which they first committed any of 20 types of crimes and to estimate their lifetime frequencies of drug and nondrug crimes. After a pretest suggested that subjects had difficulty making accurate estimates when asked open-ended questions, the researchers developed a category response set to record the frequency of specific behaviors. The response set represented an exponential scale of frequency, with nine categories ranging from "one or two times" to "more than 10,000." In this paper, the scores for prostitution, drug use, drug selling, and other illicit activities were transformed in several ways to facilitate the analysis. First, the categorical response scales were changed to midpoint means. Each of these transformed scores was then divided by the interviewee's career length for each behavior.[2] Finally, consistent with other research using these data (see Fagan, 1994), the drug use, drug selling, and other independent measures were logged to adjust their skewed distribution.[3]

RESULTS

A prostitute is defined here and throughout the remaining analysis as a female interviewee who responded positively to questions about exchanging sex for money or sex for drugs. About 55% of the sample reported no incidents of prostitution, whereas the remaining 45% reported one or more incidents.

---

[2] Career length was computed by subtracting the date respondents admitted to starting a particular behavior from the date they admitted terminating that behavior, or the date of interview if they were still continuing such behavior at the time of interview.

[3] To examine the veracity of our annualized measures, we also estimated Pearson correlations between the annualized scores and measures that asked respondents about the same activities within the past two years. The results were significant, ranging from 0.35 to 0.55.

Among the active prostitutes, the average frequency of prostitution ranged from between one to more than 600 incidents per year. Like most criminal career distributions, the largest proportion of the sample is towards the lower end of the frequency scale; however, unlike many other offense distributions, there is a more even distribution across the frequency scale, suggesting that this sample is not likely representative of all prostitutes or of any group of offenders. The sample, by design, did not target infrequent drug users who lived in working neighborhoods or in middle- or upper-class areas (Johnson et al., 1995).

With regard to the age of onset, we examined the cumulative distribution for the rate of onset into prostitution. The timing of the first incidence of prostitution ranged from below 14 to 36 years of age. What is immediately apparent is the rather late onset into prostitution by many of the women. Only half of the active prostitutes had their first incident of prostitution before age 22. Only two other illicit activities examined had similar or later onsets; these were the age they first sold drugs ($\bar{x} = 22$) and the first use of crack cocaine ($\bar{x} = 25$). For all other illicit activities, including first drug use ($\bar{x} = 16$), first property crime ($\bar{x} = 19$), and first violent crime ($\bar{x} = 19$), the respondents reported significantly earlier ages of onset ($p < .05$). One other notable finding is the rather constant increase in the rate of first-timers across the entire age range. Between ages 15 and 28, no notable age exists at which the women were at a strikingly higher risk for prostitution.

The sample's median and mean ages were about 27 years. The youngest female respondent was 16 and the oldest was 50. Just more than one in four was working a part- or a full-time legitimate job, and 45% did not complete high school. Nearly the same percentage of women never had children, had children but did not live with them, and had children living with them. Finally, approximately one out of every three women interviewed was under some form of criminal justice supervision or was in a drug-treatment facility during the study. Overall, the respondents were typically minority women (African-American or Hispanic), had no high school diploma, were unemployed, and were never married.[4]

As for the distribution of prostitution across the demographic and social characteristics of the women, there were no significant differences in the prevalence of prostitution according to the women's ethnicity, age, educational achievement, or marital status. However, the prevalence of prostitution was significantly higher among those who were not employed at the time of the interview and among those who had children but were not living with them. Given the consistent assumption that economic deprivation drives involvement in prostitution, there should have been a consistently lower prevalence of prostitution among those with more favorable levels of human capital (i.e., white, middle-aged, higher educated, employed). Although not consistently observed, it is still noteworthy that not working (often a strong indicator of a person's economic situation) is one of the few significant indicators of involvement in prostitution.

The Relationships Among Prostitution, Nondrug Crimes, Drug Use, and Drug Selling

In the succeeding analyses, we examine the multivariate effects of crime, drug use, and drug selling on the prevalence of prostitution, the lambda or average annual frequency of prostitution, and age of onset into prostitution. We begin with Table 1, which includes three incremental logistic regression models to examine the effects of several independent measures on participation in prostitution and three incremental negative binomial models to examine the net effects of the same independent measures on the annual frequencies of prostitution among active prostitutes.[5] Both the logistic and the negative binomial models are used to examine separately the factors that are related to participation in prostitution and those that are related to the lambda of prostitution. This approach is consistent with analytical procedures recommended by the NAS's Panel on Research on Criminal Careers, which argued that research should look at whether the mechanisms that propel individuals to participate in a specific criminal activity are different from the mechanisms that contribute to these individuals committing more criminal acts once they have begun (Blumstein et al., 1986).

---

[4]Further demographic comparisons between subsamples that are not reported here suggested that subjects recruited from each locale were similar with respect to race, sex, age, education, employment, and marital status.

[5]We considered using a Poisson estimator, but found substantial overdispersion.

TABLE 1 Regression Coefficients for Demographics, Drug Involvement, and Nondrug Crimes on Prostitution

	LIFETIME PREVALENCE OF PROSTITUTION (N = 311)						ANNUAL FREQUENCY OF PROSTITUTION (N = 140)					
	Model 1		Model 2		Model 3		Model 1		Model 2		Model 3	
	b	S.E.	b	S.E.	b	S.E.	b	S.E.	b	S.E.	b	S.E.
Age	−0.01	0.02	0.01	0.02	0.02	0.03	−0.03	0.03	−0.03	0.03	0.07	0.06
Ethnicity:												
White	0.48	0.42	0.51	0.46	0.47	0.47	0.61	0.70	0.40	0.74	0.37	0.71
Hispanic	0.86	0.43*	1.05	0.47*	0.90	0.48	0.05	0.41	0.01	0.47	0.07	0.49
Puerto Rican	0.52	0.31	0.69	0.35*	0.59	0.36	0.22	0.33	0.23	0.46	0.32	0.51
Highest completed grade:												
High school diploma	−0.06	0.27	0.06	0.30	0.09	0.30	−0.23	0.28	−0.11	0.37	−0.09	0.38
Some college or higher	−0.38	0.36	−0.17	0.39	0.06	0.40	0.27	0.46	0.33	0.52	0.59	0.57
Employment status:												
Part-time or more	−0.85	0.30**	−0.57	0.34	−0.63	0.31	0.12	0.60	0.43	0.62	0.67	0.59
Marital status:												
Married and cohabitation	−0.22	0.31	−0.34	0.34	−0.35	0.34	0.07	0.41	−0.06	0.48	−0.33	0.50
Separated/divorced/widowed	0.49	0.45	0.21	0.48	0.24	0.48	−0.21	0.57	−0.53	0.64	−0.43	0.70
Annual frequency (logged) of using:												
Crack			0.06	0.04	0.46	0.17			0.15	0.06**	0.54	0.27*
Heroin			−0.04	0.04	0.21	0.19			0.06	0.06	0.27	0.32
Marijuana			0.03	0.04	0.04	0.04			0.00	0.04	0.01	0.04
Annual frequency (logged) of:												
Personal crime			0.10	0.08	0.04	0.08			0.05	0.11	0.23	0.46
Property crime			0.28	0.07***	−0.07	0.31			0.02	0.12	−0.01	0.11
Drug selling			−0.12	0.04***	−0.26	0.16			−0.00	0.06	0.21	0.25
Frequency of crack use × age					−0.01	0.01**					−0.01	0.01
Frequency of heroin use × age					−0.01	0.01					−0.01	0.01
Frequency of property crime × age					0.00	0.01					−0.01	0.02
Frequency of drug selling × age					0.00	0.01					−0.01	0.01
Constant	0.61	0.60	−0.40	7.15	−1.23	1.02	5.85	0.78	4.59	1.03	1.51	1.89
Alpha (overdispersion)							2.39	0.30**	2.29	0.34**	2.23	0.33***
Initial 2 log likelihood	424.42		424.42		424.42		−773.51		−769.51		−766.74	
Model Chi-Square	19.63*		60.55***		67.01***		4125.4***		3902.5***		3803.9***	

* p < .05;   ** p < .01;   *** p < .001.

Note: Dummy variables were entered for ethnicity with African-American as the excluded group; for highest grade completed with no high school as the excluded group; and for marital status with never married as the excluded group.

The first logistic and negative binomial regressions model the effects of human capital and the demographic characteristics of the women on their participation and annual frequencies of prostitution (Models 1). The results from the logistic model show that employment significantly predicts nonparticipation (this finding is similar to the bivariate findings). Although this effect is in the expected direction, it cannot be ascertained whether these women were driven into prostitution for lack of licit employment opportunities or whether they were not working because they have chosen to prostitute. However, in the neighborhoods where these women lived, it is likely that their need to prostitute was heightened by insufficient opportunities for legitimate employment (Fagan, 1992). Another significant predictor of participation in prostitution is a woman's ethnicity. In this sample, Hispanic women were more likely to have prostituted than African Americans (the reference category), whereas White women were no more or less likely to have prostituted than were African-American women. Turning to the model for lambda, not one of these women's human capital or demographic characteristics could significantly explain the variance in the annual frequencies of prostitution.

The next set of logistic and negative binomial models examines the relationships between drug use and participation in other criminal activities while controlling for the demographic and human capital characteristics (Models 2). The logistic regression results show that frequent use of crack, heroin, or marijuana was neither positively nor negatively related to the likelihood of ever prostituting, but frequent involvement in property crimes significantly increased the likelihood of prostitution.[6] However, frequent drug selling decreased a woman's likelihood of ever prostituting. Furthermore, with these additional measures, the original significant effect of unemployment disappeared, but the significant effect of ethnicity remained. This latter result suggests that unemployment is not necessarily a risk factor for prostitution. Instead, prostitution seems to be an alternative route for women who engage in other crimes for economic gain, specifically property crimes. Although selling drugs is another illicit activity for economic gain, its negative effect on prostitution suggests that drug selling may shield some women from prostitution.

In the negative binomial model, a different but an expected result was found. This model shows that among active prostitutes, only the more frequent use of crack was related to greater annual frequencies of prostitution. As previously cited, several researchers have contended that the highly addictive nature of crack has led users to behave in ways previously unobserved among drug users (Inciardi et al., 1993; Ratner, 1993). Our finding is congruent with this pattern, particularly when crack use was juxtaposed with use of other types of drugs that did not show the same effects.

The last set of regressions in Table 1 (Models 3) models the effects of four interaction terms on prostitution: age by crack use, age by heroin use, age by property offenses, and age by drug selling. We chose to test for these particular interactions because some scholars have argued that a person's involvement with specific drugs can vary in relation to their age or cohort. In particular, Golub and Johnson (1993) have argued that the type of drug a person principally uses is strongly related to when they come of age (i.e., turn 18) because the availability and the popularity of drugs vary substantially over time. The final logistic regression results reported in Table 1 show that after specifying these interactions, only the crack-use-by-age-interaction term is significantly associated with the prevalence of prostitution.[7] The direction of the

[6]We found some evidence of multicollinearity in the regression models. All of the measures except one, the annual use of cocaine, had tolerance levels exceeding 0.6 when estimated using an ordinary least-squares (OLS) regression model. The tolerance level for cocaine was just over 0.5. This level concerned us, so we estimated several modified logistic and negative binomial regression models. Models with both crack and cocaine use included as regressors produced no significant effect for either. When only crack use was included, we found that crack was significant. When only cocaine use was included or a composite measure of cocaine and crack, these measures were not significant. Also, removing cocaine use had no effect on other coefficients or *t* test scores.

[7]Three logistic regressions, not reported, were also performed that examined the effect of drug and non-drug crimes on the prevalence and frequency of prostitution with only the women who came of age during the three major drug eras (heroin era, cocaine era, crack era). The results showed that frequent crack use increased the likelihood of prostitution among those who came of age during the crack era; this pattern was not observed, however, among women who came of age during the heroin and cocaine eras. We also ran the interactions one at a time with the full sample and again found that the age-by-crack use was the only significant interaction.

interaction term indicates that compared with older women, more frequent use of crack cocaine by younger women significantly increased their risk of prostitution. This finding is particularly interesting because neither age nor the frequency of crack use had any direct effect on the prevalence of prostitution. Thus, this final model suggests that after controlling for other factors such as the frequency of property crimes, crack cocaine use did, indeed, precipitate prostitution but only among younger women. It is also interesting to note that there are no significant interactions between crack use and age when the frequency of prostitution was modeled nor was there a significant interaction between frequent heroin use and age. Apparently, for women who came of age during the heroin era or before, more frequent use of heroin did not increase their risk of prostitution compared with those who less often used heroin.

The Relative Timing of Prostitution and Nondrug and Drug Crimes

Although Table 1 listed factors that co-occur with the prevalence and frequency of prostitution, these analyses did not distinguish the relative timing between initial participation in several illicit activities (drug use, drug selling, nondrug crimes) and initiation into prostitution. Recent studies have begun exploring the time order between nondrug crimes, drug use, and prostitution, showing mixed results. Sterk and Elifson (1990), for instance, found that three-quarters of the women in their small sample used drugs before prostitution, but among crack users, only 50% reported addiction to the drug before they started prostituting. In Miami, Inciardi (1986) found that most female addicts in his sample used heroin and committed their first crime before they prostituted, although prostitutes committed their first crimes at significantly younger ages than did nonprostitutes.

To examine the relative timing of illicit activities, Table 2 presents the relationship between age of first entry into a number of illicit activities and age of first prostitution. The model uses Cox regression, which allows us to examine the entire sample of women (instead of only those who ever prostituted) and the effects that their ages of first drug use, first drug selling, and other criminal offenses have on the risk (hazard) of entry into prostitution. Table 2 shows that of the four types of drugs examined, only the age of first crack use was positively related to the risk of prostitution. The younger the women were when they first used crack (exemplified by the positive coefficient), the younger they became involved in prostitution. Accordingly, the unique effects of crack that many ethnographers have observed may be particularly deleterious for young women (Goldstein et al.,

TABLE 2   Relationship of Age, Ethnicity, and Age of First Illicit Activities with the Age of First Prostitution ($N = 311$)

	b	S.E.	Odds ratio
Age	−0.11	0.02*	0.90
Ethnicity			
Black			
White	−0.01	0.29	0.99
Hispanic	0.28	0.19	1.33
Age at first:			
Cocaine use	−0.04	0.23	0.87
Crack use	0.39	0.24***	1.48
Heroin use	0.28	0.22	1.32
Marijuana use	0.34	0.23	1.41
Personal crime	0.15	0.21	1.16
Property crime	0.79	0.20***	2.20
Drug sold	−0.88	0.25***	0.42
Initial 2 log likelihood = 981.26			
Model Chi-square = 97.92***			

*** $p < .001$.

Note: Dummy variables were entered for ethnicity with African-American as the excluded category.

1992), who seemed to engage in prostitution more readily than did older women. Ethnographic studies of crack houses have described instances of teenage girls providing sexual favors to crack house clients in exchange for crack (Inciardi et al., 1993; Ratner, 1993).

Table 2 also shows the positive relationship between first property crime and the risk of prostitution and the negative relationship between drug selling and the hazard of prostitution. Women who started committing property crimes at younger ages also initiated prostitution at younger ages, whereas women who started selling drugs at younger ages decreased their risk of prostituting until later in their lives. This is again consistent with our earlier models of prevalence (see Table 1).

DISCUSSION

Although there have been many studies of prostitution, few have used standard quantitative methods and most of those that did were limited in their methodologies by sampling on the dependent measure or small sample sizes. This paper builds on these earlier studies by examining prostitution within the nexus of other illicit activities, such as property offenses, drug use, and drug selling, and by partitioning a prostitution career into three dimensions: the age of onset, prevalence, and the lambda or frequency of prostitution. Using these dimensions allowed us to more fully examine the nature of prostitution and its relationship to other illicit activities. The sample used is also unique among criminal career studies in that it comprises individuals who were potentially high-rate offenders and have committed various types of crimes, but were not all sampled because they were officially known offenders or because they were known prostitutes.

Results show that predictors of one dimension of a prostitution career (i.e., age of onset) were not necessarily the same predictors for another dimension (i.e., frequency), although there were similar predictors. In particular, the results show that two factors, namely, property crimes and drug selling were associated with the prevalence of prostitution (positively for property crimes and negatively for drug selling), but not directly associated with the frequency of prostitution. Alternatively, use of crack cocaine was significantly associated with the frequency of prostitution, but not the prevalence of

prostitution. These distinctions tend to support the criminal career paradigm and not the general propensity model because the latter would have argued that many illicit activities have a high degree of association regardless of the criminal dimension modeled. Moreover, our diagnostic analysis did not find strong relationships among the independent measures and only one problem with multicollinearity. This result suggests that prostitution and other criminal activities are not necessarily related to an underlying "control" or propensity trait.

The analyses also show that early involvement in property crimes significantly increased the risk of early involvement in prostitution, whereas early involvement in drug selling significantly reduced the risk of early involvement in prostitution. These and the other results show the possibility of two distinct groups of women who may have followed different pathways in illicit careers. In one group were women who used drugs and simultaneously engaged in a variety of illicit activities, including prostitution and property crimes, possibly to generate capital for drug purchases. In another group were women who specialized in drug selling and generally avoided other income-generating illicit activities like prostitution and property crimes. These different pathways are indicative of a structural-economic explanation for involvement in prostitution, in which, perhaps, because of some unmeasured opportunity structures or characteristics of the women, some women were able to specialize in drug selling that may have protected them from hustling between prostitution and property crimes.

By specifying age and drug use interactions and by modeling time-variant hazard rates, the results also demonstrate the specific effects that crack cocaine had on young women. The youngest women in our sample were at significantly greater risk for prostitution if they either frequently used crack cocaine or if they started using crack cocaine early in their lives. For the older women who were already committing a number of illicit activities and were likely using heroin and other drugs, their use of crack cocaine had little to do with their risk for prostitution. It is important to note, however, that we only presented the relative timing of events in the preceding analyses. Thus, conclusions about the structural relationship between drug use and prostitution cannot be drawn from the results. Because of the nature of our data (i.e., retrospective self-reports), we cannot address the direction of effects more explicitly.

REFERENCES

Ball, J. C., Rosen, L., Flueck, J. A., and Nurco, D. (1981). The criminality of heroin addicts when addicted and when off opiates. In J. A. Inciardi (Ed.), *The Drugs and Crime Connection*. Newbury Park, CA: Sage.

Benjamin, H., and Masters, R. E. L. (1964). *Prostitution and Morality*. New York: Julian Press.

Blumstein, A., Cohen, J., and Farrington, D. P. (1988). Criminal career research: Its value for criminology. *Criminology, 26*, 1–35.

Blumstein, A., Cohen, J., Roth, J., and Visher, C. (1986). *Criminal Careers and "Career Criminals."* Washington, DC: National Academy Press.

Cohen, L., and Vila, B. J. (1996). Self-control and social control: An exposition of the Gottredson-Hirschi/Sampson-Laub debate. *Studies on Crime and Crime Prevention, 5*, 125–150.

Darrow, W. (1988). The potential spread of HIV infection in female prostitutes. Paper presented at the American Psychological Association.

Davis, N. J. (1985). Becoming a prostitute. In J. M. Henslin (Ed.), *Down to Earth Sociology*, 5th ed. New York: Free Press.

Dean, C., Brame, R., and Piquero, A. R. (1996). Criminal propensities, discrete groups of offenders, and persistence in crime. *Criminology, 34*, 547–574.

Des Jarlais, D., and Friedman, S. (1987). HIV infection among intravenous drug users: Epidemiology and risk reduction. *AIDS, 1*, 67–76.

Dunlap, E., Johnson, B., Sanabria, H., Holliday, E., Lipsi, V., Barnett, M., Hopkins, W., Sobel, I., Randolph, D., and Chin, K. (1990). Studying crack users and their criminal careers: The scientific and artistic aspects of locating hard-to-reach subjects and interviewing them about sensitive subjects. *Contemporary Drug Problems, 17*, 121–144.

Fagan, J. A. (1992). Drug selling and licit income in distressed neighborhoods: The economic lives of street-level drug users and dealers. In A. Harrell and G. E. Peterson (Eds.), *Drugs, Crime and Social Isolation: Barriers to Urban Opportunity*. Washington, DC: The Urban Institute Press.

Fagan, J. A. (1994). Women and drugs revisited: Female participation in the cocaine economy. *Journal of Drug Issues, 24*, 179–226.

Farrington, D. P. (1989). Early predictors of adolescent aggression and adult violence. *Violence and Victims, 4*, 79–100.

Feld, S. L., and Straus, M. (1989). Escalation and desistance of wife assault in marriage. *Criminology, 27*, 141–161.

Frazier, C. E. (1978). The use of life histories in testing theories of criminal behavior. *Qualitative Sociology, 1*, 122–142.

Goldstein, P. J. (1979). *Prostitution and Drugs*. Lexington, Mass.: Lexington Books.

Goldstein, P. J., Ouellet, L. J., and Fendrich, M. (1992). From bag brides to skeezers: A historical perspective on sex-for-drugs behavior. *Journal of Psychoactive Drugs, 24*, 349–361.

Golub, A., and Johnson, B. D. (1993). Drug eras: A conceptual model for the dynamics of change in the popularity of a particular drug. Paper presented at the Society for the Study of Social Problems Annual Convention, Miami Beach, Fla.

Gottfredson, M. R., and Hirschi, T. (1990). *A General Theory of Crime*. Palo Alto, CA: Stanford University Press.

Horney, J., Osgood, D. W., and Marshall, I. H. (1995). Criminal careers in the short-term: Intra-individual variability in crime and its relation to local life circumstances: *American Sociological Review, 60*, 655–673.

Inciardi, J. A. (1986). *The War on Drugs: Heroin, Cocaine, Crime and Public Policy*. Palo Alto, CA: Mayfield.

Inciardi, J. A., Lockwood, D., and Pottieger, A. E. (1993). *Women and Crack Cocaine*. New York: Macmillan.

James, J. (1976). Prostitution and addiction: An interdisciplinary approach. *Addictive Diseases, 2*, 601–618.

Johnson, B. D., Golub, A., and Fagan, J. (1995). Careers in crack, drug use, drug distribution, and nondrug criminality. *Crime and Delinquency, 41*, 275–295.

Lewis, C., Johnson, B., Golub, A., and Dunlap, E. (1992). Studying crack abusers: Strategies for recruiting the right tail of an ill-defined population. *Journal of Psychoactive Drugs, 24*, 323–336.

Maher, L., and Curtis, R. (1992). Women on the edge of crime: Crack cocaine and the changing contexts of street-level sex work in New York City. *Crime, Law and Social Change, 17*, 221–258.

Maher, L., and Daly, K. (1996). Women in the street-level drug economy: Continuity or change? *Criminology, 34*, 465–492.

McKeganey, N., and Barnard, M. (1992). *AIDS, Drugs, and Sexual Risk: Lives in the Balance*. Buckingham, UK: Open University Press.

Miller, E. M. (1986). *Street Women*. Philadelphia: Temple University Press.

Nagin, D. S., and Farrington, D. P. (1992). The onset and persistence of offending. *Criminology, 30*, 501–523.

Ouellet, L. J., Wiebel, W. W., Jimenez, A. D., and Johnson, W. A. (1993). Crack cocaine and the transformation of prostitution in three Chicago neighborhoods. In M. S. Ratner (Ed.), *Crack Pipe as Pimp*. New York: Lexington Books.

Ratner, M. S. (1993). Sex, drugs, and public policy: Studying and understanding the sex-for-crack phenomenon. In M. S. Ratner (Ed.), *Crack Pipe as Pimp*. New York: Lexington Books.

Smith, D. A., and Brame, R. (1994). On the initiation and continuation of delinquency. *Criminology, 32*, 607–630.

Smith, D. A., Visher, C. A., and Jarjoura, G. R. (1991). Dimensions of delinquency: Exploring the correlates of participation, frequency and persistence of delinquent behavior. *Journal of Research in Crime and Delinquency, 28*, 6–32.

Sommers, I., Baskin, D., and Fagan, J. (1996). The structural relationship between drug use, drug dealing, and other income support activities among women drug sellers. *Journal of Drug Issues, 26*, 975–1006.

Stephens, R. (1972). The truthfulness of addict respondents in research projects. *International Journal of the Addictions, 7*, 549–558.

Sterk, C. E., and Elifson, K. W. (1990). *Drugs and Violence: Causes, Correlates and Consequences*. Rockville, MD: U.S. Department of Health and Human Services.

Wilson, W. J. (1987). *The Truly Disadvantaged*. Chicago: University of Chicago Press.

CHAPTER 3: DISCUSSION QUESTIONS

1. How have things changed for women in the drug economy? What are the "two social worlds" of women in the drug scene? How do things differ for men and women in the New York City drug economy?

2. According to Maher and Daly, what is the basic structure of New York City crack markets?

3. According to Fogel and Belyea, what life factors may influence risk for HIV infection? What are barriers to HIV protective practices for women in prison?

4. What does it mean that women in prison are at a "teachable moment" about HIV risk?

5. How does violence affect HIV risk behavior? How should it be handled in prevention programs?

6. What are prevalence, lambda, and age of onset as dimensions of the criminal career paradigm according to Maxwell and Maxwell?

7. How was "prostitute" defined in the Maxwell and Maxwell study?

8. What factors influenced the prevalence of prostitution? Which model of the relationship between drug use and prostitution was supported by Maxwell and Maxwell?

9. What are the limitations of each selection?

10. What are the policy implications of each selection?

CHAPTER 3: ADDITIONAL RESOURCES IN RESEARCH NAVIGATOR AND IN THE *NEW YORK TIMES*

Baker, A. (2004, March 23). Ex-prisoner tells her story, hoping to change drug laws. *New York Times*.

Bandstra, E. S., Morrow, C. E., Anthony, J. C., Churchill, S. S., Chitwood, D. C., Steele, B. W., Ofir, A. Y., and Zue, L. (2001). Intrauterine growth of full-term infants: Impact of prenatal cocaine exposure. *Pediatrics, 108*, 1309–1319.

Brown University Child and Adolescent Behavior Letter. (2004). National report examines eating disorders: Girls with eating disorders likely to abuse alcohol, drugs. *Brown University Child and Adolescent Behavior Letter, 20*, 1(3).

Dunlap, E., Golub, A., Johnson, B. D., and Wesley, D. (2002). Intergenerational transmission of conduct norms for drugs, sexual exploitation and violence: A case study. *British Journal of Criminology, 42*, 1–20.

Hanley, R. (2004, July 8). Friend tells of beatings by parolee over drugs. *New York Times*.

Harrison, L. D., Bachman, T., Freeman, C., and Inciardi, J. A. (2001). The acceptability of the female condom among U.S. women at high risk from HIV. *Culture, Health, and Sexuality, 3*, 101–118.

Luck, P. A., Elifson, K. W., and Sterk, C. E. (2004). Female drug users and the welfare system: A qualitative exploration. *Drugs: Education, Prevention, and Policy, 11*, 113–128.

Molitor, F., Ruiz, J. D., Klausner, J. D., and Mcfarland, W. (2000). History of forced sex in association with drug use

and sexual HIV risk behaviors, infection with STDs, and diagnostic medical care: Results from the young women survey. *Journal of Interpersonal Violence, 15*, 262–278.

Nyamathi, A., Longshore, D., Keenan, C., Lesser, J., and Leake, B. D. (2001). Childhood predictors of daily substance use among homeless women of different ethnicities. *American Behavioral Scientist, 45*, 35–50.

Rimer, S. (2004, April 29). At last, the windows have no bars. *New York Times*.

Surrat, H. L., Inciardi, J. A., Kurtz, S. P., and Kiley, M. C. (2004). Sex work and drug use in a subculture of violence. *Crime and Delinquency, 50*, 17–22.

Vogeltanz-Holm, N. D., Neve, R. J. M., Greenfield, T. K., Wilsnack, R. W., Kubicka, L., Wilsnack, S. C., Fleming, J. M., and Spak, F. (2004). A cross-cultural analysis of women's drinking and drinking-related problems in five countries: Findings from the international research group on gender and alcohol. *Addiction Research and Theory, 12*, 31–40.

Williams, M. L., Bowen, A. M., Elwood, W. N., McCoy, C. C., McCoy, H. V., Freeman, R. C., Weatherby, N. L., and Pierce, T. (2000). Determinants of condom use among African Americans who smoke crack cocaine. *Culture, Health, and Sexuality, 2*, 15–32.

Yacoubian, G. S. Jr., Urbach, B. J., Larsen, K. L., Johnson, R. J., and Peters, R. J. Jr., (2000). A comparison of drug use between prostitutes and other female arrestees. *Journal of Alcohol and Drug Education, 46*, 12–25.

YOUTH AND DRUGS

The use of illicit drugs has been on the rise among youth in the United States, although recent reports suggest the rates have stabilized or even begun to decline. These patterns differ by age categories, however, as there has been evidence of an increase among junior high students. Importantly, illicit drug use has been linked to suicide attempts among youth. And although the overall crime rate is decreasing in the United States, it is increasing for youth. Together, these patterns highlight the need to pay special attention to what is happening with American youth. In the three selections for this chapter, several predictable patterns in the relationship between drugs and crime for youth become clear. In the first piece, Denise Kandel, Ora Simcha-Fagan, and Mark Davies examine risk factors for drugs and delinquency as individuals move from youth to young adulthood. In a series of regression models using longitudinal data, they both confirm existing research and contribute new information about these patterns. They find that the same things predict drug use for women and delinquency for men.

Stephen Baron and Timothy Hartnagel focus on violence perpetrated by street youth. Although they find high rates of violence predicted by participation in the street subculture, they find minimal evidence that this violence is associated with the use of drugs and alcohol. They use a combination of qualitative and quantitative data and attempt to use several theories (subcultural, economic dependency and routine activities) to explain their findings. Although their respondents are all heavy users of alcohol and drugs, their

study shows that only alcohol use predicts simple assault.

Finally, Helene Raskin White and colleagues examine youth and their illegal acts committed while actually under the influence of alcohol and drugs. This piece provides a good overview of models that are often used to explain the relationship between drugs and crime. These authors also use longitudinal data, which provide greater confidence in the causality implied by their findings.

Several patterns deserve note. First, the use of drugs and alcohol is clearly related to delinquency for youth. The nature of the relationship, however, is complex and varies by type of drug and type of delinquency, life circumstances, and whether the acts occur at the same time. Second, one selection observes gender differences in both drug use and crime, but two selections sampled only males. These gender findings replicate existing research in drug studies. Third, youth behaviors are different from adults, and these behaviors may change over time. For example, as noted by Kandel and colleagues, the persistence of illicit drug use is greater than that of delinquency. Fourth, many moderating factors contribute to our understanding, including risk taking, impulsivity, peer relationships, depression, and family and lifestyle circumstances. Despite some limitations due to sampling and measurement in all the selections, each contributes yet another piece to the puzzle of understanding youth and their drug use and criminal behaviors.

12

Risk Factors for Delinquency and Illicit Drug Use From Adolescence to Young Adulthood

DENISE KANDEL

ORA SIMCHA-FAGAN

MARK DAVIES

ABSTRACT

This study examines the interrelationships and predictors of involvement in delinquent activities and illicit drug use over a nine-year interval, from adolescence (age 15–16) to young adulthood (age 24–25) in a cohort representative of adolescents formerly enrolled in grades 10 and 11 in public secondary schools in New York State (N = 1,004). Persistence of illicit drug use in this period of the life-cycle is greater than for delinquency and is higher among men than among women. Convergences and divergences in intrapersonal and interpersonal predictors of drug use and delinquency are analyzed. Adult illicit drug use is much better predicted by adolescent illicit drug use, especially among men. Among women, early drug use predicts later delinquent behavior. However, illicit drug use in the period from adolescence to early adulthood selectively predicts adult participation in one type of delinquent behavior, namely theft, among men and women, but has no effect on interpersonal aggression. Different risk factors in adolescence other than drug use predict continued delinquent involvement among men and women. In particular, depression plays an important role for women and family factors for men. Lifestyle factors subsequent to adolescence, especially failure to enter the conventional roles of adulthood, such as marriage and continuous employment, are important predictors of continued illicit drug use in adulthood but not of delinquency. Delinquency among males and illicit drug use among females appear to be subject to common etiological factors and may play similar roles in the lives of young people. Convergence between the findings and results reported by others are discussed.

The association between involvement in delinquent activities and illicit drug use has been the subject of many inquiries. That there is an association has been repeatedly established, both in representative samples of the population (see, for example, Bachman, Johnston, and O'Malley, 1981; Elliott and Huizinga, 1984; Kaplan, 1980; Jessor, Donovan, and Widmer, 1980; Jessor and Jessor, 1977; Johnson, Wish, and Huizinga, 1983; Johnston, O'Malley, and Eveland, 1978; O'Donnell et al., 1976; Robins and Wish, 1977; Thornton, 1981; Tuchfeld, Clayton, and Logan, 1982; White Johnson, and Garrison, 1983) as well as in treatment samples of drug abusers (McGlothlin, 1979; O'Donnell, 1969; Simpson and Sells, 1982) or samples of individuals arrested or incarcerated (Weitzel and Blount, 1982). Two issues have been debated. One issue, especially prominent in considering adults, pertains to the causal connection between the two behaviors, and is reflected in the

This article is based on a paper presented at the Annual Meeting of the Society for Criminology, November 1984, Cincinnati. This research has been supported by grants DA01097, DA02867 and DA03196 and by Research Scientist Award DA00081 from the National Institute on Drug Abuse, and by an award from the Catherine T. and John D. MacArthur Foundation. The research assistance of Dan Karus is gratefully acknowledged.

prevalent notion that drug use is a cause of crime (Clayton and Tuchfeld, 1982; McBride and McCoy, 1982). Earlier evaluations of drug treatment programs (see Lukoff and Kleinman, 1977) disputed that such a causal association existed, and emphasized that drug users had delinquent careers that anteceded their drug involvement and their current delinquency. Recent studies, however, that have collected more detailed descriptions of drug use and criminal activities, in particular Ball and Nurco's work (Ball, Rosen, Flueck and Nurco, 1982) and Johnson and Preble's (Johnson et al., 1983) ethnographic studies, have established that criminal activities increase on days that addicts need to buy drugs to support their addiction.

The second issue, raised more frequently in considering adolescents and preadolescents rather than adults, considers whether drug use and delinquency are part of a single syndrome, and whether developmental stages can be delineated in their respective appearance (Robins and Wish, 1977). The syndrome can reflect a clinical disorder such as conduct disorders (DSM-III, 1980; Robins, 1978), a common psychological trait (Kaplan, 1980), common social developmental processes (Hawkins and Weiss, 1985) or a particular lifestyle (Jessor and Jessor, 1977). On the basis of an extensive longitudinal national sample of adolescents, Elliott and his colleagues concluded that among adolescents who had participated both in delinquency and in illicit drug use, delinquent activities preceded experimentation with illicit drugs in half the cases, with the other half evenly divided among young people who initiated both behaviors in the same year and those who initiated drug use prior to delinquency (Elliott and Huizinga, 1984; Huizinga and Elliott, 1981). In addition to timing and sequence, common etiology and risk factors would help resolve the issue as to whether drug use and delinquency are part of a single syndrome.

It is the issues of commonalities and differences in the predictors of delinquency and drug use from adolescence to young adulthood and the role which involvement in one of these behaviors has for later involvement in the other that we address in this study. We rely on longitudinal data covering a nine-year interval collected from a cohort of young men and women in their mid-twenties, who were first studied when in high school at age 15 to 16. We are concerned with the following three issues:

1. What is the prevalence and persistence of self-reported aggressive and nonaggressive delinquent behavior and drug use among young adults?

2. To what extent do delinquency and illicit drug use predict participation in the same behavior and participation in the other behavior from adolescence to young adulthood?

3. What factors, measured in adolescence and in the transitional period from adolescence to adulthood, best predict participation in delinquency and illicit drug use in young adulthood? Are the risk factors similar or divergent for the two types of outcomes? Are the risk factors similar or divergent among men and women?

Note that we use the term delinquency to refer to a variety of self-reported antisocial acts and not necessarily to behaviors that have come to the attention of the police or the courts.

METHODS

Sample

The data derive from a follow-up cohort of young adults, who were first studied as adolescents in 1971, at ages 15–16 and reinterviewed nine years later in 1980, at age 24–25. The cohort is representative of adolescents formerly enrolled in grades 10 and 11 in public secondary schools in New York State in 1971–72. The original high school sample was a random sample of the adolescent population attending public secondary schools in New York State in Fall 1971, with students selected from a stratified sample of 18 high schools throughout the state. The target population for the adult follow-up was drawn from the enrollment list of half the homerooms from grades 10 and 11 and included students who were absent from school at the time of the initial study. The inclusion of these former absentees assures the representativeness of the sample and the inclusion of the most deviant youths. As we confirmed subsequently from data derived from school records, these absentees can be considered to be truants, as per the definition of Robins and Ratcliff (1980).[1]

With an 81% completion rate of those alive, 1,325 young adults were interviewed in 1980–81 at a mean age of 24.7 years. The longitudinal analyses are based on the 1,004 respondents who had participated in the high school survey nine years earlier and exclude the former absentees for whom adolescent data are not available. As we will see, and not surprisingly, the restricted longitudinal matched sample is less deviant in certain respects than the total cohort. (See also Kandel, Raveis, and Kandel, 1984.)

Personal interviews were carried out that took on the average two hours to administer. The interview schedule comprised almost exclusively structured items with closed-end response alternatives. An unusual component of the schedule consisted of two charts designed to reconstruct on a monthly basis the respondents' life and drug histories, respectively. In order to reduce the respondents' burden, the drug histories were ascertained only from persons who reported having used a given drug at least 10 times in their lives. Thus, measures could be obtained of the timing and number of events and of the continuity or discontinuity of participation in drugs and various social roles. Although the retrospective data have various limitations in that they are subject to distortions, such as telescoping of recall,[2] they still provide unique information that is not otherwise available.

Definitions of Delinquency and Drug Use in Adolescence and Adulthood

Delinquency. Different measures assessed delinquency in adolescence and young adulthood. In young adulthood, respondents were presented with a list of 16 acts and asked whether they had ever committed each one in their lives. If they answered in the affirmative, they were asked how many times in the past year they had done so. Most of the items were taken from the delinquency scale in the *Youth in Transition* study (Johnston, O'Malley, and Eveland, 1978). Factor analyses were carried out on 10 items. Six of the items were eliminated, either because they were extremely rare in that they were reported by less than 1% or 2% of the sample (such as arson, armed robbery and passing bad checks),[3] were considered to reflect societal reaction rather than primary deviance (trouble with the police), were closely related to drug use behavior (selling drugs), or because they were too common (having had a fight or argument with parents). Three scales were identified: (1) a scale of interpersonal aggression (alpha = .69), composed of five items: serious fight, hurt someone badly, hit instructor or supervisor, taken car, gang fight, (2) a scale of theft (alpha = .75), composed of three items, shoplifting, theft under $50, theft over $50, and (3) a scale of vandalism (or property destruction) (alpha = .51) composed of 2 items: damaged property school/work, taken car. The two scales of interpersonal aggression and theft reflect the two basic dimensions of self-reported delinquency that have been consistently identified by others using similar self-report instruments (e.g., Johnston, O'Malley, and Eveland, 1978). Since the vandalism scale had an extremely skewed distribu-

tion and included an item that also loaded on the aggression scale, it was not used in any of the analyses.

A different series of questions about delinquent involvement were included at Time 1, when respondents were in high school. They were asked about their lifetime participation in five delinquent acts (taken a car, banged up something that did not belong to you on purpose, theft over $50, held up or robbed a person, played the numbers racket) and their participation within the last three months in another set of six acts (theft under $2, theft $2–$50, been sent out of a classroom by a teacher, cheated on a class test, run away from home or stayed out all night without parent's permission, driven too fast). A factor analysis of these eleven items plus a twelfth on self-reported number of school absences during the last year indicated that they loaded on a single factor. A general delinquency scale that summated the twelve items was created (alpha = .63).

Illicit Drug Use. The use of marijuana was distinguished from the use of other illicit drugs, which include psychedelics, cocaine, heroin and non-medical use of minor tranquilizer, sedatives, stimulants, methadone in adolescence, as well as major tranquilizers and anti-depressants in young adulthood.

In adolescence, two measures were constructed that identified whether an individual had ever used any of these two classes of drugs, marijuana and other illicit drugs. In young adulthood, more differentiated variables took into account the frequency of use of each class of drugs in the last twelve months. The 8-category frequency variable ranged from used "not at all" to "every day," coded 1 through 8. If multiple illicit drugs had been used in the last year, the classification was based on the component drug used at the highest frequency.

RESULTS

Although our main interest is in the adolescent risk factors that predict participation in delinquency and drug use in young adulthood, it is useful first to consider the prevalence of these behaviors in adulthood and the stability of the two behaviors over time from adolescence to young adulthood.

The Epidemiology of Delinquency and Illicit Drug Use

Delinquent Activities in Young Adulthood. What is the prevalence of delinquent acts in young adulthood at age 24–25 among these former high school students and how much stability does it represent compared to lifetime participation in the behaviors that constitute the scales? Other investigators have noted the decline of participation in delinquent acts in late adolescence and adulthood compared to childhood and early adolescence. (See, for example, Farrington, 1983; Leober, 1985; McCord, 1980; Robins, 1966; Robins and Wish, 1977; Rutter, 1978.)

It should be noted that the levels of delinquency reported by members of the panel sample are lower than in the representative cross-section. As mentioned earlier, because we are interested in identifying antecedent risk factors, the longitudinal analyses are based on the matched longitudinal sample of individuals who had participated in the initial high school survey. These individuals are much less likely to have a history of self-reported delinquency than those who had been absent from school on the day of the high school survey. Differences are especially striking with respect to items that measure more serious behaviors, those included in the index of interpersonal aggression and serious theft over $50.00. These contrasts hold both for men and for women.

As is to be expected, a much smaller proportion of individuals have committed a delinquent act in the last twelve months compared to lifetime. However, while women are less likely than men to get initially involved in delinquent activities, once initiation has taken place, they are as likely as men to remain active participations.[4] Overall, approximately 50% of those who reported ever to have committed any type of offense also did so in the last year preceding the adult interview. These trends are illustrated more clearly in Table 1 which displays participation in at least one of the ten delinquent acts, as well as any participation specifically in theft and interpersonal aggression. In most instances, there is substantial persistence of participation among those who have ever been involved, since the proportion reporting any activity in the last year represents about 50% of those who admitted to lifetime involvement (see Robins, 1966; Robins and Ratcliff, 1980; West and Farrington, 1977). In addition to reflecting persistence of participation, these data could also be interpreted to reflect the salience of recent events or potential distortion in recall, with foreshortening of the period of recall.

Illicit Drug Use in Young Adulthood. The phenomenology of involvement in illicit drugs differs from that of participation in delinquent activities in several respects: in terms of the contrasts between the behaviors of former regular students and absentees, and the behaviors of men and women, and especially in terms of persistence over time.

Among men and women, former absentees do not differ from former regular students in their extent of current drug involvement (Table 2). The contrast with the differences between the two groups observed with respect to delinquency document the crucial role of lack of commitment to school in adolescent delinquency.

To the extent that individuals who are included at both points in time in the longitudinal survey represent a biased subsample of the age cohort, this bias occurs with respect to delinquent activities rather than with illicit drug behavior.

Persistence of the use of illicit drugs is generally much greater than persistence of commission of delinquent acts. Over 75% or more of the males who ever used one of the illicit drugs at least 10 times in

TABLE 1 Proportion of Young Adults Reporting at Age 24–25 Having Done at Least One Delinquent Act and Persistence of Involvement

	MALES			FEMALES		
	At least one act		% of ever who did so in last year	At least one act		% of ever who did so in last year
	Ever %	In last year %	%	Ever %	In last year %	%
Interpersonal aggression	38	19	50	14	8	57
Theft	40	23	58	22	9	41
Any deviant act	49	27	55	25	13	52
Total N	(446)	(446)		(558)	(558)	

TABLE 2   Last Year Frequency of the Use of Illicit Drugs in Young Adulthood at Age 24–25

	FORMER REGULAR STUDENTS		FORMER ABSENTEES	
	Marijuana	*Other Illicit Drugs*	*Marijuana*	*Other Illicit Drugs*
MEN:				
Total who used last year:	*52%*	*21%*	*52%*	*18%*
Less than once a week	24	18	17	13
1–3 times a week	15	2	17	3
4 times or more	13	1	18	3
Total N	(446)	(446)	(173)	(173)
WOMEN:				
Total who used last year:	*36%*	*10%*	*29%*	*11%*
Less than once a week	22	8	16	6
1–3 times a week	7	1.5	10	4
4 times or more	7	.5	3	.5
Total N	(558)	(558)	(148)	(148)

their lives remained active users of that drug during the year preceding the adult interview (Table 3). This compares to approximately 50% of those ever involved in delinquency, as shown in Table 1. Among women, approximately the same proportion remain participants in interpersonal aggression and continue to use other illicit drugs.

Finally, the proportion of persistent users is lower among women than men, again contrasting with the pattern for delinquency. Women are less likely than men to become deviant, but once involved in delinquency they are as likely as men to remain delinquent. With respect to illicit drugs, women are less likely to become involved and less

likely to remain users to these drugs, once initiated into their use.

Interrelationships of Participation in Delinquency and Drug Use.   Finally, confirming a consistent result of prior studies, we find that involvement in illicit drugs is related to participation in delinquency. A five-group classification of active use of illicit drugs in the last year was created that distinguished individuals who had never used these drugs, those who had used them sometime in the past but not in the past year, and among the active users those who were only using marijuana, those who were using other illicit drugs but not cocaine, with cocaine

TABLE 3   Proportion of Young Adults Reporting Having Used Illicit Drugs at Least Ten Times in Their Lives and Persistence of Use in Young Adulthood at Age 24–25

	MALES			FEMALES		
	Used		% of ever who did so in last year	Used		% of ever who did so in last year
	Ever %	*In last year* %	%	*Ever* %	*In last year* %	%
Marijuana	65	52	80	51	36	71
Other illicit drugs	28	21	75	17	10	59
Total N	(446)	(446)		(558)	(558)	

users singled out from all other users. There is a positive relationship between involvement in drugs and delinquency, with the users of illicit drugs other than marijuana more deviant than those who have used only marijuana or have used illicit drugs sometime in the past but not currently.

Mutual Effects of Delinquency and Illicit Drug Use Over Time

To what extent do delinquency and drug use in adolescence predict themselves and each other over time?

The results show certain similarities but also important contrasts between men and women.

Simple models were tested which included two adolescent predictors, the index of general delinquency and each of the two illicit drug use measures, in turn, and three outcomes in young adulthood: scores on the index of theft, the index of aggression, and alternately use of marijuana and other illicit drugs. Because of their high interrelationships, each of the two measures of illicit drug use was considered in separate models. Results of the two models are displayed in Figure 1 for men and in Figure 2 for women.

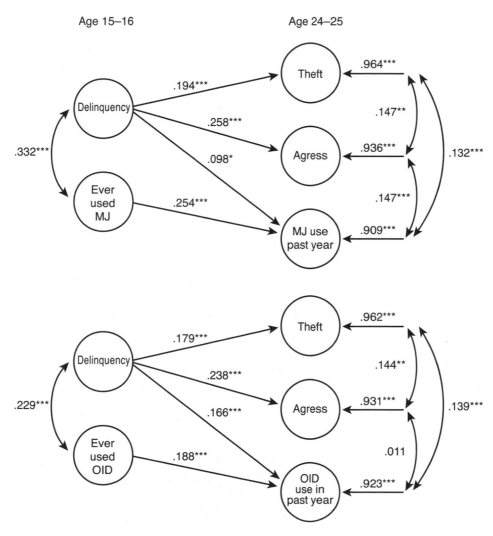

Standardized Coefficients: Lisrel Model. OID = Other Illicit Drugs
  *p < .05
 **p < .01
***p < .001

FIGURE 1   Effects of Adolescent Drug Use and Delinquency on Drug Use and Delinquency in Young Adulthood at Age 24–25, Among Men.

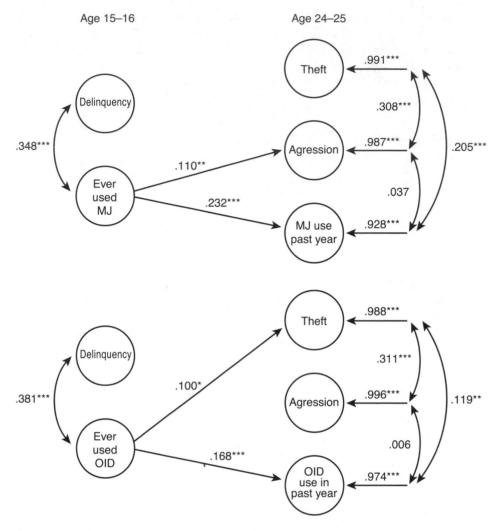

Standardized Coefficients: Lisrel Model. OID = Other Illicit Drugs
   *p < .05
  **p < .01
 ***p < .001

FIGURE 2   Effects of Adolescent Drug Use and Delinquency on Drug Use and Delinquency in Young Adulthood at Age 24–25, Among Women.

Among men, both illicit drug use and delinquency predict themselves over time, but while adolescent delinquency predicts the use of illicit drugs in early adulthood, illicit drugs does not predict later delinquency (Figure 1). This confirms the conclusions reached by a number of investigators that delinquency is a precursor to the use of illicit drugs, rather than the reverse.

However, not all these patterns hold exclusively for women. The patterns for women, however, differ in two important respects (Figure 2). One point of

similarity between women and men is that illicit drug use in adolescence predicts illicit drug use in young adulthood, and predicts it with the same intensity. Delinquency in adolescence does not predict delinquency in young adulthood, but illicit drug use does so: use of marijuana predicts interpersonal aggression and use of other illicit drugs predict participation in theft.

These causal models reflect the unique effects of adolescent behaviors on adult outcomes controlling for the other behavior in the equation, but not for any other characteristics that could also account for these relationships. There may be other important risk factors which can be identified in adolescence or between adolescence and young adulthood as singling out those individuals who will have a higher risk of becoming active participants either in delinquent activities or in illicit drug use as young adults, risk factors which may eliminate the effects of adolescent delinquency and illicit drug use identified in the simple causal models just described.

Risk Factors for Delinquency and Drug Use in Young Adulthood

In order to identify additional risk factors, a series of multiple regressions were carried out among men and women, where four different behavioral outcomes within the last year in young adulthood constituted the dependent variables: each form of delinquency, theft and interpersonal aggression, and the two forms of illicit drug use, marijuana and other illicit drugs.

Identical predictors were included in all the regressions and represented three different classes of predictor variables (1) sociodemographic characteristics, (2) variables measured in adolescence, and (3) variables measured in the intervening period between the initial survey and twelve months preceding the follow-up interview so as not to confound antecedents and consequences of the four outcomes.

Adolescent Variables (Time 1). The 15 variables measured in adolescence assessed selected aspects of the adolescent's life that, according to socialization, social learning and social control theories, could be expected to constitute positive or negative risk factors for subsequent deviant behaviors, such as illicit drug use and delinquency.

We included measures of parental models for drug use (measures of parental models for delinquency were not available), measures of parental decision-making (whether the parent was autocratic, democratic or permissive), attachment (closeness to parents,[5] score on a peer activity index[5]), commitment (commitment to school index,[5] frequency of church attendance), psychological status (whether parent or sibling were ever treated for an emotional disorder, score on index of depressive mood[5]), and delinquency (general delinquency index described above), and drug use (lifetime use of four separate classes of drugs by the time of the initial survey: cigarettes, alcohol, marijuana/hashish, and other illicit drugs). The drug variables measured early onset into the illicit drugs: 37% of the cohort members who ever

used marijuana and 20% of the users of other illicit drugs had done so by the initial survey. Parental drug use variables were restricted to use reported for a single parent: alcohol for the father and use of medically prescribed drugs by the mother, since these were found in earlier analyses to be the most important for each parent in determining their children's involvement in illicit drugs (Kandel, Kessler, and Margulies, 1978).

Intervening Variables (Adolescence to Early Adulthood). Eight intervening predictors were included in each model and measured a person's status up to the thirteenth month preceding the interview, so as not to confound determinants and consequences of the four adult outcomes under study. The non-drug variables assessed commitment to the social roles of adulthood and included whether or not the person had dropped out of high school, number of years of schooling attained, number of unemployment spells (including never worked), and whether ever married.

Little information was available on the commission of delinquent acts during the follow-up interval, except for whether or not the person had been arrested, a more serious indicator than participation in the acts included in the delinquency scales.

Three intervening drug use variables were created to characterize the cumulative degree of involvement in cigarettes, alcoholic beverages, and illicit drugs. Among individuals who had used each of twelve classes of drugs at least 10 times, the retrospective drug histories ascertained their use of that class of drug during the interval (coded for monthly intervals), the period of highest use, and the frequency of use during the highest use period. This information was used to create an adjusted cumulative measure of involvement up to the 13th month preceding the interview for each of the twelve classes of drugs inquired about in the drug histories. For each drug, the measure took into account the total number of months of use and the intensity of use. For cigarettes and alcoholic beverages, the intervening involvement variable was the total number of months of use of each class of drug weighted by the frequency of use during the period of highest use of the drug. These frequencies ranged from once a year to every day. For illicit drugs, a summary variable was created that summed the weighted total number of months for each of ten classes of illicit drugs that had been used, including marijuana. Because of the high association in the use of marijuana and other illicit drugs, and the resulting multicollinearity when separate measures for marijuana and other illicit drugs were entered in the regressions, marijuana was included in a combined illicit drug use variable. This variable was logarithm transformed to normalize its distribution.

Results of the regressions of the two delinquency scales for men and women showing only the statistically significant zero-order correlations and predictors are interesting. Although many variables have significant zero-order correlations with the four outcomes, few variables retain a uniquely significant statistical effect once other variables are simultaneously included in the model. The uniquely significant predictors of adult delinquency are different for men and women and they are different for different types of delinquency. A greater amount of the variance is explained for interpersonal aggression than for theft. For men, confirming a finding of the simpler causal model, general delinquency in adolescence is one of the strongest predictors of delinquency in young adulthood, controlling for other adolescent and intervening characteristics. The only other important factor for theft is cumulative illicit drug use in the intervening period between adolescence and young adulthood. For interpersonal aggression being a school dropout and adolescent family-related factors are important, namely family intactness and having an authoritarian mother. Cumulative illicit drug use also is an important predictor of theft for women.

The striking difference between men and women is the uniquely important role of psychological factors as predictors of subsequent delinquency among women. For women, a family history of emotional disorders and dysphoric mood in adolescence are important predictors while earlier delinquency is not. For men and women, intervening illicit drug use predicts one type of delinquency, theft, but not interpersonal aggression. For both men and women, interpersonal aggression seems to be predicted by more serious forms of prior maladjustment than those which predict theft, such as being a high school dropout for men and having had an arrest for women.

Adolescent drug use rarely is a significant predictive factor on subsequent delinquency, even when intervening variables are omitted from the regressions. The only observed effect is in predicting interpersonal aggression among women.

Different patterns characterize the predictors of illicit drug use compared with delinquency. In addition, there is a reversal in the type of adolescent factors that are respectively important for men and women. In contrast to delinquency, in predicting illicit drug use family factors are more important for women than for men. There seem to be some anomalous results in the

regressions, in particular, the negative effect of depression on the use of other illicit drugs among men and the positive coefficient of closeness to parents among women as predictors of marijuana, both opposite to what we would have predicted. In both cases, however, the zero-order correlations are not significant. For men and women, the most important predictive factors are drug use and lifestyle factors that intervene between adolescence and early adulthood. In particular, lack of participation in the conventional roles of work and marriage predict marijuana use among men and the use of other illicit drugs among men and women. Cumulative illicit drug use is a crucial factor for both types of drugs for men and women. There is also a unique cigarette use effect for men.

CONCLUSION

The risk model that we tested has greater predictive power for illicit drug use than delinquent involvement in young adulthood. Two factors may account for this differential predictability. Superior measures of the parallel intervening behavior were available for drug use than for delinquency. For delinquency, the single measure of arrest was available, while for drug use very comprehensive measures of cumulative involvement in different classes of drugs, including legal ones, could be included. However, eliminating the intervening measures of delinquency and other illicit drugs in the multiple regressions so as to render the models truly parallel conceptually across outcomes does not eliminate the differential explanatory power of the model across these outcomes. Elimination of the intervening measures of drug use and of arrest reduces dramatically the explained variance in the drug outcomes. For example, the explained variance in marijuana use in the last year preceding the interview decreases from 63% to 21% for men, and from 56% to 17% for women. The explanatory power of the models is still higher, however, for the drug outcomes than for delinquency. The explained variances are 7% and 16% for theft and interpersonal aggression among men, and 7% and 6%, respectively, among women. Explained variances for illicit drugs other than marijuana are 22% for men and 10% for women. Illicit drug behavior is better predicted than delinquency.

The lower overall predictive power of the model for delinquency as compared to illicit drug use may also be a function of developmental differences in participation in the two classes of behaviors and the particular periods in the lifecycle over which the predictions were made. In the very same period from mid-adolescence to young adulthood, involvement in delinquency declines while involvement in illicit drugs rises sharply. Indeed, prior studies have established that there is a negative exponential effect of age with delinquency, especially aggressive behaviors, from middle adolescence to early adulthood (Elliott, Knowles, and Canter, 1981; Simcha-Fagan and Silver, 1982). Thus, the initial measurements at age 15–16 in adolescence were made at a time when delinquency had already reached its peak. Delinquency measured in preadolescence seems to be most predictive of subsequent delinquency (Loeber, 1982, 1985; Loeber and Dishion, 1983; McCord, 1980; Robins and Ratcliff, 1980).

Cross-over effects are much stronger for the prediction of illicit drug use by delinquency than vice versa. Illicit drug use in the intervening period selectively predicts persistence in delinquent behavior in young adulthood among men and women; it does so for theft and has no effect on interpersonal aggression. These findings have important implications for several theoretical issues that have been raised in delinquency research. They support the distinction between overt (or "confrontive") and covert (or "concealing") delinquency emphasized by Patterson (1982) and Loeber (Loeber, 1985; Loeber and Schmaling, 1983). They also support the relationship of drug use to non-aggressive conduct disorders suggested by DSM-III (1980) and to covert delinquency, suggested by Loeber.

Different risk factors in adolescence predict continued delinquent involvement in early adulthood among men and women. In particular depression plays an important role for women and family factors for men. The significant role played by psychological distress among women suggests that a closer link exists between delinquency and psychopathology, especially depression, among women than among men. Furthermore, delinquency among males and illicit drug use among females may play similar roles in the lives of young people since they appear to be subject to common etiological factors.

Reflecting perhaps the continued initiation into illicit drugs and the sustained usage of these drugs that still occurs in the early twenties (Kandel and Logan, 1984), lifestyle factors subsequent to adolescence are important predictors of continued illicit drug use in young adulthood, but not of delinquency. More than early drug involvement in mid-adolescence, subsequent failure to enter the conventional roles of adulthood, in particular marriage and continuous employment, are important and uniquely significant predictors of continued illicit drug involvement in young adulthood.

Similarly, McCord (1981) found that the likelihoods of marriage and alcoholism were inversely related.

Despite the difficulties involved in comparing these results with those of other studies because of differences in measures, and in the subjects' age and racial background, certain convergences emerge across studies. These convergences pertain to sex differences and the importance of specific parental patterns of behaviors in fostering specific types of delinquent behaviors in their children. The greater association between psychopathology and delinquency among women as compared to men observed in the present study parallels that reported earlier by Simcha-Fagan (1979) for an urban sample ranging in age from 11 to 23 at the time of a longitudinal follow-up, despite great differences in the measures used in the two studies. Simcha-Fagan (1979) also stressed that for girls, "early severe emotional pathology seems of crucial importance" (p. 175) as an etiological factor in self-reported and official delinquency. Similarly, the greater importance of family-related factors among males as compared to females was also found in that earlier study, as in Kellam and his collaborators' follow-up of a black sample from first grade to middle adolescence (Ensminger, Kellam and Rubin, 1983).

The results also support the thesis that parental coerciveness and aggression predict interpersonal aggression in children. We found that adolescent males who reported their mothers to be authoritarian had a significantly increased risk of engaging in interpersonal aggression as young adults. Patterson (1982) emphasized that parental coerciveness toward children, especially on the part of mothers, characterized the families of the children described as "social aggressors" in contrast to "stealers." McCord (1979) found that parental conflict and aggression were related to children committing crimes against persons and not to crimes against property.

The results presented in this study are based on multiple regressions and imply that certain causal processes intervene between adolescence and early adulthood, processes that were not actually subjected to an empirical test. The regressions must be supplemented by path models that will establish not only the total unique effect of a particular variable but the various indirect and direct paths that connect different factors to each other. The lack of a measure of intervening delinquency to parallel the drug measure will be a serious limitation of these analyses, however. One hypothesis we plan to explore is the extent to which early delinquency predisposes adolescents to involvement in drug use, the latter acting as a stabilizing force in sustaining delinquent participation.

However, these data bring us slightly closer to providing an answer to the basic question with which we started this inquiry. Is there a common set of etiological factors that predict adult participation in delinquent activities and continued consumption of illicit drugs? The answer is not a simple affirmative or negative one. The answer depends on the type of delinquency, the type of drug used, and sex of the individual. For men, a common etiology is more apparent between illicit drugs and theft than between illicit drugs and interpersonal aggression. Furthermore, since the same factors that predict illicit drug use among women predict delinquency among men, these two behaviors may play similar functions in one sex as compared to the other.

NOTES

1. In the school year 1971–72, the average number of school absences reported for the former regular students who had participated in the initial survey was 12 days as compared to 19.5 days for the former absentees.

2. Although validity of recall has been previously established for reports of certain drug use patterns (Ball, 1967; Parry et al., 1970–71), underreporting, telescoping and distortions have generally been shown to affect recall of various life events (Uhlenhuth et al., 1977). However, as stressed by Featherman (1980), distortions in retrospective reports may not necessarily be greater than those in contemporaneous reports. In the earlier phase of the research carried out in high school, we found that inconsistencies in self-reported patterns of drug use over a 6 month interval were associated with light patterns of use (Single et al., 1975).

   In order to assess the validity of retrospective reports in the follow-up interviews, we relied on two strategies. We compared: (1) reports in 1980 for similar events reported on in 1971, and (2) rates of retrospective self-reported drug use for 1977 with rates for the same age cohort interviewed contemporaneously in 1977 in the General Household Survey (Fishburne et al., 1980). The majority of recalled use patterns are consistent with those reported in 1971, especially for marijuana: 79% of males and 85% of females give consistent reports, although young people who reported not using as high school students are more consistent than those who reported using. The marginal distributions in reported lifetime prevalence are identical at both points in time (27%), but only because an equal number of persons gave inconsistent reports from the initial non-using (N = 88) and using (N = 86) groups. However, while in 1971, 259 adolescents reported to have already used marijuana, in 1980, only 173 (67%) of these same persons remembered having done so. The inconsistencies are larger for cigarettes and for alcohol than for marijuana. Thus, the distributions of self-reported users in 1971 were 71% for cigarettes and 86% for alcohol, whereas only 49% and 68%, respectively, recalled being users by 1980. Most of the inconsistencies represent failures to recall Time 1 use at Time 3. Similarly, there are discrepancies in the ages of onset of use recalled in young adulthood by those who had indicated in 1971 that they were already using certain drugs, with a greater proportion reporting a later age of onset than was reported initially.

   Although there appears to be a consistent telescoping and foreshortening of time in the recall process, there must be gradual adjustments over the life span being recalled. The annual prevalence of marijuana use (44%) reported retrospectively for 1977 at age 21–22, three years prior to the 1980 interview, is almost identical to that reported contemporaneously by members of parallel birth cohorts in the General Household Survey (Fishburne et al., 1980, Table 18). In 1977, 41% of persons aged 18–21 and 36% of those 22–25 reported using marijuana in the last year. (Given the tabulations in the report on the General Household Survey, more exact age comparisons cannot be made.)

3. These deletions, however, did not result in delinquents being classified as non-delinquents since individuals who had committed one of the more serious acts had also committed one or more of the less serious ones.

4. Male absentees are also more likely than former regular students to have committed delinquent acts as young adults; the higher rates, however, do not represent substantially higher persistence but a higher initial baseline. Former absentee women, however, show less persistence than males.

5. The index of closeness to parents is the average score of two separate indices for each parent. The closeness to father index was based on four items: depending on parent for advice, feeling close to parent, willing to be like parent, and getting praise from parent (Cronbach's alpha = .84). Closeness to mother included a fifth item, frequency of talking to parent about personal problems (Cronbach's alpha = .79). The degree of peer activity index is based on five items asking about frequency of getting together with friends outside school, dating, attending parties, hanging around with a group of kids, and driving around with friends (Cronbach's alpha = .68). Depressive mood index is based on a six-item scale asking respondents how often they had been "bothered or troubled" by each of six states within the past year: feeling too tired to do things, having trouble going to sleep or staying asleep, feeling unhappy, sad or depressed, feeling hopeless about the future, feeling nervous or tense, and worrying too much about things (Cronbach's alpha = .79). The commitment to school index is the sum of the z-scores for the following items: average time spent per day on homework, grade average in previous term, educational expectations, frequency of boredom with classes, and the average number of classes cut per week (Cronbach's alpha = .60).

REFERENCES

Bachman, J. G., Johnston, L. D., and O'Malley, P. M. (1981). Smoking, drinking, and drug use among American high school students: Correlates and trends, 1975–1979. *American Journal of Public Health*, 71, 59–69.

Ball, J. C. (1967). The reliability and validity of interview data obtained from 59 narcotic drug addicts. *American Journal of Sociology*, 72, 650–665.

Ball, J. C., Rosen, L., Flueck, J. A., and Nurco, D. N. (1981). The criminality of heroin addicts when addicted and when off opiates. In J. A. Inciardi (Ed.), *The Drugs-Crime Connection*. Beverly Hills: Sage. Chapter 2.

Clayton, R. R., and Tuchfeld, B. S. (1982). The drug crime debate: Obstacles to understanding the relationship. *Journal of Drug Issues*, 12(2), 153–166.

Diagnostic and Statistical Manual of Mental Disorders, 3rd ed. (1980). (SMD-III). Washington, DC: American Psychiatric Association.

Elliott, D. S., and Huizinga, D. (1984). *The Relationship Between Delinquent Behavior and ADM Problems*. The National Youth Survey Project Report No. 28. Boulder, CO: Behavioral Research Institute.

Elliott, D. S., Knowles, B. A., and Canter, R. J. (1981). The epidemiology of delinquent behavior and drug use among American adolescents, 1976–1978. Unpublished manuscript. Boulder, CO: Behavioral Research Institute.

Ensminger, M. E., Kellam, S. G., and Rubin, B. R. (1983). School and family origins of delinquency: Comparisons by sex. In K. T. Van Dusen and S. A. Mednick (Eds.), *Prospective Studies of Crime and Delinquency*, pp. 73–97. Boston: Kluwer-Nijhoff Publishing.

Farrington, D. P. (1983). Offending from 10 to 25 Years of Age. In K. T. Van Dusen and S. A. Mednick (Eds.), *Prospective Studies of Crime and Delinquency*, pp. 17–37. Boston: Kluwer-Nijhoff Publishing.

Fishburne, P., Abelson, J., and Cisin, I. (1980). *The National Survey on Drug Abuse: Main Findings, 1979*. Washington, DC: U.S. Government Printing Office.

Hawkins, J. D., and Weiss, G. J. (1985). The social developmental model. *Journal of Primary Prevention* (in press).

Huizinga, D. H., and Elliott, D. S. (1981). *A Longitudinal Study of Delinquency and Drug Use in a National Sample of Youth: An Assessment of Causal Order*. The National Youth survey Project Report No. 16. Boulder, CO: Behavioral Research Institute.

Jessor, R., Donovan, J. E., and Widmer, K. (1980). *Psychosocial Factors in Adolescent Alcohol and Drug Use: The 1978 National Sample Study, and the 1974-78 Panel Study*. Unpublished final report. Boulder, CO: Institute of Behavioral Science, University of Colorado.

Jessor, R., and Jessor, S. (1977). *Problem Behavior and Psychosocial Development—A Longitudinal Study of Youth*. New York: Academic Press.

Johnson, B. D., Goldstein, P. J., Preble, E., Schmiedler, J., Lipton, D. S., Spunt, B., Miller, T., Duchaine, N., Kale, A., Norman, R., and Hand, D. (1983). Final report of economic behavior of street opiate users. New York Narcotic and Drug Research, Inc.

Johnson, B. D., Wish, E., and Huizinga, D. (1983). *The Concentration of Delinquent Offending: The Contribution of Serious Drug Involvement to High Rate Delinquency*. Interdisciplinary Research Center for the Study of the Relations of Drugs and Alcohol to Crime. Washington, DC.

Johnston, L. D., O'Malley, P. M., and Eveland, L. K. (1978). Drugs and delinquency: A search for causal connections. In D. B. Kandel (Ed.), *Longitudinal Surveys of Research on Drug Use*. New York: Wiley.

Kandel, D. B., Kessler, R. C., and Margulies, R. Z. (1978). Antecedents of adolescent initiation into stages of drug use: A developmental analysis. *Journal of Youth and Adolescence*, 7, 13–40.

Kandel, D., and Logan, J. A. (1984). Patterns of drug use from adolescence to early adulthood—I. Periods of risk for initiation, stabilization and decline in drug use from adolescence to early adulthood. *American Journal of Public Health*, 74, 660–666.

Kandel, D. B., Ravies, V. H., and Kandel, P. I. (1984). Continuity in discontinuity: Adjustment in young adulthood of former school absentees and school dropouts. *Youth and Society*, 13, 325–52.

Kaplan, H. B. (1980). *Deviant Behavior in Defense of Self*. New York: Academic Press.

Loeber, R. (1982). The stability of antisocial and delinquent child behavior: A review. *Child Development*, 53, 1431–1446.

Loeber, R. (1985). Patterns and Development of Antisocial Child Behavior. In G. Whitehurst (Ed.), *Annals of Child Development* (vol. 2). Greenwich, CT: JAI Press (in press).

Loeber, R., and Dishion, T. (1983). Early predictors of male delinquency: A review. *Psychological Bulletin* 94(1), 68–99.

Loeber, R., and Schmaling, K. B. (1983). *Empirical Evidence for Overt and Covert Patterns of Antisocial Conduct Problems: A Meta-Analysis*. Eugene: Oregon Social Learning Center.

Lukoff, I. F., and Kleinman, P. H. (1977). The addict life cycle and problems in treatment evaluation. In A. Schecter (Ed.), *Rehabilitation Aspects of Drug Dependence*, Chapter 10. Cleveland: CRC Press, Inc.

McBride, D. C., and McCoy, C. B. (1982). Crime and drugs: The issues and literature. *Journal of Drug Issues*, 12(2), 137–151.

McCord, J. (1979), Some Child-Rearing Antecedents of Criminal Behavior in Adult Men. *Journal of Personality and Social Psychology*, 37, 477–1486.

McCord, J. (1980), Patterns of Deviance. In S. B. Sells, R. Crandall, M. Roff, J. S. Strauss, and W. Pollin (Eds.), *Human Functioning in Longitudinal Perspective*, Chapter 12. Baltimore: Williams and Wilkins.

McCord, J. (1981). Alcoholism and criminality: Confounding and differentiating factors. *Journal of Studies on Alcohol*, 42, 739–748.

McGlothlin, W. (1979). Drugs and crime. *Handbook on Drug Abuse*. National Institute on Drug Abuse, Office of Drug Abuse Policy, Washington, DC.

O'Donnell, J. A. (1969). *Narcotic Addicts in Kentucky*. Washington, D.C.: U.S. Government Printing Office.

O'Donnell, J. A., Voss, H. L., Clayton, R. R., Slatin, G. T., and Room, R. (1976). *Young Men and Drugs: A Nationwide Survey*. NIDA Research Monograph No. 5. DHEW Pub. No. (ADM) 76–311. Washington, DC: Supt. of Docs., U.S. Government Printing Office.

Osborn, S. G., and West, D. J. (1980). Do young delinquents really reform? *Journal of Adolescence, 3*, 99–114.

Parry, H. J., Balter, M. B., and Cisin, I. H. (1970–1971). Primary levels of underreporting psychotropic drug use (with and without the use of visual aids). *Public Opinion Quarterly, 34*, 582–592.

Patterson, G. R. (1982). *Coercive Family Processes*. Eugene, OR: Castalia Publishing Company.

Robins, L. N. (1966). *Deviant Children Grow Up*. Baltimore: Williams and Wilkins.

Robins, L. N. (1978). Sturdy childhood predictors of adult anti-social behaviour: Republications from longitudinal studies. *Psychological Medicine, 8*, 611–622.

Robins, L. N., and Ratcliff, K. S. (1980). The long-term outcome of truancy. In L. Herson and I. Berg (Eds.), *Out of school*, pp. 65–83, New York: John Wiley & Sons.

Robins, L. N., and Wish, E. (1977). Childhood deviance as a developmental process: A study of 223 urban black men from birth to 18. *Social Forces, 56*, 448–473.

Rutter, M. (1978). Family, area, and school influences in the genesis of conduct disorders. In L. A. Hersov, M. Berger, and D. Shaffer (Eds.), *Aggression and Antisocial Behavior in Childhood and Adolescence*. Oxford: Pergamon.

Simcha-Fagan, O. (1979). The prediction of delinquent behavior over time: Sex specific patterns related to official and survey-reported delinquent behavior. In R. G. Simmons (Ed.), *Research in Community and Mental Health, Vol. 1*, pp. 163–181. Greenwich, CT: JAI Press.

Simcha-Fagan, O., and Silver, M. (1982). Social background, parental predispositions and delinquent behavior: An examination of the mediating effect of family socialization. Presented at the Annual Meeting of the Society of Criminology, Toronto.

Simpson, D. D., and Sells, S. B. (1982). Effectiveness of treatment for drug abuse: An overview of the DARP Research Program. *Advances in Alcohol and Substance Abuse, 2*(1), 7–29.

Single, E., Kandel, D., and Johnson, B. (1975), The reliability and validity of drug use responses in a large scale longitudinal survey. *Journal of Drug Issues, 5*, 426–443.

Thornton, W. E. (1981). Marijuana use and delinquency. *Youth and Society, 13*(1), 23–37.

Tuchfeld, B. S., Clayton, R. R., and Logan, J. A. (1982). Alcohol, drug use and delinquent and criminal behaviors. *Journal of Drug Issues, 12*(2), 185–198.

Uhlenhuth, E. H., Haberman, S. J., Balter, M. D., and Lipman, R. S. (1977). Remembering life events. In J. S. Strauss, H. Babigian, and M. Roff (Eds.), *The Origins and Course of Psychopathology*. New York: Plenum.

Weitzel, S. L., and Blount, W. R. (1982). Incarcerated female felons and substance abuse. *Journal of Drug Issues, 12*, 259–273.

West, D. J., and Farrington, D. P. (1977). *The Delinquent Way of Life*. New York: Crane Russak.

White, H. R., Johnston, V., and Garrison, C. G. (1983). The drug-crime nexus among adolescents and their peers. Paper presented at the 1983 annual meeting of the American Sociological Association, Detroit.

13

Street Youth and Criminal Violence

STEPHEN W. BARON

TIMOTHY F. HARTNAGEL

ABSTRACT

This research examines the roles of various subcultural, economic, and victimization factors in the violent behavior of 200 homeless male street youths. Findings reveal that factors associated with the street subculture, including long-term homelessness and criminal peers, increase the respondent's risk for violence on the street and provide rules concerning honor, protection, and retribution. However, the heavy use of drugs and alcohol on the street plays only a minor role in explaining violent behavior in this population, and the violence associated with these substances appears to be recreational. Findings also suggest that minimal economic resources and perceptions of a blocked opportunity structure also leave the youths at risk for various violent activities. Results also indicate that victimization on the street and a history of physical abuse in the home are related to the respondents' violent behavior. Results are discussed in terms of different types of violent behavior.

The term *street youth* usually refers to youth who have run away or been expelled from their homes and/or who spend some or all of their time in various public locations (Kufeldt and Nimmo, 1987a, 1987b; McCullagh and Greco, 1990; Smart et al., 1990). Most of these street youths are underemployed/ unemployed, often lack a permanent residence, and spend significant amounts of time without shelter (Hagan and McCarthy, 1992; Kufeldt and Nimmo, 1987a, 1987b; McCarthy and Hagan, 1991, 1992a, 1992b; Palenski, 1984; Webber, 1991). Their lives are characterized by poverty, hunger, and other conditions of extreme deprivation (Hagan and McCarthy, 1992; Kufeldt and Nimmo, 1987a, 1987b; McCarthy and Hagan, 1991, 1992a, 1992b; Palenski, 1984; Webber, 1991).

Past research suggests this population is heavily involved in criminal activity (Brennan, Huizinga, and Elliott, 1978; Janus et al., 1987; Kufeldt and Nimmo, 1987a, 1987b; McCarthy and Hagan, 1991, 1995; Palenski, 1984; Radford, King, and Warren, 1989; Rothman, 1991; Smart et al., 1990) and indicates that these activities are influenced by various family, school, and street factors (Brennan et al., 1978; Gullotta, 1979; Hagan and McCarthy, 1992; Kufeldt and Nimmo, 1987a, 1987b; McCarthy and Hagan, 1992a; Palenski, 1984; Rothman, 1991). However, McCarthy and Hagan (1991, 1992a, 1995; see also Palenski, 1984) argue that street youths' participation in crime is most likely the result of the homeless experience itself, and not the direct effect of predisposing background variables.

Yet, little research has explored just what aspects of street life lead to criminal behavior. Hagan and McCarthy (1992) suggest that at a minimum, the relationship between homelessness and crime and delinquency is poorly specified, arguing that street life is something of a "black box," and they call for researchers to demonstrate the specific conditions, experiences, and aspects of life on the street that cause delinquency.

The financial support of the Social Sciences and Humanities Research Council of Canada, the solicitor general of Canada, and the Edmonton Sociological Society is gratefully acknowledged. The authors would also like to thank James Finckenauer and the anonymous reviewers for their comments.

Limited research suggests that street youths are active participants in group fights, robbery, and other serious assaults (Baron, 1989a, 1989b, 1995; Kennedy and Baron, 1993; McCarthy and Hagan, 1991). But the specific conditions and experiences of the street leading to street youth violence are poorly understood in that most research on this population tends to focus on understanding the background factors that lead these youths to being on the street and documenting their utilitarian behaviors (theft and prostitution) once there (Brennan et al., 1978; Gullotta, 1979; Hagan and McCarthy, 1992; Kudfeldt and Nimmo, 1987a, 1987b; McCarthy and Hagan, 1991, 1992a, 1992b, 1995; Palenski, 1984; Radford et al., 1989; Rothman, 1991).

The literature does, however, point to a number of intersections between the characteristics of street youth and the conditions others argue are conducive to violent crime including poverty, unemployment, substance abuse, and victimization (Fagan and Jones, 1984; Fagan, Piper, and Moore, 1986; Hartstone and Hansen, 1984). However, a review of the other available literature reveals a historical inclination to adopt "unicausal" explanations (Fagan and Jones, 1984) of violence. The tendency has been for researchers to focus on only one of the many possible causal paths (i.e., family violence, poverty, subcultural support) while ignoring the influence of other probable factors (Fagan and Jones, 1984). As a result, the field has been left with a number of competing accounts of limited explanatory power. Further, this work has failed to explore how these frameworks work to explain different forms of violence, focusing instead on more general explanations. Finally, the applicability of findings from other populations to homeless street youths is an open issue because the street population has been all but neglected in other individual level research (Hagan and McCarthy, 1992; Inciardi, Horowitz, and Pottieger, 1993).

The current research draws from several criminological perspectives in an effort to identify the specific aspects of street life that lead to several varieties of criminal violence. Specifically, subcultural, economic deprivation and routine activities theories will be used to develop hypotheses regarding these causal processes. Furthermore, given the evidence of the effect of family abuse on later violence (Elliott, 1994; Hartstone and Hansen, 1984; Hotaling, Straus, and Lincoln, 1989; McCord, 1979; Sedgely and Lund, 1979; Smith and Thornberry, 1995; Straus, 1985; Widom, 1989), we distinguish further between prior family and recent street experiences of violent victimization as possible causal variables in the youths' street

violence. We will also explore whether four different forms of violence in this population have different antecedents. Finally, we supplement our quantitative analysis of the net effects of several predictor variables with some open-ended interview data to further elucidate these processes as seen by street youths.

THEORETICAL PERSPECTIVES

Street Subculture and Lifestyle

A popular explanation for the violent behavior of youths has drawn from a subculture of violence perspective. Fagan and Jones (1984) note that the highest rates of aggressive behavior are located in environments where aggressive role models are abundant and where aggressiveness is a positive attribute. The peer group offers a climate where violent behaviors are modeled, practiced, and reinforced. Some have suggested that the violent crime in these groups is a product of conformity to a distinctive culture. Those who are in intimate contact with groups organized in favor of violent criminal activities become exposed to definitions favorable to this unlawful behavior, and, given their extensive associations with such definitions, such individuals are likely to act in terms of them, committing violent crimes (Curtis, 1975; Gastil, 1971; Wolfgang and Ferracuti, 1967).

In this tradition, Horowitz (1983) suggests that violence revolves around insult and honor. Horowitz argues that honor is a normative code that "stresses the inviolability of one's manhood and defines breaches of etiquette, in an adversarial idiom." Honor sensitizes members of the subculture to violations that are interpreted as "derogations of the self" and must be responded to with physical violence.

At a broader level, Inciardi et al. (1993) argue that criminal behavior is a "definitional characteristic" of a street lifestyle and subculture for those who spend considerable amounts of time on the street. Over time, contacts become increasingly limited to other street people, values become altered to fit behaviors, and crime becomes an accepted part of life.

Part and parcel of this street lifestyle is the use of drugs and alcohol (Inciardi et al., 1993): substances that tend to be associated with aggressive behavior (Elliott, Huizinga, and Ageton, 1985; Fagan, 1990; Fagan et al., 1986; Harstone and Hansen, 1984; Tinklenberg, Murphy, and Pfefferbaum, 1981; White, Pandina, and LaGrange, 1987). Inciardi et al. (1993) note that substance use is a major requirement for successfully participating in the street lifestyle and reaping its benefits and satisfactions. They argue that being under the influence while committing a crime is something to be expected for those heavily involved in a street lifestyle. In fact, they suggest that the critical factor in the move from trivial to serious crime on the street is drug and alcohol use. Drugs and alcohol can directly affect crime by making risky or otherwise difficult offenses easier (Inciardi and Russe, 1977). These substances can create feelings of omnipotence, which, in tandem with the sheer youth of many street participants, can distort perceptions of risk. This suggests that the street lifestyle and the substance abuse linked to the street subculture might serve to increase violent criminal activity.

Economic Deprivation

Research assessing the capacity of these subcultural explanations to account for violent behavior has generated inconsistent results (Ball-Rokeach, 1973; Bankston and Allen, 1980; Blau and Blau, 1982; Curtis, 1975; Danziger and Wheeler, 1975; Doerner, 1979; Gastil, 1971; Hackney, 1969; Huff-Corzine, Corzine, and Moore, 1986; Loftin and Hill, 1974; Messner, 1983; Rosenfeld, 1986; Sampson, 1985; Williams, 1984), leading to a focus on structural explanations of violent behavior. A number of researchers have argued that violent behavior stems from inequality, the uneven distribution of resources, and the deprivation of some relative to others. Perceptions of inequality and relative deprivation are thought to generate feelings of resentment and hostility, which in turn stimulate impulses that are ultimately expressed as violent crime (Blau and Blau, 1982; Braithwaite, 1979; Danziger and Wheeler, 1975; Hawkins, 1983; Messner and Tardiff, 1986). Furthermore, the likelihood of aggression is increased by the chronic stress of poverty and lower class life, which further reduces the ability to cope with arousal, which in turn can generate more violence and angry aggression (Bernard, 1990).

The conditions outlined by the structural perspective can lead to the creation of an aggressive environment, particularly if the poor are socially isolated (Bernard, 1990). An atmosphere is created where there is the constant threat of physical injury or death. These realities produce additional arousal that is probably chronic, leaving a socially isolated group extremely at risk to exhibit angry aggression.

Poverty may also lead to more utilitarian types of violence. Desroches (1997) argues that robbery may be viewed as an offense that is primarily motivated by the desire or need for money. He suggests that limited access to legitimate monetary and material sources may lead to violent offenses that meet offenders' immediate requirements (Desroches, 1995).

A number of researchers have called for greater attention to be paid to the variables linking poverty, particularly unemployment, to crime (Baron and Hartnagel, 1997; Box, 1987; Box and Hale, 1985; Horwitz, 1984; Wright 1981). These scholars have pointed out that people's interpretation of their labor and life situations play a large role in shaping their responses to unemployment and poverty. These interpretations may be contingent on what people believe causes their poverty and unemployment and the actual duration of these conditions (Baron and Hartnagel, 1997; Box and Hale, 1985; Horwitz, 1984; MacLeod, 1987; Pearlin et al., 1981).

This may be most important for understanding a more utilitarian type of offense like robbery. Cloward and Ohlin (1961) argue that the failure to achieve socially approved goals can lead to alienation and a "withdrawal of attributions of legitimacy" for dominant norms. The most significant step in the development of this alienation is "the attribution of the cause of failure to the social order rather than to oneself" (Cloward and Ohlin, 1961, p. 112). In short, the link between occupational deprivation and utilitarian criminal activity may be contingent upon the degree of acceptance of the meritocratic ideology. Robbery may be more likely when persons experiencing economic deprivation and employment difficulties believe the system is at fault (Box, 1987; Hartnagel, 1990; Merton, 1957; Stack, 1984).

Routine Activities

Sampson and Lauritsen (1990; Lauritsen, Sampson, and Laub, 1991) suggest that mere opportunity can lead to an increase in crime independent of the structural or cultural conditions that might motivate individuals to engage in crime. From this perspective, violent street crime is a product of opportunity that arises in the ongoing activities that occur on the street. The probability of crime increases with the convergence in space and time of motivated offenders, suitable targets, and absent guardianship (Cohen and Felson, 1979; Felson and Cohen, 1980; Lauritsen et al., 1991; Sampson and Lauritsen, 1990; Sampson and Wooldredge, 1987). It is argued that the lifestyles that lead one to go to bars and to being on the street lead to situations in which these factors coincide to present offenders with opportunities to commit crime (Jensen and Brownfield, 1986; Kennedy and Forde, 1990a, 1990b).

Routine activities theorists suggest further that the chances of violence may increase through the "principle of homogamy" (Sampson and Lauritsen, 1990). Individuals increase their likelihood of violence the more frequently they come into contact with, or associate with, members of demographic groups that contain a disproportionate share of violent offenders. For example, young males leading "risky lifestyles" out on the street are more likely to become involved in violent altercations because they are more likely to come in contact, and associate, with other young males who are themselves involved in offending (Kennedy and Forde, 1990b; Lauritsen et al., 1991; Sampson and Lauritsen, 1990).

There is evidence to suggest that the social hazards of leading these risky lifestyles are reflected in greater risks of experiencing violent victimization. Victimization within this environment in turn leads to greater violent offending behavior (Fagan, Piper, and Cheng, 1987; Fagan et al., 1986; Singer, 1981, 1986). People are expected to legitimate more readily the use of violence because of their victimization experience (Singer, 1986), and there may also be subcultural expectations that condone retaliation (Lauritsen et al., 1991; Sampson and Lauritsen, 1990).

Another form of violent victimization takes place in the family. A consistent theme in the criminological and family violence literature is the relationship between experiencing violence in the home and later antisocial behavior (Elliott, 1994; Hartstone and Hansen, 1984; Hotaling et al., 1989; McCord, 1979; Sedgely and Lund, 1979; Smith and Thornberry, 1995; Straus, 1985; Widom, 1989). It is argued that children in these circumstances come to model the behavior of their parents (Fagan and Jones, 1984; Fagan and Wexler, 1987; Farrington, 1978; Sorrels, 1977) and adopt violence as an interpersonal strategy and/or tactic. The violent experience encourages the youths to use aggression as a means of problem solving and/or of gaining compliance from others (Fagan and Wexler, 1987; Siegal and Senna, 1994).

Abusive histories are also said to diminish people's ability to cope with stress or develop empathy for others, resulting in a greater tendency to victimize others and strike out in anger during times of stress (Siegal and Senna, 1994; Wooden, 1995). Regoli and Hewitt (1991) argue that these violent experiences also influence youths to seek out and create violent situations including joining peers who approve of, require, and encourage violence while providing a sense of belonging. Evidence also suggests that these violent experiences leave abused youths vulnerable to the aggression and violence in the larger culture (Siegel and Senna,

1994). They are more likely to be swayed by expectations for, or tolerations of, violence. This may result from the microinfluence of peers or from placement in structural locations where violence in expected.

HYPOTHESES

Drawing from these theoretical perspectives and the supporting research, we can specify several hypotheses regarding the influences of subcultural, economic, routine activities, and family abuse predictors on the violent behavior of street youth.

1. Beginning with the role of subculture, we expect that those street youths who spend more time with criminal peers will engage in more violent behavior.
2. Further, the street youth literature suggests that the condition of homelessness itself is criminogenic. Therefore, we expect that those youths who have lived on the street for a longer time period should report more violent crime net of their other experiences.
3. As part of this street lifestyle, we also anticipate that those youths who are more often under the influence of drugs and/or alcohol will be more at risk for violent behavior.
4. We also expect that long-term unemployment, living with few financial resources, the anger associated with unemployment, and perceptions of an unfair social structure will lead to more violent behavior.
5. Further, we expect that youths who have suffered violent victimization on the street will be at an increased risk for violent offending.
6. Finally, we believe that the physical abuse that characterizes many street youths' home experiences will increase these youths' violent behavior.

We will test these predictions with four specific types of violence—robbery, aggravated assaults, group fights, and simple assaults—as well as an index of general violence to assess the various processes that underlie these behaviors. We expect to discover that some predictors have stronger effects on certain offenses in that the four types of violence vary among themselves. Robbery is a utilitarian offense mainly committed for monetary gain. Group fights have a collective character that may reflect certain aspects of the street subculture including peers and conflict over status. Assaults may also involve such conflict and peer influence, though in other instances assaults may arise more in the context of alcohol and other drug use and/or the experience of violent victimization.

METHODS

A problem that plagues researchers studying street youth is the difficulty in setting an appropriate definition or criteria for selection into a study. Past research suggests that the street population is made up of a heterogeneous group of youths from preteens to mid-20s. The street is populated by students and dropouts, employed and unemployed youths, regulars who "hang out" on the street on a permanent basis, and those whose presence is sporadic (Kufeldt and Nimmo, 1987a, 1987b; McCullagh and Greco, 1990; Smart et al., 1990).

Recognizing the heterogeneity of this population, 200 male respondents were identified based on four sampling criteria.

1. Participants must be male;
2. they must be aged 24 and under;
3. they must have left or finished school;
4. they must spend at least three hours a day, three days a week "hanging around" on the street or in a mall.

The rationales for these criteria were (a) to avoid the potential ethical and methodological problems of a male researcher inquiring about intimate areas of female respondents' lives (sexual abuse, sexual assault, and prostitution);[1] (b) to cover the age range of those described as street youth (Caputo and Ryan, 1991, pp. 8–10); (c) to eliminate those not eligible for full-time employment; and (d) to obtain a sample of "serious" "at-risk" youth and avoid the "weekend warriors." Although criterion four left the door open for the inclusion of less at-risk youths, the data show the average respondent to be a full-time street youth who had been homeless for about four months in the prior year.

DATA COLLECTION

The data were collected over a six-month period from January through June of 1993 in Edmonton, Alberta, a large western Canadian city with a population of 800,000. The violent crime rate for the area in 1993 was 1,151/100,000, a number somewhat higher than the national average of 1,079/100,000 for that year (Statistics Canada, 1994). Further, the labor market at the time of data collection was extremely difficult for those younger than 24, with their unemployment rate reaching 20.2 percent in 1993.

The study took place in and around the downtown business core of the city, which is bordered by the local skid row and the "inner city." Thus, the area contained a mix of commercial and financial establishments surrounded by bars, pawnshops, hotels, shelters, detox centers, rooming houses, rundown residential units, and abandoned buildings.

Unlike other research where appropriate samples reflecting target population parameters are drawn from exhaustive population lists, the fluid and mobile nature of the street population makes estimations of composition and size a difficult if not impossible task. Therefore, the study used a snowball sampling technique. This strategy is often employed in field research of little known or hard to reach subjects (Hagan, 1993; Inciardi et al., 1991; Johnson et al., 1985; Maxfield and Babbie, 1995). This process begins with the identification of a single or small group of respondents who are then asked to identify, or recruit, other suitable candidates who might be willing to participate in the study.[2] Larger sample sizes can capture the variability of the researched population and reduce some of the sampling error inherent in this method (McCarthy, 1990).

Sample selection began with one of the researchers situating himself in this geographical area. The researcher approached potential respondents, informed them of the project, and screened them for study eligibility. Those youths meeting the selection criteria were then provided additional information on the study and invited to participate. Subsequent to granting consent, the respondents were taken to be interviewed in the more comfortable and sheltered conditions of one of the many malls in the downtown core. The interview contained a combination of forced choice and open-ended questions pertaining to the issues under study. The youths were interviewed for an average of an hour and 10 minutes and were rewarded for their participation with $10 in food coupons to a popular fast food restaurant.

Additional contacts were initiated by youths who were made aware of the researcher's presence and solicited interviews or through introductions from previously interviewed subjects. Following these advances, informed consent was obtained from each new respondent who was then interviewed and rewarded.

The researcher began and ended each day by returning to the locations where he had come into contact with previous respondents. This allowed him to follow up on the youths' situations and observe and gather more information on their behaviors, which was recorded in field notes at the end of each day. This process also filled periods of down time when there were no new people to be approached or found.

These procedures provided us with a sample of 200 youth of an average age of almost 19 ($X = 18.86$).[3] All but 15 of these youths had spent some time during the year living away from their parents, and a full three quarters of the sample had been with no fixed address during the last year ($N = 153$). Those who had been homeless had spent on average almost five months (4.93) in total living on the street in the previous year.

MEASURING CRIME

Information on a number of measures of criminal behavior including robbery, aggravated assault, group fights, and common assault was obtained via self report.[4] After each self-report item, youths who admitted to an offense were then asked in an open-ended question to explain circumstances that led to the most recent offense in each category.

The totals generated by the responses to each of the closed-ended questions revealed a large number of violent offenses (see Table 1 in brackets). An inspection of the raw frequency distributions for these various measures suggested a high degree of skewness. This condition stemmed from most respondents reporting a small number of offenses, with a few reporting large numbers of offenses. To reduce this skewness, values for each offense were converted to their natural log (see Table 1 outside of brackets). The sums of the four offense types were also aggregated to create a violent crime index, which again was subject to the log conversion procedure.

INDEPENDENT VARIABLES

Information was obtained in the interviews on a range of subcultural, economic, and victimization variables hypothesized to be important in explaining the violent behavior of street youths. To explore the effects of the

TABLE 1   Means and Standard Deviations

VARIABLE	M	SD	MINIMUM	MAXIMUM
Street subculture				
Time on street	3.77	4.02	0 (months)	12 (months)
Criminal peers	2.38	.85	1 (none)	5 (all)
Peer pressure	2.00	1.11	1 (never)	5 (always)
Alcohol use	4.10	1.82	1 (none)	7 (every day)
Drug use	4.51	2.25	1 (none)	7 (every day)
Economic deprivation				
Income	.77	.94	0 ($0)	3 ($1,000 >)
Length unemployed	8.22	3.60	0 (months)	12 (months)
Strain	1.16	.36	1 (agree)	2 (disagree)
Anger	3.17	1.23	1 (s disagree)	5 (s agree)
Victimization				
Robbed	.63	1.58	0 (times)	15 (times)
Aggravated assault	.52	1.74	0 (times)	15 (times)
Common assault	1.99	8.72	0 (times)	97 (times)
Family abuse	2.62	1.24	1 (never)	5 (always)
Dependent variables				
Robbery	.87 (47.9)[a]	1.50 (379.8)	0	8.82 (5,000)
Aggravated assault	.84 (1.8)	1.15 (41.2)	0	6.09 (442)
Common assault	1.17 (15.7)	1.43 (65.4)	0	6.62 (750)
Group fights	1.12 (10.9)	1.29 (48.5)	0	6.31 (550)
Total violent crime	2.12 (87.2)	1.73 (379.8)	0	8.73 (6,195)

[a]Numbers inside of parentheses are raw scores. Numbers outside of parentheses are the logged values of the raw scores.

street subculture, respondents were asked about the length of their homelessness, their criminal peers, and peer pressure, as well as their use of alcohol and drugs. To examine the effects of economic deprivation and reactions to structural conditions, respondents were queried about the length of their unemployment, their financial status, their anger over their unemployment, and if they felt the social structure was fair. To explore the role of victimization on subjects' violent behavior, they were asked to self-report how many times in the past year they had been the victims of a robbery, aggravated assault, and a common assault. Because we are examining different types of violent crime, it was decided to explore the effect of the various types of victimization on the various categories of violent behavior. Finally, the youths' history of physical abuse within the family was determined. The youths were also asked in an open-ended question to describe any problems they encountered in their family. The appendix describes the exact wording and response categories for all of the variables, whereas Table 1 provides a summary of their means and standard deviations.

The correlation matrix of all predictor variables[5] revealed few problems of collinearity (i.e., $r > .4$). No Variance Inflation Factor score was greater than 1.4, suggesting that the collinearity between independent variables would not significantly affect the estimates of other independent variables.

FINDINGS

Statistical analysis proceeded with all of the predictor variables simultaneously entered into multiple regression equations with each dependent variable: robbery, aggravated assault, assault, gang fights, and total violence. The results of this process are displayed in Table 2.

STREET SUBCULTURE

Beginning with an examination of the effects of the street subculture and lifestyle variables, we find that peer influence has an unanticipated effect on a variety of violent behaviors. Those youths who reported that friends never or rarely pressured them to engage in criminal activities reported greater participation in robbery, aggravated assaults, and total violent crime net of the other predictors. However, the results also reveal that those youths who reported having more

TABLE 2 Standardized Betas for Regression Models

VARIABLE	ROBBERY	AGGRAVATED ASSAULT	ASSAULT	GROUP FIGHTS	TOTAL VIOLENCE
Street subculture					
Time on street	.17**	.08	.10	.07	.14*
Criminal peers	.12	.13	.17*	.08	.15*
Peer pressure	−.20**	−.21*	−.13	−.10	−.17**
Drinking	−.03	.11	.18*	.10	.08
Drug use	.04	−.06	.06	.00	.04
Economic deprivation					
Income	−.16*	−.14*	−.19**	−.14*	−.19**
Length unemployed	.11	.08	.10	.10	.12
Strain	.17*	.12	.07	.10	.11
Anger	−.00	−.03	−.11	−.09	−.08
Victimization					
Robbed	−.04	.00	−.00	.03	−.00
Aggravated assault	.12	.25***	−.00	.27***	.16*
Common assault	.14*	.17*	.11	.02	.08
Family abuse	.24*	.16*	.13	.12	.20**
R^2	.30	.27	.24	.22	.31
Adjusted R^2	.25	.21	.18	.15	.25
$p =$	.0000	.0000	.0000	.0001	.0000
$N =$	179	179	179	179	179

*Significant at .05. **Significant at .01. ***Significant at .001.

criminal peers also indicated greater participation in simple assaults and total violent crime. These findings suggest that there is a self-selection or mutual attraction of like-minded youths to form friendships. Reiss and Farrington (1991) note that there is a strong tendency for like-minded youths to have friends whose attitudes and behaviors are congruent with their own. If this is the case, there is little need to socially coerce others into criminal behavior. Further, it is likely that on the street these youths are able to choose from a number of potential criminal peers. As Tremblay (1993) notes, a concentration of offenders increases the likelihood that a given offender will find other like offenders. Thus, violent offenders on the street should select one another as friends because of their similar conflict styles and their greater opportunities for contact and communication.

Reiss and Farrington (1991) also note that high-rate offenders tend to be criminal recruiters who take on the role of social instigator. Low-rate offenders are more likely to require pressure than are willing chronic offenders. Thus, they may recruit others for robberies and act as third parties in other situations that evolve into violence.

Although the quantitative data indicated little pressure to engage in violence, the qualitative data did suggest the presence of group norms regarding protection and guardianship. Many of the group fights described by respondents began as altercations between two disputants that escalated when youths from one group came to the aid of their friend, necessitating the inclusion of people from the other group. Similarly, there were situations where a number of youths attacked a single victim, which rallied respondents to enter the battles as guardians.

> Too many of the others so I joined in to even it up.
> Couple of buddies got into a fight. Some other
>   people jumped in on the other side.
> I was ambushed, and my friends came to help.
> Jocks came up and jumped me, so my friends
>   helped me out.

Responses also revealed that group altercations provided these youths with avenues for retribution to avenge the victimization of friends. Group members who had been robbed or who had been physically assaulted, often by more than one person, enlisted the support of their peers, and together they sought out the offenders and their groups in an attempt to even up the score.

> Somebody rolled one of my friends, so we beat the
>   shit out of them.

> My friend got rolled.
> Some people jumped a friend of mine.
> Somebody beat up one of our friends.

Finally, in their responses, the members indicated that group rivalries, including territorial and turf disputes, provided the impetus for recent group altercations. The idea that these youths would bind together and do battle for each other again suggests certain normative expectations concerning violence for group members.

> Long hairs against the skins.
> Against some bangers before NIA.
> Downtown versus Bonnie Doon.
> Turf, Northside.

These findings suggest that although the youths under study may not acknowledge peer pressure to engage in violent activities, they do enter into peer alliances and appear to give normative assent to requirements for violent participation in defense of their peers. As Thrasher (1927) and Suttles (1968) note, delinquent street groups are often formed to defend against conflict (see also Kornhauser, 1978).

Moving to other aspects of the street lifestyle, we find that the experience of homelessness is significantly related to respondents' violent behaviors. The longer youths had been without a fixed address, the greater their involvement in robbery and total violent crime in general. Spending time on the street may isolate these youths from conventional society as they become immersed in a street lifestyle. This immersion appears to provide them with access to criminal peers perhaps while breaking down standards of behavior and restrictions on the use of violence.

Furthermore, there may be cultural expectations of violence on the street. Although our quantitative analysis does not do justice to this idea, the qualitative data indicate that a great deal of street youth violence appears to be guided by rules of honor and retributive justice, characteristics often noted by researchers who argue for the existence of a subculture of violence (Horowitz, 1983; Wolfgang and Ferracuti, 1967).

If a respondent was wronged in terms of business dealings or derogations of self, he was expected to avenge this with violence. For example, when asked to explain the circumstances leading up to their most recent robbery, many youths indicated that unpaid debts led to robbery episodes. On the street, youths owed money, particularly for fronted drugs, forced victims to settle accounts by robbing them.

Screwed me over for a large amount of money.
I got ripped off. Justice must be served.
Ripped me off. Let him know you don't f*** me
  around.
Ripped me off. Show him you can't have that.

This theme of being owed money or being "ripped off" also figured prominently in explanations of the circumstances surrounding the recent aggravated assaults. Failed business transactions appeared to lead respondents to exact retribution for their losses through physical injury. Retribution for other transgressions, including informing on respondents, also figured prominently as explanations for extreme violent behavior.

Another popular explanation provided by respondents for seriously injuring others (aggravated assault) revolved around violations of honor and name calling. People who verbally offended respondents with derogatory or offensive names were attacked so severely that respondents believed their victims required medical attention.

Some guy called me a goof, so he deserved it.
'Cause a guy called me a f***ing Indian.
Name calling. Called me a goof.
Called me a homeless bastard.

In terms of explanations for recent simple assaults, the violation of honor again appears to be an important impetus for violent reactions. In this case, respondents added "the look" and people "kicking attitude" and not showing the proper respect to the list of stimuli that drew out violent reactions. Thus, whereas verbal assaults lead to severe attacks resulting in victims needing medical attention, visual assaults provoke less severe attacks.

The guy had been kicking attitude, so I solved his
  problem.
I just didn't like him. His attitude, "I'm big shit."
The guy looked at me, so I decided to punch him in
  the mouth.
Just looked at me funny. I snapped and jumped on
  him.

Together this suggests that on the street, there may exist a subculture of violence where certain verbal and visual stimuli are viewed as provocative and reacted to with violence. We would expect that those who have spent the most time on the street would be the most vulnerable for adopting these cultural expectations existing on the street (Regoli and Hewitt, 1991).

It is also true that spending a great deal of time on the street presents the respondents abundant opportunities to witness different styles of conflict management. They may learn from being on the street that violence is the method most often used to settle conflict. Furthermore, the experience of living on the street provides these youths with ample opportunities to attack attractive targets. Being on the street exposes street youths to more potential victims from which they can pick and choose according to risk and desired items.

Table 1 reveals that as full participants in the street lifestyle (Inciardi et al. 1993), street youths are heavy users of alcohol and/or drugs. However, Table 2 indicates that alcohol emerges as a significant predictor of only simple assaults, and drug use is not a significant predictor of street youth violence. The failure of drug and alcohol use to reach significance might be explained by the minimal variation in these variables due to this population's heavy substance use. This makes the significance of alcohol use in the assault model more impressive. Although the literature remains unclear about the physiological effects of these substances on violent behavior, we might speculate that these youth exhibit violent responses while using alcohol in certain settings (Zinberg, 1984) and under certain conditions. For example, the simple assault question asks, "How many times have you got into a fight for the hell of it?" This suggests that alcohol use may be linked to less serious forms of recreational violence.

The qualitative data support this speculation. When asked about their involvement in common assaults, respondents often simply indicated that they got into a fight because they were "drunk." This type of response did not regularly emerge in their explanations of other types of violence.

I was drunk, I wanted to fight.
I was drunk, so the first person I see.
Just drunk and stupid in a bar.
When I get pissed.

ECONOMIC DEPRIVATION

Moving from our exploration of the street subcultural lifestyle to the role of economic deprivation in the generation of street youth violence, we discover that poverty is consistently an important predictor. Respondents lacking financial resources were more likely to have high robbery, aggravated assault, common assault, group fight, and overall violence totals. If the others who inhabit the area of the city where the study took place suffer from similar economic situations and react in the same fashion to these situations, it is likely that our respondents are living in a milieu of angry aggression (Bernard, 1990). Therefore, conditions regarding a street subculture of violence should be tempered somewhat by the acknowledgment that a number of the described violent behaviors are the result of living under negative economic conditions. In fact, length of time on the street probably reflects to some extent the economic deprivation experienced by these youths.

In the qualitative data, many respondents indicated that they participated in fights to help relative stress and frustration that is possibly related to their poverty. Some of the respondents indicated that getting into a fight was also "something to do." Thus, for those without disposable income for leisure, violence provided a recreational avenue.

> Stress relief.
> For fun. Let some frustration off.
> Just for something to do.
> Something to do.

The qualitative data also indicate that a lack of financial resources provides an important impetus for more utilitarian violence as well. Respondents indicated that the bulk of their robberies were to obtain money and other material articles.

> Just for f***ing things, just for f***ing money.
> Needed money really really bad to get a hotel room to sleep.
> I was in need.
> Get clothes and money.

In addition to a lack of income, attitudes toward economic deprivation also proved to be a significant predictor of some violent behavior. Those youths who perceived the social structure to be blocked were more likely to rob people. From a traditional strain perspective, those youths who thought they could not get a fair shake in the legitimate labor market used violent, illegitimate means to secure monetary resources. Thus, the lack of resources and perceptions of inequality appear to stimulate impulses expressed as utilitarian violence.

We do not find the length of the respondents' unemployment to be a significant predictor of violence net of income. This likely stems from the fact that the average respondent had been without legitimate employment for 8 out of the previous 12 months. Therefore, there is little variation in most respondents' employment circumstances.

VICTIMIZATION

In our hypotheses, it was also recognized that risky lifestyles expose actors to victimization, and this experience might increase offending behavior. It appears that being the victim of an aggravated assault in particular, or to a lesser degree a simple assault, helps to explain a number of violent behaviors. Those youths who had been victims of aggravated assaults were more likely to have participated in aggravated assaults, group fights, and accumulated a greater number of overall violent behaviors; whereas the victims of common assaults tended to have higher robbery and aggravated assault totals. This suggests that victimization on the street is related to serious violent behavior. Victimizations can lead to retaliation in both the group and individual setting. Further, respondents may be learning from their victimization experiences on the street that extreme violence is an effective method of dispute settlement and conflict management. Finally, the environment of angry aggression may have left these youths seeking out their victimizers to settle the score regardless of learning experiences and subcultural expectations.

We must also acknowledge that these youths' heavy involvement in violent activity may have led to others retaliating against, and injuring, them. Similarly, assaultive behaviors require more than one person, so that the risk of injury in a dispute despite being the initial offender (striking the first blow) is at a maximum (Lauritsen et al., 1991; Sampson and Lauritsen, 1990). Thus, these offenders may have seriously injured someone in the past and then been grievously damaged in return; or they may have received their injuries in the course of battle in various individual and gang fights. Alternatively, they may have been seriously injured and sought out, either alone or with peers, to injure others. In sum, the street provides the social experiences that guide respondents' behavior as well as the locales, environments, and situations where violence is more likely.

Finally, the experience of familial physical abuse is related to a range of offenses including robbery, aggravated assault, and the total violent crime index. Youths who have experienced violent victimization in the home may be more likely to model this type of behavior and use violence as a method of gaining compliance and seriously injuring others. An indication of the impact these experiences had on the respondents is revealed in the graphic depictions of their violent home life. These episodes were not the accidental result of a parent who "inadvertently" uses too much force in physically disciplining the child. The events were serial and extremely intense and displayed a savageness that could only serve to physically damage the child. This appears to have led to long-term harm.

> Pretty much my dad beating me up and that. Basically treating me like shit.
> Yes there was problems. If we got along it was a shot in the mouth and a good boot f***.
> Just my dad was a problem. Physical abuse. Bounced me off the walls.
> The only serious problem was my stepdad. . . . My stepdad used to beat the shit out of me all the time. I couldn't beat him so . . .

Thus, a history of violent victimization seems to be a fertile breeding ground for the creation of violent offenders. This abusive experience appears to provide these youth with models of behavior that they then replicate on the street.

DISCUSSION

Our results reveal that aspects of the street subcultural lifestyle, economic deprivation, and victimization work together to explain street youth violence. For the index of total violence, being the victim of family abuse or serious assault, having few financial resources, spending more time on the street, and associating with criminal friends results in more violence.

However, the results also show that different combinations of the street subculture, economic deprivation, and victimization help to explain the different types of violent behavior. Robbery is best predicted by spending more time on the street, having few financial resources, perceptions of a lack of legitimate opportunities, and the experience of victimization in the home as well as on the street. Because robbery is usually a utilitarian or instrumental offense committed to obtain money, it is not surprising that several of these predictors reflect economic factors. Lack of income can be at least temporarily solved by robbing others. Youths who believe the social system is stacked against them can respond with violent means to obtain financial rewards denied them by the legitimate or conventional opportunity structure. Lengthy homelessness can increase the extent of material deprivation experienced by these street youths for whom robbery is a means of survival. These youths also learn from their abusive home experiences that using force is a practical and effective method of gaining compliance, increasing the odds that they will use coercion to gain financial or material rewards.

Low income is also the only consistent significant predictor across the four types of violent crime. This finding lends support to the view that extreme or absolute deprivation can lead to a variety of serious violent behaviors. The average available legal income reported by respondents was $328, and the level of state support for a single employable was $470. This suggests that even minimal amounts of legal financial resources might be able to negate the influences of deprivation on violence. However, the qualitative data suggest that such motives as retribution also play a role even in robbery and that the stresses of a life in poverty are also important in explaining nonutilitarian violence.

Predictive accuracy was weakest for group fights. In addition to low income, the only other significant predictor was serious street victimization. However, qualitative data indicate that youths with similar conflict management strategies enter into peer networks that stress norms of protection and guardianship. These norms required street youths to engage in battle over turf and group identity, to retaliate for the victimization of group members, while at the same time providing for guardianship that minimizes their own victimization. Group conflicts, then, can be distinguished from the other types of violence by the centrality of concerns over territoriality, protection, and group identity.

Aggravated assault is heavily influenced by the experience of serious street victimization and abusive family relationships. The experience of victimization in the home and on the street, along with the stresses of poverty, appear to be vital to an understanding of these serious violent behaviors. Highly injurious violence appears to be linked to retaliation and retribution in response to violence or status threats and perceived violations of honor. The experience of violence can lead to an escalation in violence, and participation in violence can in turn lead to victimization. It is likely that youths learn from these experiences that violence is a method of conflict resolution and that seriously injuring harm doers is an acceptable mode of resolving disputes.

In contrast, simple assaults do not appear to involve the experience of victimization. Rather, involvement in simple assault is best explained by alcohol use, association with criminal peers, and the stresses of poverty. It appears that street youths often become involved in these more minor incidents of violence for recreational purposes when using alcohol, or to "blow off some steam." Drinking and fighting in the company of like-minded peers appears to characterize those street youths reporting more involvement in simple assaults.

We have attempted to go beyond previous research on youth violence by focusing on a population "missing" (Hagan and McCarthy, 1992) from traditional data sources and exploring the conditions, experiences, and aspects of life on the street that can lead to violent crime. Although the street subculture, economic deprivation, and violent victimization are elements in the explanation of street violence, our research has shown that no single explanation will suffice for several different types of violence. As expected, economic factors are predominant in the case of robbery, whereas elements of a culture of violence acquired from experience with violence in the home and on the street are more applicable to group fights and serious assaults. Minor violence, on the other hand, appears to be somewhat more spontaneous and linked to excessive drinking with similarly situated peers. Because violence itself is not uniform, neither are its explanations. Future research should explore further the distinctive causes of different types of violent crime, using both at-risk and conventional samples of youth.

APPENDIX   Coding Information for Variable Indicators

INDEPENDENT VARIABLES
STREET SUBCULTURE VARIABLES

Time on the Street
"How many months in the last year (give anchor) did you live in a shelter or have no fixed address?"

Criminal Peers
"How many of your current friends have been picked up by the police?"
(1 = *none*, 2 = *a few*, 3 = *some*, 4 = *most*, 5 = *all*)

Peer Pressure
"Do you ever feel pressure from friends to undertake illegal activities?"
(1 = *never*, 2 = *a few times*, 3 = *sometimes*, 4 = *most of the time*, 5 = *always*)

Alcohol Use
"How many times in the last month have you drank alcoholic beverages?"
(1 = *never*, 2 = *once a month*, 3 = *2–3 times a month*, 4 = *once a week*, 5 = *2–3 times a week*, 6 = *4–6 times a week*, 7 = *everyday*)

Drug Use
"How many times in the last year have you used marijuana?"
(1 = *never*, 2 = *once a month*, 3 = *2–3 times a month*, 4 = *once a week*, 5 = *2–3 times a week*, 6 = *4–6 times a week*, 7 = *everyday*)

ECONOMIC DEPRIVATION AND REACTION VARIABLES

Length Unemployed
"How many months in the last year (give anchor) were you out of work?"

Income
"What is your legal income a month before deductions?" Income includes sources from both employment and state support. Recoded
(0 = 0, 1 = *1–470*, 2 = *471–999*, 3 = *1,000 and above*). Note that state support for a single employable in the area was $470 per month.

Strain
"Any person who is able and willing to work hard has a good chance of succeeding."
(1 = *agree*, 2 = *disagree*)

Anger
"I feel angry about my unemployment."
(1 = *strongly disagree*, 2 = *disagree*, 3 = *neither agree nor disagree*, 4 = *agree*, 5 = *strongly agree*)

VICTIMIZATION VARIABLES

Robbed
"How many times in the past year (give anchor) did you have physical force used against you to get your money or things?"

Aggravated Assault

"How many times in the past year (give anchor) have you been attacked with a weapon or fists/feet, injuring you so badly you needed a doctor?"

Common Assault

"How many times in the past year (give anchor) have you been physically attacked for no apparent reason?"

Family Abuse

"Did your parents or guardians ever use physical forms of discipline?" and "Have you ever been intentionally struck so hard by a parent or guardian that it caused a bruise or bleeding?"

(1 = *never*, 2 = *rarely*, 3 = *sometimes*, 4 = *usually*, 5 = *always*). The two measures were combined and divided by two (α = .8450).

DEPENDENT VARIABLES

"I would like you to think back over the last year (give anchor) and tell me how many times you have:

Robbery

used physical force (like twisting an arm or choking) to get money or things from another person?"

Aggravated Assault

attacked someone with a weapon or your fists, injuring them so badly they probably needed a doctor?"

Common Assault

got into a fight with someone just for the hell of it?"

Group Fight

taken part in a fight where a group of your friends was against another group?"

Total Violence

An aggregate of the robbery, aggravated assault, common assault, and groups offenses listed above.

NOTES

1. Both the researchers and their university's ethics committee also concluded it was improper for a male researcher to ask female respondents questions of this nature. Methodologically, the nature of the data collection (relatively short, "one-shot" interviews in a semi-public place) may have affected the validity and reliability of responses from female respondents to these questions. One potential solution was to eliminate these questions. However, past research suggested that these types of variables were particularly important in explaining the backgrounds and behaviors of both male and female street youths. Because the lack of financial support precluded hiring a female interviewer, and these questions could not be eliminated, the decision was made to restrict the sample to male street youths. Due to concerns raised in the ethics review about the sensitive nature of some of the questions bearing on physical and sexual victimization, as well as other issues raised in the interviews including substance abuse, a referral list of relevant social service agencies was a constant companion of the researcher. Despite the sensitivity of a number of the questions, the interviews proceeded without issue. The respondents seemed at ease in responding to the interview questions.

2. Upon assent, they were supplied with informed consent forms outlining study goals and apprising them of their rights within the interview situation. Subjects were notified that they were not obliged to respond to any of the questions and were provided the option to withdraw from the interview at any time. None of the youths exercised this power.

3. More than 300 youths were contacted during the course of the research. Of these youths, 220 met the study criteria. However, 20 of the eligible youths declined to participate in the interview process.

4. An extensive literature has developed on the self-report methodology indicating that its use with normal youth populations gives results that are both sufficiently accurate and fairly compatible with the conclusions drawn from analyses of arrest data (for summaries, see Elliott, Huizinga, and Menard, 1989, pp. 4–9; Hindelang, Hirschi, and Weiss, 1981, pp. 13–25; Johnson, 1979, pp. 89–93). Studies of more serious drug/crime participants consistently find that the respondents' self-reports are "surprisingly truthful and accurate" (Inciardi et al., 1993; Johnson et al., 1985). Furthermore, research has determined that self-reported delinquency measures that ask questions about serious as well as trivial offenses do not restrict response categories, do not request information beyond a one-year period, and use face-to-face interviews as opposed to paper-and-pencil written questionnaires provide the best and most complete data on serious offenders (see Huizinga and Elliott, 1986). The present research contained all of these characteristics.

5. This table is available from the authors upon request.

REFERENCES

Ball-Rokeach, S. J. (1973). Values and violence: A test of the subculture of violence thesis. *American Sociological Review, 31,* 736–749.

Bankston, W. B., and Allen, H. D. (1980). Rural social areas and patterns of homicide: An analysis of lethal violence in Louisiana. *Rural Sociology, 45,* 223–237.

Baron, S. W. (1989a). The Canadian West Coast punk subculture: A field study. *Canadian Journal of Sociology, 14,* 289–316.

Baron, S. W. (1989b). Resistance and its consequences: The street culture of funks. *Youth and Society, 21,* 207–237.

Baron, S. W. (1995). Serious offenders. "In J. Creechan and R. A. Silverman (Eds.), *Canadian Delinquency.* Toronto, Canada: Prentice Hall.

Baron, S. W., and Hartnagel, T. F. (1997). Attributions, affect and crime: Street youths reactions to unemployment. *Criminology, 35,* 409–434.

Bernard, T. J. (1990). Angry aggression among the "Truly Disadvantaged." *Criminology, 28,* 73–95.

Blau, J. R., and Blau, P. M. (1982). The costs of the inequality: Metropolitan structure and violent crime. *American Sociological Review, 47,* 114–129.

Box, S. (1987). *Recession, Crime and Punishment.* Basingstoke, UK: Macmillan.

Box, S., and Hale, C. (1985). Unemployment, imprisonment and prison overcrowding. *Contemporary Crises, 9,* 209–228.

Braithwaite, J. (1979). *Inequality, Crime and Public Policy.* London: Routledge and Kegan Paul.

Brennan, T., Huizinga, D., and Elliott, D. S. (1978). *The Social Psychology of Runaways.* Toronto, Canada: Lexington.

Caputo, T., and Ryan, C. (1991). *The Police Response to Youth at Risk.* Ottawa, Canada: Solicitor General.

Cloward, R. A., and Ohlin, L. E. (1961). *Delinquency and Opportunity.* New York: Free Press.

Cohen, L. E., and Felson, M. (1979). Social change and crime rate trends. *American Sociological Review, 44,* 588–607.

Curtis, L. A. (1975). *Violence, Race, and Culture.* Lexington, MA: D.C. Heath.

Danziger, S., and Wheeler, D. (1975). The economics of crime: Punishment or income redistribution. *Review of Social Economy, 33,* 113–131.

Desroches, F. J. (1995). *Force and Fear: Robbery in Canada.* Toronto, Canada: Nelson.

Desroches, F. J. (1997). *Behind the Bars: Experiences in Crime.* Toronto: Canadian Scholars Press.

Doerner, W. G. (1979). The violent world of Johnny Reb: An attitudinal analysis of the regional "Culture of Violence" thesis. *Sociological Forum, 2,* 61–71.

Elliott, D. S. (1994). Serious violent offenders: Onset, development course, and termination. *Criminology, 32,* 1–22.

Elliott, D. S., Huizinga, D., and Ageton, S. (1985). *Explaining Delinquency and Drug Use.* Beverly Hills, CA: Sage.

Elliott, D. S., Huizinga, D., and Menard, S. (1989). *Multiple Problem Youth: Delinquency, Substance Abuse, and Mental Health Problems.* New York: Springer Verlag.

Fagan, J. (1990). Intoxication and aggression. In M. Tonry and J. Q. Wilson (Eds.), *Drugs and Crime, Crime and Justice: A Review of Research.* Chicago: University of Chicago Press.

Fagan, J. A., and Jones, S. J. (1984). Towards an integrated model of violent delinquency. In R. Mathias, P. DeMuro, and R. S. Allinson (Eds.), *An Anthropology on Violent Juvenile Offenders,* Newark: National Council on Crime and Delinquency.

Fagan, J., Piper, E. S., and Cheng, Y. T. (1987). Contributions of victimization to delinquency in inner cities. *Journal of Criminal Law and Criminology, 78,* 586–609.

Fagan, J. A., Piper, E. S., and Moore, M. (1986) Violent delinquents and urban youths. *Criminology, 24,* 439–471.

Fagan, J. A., and Wexler, S. (1987). Family origins of violent delinquents. *Criminology, 25,* 643–669.

Farrington, D. P. (1978). Family backgrounds and aggressive youths. In L. A. Hersov, M. Berger, and D. Shaffer (Eds.), *Aggressive and Anti-Social Behavior in Childhood and Adolescence.* Oxford: Pergamon.

Felson, M., and Cohen, L. E. (1980). Human ecology and crime: A routine activities approach. *Human Ecology, 4,* 389–406.

Gastil, R. D. (1971). Homicide and a regional culture of violence. *American Sociological Review, 36,* 412–437.

Gullotta, T. P. (1979). Leaving home: Family relationships of the runaway child. *Social Casework, 60,* 111–114.

Hackney, S. (1969). Southern violence. *American Historical Review, 39,* 906–925.

Hagan, F. E. (1993). *Research Methods in Criminal Justice and Criminology,* 3rd ed. Toronto: Maxwell Macmillan Canada.

Hagan, J., and McCarthy, B. (1992). Streetlife and delinquency. *British Journal of Sociology, 42,* 533–561.

Hartnagel, T. F. (1990). Under/unemployment and crime among youth: A longitudinal study of recent high school graduates. Discussion Paper 23, University of Alberta, Centre for Criminological Research.

Hartstone, E., and Hansen, K. V. (1984). The violent juvenile offender: An empirical portrait. In R. Mathias, P. DeMuro, and R. S. Allinson (Eds.), *An Anthology on Violent Juvenile Offenders.* Newark: National Council on Crime and Delinquency.

Hawkins, D. F. (1983). Black and white homicide differentials: Alternatives to an inadequate theory. *Criminal Justice and Behavior, 10,* 407–440.

Hindelang, M. J., Hirschi, T., and Weiss, J. G. (1981). *Measuring Delinquency.* Beverly Hills, CA: Sage.

Horowitz, R. (1983). *Honor and the American Dream.* New Brunswick, NJ: Rutgers University Press.

Horwitz, A. V. (1984). The economy and social pathology. *Annual Review of Sociology, 12,* 109–158.

Hotaling, G. T., Straus, M. A., and Lincoln, A. J. (1989). Intrafamily violence, and crime and violence outside the family. In M. Tonry (Ed.), *Crime and Justice: A Review of Research.* Chicago: University of Chicago Press.

Huff-Corzine, L., Corzine, J., and Moore, D. C. (1986). Southern exposure: Deciphering the South's influence on homicide rates. *Social Forces, 64,* 906–924.

Huizinga, D., and Elliott, D. S. (1986). Reassessing the reliability and validity of self-report delinquency measures. *Journal of Quantitative Criminology, 2,* 293–327.

Inciardi, J. A., Horowitz, R., and Pottieger, A. E. (1993). *Street Kids, Street Drugs, Street Crime.* Belmont, CA: Wadsworth.

Inciardi, J. A., Pottieger, A. E., Forney, M. A., Chitwood, D. D., and McBride, D. C. (1991). Prostitution, IV drug use, and sex-for-crack among serious delinquents: Risks for HIV infection. *Criminology, 29,* 221–236.

Inciardi, J. A., and Russe, B. R. (1977). Professional thieves and drugs. *International Journal of Addictions, 12,* 1087–1095.

Janus, M. D., McCromick, A., Burgess, A. W., and Hartman, C. (1987). *Adolescent Runaways.* Toronto, Canada: Lexington.

Jensen, G. F., and Brownheld, D. (1986). Gender, lifestyles, and victimization: Beyond routine activity. *Violence and Victims, 1,* 85–99.

Johnson, B. D., Goldstein, P. J., Preble, E., Schmeidler, J. Lipton, D. S., Spunt, B., and Miller, T. (1985). *Taking Care of Business: The Economics of Crime by Heroin Abusers.* Lexinton, MA: Lexington.

Johnson, R. E. (1979). *Juvenile Delinquency and Its Origins: An Integrated Theoretical Approach.* New York: Cambridge University Press.

Kennedy, L. W., and Baron, S. W. (1993). Routine activities and a subculture of violence: A study of violence on the street. *Journal of Research in Crime and Delinquency, 30,* 88–113.

Kennedy, L. W., and Forde, D. R. (1990a). Routine activities and crime: An analysis of victimization in Canada. *Criminology, 28,* 137–152.

Kennedy, L. W., and Forde, D. R. (1990b). Risky lifestyles and dangerous results: Routine activities and exposure to crime. *Sociology and Social Research, 74,* 208–211.

Kornhauser, R. R. (1978). *Social Sources of Delinquency.* Chicago: University of Chicago Press.

Kufeldt, K., and Nimmo, M. (1987a). Kids on the street they have something to say: Survey of runaway and homeless youth. *Journal of Child Care, 3,* 3:53–61.

Kufeldt, K., and Nimmo, M. (1987b). Youth on the street: Abuse and neglect in the eighties. *Child Abuse and Neglect, 11,* 531–543.

Lauritsen, J. L., Sampson, R. J., and Laub, J. (1991). The link between offending and victimization among adolescents. *Criminology, 29,* 265–291.

Loftin, C., and Hill, R. (1974). Regional subculture and homicide. *American Sociological Review, 39,* 714–724.

MacLeod, J. (1987). *Ain't No Makin It.* Boulder, CO: Westview.

Maxfield, M. G., and Babbie, E. (1995). *Research Methods for Criminal Justice and Criminology.* Toronto, Canada: Wadsworth.

McCarthy, B., and Hagan, J. (1991). Homelessness: A criminogenic situation? *British Journal of Criminology, 31,* 393–410.

McCarthy, B., and Hagan, J. (1992a). Mean streets: The theoretical significance of situational delinquency among homeless youths. *American Sociological Review, 98,* 597–627.

McCarthy, B., and Hagan, J. (1992b). Surviving on the street: The experience of homeless youth. *Journal of Adolescent Research, 7,* 412–430.

McCarthy, B., and Hagan, J. (1995). Getting into street crime: The structure and process of criminal embeddedness. *Social Science Research, 24,* 63–95.

McCarthy, W. D. (1990). Life on the streets: Serious theft, drug selling and prostitution among homeless youth. Ph.D. dissertation, University of Toronto, Toronto, Canada.

McCord, J. (1979). Some child-rearing antecedents of criminal behavior in adult men. *Journal of Personality and Social Psychology, 37,* 1477–1486.

McCullagh, J., and Greco, M. (1990). *Servicing Street Youth: A Feasibility Study.* Toronto, Canada: Children's Aid Society.

Merton, R. K. (1957). *Social Theory and Social Structure.* Glencoe, IL: Free Press.

Messner, S. F. (1983). Regional and racial effects on the urban homicide rate: The subculture of violence revisited. *American Journal of Sociology, 88,* 997–1007.

Messner, S. F., and Tardiff, K. (1986). Economic inequality and levels of homicide: An analysis of urban neighbourhoods. *Criminology, 24,* 297–317.

Palenski, J. E. (1984). *Kids Who Run Away.* Saratoga, CA: R & E.

Pearlin, L. I., Lieberman, M. A., Menaghan, E. G., and Mullan, J. T. (1981). The stress process. *Journal of Health and Social Behavior, 22,* 337–356.

Radford, J. L., King, A. J. C., and Warren, W. K. (1989). *Street Youth and AIDS.* Ottawa: Health and Welfare Canada.

Regoli, R. M., and Hewitt, J. D. (1991). *Delinquency in Society.* New York: McGraw-Hill.

Reiss, A. J., and Farrington, D. P. (1991). Advancing knowledge about co-offending: Results from a prospective longitudinal survey of London males. *Journal of Criminal Law and Criminology, 82,* 360–395.

Rosenfeld, R. (1986). Urban crime rates: Effects of inequality, welfare dependency, region, and race. In J. Byme and R. Sampson (Eds.), *The Social Ecology of Crime.* New York: Springer-Verlag.

Rothman, J. (1991). *Runaway and Homeless Youth.* New York: Longman.

Sampson, R. J. (1985). Structural sources of variation in race-age-specific rates of offending across major U.S. cities. *Criminology, 23,* 647–673.

Sampson, R. J., and Lauritsen, J. L. (1990). Deviant lifestyles, proximity to crime, and the offender-victim link in personal violence. *Journal of Research in Crime and Delinquency, 27,* 110–139.

Sampson, R. J., and Wooldredge, J. (1987). Linking the micro- and macro-level dimensions of lifestyles routine activity and opportunity models of predatory victimization. *Journal of Quantitative Criminology, 3,* 371–393.

Sedgely, J., and Lund, D. (1979). Self-reported beatings and subsequent tolerance for violence. *Review of Public Data Use, 7,* 30–38.

Siegal, L. J., and Senna, J. J. (1994). *Juvenile Delinquency: Theory Practice and Law,* 5th ed. New York: West.

Singer, S. (1981). Homogeneous victim-offender populations: A review of some research implications. *Journal of Criminal Law and Criminology, 72,* 779–88.

Singer, S. (1986). Victims of serious violence and their criminal behaviour: subcultural theory and beyond. *Violence and Victims, 1,* 61–9.

Smart, R. G., Adlaf, E. M., Porterfield, K. M., and Canale, M. D. (1990). *Drug, Youth and the Street.* Toronto, Canada: Addictions Research Foundation.

Smith, C., and Thornberry, T. P. (1995). The relationship between childhood maltreatment and adolescent involvement in delinquency. *Criminology, 33,* 451–482.

Sorrells, J. M. (1977). Kids who kill. *Crime and Delinquency, 23,* 312–320.

Stack, S. (1984). Income inequality and property crime: A cross national analysis of relative deprivation theory. *Criminology, 22,* 222–257.

Statistics Canada. (1994). *Canadian Crime Statistics 1993.* Ottawa: Canadian Centre for Justice Statistics.

Straus, M. A. (1985). Family training in crime and violence. In A. J. Lincoln and M. A. Straus (Eds.), *Crime and the Family.* Springfield, IL: Charles C Thomas.

Suttles, G. (1968). *Social Order of the Slum.* Chicago: University of Chicago Press.

Thrasher, F. M. (1927). *The Gang.* Chicago: University of Chicago Press.

Tinklenberg, J. R., Murphy, P., Murphy, P. L., and Pfefferbaum, A. (1981). Drugs and criminal assaults by adolescents: A replication study. *Journal of Psychoactive Drugs, 13,* 277–287.

Tremblay, P. (1993). Searching for suitable co-offenders. In R. V. Clarke and M. Felson (Eds.), *Routine Activity and Rational Choice. Advances in Criminological Theory.* New Brunswick, NJ: Transaction.

Webber, M. (1991). *Street Kids: The Tragedy of Canada's Runaways.* Toronto, Canada: University of Toronto Press.

White, H. R., Pandina, R. J., and LaGrange, R. L. (1987). Longitudinal predictors of serious substance abuse and delinquency. *Criminology, 25,* 715–740.

Widom, C. S. (1989). Child abuse, neglect, and violent criminal behaviour. *Criminology, 27,* 251–271.

Williams, K. (1984). Economic sources of homicide. Reestimating the effects of poverty and inequality. *American Sociological Review, 49,* 283–289.

Wolfgang, M. E., and Ferracuti, F. (1967). *The Subculture of Violence.* London: Tavistock.

Wooden, W. S. (1995). *Renegade Kids, Suburban Outlaws.* Toronto, Canada: Wadsworth.

Wright, K. N. (1981). *Crime and Criminal Justice in a Declining Economy.* Cambridge, MA: Oelgeschlager, Gunn and Hain.

Zinberg, N. E. (1984). *Drug, Set, and Setting: The Social Bases of Controlled Use.* New Haven, CT: Yale University Press.

14

Illegal Acts Committed by Adolescents Under the Influence of Alcohol and Drugs

HELENE RASKIN WHITE

PETER C. TICE

ROLF LOEBER

MAGDA STOUTHAMER-LOEBER

ABSTRACT

This study examined the proximal effects of alcohol and drug use on adolescent illegal activity. Four years of longitudinal data from the Pittsburgh Youth Study were analyzed for 506 local male adolescents. Participants reported committing offenses against persons more often than general theft under the influence of alcohol or drugs. Aggressive acts were more often related to self-reported acute alcohol use than to marijuana use. Those who reported committing illegal acts under the influence reported committing offenses with other people and being arrested more often than those who did not. Offenses under the influence were more prevalent among heavier alcohol and drug users, more serious offenders, more impulsive youth, and youth with more deviant peers. There were no significant interaction effects of alcohol and drug use with impulsivity or deviant peers in predicting whether illegal acts were committed under the influence. The association between drug use and illegal activity during adolescence is complex.

Although several recent studies have examined the developmental or long-term associations between drug use and delinquency in adolescence (e.g., Huang et al., 2000; Kaplan and Damphousse, 1995; White and Hansell, 1996, 1998; White et al., 1999), few studies of adolescents have focused on the acute or proximal associations. Furthermore, those studies that have examined these associations have had mixed results (Altschuler and Brounstein, 1991; Hartstone and Hansen, 1984; Huizinga, Menard, and Elliott, 1989; Tinklenberg et al., 1981). The purpose of this study was to examine the proximal effects of alcohol and drug use on adolescent illegal activity using longitudinal data from a large community sample of male adolescents.

Laboratory studies of adults shed some light on this issue. These studies have found that acute intoxication by alcohol (below sedating levels) is related to aggression when an individual is provoked (Bushman, 1997; Lipsey et al., 1997). This increased aggression under conditions of alcohol intoxication in the laboratory is best explained by the fact that alcohol causes changes within a person that increase the risk for aggression, such as reduced intellectual functioning, reduced self-awareness, selective disinhibition, and

The preparation of this article was supported in part by grants from the National Institute on Drug Abuse (DA 41101 and Da/AA 03395), the National Institute on Mental Health (NIMH 50778), the Office of Juvenile Justice and Delinquency Prevention (OJJDP 96-MU-FX-0012). This article was presented at the American Society of Criminology Meeting in San Francisco in November 2000. The authors would like to thank three anonymous reviewers for their comments and suggestions.

the inaccurate assessment of risks (Chermack and Giancola, 1997; Ito, Miller, and Pollock, 1996; Parker and Auerhahn, 1998). These same alcohol-induced changes may put a person at risk for nonaggressive crimes, although less research and theorizing have been applied to psychopharmacological explanations for property crime (Goldstein, 1985; White and Gorman, 2000). In contrast, laboratory studies indicate that marijuana has the opposite effect of alcohol in that moderate doses temporarily inhibit aggression and violence (Meyerscough and Taylor, 1985; Miczek et al., 1994).

In addition to experimental research, statistics on the rates of alcohol use by adult offenders at the time of an offense provide strong support for the alcohol–violence relationship (Collins and Messerschmidt, 1993; Roizen, 1993). In one study, however, although more than 50 percent of the assaultive offenders reported drinking at the time of their offenses, 59 percent of those drinking did not think that their drinking was relevant to the commission of their crimes (Collins and Messerschmidt, 1993). In a study of incarcerated offenders, Collins and Schlenger (1988) concluded that acute episodes rather than chronic patterns of alcohol use better predict violent offending. High percentages of jail inmates have also reported being under the influence of drugs, primarily marijuana and cocaine, at the time of their offenses (Harlow, 1998). However, reports from adult offenders indicate that more violent crime than property crime is committed under the influence of alcohol alone, and more property crime than violent crime is committed under the influence of drugs alone (Franklin, Allison, and Sutton, 1992; Harlow, 1998; Miller and Welte, 1986). Valdez, Yin, and Kaplan (1997) also found that arrests for aggressive crimes were more strongly related to reports of frequent alcohol use than to testing positive for illicit drugs. In fact, persons who tested positive compared to negative for illicit drugs were less likely to be involved in aggressive crime. Therefore, laboratory and epidemiological research on adults underscores the facts that alcohol use compared to most illicit drug use is more strongly related to aggressive crime and that drug use may be more related to property crime.

The stronger association between drug use and property crime may reflect economic necessity (White and Gorman, 2000). The economic motivation model, which is an alternative perspective to the psychopharmacological model, assumes that drug users need to generate illicit income to support their drug habits (Goldstein, 1985). Support for this model comes from the literature on heroin addicts, which indicates that increases or decreases in the frequency of substance use among addicts raise or lower their frequency of crime, especially property crime (e.g., Anglin and Perrochet, 1998; Chaiken and Chaiken, 1990; Nurco et al., 1984). In contrast, self-report data do not provide strong support for an economic motivation model (White and Gorman, 2000). Intensive drug users and highly delinquent youth do not report committing illegal acts to raise money for drugs, and most report committing illegal acts for reasons completely independent of drugs (Altschuler and Brounstein, 1991; Carpenter et al., 1988; Johnson et al., 1986). In fact, much of the recent research dispels the assumption of economically motivated offending, once drug dealing is excluded (White and Gorman, 2000).

Research examining the acute effects of various drugs and their relationships with different types of illegal activity is more inconsistent for adolescents than for adults. Reports from arrested adolescents indicate a much greater overlap in the use of alcohol and drugs and less of a distinction between them in their associations with different types of offenses (Bureau of Justice Statistics, 1994; White, 1997b). For example, in one study of adolescents who were adjudicated for violent offenses, almost half had used either alcohol or drugs immediately prior to committing their offenses (Hartstone and Hansen, 1984). In this study, rates were somewhat higher for other drugs than for alcohol. In contrast, in a study of incarcerated adolescents, it was found that the acute use of alcohol either alone or in combination with other drugs was involved in more than half of the incidents of physical assault, whereas the acute use of marijuana was involved in about one fourth of such incidents (Tinklenberg et al., 1981). The researchers concluded that marijuana use was underreported in physical assault offenses in comparison to alcohol relative to their reported frequency of use in the sample. The findings for sexual assault were similar.

The few community studies of adolescents that have attempted to address this issue provide mixed support for a proximal association between alcohol and/or drug use and delinquency (Carpenter et al., 1988; Huizinga et al., 1989; White, 1997b). For example, Carpenter et al. (1988) interviewed adolescents about their use of alcohol and drugs immediately preceding offenses. Many adolescents reported that they actually moderated their use when they knew they were going to commit illegal acts. In a study of inner-city ninth graders, Altschuler and Brounstein (1991) found that only a minority of youth used drugs before committing any type of illegal act.

Huizinga et al. (1989), in a national study of adolescents, reported higher rates of acute alcohol use than drug use for all index offenses except robbery, for which the rates were equal for both substances. As these participants aged, the distinctions between using alcohol and drugs became much clearer. All categories of offenses were more strongly related to alcohol use except motor vehicle theft, which was strongly related to drug use. Overall, the association between alcohol use and violent offenses was stronger in young adulthood than in adolescence, suggesting that the nature of the relationship may change over the life course (see also Collins, 1986). In these analyses, the researchers did not control for drug use, so the differences could partly reflect the fact that alcohol use was the most prevalent substance used. However, Huizinga et al. (1989) also compared the average percentage of days when alcohol and drugs were used to the percentage of offenses committed under the influence of alcohol and drugs. They found a very strong association between alcohol use and sexual assaults. For the remaining offenses, the estimated daily use of alcohol exceeded (or was equal to for aggravated assaults) the rate at which alcohol was used prior to offense commission. Further, the use of drugs prior to offense commission was much lower than expected on the basis of average daily use. White and Hansell (1998) controlled for the prevalence of drug use in their analyses and found that alcohol was more strongly related to fighting than was marijuana. The strength of the relationship between alcohol and fighting relative to marijuana and fighting increased with age.

Overall, the extant research on acute intoxication and delinquency for adolescents is limited (Huizinga et al., 1989). Samples have been primarily restricted to arrestees and adjudicated delinquents, whose use patterns may not be generalizable to all adolescents. These youth may report drug use simply to give themselves an excuse for their illegal behavior (Collins, 1993). As well, individuals who use alcohol or drugs when committing illegal acts may be more likely to get caught (Chaiken and Chaiken, 1990; Collins, 1986). Few community samples of adolescents have been assessed in terms of their drug use prior to offense commission. Those studies that have made such assessments have been limited to only a few offenses and/or have not controlled for the type or extent of typical drug use within the analyses. That is, if delinquents are also frequent drug users, they are probably using drugs often both when they commit illegal acts and when they do not, and their drug use may be superfluous to their offense commission

(White, 1990). In addition, none of these studies has attempted to understand the possible mechanisms that account for these relationships.

One possible explanation for the association between acute alcohol and drug use and illegal activity is the psychopharmacological effects of drugs. Psychopharmacological effects of alcohol that have been postulated to increase the risks for delinquency include impairment in communication, which involves provoking others and being easily angered; increased risk taking; an unawareness of the consequences of one's own behavior; and expectancies that alcohol use causes aggression (Bushman, 1997; Chermack and Giancola, 1996; Ito et al., 1996; Parker and Auerhahn, 1998; White, 1997a, 1997b). An alternative explanation may be that the use of drugs is a social activity, and thus, while using drugs, adolescents may be in the company of peers who encourage or reinforce illegal behavior (Fagan, 1993; White, 1990). In addition, drug use may interact with an individual's personality or temperament characteristics, such as impulsivity and hyperactivity, to increase the risk for offense commission (Lang, 1993). One needs to be aware, however, that different drugs may have different moderating effects. For example, alcohol or sedative drugs may interact with temperament characteristics to increase aggression, whereas drugs such as marijuana may actually have inhibiting effects on aggression (Miczek et al., 1994).

This study examined the self-reported proximal associations between drug use and illegal activity during adolescence and explanations for these associations. It extended prior research on adolescents by including a large number of types of illegal activities, controlling for individuals' drug use in the analyses, and examining potential mechanisms that might account for a proximal association. We addressed the following questions, which have not been adequately addressed in community studies of adolescents to date: (a) Is there a difference in the types of illegal acts that are committed under the influence of alcohol and those committed under the influence of drugs? (b) Is there a difference in the rates of illegal acts committed under the influence of alcohol and those committed under the influence of marijuana? (c) Is there a relationship between using alcohol and drugs and being with others at the time of an offense? (d) Does the extent of drug involvement or the extent of offending involvement affect the likelihood of committing illegal acts under the influence of drugs? (e) Are those who commit illegal acts under the influence of drugs more likely to get arrested? and (f) Are these relationships moderated by individual hyperactivity and/or impulsivity or type of peer group?

METHOD

Design and Sample

Data were collected as part of the Pittsburgh Youth Study (PYS). The PYS is a prospective longitudinal study of the development of delinquency, substance use, and mental health problems (Loeber et al., 1998). In 1987 and 1988, random samples of first-, fourth-, and seventh-grade boys enrolled in the city of Pittsburgh's public schools were selected. Approximately 850 boys in each grade (85 percent of the target sample) were screened. About 500 boys in each grade (the 250 most antisocial and another 250 randomly selected from those remaining) were chosen for the first follow-up six months later. For the present analyses, we used only the oldest cohort ($N = 506$) because of low rates of drug use in the younger cohorts (White et al., 1999). After the first follow-up, subjects in the oldest cohort were subsequently followed up at six-month intervals for four additional assessments and then at yearly intervals for another four assessments. Attrition has remained relatively low, and 89.7 percent of the original sample was followed up at the last assessment.

For the present study, we concentrated on the last four yearly assessments because the measures of alcohol and drug use at the time of offense commission were not available prior to that. The sample was approximately 16.5 years old in the first of these four assessments ($M = 16.33$, $SD = 0.80$) and 19.5 years old at the end. Most of the analyses combined data from all four years to create a single indicator for each variable of interest. The sample was 57.5 percent African American, with the remainder almost entirely White. In addition, 36.2 percent of the boys' families received public assistance or food stamps. (For greater detail on participant selection and sample characteristics, see Loeber et al., 1998).

For these analyses we only include adolescents who had used alcohol (beer, wine, or hard liquor), marijuana, and/or other drugs (hallucinogens, cocaine, crack, heroin, PCP, and the nonmedical use of tranquilizers, barbiturates, codeine, amphetamines, and over-the-counter medications) at least once during the four-year period (i.e., at any time during the period from approximate 16.5 through 19.5 years of age). As stated earlier, it would not make sense to assess offenses committed under the influence of drugs for individuals who never used alcohol or drugs. This limited our analysis to 454 of the 506 subjects (89.7 percent).

Measures

All of the measures came from self-reports from the adolescents except for the serious offender classification scale and the measure of hyperactivity and/or impulsivity (see below). Self-reports are generally accepted as reliable and valid indicators of delinquent behavior and drug use (Farrington et al., 1996; Hindelang, Hirschi, and Weis, 1981; Single, Kandel, and Johnson, 1975). According to Elliott, Huizinga, and Menard (1989), self-reports provide a more direct, sensitive, and complete measure of various forms of deviant behavior than measures based on official law enforcement and institutional records. Self-reports also have their limitations in terms of the accuracy of recall, misunderstanding the questions, and efforts to conceal or exaggerate (Chaiken and Chaiken, 1990). When both the dependent and independent measures are assessed with self-reports, there is also a potential influence of shared method variance. Therefore, the results of this study should be evaluated in light of possible measurement limitations. (For greater detail on the advantages and disadvantages of self-report data, see Elliott et al., 1989; Farrington et al., 1996; Hindelang et al., 1981.)

Illegal Activities.[1] We examined the frequency (number of times) of commission of 19 different types of illegal acts within the past year. These behaviors were divided into general theft (i.e., theft at four levels ranging from less than $5 to more than $100, shoplifting, breaking and entering, auto theft, joyriding, and stealing from cars), offenses against persons (i.e., attacking, hitting to hurt, gang fighting, strongarming, and throwing objects at people), and miscellaneous offenses (i.e., setting fires, vandalism, credit card fraud, fencing, and check forgery) (Huizinga et al., 1989). We were primarily interested in the prevalence of each of these behaviors in any of the four years (between 16.5 and 19.5 years of age).

We also controlled for the level of serious offending by using a serious and violent offending classification scale, which is a Guttman scale that reflects the most serious offending in the past year and is based on reports from the child, parent or guardian, and teacher (Loeber et al., 1998). Serious offenders (i.e., those who engaged in breaking and entering, auto theft, prostitution, attacking with a weapon, strong-arming, hurting for sex, or forced sex) were compared to minor and moderate offenders.

Illegal Acts Committed Under the Influence. For each type of illegal act that an adolescent committed, he was asked whether he used alcohol or drugs at the time he committed the most serious occasion of that offense within the past year. Note that this measure did not assess drug use at the time of committing every illegal activity, only the most serious of each type. Thus, this measure could have underestimated the extent of acute drug involvement if alcohol or drugs were used on less serious occasions. Also note that the question did not distinguish between alcohol and other drugs.

Distinguishing Between Alcohol-Related and Marijuana-Related Illegal Acts. Although the previous questions about illegal activities could not distinguish between alcohol and other drugs, there were a few questions about illegal acts that were asked separately for alcohol and for marijuana and included in these analyses. Adolescents were asked how often in the past year they got into fights and got in trouble with the police while using alcohol and while using marijuana. For these questions, only those adolescents who used alcohol ($n = 445$) were included for the two alcohol items, and those who used marijuana ($n = 264$) were included for the marijuana items.

Illegal Acts Committed Alone or With Others. The same question that asked about using alcohol and drugs while committing the most serious offense also asked about whether adolescents were alone or with others when they committed the most serious offenses for each act.

Drug Use Measures. Frequency of alcohol use was the sum of the number of times participants used beer, wine, or hard liquor during the past year. Adolescents who used alcohol were divided into the highest quartile versus the lower three in each of the four years. Anyone who was in the highest quartile in at least one of the four years was considered a heavy alcohol users. We constructed the same measures for marijuana use.

Arrests. Each year, participants reported the number of times that they were arrested within the past year. We dichotomized this variable into those ever arrested versus those never arrested during the four-year period. Note that this variable could not be matched with each individual type of offense committed under the influence.

Hyperactivity, Impulsivity, and Attention Problems. At ages 16.5 and 17.5, primary caretakers and teachers completed the Achenbach Child Behavioral Checklist (Achenbach and Edelbrock, 1983; Edelbrock and Achenbach, 1984). Fourteen items assessing hyperactivity, impulsivity, and attention problems (e.g., is impulsive or acts without thinking, behaves irresponsibly is inattentive, is daring) were combined to form a composite scale that measured hyperactivity,

impulsivity, and attention problems (hereafter referred to as impulsivity). We took the maximum value for the two years for this analysis, and for some analyses, we divided adolescents into the top quartile versus the lower three.

Peer Deviance. Each year, participants reported the number of close friends who had committed 11 illegal acts ranging from lying and vandalism to strong-arming and attacking individuals. We took the maximum number for the four years (from 16.5 to 19.5 years of age) for this variable, and for some analyses, we divided adolescents into the top quartile versus the lower three.

RESULTS

Are There Differences by Type of Illegal Act?

Table 1 shows the percentage of the most serious of each illegal act reported to have been committed under the influence of alcohol and/or drugs. These percentages reflect the percentage of those who reported committing each offense, which could be as few as 14 subjects for credit card fraud and as many as 222 for hitting to hurt. (In fact, five offenses were committed by less than 10 percent of the sample.)

The percentages under the influence ranged from 0 percent for forging checks to 45.8 percent for strong-arming. Proportionally, the most frequent illegal acts reported to have been committed under the influence of alcohol or drugs were strong-arming, gang fighting, attacking, vandalism, and throwing things at others. For each of these, more than one third of those who committed the offense committed their most serious offenses under the influence of alcohol or drugs. Most of these activities would be considered aggressive, and thus, these data suggest that violent offenses as opposed to property offenses may be more strongly related to acute incidents of alcohol and drug use.

The least likely offenses to have been committed under the influence were white-collar offenses such as check forgery, credit card fraud, and fencing. We also examined these associations for alcohol users only to be sure that the illegal act involved only alcohol use and not other drugs. The findings were very similar, suggesting that many of the offenses committed under the influence, as shown in Table 1, were probably committed under the influence of alcohol rather than other drugs. (These data are not presented here but are available from the first author by request.)

TABLE 1 Percentage Committing Each Type of Illegal Act Under the Influence (N = 454)

ACT	n	PERCENTAGE UNDER THE INFLUENCE
Theft of < $5	63	15.9
Theft of $5 to $50	36	17.9
Theft of $50 to $100	24	26.3
Theft of > $100	59	28.8
Stealing from cars	50	20.7
Auto theft	40	32.5
Joyriding	90	26.7
Shoplifting	90	18.9
Breaking and entering	27	22.2
Vandalism	104	35.6
Gang fighting	97	42.3
Attacking	97	37.1
Hitting to hurt	222	29.3
Throwing	100	34.0
Strong-arming	24	45.8
Setting fires	18	16.7
Fencing	125	12.8
Check forgery	14	0
Credit card fraud	14	7.1
Offenses against persons	279	39.8
General theft	147	23.1

The final two lines in Table 1 summarize the difference between offenses against persons and general theft. Almost twice as many boys were ever involved in an offense against a person than were involved in a property offense.[2] Of those who committed offenses against persons, 39.8 percent reported that they were under the influence of alcohol or drugs when they committed their most serious of at least one type of personal offense. In contrast, only 23.1 percent reported that they were under the influence for their most serious occasion of any theft offense. Therefore, in answer to our first question, offenses against persons, compared to general theft, were more often reported to have been committed under the influence of alcohol and drugs.

Is There a Difference Between Alcohol and Marijuana?

If there is credence to the psychopharmacological explanation for the acute association between alcohol and drug use and offending, then there should be a stronger relationship between acute alcohol use and illegal activity than between marijuana use and illegal activity. Among those who used each substance, 23.1 percent of the alcohol users got into fights, and 17.5 percent got into trouble with the police while using alcohol, whereas 6.1 percent of the marijuana users got into fights and 10.2 percent got into trouble with the police while using marijuana. Therefore, more adolescents reported an association of alcohol than marijuana to fighting behavior, which corroborates the findings of experimental studies (White, 1997a).

Is There a Difference Between Being Alone and Being With Others?

The third question we addressed was whether those who committed offenses under the influence, compared to those who did not, would be more likely to have committed their offenses with other people. As is commonly found in delinquency research, most adolescents committed offenses with others. This ranged from a low of 62 percent for strong-arming to a high of 93 percent for breaking and entering. For 12 of the 18 illegal acts that were examined, more than 75 percent of those committing a given offense did so with someone else.[3] (These data are not shown but are available from the first author by request.)

Table 2 presents the rates of committing personal and property offenses with others while under the influence and while not under the influence of alcohol or drugs. The rates for those under the influence are shown in the first column, the rates for those

TABLE 2 Percentage Committing Illegal Acts with Others (N = 454)

ACT	THOSE UNDER THE INFLUENCE	THOSE NOT UNDER THE INFLUENCE	TOTAL
Against persons	90.8	74.6***	85.8
General theft	88.6	73.7	77.6

***$p < .001$ as determined by a chi-square analysis.

not under the influence are shown in the second column, and the rates for the total sample are shown in the third column. Participants reported that they were more likely to commit their most serious personal offenses than their most serious property offenses with others.

There was a significant association between self-reports of being under the influence of alcohol and/or drugs and committing personal offenses with other people: Of those under the influence, 90.8 percent committed personal offenses with others, whereas 74.6 percent of those not under the influence committed personal offenses with others (odds ratio [OR] = 3.4, $p < .001$). This relationship was not significant for property offenses, although the differences were almost as large as for personal offenses: 88.6 percent versus 73.7 percent (OR = 2.8, $p > .05$).

Given that illegal activity is often a peer group behavior, as is drug use, the overlap may reflect circumstantial effects. The results may also reflect group psychopharmacological effects; that is, as those in a group get high together, they motivate one another to commit illegal acts. It is also possible that youth plan to get high together intentionally to give themselves the courage or an excuse to engage in illegal acts, especially aggressive offenses (Fagan, 1993). Unfortunately, the data do not allow us to disentangle these effects.

Are There Differences Depending on Drug Use Patterns?

One explanation for the strong association between acute drug use and illegal activity is that those who use drugs often use them all the time, whether or not they commit illegal offenses. In other words, frequent drug users will be more likely to be under the influence simply by chance. Therefore, the pattern of usage is a confounding factor, and we examined the association between frequent drug use and committing offenses under the influence. For these analyses, we divided adolescents into heavy users (the top 25 percent) and light users (the remaining 75 percent). As found in previous research (White and Gorman, 2000), heavy versus light alcohol users were significantly more likely to commit both personal (OR = 6.2, $p < .001$) and property (OR = 5.2, $p < .01$) offenses under the influence. Note that 54.6 percent of the heavy alcohol users committed violent offenses under the influence, and only 29.5 percent committed property offenses under the influence. Thus, these data for heavy alcohol users support the earlier findings for all users showing a stronger relationship with personal offenses than with theft offenses for those under the influence.

On the other hand, heavy versus light marijuana users were not significantly more likely to commit either type of offense under the influence of alcohol or drugs (OR = 1.5, $p > .05$ for personal; OR = 1.5, $p > .05$ for theft). Thus, the extent of marijuana use was not related to committing offenses under the influence of alcohol or drugs. Note, however, that the rates of committing offenses under the influence were relatively high for both heavy and light marijuana users. These high rates probably reflect the fact that marijuana users were also heavy alcohol users and committed these offenses under the influence of alcohol rather than marijuana.

The results also show that heavy alcohol users were more likely to report getting into fights (OR = 6.2, $p < .001$) and into trouble with the police (OR = 3.5, $p < .001$) while using alcohol and that heavy marijuana users were more likely to report getting into fights (OR = 3.5, $p < .05$) and into trouble with the police (OR = 6.9, $p < .001$) while using marijuana. Thus, when only marijuana-related offenses are considered, the frequency of marijuana use appears to make a difference.

Is There a Difference Between Serious and Nonserious Offenders?

We were also interested in whether serious offenders were more likely to commit offenses under the influence. Serious offenders, compared to minor and moderate offenders, were more than twice as likely to commit both violent (OR = 3.3, $p < .001$) and property (OR = 2.7, $p < .05$) offenses under the influence of alcohol and/or drugs. Note that these analyses were limited to only those who used drugs, so the fact that drug use is more prevalent among serious offenders was held constant, although the analysis did not control for the fact that serious offenders may be more frequent users. Serious offenders, compared to nonserious offenders, were also significantly more likely to report getting into fights while using alcohol (OR = 4.0, $p < .001$) and marijuana (OR = 4.6, $p < .001$) and getting into trouble with the police while using alcohol (OR = 3.2, $p < .001$) but not marijuana (10.8 percent, OR = 1.2, $p > .05$).

Are Those Who Commit Illegal Acts Under the Influence More Likely to Get Arrested?

As mentioned earlier, we could not match arrests with specific illegal acts committed under the influence. Instead, we examine the percentage of youth who reported getting arrested among those who reported committing offenses under the influence and those who did not. Those individuals who committed both property (OR = 4.4, $p < .01$) and personal (OR = 4.1, $p < .001$) offenses under the influence of alcohol or drugs were at much higher risk for having ever been arrested compared to those who did not commit these offenses under the influence. As well, a much larger percentage of those who fought under the influence of alcohol (OR = 4.5, $p < .001$) and got into trouble with the police because of alcohol (OR = 7.4, $p < .001$) or marijuana (OR = 7.7, $p < .01$) had been arrested. The difference in arrest rates for those who fought versus those who did not fight under the influence of marijuana (OR = 4.0, $p > .05$) was not significant.

Given the nature of the data, we cannot conclude that the use of drugs contributed to the arrests. These differences could reflect the fact that some individuals were careless in the commission of their illegal acts because they were intoxicated. Alternatively, the differences might simply reflect the fact that arrestees are more frequent drug users.

Do Deviant Peers and Levels of Impulsivity Moderate the Effects of Drug Use on Illegal Activity?

To understand more about the mechanisms that might account for the association between acute alcohol and drug use and illegal activity during adolescence, we examined the moderating effects of impulsivity and deviant peers on committing offenses under the influence. First, we examined whether those high in impulsivity, compared to those low in impulsivity, were more likely to engage in illegal activity under the influence. Impulsivity was signifi-

cantly related to offenses against persons (OR = 2.0, $p < .05$) but not to theft (OR = 1.9, $p > .05$). It was also significantly related to fighting (OR = 2.0, $p < .01$) and getting into trouble with the police (OR = 2.2, $p < .01$) while using alcohol, but not while using marijuana (OR = 0.9, $p > .05$ for fighting; OR = 0.9, $p > .05$ for trouble with the police). Thus, impulsivity, alcohol, and violence appear to be interconnected.

Those boys with larger proportions of deviant peers were more likely to commit both personal (OR = 2.9, $p < .001$) and theft (OR = 3.9, $p > .001$) offenses while under the influence. They were also more likely to fight while under the influence of alcohol (OR = 3.8, $p < .001$) and marijuana (OR = 3.7, $p < .01$) and to get into trouble with the police while using alcohol (OR = 3.3, $p < .001$) but not marijuana (OR = 1.0, $p > .05$). Again, this strong relationship could be indicative of the fact that drug use and offending are peer group activities, and thus, there is a circumstantial association, and/or that those boys with more deviant peers are also heavier alcohol and marijuana users.

For the moderation analyses, we conducted hierarchical logistic regression analyses to test whether heavy alcohol and marijuana use, deviant peers, impulsivity, and their interactions predicted committing offenses under the influence of drugs. For these analyses, we dichotomized the predictors into the top quartile versus the rest. The odds ratios are shown in Table 3. All of the main effects variables were significant predictors of committing personal offenses while under the influence of alcohol and/or drugs, even when the other variables were held constant. Only frequent marijuana use and having many deviant peers were significant predictors of being under the influence when committing a theft. (Note that when the analyses were conducted separately for alcohol and marijuana, the findings remained the same. The results are available from the first author by request.) None of the interactions were significant. However, we were able to model only the interaction between the frequency of use with deviant peers and with impulsivity, not necessarily the interactions between acute use and these two variables.

We also tested these same models for alcohol users only and for marijuana users only using fights and trouble with the police while under the influence as the outcome variable (see Table 3). We found that frequent alcohol use and having many deviant peers significantly predicted fighting and getting into trouble with the police while using alcohol. Only frequent marijuana use significantly predicted

TABLE 3   Odds Ratios from the Logistic Regression Analyses

	MODEL					
Predictor	Persons under the Influence[a]	Theft under the Influence[b]	Fight Alcohol[c]	Police Alcohol[c]	Fight Marijuana[d]	Police Marijuana[d]
Alcohol frequency	2.8**	1.2	4.1***	2.8***	nt	nt
Marijuana frequency	2.7**	2.5*	nt	nt	5.0*	4.8**
Deviant peers	2.2*	2.9*	2.5***	2.4**	2.2	0.7
Impulsivity	1.9*	1.7	1.5	1.8	0.7	0.8
Chi-square ($df = 4$)	54.5***	17.5**	65.1***	42.5***	11.4**	12.1**

Note: nt = not tested.

[a]Based only on those who had committed offenses against persons ($n = 279$).

[b]Based only on those who had committed general theft offenses ($n = 147$).

[c]Based only on alcohol users ($n = 445$).

[d]Based only on marijuana users ($n = 264$).

*$p < .05$. **$p < .01$. ***$p < .001$.

fighting and getting in trouble with the police while using marijuana. Again, none of the interactions were significant.

DISCUSSION

In sum, the self-report data indicate that offenses against persons, compared to general theft, were more likely to be committed under the influence of alcohol or drugs. Furthermore, aggressive offenses were more often related to acute use of alcohol than marijuana. Those who reported committing offenses under the influence, compared to those who did not, were more likely to report having committed offenses with other people and having been arrested. Committing offenses while under the influence was more prevalent for those who were heavier alcohol and drug users, were more serious offenders, were more impulsive, and had more deviant peers. After controlling for levels of alcohol and drug use, both being more impulsive and having more deviant peers predicted committing personal offenses under the influence, whereas deviant peers but not impulsivity predicted committing general theft offenses under the influence. However, there were no significant interaction effects of alcohol and drug use with impulsivity or deviant peers in the prediction of whether offenses were committed under the influence.

Overall, the results of this study of adolescents support prior research on adults and indicate a stronger relationship between the acute use of alcohol and illegal activity than between marijuana use

and illegal activity, as well as a stronger relationship of alcohol use to personal offenses than to general theft (Franklin et al., 1992; Harlow, 1998; Miller and Welte, 1986; Valdez et al., 1997). These differences could reflect either differences in the psychopharmacological effects of alcohol or societal expectancies regarding alcohol use and aggression. Furthermore, individual differences in impulsivity appear to be involved in this complex association between alcohol use and aggressive offending. Note that impulsivity was measured as a broad category including hyperactivity, impulsivity, and attention problems. Future research should examine these and other temperamental traits individually to assess their role in alcohol- and drug-related offending. In addition, more research is needed to understand the situational factors that may condition the associations among impulsivity, alcohol use, and aggression (Fagan, 1993).

We could not substantiate a unique relationship between drug use and theft, as has been demonstrated for adults. Miller and Welte (1986) found that adult offenders who used only drugs when they committed their crimes compared to those who used only alcohol or used alcohol and drugs were more likely to have committed property offenses. Because we could not separate out the use of alcohol and marijuana when examining theft offenses committed under the influence, we could not address this issue. The extent of marijuana use was not related to committing general theft or personal offenses under the influence of alcohol or drugs, although among marijuana users, it was related to fighting and getting into trouble with the police while using marijuana. In the logistic regression analyses, frequent marijuana use predicted committing both personal and property offenses under the influence, whereas frequent alcohol use was not related to committing general theft offenses under the influence. Thus, in this sample, marijuana use appears to be related similarly to both general theft and to offenses against persons.

Those youth most involved in drug use and most involved in serious offending were at the greatest risk for being under the influence when they committed illegal acts. We cannot necessarily assume that this relationship is causal, however, because these individuals may have been under the influence of alcohol and/or drugs often, regardless of whether or not they were committing illegal acts (Carpenter et al., 1988; White, 1990).

The fact that personal offenses were more likely to be committed with other people when under the influence and were more strongly related to alcohol use than no marijuana use suggests that aggression occurs in social settings where alcohol is used and that alcohol may be a contributing factor (as a cause or an excuse) (Collins, 1993; Fagan, 1993). Nevertheless, large majorities of adolescents committed offenses with other individuals regardless of whether they were under the influence or not. Further, having deviant peers predicted committing offenses against persons and theft under the influence even after controls for the youth's own levels of marijuana and alcohol use. Therefore, these data suggest that peer groups may play a significant role in affecting the nature of illegal activities.

This study could not address several questions. First, for most offenses, we could not differentiate whether adolescents were under the influences of alcohol, drugs, or both when committing illegal acts. Even when we could distinguish between alcohol and drugs, we only differentiated between alcohol and marijuana, two drugs with opposite psychopharmacological associations with aggression (at least as assessed under laboratory conditions) (Miczek et al., 1994). Because the prevalence of other drug use was relatively low in this sample, we could not explore associations between other drug use and illegal activity. Future research on other samples should attempt to distinguish among different types of drugs. Second, we had data on only the most serious offenses within each behavior category, and therefore, we missed all other occasions of acute alcohol or drug use when offending. Third, we could not link specific offenses

under the influence to being arrested for those offenses. Fourth, we could not assess the interactions between acute drug use (as opposed to frequent drug use) and impulsivity or deviant peers to specify mechanisms more clearly. Also, we did not examine other factors that could condition the associations between acute drug use and offending. For example, there is substantial data to suggest that race, ethnicity, and social class are related to both offending and drug use among adolescents, although not necessarily in the same direction (Elliott, 1994; Johnston, O'Malley, and Bachman, 2000). Given that more than half this sample was African American, and over one third were at or near the poverty level, the sociodemographic characteristics of this sample may have affected the nature of the observed associations. Therefore, future research should include race, ethnicity, social class, and other potential moderators.

In spite of these limitations, this study is one of the only community studies to collect data from adolescents on the use of alcohol and drugs at the time of commission of numerous types of offenses. Further, in this study, we controlled for drug use so as not to artificially inflate associations between drug use and offending. In addition, we attempted to understand various mechanisms that could account for the associations between drug use and illegal activity.

Overall, the findings indicate a complex association between illegal activity and alcohol and drug use and raise as many questions as they answer. It appears that one single model cannot explain this relationship for all adolescents. Rather, there are some individuals for whom the acute cognitive effects of some drugs, such as alcohol, increase the propensity toward illegal behaviors, especially violence. For others, deviant behavior may lead to involvement in peer groups that provide opportunities and reinforcement for increased illegal activity and drug use. Finally, for others, shared intrapersonal and environmental factors may increase the risk for involvement in all types of deviant behavior. Harm reduction strategies may help prevent offending for those who commit illegal acts because of the acute effects of alcohol or drugs; changes in peer groups may work for the second group, and prevention programs that focus on individual and environmental risk factors will be indicated for the third group (Loeber, Stouthamer-Loeber, and White 1999; Marlatt 1998). More research is needed to prospectively differentiate these various subgroups to develop appropriate interventions.

NOTES

1. Jurisdiction in the Commonwealth of Pennsylvania changes at age 18. However, for serious offenses, juveniles can be referred to criminal court at an earlier age. Because this study focused on the period from approximately 16.5 through 19.5 years of age, some of the illegal acts reported by adolescents were delinquent offenses, and some were criminal offenses. Therefore, we use the terms *illegal act* and *offense* rather than *delinquency* or *crime* to avoid confusion regarding issues of jurisdiction.

2. The reason for the higher rate of personal offenses in this sample may reflect the fact that a relatively minor violent act, hitting to hurt, was included in the personal offense category and was reported by the greatest number of participants. Nevertheless, the inclusion of this minor violent act does not appear to have influenced the findings for the differences between personal offenses and general theft; more serious personal offenses (e.g., strong-arming and attacking) had higher rates of being committed under the influence than hitting to hurt.

3. The number of acts was reduced from 19 to 18 because gang fighting was left out of this specific analysis.

REFERENCES

Achenbach, T. M., and Edelbrock, C. S. (1983). *Manual for the Child Behavior Checklist and Revised Child Behavior Profile*. Burlington: University of Vermont Department of Psychiatry.

Altschuler, D. M., and Brounstein, P. J. (1991). Patterns of drug use, drug trafficking, and other delinquency among inner-city adolescent males in Washington, DC *Criminology, 29*, 589–622.

Anglin, M. D. and Perrochet, B. (1998). Drug use and crime: A historical review of research conducted by the UCLA Drug Abuse Research Center. *Substance Use and Misuse, 33*, 1871–1914.

Bureau of Justice Statistics. (1994). *Fact Sheet: Drug-Related Crime*. Washington, DC: U.S. Department of Justice.

Bushman, B. J. (1997). Effects of alcohol on human aggression: Validity of proposed explanations. Pp. 227–43 in *Recent Developments in Alcoholism*, vol. 13. *Alcohol and Violence*, edited by Marc Galanter. New York: Plenum.

Carpenter, C., Glassner, B., Johnson, B. D., and Loughlin, J. (1988). *Kids, Drugs, and Crime*. Lexington, MA: Lexington Books.

Chaiken, J. M., and Chaiken, M. R. (1990). Drugs and predatory crime. In M. Tonry and J. Q. Wilson (Eds.), (pp. 203–239). Chicago: University of Chicago Press.

Chermack, S. T., and Giancola, P. R. (1997). The relationship between alcohol and aggression: An integrated biopsychosocial conceptualization. *Clinical Psychology Review, 17*, 621–649.

Collins, J. J. (1986). The relationship of problem drinking to individual offending sequences. In A. Blumstein, J. Cohen, J. Roth, and C. A. Visher (Eds.), *Criminal Careers and "Career Criminals,"* vol. 2 (pp. 89–120). Washington, DC: National Academic Press.

Collins, J. J. (1993). Drinking and violence: An individual offender focus. pp. 221–35 In S. E. Martin (Ed.), *Alcohol and Interpersonal Violence: Fostering Multidisciplinary Perspectives* (NLAAA Research Monograph No. 24 (pp. 221–235). Rockville, MD: National Institute of Health.

Collins, J. J., and Messerschmidt, P. M. (1993). Epidemiology of alcohol-related violence. *Alcohol Health and Research World, 17*, 93–100.

Collins, J. J., and Schlenger, W. E. (1988). Acute and chronic effects of alcohol use on violence. *Journal of Studies on Alcohol, 49*, 516–521.

Edelbrock, C. S., and Achenbach, T. M. (1984). The teacher version of the child behavior profile: I. Boys aged six through eleven. *Journal of Consulting and Clinical Psychology, 52*, 207–217.

Elliott, D. S. (1994). Serious violent offenders: Onset, developmental course, and termination—the American Society of Criminology 1993 Presidential Address. *Criminology, 32*, 1–21.

Elliott, D. S., Huizinga, D., and Menard, S. (1989). *Multiple Problem Youth: Delinquency Substance Use and Mental Health Problems*. New York: Springer-Verlag.

Fagan, J. (1993). Set and setting revisited: Influences of alcohol and illicit drugs on the social context of violent events. pp. 161–91 In S. E. Martin (Ed.), *Alcohol and Interpersonal Violence: Fostering Multidisciplinary Perspectives* (NIAAA Research Monograph No. 24) (pp. 161–191). Rockville, MD: National Institute of Health.

Farrington, D. P., Loeber, R., Stouthamer-Loeber, M., Van Kammen, W., and Schmidt, L. (1996). Self-reported delinquency and a combined delinquency seriousness scale based on boys, mothers, and teachers: Concurrent and predictive validity for African-Americans and Caucasians. *Criminology, 34*, 501–525.

Franklin, R. D., Allison, D. B., and Sutton, T. (1992). Alcohol substance abuse, and violence among North Carolina prison admissions 1988. *Journal of Offender Rehabilitation, 17*, 101–111.

Goldstein, P. J. (1985). The drugs/violence nexus: A tripartite conceptual framework. *Journal of Drug Issues, 15*, 493–506.

Harlow, C. W. (1998). *Profile of Jail Inmates 1996*. Washington, DC: U.S. Department of Justice, Bureau of Justice Statistics.

Hartstone, E., and Hansen, K. V. (1984). The violent juvenile offender: An empirical portrait. In R. A. Mathias, P. DeMuro, and R. S. Allison (Eds.), *Violent Juvenile Offenders: An Anthology* (pp. 83–112). San Francisco: National Council on Crime and Delinquency.

Hindelang, M. J., Hirschi, T., and Weis, J. G. (1981). *Measuring Delinquency*. Beverly Hills, CA: Sage.

Huang, B., White, H. R., Kosterman, R., Hawkins, J. D., and Catalano, R. F. (2000). Developmental associations between alcohol and interpersonal aggression during adolescence. *Journal of Research in Crime and Delinquency, 38*, 64–83.

Huizinga, D. H., Menard, S., and Elliott, D. S. (1989). Delinquency and drug use: Temporal and developmental patterns. *Justice Quarterly, 6,* 419–455.

Ito, T. A., Miller, N., and Pollock, V. E. (1996). Alcohol and aggression: A meta-analysis on the moderating effects of inhibitory cues, triggering events, and self-focused attention. *Psychological Bulletin, 120,* 60–82.

Johnson, B. D., Wish, E., Schmeidler, J., and Huizinga, D. H. (1986). The concentration of delinquent offending: Serious drug involvement and high delinquency rates. In B. D. Johnson and E. Wish (Eds.), *Crime Rates Among Drug Abusing Offenders* (pp. 106–143). New York: Interdisciplinary Research Center, Narcotic and Drug Research.

Johnston, L. D., O'Malley, P. M., and Bachman, J. G. (2000). *National Survey Results on Drug Use from the Monitoring Future Study, 1975–1999.* Vol. 1, *Secondary School Students.* Washington, DC: U.S. Department of Health and Human Services, National Institutes of Health.

Kaplan, H. B., and Damphousse, K. R. (1995). Self-attitudes and antisocial personality as moderators of the drug use–violence relationship. Pp. 187–210 In H. B. Kaplan (Ed.), *Drugs, Crime, and Other Deviant Adaptations: Longitudinal Studies* (pp. 187–210). New York: Plenum.

Lang, A. R. (1993). Alcohol-related violence: Psychological perspectives. In S. E. Martin (Ed.), *Alcohol and Interpersonal Violence: Fostering Multidisciplinary Perspectives* (NIAAA Research Monograph No. 24) (pp. 121–147). Rockville, MD: National Institute of Health.

Lipsey, M. W., Wilson, D. B., Cohen, M. A., and Derzon, J. H. (1997). Is there a causal relationship between alcohol use and violence? pp. 245–82 In M. Galanter (Ed.), *Recent Developments in Alcoholism,* vol. 13, *Alcoholism and Violence* (pp. 245–282). New York: Plenum.

Loeber, R., Farrington, D. P., Stouthamer-Loeber, M., and Van Kammen, W. B. (1998). *Antisocial Behavior and Mental Health Problems: Explanatory Factors in Childhood and Adolescence.* Mahwah, NJ: Lawrence Erlbaum.

Loeber, R., Stouthamer-Loeber, M., and White, H. R. (1999). Developmental aspects of delinquency and internalizing problems and their association with persistent juvenile substance use between ages 7 and 18. *Journal of Clinical Child Psychology, 28,* 322–332.

Marlatt, G. A. (Ed.). (1998). *Harm Reduction: Pragmatic Strategies for Managing High-Risk Behaviors.* New York: Guilford.

Meyerscough, R., and Taylor, S. (1985). The effects of marijuana on human physical aggression. *Journal of Personality and Social Psychology, 49,* 1541–1546.

Miczek, K. A., DeBold, J. F., Haney, M., Tidey, J., Viyian, J., and Weerts, E. M. (1994). Alcohol, drugs of abuse, aggression, and violence. In A. J. Reiss and J. A. Roth (Eds.), *Understanding and Preventing Violence,* vol. 3 (pp. 377–468). Washington, DC: National Academy Press.

Miller, B. A., and Welte, J. W. (1986). Comparisons of incarcerated offenders according to their use of alcohol and/or drugs prior to offense. *Criminal Justice and Behavior, 13,* 366–392.

Nurco, D. N., Shaffer, J. C., Ball, J. C., and Kinlock, T. W. (1984). Trends in the commission of crime among narcotic addicts over successive periods of addiction. *American Journal of Drug and Alcohol Abuse, 10,* 481–489.

Parker, R. N., and Auerhahn, K. (1998). Alcohol, drugs, and violence, *Annual Review of Sociology, 24,* 291–311.

Roizen, J. (1993). Issues in the epidemiology of alcohol and violence. In S. E. Martin (Ed.), *Alcohol and Interpersonal Violence: Fostering Multidisciplinary Perspectives* (NIAAA Research Monograph No. 24) (pp. 3–36). Rockville, MD: National Institute of Health.

Single, E., Kandel, D. B., and Johnson, B. (1975). The reliability and validity of drug use responses in a large scale longitudinal survey. *Journal of Drug Issues, 5,* 426–433.

Tinklenberg, J. R., Murphy, P. Murphy, P., and Pfefferbaum, A. (1981). Drugs and criminal assaults by adolescents: A replication study. *Journal of Psychoactive Drugs, 13,* 277–287.

Valdez, A., Yin, Z., and Kaplan, C. D. (1997). A comparison of alcohol, drugs, and aggressive crime among Mexican-American, black, and white male arrestees in Texas. *American Journal of Drug and Alcohol Abuse, 23,* 249–265.

White, H. R. (1990). The drug use–delinquency connection in adolescence. pp. 215–56 In R. Weisheit (Ed.), *Drugs, Crime and the Criminal Justice System* (pp. 215–256). Cincinnati, OH: Anderson.

White, H. R. (1997a). Alcohol illicit drugs, and violence. Pp. 511–23 In D. Stoff, J. Brieling, and J. D. Maser (Eds.), *Handbook of Antisocial Behavior* (pp. 511–523). New York: John Wiley.

White, H. R. (1997b). Longitudinal perspective on alcohol use and aggression during adolescence. pp. 81–103 In *Recent Developments in Alcoholism: Alcohol and Violence,* vol. 13, edited by Marc Galanter. New York: Plenum.

White, H. R., and Gorman, D. M. (2000). Dynamics of the drug–crime relationship. In G. LaFree (Ed.), *Criminal Justice 2000,* vol. 1, *The Nature of Crime: Continuity and Change* (pp. 151–218). Washington, DC: U.S. Department of Justice.

White, H. R., and Hansell, S. (1996). The moderating effects of gender and hostility on the alcohol-aggression relationship. *Journal of Research in Crime and Delinquency, 33,* 451–472.

White, H. R., and Hansell, S. (1998). Acute and long-term effects of drug use on aggression from adolescence into adulthood. *Journal of Drug Issues, 28,* 837–858.

White, H. R., Loeber, R., Stouthamer-Loeber, M., and Farrington, D. P. (1999). Developmental associations between substance use and violence. *Development and Psychopathology, 11,* 785–803.

CHAPTER 4: DISCUSSION QUESTIONS

1. What are the common etiological factors that predict young adult drug use and delinquency? How do these differ for males and females?

2. What are the intervening variables in the study by Kandel and colleagues? How did they differ for delinquency and drug use models?

3. What are the three theories used by Baron and Hartnagel to examine street violence? How do they differ?

4. Why did Baron and Hartnagel exclude women from their sample? Did they provide sufficient justification? How might their findings differ had they also interviewed women?

5. According to Baron and Hartnagel, what are the factors influencing street violence? What is the role of economic deprivation in the generation of street youth violence? How did the experience of victimization affect rates of violence?

6. According to White and colleagues, what types of offenses are most likely to be committed while under the influence for youth? Why?

7. What are the limitations of each selection?

8. What are the policy implications of each selection?

CHAPTER 4: ADDITIONAL RESOURCES IN RESEARCH NAVIGATOR AND IN THE *NEW YORK TIMES*

Baron, S. W. (2003). Self-control, social consequences, and criminal behavior: Street youth and the general theory of crime. *Journal of Research in Crime and Delinquency, 40,* 403–425.

Boys, A. Dobson, J., Marsden, J., and Strang, J. (2002). "Rich man's speed": A qualitative study of young cocaine users. *Drugs: Education, Prevention, and Policy, 9,* 195–210.

Crabbe, T. (2000). A sporting chance? Using sport to tackle drug use and crime. *Drugs: Education, Prevention, and Policy, 7,* 381–391.

Ellickson, P. F., McCaffrey, D. F., Ghosh-Dasitdar, B., and Longshore, D. L. (2003). New inroads in preventing adolescent drug use: Results from a large-scale trial of project ALERT in middle schools. *American Journal of Public Health, 93,* 1830–1836.

Flaherty, J. (2004, August 1). Swiping for marijuana. *New York Times.*

Forsyth, A. J. M., and Barnard, M. (2003). Young people's awareness of illicit drug use in the family. *Addiction Research and Theory, 11,* 459–462.

Golub, A., and Johnson, B. D. (2001). Variation in youthful risks of progression from alcohol and tobacco to marijuana and to hard drugs across generations. *American Journal of Public Health, 91,* 225–232.

Hamilton, G., Cross, D., Lower, T., Resnicow, K., and Williams, P. (2003). School policy: What helps to reduce teenage smoking? *Nicotine and Tobacco Research, 5,* 507–513.

Hser, Y. I., Grella, C. E., Collins, C., and Teruya, C. (2003). Drug-use initiation and conduct disorder among adolescents in drug treatment. *Journal of Adolescence, 26,* 331–345.

Johnson, M. K. (2004). Further evidence on adolescent employment and substance use: Differences by race and ethnicity. *Journal of Health and Social Behavior, 45,* 187–197.

Lewin, T. (2003, December 9). Raid at high school leads to racial divide, not drugs. *New York Times.*

Lewin, T. (2004, January 7). Principal who invited police to school for drug raid quits. *New York Times.*

Madon, S., Guyll, M., Spoth, R. L., Cross, S. E., and Hilbert, S. J. (2003). The self-fulfilling influence of mother expectations on children's underage drinking. *Journal of Personality and Social Psychology, 84,* 1188–1205.

Markel, H. (2003, January 7). Tailoring treatments for teenage drug users. *New York Times.*

McIntosh, J., MacDonald, F., and McKeganey, N. (2003). Knowledge and perceptions of illegal drugs in a sample of pre-teenage children. *Drugs: Education, Prevention, and Policy, 10,* 331–344.

McKeganey, N., McIntosh, J., MacDonald, F., Gannon, M., Gilvarry, E., McArdle, P., and McCarthy, S. (2004). Preteen children and illegal drugs. *Drugs: Education, Prevention, and Policy, 11,* 315–327.

Newman, M. (2004, March 11). Death of girl, 16, spotlights hard drugs in New Jersey suburbs. *New York Times.*

Parker, H., and Williams. L. (2003). Intoxicated weekends: Young adults' work hard-play hard lifestyles, public health and public disorder. *Drugs: Education, Prevention, and Policy, 10,* 345–367.

Radsch, C. C. (2004, August 20). Teenagers' sexual activity is tied to drugs and drink. *New York Times.*

Rosenbaum, M. (2004). Random student drug testing is no panacea. *Alcoholism and Drug Abuse Weekly, 16,* 5–6.

Stanistreet, D., Gabbay, M., Jeffrey, V., and Taylor, S. (2005). Are deaths due to drug use among young men underestimated in official statistics? *Drugs: Education, Prevention, and Policy, 11,* 229–242.

Winter, G. (2003, May 17). Study finds no sign that testing deters students' drug use. *New York Times.*

■ ■ ■ ■ ■

RESPONSES TO DRUGS: CRIMINAL JUSTICE

There are two main societal responses to the use of illicit drugs: criminal justice and treatment. These responses are often intertwined, especially as more components of the criminal justice system incorporate treatment into their structures. They represent philosophically different approaches to drug use, however, and are therefore considered in separate chapters in this volume.

To begin the first of these two chapters, Lana Harrison provides an excellent overview of the issues involved with the criminal justice response to illicit drug use. This comprehensive examination of the "revolving door" problem for drug offenders highlights many important issues, including mandated treatment, treatment efficacy, and barriers to reintegration for released offenders. This reading sets the stage for the following reading examining specific criminal justice responses.

M. Douglas Anglin and colleagues provide evaluation data on a very important criminal justice response: the Treatment Alternatives to Street Crime (TASC) program. In TASC, individuals are diverted into community-based treatment so as to avoid becoming progressively more involved with the criminal justice system. Despite differences in application of the program, the authors find evidence for success and conclude that the TASC model is an effective one for improving delivery of treatment services. Findings in terms of criminal behaviors were more complex, but nevertheless seemed to provide evidence of improved outcomes.

In the next reading, Douglas Longshore and colleagues take the research on the criminal justice response one step further by working to develop a systematic framework for studying drug courts. Because they are a relatively new response to the drug problem, drug courts have not been systematically evaluated. Drug courts are specialty courts, much like traffic courts and family courts. They were developed

to channel drug cases out of the overburdened general court and to speed case processing. Although subject to numerous problems in theory and application, they have proved to be useful in many ways.

Finally, John Braithwaite uses two cases to illustrate and examine his innovative theory of restorative justice. Implementing this approach requires a significant change in how criminals are handled in the system. The goal is to have victims and offenders communicate with each other and find ways to rectify the social harm caused by illegal behaviors. This very new approach to criminal behavior can be applied to illicit drug use and alcoholism, as is shown in the two case studies. Many new terms are introduced in this selection, but it is well worth the effort to understand how the concepts work together to create a new system for responding to drugs and crime.

All the readings broach the complexity of dealing with drug users through the criminal justice system. For example, coerced treatment is a hotly debated issue that is central to the intersection of criminal justice and treatment. What does it mean to be "forced" into treatment? This question is grappled with by several authors. In addition, definitions of treatment and treatment success need to be reevaluated. Harrison points out that what falls under the rubric of treatment can vary from a simple drug education curriculum to a comprehensive therapeutic community. Evaluations of treatment programs can vary by definitions of what constitutes the programs. Because of variations in definitions and application, there are many inherent problems in evaluating criminal justice programs. Longshore and colleagues confront this problem directly by attempting to develop a framework that would allow for development and evaluation of programs, including drug courts and therapeutic communities. It is important to identify such effective programs because inmates have better outcomes when they receive effective treatment. In addition, as Harrison also notes, the criminal justice approach alone cannot solve the underlying problems with illicit drug use. For example, many inmates return to poverty, violence, and other social and personal problems upon release from incarceration. A continuum of criminal justice that incorporates treatment extending beyond release could work to alleviate these problems. At some point, the cost of imprisonment compared with the cost of treatment should be examined by policy makers. Research shows that treatment is cost effective compared with incarceration alone.

Finally, there is a lack of funding for treatment programs in prisons and jails. Anglin and colleagues note that the variety of criminal justice-based treatment approaches is promising. For example, TASC programs can use existing drug courts when they are available. Elements of restorative justice could be incorporated into all these approaches. Although it is difficult to integrate treatment with criminal justice, outcomes are improved when efforts are made.

15

The Revolving Prison Door for Drug-Involved Offenders: Challenges and Opportunities

LANA D. HARRISON

ABSTRACT

This article examines the role of drugs in increasing the incarcerated population in the United States. Research is increasingly demonstrating the effectiveness of treatment for incarcerated populations in reducing recidivism and drug use, especially treatment in a therapeutic community (TC). Transitional services that include TC treatment in a work release setting greatly reduce recidivism and relapse, as do aftercare services. Although treatment options are increasing in prisons, there are many more who could benefit from treatment than receive it. Much remains unknown about how to best reach drug-involved offenders to stop the revolving door of drug addiction and incarceration. This article touches on many relevant areas ripe for further research.

SCOPE OF THE PROBLEM

At the beginning of the millennium, more than 2 million people were incarcerated in the United States. This represents a tripling since 1980. Although the numbers continue to rise gradually, the bulk of the increase was realized over the decade of the 1980s as the nation engaged in the drug war. Virtually all of the increase can be attributed to drug offenses. By 1996, drug offenders comprised 60% of the federal prison population, 23% of the state prison population, and 22% of the jail population (Bureau of Justice Statistics [BJS]/Harlow, 1998; BJS/Mumola, 1999).

Mandatory minimum and three-strikes laws have contributed to some of the increase in the number of drug offenders incarcerated, but so have changes at every step of the criminal justice process. As the follow-

ing statistics illustrate, more people are being arrested on drug offenses, more of them are found guilty, a greater proportion of those found guilty are sentenced to incarceration, and they are being sentenced for lengthier periods (BJS, 1999). Arrests for drug abuse violations increased 57.5% between 1989 and 1996, rising from 654,000 in 1989 to more than 1 million in 1996. In 1996, drug offenders comprised a third of all persons convicted of a felony in state courts (BJS/Brown and Langan, 1999). The 1984 Sentencing Reform Act resulted in the proportion of drug offenders at the federal level sentenced to prison increasing from 79% in 1988 to 92% in 1998. Over the same time period, the proportion of all federal defendants sentenced to prison increased from 54% to 71% (BJS/Brown and Langan, 1999). The growth in incarceration attributed to nondrug crimes can be explained as a result of increases in the number of people sentenced to prison per arrest and lengthier sentences.

Drug offenders are frequently drug abusers, but so are a large proportion of those arrested for property or other crimes. Among the incarcerated population in 1997, more than 80% of state and 70% of federal prisoners reported past drug use (BJS/Mumola, 1999). The 1997 Survey of Inmates in State and Federal Correctional Facilities found half (52%) of state prison inmates and a third (34%) of federal prison inmates indicated they were under the influence of alcohol or drugs while committing the offense leading to their imprisonment. In this nationally representative survey, 37% of state and 20% of federal inmates reported they were under the influence of alcohol at the time of the offense, and 33% of state and 22% of federal inmates were under the influence of illicit drugs at the time of the offense (BJS/Mumola, 1999). A nationally representative survey of jail inmates in 1996 found 36% of convicted inmates were using illicit drugs at the time of their offense, compared with 27% in 1989 (BJS/Harlow, 1998).

Even more direct connections between drug use and criminal offending are evident, with one in five (19%) state prisoners reporting committing their offense to purchase drugs. Sixteen percent of federal prisoners in 1997 admitted the same—up from 10% in 1991 (BJS/Mumola, 1999). Sixteen percent of jail inmates reported the same in 1996; up from 13% in 1989 (BJS/Wilson, 2000). These statistics testify to the extent of illicit drug and alcohol abuse among the nation's population of inmates in federal and state prisons and local jails.

Several studies have more fully explored the relationship between drug using and criminal behavior to, in essence, plot the course of a criminal and drug-using career (cf. Harrison, 1992). Consistent findings across studies show that chronic users of heroin, cocaine, and crack commit a vast amount of crime. In extensive longitudinal studies of addict careers in Baltimore, for example, Nurco, Ball, and colleagues found there were exponentially higher rates of criminality among heroin users during periods of addiction than during periods of nonaddiction (Ball, Rosen, Flueck, and Nurco, 1981; Ball, Shaffer, and Nurco, 1983; Nurco, 1998). Another major series of studies was conducted by investigators in New York City interviewing hundreds of criminally active drug users recruited from the streets of east and central Harlem. The studies documented the wide range of heroin usage rates among addicts and the clear correlation between amount of heroin used and amount of crime committed (Johnson et al., 1985; Lipton and Johnson, 1998). Studies conducted in Miami, Florida, demonstrated the vast amount of crime committed by crack users (Inciardi, 1992; Inciardi, Horowitz, and Pottieger, 1993; Inciardi and Pottieger, 1986, 1991, 1998; Pettiway, 1987). Altogether, these varied findings imply that, although the use of heroin, cocaine, and other drugs does not initiate criminal careers, it intensifies and perpetuates them. And more important, reduced illicit drug use is correlated with less criminal activity.

Incarceration obviously halts the commission of crimes against society. It also severely limits access to drugs and therefore accomplishes withdrawal for most drug abusers. However, research shows that when those who were addicted to drugs before they were incarcerated return to the community, they quickly resume their addicted and criminal lifestyle. Nationally, 40% of state prisoners are expected to be released in 2000 (BJS/Beck, 2000). Adding federal offenders means more than 500,000 offenders are estimated to be released from correctional institutions in 1999 and 2000, often in large concentrations in a relatively small number of neighborhoods (Robinson and Travis, n.d.). Considering the costs to society, it is imperative to develop resources for ex-offenders and their communities. Without intervention, these inmates will invariably repeat the same types of behaviors that led to their incarceration. This is exemplified in statistics showing that in 1997, 46% of state inmates and 26% of federal inmates were on probation or parole when they were incarcerated (General Accounting Office [GAO], 2000). Addressing the treatment needs of drug-involved offenders is of critical importance in reducing the costs of the crime, including incarceration, other criminal justice costs, and social costs.

TREATMENT IN THE CRIMINAL JUSTICE SYSTEM

Because the criminal justice system deals with a large proportion of chronic drug abusers, the criminal justice system is an ideal place to organize and provide needed drug treatment services. The criminal justice system has become the largest source of mandated, or coerced, drug treatment in the United States (National Institute on Drug Abuse [NIDA], 1992). Many employed in the criminal justice system (police, judges, probation/parole officers, correctional personnel, and others) serve as major sources of referral to, and payment for, drug abuse treatment (O'Brien and McClelland, 1996). Mandated treatment within the criminal justice system can have various degrees of severity and can be imposed at different levels within the process. For example, courts may require that an offender choose between a jail sentence or treatment, a probation officer may recommend or require that the offender enter treatment, or a correctional facility may send inmates involuntarily to a prison treatment program (Farabee, Prendergast, and Anglin, 1998).

In 1997, 40% of correctional facilities nationally provided substance abuse treatment on-site to inmates. Nearly all federal prisons (94%) and 61% of state prisons provided treatment (which could include detoxification, group or individual counseling, other rehabilitation services, and methadone or other pharmaceutical treatment). *Treatment* is interpreted loosely, so various activities fall under the rubric of treatment, including drug information and education and other brief interventions. Jails and juvenile facilities lagged far behind, with only about a third providing treatment (Substance Abuse Mental Health Services Administration [SAMHSA], 2000).

In 1997, about a quarter of state and federal prison inmates reported they had participated in either professional substance abuse treatment or other treatment programs since they were incarcerated. However, only about 1 in 10 state inmates reported doing so in 1997, compared to 1 in 4 in 1991 (BJS, 1997). The percentage of federal prisoners receiving treatment in the past year also fell, but the percentage participating in self-help or peer groups and drug education classes increased. About 1 in 5 state and federal prison inmates reported participation in self-help or drug education programs in 1997, up from 1 in 10 federal prisoners and 1 in 6 state prisoners in 1991. BJS/Beck (2000) indicated that among those state prisoners due to be released in the next 12 months, only about 1 in 5 drug and/or alcohol abusers received treatment. About 1 in 3 participated in self-help, peer counseling, or other education/awareness programs.

A large proportion of probationers have conditions to their sentences required by the court or probation agency related to drug or alcohol abuse. In 1995, 41% were required to get drug or alcohol treatment. However, for many, treatment constituted attendance at 12-step meetings (i.e., Alcoholics Anonymous or Narcotics Anonymous). A nearly equal number (38%) had mandatory drug testing and/or were ordered to abstain from alcohol and/or drugs as a condition of probation (BJS/Bonczar, 1997; BJS/Mumola and Bonczar, 1998).

Although the amount of treatment available in the criminal justice system has generally increased in the 1990s, treatment need far outstrips treatment availability. There are obviously more inmates who require treatment than receive it, and much treatment is either short-term or not intensive enough to address inmates' needs. Treatment programs in correctional institutions, particularly more intensive programs, often have waiting lists. Considering the depth of the typical inmate's addiction, self-help or drug education programs are unlikely to effect long-lasting change. Nor is prison time, because 77% of state and 62% of federal inmates in 1997 had served prior sentences (GAO, 2000).

Treatment Efficacy

There now exists a body of research on the effectiveness of treatment programs (see Lipton, 1995; NIDA, 1992). The Drug Abuse Reporting Program (DARP) conducted between 1969 and 1973 was the first large-scale longitudinal study to assess treatment effectiveness. Clients admitted to publicly funded drug treatment programs, including detoxification, outpatient drug-free, methadone maintenance, and therapeutic communities (TCs), were followed 1 year after treatment. This early study found positive effects for all programs except detoxification and those who dropped out of treatment within 3 months (Simpson, Davage, Lloyd, and Sells, 1978).

A national study of treatment effectiveness, the Treatment Outcome Prospective Study (TOPS), also considered the efficacy of several treatment modalities (Hubbard et al., 1989). The study documented the progress of 11,750 clients who entered treatment for drug abuse between 1979 and 1981 in 41 programs throughout the United States. A sample of 4,270 clients in methadone maintenance, outpatient drugfree, and residential treatment programs were followed for 5 years after treatment completion. Approximately 20% of the methadone maintenance clients, 40% of the outpatient drugfree, and 50% of the residential treatment client population were involved with the criminal justice system (Hubbard et al., 1989). Substantial reductions in criminal activity accompanied treatment. The average illegal income in the year following treatment was reduced by nearly two thirds, remaining at about the same level during the 5-year follow-up period (Hubbard et al., 1989). The study also concluded that time spent in treatment was correlated with positive outcomes. There was strong evidence that criminal justice clients benefited more from longer stays in treatment than self-referrals. The study concluded treatment is economically effective, because the costs of treatment were more than recovered by the savings in crime reduction. The savings to society per day of treatment were substantially greater for clients referred by the criminal justice system than others. Improvements in other negative behaviors may further increase the cost effectiveness of drug abuse treatment for criminally involved drug abusers (Hubbard et al., 1989).

The Drug Abuse Treatment Outcome Study (DATOS) is a longitudinal study being conducted with 12,000 clients admitted to drug treatment between 1991 and 1993 in 12 cities. About 4,500 clients referred to inpatient, long-term residential, TCs, methadone maintenance, and outpatient drugfree programs are being followed up on. The 1 year follow-up data showed the percentage of outpatient treatment clients who reported using cocaine and alcohol was reduced by half, and less than 1 in 10 clients reported weekly or more frequent marijuana use (Hubbard, Craddock, Flynn, Anderson, and Etheridge, 1997).

Several studies have also been conducted on the effectiveness of in-prison drug treatment. The Stay'N Out prison TC in New York became the first large-scale study of in-prison drug treatment to show reductions in recidivism. A study of the Amity TC in California replicated the Stay'N Out findings and showed that even more positive outcomes were produced by adding aftercare TC treatment in the community (Wexler, Melnick, Lowe, and Peters, 1999). Most of the research on treatment effectiveness with incarcerated populations has addressed the effectiveness of TCs. TCs have operated in correctional institutions since the late 1960s. Their structure and discipline fits well into many correctional institutions. Inmates progress through a phase system, gaining increased responsibility. TCs are generally staffed by a mixture of recovering addicts and treatment and mental health professionals. They are generally cheaper than other residential treatment modalities, because they are less reliant on paid professional staff. Residents are involved in all aspects of governing the TC and its operations and take responsibility for their own and others' treatment. Groups and meetings provide positive persuasion to change attitudes and behaviors and also provide confrontation by peers when values or rules are violated. The typical TC is 6 to 12 months in duration, and time in treatment has long been recognized as critical to treatment success.

Delaware's Continuum of Treatment

Research from Inciardi and colleagues' longitudinal study of treatment within the Delaware criminal justice system supported the efficacy of TCs and also made a strong case for the need for treatment services to continue as the offender transitions to the community (Inciardi, Martin, Butzin, Hooper, and Harrison, 1997; Martin, Butzin, Saum, and Inciardi, 1999; Martin and Inciardi, 1993a, 1993b). The Delaware TC was established in a maximum-security prison for men in 1988. A year later, a treatment demonstration grant from NIDA was used to create a TC in a correctional work release facility. Very few offenders are paroled "to the streets" in Delaware; rather, they spend the last 6 months of their sentence in a work release facility. There, they search for and secure employment while spending nights incarcerated. The TC work release program follows a five-phase model designed to facilitate reentry into the community while inmates are undergoing intensive TC

treatment. Inmates are given increasing time away from the work release TC as they successfully work through the phase system. An aftercare component was added in 1994, although it did not become fully functional until 1997. The aftercare component entails an additional 6 months and requires total abstinence from drug and alcohol use, one 2-hour group session per week, monthly individual counseling, and urine monitoring. Graduates must return once a month to serve as role models for current work release TC clients.

As inmates completed the in-prison TC, they were ideally released to the work release TC. However, due to the shortage of treatment beds in the state, judges started sentencing offenders to the work release TC independent of whether they had completed the prison TC. Some prison inmates also requested to be placed in the work release TC. Judges also began sentencing some offenders *just* to the 6-month work release TC. This created a natural experiment allowing the research team to examine the efficacy of different doses and types of transitional treatment. A TC was also initiated in a women's prison, and a small proportion of the beds at the work release TC were designated for women. A comparison group generated from an adjacent work release program without a treatment component is also being followed over time.

Figure 1 demonstrates the effectiveness of the continuum of treatment at the 18-month follow-up. Logistic regression models controlling for possible intervening variables (gender, age, race, criminal history, previous drug use) and correcting self-report with urinalysis results found that 16% of the comparison group, 22% of the in-prison TC group, 31% of the work release TC group, and 47% of those receiving both in-prison and work release TC treatment were drug free at the 18-month follow-up. This suggests a pattern of increasing effectiveness through in-prison and work release TC treatment. This pattern is even more impressive for arrest-free status. Figure 2 shows 46% of the comparison group, 43% of the in-prison TC group, 57% of the work release TC group, and 77% of those receiving both in-prison and work release TC treatment were arrest free at 18 months (Inciardi et al., 1997). The outcome data support the improvement of a work release TC relative to an in-prison TC but suggest the strongest and most consistent pattern of success comes from the group that received TC treatment in prison and in work release. The gains of prison TC treatment were generally nonsignificant compared with the control group. However, the size of the in-prison TC group is relatively small and destined

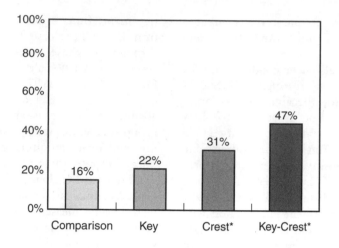

Comparison   – No TC, N = 184
Key   – In-prison TC only, N = 38
Crest   – Work release TC only, N = 183
Key-Crest   – Both TC's, N = 43

FIGURE 1   Delaware Therapeutic Continuum Assessment: Drug Free Since Release by Self-Report and Urine Test at 6- and 18-Month Follow-Up, Controlling for Other Group Differences.

Note: Adjusted percentages from logistic regression using control variables measuring gender, race, age, criminal history, and previous drug use. Data as of July 1996. TC = therapeutic community.

*Significantly different from comparison group, $p < .001$.

to remain so, because most offenders graduating from an in-prison TC get preference for a work release TC in the state of Delaware.

Other benefits of the exposure to the TC programs can be seen in some additional outcomes examined in the 18-month data. These include significant reductions in the use of injection drugs and in the amount of income from crime in the past year, fewer returns to prison for new sentences, fewer hospital stays for drug and alcohol problems, and an increased likelihood of having health insurance if working among those in the TC continuum compared with those not (Inciardi et al., 1997).

The gains made in treatment are impressive, although some will point out that even among those who got the full continuum of treatment in both the prison and work release TC, half (53%) had relapsed by the 18-month follow-up. But relapse is a high standard, in which a single incident of drug use results in permanent failure. In a groundbreaking article on treatment myths, O'Brien and McClelland (1996) compared drug addiction to other chronic diseases such as asthma, diabetes, and hypertension in which relapse may occur despite considerable improvement. They contended that treatment should be considered successful if considerable improvement occurs, even though complete remission or cure is not achieved.

With this in mind, the 18-month outcomes were reexamined in logistic regression models controlling for the same intervening variables but using a dependent variable of frequency of illicit drug use, where 0 = *no use*, 1 = *less than once a month*, 2 = *one to three times a month*, 3 = *weekly*, 4 = *several times a week*. 5 = *once a day*, and 6 = *several times a day*. Figure 3 shows the same stair-step pattern of results is achieved as shown in Figures 1 and 2. The mean frequency of illegal drug use for the comparison group was 3.29 compared with 2.45 for the in-prison TC group, 2.16 for the work release TC group, and 1.12 for those participating in both the in-prison and work release TCs. A similar pattern was evident for alcohol use, with the mean frequency of use for the comparison group 3.24, 2.26 for the in-prison TC group, 1.9 for the work release TC group, and 0.7 for those participating in both the in-prison and work release TCs. These results demonstrate the continuum of treatment was strongly related to reductions in the frequency of illicit drug and alcohol use. There are obvious gains from the in-prison TC group, to the work release TC, to those participating in both.

More recent analyses have been conducted examining the added value of aftercare. However, the treatment groups had to be organized differently. Due to the small numbers for the in-prison treatment

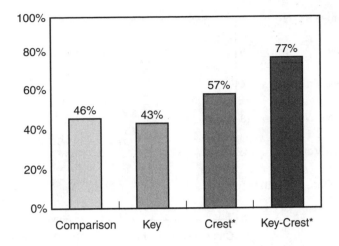

Comparison   – No TC, N = 180
Key   – In-prison TC only, N = 37
Crest   – Work release TC only, N = 179
Key-Crest   – Both TC's, N = 43

FIGURE 2   Delaware Therapeutic Continuum Assessment: Arrest Free Since Release at 6- and 18-Month Follow-Up, Controlling for Other Group Differences

Note: Adjusted percentages from logistic regression using control variables measuring gender, race, age, criminal history, and previous drug use. Data as of July 1996. TC = therapeutic community.

*Significantly different from comparison group, $p < .05$.

group, it was omitted from the analysis. Figure 4 compares work release TC dropouts with completers and those who completed both the work release TC and the 6-month aftercare program. It also compares these three groups with a comparison group that did not receive treatment. The comparison group includes those with identified drug problems attending a work release facility without a TC. Figure 4 shows the arrest-free and drug-free status of offenders 3 years after release from the work release TC. It is worth noting that even among the comparison group, many sought treatment of their own accord, although their mean frequency of treatment sessions/contacts was much lower than among those in the treatment groups.

With these groupings, using logistic regression models that control for possible intervening variables, the same stair-step pattern of positive results related to treatment involvement was achieved 3 years following treatment. The percentage completely drug free among the comparison group was 5%, 17% among the work release TC dropouts, 27% among the work release program graduates, and 35% among those who completed both the work release TC and aftercare. The arrest-free statistics show 29% of the comparison group arrest-free at the 3 year follow-up, compared with 28% of the work release TC dropouts,

55% of the work release graduates, and fully 69% of those completing both the work release and aftercare programs (Martin et al., 1999). The arrest-free statistics are more impressive than the drug-free, but again, the drug-free statistics hold the user to total abstinence for 3 years.

The analyses were repeated with the 3-year follow-up data, controlling for the same variables, to examine the impact of the work release TC treatment with and without aftercare on the frequency of drug use. Figure 5 shows the anticipated stair-step pattern of results as found in earlier analyses, with frequency of drug use strongly correlated with the continuum of treatment. The mean frequency of drug use increases at the 3-year post–TC work release relative to that at the 18-month follow-up, but the gains in treatment are evident. The data support the important role of treatment for drug-involved offenders as they transition back to the community.

The research program by Inciardi and colleagues in Delaware demonstrates the importance of treatment continuing during the transition stage to work and the free community. It is important to remember the comparison group was in work release, so the gains were the result of the TC treatment program and 6-month aftercare services. The gains made in work release even without aftercare show the value

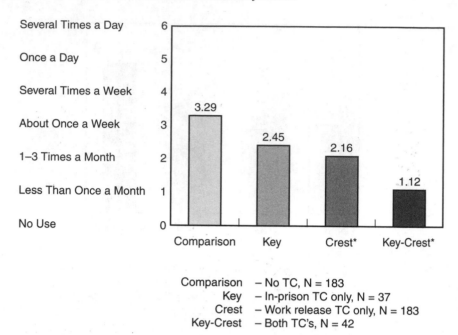

FIGURE 3 **Delaware Therapeutic Continuum Assessment: Maximum Use of Any Illegal Drug During Any Period in 18-Month Follow-Up, Controlling for Other Group Differences.**

Note: Adjusted means from regression using control variables measuring gender, race, age, criminal history, and previous drug use. Data as of July 1996. TC = therapeutic community.

*Significantly different from comparison group, $p < .01$.

of inmates' receiving treatment as they are reintegrating into the community, finding a job and housing, and spending increasing time with family and friends. Aftercare, provided when work release graduates begin living in the community, helps to further reduce relapse and recidivism. Those inmates who graduated from the 6-month aftercare programs had the greatest chances for success. This research program generally demonstrates a linear relationship between length of time and treatment and both relapse and recidivism. These findings obviate the need for transitional drug treatment services including aftercare in the community for drug-involved offenders as they exit correctional institutions.

Barriers to Reintegration

Prisoners have numerous barriers to reintegration, sans drug use, into the community. Perhaps one of the greatest insights of drug treatment is that drug abuse is a disorder of the whole person, so the whole person must be treated. Drug abuse is often regarded as a symptom of underlying problems, and those underlying problems must be treated for the individual to stop abusing drugs. This is particularly true in the case of drug-abusing offenders, who present a litany

of problems. They are disproportionately from poor families and single-headed households. More than half of state prison inmates (56%) indicated in the 1997 Survey of Inmates in State and Correctional Facilities they did not grow up with both parents, as did 46% of federal inmates. Among jail inmates in 1996, 43% lived primarily with their mother only while growing up. Nearly a quarter (22%) reported their family received welfare while they were growing up. About a third of state inmates and jail inmates had a parent or guardian who abused alcohol or drugs while they were growing up. The figure among federal inmates was 20%. About 40% of state prisoners and 26% of federal prisoners had not graduated from high school or finished a general equivalency diploma (GED). About a third of state prisoners (31%), a quarter of federal prisoners (27%), and a third of jail inmates (36%) were not working before their arrest. Among jail inmates, almost half reported incomes of $600 or less in the month before their arrest, which amounts to an annual income of less than $7,200. About a quarter (22%) received one or more kinds of financial support from government agencies in the month before arrest (BJS/Harlow, 1998).

In its first comprehensive report on mental illness in correctional institutions, the BJS identified

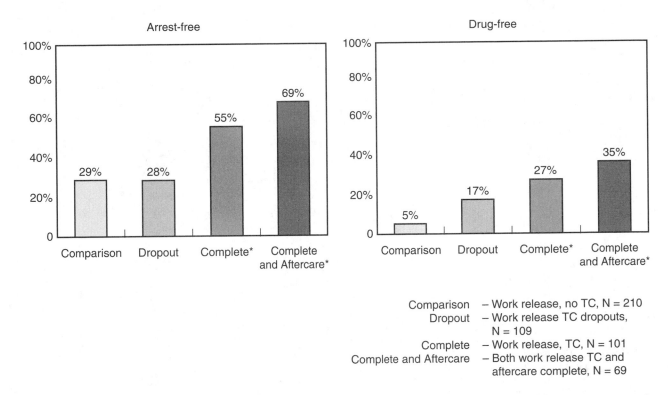

Comparison — Work release, no TC, N = 210
Dropout — Work release TC dropouts,
N = 109
Complete — Work release, TC, N = 101
Complete and Aftercare — Both work release TC and
aftercare complete, N = 69

FIGURE 4   Delaware Therapeutic Continuum Assessment: Arrest Free and Drug Free by Self-Report and Urine Test at 3-Year Follow-Up, Controlling for Other Group Differences.

Note: Adjusted percentages from logistic regression using control variables measuring gender, race, age, criminal history, and previous drug use. Data as of July 1996. TC = therapeutic community.

*Significantly different from comparison group, $p < .05$.

persons with mental or emotional problems based on personal interviews with a representative sample of offenders in federal and state prisons, sentenced jail inmates, and persons on probation (BJS/Ditton, 1999). Rates of mental illness among incarcerated offenders are double or more that found in the general population. The study found 7% of federal and 16% of state prison inmates and jail inmates either had a mental condition or had stayed overnight in a mental hospital or treatment program (BJS/Ditton, 1999). Nearly one in three (29%) White females in state prisons had a history of mental illness.

Inmates and probationers report high rates of sexual and physical abuse. Females are much more likely to report both sexual and physical abuse (BJS/Mumola, 1999). More than half (57%) of females and 16% of males in state prisons had ever been abused. Among federal inmates, 40% of females and 7% of males report being abused. Similar statistics are present among jail inmates, with 48% of females and 13% of males reporting a history of abuse (BJS/Harlow, 1998). Inmates with a history of mental illness reported higher rates of prior sexual and physi-

cal abuse: three quarters of women and a third of men. More than 40% said a parent or guardian abused drugs or alcohol while they were growing up, and more than half had a family member who had been in jail or prison (BJS/Ditton, 1999).

These statistics paint a picture of a population of incarcerees who are overwhelmingly poor, are frequently unemployable, often have mental health problems and a history of abuse, and frequently were reared by a single parent and/or a parent or guardian who abused drugs or alcohol.

Ideally, drug treatment involves habilitation in the sense that other service needs of the individual are recognized and addressed. Drug treatment rarely involves a single philosophy but rather includes a variety of techniques, interventions, and strategies within different treatment approaches. Treatment is targeted toward identifying and improving functioning of the individual on multiple levels. The goals of drug treatment, in addition to stopping drug abuse, may include helping the user to develop educational or vocational capabilities; restoring or increasing employment; reducing criminal activity; changing the drug users'

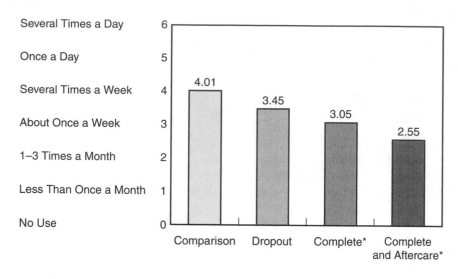

Comparison — Work release, no TC, N = 219
Dropout — Work release TC dropouts, N = 134
Complete — Work release TC, N = 111
Complete and Aftercare — Both work release TC and
aftercare complete, N = 139

FIGURE 5   Delaware Therapeutic Continuum Assessment: Maximum Use of Any Illegal Drug During Any Period in 3-Year Follow-Up, Controlling for Other Group Differences.

Note: Adjusted means from regression using control variables measuring gender, race, age, criminal history, and previous drug use. Data as of July 1996. TC = therapeutic community.

*Significantly different from comparison group, $p < .01$.

values; improving the users' family life, health, and psychological functioning; and reducing fetal exposure to drug dependence (NIDA, 1992).

Barriers to Treatment

Perhaps the biggest barrier to expanding treatment options for offenders is the belief that treatment does not work. Considering the profile of incarcerated inmates, the reductions in crime and drug use following treatment is amazing. The growing body of research on the efficacy of treatment for correctional populations has garnered some political attention. Furthermore, research demonstrating the high costs of drug abuse to society at large (Gerstein et al., 1994; Harwood, Fountain, and Livermore, 1996; Harwood, Napolitano, Kristiansen, and Collins, 1984; Rice, Kelman, Miller, and Dunmeyer, 1990) has promoted the reversal of earlier treatment policies and practices. These costs are particularly dramatic for drug-abusing offenders whose criminal activity, criminal justice costs, usually poor health status, and use of expensive public health services all put heavy burdens on the taxpayer and society. Therefore, the major impetus

for the renewed attraction of treatment alternatives in corrections came from the desire to reduce the burgeoning costs of criminal justice services and the custodial cost of health care associated with rapidly increasing numbers of incarcerated drug users with related chronic and acute health conditions (Martin and Inciardi, 1993a, 1993b).

Several studies have addressed the issue of cost effectiveness of drug abuse treatment (Apsler and Harding, 1991; Caulkins and Reuter, 1997; Harwood et al., 1996; Harwood, Hubbard, Collins, and Rachal, 1988; Hubbard et al., 1989). Hubbard and his colleagues reported the 41 programs they studied in TOPS were cost effective in reducing the costs of crime well beyond treatment costs. The landmark study to date however, may be the California Drug and Alcohol Treatment Assessment (CALDATA) study, which evaluated the cost effectiveness of publicly supported treatment programs in California (Gerstein et al., 1994). The California survey was a representative sample of the 150,000 persons in treatment in California in 1992, not just criminal justice clients. Although the scope of the study led to some problems with sample representativeness, CALDATA reported 18-month savings from treatment of $1.5 billion, with the largest savings coming from reduction in crime, followed by significant reductions in health care costs (emergency room admissions declined by a third). The study concluded that for every dollar spent on treatment, approximately $7 in future savings costs could be gained.

Moreover, it appears that service utilization is greatly reduced after clients have been treated for their drug user (Holder, 1987; Holder and Blose, 1992; Jones and Vischi, 1979). The CALDATA study (Gerstein et al., 1994) found that patients participating in residential treatment programs experienced a 40% decrease in hospitalizations (for physical health, drug overdoses, or mental health problems) following treatment. Research also shows that reductions in drug use are associated with improved hygiene, nutrition, housing, employment, and other life circumstances associated with improved health (Avants, Margolin, Koste, and Singer, 1993; Cotton, 1994) such as reductions in violence and HIV and STD risk behaviors. Therefore, a primary mechanism for reducing the health service needs of chronic drug users is to provide effective drug treatment. Furthermore, drug treatment, by virtue of reducing health risks, will reduce future costs. CALDATA has been criticized for methodological problems, particularly for relying on self-reported data about drug use, but the consistency of findings across several studies provides compelling evidence of the cost effectiveness of treatment, particularly for criminally involved offenders. But this is an area where more research is needed.

It is imperative that the policy-making community and the public at large be educated about the efficacy of treatment in reducing drug use and criminal behavior. The cost-benefit ratio cannot be ignored. The policy-making community and public must be educated that, as O'Brien and McClelland (1996) pointed out, drug abuse is a chronic, relapsing disease. Equating treatment success with no relapse fails to recognize the nature of the "disease." Instead, we need to look at a variety of indicators of treatment success such as reductions in drug use and improved social functioning, moving beyond simplistic indicators such as relapse. We also need to determine the most efficacious ways to help individuals deal with "slips" and quickly recover from such.

One example of the changing attitudes of the policy-making community was the implementation of the Residential Substance Abuse Treatment (RSAT) program. In September 1996, the Violent Crime Control and Law Enforcement Act of 1994 was amended to require that states "have a program of . . . intervention for . . . convicted offenders during periods

of incarceration [no later than September 1, 1998]." The funding for the RSAT program was $270 million divided across 5 years (1996–2000), representing the largest sum ever devoted to the development of drug treatment programs in state and local correctional facilities. Every state has applied for and is using RSAT funds to implement or expand its treatment capacity in prisons and/or jails. States are required to give preference to programs that provide aftercare services coordinated between the correctional treatment program and other human service and rehabilitation programs. However, aftercare was an unfunded mandate. A preliminary national evaluation expressed concern over the lack of aftercare, with less than half the programs having halfway houses, work release programs, or other aftercare support services (Lipton, Pearson, and Wexler, 2000).

The significance of the RSAT legislation is yet to be realized. Virtually all the programs experienced moderate to severe start-up problems, and the RSAT money to the states was only for a period of 3 years. The major problems reported by state officials were locating or constructing appropriate facilities, because the treatment programs were to be separated from the general population. They also reported significant problems recruiting appropriate staff. Administrative expedience and demands often took precedence over program operations. This includes having to accommodate the following kinds of problems: initially filling a program to capacity even if there was not sufficient staff, inexperienced staff, inmates with too little or too much time remaining on their sentence, not isolating the treatment program participants from other inmates due to overcrowding and the need to fill all available beds, and graduates' being returned to the general population at treatment completion because time remained on their sentence and there was a waiting list for the program. Even with adequate resources and excellent administrative support from the correctional system, program implementation is a difficult process, and program stability is not reached for 2 to 3 years at a minimum (Harrison and Martin, in press). Based on the limit of 3 years of RSAT funding, programs could be abandoned due to the difficulties experienced at start-up without ever having a chance to stabilize.

RECOMMENDATIONS FOR FUTURE RESEARCH

Given the enormity of the demand for treatment services among criminal justice populations, it is important to determine the most efficacious methods for responding to their needs. Research on the effectiveness of different treatment approaches and alternatives for criminal justice clients has lagged behind the implementation of new programs. Much remains unknown about how to best reach drug-involved offenders to stop the revolving door of drug addiction and incarceration.

There needs to be more research on what types of treatment programs are best suited for what types of offenders and at what stage of criminal justice processing. How well are diversion programs working, or can we identify which ones work best? Are TCs the ideal program for prisons? We need to examine the effectiveness of various treatment modalities, including the mix of elements founds in TCs and other residential and outpatient treatment programs. Findings from treatment studies suggest that a number of variables, independent of treatment modality, predict successful outcomes. Among these are degree of involvement in treatment, ethnicity, age, social support, employment, and psychological status. The role of intervening variables needs to be further examined in predicting treatment efficacy.

We need to evaluate 12-step programs, which are frequently included in most treatment programs, and which may constitute the sole treatment available to correctional populations. There are virtually no research studies evaluating the effectiveness of 12-step approaches with offender populations, either alone or as an adjunct therapy. Many treatment programs mix elements, and this was encouraged in the RSAT legislation, but there is sparse research on the effectiveness of doing so. For example, encounter groups, which have always been the purview of TCs, are frequently used in non-TC treatment programs. Furthermore, many in-prison treatment programs that consider themselves TCs have too few elements contained in typical TCs to be really characterized as such. The bottom line is that it is important to determine at what step in the criminal justice processing system intervention—and what type of intervention—is most efficacious. We need to determine the mix of treatment elements that contribute to success. And we need to invest resources and improve methods. To be really informative, treatment evaluations require several years of data. Any meaningful outcome evaluation also will require sufficient sample sizes, an appropriate comparison group, and sufficient time to conduct a prospective analysis to see if successes are maintained over a reasonable follow-up time after release from prison. Longitudinal evaluations are necessary to really evaluate programs, but they need to follow clients for a minimum of 3 years for a proper outcome evaluation (Harrison and Martin, in press).

It is important to more fully evaluate the efficacy of transitional and aftercare treatment services in the community for those leaving prison. As noted by Knight, Simpson, and Hiller (1999), Martin et al. (1999), Pearson and Lipton (1999), and Wexler et al. (1999), clients who receive aftercare do significantly better than clients who do not. These recent outcome evaluations suggest that treatment programs for inmates need a strong aftercare component and, probably, the aftercare should be tied to probation or parole stipulations. A good aftercare program is not cost-free by any means, but the cost per client will be much less than a residential treatment slot. But more needs to be known about how to improve the efficacy of aftercare.

Another area that needs to be considered is the compulsory versus voluntary nature of treatment. Whereas some researchers (e.g., Anglin and Maugh, 1992, and Salmon and Salmon, 1983, both cited in Farabee et al., 1998) have argued that coerced treatment serves as an external motivation for addicts to enter and remain in treatment, there are questions raised by other researchers (e.g., Hartjen et al., 1981, and Platt et al., 1988, both cited in Farabee et al., 1998) as to the morality and constitutionality, as well as the benefit and effectiveness, of treatment for a client who may not be motivated to change. A recent review showed treatment outcomes varied among 11 studies of mandatory substance abuse treatment, but the usefulness of the criminal justice system as a source of treatment referral, as a means of increasing program retention, was supported (Farabee et al., 1998). Compulsory treatment may be the "stick" that increases the length of time in treatment, the most consistent program characteristic associated with long-term client success. Conversely, a sentence reduction or tying sentence length of successful program completion can serve as the "carrot" that gets more offenders to volunteer for treatment.

It is important to conduct research on the efficacy of treatment options in jail settings. Jail-based offenders with substance abuse problems are a significant group, as the 1996 survey of jail inmates (BJS/Harlow, 1998) and the DUF/ADAM (Drug Use Forecasting/Arrestee Drug Abuse Monitoring) studies have made clear. However, the transient nature of jail-based populations is not conducive to a lengthy, structured treatment program. Nevertheless, large numbers of offenders in jail could benefit from treatment. The lessons from the preliminary RSAT jail-based program evaluations are that treatment modality should fit correctional mandates and jails should incorporate short-term interventions rather than long-term phased treatment (Harrison and Martin, in press).

We need to create and explore other alternatives for addressing the needs of drug-involved offenders. One promising innovation in recent years is drug courts. The first drug court was established in Miami-Dade County, Florida, in 1989 and, by the end of 1999, there were more than 425. There are different kinds of drug courts with different types of caseloads, but all try to use the court system to more effectively manage drug-involved offenders. The key elements of drug courts include integration of treatment with justice system case processing; frequent drug testing; a coordinated strategy among judge, prosecution, defense, and treatment providers to govern compliance; ongoing judicial interaction with each participant; and monitoring and evaluation to measure achievement of goals and gauge effectiveness. Offenders generally enter a drug court through a plea, a conditional plea, a contract, or some similar mechanism (see Gebelein, 2000). The offender is assessed and assigned to a treatment program. Case management is an important component of most drug courts, frequently accomplished by judges and the frequency of contact with the court. Many drug courts, however, offer more intensive case management through teaming with Treatment Alternatives to Street Crime (TASC) or similar programs that provide case management. Case managers often testify in court hearings as to offenders' status in meeting treatment goals.

One of the early measurable effects of the drug court movement was to speed case processing. This finding has been repeatedly emphasized as it conserves jail beds and results in cost savings (Belenko, 1998). Nearly every published evaluation to date has shown drug court graduates less likely to be arrested for new crimes (GAO, 1997). However, many of these studies did not have long follow-up periods. In a recent 30-month follow-up study of two Florida drug courts, graduates of a year of outpatient treatment were only about half as likely to be rearrested as nongraduates (Peters and Murrin, 2000). Based on the early evaluations showing drug courts to be successful in rehabilitating offenders, they may provide a model to help address other aspects of offender rehabilitation.

We need to continue to research the efficacy of drug courts in reducing drug abuse and recidivism. In addition to receiving drug treatment, those under drug court jurisdiction receive closer and more comprehensive supervision, including more frequent drug testing and monitoring than is available in other types of community-supervised programs. The case management aspect helps to ensure that offenders access needed services beyond drug treatment. This model, which enhances supervision and increases accountability, can help facilitate a smoother reentry for ex-offenders as they leave correctional institutions. The National Institute of Justice has helped to establish reentry courts that appear to utilize many of the elements founds in drug courts in nine states. These courts need to be evaluated to determine their efficacy in reducing offender recidivism and their cost effectiveness.

In reference to thinking innovatively, it is critically important to determine the efficacy of our policies with respect to drug offenders. Given that there is little evidence nationally that suggests any real increase in drug use, but rather evidence that points to decreases over the past two decades, where did all these drug-abusing incarcerated individuals come from? How much has the net been widened with respect to bringing more drug users to the attention of the criminal justice system, and with what overall effects? Blumstein and Beck (1999) concluded that the changes in our prison population have to do with harsher sentencing policies. And there is an increasing trend of returning parole violators to prison—54% between 1990 and 1998 (BJS/Beck, 2000). Drug offenders accounted for more than half of the total increase in parole violators returned to state prison (BJS/Beck, 2000). As Robinson and Travis (n.d.) asked, Is it really effective to reincarcerate parolees for positive drug tests? We need to review our history over the past few decades to understand what factors have led to the huge increases in incarceration, who is being incarcerated, and at what costs and benefits to society overall. The cost-benefit of policies need to be a more routine part of all evaluation research.

REFERENCES

Apsler, R., and Harding, W. M. (1991). Cost-effectiveness analysis of drug abuse treatment: Current status and recommendations for future research. In *National Institute on Drug Abuse, Drug Abuse Services research series, No. 1: Background papers on drug abuse financing and services approach.* Washington, DC: Government Printing Office.

Avants, S. K., Margolin, A., Koste, T. R., and Singer, J. L. (1993). Changes concurrent with initiation of abstinence from cocaine abuse. *Journal of Substance Abuse Treatment, 10*(6), 577–583.

Ball, J. C., Rosen, L., Flueck, J. A., and Nurco, D. N. (1981). The criminality of heroin addicts when addicted and when off opiates. In J. A. Inciardi (Ed.), *The drug crime connection.* Beverly Hills, CA: Sage.

Ball, J. C., Shaffer, J. W., and Nurco, D. N. (1983). Day-to-day criminality of heroin addicts in Baltimore: A study in the continuity of offense rates. *Drug and Alcohol Dependence, 12*(1), 119–142.

Belenko, S. (1998). *Research on drug courts; A critical review.* New York: Columbia University, National Center on Addiction and Substance Abuse.

Blumstein, A., and Beck, A. (1999). Population growth in U.S. prisons, 1980–1996. In M. Tonry and J. Petersilia (Eds.), *Prisons.* Chicago: University of Chicago Press.

Bureau of Justice Statistics. (1997). *Correctional populations in the U.S., 1995.* Washington, DC: U.S. Department of Justice, Office of Justice Programs, Bureau of Justice Statistics.

Bureau of Justice Statistics. (1999). *Felony criminal case processing, 1998.* Washington, DC: U.S. Department of Justice, Office of Justice Programs, Bureau of Justice Statistics.

Bureau of Justice Statistics/Beck, A. J. (2000). *Prisoners in 1999.* Washington, DC; U.S. Department of Justice, Office of Justice Programs, Bureau of Justice Statistics.

Bureau of Justice Statistics/Bonczar, T. P. (1997). *Characteristics of adults on probation, 1995.* Washington, DC: U.S. Department of Justice, Office of Justice Programs, Bureau of Justice Statistics.

Bureau of Justice Statistics/Brown, J. M., and Langan, P. A. (1999). *Felony sentences in state courts, 1996.* Washington, DC: U.S. Department of Justice, Office of Justice Programs, Bureau of Justice Statistics.

Bureau of Justice Statistics/Ditton, P. M. (1999). *Mental health and treatment of inmates and probationers.* Washington, DC: U.S. Department of Justice, Office of Justice Programs, Bureau of Justice Statistics.

Bureau of Justice Statistics/Harlow, C. W. (1998). *Profile of jail inmates, 1996.* Washington, DC: U.S. Department of Justice, Office of Justice Programs, Bureau of Justice Statistics.

Bureau of Justice Statistics/Mumola, C. J. (1999). *Substance abuse and treatment, state and federal prisoners, 1997.* Washington, DC: U.S. Department of Justice, Office of Justice Programs, Bureau of Justice Statistics.

Bureau of Justice Statistics/Mumola, C. J., and Bonczar, T. P. (1998). *Substance abuse and treatment of adults on probation, 1995.* Washington, DC; U.S. Department of Justice, Office of Justice Programs, Bureau of Justice Statistics.

Bureau of Justice Statistics/Wilson, D. J. (2000). *Drug use, testing, and treatment in jails.* Washington, DC: U.S. Department of Justice, Office of Justice Programs, Bureau of Justice Statistics.

Caulkins, J. P., and Reuter, P. (1997). Setting goals for drug policy: Harm reduction or use reduction. *Addiction, 92,* 1143–1150.

Cotton, P. (1994). Hindsight and new data converge on drug policy. *Journal of the American Medical Association, 272*(13), 992–993.

Farabee, D., Prendergast, M., and Anglin, M. D. (1998). The effectiveness of coerced treatment for drug-abusing offenders. *Federal Probation, 62*(1), 3.

Gebelein, R. S. (2000). *The rebirth of rehabilitation: Promise and perils of drug courts.* Washington, DC: U.S. Department of Justice, Office of Justice Programs, Bureau of Justice Statistics.

General Accounting Office. (1997). *Drug courts: Overview of growth, characteristics, and results.* Washington, DC: Author.

General Accounting Office. (2000). *State and federal prisoners: Profiles of inmates characteristics in 1991 and 1997.* Washington, DC: Author.

Gerstein, D. R., Johnson, R. A., Harwood, J. J., Fountain, D., Suter, N., and Malloy, K. (1994). *Evaluating recovery services: The California Drug and Alcohol Treatment Assessment (CALDATA).* Sacramento, CA: California Department of Alcohol and Drug Programs.

Harrison, L. D. (1992). The drug-crime nexus in the USA. *Contemporary Drug Problems, 19*(2), 203–246.

Harrison, L. D., and Martin, S. S. (in press). *Residential Substance Abuse Treatment (RSAT) for state prisoners formula grant: Compendium of program implementation and accomplishments.* Washington, DC: U.S. Department of Justice, Office of Justice Programs, and the National Institute of Justice.

Harwood, H., Fountain, D., and Livermore, G. (1996). *The economic costs of alcohol and drug abuse in the United States 1992.* Rockville, MD: U.S. Department of Health and Human Services and the National Institute on Drug Abuse.

Harwood, H. J., Hubbard, R. L., Collins, J. J., and Rachal, J. V. (1988). The costs of crime and the benefits of drug abuse treatment: A cost-benefit analysis using TOPS data. In C. G. Leukefeld and F. M. Tims (Eds.), *Compulsory treatment of drug abuse: Research and clinical practice* (pp. 209–235) (National Institute on Drug Abuse Research Monograph No. 86) (DHHS Pub. No. [ADM] 89-1578). Washington, DC: Superintendent of Documents, Government Printing Office.

Harwood, H. J., Napolitano, D. M., Kristiansen, P., and Collins, J. J. (1984). *Economic costs to society of alcohol and drug abuse and mental illness.* Research Triangle Park, NC: Research Triangle Institute.

Holder, H. D. (1987). Alcoholism treatment and potential health care cost saving. *Medical Care, 25*(1), 52–71.

Holder, H. D., & Blose, J. O. (1992). The reduction of health care costs associated with alcoholism treatment: A 14-year longitudinal study. *Journal of Studies on Alcohol, 53,* 293–302.

Hubbard, R. L., Craddock, S. G., Flynn, P. M., Anderson, J., and Etheridge, R. M. (1997). Overview of 1-year follow-up outcomes in the Drug Abuse Treatment Outcome Study (DATOS). *Psychology of Addictive Behaviors, 11,* 261–278.

Hubbard, R. L., Marsden, M. E., Rachal, J. V., Harwood, H. J., Cavanaugh, E. R., and Ginzburg, H. M. (1989). *Drug abuse treatment: A national study of effectiveness.* Chapel Hill, NC: University of North Carolina Press.

Inciardi, J. A. (1992). *The war on drugs II: The continuing grip of heroin, cocaine, crack, crime, AIDS, and public policy.* Mountain View, CA: Mayfield.

Inciardi, J. A., Horowitz, R., and Pottieger, A. E. (1993). *Women and crack-cocaine.* New York: Macmillan.

Inciardi, J. A., Martin, S. S., Butzin, C. A., Hooper, R. M., and Harrison, L. D. (1997). An effective model of prison-based treatment for drug-involved offenders. *Journal of Drug Issues, 27*(2), 261–278.

Inciardi, J. A., and Pottieger, A. E. (1986, Winter). Drug use and crime among two cohorts of women narcotics users: An empirical assessment. *Journal of Drug Issues, 16,* 91–106.

Inciardi, J. A., and Pottieger, A. E. (1991). Kids, crack and crime. *Journal of Drug Issues, 21*(2), 257–270.

Inciardi, J. A., and Pottieger, A. E. (1998). Drug use and street crime in Miami: An almost twenty-year retrospective. *Substance Use and Misuse, 33*(9), 1839–1870.

Johnson, B. D., Goldstein, P. J., Preble, E., Schmeidler, J., Lipton, D. S., Spunt, B., and Miller, T. (1985). *Taking care of business: The economics of crime by heroin users.* Lexington, MA: Lexington Books.

Jones, K .R., and Vischi, T. R. (1979). Impact of alcohol, drug abuse and mental health treatment on medical care utilization: A review of the research literature. *Medical Care, 17*(Suppl. 12).

Knight, K., Simpson, D. D., and Hiller, M. L. (1999). Three-year reincarceration outcomes for in-prison therapeutic community treatment in Texas. *The Prison Journal, 79,* 337–351.

Lipton, D. S. (1995). *The effectiveness of treatment for drug abusers under criminal justice supervision.* Washington, DC: U.S. Department of Justice, Office of Justice Programs, and the National Institute of Justice.

Lipton, D. S., and Johnson, B. D. (1998). Smack, crack and score: Two decades of NIDA-funded drugs and crime research at NDRI 1974–1994. *Substance Use and Misuse, 33*(9), 1779–1816.

Lipton, D. S., Pearson, F. S., and Wexler, H. K. (2000). *Final report: National evaluation of the Residential Substance Abuse Treatment for state prisoners program from onset to midpoint* (Rep. to the National Institute of Justice). Washington, DC: National Institute of Justice.

Martin, S. S., Butzin, C. A., Saum, C. A., and Inciardi, J. A. (1999). Three-year outcomes of therapeutic community treatment for drug-involved offenders in Delaware: From prison to work release to aftercare. *The Prison Journal, 79,* 294–320.

Martin, S. S., and Inciardi, J. A. (1993a). Case management approaches for criminal justice clients. In J. A. Inciardi (Ed.), *Drug treatment and criminal justice* (pp. 81–96). Newbury Park, CA: Sage.

Martin, S. S., and Inciardi, J. A. (1993b). A case management treatment program for drug involved prison releasees. *The Prison Journal, 73*(3/4), 319–331.

National Institute on Drug Abuse. (1992). *Extent and adequacy of insurance coverage for substance abuse services* (Institute of Medicine Rep.: Treating Drug Problems). In *Drug Abuse Services research series, No. 2, Vol. 1.* Rockville, MD: U.S.

Department of Health and Human Services; Alcohol, Drug Abuse, and Mental Health Administration; National Institute on Drug Abuse.

Nurco, D. N. (1998). A long term program of research on drug use and crime. *Substance Use and Misuse, 33*(9), 1817–1838.

O'Brien, C. P., and McClelland, T. A. (1996). Myths about the treatment of addiction. *Lancet, 347,* 237–240.

Pearson, F. S., and Lipton, D. S. (1999). A meta-analytic review of the effectiveness of corrections-based treatments for drug abuse, *The Prison Journal, 79,* 384–410.

Peters, R. H., and Murrin, M. R. (2000). Effectiveness of treatment-based drug courts in reducing criminal recidivism. *Criminal Justice and Behavior, 20*(1), 72–96.

Pettiway, L. E. (1987). Participation in crime partnerships by female drug users: The effects of domestic arrangements, drug use, and criminal involvement. *Criminology, 251,* 741–766.

Rice, D. P., Kelman, S., Miller, L. S., and Dunmeyer, S. (1990). *The economic costs of alcohol and drug abuse and mental illness: 1985* (Rep. Submitted to the Office of Financing and Coverage Policy of the Alcohol, Drug Abuse, and Mental Health Administration, U.S. Department of Health and Human Services). San Francisco: Institute for Health and Aging.

Robinson, L., and Travis, J. (n.d.). *Managing prisoner reentry for public safety.* Unpublished manuscript.

Simpson, D. D., Davage, L. J., Lloyd, M. R., and Sells, S. B. (1978). *Evaluation of drug abuse treatments based on first year follow up* (NIDA Services Research Monograph Series No. ADM 78-701). Rockville, MD: National Institute on Drug Abuse.

Substance Abuse Mental Health Services Administration. (2000). *Substance abuse treatment in adult and juvenile correctional facilities: Finding from the Uniform Facility Data Set 1997 Survey of Correctional Facilities.* Rockville, MD: Author. Available: www.samhsa.gov/csat/csat.htm

Wexler, H. K., Melnick, G., Lower, L., and Peters, J. (1999). Three-year reincarceration outcomes for Amity in-prison therapeutic community and aftercare in California. *The Prison Journal, 79,* 321–336.

16

Treatment Alternatives to Street Crime: An Evaluation of Five Programs

M. DOUGLAS ANGLIN

DOUGLAS LONGSHORE

SUSAN TURNER

ABSTRACT

In response to the increasing numbers of criminal offenders involved with drugs, the criminal justice system has sought more effective means of intervening with these offenders. One intervention approach is Treatment Alternatives to Street Crime (TASC), an offender management model that has been implemented in various forms since the early 1970s. TASC facilitates treatment for drug-using offenders as part of an overall strategy to control drug use and associated criminal behaviors. This article reviews the evolution of TASC and reports findings from an evaluation of five TASC programs. The evaluation, experimental at two sites and quasi-experimental at three, found favorable effects of TASC programs on service delivery and offenders' drug use. Findings on criminal recidivism were mixed and difficult to interpret. This article concludes with specific recommendations for improving TASC and similar programs within the criminal justice system.

Primary responsibility for suppressing drug use in the United States has become the domain of the criminal justice system (CJS). In attempting to meet this responsibility and in response to the drug-use epidemics of the 1960s, 1970s, and 1980s, police, court, prosecutorial, and corrections personnel have been overwhelmed in terms of workload, stretched resources, and limited options. Corrections departments at local, state, and federal levels have all been affected by overcrowded facilities and by high recidivism rates among drug-using probationers and parolees. The impact on the criminal justice system of the waves of these offenders has driven CJS planners and policy makers to seek solutions other than mere incarceration; thus, a trend has developed toward increasing the provision of treatment for controlling, if not resolving, offenders' drug problems.

The importance of providing treatment for drug-using offenders is amply demonstrated both by the relationship between criminal activity and the use of alcohol and other drugs and by extensive research on treatment efficacy among offenders. Most striking is the connection between drugs and crime. Numerous studies have documented the large number of crimes committed by drug-dependent offenders, particularly those who use drugs daily or almost daily. A consistent finding is that as levels of drug use increase, so does criminal activity. Similar to this, declines in drug use are accompanied by declines in crime—particularly income-generating crimes (Chaiken and Chaiken, 1982; Inciardi, 1987; Johnson and Wish, 1986; Nurco, Kinlock, and Hanlon, 1990; Speckart and Anglin, 1986). The likelihood of recidivism following release from incarceration is higher for offenders who are drug dependent than for other offenders (Bureau of Justice Statistics, 1993). Drug use also negatively affects rehabilitation regarding other social and per-

AUTHORS' NOTE: *Support for this article was provided, in part, by contract NOIDA-1-8408 from the National Institute on Drug Abuse (NIDA) and by NIDA Research Scientist Development Award DA00146 (Anglin). Thanks to Brian Perrochet for editorial assistance and Janice Pride for manuscript preparation.*

sonal problems such as unemployment, family dysfunction, or mental disorders. Thus, treating the drug-use problems of offenders may be a crucial element in any overall strategy to reduce drug use and recidivism among the offender population.

The potential benefits of treatment for drug-using offenders (and for the general population) have been substantiated by research, but achieving these benefits requires a strategy for ensuring that drug-using offenders receive appropriate treatment and are adequately supervised in order to detect drug use or crime and to institute appropriate intervention as needed. The offender management model, Treatment Alternatives to Street Crime (TASC), evolved as one such strategy. This article describes the TASC model and its most recent and comprehensive evaluation, presenting salient findings and briefly discussing the research challenges that were faced in the process of assessing the model as applied in five sites. The article recommends modifications to TASC and suggests future research that may provide additional information to improve the implementation of TASC and other offender management models designed to ameliorate problems related to drug use among offenders.

OVERVIEW OF TREATMENT ALTERNATIVES TO STREET CRIME

Description of TASC

For more than two decades, TASC programs have provided a bridge between agencies of the criminal justice system and community-based drug treatment programs in an effort to arrange rehabilitative interventions for drug-using offenders. TASC is possibly the best example of programmatic efforts to establish and promote formal coordination between criminal justice and drug treatment within local jurisdictions (Wellisch, Prendergast, and Anglin, 1993). Under TASC auspices, drug-using offenders who might progressively become more involved with the criminal justice system are offered the opportunity to enter community-based treatment. TASC identifies, assesses, and refers drug-using offenders to appropriate community treatment services as an alternative or supplement to existing criminal justice sanctions and procedures. After referring offenders to treatment, TASC monitors their progress and compliance, especially in terms of drug use (through urine testing). Dropping out of treatment or other noncompliance is treated by the courts as a violation of the conditions of release (Inciardi and McBride, 1991; Weinman, 1990). In some locales, the agency providing TASC services is also the provider of treatment services, but the two types of services are functionally distinct.

TASC programs have evolved in purpose and in content as well as in their funding support. Although the criminal justice system generally has accepted the validity and utility of diverting offenders to treatment in lieu of incarceration, the original TASC that was focused on young offenders early in their criminal careers had some pragmatic difficulties. Young first offenders tended to be marijuana users, and treatment resources in the early 1970s were designed mainly for heroin users. However, heroin-using offenders often had such extensive criminal histories that judges and prosecutors were reluctant to allow pretrial diversion. Because of these problems, TASC programs moved toward a model of flexibility when considering the point of intervention in the criminal justice process and the type of client they would serve. By 1977, TASC program clients were equally divided between pretrial diversion and posttrial sentencing (System Sciences, 1979). Other changes in the original TASC model also occurred. Posttrial but presentencing intervention was introduced, and the TASC model was expanded to include nonopiate drug users. In addition, mass urine screening became optional rather than mandatory when screening interviews were found to be as effective as urinalysis in identifying drug users. More recently, program admission criteria were expanded to include juveniles and persons dependent on alcohol. In 1996, there were an estimated 300 TASC programs in 30 states (Anglin et al., 1996).

Previous Evaluations of TASC

Initial evaluations of TASC programs across the United States were fairly positive, although they focused on operations and processes of programs rather than client outcomes. Researchers found that TASC programs were able to screen and identify large numbers of drug users in the criminal justice system (Toborg, Levin, Milkman, and Center, 1976). Furthermore, TASC was able to develop an effective linkage with the criminal justice system, increase ethnic diversity in treatment, and increase the proportion of those in drug treatment who were criminal offenders (Collins, Hubbard, Rachal, Cavanaugh, and Craddock, 1982). There was also evidence that TASC programs increased treatment retention. The Treatment Outcome Prospective Study (Hubbard et al., 1989) found that TASC clients remained in treatment longer than non–TASC clients, and the length of stay in treatment was found to be related to a more positive treatment outcome (Hubbard, Collins, Rachal, and Cavanaugh, 1988). System Sciences (1979) found that the cost to identify, assess, refer, and monitor TASC clients, plus the cost of treatment, was no more than $7,000 per client per year for the most expensive type of treatment—residential care. This was considerably cheaper than any form of incarceration.

By the late 1970s, when about 40 TASC programs were in operation, there was a consensus that TASC programs had been shown to be successful in gaining a legal and political acceptance. They were also found to be cost-effective in identifying, screening, and referring clients to treatment and retaining drug-using offenders in treatment. But, the evaluations conducted in the 1970s were process evaluations that focused on the operations of the programs; they did not include experimental designs with random assignment to determine short- or long-term outcomes among clients. The study described in this article attempted a refined research approach to more accurately reflect the effectiveness of TASC programs.

METHOD

Site Selection

This evaluation began in 1991 with funding from the National Institute on Drug Abuse (NIDA). At that time, more than 125 TASC programs operated in 25 states. They differed widely in terms of the local treatment and criminal justice ecologies in which they operated. They also differed in the clientele they targeted and in particular program activities. Given the diversity of TASC programs nationwide, a critical task was to determine both the criteria for the selection of programs for evaluation and the actual process of seeking site participation.

Potential programs were assessed for the degree to which they conformed to the TASC model as represented by the Ten Critical Program Elements and Performance Standards (Bureau of Justice Assistance, 1992) (see appendix). Programs had to include a significant number of high-risk offenders (e.g., crack cocaine users) in the client pool. We sought programs that were diverse on other dimensions as well, such as geography, time since program inception, and gender and ethnic representation in the local offender population. A sufficient client flow was necessary to provide the required number of participants during the planned fieldwork period. The program's ability to negotiate successfully with local officials to ensure their cooperation with evaluation activities was also a condition of study inclusion.

Two major limitations of this approach were that it included only TASC programs for which documented profiles were available and that some of the data on which selection was based were not current. However, because only 24 programs were large enough to meet our client-flow requirements, it is likely that only a few of the programs without profiles would have qualified in the initial screen.

We conducted a preliminary analysis of TASC programs for which profiles were available in the *TASC Resource Catalog* (Bureau of Justice Assistance, 1989). The programs were first screened for a minimum number of clients likely to be served (at least 400 clients in the 18 months of intake projected for the evaluation) to ensure a sufficient number of participants. Programs were then categorized into five regions (Northeast, Southeast, Midwest, Southwest, and West) and by offender type (juvenile or adult). We also determined which programs met the minimum requirements of the TASC Ten Critical Elements and Performance Standards.

From those programs that qualified as strong examples of the TASC model and that served large and varied types of clients, five were asked to participate in the outcome evaluation. All five programs agreed to participate. Four programs handled adult offenders; one handled juvenile offenders. We make no claim that these five programs are representative of all TASC programs in a statistical sense. Instead, we view the study as a five-site replication based on programs that conform to the TASC program model. A randomized design was practical in two of the adult programs in which the number of eligible offenders was too large for programs to handle. Thus, random assignment to TASC or to a control group was ethically permissible and politically acceptable. Comparison groups were constructed in the other two adult programs and in the juvenile program. Using local program eligibility criteria, we screened offenders into comparison groups if their current charges, drug-use histories, and other characteristics indicated that they would have been eligible for TASC if the judge or probation officer had referred them to TASC for an eligibility assessment. (Eligible cases were referred or not referred to TASC for a variety of reasons. For example, some judges were more favorably disposed to TASC than others.)

Sample

A total of 2,014 offenders agreed to participate in the outcome study and completed the intake interview. Very few (less than 1%) of the offenders refused to participate, usually on the advice of defense counsel. More than 80% were located 6 months later and completed the follow-up interview. TASC and control/comparison offenders at any site differed on very few characteristics, including drug use and drug-treatment histories. Thus, our random assignment procedure (at two experimental sites) and screening procedure (at three quasi-experimental sites) apparently succeeded in creating similar groups of TASC and control/comparison offenders. When we compared clients interviewed to those lost at the follow-up stage, no statistically significant differences emerged for the basic demographic characteristics.

Evaluation Design

Several aspects of the design were constant across sites. Offenders at each site were asked to complete the same set of intake interview forms concerning their personal backgrounds, criminal and drug-use histories, treatment histories, and other topics. Six months after their intake interviews, we attempted to relocate all offenders at each site to complete a follow-up interview in which we updated our intake information and obtained offender self-reports of the treatment services they had received in the interim. Interviewers were hired and trained by the evaluation staff, and the same quality-control procedures were applied at each site.

One important aspect of the design varied across sites. At our two experimental sites, the alternative interventions were treatment programs that offered services (counseling, urine testing, etc.) appropriate for drug-involved offenders but which did not do so under the TASC offender-management model. Thus, if it was to emerge as more effective, the TASC model would have to outperform an alternative intervention by delivering more service units, monitoring offenders more closely, or in some other way separating itself from the alternative intervention. This was a stringent criterion for success. On the other hand, because of the scientific rigor achieved with an experimental design, findings indicating a TASC program's success, even if modest, would constitute very persuasive evidence for the value of the TASC model. At our three quasi-experimental sites, the alternative intervention was routine probation. To emerge as more effective, a TASC program had to outperform "business as usual" probation in the same community. Thus, quasi-experimental sites had a less stringent criterion for success, but they also had the advantage of comparing TASC to an intervention routinely available to most offenders in the same community.

Analytic Approach

We measured TASC program outcomes in three domains: treatment services received, drug use, and criminal recidivism. TASC outcomes at any site depended partly on client population, program maturity, and evaluation design. Accordingly, in data interpretation, we believed the sensible approach was to look for patterns in findings across sites, rather than to read findings from each site in isolation. An alternative would have been to pool the data across sites, but as noted above, we view this study as a five-site replication; we wished to see if consistent findings would emerge when each site is analyzed separately. Moreover, given the diversity in offender characteristics across sites (most notably, the distinction between adult and juvenile offenders), we believed that pooling the data might obscure more than it revealed. When patterns emerged, we viewed them as evidence regarding the effectiveness of the TASC model overall—implemented with different client populations and by programs at different stages in their development.

Analyses of two outcomes—drug use and crime—were based on multivariate regression techniques. This is important for two reasons. First, adjusting for offender background characteristics related to group assignment and/or to outcome measures in a multivariate analysis enabled us to isolate potential TASC effects more clearly and reduced the possibility that preexisting differences between TASC and control/comparison offenders might account for findings. Second, by checking for interactions between group assignment and other predictor variables, we moved beyond the more common but limited analyses that deal only with main effects of an intervention. Favorable outcomes within offender subsamples might have been missed in main-effects analyses based on entire samples. Conversely, if favorable outcomes emerge in main-effects analyses, it is still important to see if these outcomes are actually confined to, or are greatest within, particular offender subsamples.

We drew up an initial list of potential covariates by identifying background characteristics related to group assignment or outcomes at any site ($r \geq .10$ or $p \leq .10$) and then merging these lists across sites. All potential covariates on this list were allowed to enter the regression equation for each site by backward stepping (the criterion for entering the equation was $p \leq .05$). If a covariate stepped in at any site, we included it among the covariates for all sites, thus standardizing the set of prediction variables across sites.

Terms for the interaction between each covariate and the outcome measure were allowed to enter the equation by forward stepping ($p \leq .01$). The procedure was more stringent for interaction terms than for main effects because interactions are often complex and difficult to interpret. Moreover, because so many potential interactions were being tested, setting the p value at .01 reduced the possibility that interactions detected in the data could have arisen by chance. We did not standardize the set of covariate interaction terms across sites. We included them on a site-specific basis only. Thus, where TASC effects were contingent on a covariate, we sought to characterize the contingency at each individual site without imposing it on the data for all sites.

Analyses were performed on an intent-to-treat basis. That is, at each site, all offenders in the TASC group were compared to all offenders in the control/comparison group regardless of the amount or dose of treatment services actually received by offenders in either group. This method is conservative. TASC effects might have appeared stronger if we had excluded TASC cases who received no treatment services after referral by TASC and cases whose dose of treatment services was less than intended or optimal.

Measures

This study made use of four types of data: (a) offender self-reports obtained in intake and follow-up interviews, (b) results of urinalysis tests performed on urine specimens voluntarily supplied by offenders at each interview, (c) treatment records, and (d) criminal justice records.

The intake interview, conducted as soon as possible after recruitment into the study, gathered self-report data on offender demographics (e.g., age, marital status, employment), drug use and crime on a monthly basis during the 6 months preceding intake, and offender attitudes and perceptions regarding crime and drug-abuse treatment. We conducted a follow-up interview 6 months after intake in which self-reported drug use and crime during the intervening period were recorded and attitudinal and perceptual measures updated. Additional information was obtained on the nature of treatment services received, their frequency, duration, and perceived value to the offender.

Outcome Variables

Services Received.   To assess services received by each offender during the 6-month period between baseline and follow-up, we included in the follow-up interview a series of questions on whether the offender received treatment or counseling services—including any urinalysis tests—from any provider. If so, the offender was asked to specify the nature of those services and how long (from first and last day) each service was provided. Possible services included drug detoxification, drug-related medical care, other medical care, urine tests to detect recent drug or alcohol use, drug counseling, legal counseling, parenting instruction, family problem counseling, AIDS prevention counseling, personal problem counseling, school counseling, school placement, job counseling, job training, job placement, and other.

It is important to remember that the time period for the follow-up interview was the window of time between the first interview and the follow-up interview 6 months later. Recruitment at sites occurred at slightly different points relative to initial TASC enrollment (e.g., at Chicago, study recruitment occurred after initial assessment and the first orientation session; in Portland, Oregon, it occurred after orientation but before formal assessment). Thus, the window periods were not directly comparable across sites. Moreover, the service window did not capture all the early services provided by TASC. However, our main concern was documenting the relative differences in treatment services (not just TASC case management functions) received by TASC offenders and control/comparison offenders within a site. For this purpose, the window of time we chose was most informative for our purposes at each site.

Drug Use.   Drug outcome measures were based on a series of drug-use questions asked of each offender. Favorable data on the reliability and validity of these measures has been reported in Chou, Hser, and Anglin (1996) and Hser, Anglin, and Chou (1992). For each month during the follow-up period, offenders were asked whether they used any nonprescription drugs. For up to four different drug types, the frequency, route of administration, and total purchase cost were asked. Monthly information was aggregated to produce global measures of drug use during the entire follow-up period. A similar set of items was asked for each of the 6 months prior to intake into the study; these composed the baseline equivalent of the outcome measures.

Number of Drug Use Days.   For the 6-month follow-up period and 6-month baseline period, the total number of days on which the offender used drugs was determined. Drug use days ranged from 0 (no drug days during the 6-month period) to 180 (every day of the 6-month period). In analyses of this variable, the raw (untransformed) value was used because the distribution met the criterion of normal distribution.

Frequency of Drug Use. In addition to the number of days during which the offender used drugs, we also gathered the frequency or total number of times drugs were used. This measure is an alternative indicator of the intensity of drug use. The frequency of drug use ranged from 0 to several thousand. Due to the extreme skewness of this variable, the natural log was used to transform data for analyses.

Number of Drugs Used. As indicated, the offender was asked information for up to four drugs used most frequently during the 6-month period. This variable ranged from 0 (no drugs used) to four. The raw number of drugs was used in analyses.

Ratio of Drug Use Days to Days at Risk. Not all offenders were at risk (on the street) throughout the measurement periods. Some were incarcerated on one or more days. The measures above do not take into account the time that offenders may be at risk for drug use. To account for this, a final measure included the number of days on which drugs were used (measure one) divided by the total number of nonincarcerated days in the 6-month period. The measure ranged from 0 (no drugs used) to 1 (drugs used on every day at risk). An arcsine transformation of the ratio was used in the analyses.

Criminal Recidivism. Self-report crime outcome measures were constructed from a series of crime commission items that were asked for each month of the follow-up period (in the same manner as the drug-use variables). For each month of the 6-month follow-up period, offenders were asked to indicate the number of times they committed any of 18 crimes (e.g., robbed a place of business; stole a car, truck, or motorcycle; possessed marijuana or hashish). The 6-month measures were summed to provide the total number of crimes committed in each of three crime categories: violent, property, and drug-related. Favorable evidence on the reliability and validity of these crime measures appears in Marquis (1981).

Data on arrests and technical violations were gathered from criminal justice records. In each site, coders abstracted information from probation files (including local and state criminal history records, or rap sheets) on the date, nature, and outcome of any arrest or technical violation that the offender experienced during the follow-up period.

Number of Violent Crimes. The total number of violent crimes self-reported by offenders across sites was very low; thus, violent crimes were considered unreliable as a major measure of crime commission for the study.

Number of Property Crimes. The range for self-reported property crimes ranged from 0 to more than 3,000 during the follow-up period. The natural log was used to transform the data for analyses.

Number of Drug-Related Crimes. The third major measure of crime was the self-reported number of drug crimes committed by the offender during baseline and follow-up periods. Drug crimes ranged from 0 to more than 7,000. The natural log for number of drug crimes was used in analyses.

Arrest or Technical Violation. Probation records were consulted to gauge the impact of TASC on officially recorded crime measures. As a measure of crime commission, officially recorded measures capture only a fraction of all behaviors. However, official records provide a good measure of the burden placed by TASC and comparison-group offenders on the criminal justice system in terms of reprocessing subsequent crimes and violations of the technical conditions of probation. Offenders were assigned a value of 0 if their probation records indicated no arrest during their follow-up periods and 1 if one or more arrests were indicated. A similar procedure was used for technical violations. If the offender's record indicated no technical violation, they were assigned 0; if one or more technical violations were indicated, 1 was assigned. The raw value was used in regression analyses (logistic regression was used because of the binary nature of both outcomes).

RESULTS

TASC program outcomes were assessed in three domains: treatment services received, drug use, and criminal recidivism.

Service Delivery

In relation to the intervention alternatives to which control/comparison offenders were assigned, TASC programs delivered more treatment services to offenders. These services were usually drug counseling, urinalysis to detect drug use, and/or AIDS education. At four of five sites, the difference in service delivery was statistically significant. At the fifth site, Canton, Ohio, it was not. However, because we used an experimental design in Canton, the TASC program there was compared to an alternative treatment provider which, although it did not conform to the TASC model of offender management, nevertheless delivered treatment. (Another limiting factor at the Canton site was the relatively small sample size.) Thus, the pattern of findings across sites suggests that the TASC model is an effective strategy for improving delivery of treatment services.

Because of recall errors, offenders' self-reports of treatment services that they received may not be totally accurate. However, we believe the difference between services received by TASC offenders and those received by control/comparison offenders is too large to be attributable to recall effects or other sources of error. Moreover, recall error is likely to have been of the same magnitude and in the same direction for both TASC and control/comparison offenders.

Drug Use

On one or more measures of drug use, TASC programs outperformed the alternative interventions at three of five sites (see Table 1). In Birmingham, drug-use reductions were greater for TASC offenders on two outcomes: drug-use days and ratio of drug days to days at risk. For example, the nonstandardized coefficient for drug-use days in Table 1 indicates that TASC offenders reported 12.5 fewer days of drug use than comparison offenders. (The p value for the ratio outcome measure is marginal.) In Canton, reductions in number of drugs used were greater for TASC offenders who scored high at baseline on number of drugs used. This interaction is depicted in Figure 1. In Chicago, drug-use reductions

TABLE 1   Drug Use Outcomes (nonstandardized regression coefficients)

			CHICAGO[a]			
			No Arrests Before Age 18	*One or More Arrests Before Age 18*		
	Birmingham	*Canton*			*Orlando*	*Portland*
Drug-use days[b]						
Group assignment (1 = TASC)	−12.51***	−1.54	−14.98***	−42.63***	6.86*	−3.24
Baseline number of drug-use days	−.01	.33***	.44***	.39***	38***	.20**
Group by baseline interaction	NA	NA	NA	NA	NA	NA
Adjusted R^2	.28	.27	.27***	.23***	.36**	.22***
N	365	134	229	163	422	330
Log frequency of drug use[c]						
Group assignment (1 = TASC)	−.32	−.52	−1.31*		.08	−.08
Baseline number of drug use	.62***	.58**	−.02		.24	.51
Group by baseline interaction	−.09	−.25*	.00		.10	−.02
Adjusted R^2	.34***	.31***	.27***		.38***	.22***
N	365	133	390		422	330
Number of drugs used[d]						
Group assignment (1 = TASC)	.00	.34*	−.19		.13	−.11
Baseline number of drugs used	.39**	1.20***	.54***		.55	.30
Group by baseline interaction	−.06	−.43***	−.18*		−.19**	.05
Adjusted R^2	.35***	.41***	.22***		.29***	.28***
N	365	133	390		422	329
Arcsine ratio of days of use to days at risk[e]						
Group assignment (1 = TASC)	−.06*	.09	.00		.02	.00
Baseline ratio of days of use to days at risk	.29**	.72***	.56***		.32**	.24
Group by baseline interaction	−.13	−.25*	−.23**		.03	−.07
Adjusted R^2	.25***	.28***	.18***		.39***	.22**
N	360	132	380		396	322

Note: TASC = treatment alternatives to street crime.

[a]Findings from the Chicago program regarding drug-use days were contingent on whether offenders had an arrest before the age of 18.

[b]Findings were adjusted for 18 covariates, not shown, in Chicago. Findings were adjusted for 19 categories, not shown, at four other sites.

[c]Findings were adjusted for 23 covariates, not shown.

[d]Findings were adjusted for 26 covariates, not shown.

[e]Findings were adjusted for 18 covariates, not shown.

*$p \leq .10$. **$p \leq .05$. ***$p \leq .01$.

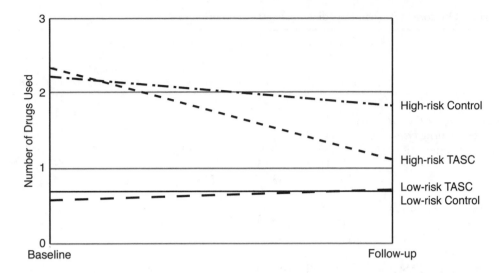

FIGURE 1   Effect of TASC on Number of Drugs Used at Two Levels of Baseline Risk, Canton.

Note: TASC = treatment alternatives to street crime.

were greater for TASC offenders on all four drug use outcomes: drug-use days, frequency of drug use, number of drugs used, and ratio of drug days to days at risk. Two effects were contingent on a level of baseline use, and one main effect was stronger for cases with an arrest prior to age 18. To illustrate this pattern of findings for Chicago, Figure 2 shows the interaction of drug-use days at baseline with group assignment (TASC vs. comparison group). No significant effects emerged in Orlando or Portland.

Crime

Evidence on new crimes, arrests, and technical violations in the 6-month follow-up period was quite mixed (see Table 2). Two TASC programs, Birmingham and Chicago, showed favorable effects on self-reported drug crimes. For example, after the logged value for drug crimes is back-translated to a raw number, the nonstandardized coefficient for Birmingham indicates 16 fewer drug crimes for TASC offenders than for comparison offenders. (The p value in Birmingham was

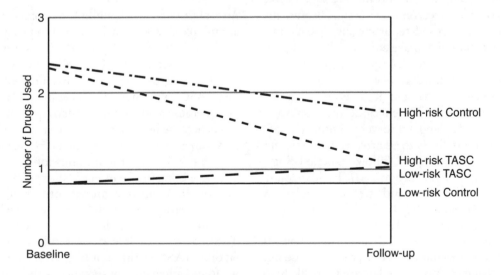

FIGURE 2   Effect of TASC on Number of Drugs Used at Two Levels of Baseline Risk, Chicago.

Note: TASC = treatment alternatives to street crime.

TABLE 2   Crime Outcomes (nonstandardized regression coefficients)

			CHICAGO[a]			
	Birmingham	*Canton*	*Fewer Than Three Prior Convictions*	*Three or More Prior Convictions*	*Orlando*	*Portland*
Number of drug crimes[b]						
Group assignment (1 = TASC)	−.19*	.13	−.16	−1.09***	.15	.13
Baseline number of drug crimes	.35***	.11	−.06	.97***	.26*	.60***
Group by baseline interaction	−.10	−.02	.12	−.48***	.00	−.29**
Adjusted R^2	.16***	.05	.13***	.28***	.27***	.14***
N	365	133	243	146	422	330
Any arrest[c]						
Group assignment (1 = TASC)	−.29	.77	−.32		.11	1.26***
−2 log likelihood	17.33**	7.33	46.36***		48.22	44.30***
N	378	132	477		470	378
Any technical violation[d]						
Group assignment (1 = TASC)	1.23**	−12.99	−.22		.41	.35
−2 log likelihood	35.33***	42.38***	34.34***		18.82*	47.64**
N	378	132	477		470	378

Note: TASC = treatment alternatives to street crime.

[a]Findings from the Chicago program regarding drug crimes were contingent on whether offenders had three or more prior convictions.

[b]Chicago findings were adjusted for 22 covariates, not shown. Findings for other sites were adjusted for 23 covariates not shown.

[c]Findings were adjusted for 10 covariates, not shown.

[d]Findings were adjusted for 9 covariates, not shown.

*$p \leq .10$. **$p \leq .05$. ***$p \leq .01$.

marginal.) In Chicago, this effect was seen only among offenders with at least three prior convictions. We found no sign that these TASC programs, compared to alternative interventions, led to greater reductions in property crime. (Data are not shown.) We were unable to examine possible effects on violent crime because the percentage of offenders self-reporting any violent crime was quite low at both the intake and the follow-up periods in the TASC and control/comparison groups.

When we examined new arrests and technical violations shown in state and local criminal justice records, we found no differences at three sites. In Birmingham and Portland, there were signs that TASC offenders were more likely to be arrested or to commit a technical violation during the follow-up period. Studies of intensive supervision programs (ISPs) have found similar effects on arrests and technical violations (Petersilia and Turner, 1990, 1993). This finding may reflect the fact that ISPs, like TASC, are meant to serve monitoring as well as rehabilitative functions. If offenders are watched more carefully, those who do not conform to requirements of the law are more likely to be detected and consequently arrested or charged with a technical violation than those under less stringent monitoring. From the standpoint of community safety, the greater likelihood of arrests and technical violations

among TASC offenders might actually be considered a sign of success, not failure.

Summary of Outcomes

An evaluation in which multiple outcomes are examined at multiple sites is virtually certain to produce complex findings. When so many comparisons are made, it is common to see some differences in the expected direction (favoring the more intensive intervention, in this case TASC) and other differences in the opposite direction. Because a few of these differences will have arisen by chance, the best approach to data interpretation is to look for patterns across sites and outcome measures.

Table 3 arrays the findings for each site in each outcome domain. An effect is shown favoring TASC (T) or the control/comparison group (C) if it appeared either in the site's sample as a whole or in a subsample. Findings for service delivery favored TASC at four of five sites. Findings for drug use favored TASC at three of five sites. At a fourth site, we found a marginally significant reduction in drug days favoring comparison offenders. Because this difference was marginal and appeared at only one site, we believe it is unreliable, and in any case, the overall pattern clearly favored TASC. Findings on

TABLE 3 **Main and Interactive Effects of TASC Programs**

OUTCOME	BIRMINGHAM	CANTON	CHICAGO	ORLANDO	PORTLAND
Service delivery	T*		T*	T*	T*
Drug-use days	T*		T*	C	
Drug-use frequency			T		
Number of drugs used	T*	T			
Days at risk ratio	T		T*		
Drug crimes	T*		T*		
Any arrest					C*
Any technical violation	C*				
Frequency of unprotected sex					T
Frequency of sex while high	T*		T*	T*	T*

Note: TASC = treatment alternatives to street crime. "T" and "C" entries denote a significant or near significant difference between TASC and control/comparison offenders overall or within at least one subsample. T means that TASC offenders outperformed the control/comparison group. C means that control/comparison offenders outperformed TASC offenders.

$p \leq .05$. Marginally significant differences, $.05 < p \leq .10$, are unmarked.

drug crimes favored TASC at two of five sites. In view of TASC's clearly favorable effect on drug use, its effect on drug crimes is quite plausible. As already noted, offenders who are monitored more closely are often more likely to be rearrested or charged with technical violations. Against this trend, self-report data showed that two TASC programs reduced drug crime.

DISCUSSION

The TASC program model includes a number of features that research and clinical experience have found to be important for drug treatment to be effective, and it is possibly the only model that combines all of these features: (a) coordination of criminal justice and treatment, (b) use of legal sanctions as incentives to enter and remain in treatment, (c) matching of offenders to appropriate treatment services, and (d) monitoring of offenders with drug testing and keeping criminal justice officials apprised of the offenders' performance. The value of TASC depends ultimately on whether handling offenders according to this model leads to greater reductions in drug use and other problem behavior than would be achieved otherwise. Our purpose was to evaluate the gains achieved when the TASC model of case management was added to the local ecology of criminal justice and treatment services.

TASC outcomes across sites were consistently favorable, although they were often modest or confined to high-risk offender subsamples. We believe the consistency of findings represents a clear signal of the effectiveness of the TASC model in different environments, in different client populations, and in tests within a highly rigorous research design. In particular, we note favorable effects at two sites in which the design was experimental and offenders were randomly assigned to TASC or an alternative treatment. TASC outperformed the alternative on one or more outcomes at each site.

Although reductions in drug use and crime were often modest, recovery from chronic and heavy drug use is an incremental process involving perhaps several cycles of drug use, treatment, abstinence, and relapse. We take a similar view of favorable outcomes found only in subsamples of TASC offenders, rather than in the samples as a whole. It is important to identify offender types for whom an intervention is more or less effective.

The pattern of findings in this study suggests that the TASC model had favorable effects among offenders whose behavior was more problematic, as indicated in baseline levels on the outcome measures or other characteristics associated with hard-core offending. This is precisely the type of offender who is most in need of intervention and who represents the greatest recurring cost to the public. Thus, the value of TASC programs might be enhanced, from the point of view of system efficacy, if offenders who are referred to TASC included a higher proportion of these more problematic offenders. Alternatively, although TASC assists local judges and probation agencies as a screening and assessment service, the fact that low-risk offenders often did no better in TASC than in alternate—and usually lower cost—placements suggests that the drug-use history threshold employed to place offenders in TASC may be too low in many jurisdictions. More careful selection and placement of high-risk offenders might extend the benefits of TASC.

Findings should be considered in light of the social and economic developments in the past two decades. When TASC began in the early 1970s, the primary illicit drug problem was heroin, treatment availability was increasing, and social services were relatively well funded. In addition, throughout the 1970s, TASC programs had more stable funding sources as well as policy and programmatic support at the federal level. The 1980s brought a dramatic shift in the environment within which TASC operated: Federal funding for TASC programs diminished and/or became less stable, cocaine replaced heroin as the nation's primary illicit drug problem, and the availability of drug treatment and other social services declined. These trends continued into the 1990s. All of these developments make it more difficult for TASC to bring about significant and enduring change in a large number of offenders. The appearance of consistent TASC effects in our evaluation is, in this context, all the more persuasive. The current context is a harsh reality for any intervention targeting drug-using offenders, not just TASC. However, TASC may be in a better position than many alternative interventions by virtue of the long experience of TASC program leaders, the well-conceived model of offender management represented in the Ten Critical Elements, and the strong links between TASC and both the treatment system and the criminal justice system.

Some of the existing constraints that may limit optimal outcomes from TASC programs are amenable to change. For example, assessment and treatment planning for offenders could be conducted during their pretrial or during-trial incarceration. Such on-site assessment would lead to several benefits, including reduction in the number of offenders who are directed to TASC but who fail to appear. If assessment indicates that TASC placement is suitable, the offender can remain incarcerated until a treatment plan and receiving facility can be arranged. Then, the offender can be immediately inducted into a treatment program without lengthy delays, during which the offender in the community can reoffend or choose not to appear once treatment arrangements have been finalized. Moreover, efforts should be implemented to integrate TASC with the drug-court movement that has received national attention in the past few years. The drug-court phenomenon has produced judicially directed interventions with goals similar to TASC. However, there is no uniform drug-court model or standard that is widely implemented, resulting in wide disparities in their philosophies, practices, and actual services provided to offenders. Where drug courts and TASC programs are geographically proximal, the courts should use the existing TASC infrastructure, which is designed and has the experience to serve drug-using offenders. In drug-court areas without an existing TASC program, judges and probation officials should consider developing one as a proven offender management structure.

Appendix TASC Critical Elements

ORGANIZATIONAL ELEMENTS

1. A broad base of support from the criminal justice system with a formal system for effective communication
2. A broad base of support from the treatment system with a formal system for effective communication
3. An independent TASC unit with a designated administrator
4. Required staff training, outlined in TASC policies and procedures
5. A system of data collection for both program management and evaluation

OPERATIONAL ELEMENTS AND PERFORMANCE STANDARDS

6. Explicit and agreed on eligibility criteria
7. Screening procedures for the early identification of eligible offenders
8. Documented procedures for assessment and referral
9. Documented policies, procedures, and technology for drug testing
10. Procedures for offender monitoring with established success/failure criteria and constant reporting to criminal justice referral source

Source: Bureau of Justice Assistance (1992).

REFERENCES

Anglin, M. D., Longshore, D., Turner, S., McBride, D., Inciardi, J., and Prendergast, M. (1996). *Studies of the functioning and effectiveness of treatment alternatives to street crime (TASC) programs* [Final report]. Los Angeles: UCLA Drug Abuse Research Center.

Bureau of Justice Assistance. (1989). *Treatment alternatives to street crime. TASC programs: Resource catalog.* Washington, DC: Bureau of Justice Assistance, U.S. Department of Justice.

Bureau of Justice Assistance (1992). *Treatment alternatives to street crime. TASC programs: Program brief* (NCJ Publication No. 129759). Washington, DC: Bureau of Justice Assistance, U.S. Department of Justice.

Bureau of Justice Statistics. (1993). *Drug and crime facts, 1992* (NCJ-139651). Washington, DC: Bureau of Justice Statistics, U.S. Department of Justice.

Chaiken, J. M., and Chaiken, M. R. (1982). *Varieties of criminal behavior* (RAND Publication No. R-2814). Santa Monica, CA: RAND.

Chou, C. -P., Hser, Y. -I., and Anglin, M. D. (1996). Pattern reliability of narcotics addicts' self-reported data: A confirmatory assessment of construct validity and consistency. *Substance Use and Misuse, 31*(9), 1189–1216.

Collins, J. J., Hubbard, R. L., Rachal, J. V., Cavanaugh, E. R., and Craddock, S. G. (1982). *Criminal justice clients in drug treatment.* Research Triangle Park, NC: Research Triangle Institute.

Hser, Y. -I., Anglin, M. D., and Chou, C. -P. (1992). Reliability of retrospective self-report by narcotics addicts. *Psychological Assessment, 4*(2), 207–213.

Hubbard, R. L., Collins, J. J., Rachal, J. V., and Cavanaugh, E. R. (1988). The criminal justice client in drug abuse treatment. In C. G. Leukefeld and F. M. Tims (Eds.), *Compulsory treatment of drug abuse: Research and clinical practice* (NIDA Research Monograph 86, pp. 57–80). Rockville, MD: National Institute on Drug Abuse.

Inciardi, J. A. (1987). Heroin use and street crime. In C. D. Chambers, J. A. Inciardi, D. M. Petersen, H. A. Siegal, and O. Z. White (Eds.), *Chemical dependencies: Patterns, costs, and consequences.* Athens: Ohio University Press.

Inciardi, J. A., and McBride, D. C. (1991). *Treatment alternatives to street crime: History, experiences, and issues* (DHHS Pub. No. ADM 92-1749). Rockville, MD: National Institute on Drug Abuse.

Johnson, B., and Wish, E. (Eds.). (1986). *Crime rates among drug-abusing offenders: Final report to the National Institute of Justice.* New York: Narcotic and Drug Research.

Marquis, K. H. (1981). *Quality of prisoner self-reports: Arrest and conviction response errors.* Santa Monica, CA: RAND.

Nurco, D. N., Kinlock, T. W., and Hanlon, T. E. (1990). The drugs-crime connection. In J. A. Inciardi (Ed.), *Handbook of drug control in the United States* (pp. 71–90). Westport, CT: Greenwood Press.

Petersilia, J., and Turner, S. (1990). *Intensive supervision probation for high-risk offenders: Findings from three California experiments* (RAND Publication No. R-3936-NIJ/BJA). Santa Monica, CA: RAND.

Petersilia, J., and Turner, S. (1993). Intensive probation and parole. In M. Tonry (Ed.), *Crime and justice: A review of research* (Vol. 17, pp. 281–335). Chicago: University of Chicago Press.

Speckart, G. R., and Anglin, M. D. (1986). Narcotics and crime: A causal modeling approach. *Journal of Quantitative Criminology, 2*, 3–28.

System Sciences. (1979). *Evaluation of treatment alternatives to street crime: National evaluation program, phase II report.* Washington, DC: National Institute of Law Enforcement and Criminal Justice.

Toborg, M. A., Levin, D. R., Milkman, R. H., and Couter, L. J. (1976). *Treatment alternatives to street crime (TASC) projects: National evaluation program, phase I summary report.* Washington, DC: Government Printing Office.

Weinman, B. (1990). Treatment Alternatives to Street Crime (TASC). In J. A. Inciardi (Ed.), *Handbook of drug control in the United States* (pp. 139–150). New York: Greenwood.

Wellisch, J., Prendergast, M., and Anglin, M. D. (1993). Criminal justice and drug treatment systems linkage: Federal promotion of interagency collaboration in the 1970s. *Contemporary Drug Problems, 20*, 611–650.

17

Drug Courts: A Conceptual Framework

DOUGLAS LONGSHORE

SUSAN TURNER

SUZANNE WENZEL

ANDREW MORRAL

ADELE HARRELL

DUANE McBRIDE

ELIZABETH DESCHENES

MARTIN IGUCHI

ABSTRACT

Structural and process characteristics of drug courts may have a major influence on offender outcomes. However, despite the existence of dozens of outcome evaluations in the drug court literature, it is impossible to draw clear conclusions regarding variability in outcomes in relation to drug court characteristics. We describe existing approaches to the description of drug court structure and process and argue that a new approach is needed. To address that need, we propose a conceptual framework of five drug court dimensions: leverage, population severity, program intensity, predictability, and rehabilitation emphasis. These dimensions, each scorable on a range from low to high, lend themselves to a systematic set of hypotheses regarding the effects of structure and process on drug court outcomes. Finally, we propose quantitative and qualitative methods for identifying such effects.

INTRODUCTION

Drug courts have proliferated as a greater number of criminal court judges and observers have come to see traditional jurisprudence as merely a revolving door for drug-using offenders. Under the direct supervision of a judge, offenders in drug court receive regular drug tests to monitor abstinence, drug abuse treatment, and other interventions intended to address more effectively the underlying causes of their criminal conduct. Given the large number of drug courts in the U.S. today, it is not surprising that their structure and processes vary widely. Some handle only first-time, minor offenders. In others, a broader or more serious range of offenders is eligible to participate. Some drug courts accept offenders before a plea is entered, whereas others take offenders only post-plea.

Some are quick to apply punitive sanctions, including discharge from drug court and imposition of sentence, when participants continue to use drugs. Other courts view occasional lapscs as a part of recovery and will retain drug-positive participants so long as they attend treatment and commit no new crimes.

Judges, court administrators, drug court advocates, and legislators are keenly interested in knowing how drug court structure and process influence offender outcomes because "[d]ifferent approaches . . . can result in significantly different outcomes and are . . . likely to require different types and levels of resources" (Drug Courts Program Office, 1998, p. 4). However, despite the existence of dozens of outcome evaluations in the drug court literature, it is impossible to draw clear conclusions on this issue.

The RAND Criminal Justice Program recently completed a study of 14 "implementation courts" funded by the Drug Courts Program Office at the National Institute of Justice in the 1995–96 funding cycle. Our purpose was to describe court structure and process and to assess the feasibility of rigorous outcome evaluation at each drug court. We reviewed internal evaluations of the 14 drug courts; examined data archives and management information systems, planned or in place; and interviewed local judges, court administrators, prosecutors, defense attorneys, service providers, and drug court evaluators. Our findings are reported in Turner et al. (2000).

In this paper we describe existing approaches to the characterization of drug court structure and process and argue that a new approach is needed. We then describe the five drug court dimensions that comprise the conceptual framework we developed in our evaluation. This framework is based on the "therapeutic jurisprudence" perspective (Hora, Schma, and Rosenthal, 1999) and draws upon the criminal justice literature and our experience in evaluating drug courts and other criminal justice interventions. The five dimensions are: *leverage*, *population severity*, *program intensity*, *predictability*, and *rehabilitation emphasis*. These dimensions, each scorable on a range from low to high, lend themselves to a systematic set of hypotheses regarding the effects of structure and process on drug court outcomes. Finally, we propose quantitative and qualitative methods for identifying such effects. While the framework is preliminary and subject to revision, we believe it can help to improve our understanding of what drug court characteristics matter and why.

BACKGROUND

The evaluation literature on drug courts indicates that they succeed in placing offenders in treatment and keeping them there; that monitoring of drug court participants is, as intended, more intensive than monitoring of offenders placed in other forms of community supervision; that drug use and criminal behavior are sharply curtailed when offenders participate in drug court; and that offenders who complete drug court may be less likely than noncompleters to recidivate (Belenko, 1998; Harrell, 1999). These findings are encouraging for drug courts as a class. However, because drug courts differ in target population, sanctioning protocol, and many other characteristics, it is important to know whether particular drug court characteristics are more or less effective than others.

What approaches can be used to encompass the range of structural and process characteristics of drug courts and to link those characteristics to outcomes? The most straightforward approach is a literature review, in which drug court evaluations are collated and synthesized with specific questions regarding structure and process in mind. But structure and process are not described fully, if at all, in many drug court evaluations, and the information they do provide is often not amenable to comparison (Goldkamp, 1999). For example, to see if outcomes differ between pre-plea and post-plea drug courts, we might scan the literature for evaluations of each. But pre- and post-plea drug courts will differ on other characteristics as well, and because the set of such characteristics is so numerous and open-ended, any given study, no matter how well-designed, will have measured and reported only some of them. Even as new studies become available, coverage of structural and process factors is not likely to be systematic. Measurement strategies will differ (Drug Courts Program Office, 1998), and coverage of the relevant factors will depend on resources available and evaluation priorities. Finally, research on drug courts has not been guided by any unifying conceptual framework for studying structure and process (Harrell, 1999). No one has formulated and tested specific hypotheses for how and why various drug court characteristics might influence outcomes.

An alternative to relying on finished evaluations is to use the raw data being compiled by the Drug Court Clearinghouse and Technical Assistance Project at American University. The database includes a great deal of descriptive information on drug court structure and process, such as program goals, costs, and funding sources; participant eligibility criteria; screening and assessment procedures; number and duration of program phases; services available; frequency of urine testing and court appearances; and requirements for program completion. The database has two major limitations, however. First, much of the data describe what Chen (1990) calls the normative, as opposed to the actual, implementation environment. That is, the database contains information on how drug courts are designed to operate rather than how they actually operate. Considerable discrepancies may exist between programs as intended and programs as implemented (Chen, 1990). Second, although the database provides an extensive and very useful listing of program characteristics, it has no organizing theoretical or conceptual scheme. It offers no guidance for identifying which of the many characteristics in the database ought to matter, i.e., which ones, taken singly or in combination, are likely to have a substantial effect on outcomes and why.

The best-known conceptualization of drug courts may be the "ten components" specified by the National Association of Drug Court Professionals (Drug Courts Program Office, 1997). These include, for example, frequent drug/alcohol testing, ongoing interaction between judge and participant, and prompt identification and placement of eligible offenders. The components offer a systematic view of drug court structure and process. However, their purpose is prescriptive; they are a minimum set of precepts that any drug court should follow. They are not a framework for assessing alternative drug court models when each model is (or in principle could be) congruent with the ten components. For example, they do not speak to the relative effects of pre- versus post-plea drug courts and do not tell us anything about levels of intensity (how much drug testing is "frequent" enough, and what is the right amount of "ongoing interaction" between judge and participant).

Similarly, Goldkamp (1999) has specified a "descriptive typology" based on seven dimensions of drug court. These include, for example, the target problem (e.g., heroin addiction or misdemeanor property crime); processing focus and adaptation (indicated by stage of intervention, geographic area covered by the court, method by which the drug court is integrated with other criminal justice agencies, and administrative approach); structure and content of treatment; and extent of system-wide support for the drug court among other criminal justice, health, and social service agencies. As it stands, this typology cannot be straightforwardly applied in analyses of drug court structure and process. One of the dimensions, extent of system-wide support, is a contextual characteristic, not an aspect of structure or process. (We do not mean to suggest that system support is irrelevant to drug court outcomes, but rather that it is outside the scope of characteristics directly defining what happens to drug court participants.) More important, while hypotheses are implicit in some dimensions (e.g., outcomes should be better when a drug court is well-integrated with other criminal justice agencies), Goldkamp did not propose an explicit, systematic set of hypotheses for how and why each dimension might be related to drug court outcomes. Finally, while the indicators or aspects cited under each dimension in Goldkamp's typology suffice for purposes of broad definition and illustration, they are not spelled out well enough (and apparently were not intended) to serve as a basis for formal comparisons of drug courts. Examples of this limitation arise with respect to the dimension called "processing focus and adaptation." Goldkamp did not enumerate the range of choices available as the "method by which drug court is integrated with other criminal justice agencies," did not say how or why drug court outcomes might vary in relation to their geographic coverage, and did not specify the set of "administrative approaches" he had in mind or how they might affect outcomes.

CONCEPTUAL FRAMEWORK

We have argued that drug court research currently has no unifying perspective (or, short of that, a set of competing perspectives) regarding the structural and process characteristics of drug courts. For maximum value, such a perspective must have five features. First, it must be systematic; it must cover all relevant drug court characteristics. Second, it must be parsimonious. That is, while covering all relevant dimensions, it must also be simple enough to be manageable in analysis. Third, measures of each characteristic must be amenable to direct comparison across drug courts. Fourth, measures must reflect structure and process as actually implemented—not simply as planned, intended, or drawn up in memos and protocols. Fifth, a conceptual perspective on drug courts should lead to hypotheses that are testable and relevant to policy and practice. For example, are outcomes more favorable in drug courts quick to impose severe consequences for noncompliance than in courts more patient with noncompliance? One hypothesis is that the former sort of drug court is more effective with serious offenders but not with first-time or lightweight offenders, for whom a more gradual approach might suffice to produce compliance. As a final comment on hypotheses, we note that hypothesis testing is more straightforward if drug court characteristics are conceptualized and measured with directionality, e.g., from less to more or low to high. Directionality is descriptive only; it does not imply quality. For example, a drug court scored high on Goldkamp's "target problem" dimension is serving a more severe class of drug-using offenders than a court scored low, but the high score does not mean the court is run more professionally.

In the conceptual framework proposed here, we have tried to address, or at least to begin addressing, each of the requirements above. The framework has five dimensions: leverage, population severity, program intensity, predictability, and rehabilitation emphasis. The first two dimensions are structural characteristics of drug court. *Leverage* refers to the nature of consequences faced by incoming participants if they later fail to meet program requirements and are discharged from drug court. *Population severity* refers to characteristics of offenders deemed eligible to enter drug court. The other three dimensions are process characteristics. They describe what happens to participants as they proceed through the drug court program.

In developing the framework, we attempted to make explicit a set of structural and procedural precepts implied in the emerging criminal justice perspective known as "therapeutic jurisprudence" (Hora, Schma, and Rosenthal, 1999). In this perspective, formalistic application of the law is de-emphasized, and greater attention is paid to the consequences of legal decisions and procedures. We also took account of the NADCP's ten components (Drug Courts Program Office, 1997); "think pieces" on drug court by Goldkamp (1999), Harrell (1999), and the Bureau of Justice Assistance (1993); reviews of the drug court literature (Belenko, 1998; Inciardi, McBride, and Rivers, 1996; Terry, 1999; U.S. General Accounting Office, 1997); published and unpublished evaluations of individual drug courts; and literature on criminal deterrence. For ideas regarding empirical indicators, we consulted the database compiled by Drug Court Clearinghouse and Technical Assistance Project at American University, drug court monitoring guidelines such as those from the Drug Courts Program

Office (1998), and data we obtained from drug courts participating in our evaluation. In this section, we describe the five dimensions and offer examples of empirical indicators for each.

Leverage

Leverage refers to the seriousness of consequences faced by participants who fail to meet program requirements and are discharged from drug court. Leverage depends, perhaps heavily, on the court's entry point—pre-plea, post-plea, or probation. In pre-plea or deferred prosecution courts, entry to the program occurs before an offender is required to enter a plea. Upon completion of all program requirements, the charge is reduced or dropped. Pre-plea courts may have limited leverage because participants have not pleaded guilty and may have no sentence pending. Moreover, after pre-plea participants are discharged for noncompliance, the case may be too "cold" to re-open. In post-plea or deferred judgment courts, however, entry to the program occurs only after an offender pleads guilty. Upon program completion, the plea can be stricken and the case dismissed or expunged. But if an offender fails the program, his/her case moves directly to sentencing and possible incarceration. Thus the stakes may be high, and leverage strong, in a post-plea drug court. Finally, in probation drug courts, participants have a conviction and are entering drug court in lieu of incarceration or other sanction. Probation drug courts may have varying degrees of leverage, depending on the seriousness of consequences for program failure in relation to the seriousness of the sanction otherwise awaiting the participant. In any event, it is important to distinguish the consequences of program discharge, i.e., what happens after offenders fail drug court, from the consequences they face during participation in drug court. The leverage dimension is based on the former. The latter is addressed below.

The simplest and most objective indicator of leverage is the percentage of participants who come to the drug court at the pre- or post-plea entry point. The percentage is of course 100% in courts with only one or the other entry point, but many courts accept a mix of pre- and post-plea cases. The subjective aspect of leverage, i.e., participants' perception of it, may also be important, especially for courts accepting cases on probation. What do participants believe is likely to happen if they are discharged for program failure? What is the perceived aversiveness of those consequences? We therefore propose both objective and subjective indicators of leverage.

Our hypothesis is that, other characteristics being equal, outcomes will be more favorable when drug courts have greater actual or perceived leverage over participants. However, courts may be designed for greater leverage when the eligible population includes more serious offenders (Drug Strategies, 1997). Thus, the leverage hypothesis may need to be tested within categories of participants. How does the drug court's degree of leverage affect outcomes among minor offenders, and, separately, how does it affect outcomes among serious offenders or among offenders with more at stake (e.g., those who stand to lose their professional license or certification if they have a criminal conviction on record)?

Population Severity

This dimension is based on a distinction between drug courts set up to target a hardcore population of addicted and persistent offenders (one extreme) and drug courts dealing with offenders whose offense history is short and relatively minor and whose drug use is "recreational" (the other extreme). The latter may be routed to drug court not so much because they need intensive treatment/supervision but because the local criminal justice system views the drug court as a welcome new resource for processing cases. This possibility is perhaps most apparent when the target population is first-time or minor offenders, system resources are stretched thin, and prosecutors are using the drug court essentially as a way to move cases through the system. Of course many drug court populations fall between the high- to low-severity extremes (Center on Substance Abuse Treatment, 1996; Harrell, 1999; U.S. General Accounting Office, 1997).

Because eligibility for drug court and, more importantly, the participants' likelihood of success may depend on lifetime patterns of drug use and crime as well as on the instant offense, we believe that both current and lifetime indicators of misconduct should be used in gauging population severity. Current drug use severity can be assessed as the percentage of drug court cases who meet clinical criteria for drug abuse or dependence. This percentage can be found in records of formal screening/diagnostic assessments employed by the drug court and/or inferred from proxy variables such as frequency of recent use and self-reported need for treatment. Indicators of lifetime drug use severity, such as average number of prior treatment episodes among drug court participants, are also relevant. Criminal severity can be inferred from the ratio of felonies to misdemeanors among current charges faced by participants on the caseload and the same ratio in their criminal records. (Current charges and officially recorded charges may not accurately reflect the seriousness of acts committed by an individual participant, but they do provide an accurate overall population severity measure, useful for comparison purposes.) Additional indicators are the ratio of cases charged only with drug possession to cases charged with nondrug offenses and, for a more detailed look at criminal severity, a score reflecting the overall seriousness of current and past offenses committed by the drug court's offender population. A crime index like the one in McBride (1981) can be used for this purpose. Listed in order from high to low seriousness, his crime categories are: (1) serious crimes against the person (murder, rape, manslaughter, aggravated assault); (2) less serious crimes against the person (e.g., simple assault); (3) robbery; (4) property crime; (5) drug law violations; (6) income-producing victimless crimes (e.g., gambling); and (7) other (e.g., vagrancy, desertion, and technical violations of parole or probation).

Some readers may wish to consider additional indicators of population severity, such as age, gender, or employment history. Moreover, percent of participants with serious mental disorder and percent homeless may be germane for courts handling populations with a nonnegligible number of such participants. While not meaning to ignore the potential importance of such indicators, we suggest that some may be sufficiently reflected in participants' drug use and crime. In any case, we propose an initial focus on drug use and crime because these are the two severity indicators most clearly and broadly relevant to decisions regarding how to set up a drug court—what population to target and what services to provide.

Our "main effects" hypothesis is that courts structured to deal with more serious offenders will have worse outcomes. However, the influence of population severity on outcomes may depend on other dimensions in the framework. For example, as suggested above, outcomes for a more severe population may be favorable in courts that have strong leverage over participants but less favorable in courts where leverage is weaker. In addition, outcomes for a more severe population may be better when program requirements are intensive enough (see below) to have an impact on hardcore offenders.

Program Intensity

This dimension refers to requirements for participating in and completing drug court. These always include urine testing, court appearances, and drug abuse treatment (Harrell, 1999). Other obligations may be imposed as well, such as employment, suitable housing, completion of a G.E.D., and payment of fines or restitution. It is important to note that intensity does not refer to requirements actually met by the participant. That is affected by self-selection. Neither does intensity refer to what happens to the noncompliant participant. That too is affected by self-selection in that additional requirements are triggered by actions of the participant. Instead, we mean to focus cleanly on a dimension of drug court itself: what participants understand to be the minimum requirements for program completion.

Indicators of intensity include the required frequency of urine testing and court appearances, required hours of treatment and other required services, and fine and restitution amounts. Programs vary in duration (typically 12 to 18 months, sometimes longer) and are often broken into phases—more intensive at first and less intensive for compliant participants near program completion. It may therefore be important to measure intensity on a per-month or per-phase basis and to take overall duration into account as well. For intensity data, it may be misleading to rely solely on written or standard protocols. These may not reflect the requirements to which many or most participants are actually held.

Our hypothesis is that drug courts with more intensive requirements will show more favorable outcomes. However, along with a main effect of intensity, there may be contingent effects. For example, a high degree of intensity may be required for success with a more severe population whereas low or moderate intensity may suffice for less severe offenders. We also expect that program intensity will be associated with population severity. Courts with more intensive programs are likely to be more acceptable to offenders facing a harsher traditional sanction than to those facing a lighter one because the aversiveness of participating in a high-intensity program might appear to outweigh the aversiveness of a lighter traditional sanction.

Predictability

This dimension reflects the degree to which participants know how the court will respond if they are compliant or noncompliant (Harrell, 1999). Goldkamp's (1999) concept of client accountability is similar, but he was referring to the kinds of responses used by a drug court to reward good performance and discourage poor performance. We refer to the predictability or certainty of these responses. The literature on criminal deterrence shows that sanctions are more effective if more certain and more swift (Blumstein, Cohen, and Nagin, 1978; Nagin, 1998). Behavioral research also suggests that sanctions are more effective when people believe they have the opportunity to behave as desired and thus avoid the sanction. Absent this perception, the participant's response may be "learned helplessness" (Seligman, 1975). Marlowe and Kirby (1999) have developed a number of insights from behavioral research specifically with respect to drug courts. They argue, for example, that the court's expectations should be clear, that actions taken by the court should be consistent with expectations, and that delivery of sanctions should be "regular and immediate" (see also Drug Courts Program Office, 1998; National Drug Court Institute, 1999).

The range and frequency of rewards for good behavior may vary among drug courts, and the rate at which sanctions become more punitive (as in a "graduated sanctions" strategy) may be slow or fast. Those aspects of drug court are captured in the dimension we call *rehabilitation emphasis* (see below). The ultimate sanction, for program failure, may or may not be dire; that is captured in *leverage*. *Predictability* has to do with whether participants know what the court's expectations are, believe their behavior will be detected by the court, and know with high probability how the court will respond to their behavior.

Indicators of predictability may be drawn from court records. For instance, the court's various responses (e.g., counsel, warning, or a brief jail sentence) to the first positive urinalysis test can be tabulated for all cases with at least one positive test, its responses to the second positive test can be tabulated for all cases with at least two positive tests, and so on. Courts with less variability in their responses to each positive test are more predictable; participants are more likely to know what will probably happen to them if they test positive once, twice, and so on. Additional indicators of predictability are the percentage of all positive tests that triggered some sort of response and, more broadly, the percentage of participants for whom the recorded series of responses (both rewards and punishments) conforms to the stipulated protocol. At the participant level of analysis, one indicator of predictability is whether responses to multiple positive drug tests steadily increase in severity. Regarding the swiftness of response, one can measure the time elapsed between drug use and detection, the time elapsed between detection and response, and the time elapsed between other noncompliance (e.g., failure to appear in court) and response (e.g., contact with case manager or arrest).

Of course, it is also possible to assess predictability by asking participants, at the outset of their enrollment in drug court and periodically thereafter, to report their views on how likely the various rewards and punishments are and how swiftly they will occur. Participants' perceptions of procedural fairness—whether the court "plays favorites" or is easily manipulated—may also be relevant (Harrell, 1999; Tyler, 1988, 1994). If the court's rulings conform to expectations laid out in advance and are consistent across similar cases, participants are likely to view the court as predictable. The obvious advantage of participant surveys is that they provide direct evidence of predictability as perceived. Our hypothesis is that drug court outcomes are more favorable when rewards and sanctions are more predictable.

Rehabilitation Emphasis

The final dimension in our framework is the emphasis placed on rehabilitation as against other court functions, including case processing and punishment. This dimension takes on particular significance in light of legal philosophies known as restorative justice (Braithwaite, 1999; Kurki, 1999) and therapeutic jurisprudence (Wexler and Winick, 1991), in which criminal justice is viewed more as a therapeutic tool and less as a formalistic and essentially punitive one. To a greater or lesser degree, most drug courts reflect these philosophies (Hora et al., 1999).

Consider the distinction between expedited drug case management courts and drug treatment courts. The former employ innovative procedural rules tailored to drug-using offenders. The latter focus on offenders' needs for drug abuse treatment and other services. Procedures are less formal in drug treatment courts, and prosecutors and defense attorneys are collaborative or at least less adversarial. It is likely that, compared to expedited drug case management courts, drug treatment courts place more emphasis on rehabilitation (Hora et al., 1999). However, it is also likely that the emphasis on rehabilitation varies considerably even within the range of courts that call themselves or operate as drug treatment courts.

Indicators of rehabilitation emphasis may include the degree to which all actors (especially defense attorneys and treatment providers) are involved in deciding how to handle cases, both in review sessions and, more visibly, in court; degree to which time and other resources are devoted to multiple needs of participants; degree to which the judge and other actors take a therapeutic, as distinct from a legalistic, view of their roles; number of positive drug tests typically allowed before the court imposes an intermediate sanction (e.g., brief jail stay) or discharges the participant; whether participants who fail the program are later allowed to re-enter, the stringency of re-entry criteria, and the ratio of re-entry offenders to the total offender population. Satel's (1998) observational indicators of drug court dynamics also seem on point. These include, for example, the extent to which judges speak directly to participants and listen to what participants have to say; the amount of time spent by the judge with each participant; and proximity of participants to the bench. Our hypothesis is that outcomes are more favorable when drug courts place more emphasis on rehabilitation.

METHOD

To make hypothesis testing more straightforward, we have conceptualized the five dimensions as directional; they range from low to high. As indicated above, we view this range as descriptive, not evaluative. Herein we propose a method for scoring drug courts on these five dimensions. We also propose two methods for analyzing scores.

Scoring

As scores, we propose simple numerical ratings—low (1), moderate (2), or high (3). Indicators such as those cited above can serve as the raw data from which to derive scores. These indicators vary by source. Many are available in the American University database; others are available in case records and administrative documents at individual drug courts and from prior evaluation reports. Still others require primary data collection via interviews and observation. Indicators also vary in other ways. Some are quantitative; others, qualitative. Some are objective and clear in meaning; others are subjective and have to be interpreted with an awareness of their source and in context.

Scoring should probably begin with indicators that are objective and most easily compared. For example, number of drug tests and number of court appearances are objective indicators of drug court intensity. They are also easy to compare; across drug courts, the average number of tests required for participants (not just the number specified in the protocol) typically ranges from as few as one or two per month to as many as two or three per week, whereas the average number of required court appearances might range from one per month to one per week. Courts averaging only one or two drug tests per month and only one court appearance per month can provisionally be scored low; courts averaging two to three drug tests and one court appearance per week, high; and courts falling somewhere in between, moderate. Raters can then turn to additional indicators, which, although less objective or not so readily comparable, help to verify the overall score and provide a proper context for interpreting the various indicators as a set. The important overall point is that scoring does not require that all indicators be available and unambiguous. Researchers need only to have enough data to converge upon a score. In social science evaluation, this method is often called data triangulation (Greene and McClintock, 1985).

The method we propose may actually help to overcome the weaknesses of disparate and incomplete raw data. In an interpretive approach, individual data elements can be compared, weighed against others, and read in context before they are synthesized into an overall score on each dimension. To guard against the problem of unreliable scoring (e.g., different raters might derive different scores from the same indicators), steps in the scoring procedure should include inter-rater consistency checks and cross-validation.

Analytic Procedures

The choice of analytic procedure depends on how many courts are included in the dataset. With a sufficient number of courts, the dataset can be analyzed by means of quantitative techniques such as logistic or least squares regression and analysis of variance. The analyst can explore the importance of any given dimension by testing it as a predictor of drug court outcomes in simple regression, for example, and gauge the relative importance of all dimensions by testing them in a multivariate framework. Moreover, by adding interaction terms to the set of predictors, the analyst can see how particular combinations of drug court characteristics are associated with outcomes. Because such techniques are widely known, we do not offer any further comment on them.

If the number of courts in the database is not sufficient for quantitative analysis, an alternative procedure, known as the cumulative case study method, is

available (see Campbell, 1975; Cook, Leviton, and Shadish, 1985; Greene, 1980; U.S. General Accounting Office, 1987). Because many readers may be unfamiliar with the method, we describe it here in some detail. First, a hypothetical bivariate relationship is specified between a drug court dimension and an outcome. For example, one hypothesis is that high leverage leads to high rates of gainful employment. Second, the dataset is queried to identify courts with scores wide apart on each. Suppose, for example, that Drug Court A is found to be high on leverage and high on employment, while Drug Court B is low on both of these. This pattern of scores would be consistent with the hypothesis that high leverage boosts employment among participants. The hypothesis will gain strength if, in a third step, several additional courts are found in which the direction of this relationship is the same and few or no courts in which it is reversed.

Analysis will often entail a final step in which possible interactions between dimensions and other explanatory factors are taken up for consideration. For example, is high leverage associated with a high participant employment rate whether drug court intensity is high or low, or do high leverage and high intensity combine for an enhanced effect on employment? Additional explanatory factors, outside the realm of drug court structure and process, may also pertain. If the outcome of interest is employment, a low rate of employment in the local community may undermine the effect of drug court on this outcome. Low employment suggests low job opportunity, and high leverage might have little or no impact on participants' employment in that circumstance. To explore this possibility, data on local employment rates can be added to the dataset. Researchers can then scan the data to find Drug Court C, which, like Drug Court A, is high on leverage; but, like Drug Court B, is located in a community with a low overall employment rate. If employment is high in Drug Court C, despite the local unemployment problem, such evidence strongly supports the hypothesis that leverage boosts employment. Finding that employment is low in Drug Court C, as in Drug Court B, is inconsistent with that hypothesis.

While the cumulative case study method lacks the power and persuasiveness of multivariate techniques, it can serve to move the examination of drug court characteristics from an ad hoc descriptive level to an explanatory level. It is important to note, moreover, that hypothesis testing can be bivariate (one drug court dimension and one outcome at a time) and that tests of other explanatory factors can be based on a relatively small number of courts. Analyses will be more persuasive when the separation between courts on the dimensions and outcomes of interest is fairly wide and when the number of courts available for analysis is greater.

Finally, using either the cumulative case study method or quantitative techniques, we may be able to identify discrete drug court types or models by examining patterns of scores on two or more dimensions. For example, as we mentioned above, courts high on population severity may tend to exert more leverage. They may also be high on intensity and predictability but low on rehabilitation emphasis. A pattern of this sort would suggest drug courts set up to handle a hardcore drug-using population by means of close monitoring, strict enforcement, and relatively little tolerance for continued drug use. If such patterns can be detected in the dataset, research on drug court effectiveness will be possible at the model level of analysis. In addition, practitioners who wish to consider different drug court options will be able to specify a particular model (i.e., a configuration of two or more dimensions) and query the dataset to see what outcomes are associated with that model.

CONCLUSION

It is important to be able to examine relationships between structural and process characteristics of drug courts and outcomes. Without this capability, it is not possible to identify the particular aspects of drug court that explain its outcomes or to compare alternative models of drug court (Goldkamp, 1999). We have proposed a conceptual framework meant to focus, in a simple but comprehensive way, on crucial structural and process dimensions of drug courts. These dimensions, scorable on a low-to-high range, lend themselves to a systematic set of hypotheses regarding the effects of structure and process on drug court outcomes. In three particular ways—the systematic conceptual view of drug courts, the directionality of the five dimensions, and formulation of explicit hypotheses—we believe the framework can help to improve our understanding of what drug court characteristics matter and why.

Testing hypotheses regarding the effects of drug court structure and process will, of course, require specification of the outcomes of primary interest and methods for measuring them. Having chosen to focus on drug court structure and process, we do not offer extended comment on drug court outcomes except to

echo the prevailing view that more work on this topic is needed (Belenko, 1998; Drug Courts Program Office, 1998; U.S. General Accounting Office, 1997). Some outcomes (e.g., the percent of participants who enter the recommended treatment and the average proportion of treatment sessions attended by participants) may be easy to document. Program retention rates, on the other hand, are interpretable only when linked to a timeframe (e.g., retention for 30, 60, 90, or 180 days). Program completion rates are comparable across drug courts only if defined as the percent of all offenders accepted into drug court who stayed long enough to complete each program requirement. Measuring drug use and recidivism is perhaps most difficult. For example, the percent of participants who test positive while in the program depends, in part, on how frequently they are tested; thus, as an outcome indicator, percent drug-positive must be adjusted for testing frequency. In addition, indicators of post-program success depend on when the follow-up is done (how long program participants were "at-risk"). For these reasons, developing an appropriate set of drug court outcome dimensions and indicators for each requires a strategy much like the one we used with respect to drug court structure and process. Outcome dimensions need to be comprehensive yet manageably few in number; comparable across courts; and scored in a global, interpretive way.

Readers may believe that our framework fails to account for all relevant characteristics of drug courts. We acknowledge this possibility. However, we wanted to keep the framework simple and focused on drug court structure and process. Thus, we did not consider "external" or contextual factors such as system-wide support for the drug court or incentives/disincentives influencing an offender's decision to enter drug court. There are of course many "internal" drug court characteristics, such as years of staff experience or the ratio of staff to participants, that might influence drug court outcomes. Why are these not covered in our framework? First, we wanted to characterize drug courts at a conceptual rather than an operational level. Second, while any number of additional characteristics may be important to drug court outcomes, we believe that their influence occurs via dimensions in the framework. A high staff-to-participant ratio, for example, is relevant to the extent that it affects drug court intensity and/or predictability.

In our ongoing research, we expect to re-assess the framework periodically on conceptual grounds (e.g., dimensions may need to be added or redefined) as well as operational grounds (e.g., it may be necessary to improve inter-rater reliability). Thus, while the framework reflects our current judgment of what drug court characteristics matter and why, it remains preliminary.

Acknowledgments

The research described in this report was supported by grant #98-DC-VX-K003 from the National Institute of Justice with funds transferred from the Drug Court Program Office, United States Department of Justice. Points of view are those of the authors and do not necessarily reflect the official position or policies of the National Institute of Justice or the Drug Court Program Office.

REFERENCES

Belenko, S. (1998). Research on drug courts: A critical review. *National Drug Court Institute Review, I,* 1–42.

Blumstein, A., Cohen, J., and Nagin, D. (Eds.). (1978). *Deterrence and incapacitation: Estimating the effects of criminal sanctions on crime rates.* Washington, DC: National Academy Press.

Braithwaite, J. (1999). Restorative justice: Assessing optimistic and pessimistic accounts. In M. Tonry (Ed.), *Crime and justice: A review of research* (pp. 1–127). Chicago: University of Chicago Press.

Bureau of Justice Assistance. (1993). *Special drug courts* (Program Brief, NCJ 144531). Washington, DC: U.S. Department of Justice, Office of Justice Programs.

Campbell, D. T. (1975). "Degrees of freedom" and the case study. *Comparative Political Studies, 8,* 178–193.

Center for Substance Abuse Treatment. (1996). *Treatment drug courts: Integrating substance abuse treatment with legal case processing* (DHHS Publication No. SMA 96-3113). Treatment Improvement Protocol (TIP) Series 23. Rockville, MD: U.S. Department of Health and Human Services.

Chen, H.-T. (1990). *Theory-driven evaluations.* London: Sage Publications.

Cook, T. D., Leviton, L., and Shadish, W. R. (1985). Program evaluation. In G. Lindzey and E. Aronson (Eds.), *Handbook of social psychology* (3d ed.). New York: Random House.

Drug Courts Program Office. (1997). *Defining drug courts: The key components.* Washington, DC: Office of Justice Programs, U.S. Department of Justice.

Drug Courts Program Office. (1998). *Drug court monitoring, evaluation, and management information systems* (NCJ 171138). Washington, DC: Office of Justice Programs, U.S. Department of Justice.

Drug Strategies. (1997). *Cutting crime: Drug courts in action.* Washington, DC: Drug Strategies.

Fiscella, K., Franks, P., Gold, M. R., and Clancy, C. M. (2000). Inequality in quality: Addressing socioeconomic, racial, and ethnic disparities in health care. *Journal of the American Medical Association, 283*(19), 2579–2584.

Goldkamp, J. S. (1999). Challenges for research and innovation: When is a drug court not a drug court? In W. Clinton Terry (Ed.), *The early drug courts: Case studies in judicial innovation* (pp. 166–177). Thousand Oaks, CA: Sage Publications.

Greene, D. (1980). Inductive analysis of multiple case study data. Paper presented at the Annual Meeting of the American Educational Research Association, Boston, MA.

Greene J., and McClintock, C. (1985). Triangulation in evaluation. *Evaluation Review, 9,* 523–545.

Harrell, A. (1999). Understanding the impact of drug courts. Unpublished paper.

Hora, P. F., Schma, W. G., and Rosenthal, J. T. A. (1999). Therapeutic jurisprudence and the drug treatment court movement: Revolutionizing the criminal justice system's response to drug abuse and crime in America. *Notre Dame Law Review, 74,* 439–538.

Huddleston, C. W. (1999). Commentary: Jail-based treatment and re-entry drug courts: A unique opportunity for collaboration and change. *National Drug Court Institute Review, II,* 87–106.

Inciardi, J. A., McBride, D. C., and Rivers, J. E. (1996). *Drug control and the courts.* Thousand Oaks, CA: Sage Publications.

Kurki, L. (1999). *Incorporating restorative and community justice into American sentencing and corrections* (NCJ 175723). Washington, DC: National Institute of Justice.

Marlowe, D. B., and Kirby, K. C. (1999). Effective use of sanctions in drug courts: Lessons from behavioral research. *National Drug Court Institute Review, II,* 1–15.

McBride, D. (1981). Drugs and violence. In J. A. Inciardi (Ed.), *The drugs–crime connection.* Beverly Hills, CA: Sage Publications.

Nagin, D. S. (1998). Criminal deterrence research at the outset of the twenty-first century. In M. Tonry (Ed.), *Crime and justice: A review of research* (Vol. 23) (pp. 1–42). Chicago: University of Chicago Press.

National Drug Court Institute. (1999). *Drug courts: A research agenda.* Alexandria, VA: National Drug Court Institute.

Satel, S. (1998). Observational study of courtroom dynamics in selected drug courts. *National Drug Court Institute Review, I,* 43–72.

Seligman, M. E. P. (1975). *Helplessness.* New York: W. H. Freeman and Co.

Terry, W. Clinton (Ed.). (1999). *The early drug courts: Case studies in judicial innovation.* Thousand Oaks, CA: Sage Publications.

Turner, S., Longshore, D., Wenzel, S., Fain, T., Morral, A., and Iguchi, M. (2000). Drug court evaluation II: Creating a drug court typology and assessing program evaluability. Final report in progress.

Tyler, T. (1988). What is procedural justice—criteria used by citizens to assess the fairness of legal procedures. *Law and Society Review, 22,* 103–135.

Tyler, T. (1994). Psychological models of the justice motive: Antecedents of distributive and procedural justice. *Journal of Personality and Social Psychology, 67,* 850–863.

U.S. General Accounting Office. (1997). *Drug courts: Overview of growth, characteristics, and results* (GAO/GGD-97-106). Washington, DC: U.S. General Accounting Office.

U.S. General Accounting Office. (1987). *Case study evaluations* (PEMD Transfer Paper 9). Washington, DC: U.S. General Accounting Office.

Wexler, D. B., and Winick, B. J. (1991). Therapeutic jurisprudence as a new approach to mental health law policy analysis and research. *University of Miami Law Review, 979.*

18

Restorative Justice and a New Criminal Law of Substance Abuse

JOHN BRAITHWAITE

ABSTRACT

The healing process of restorative justice might contribute to the treatment of substance abuse because it can deliver the love and caring to motivate holistic change in a life. Restorative justice is about repairing injustice, and there are important ways that substance abuse is implicated in the generation of injustice. Some case studies illustrate how (a) a restorative approach to substance abuse can catalyze confrontation of a profound community injustice and (b) confronting injustice can help tackle substance abuse. At present, most restorative justice programs fail to achieve either dynamic, sweeping substance abuse under the carpet. Criminalization of the harm caused by substance abuse (e.g., burglary to support a heroin habit) may be an effective way of reducing substance abuse when it is used to trigger well-designed restorative processes. The research and development needed to test this hypothesis is outlined.

SUBSTANCE ABUSE AND INJUSTICE

In restorative justice processes, stakeholders sit in a circle and discuss how to restore the victimized, the victimizers, and the community following an injustice. Restorative justice means a process where all the stakeholders affected by an injustice have an opportunity to discuss its consequences and what is to be done to right the wrong. Is substance abuse an injustice? This is a hard question, one on which Philip Pettit and I have had a little to say in the past (Braithwaite and Petit, 1990, pp. 92–100). The contribution of this article will not be to wade into those philosophical issues. Let me simply assert that substance abuse can be a source of profound injustice. Substance abuse by a family member can destroy the life of another family member in a way that is painfully unjust. Recognition by a substance abuser of the injustice caused by stealing from friends and family, lying, or other untrustworthy behavior is often the kind of recognition of injustice that motivates change through restorative processes.

In some restorative conferences I have convened or seen, victims (of theft) bearing the burden of injustice out of love for the offender, offering support from one friend or family member to another, moved substance abusers to want to be part of healing the relationships. Because substance abusers routinely steal from loved ones and friends who protect them by declining to lodge complaints and because abusers often suffer unacknowledged shame for putting their loved ones in this position, restorative justice programs outside the state criminal justice system can provide an opportunity for these hurts to be healed. The hope is that the process of confronting hurts and acknowledging shame to loved ones they care about will motivate a commitment to rehabilitation in a way that meetings with more unfamiliar victims would not.

There is much evidence reviewed by Muck et al. (2001) that prevention of problems such as substance abuse and crime can work. There is also a lot of evidence that mostly it does not. My hypothesis is that the key reason for the gap between preventive promise and the reality of practice is motivation. The person with the substance abuse or crime problem is not motivated to change. This hypothesis is implicit in Prochaska, DiClemente, and Norcross's (1992) six-stage model of how people move out of addictive behaviors. The first three stages involve moving from having no intention to change, to becoming aware that there is a problem, to motivation to take action. Furthermore, my hypothesis is that love is a source of acknowledgment and motivation, as is empathic engagement with the injustices that others suffer. The empirical evidence is that the experience of love is a key ingredient in successful restorative justice processes in a way that it is not an important ingredient of successful court cases (Ahmed, Harris, Braithwaite, and Braithwaite, 2001), that empathy is greater in restorative justice conferences than in court cases (Ahmed et al., 2001), and that empathy predicts success in restorative justice processes (Maxwell and Morris, 1999). Redemption rituals assist motivational transformation (Maruna, 2001), and redemption is earned through repairing injustice (Bazemore, 1999).

In such rituals, old debates about whether it is right to blame or punish people for substance abuse are not relevant. In restorative justice processes, it is just fine to allow those who are responsible for injustice to believe "It is not my fault, but it is my responsibility" (Brickman et al., 1982). It becomes morally possible for poverty and drugs to be blamed for past errors. This follows Jesse Jackson's political prescription: "You are not responsible for being down, but you are responsible for getting up." For the victim of substance abuse, the "liberating life narrative" (Henry and Milovanovic, 1996, p. 224) that restorative justice might draw out can be about action under the influence of a drug as "not the real me." Maruna (2001) defined an archaeology of hope as one that motivates a restorying (Zehr, 2000) of the self as basically good. Maruna found empirically that desistance from crime is associated with a restorying that in cases of substance abuse means redefining the self as "not like that anymore," "not like I was when the drug had hold of me." Maruna also found that in redemption rituals, a recurrent feature of finding the "real me" (and of desistance) is a desire to help others suffering the same struggles. For example, one of the things I have seen happen in a conference I have convened is a young substance abuser urging an adult neighbor (who he loved and had victimized by burglary) to try one of the programs he had experienced for her minor problem of substance abuse. She agreed to do so! Just as one of the best ways to learn is to teach, Maruna's research shows that one of the best ways to be helped is to help.

So, restorative justice sidesteps questions of whether it is right or wrong to punish substance abuse with the following move. If substance abuse is part of the story of injustice, part of what it is important to understand to come to terms with the injustice, then both the substance abuse and the injustice it causes are likely to be among the things participants will wish to see healed in the restorative process. Another thing they might want to see healed is hurt and injustice arising from attempts to punish substance abuse. I have seen conferences in Australia on marijuana use where much of the discussion was around the inappropriateness of the police intervening through threatening to invoke the criminal law against the marijuana use. Justice under the restorative model is an emergent property of deliberative democracy. Citizens are given a space where they can contest laws they believe to be unjust or laws that might be just in some abstract sense but unjust in the practice of their enforcement in a particular context.

Because citizens discover through deliberation whether they feel something should be done about a particular injustice, restorative justice builds democratic commitment to doing those things. The story about restorative justice building motivation to repair the harm is therefore a relational one, not just one of the individual psychology of being moved by the revelation of injustice. Those invited into the restorative justice circle are those who enjoy the most respect, trust, and love from victims and offenders. When those we most respect sit and work through with us the reasons why something should be done to repair a harm, the collective quality of the resolve means that we will be more committed to it. We know we enjoy collective support for the resolve to embark on drug rehabilitation or to do something else (Cullen, 1994). We make a personal choice to commit to the remedy based on a process that motivates this commitment and delivers collective support to us to stick with it and to offer all manner of practical help along the way. The ideal of relational transformation is that through empowerment and recognition, all parties to the conversation acquire compassionate strength to deal with problems as they choose (Bush and Folger, 1994).

The fundamental decency of the normative commitment to deliberative democracy in restorative justice therefore bears a causal connection to the effectiveness of restorative justice in motivating the free choice to restore. These are the core theoretical claims advanced here.

CRIME AS AN OPPORTUNITY TO CONFRONT SUBSTANCE ABUSE

We know it takes an enormous amount of personal commitment and help from others to turn around a serious problem of substance abuse. We know that people in the grip of an addictive substance drift rather than confront the issues in their lives. It takes something special to shake the person out of this drift. Arrest for a crime has the potential for that special drama. For minor crimes, the production-line processing in a few minutes before a lower court, transacted in the technocratic language of lawyers, has been stripped of drama, especially for repeat players. Restorative justice processes have much more hope of a ritual impact that might shake a substance abuser out of drift. First there is more time—time for greeting, for building up the story of how this happened, for drawing out who has been hurt by the police being dragged into the life of the family, time for tears, and for offering a tissue or a hug in response. With drunk driving, there is time for talking about how lives actually are shattered by drunks who drive cars. Restorative justice is partly about returning ritual to criminal process, ritual that requires taking stock rather than perpetuating drift (Braithwaite and Mugford, 1994).

When a restorative justice conference is held for a teenage heroin abuser who commits a burglary, the conference can be an opportunity for the parents of the child to cry out for help. They can emerge from the conference as the bigger victims than the folk whose house was burgled. It becomes clear that the consequences of the specific burglary are minor in comparison to the way a number of lives are being destroyed by the young person's attachment to heroin. The most important thing that happens at the conference is that the child has to sit and listen as a number of people express concern about the suffering not only the offender but also his or her parents and other family members are going through. Often the conference has no effect on the subsequent course of events, however, because it too quickly moves from the communal recognition of deep suffering to what is to be done to fix the more tractable problem of the losses suffered by the burglary victim. Everyone looks the problems of the substance abuser's family in the face, then turns away for fear that they will be saddled with the enormity and seeming impossibility of dealing with them. Instead, they settle for the comfortable denial that by agreeing on a few practical things for the offender to do to help the victim, some justice has been done, and perhaps this will get through to the offender. This seems unlikely for an unemployed offender with a heroin habit that must be paid for somehow.

The alternative is to promote restorative justice as a safe and special opportunity for the loved ones of a person with a substance abuse problem, an opportunity to talk openly about all the dimensions of the problem.

The pitch would be that the normal reason for not talking openly about an illicit drug problem—that it would bring trouble from the police—is moot because there is already trouble with the police and the police undertake not to lay any additional charges because of drug offenses disclosed at the conference. Indeed, the fact that things have gotten to the point of trouble with the police becomes the occasion for admitting the need for getting into the open all the harms and hurts at issue. The ritual importance of a criminal arrest can also be an excuse for bringing a lot of supporters of the offender into the circle, not just a few. In the facilitator's preparation for the conference, some of those supporters might have been persuaded to offer to do some little things for the family. When others see that there are many potential helpers in the circle, some of whom are already offering help, they will be more likely to take the risk of getting involved, to overcome the fear that if they do they may be overwhelmed by the scope of the problems. Just as abuse begets abuse, so can help beget help, strength beget strength.

Of course the other reason families do not want to openly discuss the substance abuse of one of their members, even for licit drugs, is that it brings shame on the family. Here we need to educate the community that acknowledging shame is healthy and helps us discharge shame. Shame acknowledgment also tends to elicit forgiveness and needed help from others. This forgiveness also helps us to discharge shame, to put it behind us. Eliza Ahmed (2001) showed that acknowledging shame for school bullying helps prevent further bullying. Loved ones of a drug abuser who seize the opportunity of a ritual encounter to acknowledge shame over some of the things associated with the drug abuse can also be role models for a substance abuser who is resisting shame acknowledgment, who prefers denial or discharging of shame in anger. All this adds up to the virtue of persuading families that a restorative justice circle provides them a confronting yet supportive context where it is in their interests to acknowledge the shame members of the family are feeling.

Most heroin addicts eventually get into trouble with the law. Most alcoholics, particularly in a society such as Australia that has random breath testing of drivers, eventually get into trouble with the law. Indeed, one of the strongest policy arguments for random breath testing of drivers is that it gives the community a principled excuse for confronting serious alcohol abuse. Even more controversially, laws criminalizing smoking in the vicinity of babies or children who are too young to resist this imposition on the health of their environment might give families an opportunity to communicate their fears about the health effects of tobacco, to offer emotional support in the struggle to give up the drug. This does not imply a need to report such a crime to the police. A better approach is for a relative who is concerned about the health of the baby to use the fact that such conduct has been criminalized as a moral resource to insist on a restorative justice conference coordinator in civil society helping the family to confront her fears for the baby. This is a new strategy of the criminal law as a weapon against drug abuse. Instead of being about deterring substance abuse, this restorative strategy is about exploiting the criminalization of the effects of substance abuse to provide an occasion for a ritual confrontation of the substance abuse itself.

Such a new criminal strategy offends liberal sensibilities. Liberals will be offended by any overreach of the criminal law into regulating the right of people to go to hell in their own fashion. Yet one can be a liberal opponent of criminalizing victimless crime while supporting the criminalization of effects or forms of substance abuse that do endanger others. We can be opposed to prohibition and support drunk driving laws. And if we support drunk driving laws, we can support the right of stakeholders to advance their proposed solution to the problem in a specific case. In saying that we think stakeholders such as accident victims, family members, or drinking mates of drunk drivers should have a right to use the ritual occasion of a restorative justice conference to seek to persuade someone to moderate or desist from substance abuse, this does not mean we think they have a right to enforce their preferred solution. All they are given is a ritual opportunity to put their case to the offender. If everyone else in the circle agrees with a proposed program of moderation or rehabilitation, under the philosophy of restorative justice, the offender has a right to say no and take whatever consequences a court might seek to impose if he or she cannot persuade the conference that its proposal is inappropriate. The new criminal strategy proposed is therefore not a threat to freedom because the restriction of freedom involved is not a matter of legal enforcement but of deliberative discussion constrained by a veto right for the person whose freedom is at risk. However, the criminalizing of effects of substance abuse that do have victims is used unapologetically to advance the regulation of substance abuse by deliberative democracy, to give those victims a special opportunity to make a case for an agreement for drug rehabilitation.

Now we will develop these ideas by considering what may be some successes and failures of restorative justice in confronting substance abuse. They will all be cases of alcohol abuse. The implications may be of general import to all kinds of substance abuse. First, we will deal with a case study where confronting substance abuse led to the confrontation of injustice (sexual assault) and then a case where the deliberative confrontation of injustice (domestic violence) led to the successful confrontation of substance abuse. Then I will consider a case where a failure to confront underlying substance abuse led to a failure to confront the injustice.

SUBSTANCE ABUSE CONFRONTED, SEXUAL ABUSE CONFRONTED

Healing circles in the Manitoba Ojibway community of Hollow Water were convened to deal with community concerns about an epidemic of alcohol abuse. As citizens sat in these circles discussing the alcohol problems of individual people, they realized in 1986 that there was a deeper underlying problem, which was that they lived in a community that was sweeping the sexual abuse of children under the carpet. Through setting up a complex set of healing circles to help one individual victim and offender after another, in the end it had been discovered that a majority of the citizens were at some time in their lives victims of sexual abuse.[1] Most of the leading roles in this process were taken by women of Hollow Water (Bushie, 1999). Fifty-two adults out of a community of 600 (Jaccoud, 1998) formally admitted to criminal responsibility for sexually abusing children, 50 as a result of participating in healing circles, 2 as a result of being referred to a court of law for failing to do so (Lajeunesse, 1993; Ross, 1996). Ross (1996) claimed that the healing circles have been a success because there have been only two known cases of reoffending. Tragically, however, there has been no genuinely systematic outcome evaluation of Hollow Water. So we do not have data on pre- and post-levels of either alcohol abuse or sexual abuse.

What is more important than the crime prevention outcome of Hollow Water is its crime detection outcome. When and where has the traditional criminal process succeeded in uncovering anything approaching 52 admissions of criminal responsibility for sexual abuse of children in a community of just 600? Before reading about Hollow Water, I had always said that the traditional criminal investigation and trial process is superior to restorative justice processes for justly getting to the truth of what happened. Restorative justice processes were only likely to be superior to traditional Western criminal process when there was a clear admission of guilt. The significance of Hollow Water is that it throws that position into doubt.

In his discussion of the Hollow Water experience, Ross (1996) emphasized the centrality of restoring communities for restoring individuals:

> If you are dealing with people whose relationships have been built on power and abuse, you must actually show them, then give them the experience of, relationships based on respect . . . [so] . . . the healing process must involve a healthy group of people, as opposed to single therapists. A single therapist cannot, by definition, do more than talk about healthy relationships. (p. 150)

Ross also found special virtue in the participation of healed victims and healed victimizers of sexual abuse who can cut through the (often shared) neutralizations that they had to cut through in confronting their own abuse.

> In Hollow Water, ex-offenders are not shunned forever, but seen as important resources for getting under the skin of other offenders and disturbing the webs of lies that have sustained them. Better than anyone, they understand the patterns, the pressures and the ways to hide. As they tell their personal stories in the circle, they talk about the lies that once protected them and how it felt to face the truth about the pain they caused. (p.183)

Indeed, at Hollow Water, before they met their own victim in a healing circle, sexual abusers met other offenders and other offenders' victims who would simply tell their stories as a stage in a process toward breaking down the tough-guy identity that pervaded the dominating relationship with their own victim. Note what an interesting strategy this is from a defiance theory perspective (Sherman, 1993). Averting defiance is about getting offenders to put their caring identity rather than their defiant self in play.

I find the fundamental hypotheses to take away from Hollow Water to be that

- abuse of substances and abuse of people is a vicious circle,
- communal caring for people and effective confrontation of abuse is a virtuous circle,
- by confronting abuse of substances communally we might confront abuses of people that have been swept under the carpet.

If there is in play here a virtuous circle of healing begetting healing that has flipped the vicious circle of hurt begetting hurt, it follows that by confronting communally the abuse of people, we might effectively deal with the abuse of substances. Our next Canadian case study is about just that.

VIOLENCE CONFRONTED, SUBSTANCE ABUSE CONFRONTED

The award-winning Health Canada video *Widening the Circle: The Family Group Decision Making Experience*, based on the work of Gale Burford and Joan Pennell (1998) with family violence in Newfoundland and Labrador, shows how to advance best restorative justice practice in a number of respects. We see on the video the family sit in the circle and discuss the problems they share as an extended family. A social worker puts up on butcher paper the range of options available locally for dealing with family violence and other problems (including substance abuse) that the family identifies as concerns. Later the experts leave but are called in to explain some other kinds of treatment options that the family thinks might help in their situation.

The hypothesis here is that the plurality of deliberation in restorative justice conferences will increase the effectiveness of rehabilitation programs. This plurality would push out one-size-fits-all pet psychotherapeutic programs often spewed up by state monopolies of welfare provision. The experts under the restorative model have to persuade the affected communities of care that this really will be the best option for them. Most critically, they must persuade the offender or the victim who is to be helped. We hypothesize that this will increase the odds of the help being effective (in comparison with coerced help). Although the evidence is not clear that this hypothesis is correct, it is far more clear that commitment to rehabilitation in a context of family and community support is more effective (Cullen, 1994).

Burford and Pennell's (1998) research found a marked reduction in both child abuse/neglect and abuse of mothers/wives after the intervention. A halving of abuse/neglect incidents was found for 32 families in the year after the conference compared to the year before, whereas incidents increased markedly for 31 control families. Pennell and Burford's (1997) research is also a model of sophisticated process development and process evaluation and of methodological triangulation. Although 63 families might seem modest for quantitative purposes, it is actually a statistically persuasive study in demonstrating that this was an intervention that reduced family violence. There were actually 472 participants in the conferences for the 32 families, and 115 of these were interviewed to estimate levels of violence affecting different participants (Pennell and Burford, 2000). Moreover, within each case a before and after pattern is tested against 31 different types of events (e.g., abuse of child, child abuse of mother, attempted suicide, and father's keeping income from mother) where events can be relevant to more than one member of the family. Given this pattern matching of families × events × individual family members, it understates the statistical power of the design to say it is based on only 63 cases. The Newfoundland and Labrador conferences were less successful in cases where young people were abusing their mothers, a matter worthy of further investigation.

Burford and Pennell (1998) also found reduced drinking problems after conferences. Although dealing with substance abuse was not a principal objective of this program, the empirical findings do support the hypothesis that communally confronting the abuse of people can assist with confronting abuse of substances. Also beyond the positive effects on the direct objective of reducing violence, the evaluation found a posttest increase in family support, concrete (e.g., babysitting) and emotional, and enhanced family unity, even in circumstances where some conference plans involved separation of parents from their children. The philosophy of this program was to look for strengths in families that were in very deep trouble and build on them. This seemed to deliver high levels of participant satisfaction. In Pennell and Burford's (1995) conferences, 94% of family members were "satisfied with the way it was run," 92% felt they were "able to say what was important," and 92% "agreed with the plan decided on." My diagnosis is that the key to the success of the Newfoundland and Labrador programs was the depth of the empowerment of families to define what were the important problems to put in the center of the circle. The hypothesis is that where substance abuse is one of the underlying problems with abuse of people, family members will know this. If the process is rich in the way it empowers them, they will target the substance abuse as a problem they need to commit collectively to solve. Our next case study is a restorative justice failure story where communal empowerment was too constrained to allow this to occur.

SUBSTANCE ABUSE NOT CONFRONTED, DRUNK DRIVING NOT EFFECTIVELY CONFRONTED

Sherman, Strang, and Woods (2000) recently reported that whereas the RISE violence restorative justice experiment in Canberra, Australia, reduced reoffending by 38 crimes per 100 per year, restorative justice increased drunk driving reoffending by 6 crimes per 100 offenders per year. I will put aside here possible reasons for the success of the violence experiment and focus on possible reasons for the failure of the drunk driving experiment in which 450 offenders were randomly assigned to a restorative justice conference and 450 randomly assigned to court. Perhaps the most likely reason for the failure of the RISE drunk driving experiment is about the incapacitative effects of license suspensions being available in court cases and not in cases assigned to the restorative justice conferences. Certainly the pattern of early analyses fits this interpretation (Sherman et al., 2000).

Perhaps, then, if only conferences were put on a level footing with courtroom adjudication by empowering conferences to suspend driving licenses, conferences would prevent more drunk driving than court processing. But there seem to be other reasons why the drunk driving experiments might not have had the success reported in other restorative justice evaluations (Braithwaite, 2001a). One is that the drunk driving cases were all ones where there was no victim. They were all detected by roadside stops and random breath tests. To assure homogeneity, the rare cases where the driver had hit someone or something were excluded. So the emotional power that comes of hearing from a victim of the consequences that were suffered as a result of the wrongdoing was missing from these conferences.

But the other deficiency I observed in these conferences that is theoretically relevant here arose from a decision by the police who convened these conferences that the offense being dealt with was drunk driving and conferences should be prevented from delving critically into aspects of the life of the offender that were not specifically implicated in the offense. This constraint was motivated by admirable liberal anxieties about averting the overreach of the criminal law (Morris and Hawkins, 1969). Yet the problem can be read as an underreach of citizen empowerment rather than an overreach of the law. What I and others (Retzinger and Scheff, 1996) observed to happen in drunk driving conferences was that when the conference would begin to struggle with confronting an underlying alcohol problem, the police convener of the conference would intervene with a constraining comment such as "It's not a crime to drink. We only break the law when we get behind the wheel of a car after drinking too much." At times, the consequences of this policy against net widening were palpably sad. There would seem to be a mother or other loved one in the conference who was deeply concerned about the effect that excessive drinking was having on the life of the offender and the family and who wanted to talk about this. Because of interventions such as that quoted earlier, these loved ones were denied the space to put this problem in the center of the circle. It was sad at times to watch the lost opportunity. Drinking mates, who often themselves had serious alcohol problems, rallying around the offender were also a big part of the problem (Inkpen, 1999). They would conspire with the police to prevent the needed net widening that would have occurred had there been undominated empowerment of the loved one who wanted to put confrontation of substance abuse on the conference agenda. The worst patterns of drunk driving arise in the lives of people who are chronically under the influence of alcohol. If you are drunk every day, in a sense you have to make a choice between drunk driving and abstaining from driving altogether. A criminal justice program that fails to confront the substance abuse problem that underlies these, the worst cases of repeat offending, is bound to have a limited effect on repeat offending. In the case of the RISE experiment, the effect was too limited to outweigh the increase in reoffending caused by not being able to suspend licenses. It must be said, however, that this is a speculative interpretation of the failure of this RISE experiment that needs more detailed empirical exploration.

CRIMINALIZING THE HARM, NOT THE ABUSE

A fundamental hypothesis to develop empirically through an ambitious program of research is that drug rehabilitation can work but that we can widen and deepen the front on which it works by making restorative justice the primary vehicle for collective choice of rehabilitative programs and follow-up of their completion (as in the Hollow Water and Newfoundland case studies). This is because restorative justice delivers superior commitment and superior follow-through compared to the professionalized therapeutic state (Braithwaite, 2001a). It is also more democratically decent. In Latimer, Dowden, and Muise's (2001)

meta-analysis of restorative justice programs, the effect size for compliance with restitution agreements was .33, meaning approximately one third higher compliance for restorative justice cases than for comparison groups. The collective commitment of loved ones to ensure that the offender honors an agreement is more effective than the enforceable orders of a court. The importance of this strength of restorative justice in building motivation to follow through on commitments is underlined by the Williams, Samuel, and Addiction Centre Adolescent Research Group (2000) literature review conclusion that key issues treatment programs must address are treatment dropout and the maximization of treatment completion.

Under such a dispensation, the new role for the criminal justice system is to trigger restorative justice, to use the crisis of laying charges to ask families to work together to face their problems—or else. The criminal justice system is not a useful instrument for the control of substance abuse. But its usefulness as an or else to programs that are extremely useful, as the gravitas in the catalysis of crisis, is sadly underdeveloped in theories of drug rehabilitation. This does involve a kind of criminal justice coercion of democratic deliberation—offering a conference as an alternative to a criminal trial.

It has been argued that there is a reciprocal relationship between substance abuse and abuse of people. Obversely, getting motivated to help others helps substance abusers to get on top of their abuse, to find their redemption narrative (Maruna, 2001). Empathic experience of the injustices suffered by others as a result of the substance abuse—the "just and loving gaze" of those who have been hurt (Drummond, 1999)—nurtures that motivation to help others. The restorative justice philosophy sidesteps debates about whether it is right or wrong to punish substance abuse. What is morally required is that those who are hurt by substance abuse are given a chance to explain their hurts and needs, what problems they would like to see solved. Restorative families can learn to do this without help from the state. Sadly, the worse the substance abuse is, the more likely state intervention will be needed to jolt the drift of the abuser. And the more likely the state will get involved because the most devastated abusers of drugs such as heroin and alcohol do eventually tend to hit serious trouble with the police. The shock to a family of this happening for the first time to one of its young members is a special opportunity when it is the substance abuse that underlies the trouble. The opportunity is that the trouble with the law gives loved ones who wish to make an issue of the harm the substance abuse is doing a ritual space, a solemn and serious dialogue it is hard not to listen to.

Hence, what the criminal justice system can offer beleaguered families of substance abusers is not deterrence of abuse but the gravitas to trigger a ritual moment in which people can be gathered and things said that it is otherwise difficult to say. People need a lot of support to make the move from incessant and ineffective nattering at the substance abuser, who drifts through the natter (Patterson, 1982), to solemn commitment to a plan of action to deal with the abuse and its consequences. The fear we have of being overwhelmed by the problems if we offer help can best be overcome by a collective process where many are encouraged to offer help. Agreements articulated collectively with those we love and depend on most have the best prospect of sticking.

Unfortunately, restorative justice in practice, as illustrated by the RISE drunk driving experiment, still typically shies away from underlying problems of substance abuse, spurning the help desperate family members need, smugly satisfied with a bit of repair for a victim or a dose of community service that at least keeps the offender out of prison for the moment. The Hollow Water and Newfoundland family group decision-making programs show that simultaneously serious confrontation of abuse of persons and of substances is possible—with powerful results. This requires a depth of communal empowerment and some serious back-up of state resources. It probably also requires preconference meetings with an offender and his or her loved ones that encourage them to look holistically at the individual and collective life at risk—to discourage them from just sweeping an underlying substance abuse problem under the carpet. This strategy also establishes restorative justice as a framework where rehabilitative options are available for choice by the community of care.

The key institutional questions are therefore not about whether to punish but about how to trigger and support problem-solving dialogue where the people who count in this particular life have a voice. It is certainly a good democratic thing if this group of people also decide to turn their private troubles into a public issue by getting involved with drug law reform, campaigns for funding more rehabilitative options, and so on. Here the institutional challenge is to create a space where that is a democratic option that citizens will occasionally be motivated to take up but not an expectation. The expectation is that normally the overwhelmed families will do well to come to grips with their private troubles. The democratic aspiration is mostly more banal—to give beleaguered people a deliberative space that they actually lack to roundly discuss a central

problem in their little lives. The systematic evidence of satisfaction with participation in restorative justice processes after loved ones are arrested is that citizens of all types, but especially mothers, appreciate and use this bit of voice (Braithwaite, 2001a).

The new criminal justice of substance abuse is therefore to move resources from state punishment of drug criminals to restorative justice processes backed up by well-resourced rehabilitative options. These conferences are triggered when the substance abuse becomes serious enough to cause real crime such as burglary, assault, pushing drugs to others, drunk driving, and even what I provocatively suggest should be the crime of blowing cigarette smoke in the face of one's children. The crime that has a victim becomes a ritual occasion for loved ones to confront the substance abuser's victimization of himself and collateral victimization of his family. The criminal law can make a very major contribution to reducing drug abuse by catalyzing loving concern that confronts substance abuse instead of nattering at it, that delivers an empathy, practical help, and support that motivates substance abusers to jettison fatalistic scripts, rediscover what they perceive to be their real selves, to restory their lives as lives where they are in control.

Some would say this program of criminal justice reform could be implemented by drug courts. Perhaps a lot of it could. That is an empirical question. Family empowerment and love seem to me the crucial ingredients for success, and a court controlled by a judge seems an unlikely context for these to flourish. All the criminal justice system needs to provide is the gravitas, perhaps even the sword of Damocles (Braithwaite, 2001a), to trigger the ritual moment where the just and loving engagement of family and friends might motivate rehabilitative resolve, might build out from their strengths. Before it escalates from help to desperate resort to the sword of Damocles, however, it may do better by escalating to even more support and help. These too are empirical assertions that demand much more rigorous testing. First, however, I suspect we need more qualitative research and development on how to prevent restorative justice processes from sweeping substance abuse under the carpet when it is a driver of criminal behavior.

SYNERGIES WITH CIVIL SOCIETY PROGRAMS

The suffering of victims of the harms inflicted by drug abusers often runs very deep. These victims desperately need vindication of that suffering, especially if they are loved ones of the abuser who need to keep finding the compassionate strength to provide support. Although they may be parents of the offender, they are victims of serious crimes and should not be seen as anything less. The wonderful opportunity with such victims is that they are often not retributive victims. They want to forgive and help. Publicly funded restorative justice programs in civil society should be available to support them as victims. Without involving the police, such programs can convene restorative justice circles to help heal the hurts of victims. The crisis that provides motivation and ritual moment in this scenario is not trouble with the police, but it is still the recognition that someone has been a victim of a serious crime (that he or she does not wish to report to the police). Just because a citizen does not want to report a loved one to the police, this does not mean he or she should be left to suffer alone as a victim of serious crime. The victim right of community support for repair of the harm suffered can be honored without resort to the criminal process. My hypothesis is that honoring this victim right in civil society can create a special kind of opportunity for confronting abuse of persons to lead to the confrontation of abuse of substances.

A second kind of civil society program I have advocated for confronting drug abuse that involves no connection with criminal justice is youth support circles (Braithwaite, 2001b). These are universal programs oriented to the educational development of young people. The circle keeps meeting with each young person in a school until he or she finds a place in a tertiary institution or a job. They are not problem-centered circles so much as development-centered circles, although they can deal with a specific problem such as drug abuse if it comes up as an obstacle to educational and vocational development. Part of the idea of this kind of circle is that because it is universal, it is less stigmatizing than other approaches to life problems. It is about building the excellence of the problem-free children as well as tackling the obstacles that confront the weakest ones. The most disadvantaged children would benefit most, however, because they most desperately need an outside adult or older pupil who can spend a couple of hours a week with them on their math homework. They most need a middle-class friend with the contacts to help them get a job on graduation. Retirees as well as older buddies are seen as especially valuable resources for challenges that single mothers in particular are overwhelmed in meeting.

Finally, there is a case for another kind of civil society program that takes referrals from the police. Good police services get to know the names of offenders who are supporting an addiction by selling drugs themselves or by persistent property crime. They target them and eventually catch them. Once the police have possession of this intelligence, I have suggested an alternative to targeting and arrest. This is prearrest conversations with such offenders that their pattern of offending is known to the police. They are advised that a judge has approved that there is "reasonable suspicion" for their being targeted for special surveillance. However, they are given the opportunity to get off this targeting program before it succeeds in arresting them by participating in a healing circle with their loved ones about the problems that are besetting their life (Braithwaite, 2001a). The same kinds of conversations are advocated in Braithwaite (2001a) for targeted organized criminals who market drugs, drawing on experience with gang retreats and gang surrenders in Papua New Guinea (Dinnen, 2001) and some of the Giuliani strategies for cleaning up the Mafia in New York (Jacobs, 1999). The Papua New Guinea restorative justice initiatives with organized crime are often brokered by the church, although often with state participation at a level as high as the prime minister. Whether we are thinking about drug barons or street-level addicts, when the police do prearrest targeting they can refer the case to a restorative justice process run totally in civil society rather than convene it themselves.

CONCLUSION

The orienting empirical insight in this article is that abuse of substances causes abuse of people and vice versa. Abuses of people but not abuses of drugs are appropriate for criminalization. A direct focus on the criminal abuse of people is therefore advanced as a promising indirect way of confronting substance abuse. Arrest for a burglary can supply an occasion of crisis in a life and a moment of ritual that is a special opportunity for creating the motivation and social support normally lacking for confronting substance abuse. Equally, a friend of a substance abuser who has something important stolen but who does not want to report the abuser to the police can trigger the crisis by saying she might go to the police unless the offender joins him or her in a restorative justice circle convened in civil society. Or, the police can create a prearrest crisis by communicating their targeting decisions to targets instead of treating them as secret. Finally, universal youth development circles that are not only prearrest but preproblem could be useful both to prevent the reasons for substance abuse before they arise and to deal with them when they first arise in a minimally stigmatizing fashion. The possible synergies between these four different kinds of restorative justice programs is the stuff of an exciting research and development program that comes at the substance abuse problem from a fresh angle that has deep theoretical roots for its effectiveness claims.

NOTE

1. LaPrairie (1994) in a study of this problem in another context found that 46% of inner-city native people in Canada had experienced child abuse. For an outline of the Hollow Water procedures for dealing with sexual abuse, see Aboriginal Corrections Policy Unit (1997a, 1997b). At Canim Lake, the site of another innovative Canadian First Nations healing circle approach to sexual abuse, "The research showed us that up to eighty percent of our people had been sexually abused at one point in their lives" (Warhaft, Palys, and Boyce, 1999, p. 171).

REFERENCES

Aboriginal Corrections Policy Unit. (1997a). *The four circles of hollow water* (Aboriginal Peoples Collection). Ottawa, Canada: Solicitor General.

Aboriginal Corrections Policy Unit. (1997b). *Responding to sexual abuse: Developing a community-based sexual abuse response team in Aboriginal communities.* Ottawa, Canada: Solicitor General.

Ahmed, E. (2001). Part III—Shame management: Regulating bullying. In E. Ahmed, N. Harris, J. Braithwaite, and V. Braithwaite (Eds.), *Shame management through reintegration.* Cambridge, UK: Cambridge University Press.

Ahmed, E., Harris, N., Braithwaite, J., and Braithwaite, V. (2001). *Shame management through reintegration.* Cambridge, UK: Cambridge University Press.

Bazemore, G. (1999). Communities, victims, and offender rehabilitation: Restorative justice and earned redemption. In A. Etizioni (Ed.), *Civic repentance* (pp. 45–96). Lanham, MD: Rowman and Littlefield.

Braithwaite, J. (2001a). *Restorative justice and responsive regulation.* New York: Oxford University Press.

Braithwaite, J. (2001b). Youth development circles. *Oxford Review of Education, 27,* 239–252.

Braithwaite, J., and Mugford, S. (1994). Conditions of successful reintegration ceremonies: Dealing with juvenile offenders. *British Journal of Criminology, 34,* 139–171.

Braithwaite, J., and Pettit, P. (1990). *Not just deserts: A republican theory of criminal justice.* Oxford, UK: Oxford University Press.

Brickman, P., Rabinowitz, V., Karuza, J., Coates, D., Cohn, E., and Kidder, L. (1982). Models of helping and coping. *American Psychologist, 37,* 368–384.

Burford, G., and Pennell, J. (1998). *Family group decision making project* (Outcome report, Vol. I). St. John's, Canada: Memorial University of Newfoundland, School of Social Work.

Bush, R. A., and Folger, J. P. (1994). *The promise of mediation: Responding to conflict through empowerment and recognition.* San Francisco: Jossey-Bass.

Bushie, B. (1999). *Community holistic circle healing: A community approach* (Proceedings of Building Strong Partnerships for Restorative Practices Conference, Burlington, VT). Pipersville, PA: Real Justice.

Cullen, F. T. (1994). Social support as an organizing concept for criminology: Presidential address to the academy of criminal justice sciences. *Justice Quarterly, 11,* 527–559.

Dinnen, S. (2001). *Law and order in a weak state: Crime and politics in Papua New Guinea.* Honolulu: University of Hawaii Press.

Drummond, S. G. (1999). *Incorporating the familiar: An investigation into legal sensibilities in Nunavik.* Montreal and Kingston, Canada: McGill-Queen's University Press.

Henry, S., and Milovanovic, D. (1996). *Constitutive criminology.* Thousand Oaks, CA: Sage.

Inkpen, N. (1999). *Reintegrative shaming through collective conscience building.* Unpublished doctoral dissertation, Australian National University.

Jaccoud, M. (1998). Restoring justice in native communities in Canada. In L. Walgrave (Ed.). *Restorative justice for juveniles: Potentialities, risks and problems for research* (pp. 285–299). Leuven, Belgium: Leuven University Press.

Jacobs, J. B. (1999). *Gotham unbound: How New York City was liberated from the grip of organized crime.* New York: New York University Press.

Lajeunesse, T. (1993). *Community holistic circle healing: Hollow Water first nation* (Aboriginal Peoples Collection). Ottawa, Canada: Supply and Services.

LaPrairie, C. (1994). *Seen but not heard: Native people in the inner city, Report 3: Victimisation and domestic violence.* Ottawa, Canada: Department of Justice.

Latimer, J., Dowden, C., and Muise, D. (2001). *The effectiveness of restorative justice practices: A meta-analysis.* Ottawa, Canada: Department of Justice.

Maruna, S. (2001). *Making good: How ex-convicts reform and rebuild their lives.* Washington, DC: American Psychological Association.

Maxwell, G. M., and Morris, A. (1999). *Reducing reoffending.* Wellington, New Zealand: Victoria University of Wellington, Institute of Criminology.

Morris, N., and Hawkins, G. (1969). *An honest politician's guide to crime control.* Chicago: University of Chicago Press.

Muck, R., Zempolich, K. A., Titus, J. C., Fishman, M., Godley, M. D., and Schwebel, R. (2001). An overview of the effectiveness of adolescent substance abuse treatment models. *Youth and Society, 33,* 143–168.

Patterson, G. R. (1982). *Coercive family process.* Eugene, OR: Castalia Publishing Co.

Pennell, J., and Burford, G. (1995). *Family group decision making: New roles for "old" partners in resolving family violence* (Implementation Report Vol. 1). St. John's, Canada: University of Newfoundland, School of Social Work, Family Group Decision Making Project.

Pennell, J., and Burford, G. (1997). *Family group decision making: After the conference—Progress in resolving violence and promoting well-being.* St. John's, Canada: University of Newfoundland, School of Social Work, Family Group Decision Making Project.

Pennell, J., and Burford, G. (2000). Family group decision making: Protecting children and women. *Child Welfare, 79,* 131–158.

Prochaska, J. O., DiClemente, C. C., and Norcross, J. C. (1992). In search of how people change. *American Psychologist, 47,* 1102–1114.

Retzinger, S., and Scheff, T. J. (1996). Strategy for community conferences: Emotions and social bonds. In B. Galaway and J. Hudson (Eds.), *Restorative justice: International perspectives.* Monsey, NY: Criminal Justice Press.

Ross, R. (1996). *Returning to the teachings. Exploring Aboriginal justice.* New York: Penguin Books.

Sherman, L. W. (1993). Defiance, deterrence and irrelevance: A theory of the criminal sanction. *Journal of Research in Crime and Delinquency, 30,* 445–473.

Sherman, L. W., Strang, H., and Woods, D. (2000). *Recidivism patterns in the reintegrative shaming experiments* [Online]. Available: http://www.aic.gov.au/rjustice/rise/recidivism/index.html

Warhaft, E. B., Palys, T., and Boyce, W. (1999). "This is how we did it": One Canadain First Nation community's efforts to achieve Aboriginal justice. *Australian and New Zealand Journal of Criminology, 32,* 168–181.

Williams, R. J., Samuel, C. Y., and Addiction Centre Adolescent Research Group. (2000). A comprehensive and comparative review of adolescent substance abuse treatment outcome. *Clinical Psychology: Science and Practice, 7,* 138–166.

Zehr, H. (2000, September). *Journal of belonging.* Paper presented at the Fourth International Conference on Restorative Justice, Tuebingen, Germany.

CHAPTER 5: DISCUSSION QUESTIONS

1. According to Harrison, why are growing numbers of people in prison for drug-related offenses when the overall trend has been less drug use in society?

2. What are the details of the TASC evaluation presented by Anglin and colleagues? What were the domains examined in the TASC evaluation?

3. What are the five dimensions of the conceptual framework of drug courts posed by Longshore and colleagues? How do they differ?

4. What are the basic premises of restorative justice? How is shame used in restorative justice?

5. How realistic is it that restorative justice will receive support and be implemented in the United States?

6. What are the limitations of each selection?

7. What are the policy implications of each selection?

CHAPTER 5: ADDITIONAL RESOURCES IN RESEARCH NAVIGATOR AND IN THE *NEW YORK TIMES*

Anderson, T. L., Rosay, A. B., and Saum, C. (2002). The impact of drug use and crime involvement on health problems among female drug offenders. *Prison Journal, 82,* 50–68.

Cardwell, D. (2004, May 21). Dozens indicted in crackdown on a Brooklyn drug ring. *New York Times.*

Cope, N. (2000). Drug use in prison: The experience of young offenders. *Drugs: Education, Prevention, and Policy, 7,* 355–366.

Davey, M. (2003, June 17). Texas frees 12 on bond after drug sweep inquiry. *New York Times.*

Farabee, D., Prendergast, M., Cartier, J., Wexler, H., Knight, K., and Anglin, M. D. (1999). Barriers to implementing effective correctional drug treatment programs. *Prison Journal, 79,* 150–162.

Hagan, J., and Coleman, J. P. (2001). Returning captives of the American war on drugs: Issues of community and family reentry. *Crime and Delinquency, 47,* 352–367.

Hanlon, T. E., and Nurco, D. N. (1999). The relative effects of three approaches to the parole supervision of narcotic addicts. *Prison Journal, 79,* 163–181.

Hernadez, D. (2003, July 3). 7 jail workers face bribery and drug charges. *New York Times.*

Herszenhorn, D. M. (2003, August 9). City is ordered to reinstate teacher arrested for drugs. *New York Times.*

Inciardi, J. A., Martin, S. S., and Butzin, C. A. (2004). Five-year outcomes of therapeutic community treatment of drug-involved offenders after release from prison. *Crime and Delinquency, 50,* 88–107.

Krebs, C. P. (2002). High-risk HIV transmission behavior in prison and the prison subculture. *Prison Journal, 82,* 19–49.

Lay, D. P. (2004, November 18). Rehab justice. *New York Times.*

Lichtblau, E. (2003, February 25). Raids put drug-paraphernalia traffickers out of business. *New York Times.*

Liptak, A. (2003, October 26). Alabama prison at center of suit over AIDS policy. *New York Times.*

Lock, E. D., Timberlake, J. M., and Rasinski, K. A. (2002). Battle fatigue: Is public support waning for "war"-centered drug control policies? *Crime and Delinquency, 48,* 380–398.

Maxwell, S. R. (2000). Sanction threats in court-ordered programs: Examining their effects on offenders mandated into drug treatment. *Crime and Delinquency, 46,* 542–563.

McElrath, K. (2001). Book review: Race and drug trials: The social construction of guilt and innocence, by Anita Kalunta-Crumpton. *British Journal of Criminology, 41,* 212–214.

Reuters. (2003, August 21). Rumsfeld cites drug problem in hemisphere. *New York Times.*

Risen, J. (2004, January 8). Interruption of effort to down drug planes is disclosed. *New York Times.*

Romero, S., and Liptak, A. (2003, April 2). Texas court acts to clear 38, almost all black, in drug case. *New York Times.*

Staples, B. (2004, March 21). Life on the outside: The other lockup. *New York Times.*

Steinhauer, J. (2004, June 25). Drug and sex offenders face restrictions on public housing. *New York Times.*

von Zielbauer, P. (2003, November 9). Court treatment system is found to help drug offenders stay clean. *New York Times.*

RESPONSES TO DRUGS: HARM REDUCTION AND TREATMENT

As noted in the Introduction, one of the most important developments in the area of drug research and policy is the exploration of harm reduction as a response to drugs. This chapter includes selections that describe harm reduction and its approach to drug use. Not all treatment responses explicitly incorporate elements of the harm-reduction philosophy, but all implicitly do so. Several of the articles in Chapter Five examined the intersection of criminal justice and treatment. This chapter focuses on broader treatment issues.

Peter Reuter and Robert MacCoun discuss programs designed to provide monetary and social support for individuals addicted to drugs and alcohol. In particular, they focus on the Supplemental Security Income revisions that dropped these people from the list of those eligible to participate in receiving benefits. Although keeping these people on the list might reduce community harm, Reuter and MacCoun argue that it is likely to increase some individual harm because the program does not address the underlying structural and individual causes of drug and alcohol addiction. They contend that international approaches that incorporate broader harm-reduction policies are more successful.

Margaret Kelley, Sheigla Murphy, and Howard Lune examine the effect of a harm-reduction approach to injection drug use by using qualitative methods to evaluate a syringe exchange program. One prominent assumption about injection drug users (IDUs) is that because they are addicted to drugs, they are also unable and unwilling to take action to protect themselves from drug-related harm. The authors find that IDUs in their sample benefited from a culture of harm reduction that grew out of the ideology of needle exchange. Individual users were capable of passing on information about how to

reduce risk, and those newer users who received this information exhibited less risk. Although it is not a traditional treatment approach to drug use, syringe exchange is a harm-reduction policy that helps users minimize risk from their illicit drug use.

Philippe Bourgois focuses specifically on the pros and cons of methadone maintenance treatment for heroin users, one of the earliest harm-reduction approaches put in place in the United States. Using a qualitative ethnographic technique gather data, Bourgois is able to provide rich, detailed descriptions of the experience of methadone clients. Because of the contradictions built into the current structure of methadone delivery, he claims that methadone is not a "magic bullet" solution to heroin addiction. In fact, there are many negative side effects of methadone. Many of the problems with methadone treatment can be seen in the treatment for other types of drug addictions because the ideology of many types of treatment programs is to punish addicts rather than to support them. This theoretical piece is a powerful overview of the contradictions in treatment ideology in the United States today.

The final article, by Yih-Ing Hser and colleagues, examines treatment for methamphetamine users. The authors recognize the paucity both of treatment options and of research in this area. They use a quantitative approach to data collection and analysis. As has been shown in other research, their results indicate that while in treatment, criminal behavior is reduced. These findings are very important because so little is known about treatment for methamphetamine users. In conclusion, even inadequate treatment is providing encouraging results.

Several themes emerge in the articles in this chapter. First, autonomy and power are two things that drug users lack and are perhaps seeking through their drug use. Current treatment approaches do not encourage autonomy and power for their clients. Research has shown that many drug treatment clients fare better when they have a say about their participation in treatment programs. Second, treatment approaches that dichotomize success ignore the complex lived experience of drug use. In other words, abstinence, while a valid goal, is not easily achieved by many users. Treatment programs incorporating harm-reduction policies that recognize that relapse is common are more likely to be successful because many users require more than one attempt at treatment. Third, treatment programs vary significantly in their ideologies and structures. Methadone, for example, takes many forms depending on funding sources and is, in fact, illegal in eight states. Regional and cultural differences in drug use are often not accounted for in treatment plans. Part of their variation is based on whether their goal is to punish or treat their clients. Fourth, as noted in Chapter Five, several articles provide additional evidence that treatment reduces criminal behaviors for drug users. Fifth, there is often a paucity of treatment options for individual drugs of abuse, and most treatment programs are not well equipped to deal with polydrug use. The vast majority of individuals who report abusing drugs do not receive treatment. Finally, all the selections suggest that alternative approaches are necessary because no one treatment modality can possibly work for every person addicted to drugs, with several sources even suggesting that heroin prescription is appropriate for some clients.

19

Harm Reduction and Social Policy: Should Addicts Be Paid?

PETER REUTER

ROBERT J. MacCOUN

ABSTRACT

Harm reduction principles have not been applied to social policy programs that affect drug users. This paper considers whether income supports for the drug-dependent poor might be harm reducing, given that a principal harm related to drug dependence is crime committed to finance drug use. We examine the political fate of the principal income support program in the United States that targeted the drug dependent. Revelations that the money was being used in part for the purchase of drugs has led to a scaling back and tightening of the program. We suggest that the program might have been more effectively defended if attention had been paid to community harms rather than only to drug consumption by recipients. European and Australian governments provide income support which is no doubt also used for drug consumption, but in the context of universalist income support programs they do not require a harm reduction defense. We conclude that great potential for reducing drug-related harm may fall well outside the domain of targeted drug policy, whether of the supply reduction, demand reduction or harm reduction variety.

INTRODUCTION

The usual account of why nations suffer from drug problems includes frequent reference to adverse social conditions. Anomie in modern societies; the failure of educational systems to provide youth with a sense of optimism and skills to succeed in postindus-trial society; and discrimination against minorities are just some of the factors that are mentioned [1].

Yet debate about drug policy starts with an implicit assumption that it is policies and programs targeted specifically against drug use and related problems which is most worthy of our attention in trying to reduce society's drug problems. (For example, in the collection of papers from the 3rd International Conference on Harm Reductions [2], only Berridge gave serious attention to any policies that were not specific to drug users.) Perhaps this reflects the bias of experts. As has been said in the context of AIDS policy: "The penchant of medical experts is to define problems in terms that can be solved only by them" [3, p. 376].

This paper is a brief effort to scrutinize this assumption about the centrality of drug policy by examining state income supports for those impoverished by expensive drug dependence. Such income support almost certainly increases drug use; it may on the other hand reduce crime and thus be net harm reducing. We will examine some of the basic issues by focusing on the functioning and fate of a US income support program specifically targeted on drug abusers and then briefly compare it to the more universalist income support addicts receive in Europe and Australia.

Defining Harm Reduction

Harm reduction is not a policy or program; it is instead a goal for policies and programs. We interpret harm reduction to be a willingness to trade potential increases in drug use for potential declines in aggregate

Reuter, P. and R. J. MacCoun (1996). *Drug and Alcohol Review.* 15(3):225–230. © 1996 by Taylor & Francis, Ltd. (http://www.tandf.co.uk/journals).

drug-related harms. ("[T]he essential feature of harm reduction is that it involves an attempt to ameliorate the adverse health, social or economic consequences of mood-altering substances without necessarily requiring a reduction in the consumption of these substances" [4, p. vi].) The measure of use normally referred to is *prevalence*. Needle exchange might still be an attractive harm reduction program, even if the gains in HIV control were accompanied by some modest increase in the prevalence of drug use; it would depend *inter alia* on the magnitude of the effects. Fortunately it does not seem to induce greater use, so the tension does not have to be resolved.

We wish to make a modest terminological extension that might be controversial. The increase in use potentially being traded against reduction in harm might be *quantity per use* or *frequency per user*, as well as number of users. If needle exchange led to addicts consuming, on average, more heroin or continuing their careers longer because of reduced health concerns, it might still be a harm reduction program. It would be an empirical issue, in which one is forced to weigh those undesirable consequences against reductions in the spread of HIV and other blood-borne diseases.

More controversially we wish to distinguish, as we have in previous articles [4], between "micro" and "macro" harm reduction. Micro harm reduction focuses on the individual user or individual use session and asks of a program whether it will raise or lower the damage that user suffers. Macro harm reduction takes account of the connection between prevalence/consumption and harms (this distinction is similar to one offered by Strang [5], who uses the terms "individual" and "public health" rather than micro and macro) and generates a tougher criterion; does an intervention raise or lower harm to society? Harms per user might decline but total harms might still rise. The following discussion uses the macro-harm criterion throughout.

Linking Income Support to Crime

The high criminality of drug addicts appears to be mostly a function of the enforcement of drug laws and other conditions of drug use that have been created in modern industrialized societies, rather than of the drugs themselves. In particular, the extraordinary expense of heroin and cocaine drives both user and seller crime rates. Dependent users, for many reasons, are unable to maintain substantial legitimate earnings but have relatively expensive habits that require urgent satisfaction.

In the United States, crime is probably the dominant community harm associated with drug addiction [6]; certainly it is the most salient. Reducing the absolute poverty of drug addicts might reduce their criminal activity. Crime is inherently risky, whether of liberty, property or physical safety. Liberty, and probably physical safety, are more valued when one is less poor. Although it may have other charms for some perpetrators [7], the principal motivation for property crime is economic. It is a reasonable but unproven conjecture that a higher state benefit check will lower addict crime.

A few descriptive studies in different nations have provided data on the sources of income of those dependent on heroin or cocaine and thus provide some information on the relationship between government income support and crime rates. A recent Australian study [8] found generous benefits might be associated with low criminal participation. In the United States, Johnston et al. [9] found that a sample of heroin addicts received very little from government programs and were primarily dependent on crime for their income. Needle and Mills [10] reported slightly more government income for a later sample, including cocaine dependent users, and somewhat less property crime. More ambiguous data come from Amsterdam [11] and Oslo [12]. In both cities benefits were broad but shallow and the sample was more involved in property crime and dealing than was the Australian sample but less than the US sample.

The evidence from these studies is mixed. None specifically analyzed the relationship between government support and crime and there are many differences across nations in the conditions of addiction (e.g. the cost of drugs, strength of family ties, tightness of labor markets) that might account for observed variation. None the less, it remains plausible that government funding of addicts might reduce their involvement in criminal activities, other than drug purchases.

Targeting Income Support

Clearly a program labeled as "income support for addicts" is unlikely to be politically viable; instead addicts need to be included among those with a more general claim on society, either because they are poor or because they are disabled and poor. This section considers the fate of a US program aimed at the disabled poor.

Supplemental Security Income (SSI), a US means-tested program created in 1972, provides income for people who are needy and aged, blind or disabled. In 1992, 5.6 million persons (about 2% of the total population) were recipients of SSI, which provided an average of about $650 per month [13, Section 9]. From the beginning drug addiction or alcoholism (DA&A) was included as a disability, along with various physical and mental handicaps.

However, DA&A recipients were singled out: "The objective of the SSI DA&A program is to rehabilitate addicts to be productive members of society and remove them from the SSI disability rolls" [14, p. 4]. Hence those receiving SSI because of alcoholism or drug dependence are, in principle, required to be in treatment for that dependence; they are also required to have a custodian ("representative payee") who receives the money. Other disability groups are subject to less stringent time and treatment requirements.

In 1983, 10 years after its creation, the enrollment in DA&A was minuscule, only 3,000. Then two states, California and Illinois, discovered that they could shift significant numbers of state welfare recipients on to the federal rolls. Enrollment rose to 20,000 recipients in 1990 and then 80,000 in 1994 [15]. Without a change in rules it was estimated that the figure would rise to over 200,000 by the year 2000 [16]. If one included those with DA&A as secondary diagnosis, the figure for 1994 was 250,000.

Few of those receiving SSI DA&A funds were in fact in treatment; most of the custodians were family members who probably made little effort to monitor the use of the income. Of those enrolled in June 1990, 70% were still receiving DA&A payments in February 1994; another 6% were receiving SSI payments under some other disability classification. Of the remainder, half (12% of the total) were deceased. Only 1% left the SSI rolls because of significant improvement in their earnings or medical status [15]. Clearly the program was not meeting the goal of helping addicts in their transition to sobriety and self-support.

The media reported horror stories of government checks being turned over to the local bar owner or drug dealer for purchase of alcohol or drugs [17, pp. 10–11]. The problem was exacerbated by the fact that, in the interests of fairness and recognizing the innate slowness of the bureaucratic process, SSI applicants received an initial lump sum payment covering the months from first filing of a claim to time of enrollment. This could amount to $5,000 or more and these initial payments generated the most egregious incidents.

A little research evidence supports these fears. Shaner et al. [18] found that the arrival of SSI checks, or checks from another similar program administered by the Veterans Administration (VA), coincided with increases in cocaine use and symptom severity in a sample of cocaine-dependent schizophrenic veterans. "The troubling irony is that income intended to compensate for the disabling effects of severe mental illness may have the opposite effect" (p. 777). Satel, commenting on Shaner's findings, noted that "[a]lthough the authors caution against over-generalizing from their results, my own clinical experiences and those of my colleagues have persuaded me that mentally-ill recipients of disability payments who abuse drugs are likely to subsidize their addictions with public funds" [19, p. 795].

Not surprisingly, the program has recently come under strong attack in Congress. As one Congressionally sponsored analysis concluded: "[The program] results in a perverse incentive that affronts working taxpayers and fails to serve the interests of addicts and alcoholics" [20]. The SSI rules have been altered so that DA&A recipients must leave the SSI rolls within 3 years; the representative payee and treatment enrollment requirements are being rigorously enforced. Ironically, most of those forced off the DA&A rolls will probably find their way back to the SSI rolls for some other disability, in which case even the minimal effort to prevent misuse of their government supports (requiring participation in treatment, use of responsible payee) will be missing.

Assessing the DA&A Program

The program, even without its special requirements, has a defensible basis. It accepts that dependence on alcohol or other psychoactive substances is a disability and that a humane society, whatever it may do to reduce the prevalence of such disabilities, must provide assistance to those who become afflicted. In terms of reducing drug-related harms, the principal harm being targeted is crime, as experienced by both the dependent user and society. The payments for heroin addicts should reduce their need to commit income generating crimes precisely because it allows them to make such purchases with their higher government-supported income, money being fungible. The test of the program, putting values issues aside for the moment, is whether the potential reductions in crime outweigh the increased drug use, lower participation in treatment, and prolonged drug using careers.

However, because it was developed as part of a comprehensive plan for supporting the "deserving poor" (a concept particularly prominent in American discourse), it is vulnerable in a way that it might not be if it were explicitly a harm reduction program. The "deserving" poor do not commit crimes although, alas, they have been known to spend their money on the wrong goods, such as alcohol and cigarettes, so that much income support is provided in kind, such as Food Stamps and medical insurance. The Shaner study and later commentaries made no effort to examine whether the payments had any effect on the criminality of the recipients; they showed only that, as compared to periods when they were poor, those in treatment were more likely to increase drug use and suffer more acute problems as a result of the payments. As is often the case with treatment program evaluations, the focus was on the welfare of the patients rather than the welfare of the community as a whole.

The DA&A's original requirements, if strengthened, seem a plausible way of avoiding the problem of government financing drug consumption. Treatment could be provided either directly through the Social Security Administration or as a companion entitlement, administered by another agency while the representative payee requirement could be given more credibility by having the treatment program itself act on behalf of the patient, thus assuring continued treatment enrollment.

However, a large literature [21] shows that most of those dependent on drugs such as cocaine and heroin have a lifetime, chronic, relapsing condition. Even those treatment subjects who greatly reduce their drug use do not do well in the labor market; for example, Hser, Anglin and Powers [22] found that 32% of the inactive users in their 24-year longitudinal study were unemployed at the time of the most recent interview. Most evaluations find that it is reductions in crime that generate most of the economic benefits of treatment, not increased earnings [23]. Success in treatment would move them from the "poor addict" category to the "poor recovering addict" category, still requiring government support.

More importantly, we are skeptical that the toughened program could benefit large numbers. The increased incentive for continued treatment participation provided by benefit payments will plausibly raise treatment enrollment and completion rates, but it is difficult to believe that modest financial support goes to the heart of relapse, which lies in the attraction of self-medication, the difficulty of abstinence in face of external cues, and so on. A tough program would be a program that left most addicts without support.

CONCLUSION

In the United States the finding that income support increased drug use was enough to curtail the principal program aimed at providing such support to addicts. The DA&A program's weakness was that it singled out drug addiction as a justification for income support; in the context of income support for the disabled, there was no other way of providing such money. The European and Australian approach, providing such support in the context of a universalist program for the poor, is more robust. Outside the United States, there is little examination of why an individual is in need of support, so that addicts are not privileged, merely not penalized. In the US context, where there is no commitment to long-term support for males who are not disabled, this is not an option.

Is such support harm reducing? Empirically this is a very complex question; the income may reduce crime by the dependent user but it may worsen the recipient's health, precisely because it increases his consumption of harmful drugs. Moreover, it will raise the income of dealers, a harm in itself. For Europeans these issues are irrelevant; the program is supported by other more broadly held values.

In the United States, income support for addicts will require a harm reduction defense if it is to survive at all. Addiction, certainly to psychoactive substances, is seen by many Americans (including politicians) as voluntary and curable [24], whatever the evidence from research and treatment experience. In an era when the poor in America are stigmatized merely for being poor, the addicted poor are clearly doubly stigmatized, and hence unable to muster political support. It may well be that just as harm reduction outcomes should be judged in aggregate social terms, harm reduction policies should be *implemented* at an aggregate social level. Evidence for weak effects of modest income support aimed at a small group of hard core adult addicts may tell us very little about the potential effects of economic support concentrated on other segments of high risk neighborhoods—on infant health, on early parenting, on adolescent job opportunities, on small business development, and so on. Calling such interventions "harm reduction" might seem to stretch the term beyond any useful meaning, but our point is that great potential for reducing drug-related harm may fall well outside the domain of drug policy, whether of the supply reduction, demand reduction or harm reduction variety.

Acknowledgments

Paper prepared for presentation at the 7th International Conference on the Reduction of Drug-Related Harm, Hobart, Australia, March 1996. The research reported here was supported by a grant from the Alfred P. Sloan Foundation to the Drug Policy Research Center at RAND. The general topic was suggested by Alex Wodak. We appreciate helpful comments from Jane Muldoon, Sally Satel and Gene Smolensky and from participants in a seminar at the School of Public Affairs at the University of Maryland.

REFERENCES

[1] Currie, E. (1993). *Reckoning: Drugs, the cities, and the American future.* New York: Hill and Wang.

[2] Heather, N., Wodak, A., Nadelmann, E., and O'Hare, P., (Eds.) (1993). *Psychoactive drugs and harm reduction: From faith to science.* London: Whurr.

[3] Kirp, D., and Bayer, R. (1992). *AIDS in the industrialized democracies.* New Brunswick, NJ: Rutgers University Press.

[4] MacCoun, R. J., and Caulkins, J. (1996). Examining the behavioral assumptions of the National Drug Control Strategy. In W. K. Bickel and R. J. DeGrandpre (Eds.), *Drug policy and human nature: Psychological perspectives on the prevention, management, and treatment of illicit drug use.* New York: Plenum Press.

[5] Strang, J. (1993). Drug use and harm reduction: Responding to the challenge. In N. Heather, A. Wodak, E. Nadelmann, and P. O'Hare (Eds.), *Psychoactive drugs and harm reduction: From faith to science.* London: Whurr.

[6] Rice, D., Kelman, S., and Miller, L. (1990). *The economic costs of alcohol and drug abuse and mental illness, 1985.* Rockville, MD: Alcohol, Drug Abuse and Mental Health Administration.

[7] Katz, J. (1989). *Seductions of crime.* New York: Basic Books.

[8] Loxley, W., Carruthers, S., and Bevan, J. (1995). *In the same vein: First report of the Australian study of HIV and injecting drug use.* Perth: Australian National Center for Research into Prevention of Drug Abuse, Curtin University.

[9] Johnston, B., Goldstein, P., Preble, E., et al. (1985). *Taking care of business: The economics of crime by heroin abusers.* Lexington, Mass: Lexington Books.

[10] Needle, R. and Mills, A. (1994). *Drug procurement practices of the out-of-treatment chronic drug abuser.* Rockville, MD: National Institute on Drug Abuse.

[11] Grapendaal, M., Leuw, E., and Nelen, H. (1992). Drugs and crime in an accommodating social context: The situation in Amsterdam. *Contemp. Drug Problems, 19,* 303–326.

[12] Bretteville-Jensen, A. L., and Sutton, M. (1996). The income-generating behavior of injecting drug users in Oslo. *Addiction, 91,* 63–80.

[13] U.S. Congress, House of Representatives, Committee on Ways and Means. (1993). *Overview of entitlement programs.* Washington, DC: Government Printing Office.

[14] U.S. General Accounting Office. (1994). *Social Security: Major changes needed for disability benefits for addicts.* Washington, DC.

[15] U.S. Department of Health and Human Services. (1994). *SSI payments to drug addicts and alcoholics: Continued dependence. An expanded analysis.* Office of the Inspector General, Washington, DC.

[16] Ross, J. (1995, January 27). Supplemental security income: Recent growth in the Rolls raises fundamental program concerns. Testimony before House Ways and Means Committee, Subcommittee on Human Resources.

[17] Wright, C. (1995). *SSI: The black hole of the welfare state.* Policy Analysis, no. 224. Washington, DC: Cato Institute.

[18] Shaner, A., Eckman, T. A., Roberts, L. J., et al. (1995). Disability income, cocaine use, repeated hospitalization among schizophrenic cocaine abusers—a government sponsored revolving door? *N Engl J Med, 333,* 777–783.

[19] Satel, S. (1995). When disability benefits make patients sicker. *N Engl J Med, 333,* 794–796.

[20] Solomon, C. (1995). *Supplemental Security Income (SSI) drug addicts and alcoholics: Welfare reform in the 104th Congress.* Washington, DC: U.S. Congressional Research Service.

[21] Anglin, M. D., and Hser, Y-I. (1993). Treatment of drug dependence. In M. Tonry and J. Wilson (Eds.), *Drugs and crime.* Chicago: University of Chicago Press.

[22] Hser, Y., Anglin, M. D., and Powers, K. (1993). A 24-year follow-up of California narcotics addicts. *Arch Gen Psychiatr, 50,* 522–584.

[23] Gerstein, D., Johnson, R., Harwood, H., et al. (1994). *Evaluating recovery services: The California drug and alcohol treatment assessment.* Sacramento, CA: California Department of Alcohol and Drug Programs.

[24] Weiner, B., Perry, R. B., and Magnusson, J. (1988). An attributional analysis of reactions to stigma. *J Personality Social Psychol, 55,* 738–748.

20

A Cultural Impact of Needle Exchange:
The Role of Safer-Injection Mentors

MARGARET S. KELLEY

SHEIGLA MURPHY

HOWARD LUNE

ABSTRACT

We examine one way in which needle-exchange services in the San Francisco Bay Area have affected needle-sharing and sexual-risk behaviors for injection drug users. We interviewed, qualitatively and quantitatively, 244 participants. Our analysis focuses on comparisons in HIV/AIDS-risk behaviors for a subcategory of "new" injectors: those initiating after the introduction of needle-exchange services in 1988 (n = 57). We found that some new injectors benefited from the presence of "safer-injection mentors." That is, those with someone to teach them harm reduction from their initiation of injection drug use were somewhat more likely to report safer injection practices at the time of interview. We also found that the mentoring process included sharing of information about needle-exchange services. Our results point to evidence of the effectiveness of needle-exchange services in contributing to a culture of harm reduction for injection drug users.

There is disagreement over the role and efficacy of harm-reduction education generally, and of needle-exchange programs in particular, within the field of HIV studies. Considerable evidence shows that (a) injection drug users (IDUs) actively seek and respond to health information; (b) IDUs, in some cases, have organized and engaged in high-risk activism to protect the lives and interests of drug users; (c) IDUs have been active volunteers in street outreach and needle-exchange operations, encouraging other users to participate in needle exchange and related risk-reduction programs; and (d) knowledgeable IDUs have provided information about health maintenance and risk reduction to other users outside of the needle-exchange setting.

Prevention studies and assessments of interventions find that even where HIV-risk behaviors are reduced, people continue to engage in them to some degree. It is not difficult to see why some IDUs do this. Illicit drug use is already inherently dangerous, and physically, emotionally and socially destructive. It often costs users their families, homes and jobs, while exposing them to risk of disease, arrest, and violence. The additional, rather vague threat of HIV/AIDS alone is not going to keep IDUs from injecting. Furthermore, many risk activities are actively encouraged by the legal sanctions against drug use. Users cannot afford to be caught carrying injection equipment, so they do not carry clean needles (Murphy, 1987). Increased police surveillance has been associated with higher-risk drug use, while reduced attention to paraphernalia laws has led to greater risk reduction (Case et al., 1998; Groseclose et al., 1995). Clearly, prevention education is not sufficient to eliminate risk behaviors for IDUs. The more relevant question is *Under what circumstances will IDUs inject more safely?*

We are interested in why and how IDUs learn and teach harm-reduction behaviors. We address the complex relationship between needle exchange and changes in risk behaviors from the perspectives of a subset of 57 IDUs. These IDUs all began injecting after 1988, subsequent to the introduction of needle exchange in the community. The gap between knowledge and behavior change may be at least partially explained by what our qualitative interviews reveal as a developing "culture of harm reduction," initiated by "safer-injection mentors" and facilitated by the material condition of needle exchange in the community. According to Erickson, "the future of success of harm reduction as a unifying concept will depend on its innovative application . . . and careful evaluation of its effectiveness in a variety of cultural contexts" (Erickson, 1999, p. 1). We believe our results offer important insights into the qualitative impact of needle-exchange programs and contribute to the understanding of risk perception and risk management for this population.

NEEDLE EXCHANGE AND CULTURAL ACTIVISM

Most forms of injecting drug use are felony offenses in the United States. In addition, they are highly stigmatized, inherently dangerous, and harshly punished. These facts, along with the social marginality of many IDUs, contribute to keeping the social organization of drug users limited and underground (Henman et al., 1998). Nonetheless, in the early years of HIV/AIDS many active and former drug users participated in the political and legal challenges that brought needle exchange to this country.

Research indicates that despite the risk of arrest and even targeted harassment by police for participating in organized HIV/AIDS risk-reduction activities (Case et al., 1998), IDUs are not significantly more antisocial than others or less able to learn and change. But it was this public perception that initially led to the development of drug-user organizations. It has been recognized that these user organizations contributed in many countries to more effective HIV-prevention policies for drug users (Friedman et al., 1993). IDUs in Amsterdam organized the world's first needle exchange. Prior to the establishment of the needle-exchange waiver system in the state of New York, and to a lesser extent since then, IDUs have participated in the operation of "underground" needle exchanges. Each of the five initial needle exchanges in New York City to receive state waivers had begun as an underground exchange program, managed by users and needle-exchange advocates without support from public health officials. Since that time, IDUs have participated in the advisory boards of many of the existing needle exchanges, and their participation

is presently a requirement of the state health department in New York (Henman et al., 1998). Implicit in this work has been the collaboration of IDUs with the public health sector. Public health interventions have taken the form of prevention campaigns employing the media, educational groups or seminars, and street outreach workers. However, it has been amply demonstrated that an individual's knowledge of high-risk behaviors alone is insufficient to ensure cessation of risky activities (Davis-Berman and Brown, 1990; Friedman et al., 1992b; Inciardi, 1990; Murphy, 1987; Murphy and Waldorf, 1991; Otomanelli et al., 1990; Page et al., 1991). IDUs and their advocates have been on the cutting edge of initiatives to change the behavior of other drug users.

One of the extrainstitutional innovations generated by needle-exchange participants is satellite, or secondary, exchange. Key IDUs may identify themselves to the program as representatives of a user collective and thereby make special arrangements to exchange needles in quantities of one or two hundred at a time (Grund et al., 1992). Although secondary exchange is formally restricted by the one-for-one policies of most United States exchange sites, users purchase or collect used needles from their associates in order to increase the number of clean needles available to them (Guydish et al., 1998). Almost 10% of the regular participants at a Baltimore needle exchange were characterized as secondary exchangers. The Baltimore study concluded that "satellite exchangers provide a natural extension of [needle-exchange programs] that further their outreach into otherwise underserved groups" (Valente et al., 1998, 95). Studies of San Francisco's Prevention Point found that over one-third of participants surveyed were involved in secondary exchange (Guydish et al., 1998; Murphy et al., 1996; Murphy et al., 2004).

In a more formally constituted initiative in New York, researchers and advocates for drug users operated a project from 1988 to 1989 to support self-organization against HIV/AIDS among drug injectors. Although the organizational efforts did not achieve stability, a follow-up study found that those injectors who had participated in group meetings not only significantly reduced their own risk activities, but remained active in encouraging behavioral change among others (Friedman et al., 1992a).

Research into needle-exchange operations has affirmed the role of an active minority of IDUs as organizers, activists, and outreach workers (Abdul-Quader et al., 1999; Centers for Disease Control and Prevention, 1995; Henman et al., 1998). IDU volunteers attempt to form a "bridge" to health services for needle-exchange participants. A study of 55 needle-exchange programs in the United States identified a variety of behavioral and health benefits sought by participants from the programs, including provision of latex condoms (82%), HIV counseling and testing (42%), tuberculin skin testing (22%), primary health care (18%), and directly observed tuberculosis therapy (11%) (Centers for Disease Control and Prevention, 1995).

NEEDLE-REUSE ETIQUETTE

There is a long-standing sociological tradition of examining induction to drug use that highlights the strong social and interactional elements of learning to use drugs (Becker, 1953; Coggans and McKellar, 1994; Crisp et al., 1997; Hirsch et al., 1995). The norms of using drugs and sharing needles are differentiated by situation and social category of the user (Crisp et al., 1997; Murphy, 1987). Social and political structures have been found to have profound effects on the physiological experience of drug use (Bunce, 1979). Two important cultural factors that help determine order of injection are who owns the injection equipment and who paid for the drugs, though individual assertiveness and other social relations are able to overcome these prioritizing factors (Crisp et al., 1997). Cultural belief systems influence both the learning of technique and motivation (Becker, 1953), and these belief systems are well understood by members of the group.

Cultural interpretations may minimize or overlook practical considerations, since patterns of equipment sharing are more complex than serving as rituals of power. Even the term "sharing" when referring to the reuse of others' equipment implies that users freely chose when and with whom to share. Underlying this decision process, however, is the fact that "syringes are shared because they are scarce, and they are scarce because they are illegal to possess without medical justification" (Koester, 1994, p. 287). Needle exchange is one material condition that facilitates a new etiquette of safer injection because it addresses this scarcity of needles. Given both the social and the legal dimensions of syringe reuse, we examine the new etiquette of injection drug use and the activism of drug users in teaching safer injection.

METHODS AND PROCEDURES

We conducted a three-year process evaluation of Prevention Point, the needle-exchange program in San Francisco.[1] Prevention Point began illegal distribution of needles and other harm-reduction materials in San Francisco in 1988.[2] Rapid expansion and community need led Mayor Frank Jordan and San Francisco's Board of Supervisors to declare a state of medical emergency in March 1993, allowing the city to circumvent California's prescription and paraphernalia laws, although it did not minimize the illegality of possession of syringes. It also allowed San Francisco's Department of Public Health to fund Prevention Point and allow needle-exchange volunteers and staff to exchange syringes. At the time of data collection, Prevention Point operated eight sessions, Monday through Friday. Program staff at all sites dispensed needles, cotton, alcohol wipes, and condoms. In addition, treatment and medical referrals and HIV/AIDS information were available upon request. The program model was one of low centralization and low formalization (Murphy et al., 1996; Wenger et al., 1996). Providers participated in the development and management of the organization. They required very little from clients in terms of their continued participation.

We use multiple data sources to triangulate on the key variables. Data collection included participant observation, indepth life-history interviews, and a closed-ended quantitative instrument. Here we use the quantitative data to define the phenomena and the interviews to explore their meaning to the people who are engaging in making these decisions about risk. We completed data collection in September 1995 with a total of 244 study participants recruited from eight needle-exchange sites. We selected our study participants using maximum-variation sampling, which aims at capturing the central themes that cut across a great deal of participation variation. The logic of maximum-variation sampling presumes that any common patterns emerging from great variation are of value in understanding the core experiences of program participants (Patton, 1987). Our sampling strategy was informed by intensive field work at all participating needle-exchange sites, for the reason that "by including in the sample individuals the evaluator determines have had quite different experiences, it is possible to describe more thoroughly the variation in the group and to understand variations in experiences" (Patton, 1987, p. 54).

We sought to maximize variation in age, sex, and race. We also used this method to maximize variation in drug of choice by recruiting heroin, speed, and cocaine users. The demographic variables were not necessarily predicted to explain differences in outcome measure of harm-reduction activity. All subjects were similar in key ways: They were regular injectors of illegal drugs; and they had either participated in a needle exchange or knew of needle exchange. Many kept a schedule to exchange needles for their own safety and the safety of others. But they were not all from one neighborhood, one ethnic background, or one supposed drug "subculture."

Experienced field workers approached needle-exchange participants and screened volunteer respondents for inclusion in the study. Interview appointments were made with those who met the criteria. Interviews took place either in the field office or out in the field, depending on which was more convenient for the study participant. Interviews were tape recorded and lasted two to four hours. Participants were paid $50 for their time. All participants were informed about their rights and protection of confidentiality.

We identified those study participants with mentors from the interview transcripts during content analysis. Many questions were asked about the process of becoming an injector and the people involved in the transition. Safer-injection mentors were friends or relatives of injecting drug users who taught them safer methods for injecting drugs and influenced their attitudes about reducing drug-related harms. Mentors were experienced injectors who were knowledgeable about HIV-prevention techniques and took the time to share this information with less knowledgeable and less experienced injectors. This knowledge consisted of more than the logistics of injecting. Rather, it consisted of techniques of *safer* injecting. Those without mentors were not social isolates, but they did lack a personal relationship with someone who was willing and able to share information about HIV prevention. We adopted the term "mentor" from the words of Tim, a 35-year-old white man, as his experience captures that of many others:

> Well, both my brothers use drugs. Michael, my brother on the West Coast, has always in many ways been kind of like my mentor. He and I are very close, and he taught me a lot about my attitudes and thoughts. And we discussed injecting one time. And in fact, if you're going to use heroin, that's probably the easiest way on the body to do it, as long as you know what you're doing. About a year and a half ago, I started using that as my way of choice of doing it. (322)

Study participants were classified as having a mentor based on their initial injection experience. These mentoring relationships were usually defined as ongoing affiliations, with participants continuing to have contact with the person who mentored them through the time of data collection.

In the following we use the quantitative information to summarize the risk behaviors for the subsample. While we report the results of some significance tests (including non-parametric tests and odds ratios), we realize that these are preliminary, considering the small quota sample. Because our focus is on the qualitative nature of the relationships, we weave in the qualitative results to provide context and meaning of these behaviors. Our analysis is limited by the nature of the data collection. Therefore our results are only representative of the population under study.

FINDINGS

Description of the Study Population

We compared risk behaviors for those with and without mentors for only those injectors who initiated injection after needle-exchange services were made available in the community. The two groups did not differ significantly by demographic characteristics. There were 24 women and 33 men in the subsample. Of these, females were less likely to report having a mentor. The overall average age was 28.3. The majority of both groups were white, followed by African-American and other ethnicities. The respondents reported an average of 12.5 years of education. Two-thirds of those with mentors used heroin as their drug of choice, while 47% of those without mentors reported heroin as their primary drug. Speed was the next most common primary drug, followed by cocaine. The overall average period of time for injecting was 2.26 years.

The overall serostatus rate was quite low for the subsample of new injectors, with only three reporting as positive (11 had not been tested or did not know the results). However, because rates often follow risky behavior, we can learn a lot about potential conversions by examining other risk behaviors. We next review needle-sharing behaviors and sexual-risk behaviors for the subset of new injectors, comparing those with and without mentors. Part of this review is spent examining the context of needle sharing, including the makeup of sharing partners, and needle-exchange participation. We then describe in detail the experience of mentoring and conclude with a discussion of the implications of our findings about the nature of mentoring for this at-risk population.

Sharing Needles and Other Injection Equipment

The following table provides the results for comparisons of recent risk behaviors by mentor status. Slightly fewer of those with mentors reported having shared needles in the six months prior to the interview. Of those sharing in the past six months, there was a significant difference in the mean number of times shared, with 8.8 times for those with mentors compared to 27.4 for those without mentors. There was also a significant difference for having shared in the past 30 days, with those without mentors being over three times as likely to have shared a needle (OR 3.50, 95% CI 1.102–11.116).

In addition to sharing needles, there are other high-risk injection behaviors, such as sharing cookers, failing to clean injection sites, and going to shooting galleries. Our most interesting finding is that those with mentors reported more often cleaning their skin before injecting (OR 3.45, CI .819–14.525). Supplies for cleaning injection sites were available at all needle exchanges. Overall, very few new injectors had used a shooting gallery in the past six months. Finally, those without mentors shared more days for all types of drugs. The only significant differences in sharing needles were when injecting speed. Many of the non-significant findings were due to small cell sizes, but they are in the expected direction. For example, while days injecting heroin were nearly the same for those with and without mentors, those with mentors shared fewer days (30.3 compared to 52.0).

Interviews with IDUs in our study population revealed reasonably consistent knowledge about HIV/AIDS and differences in the use of that knowledge. As expected, the new injectors in general had high knowledge of risk behaviors and of how to reduce personal harm related to drug injecting, likely resulting from the growing availability of information about needle exchange and risk reduction. Many of our study participants reported that they did not share needles at all. Others shared only with their current sex partner. For example, Jessica (344), a 20-year-old white woman, left home when she was 17 and found her way to New York City. While there, she started snorting cocaine and heroin, eventually transitioning to heroin injection. She had learned about AIDS while in high school and already knew she should not share injection equipment. However, she did share with her current boyfriend.

Having a mentor did not guarantee continued safer injection. Alan (343), a 20-year-old white man, was in elementary school when his uncle died of AIDS and his mother talked to him about HIV transmission for the first time. When he first began injecting drugs, after learning about the risks from his mother, he would buy clean needles on the street. But he occasionally shared them with his girlfriend, figuring that since they were not using condoms, they might as well share needles.

Jack, a 43-year-old white man, shared needles but always made sure his partner bleached them first. His partner of 10 years always injected for Jack first before injecting himself. They both took care to minimize their risk. Jack described the meticulous bleaching process:

> He gets out a little thing of bleach, and a cup of water there, he'll take the needle and he'll throw the bleach into the syringe, and squirt it out, and

TABLE 1   Recent Risk Behaviors by Safer-Injection Mentor Status (past 6 months)

	MENTOR $n = 27$	NO MENTOR $n = 30$	SIGNIFICANCE
Shared Needle	55.6%	60.0%	NS
Mean Times Shared Needle	8.8	27.4	$p = .067$
Shared Needle (30 days)	22.2%	50.0%	Cramer's V = .288 $p = .030$
Shared Cooker	59.3%	63.3%	NS
Used Shooting Gallery	7.4%	13.3%	NS
Cleaned Skin	88.9%	69.0%	Cramer's V = .243 $p = .069$
Mean Days Shared Heroin	30.3	52.0	NS
Mean Days Shared Cocaine	6.0	37.0	NS
Mean Days Shared Speed	10.4	45.6	$p = .049$

he'll do that about three times, and then he'll rinse it out with water around three times. . . . Usually when he gets through, when we get through, he'll bleach and clean it before he puts it up. But then he'll still go ahead and clean it again before we use it. He's very careful. (305)

Although Jack had not been tested for HIV, his partner had tested negative several times, and they had been monogamous for more than six years.

Matthew (263), a 38-year-old African-American man, had been injecting drugs for four years. Prior to that he dealt drugs and saw many other drug users engage in high-risk behaviors such as sharing cotton, cookers and needles. He also saw many of them suffer the consequences of sharing when they seroconverted or caught other diseases. He learned about the risks of sharing from his brother and later from educational programs in prison. As a result, he never shared needles, cotton, or water.

These and other stories about sharing point to the complex relationship between risk-reduction measures and the negotiated risk of consenting to share injection equipment, especially with sex partners.

Sexual Behaviors

Many sexual-risk behaviors varied but were not significantly different for the two groups. Those with mentors reported fewer partners for both the past five years and in the past six months. In addition, fewer mentored participants reported sharing sex toys or having sex that involved bleeding, but the differences were not significant. In further analyses, when dichotomized as "never" versus "at least sometimes" using condoms or latex protection during sexual activity, those with mentors were much more likely to use condoms. That is, new injectors with mentors were 3.3 times as likely to at least sometimes use latex protection during sex (OR 3.30, 95% CI .91–12.16). It is possible that the advice of a safer-injection mentor, coupled with needle-exchange services, spilled over into reducing risky sexual behaviors.

Kelly, a 26-year-old Native American new injector with a mentor, understood safe sex to mean using a condom. She then explained about her needle sharing and sexual relationships:

> I guess I do sort of have a false sense of security. Even with my boyfriend, when we were shooting up, we never shared a needle . . . even though we'd have unsafe sex. But I would never in a million years share needles with somebody. (271)

Kelly compared sharing needles to "playing Russian Roulette." She believed it was "ten times worse than having unsafe sex," because she could see the blood involved in the sharing of needles, and she believed it was statistically easier to get HIV through sharing than through unsafe sex.

Needle Exchange

Most of the new injectors with mentors heard about needle exchange from friends or family (77.8%). While the majority of those without mentors were also likely to hear about needle exchange from friends or family, they reported a higher rate of learning about needle exchange from service providers or the media (36.6%). Those with mentors reported overall fewer barriers to needle exchange: 2.4 compared to 3.0 for those without mentors (although not significant). Cara, a 24-year-old white woman, did not have a safer-injection mentor and did share needles with her current sex partner. They did not use the needle-exchange program, for practical reasons. She described their needle sharing:

> I'll use it and hand it to him and he uses it. We'll have rigs that either one of us has used that we keep in the same bag and we'll just take one, ones that have been used, before we use again. Because we're so far away from the needle exchange. (120)

All needle-exchange sites distributed information about all kinds of risk involved with drug injection. Respondents reported learning about risks with sharing injection equipment other than needles from needle exchange. For example, Brad, a 26-year-old white man, remembering his first experience with needle exchange, said:

> I figured there would be some place to throw your old [needles]. And you would form a line. It was a little different. I didn't expect that they would give out all the accouterments. Bleach and condoms even, and alcohol wipes and cotton, but it's cool. (125)

An Emerging Culture of Harm Reduction

Almost half of the new injectors we interviewed explained that when they first learned to inject drugs, they also learned the basics of safer injection practices (n = 27). These new injectors with "safer-injection mentors" in our study population were somewhat more likely to be white men less than 44 years old.

The new injectors identified friends, family, and lovers as responsible for sharing specific and detailed information about reducing risk when injecting. Safer-injection mentoring was most often initiated by other new injectors rather than by someone who had been injecting for a long time. For example, Monique (133), an 18-year-old white woman, learned about HIV-risk reduction and safer injection from her boyfriend. From the very beginning of her injection drug use, she knew how to reduce her drug-related harm by not sharing or by bleaching the syringe if she did share.

Mentors were often friends of the respondents. Richard (226), a 24-year-old white man, learned generally about HIV long before he started injecting heroin. He described how he was taught by a close friend to clean his injection equipment from the first time he injected, and he was also taught not to share needles. He believed this was partly because one of the people who taught him how to inject was HIV-positive. Jeff (113), a 27-year-old white man, explained that some friends taught him the logistics of how to inject properly (measuring the drug, etc.) and also taught him safer injection practices, such as how to mark his syringes and keep them separate from others' syringes, how to bleach his needles, and where to go to exchange his syringes.

There were, of course, some new injectors without mentors who took safety precautions. Marcus, a 21-year-old white man, never shared needles and was irritated by assumptions about IDUs being careless and taking risks. He said:

> Most people that use needles that I've come in contact with, contrary to what people think about junkies, they don't share needles. You know, it's mostly the people that live on the streets . . . well, I don't even want to say that, 'cause that's just another stereotype. Most people I've come in contact with just don't share needles . . . it's just an unwritten law. (244)

Shane, a 36-year-old white man, reported that a friend fixed him the first time and insisted on safe practices. He explained:

> Yeah. He taught me. And not only him, but another friend of mine as well, who was a nurse, taught me. And I feel like I learned from the best. (280)

These and other study participants who learned safer injection techniques from their friends and family reflect the development of a harm-reduction culture that can be passed on among injector cohorts. Our qualitative interviews indicate that safer-injection mentoring is indeed more than a possibility for drug-injecting populations, and is in fact already happening informally. As shown in other studies, there is an important role for IDUs in teaching each other the skills and methods of harm reduction. As one respondent put it, "You got to have somebody takin' care of you."

One result of the mentoring culture was a change in the etiquette of needle sharing. That is, the process of learning to enjoy the physiological effects of the drug was coupled with users' knowing they were protected from HIV/AIDS and other communicable diseases. Where previous research has found that neophyte users are the most likely to share (Murphy, 1987), we found a new pattern, with new users learning how *not* to share. The learning of risk-reduction behaviors by this population is a positive move toward reducing harm associated with drug injection. Needle exchange does not serve to initiate users, but it can decrease risk among those who do transition to injection drug use. At the same time, the lack of an initial mentor does not mean the respondents were not capable of learning to be safer, as indicated by those who did not share needles in the months prior to the interview.

DISCUSSION

Despite research findings to the contrary, some have implied that drug injectors are not likely to pass on risk-reduction information to their peers. According to Bloor,

> [t]he drug-injecting population has previously proved very unstable, future waves of injecting have not been predicted, and there has been limited overlap between successive waves of injectors—implying the lessons of HIV risk reduction will have to be repeated and learnt anew. (Bloor, 1995, p. 123)

Such speculation about drug-injecting populations may be preliminary, considering that most communities in the United States do not have stable and reliable risk-reduction tools, including needle exchange and other educational materials.[3] Other research follows the body of research pointing to the willingness and ability of active drug users being "competent collaborators" in public health programs designed to reduce their risk (Broadhead et al., 1998; Heckathorn et al., 1999; Henman et al., 1998; Sergeyev et al., 1999). Their increased "legitimacy and sense of personal worth" resulting from organizing create an opportunity to maximize harm-reduction networks (Henman et al.,1998, p. 397).

We began this exploratory and qualitative investigation by seeking detailed descriptions of the experiences of a subset of newer injectors in our sample. We found that their experiences varied by a number of factors, including the presence of safer-injection mentors. Those study participants with mentors reported fewer injection-risk and sexual-risk behaviors. Our contribution to the research has been the identification of an important element in the incorporation of needle exchange into communities. The role of the safer-injection mentor is one that highlights the potential of engaging drug users to spread safer-injection information. While others have reported similar findings about the networks of drug users and the capability of IDUs to participate in formal outreach efforts (Broadhead et al., 1998; Friedman et al., 1992a; Heckathorn et al., 1999; Sergeyev et al., 1999), our research focuses on the informal sharing of information that IDUs initiate without official incentive—their only motive that of keeping each other alive.

These mentors were instrumental in getting new injectors to utilize needle-exchange services and to implement safer injection practices from the beginning stages of drug use. Knowledge did not necessarily translate into behaviors for our study participants. Although overall new injectors who were trained from their initiation to injection drug use to follow safe regimens regarding needle sharing did demonstrate fewer risk incidents for needle sharing, some risk incidents did occur. We found that some of our study participants congregated in very different social groups, but that others were initiated into the larger needle-exchange circle and taught a new etiquette of safer injection. The presence or absence of mentoring, in fact, might be an indirect measure of social integration for the injectors engaging in fewer risk behaviors.

Respondents with regular and manageable access to harm-reduction tools attempted to use those tools to stop the transmission of HIV. By the time the new injectors reach drug-use maturity, with continued access to harm-reduction measures such as the needle-exchange program in conjunction with educa-tion and information opportunities, the culture of harm reduction may be widespread and deeply entrenched in drug-using circles. Based on our findings, we believe that needle-exchange programs, as modeled in the San Francisco Bay Area, facilitate changing norms and actively encourage a culture of harm reduction rather than a culture of risk. In addition, according to our study participants, the Prevention Point needle-exchange program has made an impact on the needle-sharing behaviors of our study population. Those study participants who were new injectors who also had safer-injection mentors exhibited lower risk for both injection-risk and sexual-risk behaviors. The new etiquette, comprised of safe injecting and cultural activism, reflects the culture of harm reduction surrounding injection drug use.

Our findings about the culture of harm reduction among IDUs suggest numerous areas for future research and hypotheses testing. For example, what social mechanisms encourage new injectors to participate in sharing safer injection practices and information with other injectors? A growing area of research in drug studies focuses specifically on the conditions of transition to injection (Kelley and Chitwood, 2004; Neaigus et al., 1998). This focus should include general network analysis as well as contextual analysis of the process of mentoring. Our exploratory results should be taken into account in future studies intended to solicit deeper understanding of social networks, mentoring, and the negotiation of risk. How do respondents arrive at the point of willingness to commit to safer-injection practices? What are the components of social integration that tie the safer-injecting mentors to other injectors? What is the role of secondary exchangers in expanding this culture? Probably most significantly, what are the social processes that enable IDUs to formally organize around health and safety issues in a political environment hostile to their social status? Many of these questions are already the focus of study in places such as Britain, Australia, and many European countries where needle exchange has long been instituted. These processes should be clearly addressed in research in the United States.

NOTES

1. This was a NIDA-funded study, "AIDS Prevention: An Ethnography of Needle Exchange" (RO1 DA08322), Sheigla Murphy as principal investigator, The Institute for Scientific Analysis. As of this writing, Prevention Point has been renamed San Francisco's HIV Prevention Project. The study participants have been assigned pseudonyms to protect their confidentiality.

2. Bleach distribution was begun in the San Francisco Bay Area in 1986 by community health outreach workers.

3. Although continuing to increase in number, at the time of data collection there was a limited number of exchange programs in the United States. In a review of the national profile of needle-exchange programs, it was found that between 1994 and 1996 there was a 54% increase in the number of cities operating a needle-exchange program (a total of 87 programs responded to an inquiry for information) (Paone et al., 1999).

REFERENCES

Abdul-Quader, A., Des Jarlais, D., Chatterjee, A., Hirky, E., and Friedman, S. (1999). Interventions for injecting drug users. In L. Gibney, R. J. Diclemente, and S. H. Vermund (Eds.), *Preventing HIV in Developing Countries: Biomedical and Behavioral Approaches* (pp. 283–312). New York: Plenum Press.

Becker, H. (1953). Becoming a marijuana user. *American Journal of Sociology*, 59, 235–243.

Bloor, M. 1995. *The sociology of HIV transmission.* Thousand Oaks, CA: Sage.

Broadhead, R. S., Heckathorn, D. D., Weakliem, D. L., Anthony, D. L., Madray, H., Mills, R. J., and Hughes, J. (1998). *Harnessing peer networks as an instrument for AIDS prevention: Results from a peer-driven intervention.* Paper presented at the American Sociological Association annual conference, San Francisco, CA.

Bunce, R. (1979). Social and political sources of drug effects: The case of bad trips on psychedelics. *Journal of Drug Issues*, 2, 213–233.

Case, P., Meehan, T., and Jones, T. S. (1998). Arrests and incarceration of injection drug users for syringe possession in Massachusetts: Implications for prevention. *Journal of Acquired Immune Deficiency Syndromes and Human Retrovirology*, 18 (Supplement 1): S71–S75.

Centers for Disease Control and Prevention. (1995). Syringe exchange programs—United States, 1994–1995. *Morbidity and Mortality Weekly Report*, 44 (37), 684–685, 691.

Coggans, N., and McKellar, S. (1994). Drug use amongst peers: Peer pressure or peer preference? *Drugs: Education, Prevention and Policy*, 1(1): 15–26.

Crisp, B. R., Barber, J. G., and Gilbertson, R. (1997). The etiquette of needle-sharing. *Contemporary Drug Problems*, 24, 273–291.

Davis-Berman, J., and Brown, D. (1990). AIDS knowledge and risky behavior by incarcerated females: IV and non IV-drug users. *Sociology and Social Research*, 75(1), 8–16.

Erickson, P. G. (1999). Introduction: The three phases of harm reduction. An examination of emerging concepts, methodologies, and critiques. *Substance Use and Misuse*, 34(1), 1–7.

Friedman, S. R., de Jong, W., and Wodak, A. (1993). Community development as a response to HIV among drug injectors. *AIDS*, 7 (Supplement 1), S263–S269.

Friedman, S., Des Jarlais, D. C., Neaigus, A., Jose, B., Sufian, M., Stepherson, B., Mota, P., and Manthei, D. (1992a). Organizing drug injectors against AIDS: Preliminary data on behavioral outcomes. *Psychology of Addictive Behaviors*, 6 (2), 100–106.

Friedman, S. R., Neaigus, A., Des Jarlais, D. C., Sotheran, J. L., Woods, J., Sufian, M., Stepherson, B., and Sterk, C. E. (1992b). Social intervention against AIDS among injecting drug users. *British Journal of Addiction*, 87, 393–404.

Groseclose, S. L., Weinstein, B., Jones, T. S., Valleroy, L. A., Fehrs, L. J., and Kassler, W. J. (1995). Impact of increased legal access to needles and syringes on practices of injecting-drug users and police officers—Connecticut, 1992–1993. *Journal of Acquired Immune Deficiency Syndromes and Human Retrovirology*, 10(1), 82–89.

Grund, J., Blanken, P., Adriaans, N., Kaplan, C., Barendregt, C., and Meeuwsen, M. (1992). Reaching the unreached: Targeting hidden IDU populations with clean needles via known user groups. *Journal of Psychoactive Drugs*, 24(1), 41–47.

Guydish, J., Bucardo, J., Clark, G., and Bernheim, S. (1998). Evaluating needle exchange: A description of client characteristics, health status, program utilization, and HIV risk behavior. *Substance Use and Misuse*, 33(5), 1173–1196.

Heckathorn, D. D., Broadhead, R. S., Anthony, D. L., and Weakliem, D. L. (1999). AIDS and social networks: HIV prevention through network mobilization. *Sociological Focus*, 32(2), 159–179.

Henman, A. R., Paone, D., Des Jarlais, D. C., Kochems, L. M., and Friedman, S. R. (1998). Injection drug users as social actors: A stigmatized community's participation in the syringe exchange programmes of New York City. *AIDS Care*, 10(4), 397–408.

Hirsch, M. L., Conforth, R. W., and Graney, C. J. (1995). The use of marijuana for pleasure: A replication of Howard S. Becker's study of marijuana use. In J. A. Inciardi and K. McElrath (eds.), *The American drug scene* (pp. 34–41). Los Angeles, CA: Roxbury Publishing Company.

Inciardi, J. (1990). HIV, AIDS and intravenous drug use: Some considerations. *Journal of Drug Issues*, 20, 181–194.

Kelley, M. S., and Chitwood, D. (2004). Effects of drug treatment for heroin sniffers: A protective factor against moving to injection? *Social Science and Medicine*, 58(10): 2083–2092.

Koester, S. K. (1994). Copping, running, and paraphernalia laws: Contextual variables and needle risk behavior among injecting drug users in Denver. *Human Organization*, 53(3), 287–295.

Murphy, S. (1987). Intravenous drug use and AIDS: The social economy of needle sharing. *Contemporary Drug Problems*, 14(3), 373–393.

Murphy, S., Kelley, M. S., and Lune, H. (2004). The Health Benefits of Secondary Syringe Exchange. *Journal of Drug Issues*, 34(2): 245–268.

Murphy, S., and Waldorf, D. (1991). Kicking down to the street doc: Shooting galleries in the San Francisco Bay area. *Contemporary Drug Problems*, 28(1), 9–29.

Murphy, S., Wenger, L., and Kelley, M. S. (1996). *An ethnographic study of needle exchange. San Francisco, Institute for Scientific Analysis.* Final Report to the National Institute on Drug Abuse.

Neaigus, A., Atillasoy, A., Friedman, S. R., Andrade, X., Miller, M., Ildefonso, G., and Des Jarlais, D. C. (1998). Trends in the noninjected use of heroin and factors associated with the transitions to injecting. In J. A. Inciardi and L. D. Harrison (Eds.), *Heroin in the age of crack cocaine*, (pp. 131–159). Thousand Oaks, CA: Sage.

Otomanelli, G., Kramer, T., Bihari, B., Fine, J., Heller, S., and Mosely, J. (1990). AIDS-related risk behaviors among substance abusers. *International Journal of the Addictions*, 25, 291–299.

Page, J., Smith, P., and Kane, N. (1991). Shooting galleries, their proprietors, and implications for prevention of AIDS. *Drugs and Society 5*, 69–85.

Paone, D., Clark, J., Shi, Q., Purchase, D., and Des Jarlais, D. C. (1999). Syringe exchange in the United States, 1996: A national profile. *American Journal of Public Health*, 89(1), 43–46.

Patton, M. (1987). *How to use qualitative methods in evaluation*. Beverly Hills: Sage.

Sergeyev, B., Oparina, T., Rumyantseva, T. P., Volkanevskii, V. L., Broadhead, R. S., Heckathorn, D. D., and Madray, H. (1999). HIV prevention in Yaroslavl, Russia: A peer-driven intervention and needle exchange. *Journal of Drug Issues*, 29(4), 777–803.

Valente, T. W., Foreman, R., Junge, B., and Vlahov, D. (1998). Satellite exchange in the Baltimore needle exchange program. *Public Health Reports*, 113 (Supplement 1), 90–96.

Wenger, L., Murphy, S., and Kelley, M. S. (1996). *Barriers to needle exchange for San Francisco Bay area injection drug users*. Paper presented at the North American Syringe Exchange Conference, Milwaukee, Wisconsin.

21

Disciplining Addictions: The Bio-Politics of Methadone and Heroin in the United States

PHILIPPE BOURGOIS

ABSTRACT

Biomedical understanding of methadone as a magic-bullet pharmacological block to the euphoric effects of heroin is inconsistent with epidemiological and clinical data. An ethnographic perspective on the ways street-based heroin addicts experience methadone reveals the quagmire of power relations that shape drug treatment in the United States. The phenomenon of the methadone clinic is an unhappy compromise between competing discourses: A criminalizing morality versus a medicalizing model of addiction-as-a-brain-disease. Treatment in this context becomes a hostile exercise in disciplining the unruly misuses of pleasure and in controlling economically unproductive bodies. Most of the biomedical and epidemiological research literature on methadone obscures these power dynamics by technocratically debating dosage titrations in a social vacuum. A foucaultian critique of the interplay between power and knowledge might dismiss debates over the Swiss experiments with heroin prescription as merely one more version of biopower disciplining unworthy bodies. Foucault's ill-defined concept of the specific intellectual as someone who confronts power relations on a practical technical level, however, suggests there can be a role for political as well as theoretical engagement with debates in the field of applied substance abuse treatment. Meanwhile, too many heroin addicts who are prescribed methadone in the United States suffer negative side effects that range from an accentuated craving for polydrug abuse to a paralyzing sense of impotence and physical and emotional discomfort.

In a halting voice, over the long-distance telephone lines between New York and California, Primo, the manager of the crack house I had lived next to for almost four years in East Harlem admitted that he was taking 80 milligrams of methadone every day. Profoundly embarrassed, Primo asked me not to mention his new methadone addiction in the epilogue to the book that I was preparing at the time of that telephone call (Bourgois, 1995).[1]

The news that Primo was physically addicted to methadone was counterintuitive to me: By conventional standards, Primo had turned his life around in the year prior to that telephone conversation. He had stopped selling crack; he had found legal employment as a summer replacement porter for the mafia-controlled union[2] that represents service workers in primarily luxury apartment buildings; and he had stopped drinking alcohol and sniffing cocaine. In contrast, during the almost six years I had known him as a crack dealer, Primo had sniffed heroin and cocaine without ever developing a physical addiction to heroin.

Contradictorily, therefore, Primo's new legal $500/week job (a large sum by inner-city working-class standards in the 1990s) provided him with enough stable money, and enforced a sufficiently regular schedule for him to develop a physical addiction to heroin. Previously as a crack dealer his unsteady income and work schedule had prevented him from using heroin on a daily basis. He had consumed drugs solely on a binge/party basis depending upon how much money he had earned on a particular night of dealing. As a stable working class wannabe union member, Primo began sniffing two $10 bags of heroin every weekday before and during work, and six-to-eight bags each weekend to celebrate.

When Primo's union laid him off at the end of the summer he suddenly ran out of money and discovered that he "had a monkey—King Kong—on [his] back." He attempted to quit "cold turkey," but two days later in the midst of wrenching opiate withdrawal symptoms he received a phone call from the union offering to rehire him. They had laid him off simply to prevent him from having the seniority to qualify for union membership. In order not to lose this opportunity for well-remunerated—even if unstable—legal employment, Primo immediately enrolled in the methadone clinic that was located next to the luxury condominium where he mopped and hauled garbage.

Because Primo was legally employed, the methadone clinic offered him preferential hours—a 45-minute window of time—to receive his medication, during his lunch hour. For the next three years, Primo became a very stable porter despite the fact that he was laid off for at least 2 weeks every three months in order to prevent him from qualifying for seniority and health benefits. Because of his methadone addiction, Primo would travel downtown past his site of employment every day at lunch hour to continue receiving his medication even during the weeks when he was laid off. This provided Primo with the opportunity to verify in person with management on the up-to-the-minute flexible labor needs of the apartment complex.

The symbiotic relationship between Primo's methadone addiction and his reliability at work fell apart when his conveniently located methadone clinic closed down due to budget cuts and neighborhood gentrification. He began arriving late from his lunch break due to the distant commute to his new ghetto-located clinic. His counselor promptly shifted Primo to LAAM, an experimental, longer-acting (and consequently even more physically addictive) opiate substitution product. The pharmacology of LAAM only obliged Primo to visit his dispensing clinic twice a week—and one of those medication sessions could be coordinated with his day off from work.

Several months later, when Primo asked to be detoxed gradually from LAAM he was told that there was no precedent for quitting LAAM and that he would have to be switched back to methadone. He could not afford to return to methadone, however, as it made him late for work.

BIOPOWER, POWER/KNOWLEDGE, AND THE SPECIFIC INTELLECTUAL

This paper draws on Michel Foucault to argue that methadone maintenance, the largest biomedically-organized and federally controlled drug treatment modality in the United States, affecting approximately 115,000 heroin addicts, represents the state's attempt to inculcate moral discipline into the hearts, minds, and bodies of deviants who reject sobriety and economic productivity. Surprisingly, Foucault has relatively rarely been applied to studying illegal psychoactive drugs or to critiquing the social science and biomedical literatures on the subject (for some exceptions see Bourgois, Lettiere, and Quesada, 1997; Friedman and Alicea, 1995; Moore and Wenger, 1995; O'Malley and Mugford, 1992; Smart, 1984). Foucault's concepts of (1) biopower, (2) the disciplinary power/knowledge nexus, and (3) the political utility of the specific intellectual offer a means for critiquing the moral imperatives that drive most drug policy under the rubric of quantitative evidence-based science and health promotion.

To summarize briefly, Foucault's term biopower refers to the ways historically entrenched institutionalized forms of social control discipline bodies. The biopolitics of substance abuse include a wide range of laws, medical interventions, social institutions, ideologies, and even structures of feeling (Ong, 1995; Caputo and Yount, 1993; Foucault, 1982, pp. 208–226; Williams, 1977; Rabinow (ed.), 1984, pp. 258–272). The definition of methadone maintenance as "drug treatment" is a particularly concrete example of biopower at work. The state and medical authorities have created distinctions between heroin and methadone that revolve primarily around moral categories concerned with controlling pleasure and productivity: legal versus illegal; medicine versus drug. The contrast between methadone and heroin illustrates how the medical and criminal justice systems discipline the uses of pleasure, declaring some psychoactive drugs to be legal medicine and others to be illegal poisons. Ultimately, it can be argued that the most important pharmacological difference between the two drugs that might explain their diametrically opposed legal and medical statuses is that one (heroin) is more pleasurable than the other (methadone).

By interweaving fieldwork descriptions and street conversations of inner city-based heroin addicts this paper offers an ethnographic critique of methadone treatment programs in the United States. More importantly, it links the on-the-ground flesh-and-blood contradictions of methadone versus heroin addiction to the academic, medical, and social service discourses that constitute what Foucault would identify as the power/knowledge nexus of the science of substance abuse treatment. In Foucault's framework, power and knowledge constitute one another, and in that process they set the parameters for disciplining social life. He argues that academic, medical, and juridical fields of study and practice emerged historically as central components of social control through the construction of epistemological frameworks defined as legitimate science and health (Foucault, 1981). Concretely, in the case of methadone, competing scientific, political, and populist discourses mobilize an avalanche of objective, technical and rigorously quantified data that render them oblivious to their embroilment in a Calvinist-Puritanical project (Weber, 1958) of managing immoral pursuits of pleasure and of promoting personal self-control in a manner that is consonant with economic productivity and social conformity.

A theoretically informed ethnographic approach, in contrast, can offer specific practical insights into the slippery and often contradictory ways power operates in the health sciences. In this vein, in an attempt to take Foucault out of a theoretical realm that often paralyzes political or even practical engagement, I will render him "specifically applied" by addressing the relative pharmacological merits of heroin versus methadone from the perspective of harm/risk reduction, despite the conundrum of falling into the power/knowledge trap of drug treatment debates that camouflage moral judgements behind medical objectivity. I hope to contribute, however humbly, to Foucault's political challenge of developing technically useful, applicable "specific knowledges" around the controlling micro-practices and discourses that engulf our everyday lives and desires (Rabinow (ed.), 1984, pp. 67–75). At the same time, it is important to be aware that the role of what Foucault calls the "specific intellectual" who engages ". . . real, material everyday struggles" and poses concrete alternatives through technical positioning can be treacherous (ibid., p. 68). In an attempt to reduce structurally imposed social suffering by applying one's knowledge to promote one particular drug treatment modality or public policy over another, the specific intellectual risks merely tinkering with the efficiency of biopower and missing the more complicated picture of the multi-faceted ways power operates. Even the best of intentions to help or to serve the socially vulnerable can also simultaneously perpetuate—or even exacerbate—oppression, humiliation and dependency of one kind or another. Nevertheless, in this paper I raise the politically taboo possibility that heroin may be less harmful than methadone. In fact, contrary to the standard biomedical definition of the two drugs as incompatible pharmacologically, they may actually be complementary to one another in the context of treatment.

FROM "DOPE" TO "MEDICATION"

Both heroin and methadone addicts are physiologically addicted to a drug that alters their metabolisms and their states of consciousness. A heroin addict however, is defined—and often acts—as a self-destructive, irresponsible criminal. A long-term methadone addict, in contrast, is defined—and often acts—as a worthy, well-disciplined citizen/patient who is dutifully on the road to recovery from substance abuse. Methadone addicts are referred to as "patients," "clients" and even "consumers." In contrast heroin addicts are "criminals," "sociopaths," "deviants," or at best "sick."

An ethnographer who watched the introduction of methadone maintenance as the primary treatment modality in New York City from 1973 to 1975 astutely noted: "The 'dope' became 'medication,' the 'addict' became a 'patient,' 'addiction' became 'treatment' . . ." (Agar 1977, p. 176; see also Agar and Stephens, 1975). This dramatic metamorphosis was made possible in the United States by the biomedical theories of two doctors in the late 1960s. They redefined heroin addiction as an objective, identifiable "metabolic disease." It became a physiological imbalance at the level of the brain's synapses requiring medical stabilization through pharmacological intervention (Dole and Nyswander, 1967).

Like heroin and cocaine which were originally hailed as cures for morphine addiction in the 1800s when they were first synthesized, methadone in the Post-World War II era is considered to be a cure for heroin addiction. The specific biomedical term for the way methadone intervenes pharmacologically in the brain's synapses is as an "opiate agonist." It blocks both the pleasure and the pain that heroin produces by generating alternative sensations of its own at the "μ" opioid receptor sites in the brain's synapses. According to the biomedical paradigm:

> Methadone is a slow-onset, long-acting, mu opiate receptor agonist that reduces the craving for heroin and largely prevents the reward or euphoria if the patient slips and takes a dose of an opiate. (O'Brien, 1997)

In other words methadone is a biomedical technology that facilitates a moral block to pleasure.

Ironically, methadone's effectiveness at blocking opiate-driven euphoria is predicated upon methadone being more highly physically addictive than heroin or morphine. Most methadone addicts develop such a rapid physical tolerance to the drug that they are no longer able to feel significant pleasurable effects from its consumption after only a few weeks of daily consumption. By stimulating the neurotransmitters in the brain synapses so intensively that they cannot process the electromagnetic signals for feeling the euphoria that heroin consumption triggers, methadone is supposed to enable addicts to reorganize their lives productively and healthfully. They can no longer nod away their days in unemployed bliss (or agony); they are no longer constrained to engage in risky injection practices (Ball et al., 1988), or to pursue illegal income-generating strategies. Indeed, for a significant minority of heroin addicts methadone maintenance stabilizes their lives and enables them to withdraw completely from street-based substance abuse. For the majority, however, the effects of methadone maintenance are much more mixed, and for some they are virulently counter-productive.

ETHNOGRAPHIC DISSONANCE

Long-term participant-observation ethnographic fieldwork among middle-aged homeless addicts in San Francisco and among younger heroin addicts in East Harlem and Montreal demonstrates that the official biomedical discourse on methadone makes little sense pharmacologically or socially—at least for the majority of opiate addicts one encounters on the street.

My decade-long archive of fieldwork notes on street drugs contains dozens of matter-of-fact references to methadone addicts and users "nodding out," "throwing up from overdoses," and aggressively and gleefully consuming cocaine, wine, prescription pills, and even heroin to augment the euphoria of their opiate agonist:

East Harlem, 1989:
Stumbling like a drunk; slurring his words; drooling and nodding, Tito almost in tears begged me to give him $10 to buy some powder cocaine, "Para arreglarme [to straighten myself out]." As a street dealer Tito has a big heroin habit. He claims that it is over $60 a day.

Today was Tito's first day of methadone maintenance, and the 35 mg initial dose that they gave him was knocking him off his feet. I felt sorry for him because he reports to work [selling heroin on 124th St.] at 3:00 p.m. He will be fired—or worse—if he arrives stumbling, slurring, and nodding.

A fieldwork note in a very different setting at a Montreal methadone clinic describes my concern when an HIV-positive transgender heroin addict threw up all over my feet. Once again methadone's interference with the addict's capability to perform his/her job emerges as the primary concern and justifies a craving for cocaine.

Montréal, March 1997:
Annie's body simply could not tolerate the 35 mg initial dosage the clinic doctors had prescribed. She could barely stand up, but it was past the clinic's closing time and she had to leave.

When we stepped outside, slipping and sliding on the ice and snow on our way to the prostitute stroll where she was looking for work well after midnight in below-zero weather I offered to pay for a hotel room for her.

She replied with a sigh, "No thanks, what I really need is a shot of coke to straighten me out. I have to get back to work."

Biomedical treatment experts would explain away these ethnographic vignettes as portraying the initiation phase of methadone treatment prior to dosage stabilization. Their explanations certainly sound biomedically convincing. Nevertheless, on dozens of occasions I watched Primo, the former crack dealer now working as a building porter, nod blissfully after sniffing a small $10 packet of heroin even after his methadone clinic had increased his daily dose to the maximum allowable level of 120 mgs per day.

East Harlem, July 1996:
I read Papito, (Primo's 12-year-old son) the passages in my book where his father talks of not having money to buy him a birthday present. Primo nodded out in the middle of my reading and even dropped his slice of pizza; his mouth drooped open drooling ever-so-slightly.

Later Primo insisted that he had not consumed any extra heroin that day. He claims that the nodding was strictly due to the methadone. His wife confided to me disgustedly, however, that Primo has "been sniffing dope on the sneak-tip." His son Papito, who is not supposed to know anything about his father's methadone addiction, looks profoundly depressed to me.

Primo's wife might not be right because three months later Primo apologized to me for not being able to comment on the manuscripts I had given him, claiming that he always nods out whenever he starts to read. "I can only just barely even watch television . . . I hate methadone!"

As Primo's addiction illustrates, methadone maintenance treatment is often experienced as a hostile and/or arbitrary forum for social control and enforced dependency among street addicts. It seeps into the fabric of one's most intimate relationships, distorting (in Primo's case) respectful interaction with children, wives, intellectual friends. Methadone addiction elicits a panoply of practices ranging from resistance, anger and depression, to compliance and relief as the following notes from another telephone conversation with Primo document:

East Harlem, April 1997:

Primo told me that not a day passes without him thinking about his mother who died of AIDS over a year ago. He was laid off from his porter job and has not been called back in over two months—his longest hiatus of unemployment yet.

To make matters worse the New York City Housing Authority has set a court date to evict him from his mother's apartment where he has lived all his life and where she died. Primo has a past felony record and Public Housing now has a "one-strike-you-are-out" ruling. To top it off last week his methadone clinic raised him another 10 milligrams because of a dirty urine.

One of Primo's sisters offered to allow him to live with her in New Jersey, where he can work with a cousin who is a contractor. Primo cannot move in with his sister, however, because New Jersey does not give methadone to New York emigrants.

Primo is too embarrassed to tell his sister about his methadone addiction, as a result his sister and everyone are convinced he is being a flake who does not want to work or turn his life around.

Last week Primo's counselor threatened to discontinue him because he has not obtained an updated tuberculosis test. He also owes $1,000 to the program in lapsed monthly payments. For some reason, however, the dispenser did not "write him up" and he has been "getting dosed" despite nonpayment.

Once again, we see how profoundly methadone articulates in Primo's case with his structurally exacerbated depression to affect intimate definitions of self-respect. The political economic constraints limiting Primo's life chances (i.e., unemployment, felony record, medical bills, housing market, etc.) are already overwhelming, and methadone's rigid institutional regulations further curtail his options for autonomous change. They even isolate him from his kin-based social support network at a time of personal despair when threatened by homelessness. The ethnographic literature on methadone confirms widespread resentment as well as a passive self-deprecating obedience on the part of structurally vulnerable methadone addicts (cf. Rosenbaum and Murphy, 1984). One study quotes addicts as referring to their relationship to methadone as "a ball and chain" (Johnson and Friedman, 1993, p. 37); other researchers cite methadone addicts as complaining of "feeling like automatons," and of "becoming robotic" (Uchtenhagen, 1997; Koester et al., 1999). In Denver street addicts had nicknamed methadone "methadeath" (Koester et al., 1999).

FEDERAL BIOMEDICAL VERSUS POPULIST PROHIBITIONIST AND ABSTINENCE DISCOURSES ON METHADONE

The biomedical discourse of addiction as a disease is promoted at the federal level through the National Institutes of Health (NIH), which officially declared methadone maintenance to be the most effective modality for treating heroin addiction in the 1980s and 1990s. Their conference titles and publications invariably display the aggressive/defensive slogan "Treatment Works," for the benefit of congressional budget committees and a tax paying public which prefers to punish criminals than to treat them. Methadone is especially appealing to treatment scientists because the biomedical world is dedicated to solving complex social ills by developing laboratory-based, high-tech potions that promise quick-fixes and easily replicable efficient outcomes. Methadone is understood to be the technocratic magic bullet that can resolve social, economic, and human existential quandaries by intervening almost surgically at the level of the brain's synapses. Indeed methadone has become the model for all drug treatment: short-circuiting pleasure sensations within the brain's synapses. Hundreds of millions of dollars have been spent on laboratory research to develop similar magic bullets to combat addiction to other street drugs (cf. Balter, 1996).

The federal U.S. commitment to methadone was formally reconfirmed in 1998 by a NIH National Consensus Development Panel (NCDP), entitled "Effective Medical Treatment of Opiate Addiction." The biggest opponent to the NIH biomedical discourse celebrating methadone treatment comes from the "Just-Say-No-To-Drugs" moral abstinence discourse (see critique by Rosenbaum, 1995) that dominates the U.S. Congress, law enforcement, popular culture, churches, 12-step recovery programs, and the health fad movements (from aerobics and cholesterol monitoring to new-age holism). The Just-Say-No camp is oblivious or else hostile to the "addiction is a metabolic disease" discourse of doctors who prescribe methadone and attempt to control and rehabilitate bodies through pharmacological therapeutics. Instead they exhort citizens to personal abstinence based on individual willpower and spirituality.

The healthist/abstinence discourse (Crawford, 1984) complements a third influential position that criminalizes drugs. The criminal emphasis is so hegemonic in the United States that the biomedical disease model can only resist it passively. Indeed one of the self-proclaimed yardsticks for the success of methadone treatment is that it reduces crime. There is room for a "good-cop/bad-cop" complementarity between the biomedical and the criminal discourses since criminals can be both punished and rehabilitated.[3] The healthist vision, on the other hand, tolerates no pharmacological tempering whatsoever with addicted brains. Methadone patients, for example, are not usually welcome at 12-step Narcotics Anonymous meetings.

The 1998 National Consensus Development Panel document promoting methadone was primarily concerned with arguing against the prohibitionist criminalizing discourse of the drug warriors who dominate Congress and the U.S. criminal justice apparatus. To gain credibility, despite being federally-convened and funded, the authors introduced themselves as "a non-advocate, non-federal panel of experts." They directed their most pointed criticism at "unnecessary federal regulation" which they considered "a major barrier to providing methadone maintenance treatment" (NCDP, 1998; CESAR Fax, 1997). Using the twentieth century language and values of biopower, the consensus panel's arguments in favor of methadone emphasize its impact on health, mortality, productivity, and morality. Their summary presents methadone as being "effective in reducing illicit opiate drug use, reducing crime, enhancing social productivity and reducing the spread of viral diseases such as acquired immunodeficiency syndrome (AIDS) and hepatitis" (NCDP, 1998, p. 1937). The consensus document specifically notes that the death rate of heroin addicts is "more than 3 times greater than that experienced by those engaged in MMT [methadone maintenance treatment]" (NCDP, 1998, p. 1939). In a special section entitled "Joblessness" the report assures readers that methadone addicts have superior citizenship qualities as measured according to the most objective index available in the late twentieth century:

"Persons dependent on opiates who are in MMT earn more than twice as much money annually as those not in treatment" (NCDP, 1998, p. 1939). It is disconcerting to contrast the statistical certainties of the NIH consensus statement to the ways Primo, Tito and Annie in the preceding ethnographic vignettes explain their lived experiences on the street of the interface between methadone and employment/income generation.

LOCAL DISCOURSES ON METHADONE: NEW YORK VERSUS SAN FRANCISCO

The tension between the medical, the prohibitionist, and the abstinence discourses play themselves out in the all-American terrain of states' rights. In eight states methadone treatment is illegal. Even where it is legal, however, dramatically different local cultures of treatment have emerged depending upon local constellations of forces between the medical and criminal justice establishments, the size of the street addict population, and the cultural politics of the region. In New York City (and in general along the Eastern Seaboard) the biomedical model of substance abuse as a metabolic disease requiring pharmacological intervention dominates. Long-term methadone maintenance is relatively easy to obtain. Methadone treatment is a multi-million dollar treatment and research for-profit industry located at dozens of accessible, usually federally-subsidized clinics and research hospitals.

In contrast, San Francisco is dominated by an almost New Age (but profoundly Puritanical) celebration of healthy, drug-free bodies. There is even a cultural nationalist, identity politics conspiracy theory discourse that equates methadone to genocide against people of color. Methadone, in short, is morally suspect and access to long-term maintenance clinics is extremely limited (see critique by Rosenbaum, 1995). Methadone maintenance is provided preferentially to heroin addicts with terminal or dangerously contagious disease like Tuberculosis and HIV who need to be carefully monitored and controlled. As a compromise for the long lines of addicts seeking any kind of treatment whatsoever, a panoply of badly organized for-profit and sometimes corrupt 21-day detox venues have emerged (National Alliance of Methadone Advocates, 1997). They prescribe methadone on a temporary basis at low doses that do not exceed 40 mgs per day despite the fact that biomedical researchers insist that 60 to 80 mgs is the minimum effective dose to block the brain's synapses. In fact, some epidemiological studies conclude that the minimum effective dosage is as high as 80–120 mgs (Caplehorn et al., 1993; Cooper, 1989; D'Aunno and Vaughn, 1992; Dole and Nyswander, 1982).

The San Francisco treatment community's pure body discourse can be read between the lines of the handout published by the City's Public Health Service listing the rules governing access to methadone treatment clinics:

> Maintenance Program 1 . . . No Waitlist. Languages: English, Egyptian, and Norwegian. Requirements: to be eligible you need to have one failed detox attempt and at least one year of heroin addiction (that you can prove—from a medical record, police record, etc.). You will also need a TB test, a Syphilis test, and a general physical. MediCal accepted.

> Maintenance Program 2 . . . Waitlist varies depending on your health. Preference is given to people who are seriously ill. Requirements: letter of diagnoses of HIV positive or *active* TB (not just skin-test positive). If you are not ill you may need to detox several times. (7-day wait to get back on detox).

> Maintenance Program 3 . . . Requires several years of heroin addiction and previous failed detox attempts . . . If you have recently been in another methadone detox you must wait: 7 days for a $225 slot; 28 days for a $100 slot . . . Bring proof of income . . . and a *MONEY ORDER* for the price of the detox (no cash or personal checks accepted) [Original emphasis].

This handout sheet full of byzantine rules that counselors, community-based health outreach workers, and harm reduction activists are supposed to use to facilitate street addicts into recovery is a good example of multiple discourses (puritanical, healthist and culturally correct) run amok in a for-profit medical economy with a decaying public health sector (see Crawford, 1994; Rosenbaum and Murphy, 1987a; Murphy and Rosenbaum, 1988). The primary fear of treatment centers which promote a healthist abstinence discourse is that individuals who are not truly heroin addicts will wheedle their way into methadone addiction—or worse yet, that individuals who actually enjoy methadone may become addicted to methadone for its latent euphorigenic properties (Spunt et al., 1996). The front-line service providers who treat street addicts, consequently, focus their energy on hair-splitting triages between healthy and unhealthy bodies (i.e., being positive for the TB skin test vs. having active TB; or between accepting money orders instead of MediCal Cards and cash). At the same time in tune with Californian identity politics they even strive to stretch cultural categories (Egyptian and Norwegian!) to promote diversity goals.

COMPUTERIZED BIOPOWER: AN ETHNOGRAPHIC CONVERSATION AT THE CLINIC

On the ground San Francisco's panoply of methadone detox versus maintenance rules promote confusion, mistrust, hostility and even rage. We filmed and tape recorded the following conversation outside a private, for-profit methadone clinic that costs $12 a day—and where cash is eagerly accepted by the staff.

Tenderloin, San Francisco, November 1996

Max: Just now when I was in the hospital for three-and-a-half weeks they were giving me so much methadone per day, that by the time I got out of the hospital I was actually hooked on it.

So now I'm on a detox. I'm trying, but the last three days have been real hard because the dose they've been giving me is cut way down now. I mean, I could hardly walk this morning. But I'm still gonna try to hang in there.

I had to wait for my dose until 8:00 because I ain't working. Monday through Friday they open at 6:00–6:30 for the workers. People who ain't working have to wait. Then they take a break at 9:45 and reopen again at 11:00 and close at 1:30. Sound weird?

Philippe: How does methadone work for you?

Max: It sort of stops you from craving the heroin, which is the hard part. Or craving the methadone like I do right now cause I've been so used to drinking it every day. But it has kept me off the heroin.

Philippe: But wasn't that heroin that you just shot a half hour ago?

Max: Today I broke down and fixed some dope because I was sick. I told them yesterday at the office [pointing to the doorway of the clinic] that I've been starting to feel really ill for the last three days.

But there's nothing they can do about that. Unless I had the money to pay to keep myself on the methadone—thirty or forty milligrams, which would be fine. I could maintain on that. It would cost $12 a day.

But it's the whole idea of the methadone . . . Got cigarettes?

Philippe: What happens to your body when you need methadone?

Max: Well, it's sort of the same let-down as when you don't have heroin. You're edgy; you're uptight; you don't feel good. You go to the toilet a lot. You'll start throwing up. It comes out everywhere. Your eyes water; your nose runs. You throw up a lot. You can't sleep.

Watch out! [Rapidly passing car forces cameraman onto the sidewalk] I don't know how many days that goes on for on methadone, 'cause I've never done it all the way before.

[Door to the methadone clinic slams amidst shouting and cursing] Sid looks like he might be a little upset or something.

Philippe: [Ignoring Sid's shouts] How many times have you been on methadone detox?

Max: Oh, gee whiz. I don't know, 15 times over the years. Something like that. [Sid shouting even louder in the background] Maybe 20 times over the past five years.

But methadone works if you let it work for you. It will cut your habit down. You just have to be a little bit stronger than I am.

It's just that it's easy to get hooked on and they cut you down in 21 days, and that's really too fast.

Here—ask Harry. He's been on methadone for a year and a half. I'm gonna go see what's with Sid.

Harry: Yeah, I've been staying clean. I'm on 80 milligrams. The stuff works. On methadone you're just like normal. You wake up: you're not sick at all. I mean, hey, you feel normal. I can get up; smile; brush my teeth and eat; go to work—if I worked. I can do things I'm supposed to do: I can shave; change clothes; wash clothes.

On heroin you don't even feel like getting out of bed. You're so sick you'll go grab a gun and start robbin'. You gotta pull your gun out of the closet and put it in peoples' faces and hurt 'em.

I was tired and frustrated of that shit. On the methadone I'm just like normal.

Philippe: What happens when you chip [occasionally inject heroin] on methadone?

Harry: It's a waste of money. You won't even feel the heroin unless you do a whole bunch of it. You know who invented methadone?

Sid: [Hurrying over to us] We gotta get out of here [pointing to the agitated security guard in the doorway of the clinic]. King Kong over there has a hair up his ass.

[The security guard starts walking towards us]. C'mon, let's go—quick. The asshole thinks he owns this f***ing place. [We scramble into the van carrying the camera equipment with the security guard cursing at us through the window].

Harry: [Inside the van] [embarrassed] I hope you can edit all that out? So I was tellin' you about who invented methadone.

Sid: [muttering out the window at the security guard who is slowly walking back to the clinic's entrance surveying the block for other loiterers] F****in' bastard.

Harry: I was saying that I heard that Hitler was behind methadone in the beginning. I don't know the whole story but I heard it used to be called "Adolphine" after Adolph Hitler.[4]

Philippe: [Driving away from the methadone clinic] Sid, what's the matter?

Sid: They breathalyzed me. I had too much alcohol on my breath . . . Just over the limit. One f***ing point over the limit. They didn't serve me.

Max: Did you lose your money?

Sid: Yeah. They would've given me a half a dose but the doctor isn't in now, so I woulda' had to wait a half hour. But I gotta get to work. I'm supposed to paint a sign today.

I lost $12! They used to f***ing give the money back, you know? Now they say it's in the computer. Like they can't f***ing erase the computer, you know?

Bullshit man, that's another scam of theirs. They're just legalized dope dealers. They could give a f*** less about people.

Harry: [Calmly] Well it must go to a main terminal.

Sid: No, somebody got a hair up their ass in there and decided they was gonna punish people for drinking.
[Everyone talking at once]

Jim [Anthropologist colleague driving the van]: That's biopower, Philippe!

Sid: [Interrupting] Look what they did to you [pointing to Harry] last month. They cut you way down; made you real sick for a while . . .

Harry: [Angrily excited] That was for a whole week—just for drinking.

Max: [In a low awesome voice whispering to Philippe] At 80 milligrams! You don't know how wrong that is.

Sid: They got complete control of your f****ing life.

Max: [Normal tone] That stuff is strong, man. It's stronger than heroin.

Sid: [Loud] That f***ing bitch! That's why I'd never get on maintenance again. It's like being in prison. I can't stand that.

They got you scared all the time. They threaten you: "Do this" and "Do that". And they f*** with you all the time. You know, f***in' following the rules.

And then when they get a little hair up their ass about something, they gonna cut you down.

[Wagging his head and talking in an abrasive falsetto] "We're gonna cut you off." That shit, is life and death, man.

Max: They just did it to me man. They been dropping me in just a few days. The last few mornings I been feeling really bad.

Philippe: What's your dose? How many milligrams are you on?

Max: They don't tell you how much they're giving you. But this guy I know at the clinic, he told me he started me at 40.

Then I asked for three raises. Three days in a row. So I must have been at 50—between 50 and 60.

Now they're dropping me down and it's been a week and a half, and the last three days I could feel the difference—a lot!

I wake up at about 3:00; and I lay there; just waiting till 7 or 8:00. I could hardly walk this morning!

Harry: Yeah, I could see you, goin' into convulsions, seizures. That could kill a person.

Sid: [still shouting] It does! It has. I'm tellin' you. Our bodies just can't take it anymore.

THE BIRTH OF THE METHADONE CLINIC

Despite the federal government's solid commitment through the NIH to the biomedical disease model of addiction, the public health establishment at the federal level bows to pressure from more prohibitionist criminalizing discourses on addiction spearheaded by Republicans in Congress and law enforcement agencies. Promoters of methadone, consequently, defensively focus much of their energy to ensure that legal methadone destined for treatment is not diverted illegally to thrill seekers. They also have to monitor that methadone is not supplemented with other illegal drugs that intensify its latent or frustrating euphorigenic qualities. The result is a panoply of repressive federal, state, and local regulations on methadone treatment at specially licensed methadone clinics like the ones documented in the outreach handouts cited earlier and in the videotaped conversation just above.

Psychosocial treatment is subordinated to repression of criminal behavior at most methadone clinics. To prevent patients from re-selling their doses on the street, addicts are forced to come to their clinic in person every day (hence Primo's problem with tardiness at work when his clinic changed locations) to receive their liquid dose of methadone which they are then forced to swallow under the watchful eye of a dispenser. This requirement of daily attendance is probably the single most resented regulation of methadone treatment, and according to one study significantly interferes with treatment retention rates (Rhoades et al., 1998). Exceptionally compliant addicts are rewarded for good behavior with the privilege of "take-home doses." Run-of-the-mill addicts only receive eminently re-saleable "take-homes" on Sundays. Despite all these micro-logistical precautions, doses of liquid methadone smuggled out of clinics in throats and cheeks or as privileged take-homes can be purchased on the blocks surrounding large methadone clinics in most large cities.

The complicated micrologistics for overseeing the consumption of methadone in order to prevent illegal methadone ingestion and to discourage ongoing poly-substance abuse by recovering addicts has given birth to a culture of the methadone clinic. Most of the approximately 115,000 addicts on methadone maintenance in the United States during the 1990s were granted only limited "take-home" privileges. Consequently virtually every day they are forced to converge on methadone clinics to drink their medication in a supervised setting.

One of the explicit therapeutic goals of methadone maintenance treatment is to sever an opiate addict's social relationship to the criminal economy and to the street-based substance abuse community. Ironically, however, for most patients, it accomplishes much the reverse. The ethnographic literature on methadone clinics from the 1970s confirms how the multi-million dollar, federally-subsidized institution of methadone clinics in the cities that initiated large maintenance programs created an active culture of "broken down, toothless garbage heads" (as Primo refers to his colleagues at the clinic he attends). The intense policing and disciplining of methadone combined with its frustrating euphorigenic qualities render it a drug of last resort for tired, elderly, heroin addicts no longer capable (or willing) to generate sufficient income in the underground economy. Symbolic interactionists, ethnomethodologists and other empirically descriptive ethnographers consistently document methadone addicts as being at the bottom of the status hierarchy of street-based drug abusers (Goldsmith et al., 1984; Hunt et al., 1985; Preble and Miller, 1977; Agar, 1977). Institutionally autonomous street-based addicts contrast themselves to "those lame methadone winos" (Preble and Miller, 1977). Hence the term "righteous dope fiends" to identify heroin addicts who are determined to die as outlaws with their boots on (Sutter, 1966; see also Finestone, 1957; Preble and Casey, 1969).

BIOPOWER IN ACTION

The repressive micro-logistics of methadone administration at clinics offers a graphic image of Foucault's concept of biopower unfolding in a very concrete setting: On any given day throughout the United States dispensers are cursing recalcitrant addicts, ordering them to open their mouths and move their tongues to make sure they have swallowed all of their "medication." As we experienced in the videotaped conversation outside the San Francisco methadone clinic security guards regularly patrol the block in front of clinics to chase away loiterers who might be reselling or buying smuggled methadone, or who might be selling methadone-enhancing substances. In short, there is a very intense policing, medical disciplining, and social dividing of bodies at the methadone clinic.

Methadone clinics, like most out-patient drug treatment programs, are required to submit their clients to random urine tests to verify polypsychoactive substance consumption and continued illegal opiate use. Indeed, studies measuring continued consumption of illegal substances by methadone addicts offer figures that range from 16 to 60% (Caplehorn et al., 1993; GAO, 1990). By strategically varying, supplementing, or destabilizing the effects of their dose with poly-drug consumption, methadone addicts can augment the otherwise marginal or only ambiguously pleasurable effects of methadone. Ethnographers working in the early years of methadone maintenance noted that a significant number of addicts actually managed to enjoy the methadone high (Agar and Stephens, 1975; Stephens and Weppner, 1973). As noted in the fieldwork vignettes from East Harlem and Montreal, street addicts report that cocaine mixes well with methadone, especially at high doses (Hunt et al., 1984; Hunt et al., 1986; Rhoades et al., 1998; Strug, 1985). Cocaine, in its smokeable base form known as crack, can be cheaply combined with methadone to approximate the *recherché* speedball effect: a contradictory roller-coaster high where the sedative effects of the opiate interact with the stimulating effects of cocaine (see Bourgois, 1998). Valium is also said to enhance the otherwise often frustrating or subtle euphorigenic sedative effects of methadone. The most common substance abused by methadone addicts, however, continues to be fortified wine (Preble and Miller, 1977; Valentine, 1978). The appeal of combining cocaine, alcohol, and benzodiazepines with methadone can be particularly noxious for pregnant heroin addicts who are mandated into treatment, as poly-drug consumption is usually more detrimental to fetal development than heroin alone (Chavkin and Breitmart, 1997).

An intense struggle unfolds inside methadone clinics over the dosage levels provided to addicts. Many addicts like Max in San Francisco want higher doses in order to "stay well"—or more surreptitiously in order to feel more strongly the usually frustratingly mild euphoric effects of a stable dose of methadone. Other addicts like Primo in New York want lower doses in the hope of becoming "drug free"—or more surreptitiously in order to be able to feel the euphoria of an occasional illegal supplementary consumption of a bag of street heroin.

Dosage levels are further complicated by the pharmacological fact that methadone is dangerous. Even heroin addicts with large addictions can be overdosed and killed when first prescribed methadone.

By law they have to be started at low levels. Their dosages are then raised by 10 or 5 milligram increments depending upon the evolution of their "tolerance levels." Furthermore, individual metabolisms vary considerably, allowing patients to achieve different balances of forbidden euphorigenic feelings as Primo's case illustrates. He continues to "nod out" despite having been maintained at high dosages for several years. Similarly both Annie the transvestite from Canada, and Tito the street dealer in East Harlem stumbled about the streets throwing up after taking only relatively low doses of methadone yet having high tolerances to heroin. The most common scenario around dosage levels in maintenance clinics is the experience of Primo, whose dosage was raised every time he gave a "dirty urine" sample until, against his will, he was brought up to 120 milligrams, which is such a high level of dosage that his clinic must request special Federal/State authorization.

As the conversation and events videotaped outside the San Francisco methadone clinic demonstrate, it only takes a few minutes inside (or outside) a methadone clinic to realize that what the scientific biomedical treatment community refers to as "effective methadone dosage" level has little to do with technocratic pharmacological logics and much more to do with naked power relations. Dosage is determined by a struggle over pleasure, pain, and compliant social control. For example: (1) Max, who was suffering from methadone withdrawal symptoms, had been on a blind dose since inadvertently becoming addicted to methadone in the hospital; he begged for a higher dosage, but was unwilling to pay for it and instead was rapidly detoxed; in response he spent what money he had on street heroin. (2) Sid failed his alcohol breathalyzer test and was refused his 40 milligram dose (after paying for it). (3) Harry, at 80 milligrams, had his dose lowered for a week for failing to follow the clinic's rules limiting alcohol consumption. Given Harry's high dosage addiction it is not coincidental that he was the only person who at least partially defended the clinic's administrative computerized tracking system. ("Well it must go to a main terminal"). He was also embarrassed for the sake of the clinic when we filmed our flight from the aggressive security guard. ("I hope you can edit all that out.") Six months later when Harry died, grotesquely bloated from liver disease, his heroin addict friends (Sid, Max, etc.) were convinced that the rapidity and the painfulness of his decay was caused by the high daily dose of methadone he had been consuming over the last two years.

DISCIPLINING THE DOSAGE: BIOMEDICINE'S POWER/ KNOWLEDGE NEXUS

Just as the birth of the methadone clinic offers a graphic example of bio-politics in action around the state-mediated struggle to create disciplined and addicted—but heroin-free—subjects, so too the literatures on methadone in the field of substance abuse treatment and research offer a classic case study of Foucault's understanding of the disciplinary impact of the power/knowledge nexus. Relative dosage levels emerge as the central focus of the biomedical scientific debate on methadone's effectiveness. Indeed, much of the discussion is reduced to a technocratic concern with finding the adequate dosage level.

Large, epidemiological surveys of methadone treatment clinics consistently produce anomalistic data that one would think might question the scientific coherence of methadone treatment. The disconcerting empirical outcomes of methadone treatment, however, are successfully explained away as caused by "inadequate dosages" (GAO, 1990; D'Aunno and Vaughn, 1992; Dole, 1989; Dole and Nyswander, 1982). The literature describes dosage level as a purely pharmacologically-determined objective variable. It is oblivious to the fact that recalcitrant addicts like Max, Sid, and Harry in San Francisco or Primo in New York are violently physically disciplined—if not fully controlled—at the capillary brain synapse level by manipulations in their dosage levels. As our ethnographic vignettes document, methadone addicts who fail to obey clinic rules (i.e., stay sober, make payments, arrive on time etc.) are purposely sent either into paroxysms of debilitating whole body pain (i.e., Max, Harry, and Sid), or else into drooling oblivion (i.e., Primo) by punitive decreases or increases in their dosage levels. Instead, the power/knowledge logic of biomedicine frames these conflicts strictly in terms of a technocratic search for the correct dosage. In the literature no mention is ever made of the types of concerns and rages expressed on video as we fled from the San Francisco methadone clinic. The technocratic search for determining the appropriate dosage level obscures the repressive fact that addicts like Max, Sid, and Harry are terrified of being thrown into violent withdrawal symptoms by a sudden decision of the clinic doctor or the nurse dispenser. Similarly, the dosage debate erases any scientific documentation of the humiliation experienced by Primo and his 12 year-old son when Primo, who had been raised against his will to 120 milligrams, nodded and drooled into his pizza in the midst of an intensely personal conversation with his son.

Not surprisingly, in epidemiological studies the single most significantly correlated variable for compliance among methadone addicts is a high dose level (D'Aunno and Vaughn, 1992). The literature, however, avoids the obvious explanation for why there should be such a strong correlation between high dosage level and patient compliance. It is just accepted as a pharmacological fact which is as neutral and as precise as might be the correct dose of antibiotics for a blood infection (cf. Maremanni et al., 1994). Researchers are so uncritically immersed in the disciplining parameters of their biomedical framework that they fail to recognize that it is the painfully physiologically addictive properties of methadone that reduce even the most oppositional outlaw street addicts (like Primo in East Harlem or more broken-down Harry in San Francisco) into stable patients once their bodies have built up a large enough physical dependence on methadone to make it too physically painful for them to misbehave.

Some of the most revealing large-scale studies of dosage levels at methadone clinics have been conducted by a social worker at the University of Chicago, who receives multi-million dollar federal grants to distribute a relatively simple, self-descriptive questionnaire to random national samples of hundreds of different methadone clinics. The responses demonstrate that average dosage levels fluctuate wildly across the nation. In other words the statistics reveal that there is no biologically coherent rhyme or reason to the way methadone is prescribed across the United States. Most clinics administer an average dose that is considerably lower than the dose that is considered by treatment researchers to be the minimum necessary dosage for effectively maintaining clients in compliant treatment (i.e., under 60 milligrams). A full 25% of the clinics surveyed set an upper maximum dose limit 10 milligrams below the 60 milligram minimum (D'Aunno and Vaughn, 1992, p. 256).

The apparent biomedical dosage inadequacy of most methadone maintenance treatment clinics is, once again, an expression of the competition of contradictory discourses: the criminalizing and healthist versions of biopower that dominate in law enforcement, and popular culture, versus the "addiction-is-a-disease" model that prevails in the biomedical establishment and emphasizes the pharmacological control of bodies. This contradiction is reflected in the imposition by the legislature of repressive legal regulations that discourage high dosage prescriptions of methadone despite the emphatic consensus of federally-funded drug researchers that the biggest

problem with most methadone clinics is the inadequately low doses they administer. Federal law requires clinic doctors to obtain special permission to prescribe more than 100 milligrams of methadone and further limits the rights of addicts with 100 milligram habits from having access to "take home" doses (Dole and Nyswander, 1982; Newman, 1987). High doses, of course, are especially susceptible to profitable diversionary resale since most individuals consuming methadone for the first time only need 20 milligrams to experience euphoria—complete with stumbling, nodding and drooling as the cases of Annie, the Canadian transvestite and Tito, the East Harlem heroin seller illustrate. At the same time because of federal pressure for "adequate doses" to produce compliant (i.e., thoroughly addicted) patients, more clinics are increasing dosage levels to the maximum level allowed (D'Aunno et al., 1997). Dissatisfaction by doctors over average low dosage levels at clinics across the country is confirmed repeatedly in the most prestigious medical journals. They regularly run editorials calling for less federal regulation to enable more accurate and higher dosage levels (cf. Cooper, 1989; D'Aunno and Vaughn, 1992; Dole, 1989; Dole and Nyswander, 1982). In contrast, federal publications such as a 1990 report by the Government Accounting Office call for greater central government supervision but also ironically in the name of ensuring more accurate, higher doses—precisely what the doctors who protest Federal regulations also want (GAO, 1990).

These convoluted political and moral tensions, anxieties and internal inconsistencies over dosage levels often manifest themselves at the clinic level with clients being denied access to information on their dosage level. In fact, clients are at best politely ignored when they report dramatically negative physical symptoms in response to dosage changes—hence, Max's description of his withdrawal experience outside the San Francisco clinic. Treatment scientists assert that patients should not "have a consultative influence on the determination of their dosage" (D'Aunno and Vaughn, 1992). Detoxification clinics which tend to be more moralistic and healthist usually prescribe the lowest average dose levels and they are the least likely to allow addicts to know their dosage for fear of being manipulated into prescribing excessively high doses that might produce euphoria or might provide opportunities for smuggling out underground economy doses in cheeks or jowls. Significantly, these pro-abstinence clinics are "the least influenced by government regulation" (D'Aunno and Vaughn, 1992, p. 257).[5] Federal regulation, although heavily concerned with criminalizing substance abuse, promotes control and compliance through the biomedical venue of prescribing high doses for long – even unlimited – periods of time (Maremmani et al., 1994).

In addition to the dramatic statistics on ineffective dosage levels at clinics all across the United States (D'Aunno and Vaughn 1992; GAO 1990), the epidemiological and survey literature also confronts the medical illogic of the surprisingly unpleasant side effects of methadone consumption. For example, one study reveals that 80% of a random sample of 246 addicts complained of a wide range of some dozen different types of complications caused by methadone ingestion. The primary ones were "sexual dysfunction," "constipation," and "muscle and bone aches." A considerable number of patients suffered from "psychological distress," "impotence," and "libido abnormalities;" others experienced more routine "nausea," "vomiting," and "appetite abnormalities" (see review by Goldsmith et al., 1984; and see discussion by Rosenbaum and Murphy, 1987b). Significantly, once again, studies documenting the negative side effects of methadone almost inevitably conclude that the long list of complaints made by the majority of addicted methadone consumers is "related to dosage acclimatization" problems. Once again the power/knowledge nexus manages to focus the problematic dimensions of methadone as a treatment modality onto the technical question of adequate dosage level. Most importantly, addicts are held responsible for causing these dosage inconsistencies by continuing surreptitiously to consume other euphorigenic drugs which exacerbate methadone's unpleasant range of side effects.

THE MEDICAL PRESCRIPTION OF HEROIN IN SWITZERLAND

Given that the side effects of methadone are dramatically more unpleasant than those of heroin (Uchtenhagen, 1997) one wonders why methadone "cures" while heroin "sickens." Foucault's insights into the ways illegalities shape delinquency and his documentation of how the modern prison has failed to curb crime since the first day of its inception sheds insight into how it has been possible for methadone to have such a mediocre clinical treatment record for so many years yet continues to be considered the most effective treatment modality available for heroin. Foucault argues that prisons were not meant to eliminate criminal behavior, otherwise they would have long since disappeared since they produce recidivism

and criminal subcultures. Instead prisons, like methadone clinics, distinguish, divide, and distribute illegalities, thereby differentiating them in various manageable forms (Foucault, 1979; Rabinow, 1998).

Oblivious to Foucault's critiques of state-sponsored medicalized control, Swiss substance abuse prevention researchers dedicated themselves very pragmatically to studying the internationally taboo question of whether heroin works better than methadone as a treatment modality. They launched a large pilot program for the medical prescription of heroin to stabilize chronic heroin addicts. Fully subscribing to the positivist natural science model of evidence-based epidemiological clinical trials that measure objective health outcomes, the Swiss conducted a large double-blind study involving 1,146 randomly selected heroin addicts whom they alternately treated with heroin, methadone, and morphine, both intravenously and orally (Uchtenhagen, 1997). The side effects of methadone were so much worse than those of morphine and heroin that the biggest administrative problem of the study was the high attrition rates of the control subjects who were prescribed methadone instead of heroin or morphine (Uchtenhagen, 1997). The research documented statistically that addicts who were medically prescribed heroin became more socially functional according to the classic biomedical and criminological indexes that measure health status as well as social compliance: mortality, hospitalization, psychological distress, criminal activity, legal employment, abstinence from the consumption of illegal drugs, etc. (Uchtenhagen, 1997). Compared to the addicts placed on methadone or morphine maintenance, those who consumed medically prescribed heroin were healthier, "less depressed"; "less anxious"; and "less prone to delirium." They were also "better housed," "more employed," used "less welfare," and "decreased their street contacts more" as well as their "sensations of automatism." Those prescribed heroin also used less illegal heroin and cocaine. Most dramatically, medically-stabilized heroin addicts decreased their participation in crime sevenfold.

The Swiss document concludes matter-of-factly that medically prescribed heroin is a better treatment modality than methadone or morphine. Their research design includes no qualitative component and is exclusively composed of rigorously quantified statistical correlations. The findings not only contradict the legal and moral discourses of the U.S. medical establishment and law enforcement institutions but also contradict the very core of the U.S. biomedical understanding of the pharmacological mechanism that defines methadone as an agonist block to heroin-induced pleasure sensations inside the brain's synapses. The Swiss addicts were allowed to complement their treatment medication with other psychoactive drugs and Table 6 of the final report documents that methadone (by a factor of 257%!) was the drug that was most frequently voluntarily combined with intravenous heroin by study participants in the clinic. Even when participants had the choice of augmenting their base prescription of intravenous heroin with unlimited quantities of heroin, morphine, cocaine or methadone in either injectable, oral, or smokeable form, a plurality chose oral methadone as a supplement to heroin. Most significantly those addicts who achieved stable employment were the ones who most frequently requested a supplement of oral methadone to complement their stable prescription of heroin in order to limit the number of times per day they had to interrupt their work schedule to inject. This offers a dramatic contrast to the U.S. biomedical treatment model's understanding of methadone which asserts that it is pharmacologically incompatible with heroin, and that most problems with methadone treatment can be attributed to inadequate dosage levels. The homologous biomedical Swiss model comes to precisely the opposite conclusion: Low doses of methadone in combination with heroin are the most effective way to rehabilitate formerly hard-core, anti-social addicts.

ENGAGING FOUCAULT WITH HARM/RISK REDUCTION

In 1997 the Swiss government conducted a referendum in which well over 60 percent of the population voted to legalize the medical prescription of heroin. It is ironic that Switzerland, historically the cradle of Calvinism, should be the first country in the industrialized world officially to abandon the criminal repression of heroin. Does this contradict the interpretation that a Calvinist-Puritanical morality that identifies pleasure with sinfulness and idleness (Weber, 1958) motivates government drug policy to criminalize the pursuit of pleasure? Or is the Swiss championing of the medical prescription of heroin the ultimate expression of an efficient and highly technified biopower in pragmatic practice? Indeed, the medical prescription of heroin can be understood as an extraordinarily effective method of social control—far more efficient than the prescription of methadone. It is easier to integrate stabilized, mildly

euphoric heroin addicts into the lowest-tiers of the legal labor force than it is to bully frustrated, depressed, oppositional methadone addicts into social compliance. Within the biomedical paradigm of finding technological magic-bullet solutions to complicated chronic social problems, the pharmacology of heroin allows for greater social engineering at a much cheaper cost. It is precisely the unambiguously euphoric effects of heroin, combined with its relative lack of negative side effects, that makes heroin such an effective agent of biopower once it is directly administered by the state through medical treatment clinics.

It would be tempting to conclude somewhat sanctimoniously with the foucaultian insight that disciplinary power is omnipresent—if not omnipotent—no matter what discourse happens to dominate treatment or criminal justice policy. Indeed, mixing foucaultian metaphors, disciplinary power can be understood literally and figuratively to be as capillary-like as the medicines that are used to rehabilitate the unruly bodies of self-destructive street addicts. This article, however, began with a promise to break with much of the tradition of second generation foucaultian scholarship and instead to heed Foucault's personal example along with his more humble call for "specific intellectuals" to take political positions on the "technicoscientific" practical details at the interstices of the public policies that discipline citizens' lives [Rabinow (ed.), 1984, p. 71]. Otherwise, Foucault's theoretical understanding of the way power permeates truth, knowledge and even oppositionality, leads to paralysis. The ethnographic method is well suited to the challenge of politically engaging Foucault's critical insights and rendering them concretely relevant. Consequently, the technocratic—even bio-moral—question of what combination of drugs, laws and medical/health discourses might produce less social suffering on the street needs to be taken seriously.

In this practical vein, the risk/harm reduction paradigm represents an interstice between the state and the medical apparatuses where specific foucaultian critiques of drug policy can become concrete. The first step is to suggest that according to a wide range of quantifiable measurements heroin appears to be a less harmful and more socially useful drug than methadone. More precisely, the drug combination that the Swiss study stumbled upon—i.e., low doses of methadone supplemented by strategic injections of pharmaceutically pure heroin—can be identified as an especially effective magic-bullet-like potion for stabilizing heroin addicts who want to enter the labor market. Ironically, once again, this directly contradicts the U.S. biomedical establishment's understanding for why methadone is effective in drug treatment as an opiate agonist which by its pharmacological definition is supposed to be incompatible with heroin consumption.

More important, however, than arguing over the relative effectiveness of the precise balance of milligrams of one opiate versus another is the political and intellectual urgency of debunking the power/knowledge dead-end that has confined discussions of drug treatment effectiveness to technical debates over dosage titrations. The bio-politics of methadone revolve around a political economy of human dignity that is both cultural and economic. It is no coincidence that virtually every single ethnographic description or conversation cited in this text articulates methadone consumption with the central problem of employment and income generation: from Primo's almost caricatural case of unsuccessfully negotiating sobriety and stable employment at the margins of New York's legal labor market, to the more violently tenuous attempts of Annie the Canadian transvestite and Tito the East Harlem heroin seller to consume cocaine in order to render themselves fit to continue working at the entry levels of the underground economy. Less dramatically, at the San Francisco methadone clinic Max's status of being unemployed forced him to endure painful withdrawal symptoms for two extra hours each morning. Sid, on the other hand, when he failed the breathalyzer test at that same clinic had to forgo waiting for the doctor to prescribe him a half dose of methadone in order to return to his sign-painting job on time.

From a less economically-oriented political economy perspective, the search for cultural respect emerges as another central facet complicating methadone's acceptability on the street. Indeed, virtually all the ethnographic accounts from the first decades of methadone studies identify the drug's unsatisfactory location in street-based status hierarchies. More intimately, the research from the 1980s cites the unpleasant physical and emotional effects and context of methadone consumption at user-unfriendly clinics. In this polarized context, medicalized heroin, precisely because of the pleasure it provides to its consumers, offers the opportunity of metamorphosing a larger percentage of depressed self-destructive, often-violent street-relegated outlaws into relatively reliable, low wage laborers—or at worst into harmless, complacent, inexpensive beneficiaries of public sector largess.

We need to de-exoticize how we think about drugs. The dramatic social transformation of heroin from drug to medicine in the Swiss experiments was accomplished merely by the juridical act of legalizing—or at least medicalizing—heroin-cum-methadone addiction. Perhaps, more important from a humanitarian risk reduction perspective, medicalized heroin would also certainly result in dramatic reductions in HIV, hepatitis, abscesses, tuberculosis and other new epidemics of self-administered social suffering which plague inner cities. The most significant effect would be a massive reduction in the numbers of incarcerated inner-city youth—the most dramatic outcome of U.S. drug and social welfare policy at the close of the twentieth century.

ACKNOWLEDGMENTS

This research and writing was financed by the National Institute of Drug Abuse (NIDA) grant #R01-DA10164. Preliminary fieldwork funding was received from NIDA's Epidemiological Working Group #NO1-DA-3-5201 and Public Service Contract #263-MD-519210 administered by the Community Research Branch at NIDA. Limited fieldwork was also conducted in Montreal on a Public Service Contract with the Canadian Ministry of Health and on NIDA grant #R01-DA11591. The fieldwork material drawn from East Harlem was funded by NIDA grant #R03-DAO6413-01, The Harry Frank Guggenheim Foundation, The Russell Sage Foundation, The Wenner-Gren Foundation for Anthropological Research, The Social Science Research Council, and the US Census Bureau. Paul Rabinow, Nancy Scheper-Hughes, and, especially, James Quesada (who is also an ethnographic collaborator in my San Francisco fieldwork) provided me with useful critiques on early versions of this article. I thank my other ethnographic collaborators in San Francisco especially Jeff Schonberg, Joelle Morrow, Ann Magruder, and Dan Ciccarone. Since 1994 for varying lengths of time and intensity Mark Lettiere, Charles Pearson and Raul Pereira also participated in the ethnographic research in San Francisco. Jerry Floersch introduced me to Foucault's concept of the "specific intellectual." Merrill Singer and three additional anonymous reviewers for *Culture, Medicine, and Psychiatry* forced me to tighten and clarify my argument, and to take a more clearly engaged stand. (Anonymous reviewer #2 incited the Foucaultian metaphor of "capillary-like power.")

NOTES

1. Of course I respected Primo's request to make no mention of his methadone addiction in my book. Surprisingly, given the often painful material presented in the book, this was the only major fact that any of the characters who previewed *In Search of Respect: Selling Crack in El Barrio* asked me to omit from the text. It illustrates the profound stigmatization of methadone in street culture. Three years later when I asked Primo why he was willing to be part of this current article on methadone he laughed politely:

   Methadone sucks. I hate it. Plus, I like helping you out with my stories—you know that. I mean it might help some knucklehead out there not to do wrong.

   Also, [long pause] I don't mean to disrespect you Felipe—but nobody really reads the shit you write—at least not nobody I know.

2. The president of Primo's union local (32B-32J) of the Service Employees International was the highest-paid labor leader in the nation in the mid-1990s with an annual salary of $412,000. (Daily News, p. 70, by Dave Saltonstall. April 11, 1995.)

3. See Smart, 1984, for a discussion of the interface between British medical and criminal discourses on drugs.

4. In fact, methadone's evil conspiracy creation story is even more dramatic in real life. Methadone was invented by IG Farbinindustrie, the chemical conglomerate that is better known for having been the prime employer of slave laborers at Auschwitz during the Holocaust. Their product was seized as a spoil of war by the United States and first marketed by Eli-Lilly Pharmaceuticals under the trade name "Dolophine" not "Adolphine" (www.drugtext.nl/library/books/methadone).

5. The more morally repressive, low-dose, "ineffective" clinics also treat the highest proportions of African American addicts. Surprisingly, this correlation is not explored empirically or theoretically in the epidemiological literature despite the proxy measurement it provides on differential access to biomedical facilities by race due to government regulation.

REFERENCES

Agar, M. (1977). Going through the changes: Methadone in New York City. *Human Organization, 36*(3), 291–295.

Agar, M., and Stephens, R. C. (1975). The methadone street scene. *Psychiatry, 38*, 381–387.

Ball, J., Lange, C., Myers, P., and Friedman, S. R. (1988). Reducing the risk of AIDS through methadone maintenance treatment. *Journal of Health and Social Behavior, 29*, 214–226.

Balter, M. (1996). New clues to brain dopamine control, cocaine addiction. *Science, 271*(5251), 909.

Bourgois, P. (1998). Just another night in a shooting gallery. *Theory, Culture, and Society, 15*,(2).

Bourgois, P., Lettiere, M., and Quesada, J. (1997). Social misery and the sanctions of substance abuse: Confronting HIV risk among homeless heroin addicts in San Francisco. *Social Problems, 44*(2), 155–173.

Caplehorn, J., Bell, J., Kleinbaum, D., and Gebski, V. (1993). Methadone dose and heroin use during maintenance treatment. *Addiction, 88*, 119–124.

Caputo, J., and Yount, M. (1993). Institutions normalization and power. In J. Caputo and M. Yount (Eds.), *Foucault and the Critique of Institutions* (pp. 3–26). University Park, PA: Pennsylvania State University Press.

CESAR Fax. (1997). NIH-sponsored independent consensus panel calls for increased availability of methadone treatment with less government regulation. December 1, 1997, 6(47).

Chavkin, W., and Breitbart, V. (1997). Substance abuse and maternity: The United States as a case study. *Addiction, 92*(9), 1201–1205.

Cooper, J. (1989). Methadone treatment and acquired immunodeficiency syndrome. *Journal of the American Medical Association, 262*(12), 1664–1668.

Crawford, R. (1984). A cultural account of "health": Control, release, and the social body. In John McKinley (Ed.), *Issues in the Political Economy of Health Care* (pp. 60–103). New York: Tavistock Publications.

D'Aunno, T., and Vaughn, T. (1992). Variations in methadone treatment practices. *Journal of the American Medical Association, 267*(2), 253–258.

Dole, V. (1989). Methadone treatment and the acquired immunodeficiency syndrome epidemic. *Journal of the American Medical Association, 262*(12), 1681–1682.

Dole, V. P., and Nyswander, M. E. (1967). Heroin addiction: A metabolic disease. *Archives of Internal Medicine, 120*, 19–24.

Dole, V. P., and Nyswander, M. E. (1982). Performance-based rating of methadone maintenance programs. *New England Journal of Medicine, 306*(3), 169–172.

Finestone, H. (1957). Cats, kicks, and color. *Social Problems, 5*(1), 3–13.

Foucault, M. (1982). The subject and power. In H. L. Dreyfus and P. Rabinow (Eds.), *Michel Foucault: Beyond Structuralism and Hermeneutics* (pp. 208–226). Chicago, IL: University of Chicago Press.

Foucault, M. (1981). *Power/Knowledge: Selected Interviews and Other Writings, 1972–1977*. Colin Gordon (ed). New York: Pantheon/Random House.

Foucault, M. (1979). *Discipline and Punish: The Birth of the Prism*. New York: Vintage Books.

Friedman, J., and Alicea, M. (1995). Women and heroin: The path of resistance and its consequences. *Gender and Society*, 9(4), 432–449.

General Accounting Office. (1990). Methadone maintenance: Some treatment programs are not effective; greater federal oversight needed. Report to the Chairman, Select Committee on Narcotics Abuse and Control, House of Representatives.

Goldsmith, D., Hunt, D., Lipton, D., and Strug, D. (1984). Methadone folklore: Beliefs about side-effects and their impact upon treatment. *Human Organization*, 43, 330–340.

Gourevitch, M. (1997). Methadone treatment in the United States. Paper presented at Joint U.S. (NIH)-Russia Seminar on HIV Prevention Among Drug Users. Pavlov Medical University, St. Petersburg, Russia, Oct. 6–8.

Hunt, D., Strug, D., Goldsmith, D., Lipton, D., Spunt, B., Truitt, L., and Robertson, K. (1984). An instant shot of "aah": Cocaine use among methadone clients. *Journal of Psychoactive Drugs*, 16(3), 217–227.

Hunt, D. and Lipton, D. (1986). The costly bonus: Cocaine related crime among methadone treatment clients. *Advances in Alcohol and Substance Abuse*, 6(2), 107–122.

Hunt, D., and Lipton., D. (1985). It takes your heart: The image of methadone among street addicts and its effect on recruitment and methadone treatment. *International Journal of the Addictions*, 20(11 and 12), 1751–1771.

Johnson, P., and Friedman, J. (1993). Social versus physiological motives in the drug careers of methadone clinic clients. *Deviant Behavior*, 14, 23–42.

Koester, S., Anderson, K., and Hoffer, L. (1999). Active heroin injectors' perceptions and use of methadone maintenance treatment. *Substance Use and Misuse*.

Lupton, D. (1997). Foucault and the medicalisation critique. In A. Petersen and R. Burton (Eds.), *Foucault, Health and Medicine* (pp. 94–110). London: Routledge.

Maremmani, I., Nardini, R. R., Zolesi, O., and Castrogiovanni, P. (1994). Methadone dosages and therapeutic compliance during a methadone maintenance program. *Drug and Alcohol Dependence*, 34, 163–166.

Moore, L., and Wenger, L. (1995). The social context of needle exchange and user self-organization in San Francisco: Possibilities and pitfalls. *Journal of Drug Issues*, 25(3), 583–598.

Murphy, S., and Rosenbaum, M. (1988). Money for methadone 2: Unintended consequences of limited duration methadone maintenance. *Journal of Psychoactive Drugs*, 20(4), 397–402.

National Alliance of Methadone Advocates. (1997). California methadone clinics target of fraud probe; clinic reveals patient records to DEA, patients arrested. www.ndsn.org/AUGUST97/FRAUD.html

National Consensus Development Panel. (1998). Effective medical treatment of opiate addiction. *Journal of the American Medical Association*, 280(22), 1936–1943.

Newman, R. (1987). Methadone treatment: Defining and evaluating success. *New England Journal of Medicine*, 317(7), 447–450.

O'Brien, C. (1997). A range of research-based pharmacotherapies for addiction. *Science*, 278, 66–70.

O'Malley, P., and Mugford, S. (1992). Moral technology: The political agenda of random drug testing. *Social Justice*, 18, 122–146.

Ong, A. (1995). Making the biopolitical subject: Cambodian immigrants, refugee medicine, and cultural citizenship in California. *Social Science and Medicine*, 40(9), 1243–1257.

Preble, E., and Casey, J., Jr. (1969). Taking care of business—the heroin user's life on the street. *International Journal of the Addictions*, 4(1), 1–24.

Preble, E., and Miller, T. (1977). Methadone, wine and welfare. In R. S. Weppner (Ed), *Street Ethnography*. Los Angeles: Sage.

Rabinow, P. (1998). Discussant's comments on the panel "Foucault in the Social Sciences," at the 69th Annual Meetings of the Pacific Sociological Association. San Francisco, April 16.

Rabinow, P. (Ed.) (1984). *The Foucault Reader*. New York: Pantheon Books.

Rhoades, H., Creson, D., Elk, R., Schmitz, J., and Grabowski, J. (1998). Retention, HIV risk, and illicit drug use during treatment: Methadone dose and visit frequency. *American Journal of Public Health*, 88(1), 34–39.

Rosenbaum, M. (1995). The demedicalization of methadone maintenance. *Journal of Psychoactive Drugs*, 27(2), 145–149.

Rosenbaum, M., and Murphy, S. (1987a). Money for methadone: Preliminary findings from a study of Alameda County's new maintenance policy. *Journal of Psychoactive Drugs*, 19(1), 13–19.

Rosenbaum, M., and Murphy, S. (1987b). Not the picture of health: Women on methadone. *Journal of Psychoactive Drugs*, 19(2), 217–226.

Rosenbaum, M., and Murphy, S. (1984). Always a junkie? The arduous task of getting off methadone. *Journal of Drug Issues*, 16(4), 527–552.

Smart, C. (1984). Social policy and drug addiction: A critical study of policy development. *British Journal of Addiction*, 79, 31–39.

Soloway, I. H. (1974). Methadone and the culture of addiction. *Journal of Psychedelic Drugs*, 6(1), 1–99.

Spunt, B., Hunt, D., Lipton, D., and Goldsmith, D. (1986). Methadone diversion: A new look. *Journal of Drug Issues*, 16(4), 569–583.

Stephens, R., and Weppner, R. (1973). Legal and illegal use of methadone: One year later. *American Journal of Psychiatry*, 130, 1391–1394.

Strug, D. (1985). Patterns of cocaine use among methadone clients. *International Journal of the Addictions*, 20(8), 1163–1175.

Sutter, A. G. (1966). The world of the righteous dope fiend. *Issues in Criminology*, 2(2), 177–222.

Uchtenhagen, A. (1977). *Rapport de synthese PROVE*. Zurich: Institut fur Suchtforschung in Verbindung and Institut fur Sozial-Und Praventivmedizin, Universitat Zurich.

Valentine, B. (1978). *Hustling and other hard work: Lifestyles in the ghetto*. New York: Free Press.

Weber, M. (1958). *The Protestant Ethic and the Spirit of Capitalism*. Upper Saddle River, NJ: [1905] Prentice-Hall.

Williams, R. (1977). *Marxism and Literature*. Oxford: Oxford University Press.

22

Longitudinal Patterns of Treatment Utilization and Outcomes Among Methamphetamine Abusers: A Growth Curve Modeling Approach

YIH-ING HSER

DAVID HUANG

CHIH-PING CHOU

CHERYL TERUYA

M. DOUGLAS ANGLIN

ABSTRACT

The present study examined a sample of 205 amphetamine and methamphetamine (A/M) abusers in drug treatment programs across Los Angeles County. Data were collected during face-to-face interviews using a natural history interview instrument. We applied a series of growth curve models to investigate treatment effects on A/M use and criminal involvement during a 36-month period (24 months before and 12 months after the referent treatment admission). The modeling results showed strong concurrent treatment effects in reducing A/M use and criminal involvement (e.g., being in treatment was associated, on average, with a decrease of 4.65 to 5.14 days of A/M use per month and of 1.74 crimes per month). A longer length of cumulative time in treatment (either within single episodes or across multiple episodes) was associated with a lower level of A/M use during the initial month of the 36-month period and with a slower rate of decreased use in subsequent months. Cumulative treatment was not associated with trajectories of the criminal measures. The study findings provide some support for treatment effectiveness in decreasing A/M use among A/M abusers treated in

community treatment programs. Longitudinal models allow opportunities to reveal the dynamic relationships between treatment and outcome.

INTRODUCTION

While abuse of amphetamine/methamphetamine (A/M) has been a significant and persistent problem in the United States since the late 1960s, it was long considered a more regional phenomenon (Anglin, Kalechstein, Maglione, Annon, and Fiorentine, 1998). Although in the past decade there has been an upsurge of A/M use in many parts of the country, the effectiveness of treatment for A/M abuse remains understudied (Anglin and Rawson, 2000). California has one of the highest concentrations of A/M use in the country, and the rates of A/M abuse and related problems are still increasing. For example, between 1992 and 1998, admissions to publicly funded treatment for A/M increased 226% in California, 333% in Los Angeles County, and at an even higher rate (up to 600%) in other major California counties. Between

1991 and 1994, the number of methamphetamine-related deaths almost tripled from 151 to 433, with increases of 238% in San Diego, 144% in San Francisco, and 113% in Los Angeles according to the Drug Abuse Warning Network (DAWN) (Morbidity and Mortality Weekly Report [MMWR], 1995). The increasing use of A/M and the severe consequences associated with its use have heightened the need for effective strategies to address A/M abuse (Rawson, McCann, Hasson, and Ling, 2000).

Limited data are available on treatment outcomes among A/M abusers. In a randomized clinical trial using imipramine to treat a small sample of 32 outpatient methamphetamine-dependent clients, Galloway, Newmeyer, Knapp, Stalcup, and Smith (1996) found few differences in methamphetamine use among the treatment (150 mg/day of imipramine) and control (10 mg/day of imipramine) groups, although subjects in the treatment group had significantly longer retention than did those in the control group (means of 33 and 10.5 days, respectively). Baker, Boggs, and Lewin (2001) conducted a randomized controlled trial among 62 regular users of amphetamine to test the feasibility of brief cognitive-behavioral interventions. They found a significant decrease in amphetamine use among the sample overall at the 6-month follow-up, although differences observed between the intervention groups were inconclusive. Huber, Rawson, and Shoptaw (1997) reported a comparison between 500 methamphetamine patients and 224 cocaine patients. The study indicated that although there were substantial demographic and drug history differences, the treatment response as defined by the amount of treatment services received, the duration of treatment participation and frequency of methamphetamine use measured by urinalysis, were virtually identical for the two groups of stimulant users. The only longer-term follow-up study of methamphetamine users available in the literature was reported by Rawson, Huber et al. (2002). They examined the outcomes of a sample of 114 methamphetamine users two to five years after outpatient treatment and found a significant reduction in self-reported methamphetamine use during the follow-up. Similar decreases were shown in the self-report of other drugs, and substantial improvement in employment status and a reduction in the number of individuals experiencing paranoia were also found at follow-up. Although there is currently a rapidly emerging wealth of information from animal and human brain research that has led to remarkable changes in the way methamphetamine addiction is understood (Rawson, Anglin, and Ling, 2002) and from several ongoing studies funded by National

Institute on Drug Abuse (NIDA) and Center for Substance Abuse Treatment (CSAT) to evaluate the efficacy of treatments for stimulant-using populations and the associated outcomes, results of these studies are not currently available. Furthermore, little is known about the long-term functioning of methamphetamine users following treatment.

The present study takes advantage of data collected from a subset of A/M abusers in a representative sample of patients recruited from an extensive treatment system in a large metropolitan area in California. Longitudinal data on drug abuse treatment utilization, A/M use, and criminal activities over an extended period of time were retrospectively recalled; these "natural history" data permit a longitudinal characterization of the patterns of drug use and treatment. The present article reports the results of an examination of the longitudinal patterns of treatment utilization and associated outcomes of 205 A/M abusers. We applied growth curve models to investigate the effects of treatment on A/M use and criminal involvement over time. Specifically, we tested the concurrent treatment effects (effects on outcomes while in treatment) and the cumulative treatment effects (effects of the cumulative length of time in treatment on the trajectory of outcomes) on A/M use and criminal activity among A/M abusers.

METHODS

Study Design

The study examined 205 amphetamine/methamphetamine (A/M) abusers recruited while they were in drug treatment. These A/M patients were part of a larger prospective study on processes and outcomes of drug treatment that recruited 565 patients from 19 different treatment facilities in 1995. These treatment programs were selected by stratified random sampling to represent all treatment modalities currently available for substance abuse treatment in Los Angeles County. The service modalities included outpatient drug free/day treatment (11 sites), residential (4 sites), inpatient/detoxification (2 sites), and methadone maintenance (2 sites). Within each treatment modality, programs were randomly selected. Additionally, programs that served women were oversampled.

Approximately 30 patients were randomly selected from each participating program. For programs with 30 or fewer patients, all who were enrolled in the treatment program were selected for participation; consecutively enrolled patients were subsequently sampled until 30 cases were obtained for each site. Patient drug use and related behaviors were assessed both at baseline and at one-year follow-up. A total of 565 patients were recruited at baseline and 511 completed follow-up interviews. The reasons for attrition included death (7), refusal (11), and either relocation out of the area or unable to locate (36).

Participants

The present analytic sample included 205 patients who reported amphetamine or methamphetamine (A/M) as their primary drug problem or the drug they used regularly (i.e., using A/M on a weekly or more frequent basis). Overall, the sample was 46.8% male and 64.9% White, 9.8% Black, 17.1% Hispanic, and 8.3% other ethnicity/race. The mean age of the sample at the time of the baseline interview was 33.9 years old (SD = 9.0). Of these, 73.6% had a high school or higher level of education, but only 26.3% were employed at the time of the baseline interview. About one quarter of them were married or living as married. These characteristics were similar to those of the overall sample, except that the analytic sample was younger (mean age of the overall sample was 35.9 [SD = 9.2]) and consisted of more Whites and fewer Blacks (ethnic distribution for the overall sample was 40.0% White, 33.3% Black, 18.6% Hispanic, and 8.1% other).

The mean age of first A/M use was about 18.7 years (SD = 5.9), regular use was approximately 20.7 years (SD = 6.7), and first treatment entry was around 27.7 years (SD = 8.2). These subjects reported regular use of other substances: 78.5% marijuana, 60.0% cocaine/crack, 34.7% heroin, and 81% alcohol. Of these, 26.1% reported A/M use by injection. A high percentage of the patients (87.8%) also reported having an arrest record. The mean age of first arrest was 19.0 years old (SD = 6.5). The mean number of arrests was 8.3 (SD = 12.5), with the majority of patients (51.2%) having 1 to 5 arrests prior to the referent treatment.

Fieldwork Procedures and the Natural History Instrument

At the baseline of this study, all participants were asked to complete a structured interview conducted by UCLA-trained interviewers at the treatment facility. The baseline face-to-face interview, for which participants received monetary compensation, took approximately 45 minutes to complete. The face-to-face follow-up interviews were conducted one year after the baseline at UCLA or at a location more convenient for the participants. The Natural History Instrument (NHI, described below) was administered

during the follow-up interview, which took approximately two to three hours to finish. Participants were paid for completing the interview. Subjects were given written assurances of confidentiality prior to each interview.

The interview protocol for administering the NHI was in part adapted from that of Nurco and colleagues (1975). Subjects were aware that the interviewer already knew their official history of criminal activity and legal status from information obtained independently from California criminal justice system records and could use this information to verify their self-reports of criminal activity and legal status. The NHI consists of a set of "static" and a set of "dynamic" forms that permit the capture of longitudinal, sequential data on drug use, criminal, and treatment careers (see McGlothlin, Anglin, and Wilson [1977] for a detailed description). The static forms collect background information on the subject and are administered once during the interview. The dynamic forms are designed to collect data on the drug use histories of the subjects as well as data on events that might have shaped, or have been shaped by, drug use. The dynamic forms collect chronological data on a month-to-month basis on drug and alcohol use, crime and delinquency, incarcerations, employment, medical and psychiatric status and service utilization, and drug treatment. The dynamic part of the interview consists of the repeated administration of these forms for as many life segments (defined by major changes in lifestyle) as necessary. The dynamic part of the NHI is initiated at one year prior to the subject's first use of his or her primary drug until the time of interview. The NHI procedures include construction prior to the interview of a timeline or a life history calendar where critical events (e.g., arrests, periods of incarceration) are noted to facilitate the subject's recall. Information on the timeline is collected in whole months using the 15th as the cut-off mark to determine whether it should be included with the previous or next month. Additionally, data on the incarceration of 30 days or longer are filled out first and no other events (e.g., employment) can overlap with the incarceration periods. Other institutionalized periods (e.g., inpatient drug treatment lasting 15 days or longer) are then filled out, followed by primary drug and other measures. Because the unit of NHI data is "month," the order and duration of individual events cannot be distinguished within a month. Using the NHI, behaviors and activities chronologically recorded over the drug use career allow the specification of timing of individual treatment episodes and associated events so that sequential patterns and associated precedents and consequences can be examined.

The reliability and validity of the NHI data have been thoroughly examined using two face-to-face interviews conducted 10 years apart among a sample of heroin users (Anglin, Hser, and Chou, 1993; Hser, Chou, and Anglin, 1992; Chou, Hser, and Anglin, 1996). Briefly, the rates of congruence between self-reported current opiate use and urinalysis among those who provided a urine specimen were 73.7% at the first interview and 85.8% at the second interview. Test-retest reliability of self-report data during the four-year overlap period was investigated. Pearson test-retest correlation for measures of narcotics use was .71 for abstinence and .63 for daily use. The correlation coefficients of intervariable relationships, based on 46 variables measured at two interviews 10 years apart, ranged as high as 0.86 and 0.90, depending on the period assessed.

Data and Measures

Lifetime measures of drug abuse treatment utilization prior to the referent treatment were collected at the baseline when the patients were sampled. These descriptive measures include ever-in-treatment, number of treatment episodes, type of treatment modality, and age when first entered treatment.

To investigate the dynamic relationships between treatment and outcomes (A/M use and crime) over time, we included in the models the natural history data of monthly measures of A/M use, criminal involvement, and treatment participation over a 36-month period—24 months before and 12 months after the referent treatment admission, as a majority of patients had used A/M at least 2 years prior to the referent treatment. Amphetamine/Methamphetamine (A/M) use was measured by the number of days per month using A/M. Levels of A/M use were originally collected using a 7-point scale (from 6 = daily use to 0 = no use), but the measure was converted to specify the number of days of A/M use during each month (i.e., daily use equaled 30 days, number of days per week was multiplied by 4, number of weekends was multiplied by 2, number of days per month was multiplied by 1, number of days per year was divided by 12, and number of days per segment was divided by the number of months in the segment). Criminal involvement was measured by two variables: the number of times per month crimes (e.g., robbery, burglary, forgery, prostitution, but excluding drug dealing) were committed and whether or not any crimes (all crimes including drug dealing; measured as yes/no dichotomy) were committed. Treatment status was dichotomously (1 = yes/0 = no) measured for each month during the

36-month observation period. Cumulative treatment length was calculated using the total months in treatment summed over the 36-month period.

To control for potential confounds, the following covariates were considered: demographics (gender, ethnicity, years of education, marital status), use severity (years between first use of A/M to the time of the baseline interview), and injection use (yes/no).

Analytic Methods

We applied the growth curve modeling (GCM) approach to examine longitudinal treatment effects. The GCM is a multilevel approach that treats longitudinal data to be analyzed as hierarchically structured data, and nests repeated measures within a subject. The GCM has the advantage over traditional simple group comparisons in that it can appropriately control for intracorrelation among repeated measures across time. A longitudinal treatment evaluation model can be built to test different aspects or measures of treatment utilization over time. The GCM developed for this study consists of models for two levels. The level 1 model was developed to describe the growth profiles for each individual using repeated measures taken for each month across 36 months of A/M use. The level 2 models were specified to investigate the factors that may affect the variation of growth profiles among the subjects.

Specifically, we modeled treatment effects in two ways. The concurrent treatment effect examined whether outcomes changed (i.e., reduced A/M use and crime) when patients were in treatment relative to when they were not. Treatment status was modeled as a level 1 independent variable and can be considered as a time-variant variable (a status that changes with time). The cumulative treatment effect investigated the effect of the cumulative length in treatment on the trajectory of the outcome measures across individuals. The cumulative length in treatment was modeled as a level 2 independent variable.

A separate model was tested for both concurrent treatment effect and cumulative treatment effect associated with each outcome measure. Under the linear growth assumption, each individual's outcome trajectory over time is characterized by the intercept and slope, which may be regarded as responses in regression models. For each model, we examined whether intercepts were significant. If the initial status (e.g., A/M use levels in the first month) differed significantly between individual patients, we conducted regression analyses with intercepts as outcomes using patient characteristics to predict variation in a patient's A/M use level. If the slopes varied between individuals, we conducted regression analyses with slopes as outcomes to explore individual patient variables that may account for the variation in the slopes. The level 1 effects are subject mean centered and level 2 effects are grand mean centered. With subject mean centered, the effect of a particular predictor variable is relative to the mean for each individual subject. With grand mean centered, the effect of the predictor variable is relative to the overall effect in the outcome status for all the observations from all subjects.

We applied HLM/2L to test all our models (Bryk, Raudenbush, and Congdon, 1996), in which random effect parameters are also included. Models with a dichotomized dependent variable (e.g., any crime) were tested using regression with logistic transformation on the dichotomized variable, and models with a continuous dependent variable (e.g., days using A/M, number of crimes) were tested using a linear regression, all within the context of HLM.

RESULTS

In presenting all of the modeling results, we first report models without covariates (gender, ethnicity, years of education, marital status, use severity, and injection

use), followed by results of models that incorporate these covariates as level 2 or between-subject variables in both the intercepts and slopes for A/M use.

Descriptive Statistics on Longitudinal Patterns of Treatment Utilization

A majority of the study participants (73.2%) reported having a treatment history, with the mean number of prior treatment episodes being 3.7 (SD = 4.4). These prior treatments included various modalities (outpatient drug-free, inpatient, residential, and methadone maintenance). Over the 36-month period examined in the model, the mean number of treatment episodes was 1.4 (SD = 0.8) over a mean total months of 14.0 (SD = 9.1). The most commonly used modality during the 36-month period was outpatient drug-free programs (71.2%). As for the referent treatment from which the patients were sampled, the majority of patients were enrolled in either outpatient drug-free treatment (56.6%) or residential treatment programs (26.3%).

Growth Curve Modeling Results

The percentages of patients using A/M, committing crimes, and in treatment over the 36-month period are graphed in Figure 1. As expected, the percentage

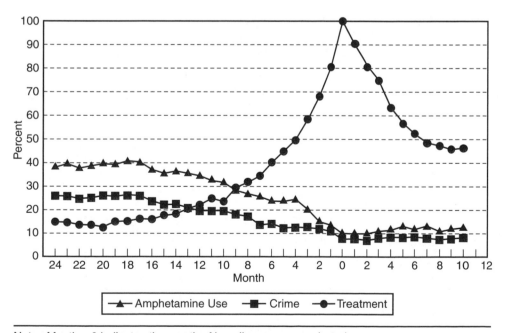

Note: Month = 0 indicates the month of baseline survey conducted

FIGURE 1   Percentage of Patients Reporting Amphetamine Use, Criminal Activity, and Treatment Over Time.

of patients in treatment peaked at the baseline of the study when the sample was recruited; the time period that patients were in treatment before the baseline and the time period they were in the referent treatment program varied. The trajectory for both A/M use and criminal involvement appeared to be linear over time, with the trajectory of A/M use having a steeper slope.

Concurrent Treatment Effects.   We tested concurrent treatment effects by incorporating treatment status as a level 1 independent variable (i.e., treatment status changes with time) to examine its effect on outcomes during the same time periods. Without covariates (Table 1), the group reported spending an average of 10.75 days using A/M during the initial month of the 36-month period, with decreased days

TABLE 1   HLM Modeling Results on Concurrent Treatment Effects ($N = 205$)

(Treatment status as level 1 independent variable)

MODEL WITHOUT COVARIATES		MODEL WITH COVARIATES	
Coefficient (standard error)		*Coefficient (standard error)*	
MODEL 1.1: A/M USE AS DEPENDENT VARIABLE[a]			
Intercept	10.75 (0.98)**	Intercept	13.21 (1.97)**
Time	−0.18 (0.03)**	Black	−9.46 (3.39)**
Treatment status	−4.65 (0.63)**	Time	−0.22 (0.06)**
		Treatment status	−5.14 (1.29)**
RANDOM EFFECT (VARIANCE COMPONENT)			
Intercept	189.84**		179.99**
Time	0.19**		0.19**
Treatment status	70.33**		68.99**
MODEL 1.2: CRIME LESS DEALING AS DEPENDENT VARIABLE[b]			
Intercept	3.13 (0.72)**		3.17 (0.94)**
Time	−0.03 (0.02)		−0.03 (0.02)
Treatment status	−1.74 (0.44)**		−1.74 (0.44)**
RANDOM EFFECT (VARIANCE COMPONENT)			
Intercept	103.06**		102.17**
Time	0.06**		0.06**
Treatment status	34.08**		34.10**
MODEL 1.3: ANY CRIME AS DEPENDENT VARIABLE[b,c]			
Intercept	−1.40 (0.42)**		−1.07 (0.69)**
Time	−0.12 (0.02)**		−0.12 (0.02)**
Treatment status	−1.83 (0.23)**		−1.85 (0.24)**
RANDOM EFFECT (VARIANCE COMPONENT)[d]			
Intercept	25.93**		26.51**
Time	0.05*		0.05**

[a]Covariates (level 2) (i.e., gender, ethnicity, education, marital status, use severity, injection) were included in both intercept and slope models.

[b]Covariates (level 2) (i.e., gender, ethnicity, education, marital status, use severity, injection) were included only in intercept models.

[c]Dependent variable (any crime) is a dichotomous measure.

[d]Random variance component of treatment slope is not significant and, therefore, is not included.

*$p < .05$, **$p < .01$

of use (on average, .18 days per month) after the initial month. However, being in treatment was associated with a reduction of 4.65 days of A/M use per month. In terms of criminal activities, the group's mean number of crimes (excluding drug trafficking) committed was 3.13 during the initial month and decreased by .03 each subsequent month. Being in treatment, on average, was associated with a reduction of 1.74 crimes. Similarly, the odds of committing any crime (including drug trafficking) when A/M abusers were in treatment was .04 (times (= $e^{-1.83-1.4}$) that of committing any crime when not in treatment.

Generally speaking, with or without covariates, being in treatment was significantly associated with reductions in A/M use ($\beta = -4.65$ and -5.14 respectively), the frequency of committing crimes (excluding dealing) ($\beta = -1.74$ for both), and likelihood of participation in any crime activity ($\beta = -1.83$, and $\beta = -1.85$). The estimates of variance-covariance components (e.g., random effects of intercept, time slope, and treatment slope) in all these models were significant. This implies that the HLM model with random effect parameters is appropriate for the data fitting. Ethnicity (Blacks versus Whites) was the only covariate that was significant. Initial A/M use was significantly lower among Black patients than White patients ($\beta = -2.91$, $p < .01$). However, there were no differences in treatment effects among ethnic groups in the frequency of committing crimes and the likelihood of participation in any crime.

Cumulative Treatment Effects. We examined cumulative treatment effects on outcomes by modeling the cumulative length of treatment as a level 2 independent variable, and the results are shown in Table 2. In terms of A/M use, the average number of days using A/M was about 10.6 days during the first month of this 36-month period and decreased .3 days each month thereafter (e.g., to an average of 10 days of use on the third month). There were significant random variations both in the intercept (initial status) and slope (change over time). When considering covariates, patients who had longer stays in treatment used A/M, on average, for fewer days (.37 day) in the initial month, but had slower decreasing rates of use over time (.34 − .008 = .332 days per month) than those who had shorter treatment stays (.34 days per month). In contrast, although criminal activities also showed decreasing trajectories, both the intercepts and slopes were not affected by the length of stay in treatment.

The only significant covariate in the intercept model of A/M use was ethnicity (Blacks relative to Whites). However, ethnicity was not significant in the slope model. On average, Black patients used 8.6 fewer days of A/M than White patients initially, and had the same decreasing rate in A/M use over time as the White patients.

DISCUSSION

The present study provides some encouraging findings in support of treatment effectiveness among A/M abusers. Concurrent treatment effects were demonstrated for both A/M use and crime reduction, which are consistent with most of the literature assessing general treatment effectiveness. On average, these A/M abusers used A/M 11 to 13 days during the initial month of the 36-month period examined, but reduced their use to 6 to 7 days per month while in treatment (i.e., being in treatment was associated with a reduction of 4.65 days to 5.14 days of use). Similarly, A/M abusers reported committing an average of 3 crimes (excluding drug trafficking) per month initially, but reduced this amount to 1.4 crimes per month (i.e., a reduction of 1.7 crimes per month) when they were in treatment. The odds of committing any crime (including drug trafficking) was .22 (= $e^{-1.4}$) initially, but was reduced to .04 (= $e^{-1.40-1.83=-3.23}$) while in treatment.

Modeling results of the cumulative treatment effectiveness showed a negative association between cumulative treatment and A/M use in the intercept model and a positive association in the slope model. In other words, A/M abusers who stayed in treatment longer were using at a less severe level initially, and they decreased their A/M use at a slower rate than those who spent less time in treatment. The negative association between initial use and cumulative treatment length appears to be consistent with the concept that patients with more favorable prognosis (e.g., better functioning, higher treatment motivation) are more likely to stay longer in treatment (Simpson, Joe, and Brown, 1997; Anglin and Hser, 1992). The slower rates of improvement (decreasing A/M use) for patients staying longer in treatment are subject to several possible interpretations. One explanation could be that patients with lower levels of problem severity had less room to improve and therefore improved at a slower pace. Alternatively, it could be that these patients stayed longer because they took a longer time to get their drug use level under control. On the other hand, we found that Black patients had a significantly lower level of use at initial status, but a similar decreasing rate of A/M use as White patients. Thus,

TABLE 2   HLM Modeling Results of Cumulative Treatment Effects ($N = 205$)

(Cumulative treatment length as level 2 independent variable)

MODEL WITHOUT COVARIATES		MODEL WITH COVARIATES	
Coefficient (standard error)		*Coefficient (standard error)*	

MODEL 2.1: A/M USE AS DEPENDENT VARIABLE[a]

Intercept	10.57 (0.99)**	Intercept	11.96 (1.99)**
Time	−0.29 (0.03)**	Black	−8.58 (3.33)*
		Cumulative treatment	−0.37 (0.11)**
		Time	−0.34 (0.07)**
		Cumulative treatment	0.008 (0.004)*

RANDOM EFFECT (VARIANCE COMPONENT)

Intercept	196.17**		174.97**
Time	0.22**		0.21**

MODEL 2.2: CRIME LESS DEALING AS DEPENDENT VARIABLE[a]

Intercept	3.08 (0.71)**	Intercept	2.31 (1.50)
Time	−0.08 (0.02)**	Cumulative treatment	0.08 (0.08)
		Time	−0.05 (0.05)
		Cumulative treatment	−0.004 (0.002)

RANDOM EFFECT (VARIANCE COMPONENT)

Intercept	102.92**		101.04**
Time	0.10**		0.10**

MODEL 2.3: ANY CRIME AS DEPENDENT VARIABLE[b]

Intercept	−1.53 (0.43)**	Intercept	−1.36 (0.97)
Time	−0.14 (0.02)**	Cumulative treatment	−0.003 (0.06)
		Time	−0.13 (0.05)**
		Cumulative treatment	−0.003 (0.003)*

RANDOM EFFECT (VARIANCE COMPONENT)

Intercept	28.34**		30.49**
Time	0.06**		0.06**

[a]Covariates (level 2) (i.e., gender, ethnicity, education, marital status, use severity, injection) were included in both intercept and slope models.

[b]Dependent variable (any crime) is a dichotomous measure.

*$p < .05$, **$p < .01$

the rate of change cannot be entirely explained by initial use level. Future studies with more detailed information on treatment processes may provide additional insight into this issue. In terms of criminal activities, the study did not find significant associa-

tions between cumulative treatment and trajectories of the criminal activity measured by either crime times or any crime.

In addition to the findings discussed above, which are uniquely revealed by the application of the growth curve modeling in the examination of longitudinal treatment effects, the descriptive statistics of the present study confirmed some previous findings. For example, this sample of A/M abusers had a disproportionately high rate of White patients (65%), compared to the 40% White in the original overall sample, but a comparable rate among A/M treatment admissions across Los Angeles County—approximately 67% being White. Most patients were polydrug users (e.g., used cocaine, heroin, marijuana, or alcohol in addition to A/M on a regular basis). Many of them reported having had prior treatment and criminal justice system interactions, which are characteristics similar to those A/M abusers observed in the general treatment samples (Anglin and Rawson, 2000).

Many subjects in our sample also reported regular use of other drugs such as cocaine. In a preliminary analysis of the data, we have found that cocaine use was negatively related to A/M use, but this relationship became insignificant when other covariates were considered in the model. Because the inclusion of cocaine use (with or without considering these other covariates) did not affect the treatment effect on A/M, we did not report modeling results that include cocaine use. Future studies focusing on the relationships among use of A/M and other drugs may shed light on the dynamics involved in the use of different types of drugs.

The present study has a number of limitations. The study is not based on an experimental study design, and thus, positive effects associated with treatment status observed in the present study cannot be definitively attributed to treatment. A related issue is that our model did not include in-depth measures of specific therapeutic methods that may be relevant to treatment effectiveness. In fact, our study sample was recruited from community treatment programs; many of these programs provide generic treatment services not necessarily designed specifically to treat A/M abuse. However, in addition to providing some findings consistent with the literature regarding the effectiveness of the community treatment programs, the present study also highlighted some interesting observations (e.g., differential rates of improvement over time for patients staying in treatment for different time periods) and suggests issues that need further investigation, perhaps in future experimental studies. Another limitation is that the study data relied on retrospective recall over an extended period of time. Our NHI instrument is designed to cover data recalled over a long period of time. In order to maintain adequate reliability and validity of the recall, data are recorded on a month-to-month basis. Thus, it is not possible for us to conduct analyses based on more precise measures such as days in treatment or to control for at-risk time (e.g., adjusting for days incarcerated) during a particular month. Few drug treatment evaluation studies have long-term follow-up assessments and even fewer have frequent assessments (McKay and Weiss, 2001). Using natural history data retrospectively recalled represents a cost efficient alternative means of conducting such a longitudinal evaluation. Future studies using frequent, repeated assessments over extended periods of time should attempt replication or validation of the present findings.

Despite these study limitations, findings of the present study are fairly consistent, confirming those generally found in the literature and, more importantly, provide detailed and quantified measures of the time course of treatment effects. Given the dearth of data on amphetamine/methamphetamine abuse, the present study provides some initial evidence of treatment effectiveness, even though at a global level. Future studies examining promising treatment approaches for A/M users will facilitate the development of improved treatment services. Additionally, future studies can replicate and expand these findings using these models to examine longitudinal patterns of treatment effects as new or longer-term treatment outcome data become available.

ACKNOWLEDGMENTS

The study was supported in part by the National Institute on Drug Abuse (NIDA; Grant No. DA08757) and the Center for Substance Abuse Treatment (CSAT), Substance Abuse and Mental Health Services Administration (SAMHSA), Department of Health and Human Services (Contract No. 270-97-7011). The authors are also supported by career development awards from NIDA (K02DA00139 for Dr. Hser and K02DA00146 for Dr. Anglin). The content of this publication does not necessarily reflect the views or policies of the Department of Health and Human Services, nor does mention of trade names, commercial products, or organizations imply endorsement by the U.S. Government. The authors thank the review comments provided by the Persistent Effects of Treatment Studies (PETS) team on an earlier version of the paper and the publication support provided by staff at the UCLA Drug Abuse Research Center.

REFERENCES

Anglin, M. D., and Hser, Y.-I. (1992). Drug abuse treatment. In R. C. Watson (Ed.). *Drug and alcohol abuse reviews* (pp. 1–36). Totowa, NJ: Humana Press, Inc.

Anglin, M. D., and Rawson, R. A. (Eds.). (2000). The CSAT methamphetamine treatment project. *Journal of Psychoactive Drugs, 32*(2).

Anglin, M. D., Hser, Y.-I., and Chou, C. (1993). Reliability and validity of retrospective behavioral self-report by narcotics addicts. *Evaluation Review, 17,* 308–323.

Anglin, M. D., Kalechstein, A., Maglione, M., Annon, J., and Fiorentine, R. (1998). *Epidemiology and treatment of methamphetamine abuse in California: A regional report.* National Evaluation Data and Technical Assistance Center (1998, February).

Baker, A., Boggs, T. G., and Lewin, T. J. (2001). Randomized controlled trial of brief cognitive-behavioral interventions among regular users of amphetamine. *Addiction, 96,* 1279–1287.

Bryk, A. S., Raudenbush, S. W., and Congdon, R. T. (1996). *HLM: Hierarchical linear and nonlinear modeling with the HLM/2L and HLM/3L programs.* Chicago: Scientific Software International.

Chou, C-S, Hser, Y.-I., and Anglin, M. D. (1996). Pattern reliability of narcotics addict's self-reported data: A confirmatory assessment of construct validity and consistency. *Substance Use and Misuse, 9,* 1189–1216.

Galloway, G. P., Newmeyer, J., Knapp, T., Stalcup, S. A., and Smith, D. (1996). A controlled trial of imipramine for the treatment of methamphetamine dependence. *Journal of Substance Abuse Treatment, 13*(6), 493–497.

Hubbard, R. L., Marsden, M. E., Rachal, J. V., Harwood, H. J., Cavanaugh, E. R., and Ginzburg, H. M. (1989). *Drug abuse treatment: A national study of effectiveness.* Chapel Hill: University of North Carolina Press.

Huber, A., Rawson, R. A., and Shoptaw, S. (1997). *Methamphetamine and cocaine users response to outpatient treatment.*

Paper presented at the Western regional conference on methamphetamine, San Francisco, California.

Morbidity and Mortality Weekly Report. (1995). Increasing morbidity and mortality associated with abuse of methamphetamine—United States, 1991–1994. *Morbidity and Mortality Weekly Report, 44*(47). 882–886.

McGlothlin, W. H., Anglin, M. D., and Wilson, B. D. (1977). *An evaluation of the California Civil Addict Program.* (DHEW Publication, No. ADM 78-558). Washington, DC: U.S. NIDA Services Research Monograph Series, Government Printing Office.

McKay, J. R., and Weiss, R. V. (2001). A review of temporal effects and outcome predictors in substance abuse treatment studies with long-term follow-ups; Preliminary results and methodological issues. *Evaluation Review, 25*(2), 113–161.

Nurco, D. N., Bonito, A. J., Lerner, M., and Balter, M. B. (1975). Studying addicts over time: Methodology and preliminary findings. *American Journal of Drug and Alcohol Studies, 2*(2), 183–196.

Rawson, R. A., Anglin, M. D., and Ling, W. L. (2002). Will the methamphetamine problem go away? *Journal of Addictive Diseases, 21*(1), 5–19.

Rawson, R. A., Huber, A., Brethen, P., Obert, J., Gulati, V., Shoptaw, S., and Ling, W. (2002). Status of methamphetamine users 2–5 years after outpatient treatment. *Journal of Addictive Diseases, 21*(1), 107–119.

Rawson, R. A., McCann, M. J., Hasson, A. J., and Ling, W. (2000). Addiction pharmacotherapy 2000: New options, new challenges, *Journal of Psychoactive Drugs, 32*(4), 371–378.

Simpson, D. D., Joe, G. W., and Brown, B. S. (1997). Treatment retention and follow-up outcomes in the drug treatment abuse outcome study (DATOS). *Psychology of Addictive Behaviors, 11,* 294–307.

CHAPTER 6: DISCUSSION QUESTIONS

1. What is harm reduction?

2. What is SSI and should it include drug users? Why or why not? According to Reuter and MacCoun, how is this policy affected by harm-reduction ideas?

3. According to Kelley, Murphy, and Lune, what does it mean to have a safer-injection mentor? How do mentors contribute to a culture of harm reduction? What is the new etiquette of drug injection?

4. What is the theoretical basis of the Bourgois reading?

5. What are some of the main concerns Bourgois expresses about methadone, based on ethnographic fieldwork with methadone clients?

6. According to Bourgois, what are some of the regional variations in methadone treatment?

7. How does the power/knowledge nexus frame dosage at methadone clinics?

8. According to Bourgois, what would happen if we "de-exoticize how we think about drugs"?

9. What is a natural history interview as described by Hser and colleagues?

10. What is a growth curve modeling approach to data analysis? Why is it important?

11. What are the various types of treatment programs that drug users might encounter?

12. According to Hser and colleagues, what are the concurrent and cumulative treatment effects for methamphetamine users? Why did they have different effects? How did they vary by race?

13. What are the limitations of each selection?

14. What are the policy implications of each selection?

CHAPTER 6: ADDITIONAL RESOURCES IN RESEARCH NAVIGATOR AND IN THE *NEW YORK TIMES*

Belluck, P. (2003, February 2). Overdoses and deaths from abuse of drug methadone are up. *New York Times*.

Belluck, P. (2003, February 2). Using methadone in Maine, for good and at times bad. *New York Times*.

Belluck, P. (2003, February 9). For drug abusers, methadone has become a double-edged sword. *New York Times*.

Belluck, P. (2003, February 9). Methadone grows as killer drug. *New York Times*.

Broadhead, R. S., Heckathorn, D. D., Altice, F. L., van Hulst, Y., Carbone, M., Friedland, G. H., et al. (2002). Increasing drug users' adherence to HIV treatment: results of a peer-driven intervention feasibility study. *Social Science and Medicine, 55*, 235–246.

Broadhead, R. S., and van Hulst, Y. (1999). The impact of a needle exchange's closure. *Public Health Reports, 114*, 439–447.

Copeland, L. (2004). The drug user's identity and how it relates to being hepatitis C antibody positive: A qualitative study. *Drugs: Education, Prevention, and Policy, 11*, 129–147.

Feuer, A. (2004, July 17). Hepatitis C outbreak adds a new woe to drug centers. *New York Times*.

Hser, Y.-I., Grella, C. E., Collins, C., and Teruya, C. (2003). Drug-use initiation and conduct disorder among adolescents in drug treatment. *Journal of Adolescence, 26*, 331–345.

Hser, Y.-I., Joshi, V., Anglin, D. M., and Fletcher, B. (1999). Predicting posttreatment cocaine abstinence for first-time admissions and treatment repeaters." *American Journal of Public Health, 89*, 666–671.

Ives, N. (2003, September 4). Drug maker sounds the alarm on drug abuse. *New York Times*.

Kelley, M. S., and Chitwood, D. D. (2004). Effects of drug treatment for heroin sniffers: A protective factor against moving to injection? *Social Science and Medicine, 58*, 2083–2092.

Kershaw, S., and Davey, M. (2004, January 18). Plagued by drugs, tribes revive ancient penalty. *New York Times*.

Krauss, C. (2003, May 18). Canadian mayor pushes for treatment centers for drug users. *New York Times*.

MacCoun, R. (1999). What harm reduction is and isn't. *American Psychologist, 54*, 843–844.

Perez-Pena, R. (2003, August 11). New drug promises shift in treatment for heroin addicts. *New York Times*.

Terry-McElrath, Y. M., and McBride, D. C. (2004). Local implementation of drug policy and access to treatment services for juveniles. *Crime and Delinquency, 50*, 60–87.

Turner, W., and Wallace, B. (2003). African American substance use. *Violence Against Women, 9*, 576–589.

Vega, C. M. (2003, January 6). Cash-for-sterilization plan starts slowly in New York. *New York Times*.

Whiteacre, K. W., and Pepinsky, H. (2002). Controlling drug use. *Criminal Justice Policy Review, 13*, 21–31.

TOPICS IN DRUGS AND CRIME RESEARCH

With an active and interdisciplinary field such as drug studies, it is possible to identify any number of current and hot topics that are leading the field in new directions. This chapter contains just a sampling of topics, including the examination of the victimization of drug users, syringe exchange and trends in crime, drug trafficking, and the drug marketplace.

The contribution by Karen McElrath, Dale Chitwood, and Mary Comerford offers a unique perspective on the drugs–crime relationship by focusing on victimization among injection drug users, a group known to commit a disproportionate amount of crime. The article approaches victimization from routine activities theory. This theory predicts that victimization is more likely to occur when a motivated offender converges in time and space with an attractive and unguarded target. People's daily activities contribute to or diminish their risk of becoming crime victims. Demographic variables affect victimization because of role expectations and behaviors that are associated with various demographic groups. Using logistic regression procedures, the authors examine the primary dependent variables of violent victimization and property victimization. They find little evidence that involvement in violent crime increases risk for violent victimization; property offenders are, however, more likely to be victims of violence. Overall, drug lifestyle activity increases the risk of victimization.

Syringe exchange programs have been around for quite some time, yet they are still hotly contested in many communities. The selection by Melissa Marx and colleagues tackles an important concern: Do these programs increase crime? The authors use quantitative data collected in Baltimore and compare areas of the city that have syringe exchange programs with those that have none. They use a variety of arrest charges to compare crime rates before and after introduction of the programs. Their findings indicate that there were increases in drug-related arrests across the city, but they did not vary by proximity to a syringe exchange program. These findings contribute to the body of evidence that harm-reduction efforts that target individual users might also provide benefits to the community at large.

Lana Harrison and Nancy Kennedy investigate the effect of drug trafficking on levels of drug use. Although it is often assumed that high-traffic areas foster higher levels of drug use, these authors find just the opposite in the U.S. Southwest. In this quantitative article, they find few differences in illicit drug use between the U.S. Southwest and the rest of the country. In conclusion, for numerous reasons, availability of drugs does not translate into higher rates of use.

Lise-Marie VanNostrand and Richard Tewksbury's contribution is qualitative in nature and is a nice complement to research examining the social impact of drug use. Here, the authors explore the "motives and mechanics" of dealing drugs. They argue that this research is important because without understanding why and how drug dealers operate we will never be able to fully address the demand side of the drug market. Their findings shed light on the experiences of cocaine dealers in a midsized midwestern city who had been referred to a drug court. Although the sample is limited by these parameters (for example, it is likely that dealers with violent crimes were not diverted to the specialty drug court), it is unique in what it can offer from the perspective of dealers. They find that there are rational reasons offered for participating in drug dealing, including financial gain, greed, and desire for the concomitant lifestyle. In addition, the authors provide insight about how drug dealers successfully operate their business while limiting contact with the police. Although the study does not focus specifically on the drugs–crime link, the authors show why and how people participate in an illegal enterprise. In addition, the respondents were all in contact with the criminal justice system as dealers and not just as users of illicit drugs. The findings are significant in a number of ways. Although the authors do not explicitly frame the findings in terms of sociological theories of addiction and criminal behavior, it is possible to extrapolate to some of them, especially using anomie to explain goals of financial success.

23

Crime Victimization Among Injection Drug Users

KAREN McELRATH

DALE D. CHITWOOD

MARY COMERFORD

ABSTRACT

This study uses routine activity theory to examine violent and property crime victimization among a sample of 308 injection drug users (IDUs). We estimate prevalence rates and identify factors that contribute to the victimization of IDUs. The findings suggest that victimization rates of IDUs were much higher than rates found for the general urban population. Generally, crime involvement did not contribute significantly to victimization risk. Use of crack-cocaine increased the likelihood of property crime victimization whereas heroin use decreased the probability of both violent and property crime victimization. Other drug lifestyle activities (i.e., waiting in uncomfortable situations to buy drugs) also affected victimization risk. Finally, the results suggest that victimization differed by age and by gender, despite controls for drug use and drug lifestyle activities. Explanations for these results are offered.

INTRODUCTION

Research that investigates the correlates of criminal victimization is guided often by routine activities theory. This theory predicts that victimization is more likely to occur when a motivated offender converges in time and space with an attractive and unguarded target (Cohen and Felson, 1979). Central to this theory is that the daily activities of persons contribute to or diminish their risk for becoming crime victims. For example, the probability increases for becoming a crime victim with increased nightly leisure activities

(Gottfredson, 1984; Sampson and Lauritsen, 1990) or empty households (Sampson and Woolredge, 1987). These situations enhance the risk of victimization because they offer fewer capable guardians.

Demographic attributes also are said to affect victimization because of role expectations and behaviors that are associated with various demographic groups (Meier and Miethe, 1993, p. 466). Several studies have investigated the relationship between victimization and gender, race or ethnicity, or age. Many studies find that males are more likely than females to be the victims of assault and/or robbery (Kennedy and Forde, 1990; Lauritsen et al., 1991; Miethe and Meier, 1990; Sampson and Lauritsen, 1990), motor vehicle theft (Kennedy and Forde, 1990), and larceny and vandalism (Lauritsen et al., 1991). According to one study, however, females are significantly more likely than males to be victimized by personal theft and by burglary (Miethe and Meier, 1990). In other studies the relationship between gender and victimization diminishes when crime involvement is controlled (Jensen and Brownfield, 1986; Lauritsen et al., 1991).

Studies that investigate the link between race or ethnicity and victimization report mixed findings. Bivariate analyses suggest that African Americans and Hispanics are victimized more often than white non-Hispanics (Bureau of Justice Statistics, 1995). Some multivariate studies, however, reveal a more complex relationship between race and victimization; that is, African Americans report lower rates of victimization than whites for some crimes, higher rates for other crimes, but race has no effect on victimization for several other offense categories (Lauritsen et al., 1991). Other studies find very weak relationships between race and victimization (Cohen et al., 1981).

Research indicates that younger persons experience greater victimization than older persons (Bureau of Justice Statistics, 1995; Cohen et al., 1981; Kennedy and Forde, 1990; Sampson and Lauritsen, 1990). However, the age-victimization link might also be contingent on the type of crime victimization. For example, Miethe and Meier (1990) report an inverse relationship for assault but find no significant relationship between age and burglary or personal theft victimization.

Criminal involvement is linked with victimization; persons who engage in criminal activity experience a higher rate of victimization than persons who are not involved in crime (Lauritsen et al., 1991; Sampson and Lauritsen, 1990). Crime-involved persons might be viewed by offenders as attractive targets because offenders might believe that victim-offenders are less likely to report the crime to police and, if reported, victim-offenders are likely to be viewed by police as having little credibility.

Crime victimization also is linked with substance abuse. Alcohol significantly increases women's risk for sexual assault (Schwartz and Pitts, 1995) and cocaine use, primarily through its psychopharmacological effects, is associated with both participation in and victimization by violent activity (Goldstein et al., 1991). One study found evidence of cocaine in the bodies of 31% of homicide victims in New York City (Tardiff et al., 1994).

Persons who engage in illicit drug use may serve as attractive targets because persons under the influence might lack the ability to physically resist offenders; Hough (1987), for example, suggests that potential offenders are attracted by easy targets. In areas where drugs are bought and sold, persons who frequent these places may be viewed as attractive crime targets because it is believed that they carry valuable items such as money or drugs. In many instances these potential victims lack capable guardians who might otherwise serve as protectors against or deterrents to crime. Also, buyers of drugs are unlikely to report to police a robbery, theft, assault, or other crime that occurred when the victim was using (Goldstein, 1985) or in the act of buying drugs. To do so might implicate buyers in the illegal enterprise and buyers who report crime also risk the stigmatic street label of informant.

Some studies find that structural factors, such as neighborhood crime rate, are linked with individual risk of victimization. For instance, Sampson and Lauritsen (1990) report that area violence rate is a significant predictor of assault and acquaintance-violence victimization but that area violence has no significant effect on stranger-violence victimization. A second study finds that respondents who view their neighborhoods as unsafe at night are significantly more likely to be victimized than respondents who feel safe (Miethe and Meier, 1990).

To date, most victimization studies use data collected from the general population of adults or youth. Fattah (1993), however, suggests that certain groups experience higher rates of victimization than other groups. For example, ethnographic accounts suggest that drug users as a group experience frequent victimization (Goldstein et al., 1991; Inciardi et al., 1993; Maher and Curtis, 1995). The routine drug-related activities of IDUs make them attractive targets because these activities often occur without the presence of capable guardians.

The present study examines victimization among injection drug users (IDUs), a group known to commit a disproportionate amount of crime (Ball, 1991; Inciardi, 1979; Speckart and Anglin, 1986). We estimate the victimization rate for a sample of IDUs and examine factors that contribute to their crime victimization.

METHODS

Between June 1987 and August 1988, 601 African-American, Hispanic, and white or non-Hispanic respondents who were clients of methadone and inpatient drug treatment clinics in Miami, Florida, were enrolled in an epidemiological panel study of HIV infection and associated risk behaviors. Study eligibility included having injected one or more drugs some time since January 1, 1978. All study subjects participated on a voluntary basis, gave informed consent, and were paid $20 at the completion of each data collection session. The study was confidential, and assurances were made that data would not be disclosed to anyone, including treatment staff. Subjects were followed at 6-month intervals.

At each data collection point, participants were administered a structured interview that asked subjects about demographic information, history of drug use, drug injection practices, and sex behavior histories. A supplemental interview was administered to subjects whose follow-up interviews were scheduled between January and September 1994 ($N = 311$). Questions addressed respondents' crime victimizations, their criminal behaviors, and other lifestyle activities during the previous 6 months. Data from this collection point served as the basis for the present study.

The two interviewers who collected the data had extensive knowledge about local street culture and had interviewed subjects at several previous data collection points. Calendars were used to aid recall about respondents' behaviors during the 6-month period before the interview; a previous study of these respondents' reports of drug use found that reliability was quite high even when respondents were asked about behaviors 12 and 18 months after the 6-month retrospective period (McElrath et al., 1994).

We examined two dependent variables in this study: violent victimization and property victimization. Violent victimization included incidents of robbery, assault (attack), threats of assault, or rape. Property victimization included reports of burglary, personal larceny, motor vehicle theft, theft from a motor vehicle, or being cheated out of drugs or money. We chose binary measures of victimization because most persons who reported being victims had been victimized one time only during the 6-month period before the interview.

Questions about victimization described the offenses but did not include the word "victim." Nor did we use crime labels, e.g., robbery, in the event that these labels did not have a shared definition among subjects. Victimization questions are included in the Appendix.

Routine activity theory predicts that lifestyle and demographic variables contribute to victimization. Several variables were included to account for respondents' lifestyles. Variables were coded based on the presence (coded 1) or absence (coded 0) of the trait.

Use of heroin and use of powder cocaine were binary variables. We also used a binary variable to measure whether cocaine users "always or almost always" used crack-cocaine or used it less frequently. Alcohol use was measured by whether respondents consumed at least two drinks per day. Drug treatment exposure during the past 6 months was measured by three categories; no treatment, 1 to 3 months, and 4 to 6 months of treatment.

Selling drugs and engaging in prostitution or other sex-for-drug exchanges are behaviors that often occur without the presence of capable guardians. Moreover, these activities contribute to the perception of target attractiveness in that participants are likely to be carrying valuable items, such as drugs or cash. We used binary measures for these variables.

The source from which injection equipment (works) is purchased varies among IDUs. When works are purchased from street suppliers capable guardians are perhaps less likely to be present, therefore, we used a binary variable to indicate whether respondents purchased works from a street supplier or from another source, i.e., shooting gallery, pharmacy, other medical source, or friends or relatives. We also included a variable that measured whether respondents had waited with people whom they did not like or had been in uncomfortable situations in order to obtain drugs.

We included two binary measures of crime *committed* by subjects in the previous 6 months. We excluded drug sales and prostitution from the crime measures because we treated them as separate variables (discussed above). One crime variable measured violent crime involvement and the second variable measured property crime involvement. Although we have no information on the time order of crime and victimization events, other researchers suggest that criminal activity more often leads to crime victimization rather than the reverse (Sampson and Lauritsen, 1990), and that crime involvement can be viewed as a "type of routine activity" (Jensen and Brownfield, 1986, p. 87).

Demographic variables included gender (male), age (less than 30, 30 to 40, and over 40 years) and ethnicity (Hispanic, white non-Hispanic, and African-American). Three respondents were of "other ethnic" groups and we deleted these cases from the present analysis.

Routine activity theory predicts that victimization is more likely to occur in the absence of capable guardians and when potential victims are viewed as attractive targets. Several behaviors that are associated with illicit drug use occur in an environment in which there are no capable guardians and in which potential victims are viewed as attractive targets because they are believed to carry cash or drugs. Accordingly, we test seven hypotheses:

1. The probability of being victimized will increase with crime involvement,
2. respondents who engage in sex-for-drug exchanges will more likely be victimized than respondents who do not engage in these behaviors,
3. respondents who sell or distribute illicit drugs will more likely be victimized than respondents who do not sell or distribute illicit drugs,
4. drug and alcohol use will increase the probability of crime victimization,

5. respondents who purchase works from street suppliers will more likely be victimized than respondents who obtain works from other sources,

6. respondents who wait in uncomfortable situations to buy drugs will experience a greater likelihood of victimization than respondents who do not encounter these situations, and

7. persons exposed to treatment will have lower rates of victimization than persons not exposed.

RESULTS

Table 1 provides summary data that describe the sample of IDUs. The data show that 15.3% of respondents had been victims of violent crime and nearly one-fourth of the sample (23.4%) had been victimized by property crime in the 6 months preceding the interview.

A total of 8.1% respondents had committed at least one violent crime during the past 6 months and 11.0% had committed one or more property crimes. Only 5.5% reported that they had engaged in prostitution or sex-for-drug exchanges and 9.4% reported selling or distributing illicit drugs during the 6-month period before the interview.

Twenty-four percent of the respondents had used heroin and 31.8% had used cocaine. Among cocaine users, 17.2% reported that they "always or almost always" used crack-cocaine rather than cocaine powder. About one-fifth of the sample (19.4%) had consumed at least two drinks per day. Most respondents had not been exposed to drug treatment during the past 6 months (56.8%). About one-fifth (20.2%) had been exposed to between 1 to 3 months of

TABLE 1   Summary Data for Injection Drug Users in Sample ($n = 308$)

VARIABLE	PERCENTAGE
Victimized by:	
Violent crime	15.3
Property crime	23.4
Crimes committed:	
Violent crime	8.1
Property crime	11.0
Sex-for-drug exchange	5.5
Sold or distributed drugs	9.4
Drug and alcohol use:	
Heroin	24.0
Cocaine	31.8
Always used crack-cocaine	17.2
Alcohol, two or more per day	19.4
Treatment exposure:	
None	56.8
1 to 3 months	20.2
4 to 6 months	23.0
Waited in uncomfortable situations to buy drugs	11.4
Works from street supplier	10.7
Male	63.3
Age	
Less than 30 years	17.5
30 to 40 years	68.2
Over 40 years	14.3
Ethnicity:	
White Hispanic	11.7
African-American	24.0
White non-Hispanic	64.3

treatment and 23.0% had received treatment for at least 4 of the 6 months. A total of 11.4% of the sample reported waiting in uncomfortable situations to obtain drugs and 10.7% had purchased works from street suppliers.

Males accounted for 63.3% of the sample and the majority of respondents (68.2%) were between 30 and 40 years of age. Most of the subjects were white non-Hispanic (64.3%); African-Americans accounted for 24.0% of the sample and white Hispanics accounted for 11.7%.

For several years, the Bureau of Justice Statistics has reported findings from the National Crime Victimization Survey (NCVS).[1] In Table 2, we provide victimization rates of IDUs in this study and national victimization rates among urban residents in 1993 (Bureau of Justice Statistics, 1995, p. 4). We recognize that the comparison is crude for several reasons: (1) questions were worded slightly differently, (2) the NCVS data are based on annual (1993) estimates whereas the IDU data are based on victimizations occurring over a 6-month period in 1994, hence the IDU data are likely to be underestimated, and (3) for some offense categories NCVS estimates are reported per household rather than per person.

Striking differences are observed between the two groups. The rate of victimization among IDUs was substantially higher than the rate for urban residents for each offense category that allowed for comparison. For example, the robbery rate for IDUs was 84.4 (number of IDUs robbed per 1,000 IDUs) and the robbery incident rate was 142.9 (number of robbery incidents per 1,000 IDUs) compared with 10.9 per 1,000 urban residents. Among IDUs, the burglary rate was 113.6 and the burglary incident rate was 441.6 compared with a burglary rate of 84.4 among urban residents. The larceny rate among IDUs was 107.1 and the larceny incident rate was 243.5; in contrast, the larceny rate among urban residents was 4.6. Rates for rape and for motor vehicle theft also were higher among IDUs.

Multivariate results were derived from logistic regression and are presented in Table 3. The equation estimating violent victimization produced four significant coefficients.

First, subjects' involvement in property crime contributed significantly to violent crime victimization.

TABLE 2   Victimization Rates (per 1,000 persons) for Injection Drug Users and General Urban Population

	INJECTION DRUG USERS				
	Numbers of Incidents	*Incident Rate*	*Number of Persons*	*Person Rate*	*NCVS Rate*
Completed robbery	44	142.9	26	84.4	10.9
Completed rape	7	22.7	2	6.5	3.4
Completed attack[a]	21	68.2	12	39.0	—
Aggravated					15.2
Simple					39.6
Threatened attack[a]	96	311.7	36	116.9	—
Completed motor vehicle theft[b]	20	64.9	14	45.5	34.3
Completed theft from motor vehicle[b]	52	168.8	25	81.2	—
Completed burglary[b]	136	441.6	35	113.6	84.4
Completed personal larceny[c]	75	243.5	33	107.1	4.6
Completed cheated or tricked out of drugs or money	77	250.0	23	74.7	—

[a]Simple and aggravated assaults are combined for injection drug user data.

[b]For these offenses National Crime Victimization Survey (NCVS) data reflect rate per household rather than rate per person. Because the IDU data do not reflect rate per household, the rate for injection drug users is likely to be underestimated.

[c]Includes personal larcenies with and without contact.

Note: NCVS = National Crime Victimization Survey.

TABLE 3   Logistic Regression Results of Crime Victimization

	VIOLENT VICTIMIZATION			PROPERTY VICTIMIZATION		
	Odds Ratio	95% Confidence Interval		Odds Ratio	95% Confidence Interval	
Violent crime committed	3.19	1.00;	10.22	1.48	.48;	4.49
Property crime committed	7.22	2.33;	10.23	2.29	.95;	5.52
Engaged in prostitution	.94	.20;	4.48	1.63	.46;	5.78
Sold or distributed drugs	.46	.12;	1.84	1.43	.50;	1.41
Drug and alcohol use:						
Heroin	.19	.05;	.68	.31	.12;	.82
Cocaine	1.43	.46;	4.45	.71	.27;	1.88
Crack-cocaine	3.08	90;	10.52	4.18	1.39;	12.59
Alcohol, two per day	.90	.32;	2.59	1.01	.45;	2.30
Treatment exposure[a]						
1 to 3 months	.79	.26;	2.42	1.47	.66;	3.25
4 to 6 months	1.52	.56;	4.10	1.76	.81;	3.82
Waited in uncomfortable situations to buy drugs	6.11	1.87;	19.93	4.94	1.79;	13.64
Works from street	1.65	.42;	6.49	2.80	.97;	8.06
Age[b]						
30 to 40	.51	.14;	1.80	.72	.33;	1.57
Over 40	.16	.03;	.87	.75	.25;	2.29
Male	.99	.49;	2.23	.50	.27;	.96
Ethnicity[c]						
African-American	1.15	.45;	2.94	1.05	.49;	2.23
White Hispanic	.87	.23;	3.29	1.01	.38;	1.05
Model chi-square	74.51			59.54		

[a]Reference category is no treatment.

[b]Reference category is younger than 30.

[c]Reference category is white non-Hispanic.

Notes: For logistic regression, confidence intervals that contain the value of 1.00 indicate a non-significant regression coefficient at alpha .05.

Persons who had committed property offenses were about seven times more likely than non-offenders to be victimized by violent crime. Violent victimization risk was not affected significantly by violent crime involvement.

Drug use also was related significantly to violent victimization but not in the direction hypothesized; respondents who reported using heroin were less likely to be victimized by violent crime compared to non-users. Use of cocaine powder, crack-cocaine, or alcohol did not contribute significantly to victimization risk.

Respondents who waited in uncomfortable situations to obtain drugs were about six times more likely to be victimized by violent crime than subjects who had not encountered these situations. Finally, persons over the age of 40 years were about six times less likely (1/.16) to be victimized by violent crime than persons younger than 30 years.

Results from the second equation show that crime involvement was not related significantly to property crime victimization. Heroin users, again, were less likely to be victimized; however, crack-cocaine users were approximately four times more likely than non-users to be victimized by property crime. Persons who had waited in uncomfortable situations to obtain drugs were about five times more likely than other persons to be victimized by property crime. Finally, the data show that females were twice as likely as males (1/.50) to be victims of property crime.

DISCUSSION

The primary questions addressed in this study were as follows. (1) To what extent are injection drug users victimized by crime? (2) What factors (activities) contribute to victimization among IDUs? The results of this study suggest that IDUs are a population vulnerable to crime victimization and that some crime involvement, some drug use, and routine activities that characterize drug use lifestyle contribute to the victimization of IDUs. We discuss and offer explanations for these results.

Victimization rates of IDUs are substantially higher than rates found for the general urban population. Routine activity theory predicts that crime will occur when suitable targets are visible and accessible to motivated offenders. The high victimization rate observed with the sample of IDUs suggests that: (1) drug users are exposed to a large pool of motivated offenders, (2) drug users are viewed as attractive targets, and (3) few, if any, capable guardians are present when drug users encounter motivated offenders.

The financial and emotional costs of crime victimization are considerable (National Institute of Justice, 1996). For drug user-victims these costs are likely to magnify to the extent that drug users have less access to victim-assistance programs that are designed to aid recovery. Victimization rates among IDUs never-in-treatment might actually be higher than the rates observed here; this sample of IDUs was drawn in 1987 from a treatment population and several had been exposed to treatment during the 6-month study period. Although treatment status had no effect on victimization we did not measure treatment modality.

We found little evidence that involvement in crime increases risk for violent victimization; the likelihood of victim-precipitated violent crime, e.g., non-stranger homicide (Luckenbill, 1990), and non-sexual assault or battery (Felson and Steadman, 1983) was not supported by these data. Perhaps violent offenders in this sample were viewed as aggressors or were feared by others so that risk for violent victimization is minimal. These data showed that property offenders were at greater risk for violent victimization. Perhaps the violence inflicted on these persons was retaliatory, arising out of some previous theft-related offense by the victim.

We found that crack-cocaine use significantly increased the risk for property crime victimization. Because crack-cocaine users consume the drug often (Pettiway, 1995), it is possible that the drug-seeking behavior associated with crack-cocaine places users in contact with a larger pool of motivated offenders.

For both types of crimes, heroin users reported being victimized less often than non-users. Previous research suggests that heroin users are less often than other users to be involved in homicides (Goldstein et al., 1992) and heroin users also might seek to avoid potentially violent situations, thus, reducing their risk for victimization. Further, heroin users are known to have "running partners" so that perhaps these partners act as guardians against property and violent crime.

We found evidence that drug lifestyle activity increases the risk for violent and property victimization. Specifically, persons who wait in uncomfortable situations to buy drugs significantly increase their risk for victimization. Purchasing drugs often occurs in hidden places, e.g., in homes, alleys, restrooms, or behind buildings where stranger guardians are not likely to be present. Unless the potential victim is accompanied by a second person who acts as a capable guardian, the risk increases for victimization.

We found that two demographic variables contributed to crime victimization, despite controls for criminal activity and other lifestyle variables. Similar to other research findings (Miethe and Meier, 1990), older persons in this sample were significantly less likely than younger persons to be victimized by violent crime. It is possible that older IDUs have developed the street skills necessary to avoid violent victimization.

This study also finds that females were more likely than males to be victimized by property crime. Perhaps females were less likely to be guarded than males and, thus, were more likely to be viewed as attractive targets. The environment in which drugs are purchased may be riskier for women, particularly if the seller is male. It is possible that in this context, women are victimized simply because they are viewed as easy targets who pose less risk to motivated offenders.

Study limitations must be considered before conclusions are drawn from this study. First, no information was available about the sequencing of victimizations and other behaviors. It is possible that victimization preceded, occurred in the same episode with, or followed the occurrence of these lifestyle and drug use events. Skogan (1981), for example, suggested that persons might alter their activities as a result of being victimized.

Second, this study examined a select group of behaviors associated with drug seeking and use activities of IDUs. It was not possible to account for all lifestyle activities. Neither did we examine routine activities that were unrelated to drug use. Third, we did not investigate "risk management," that is, protective behaviors in which persons engage to minimize the risk of victimization exposure or vulnerability in the presence of motivated offenders (Skogan and Maxfield, 1980). Risk management tactics may have included carrying a weapon or displaying street skills that show toughness.

Fourth, we did not attempt to assess the relationship between victimization and neighborhood crime levels (Sampson and Woolredge, 1987). Some research suggests that offenders do not travel long distances to victimize (Brantingham and Brantingham, 1984); however, the victim's activities outside the home neighborhood may relate more to victimization than activities within this neighborhood (Skogan, 1981). Many IDUs purchase and use drugs outside their home neighborhood and the detail necessary to assess time at risk in a variety of neighborhoods was beyond the scope of this project.

ACKNOWLEDGMENTS

This study was supported by grant DA04433 from the National Institute on Drug Abuse and by a faculty research award from the University of Miami.

NOTES

1. The National Crime Victimization Survey was formerly the National Crime Survey.

REFERENCES

Ball, J. C. (1991). The similarity of crime rates among male heroin addicts in New York City, Philadelphia and Baltimore. *Journal of Drug Issues, 21,* 413–427.

Brantingham, P. J., and Brantingham, P. L. (1984). *Patterns in Crime.* New York: Macmillan.

Bureau of Justice Statistics. (1995). *Criminal Victimization 1993.* Washington, DC: United States Department of Justice.

Cohen, L. E., and Felson, M. (1979). Social change in crime rate trends: A routine activity approach. *American Sociological Review, 44,* 588–608.

Cohen, L. E., Kluegel, J. R., and Land, K. C. (1981). Social inequality and predatory criminal victimization: An exposition and test of a formal theory. *American Sociological Review, 46,* 505–524.

Fattah, E. A. (1993). The rational choice/opportunity perspectives as a vehicle for integrating criminological and victimological theories. In R. V. Clarke and M. Felson (Eds.), *Routine activity and rational choice,* (pp. 225–258). Brunswick: Transaction.

Felson, R. B., and Steadman, H. J. (1983). Situational factors in disputes leading to criminal violence. *Criminology, 21,* 59–74.

Goldstein, P. J. (1985). The drugs/violence nexus: A tripartite conceptual framework. *Journal of Drug Issues, 14,* 493–506.

Goldstein, P. J., Bellucci, P. A., Spunt, B. J., and Miller, T. (1991). Volume of cocaine use and violence: A comparison between men and women. *Journal of Drug Issues, 21,* 345–367.

Goldstein, P. J., Brownstein, H. H., and Ryan, P. J. (1992). Drug-related homicide in New York: 1984 and 1988. *Crime and Delinquency, 38,* 459–476.

Gottfredson, M. (1984). *Victims of crime: The dimensions of risk.* London: Her Majesty's Stationery Office, Home Office Research Study number 81.

Hough, M. (1987). Offenders' choice of target: Findings from victim surveys. *Journal of Quantitative Criminology, 3,* 355–369.

Inciardi, J. A. (1979). Heroin use and street crime. *Crime and Delinquency* (July), 335–346.

Inciardi, J. A., Lockwood, D., and Pottieger, A. E. (1993). *Women and crack-cocaine.* New York: Macmillan.

Jensen, G. F., and Brownfield, D. (1986). Gender, lifestyles, and victimization: Beyond routine activity theory. *Violence and Victims, 1,* 85–99.

Kennedy, L. W., and Forde, D. R. (1990). Routine activities and crime: An analysis of victimization in Canada. *Criminology, 28,* 137–152.

Lauritsen, J. L., Sampson, R. J., and Laub, J. H. (1991). The link between offending and victimization among adolescents. *Criminology, 29,* 265–291.

Luckenbill, D. F. (1990). Criminal homicide as a situated transaction. In D. H. Kelly (Ed.), *Criminal Behavior,* 2nd ed. (pp. 280–292). New York: St. Martin's.

Maher, L., and Curtis, R. (1995). In search of the female urban "gangsta": Change, culture, and crack cocaine. In B. R. Price and N. J. Sokoloff (Eds.), *The criminal justice system and women: Offenders, victims, and workers,* 2nd ed. (pp. 147–166). New York: McGraw-Hill.

McElrath, K., Chitwood, D. D., Griffith, D. K., and Comerford, M. (1994). The consistency of self-reported HIV risk behavior among injection drug users. *American Journal of Public Health, 84,* 1965–1970.

Meier, R. F., and Miethe, T. D. (1993). Understanding theories of criminal victimization. In *Crime and justice: A review of research* (vol. 17, pp. 459–499). Chicago: University of Chicago Press.

Miethe, T. D., and Meier, R. F. (1990). Opportunity, choice, and criminal victimization: A test of a theoretical model. *Journal of Research in Crime and Delinquency, 27,* 243–266.

National Institute of Justice. (1996). *Victim costs and consequences: A new look.* Washington, DC: National Institute of Justice.

Pettiway, L. E. (1995). Copping crack: The travel behavior of crack users. *Justice Quarterly, 12,* 497–524.

Sampson, R. J., and Lauritsen, J. L. (1990). Deviant lifestyles, proximity to crime, and the offender-victim link in personal violence. *Journal of Research in Crime and Delinquency, 27,* 110–139.

Sampson, R. J., and Woolredge, J. D. (1987). Linking the micro- and macro-level dimensions of lifestyle-routine activity and opportunity models of predatory victimization. *Journal of Quantitative Criminology, 3,* 371–393.

Schwartz, M. D., and Pitts, V. L. (1995). Exploring a Feminist routine activities approach to explaining sexual assault. *Justice Quarterly, 12,* 9–31.

Singer, S. I. (1981). Homogeneous victim-offender populations: A review and some research implications. *Journal of Criminal Law and Criminology, 72,* 779–787.

Skogan, W. (1981). Assessing the behavioral context of victimization. *Journal of Criminal Law and Criminology, 72,* 727–742.

Skogan, W., and Maxfield, M. (1980). *Coping with crime: Victimization, fear and reactions to crime in three American cities.* Chicago: Northwestern University Research Report.

Speckart, G. R., and Anglin, M. D. (1986). Narcotics and crime: A causal modeling approach. *Journal of Quantitative Criminology, 2,* 3–28.

Tardiff, K., Marzuk, P. M., Leon, A. C., Hirsch, C. S., Stajic, M., Portera, L., and Hartwell, N. (1994). Homicide in New York City: Cocaine use and firearms. *Journal of the American Medical Association, 272,* 43–46.

VICTIMIZATION QUESTIONS

At this time, I would like to ask you about things that might have happened to you in the last 6 months. In the past 6 months, how many times has someone:

1. Taken money or property from you by force or threat of force?
2. Taken your car or truck without your permission?
3. Taken money or property from your car or truck without your permission?
4. Taken money or property from your home or place of business?
5. Taken money or property from your pocket or purse without your permission?
6. Physically hurt you?
7. Threatened you with physical harm?
8. Forced you to have sex with them?
9. Cheated or tricked you out of drugs or money?

24

Trends in Crime and the Introduction of a Needle Exchange Program

MELISSA A. MARX

BYRON CRAPE

RONALD S. BROOKMEYER

BENJAMIN JUNGE

CARL LATKIN

DAVID VLAHOV

STEFFANIE A. STRATHDEE

ABSTRACT

This study sought to determine whether introduction of a needle exchange program would be associated with increased crime rates. Trends in arrests were compared in program and nonprogram areas before and after introduction of a needle exchange program in Baltimore. Trends were modeled and compared via Poisson regression. No significant differences in arrest trends emerged. Over the study period, increases in category-specific arrests in program and nonprogram areas, respectively, were as follows: drug possession, 17.7% and 13.4%; economically motivated offenses, 0.0% and 20.7%; resistance to police authority, 0.0% and 5.3%; and violent offenses, 7.2% and 8.0%. The lack of association of overall and type-specific arrest data with program implementation argues against the role of needle exchange programs in increasing crime rates.

Needle exchange programs have been implemented to help reduce transmission of HIV and other blood-borne pathogens among injection drug users[1-4] and to increase the frequency of drug abuse treatment referrals[5] among addicted individuals. Studies have shown that needle exchange programs do not increase rates of drug use[6] or increase numbers of discarded needles or syringes[7]; because drug use has been associated with crime,[8,9] however, there are concerns that crime rates may increase in areas surrounding needle exchange programs after their introduction.[10,11] We examined trends in arrests in Baltimore City before and after the opening of a needle exchange program.

Marx, Melissa A., Byron Crape, Ronald S. Brookmeyer, Benjamin Junge, Carl Latkin, David Vlahov, and Steffanie A. Strathdee. 2000. Trends in Crime and the Introduction of a Needle Exchange Program. *American Journal of Public Health.* 90 (12): 1933–1935. © 2000 by APHA.

METHODS

Study Population

In 1997, Baltimore City had 657,250 residents; the average age of these residents was 35 years, and 60% were African American.[12] Approximately 50,000 Baltimore residents regularly used illicit drugs at that time, a substantial proportion of whom injected.[13]

In August 1994, the Baltimore City Health Department opened a needle exchange program housed at 2 locations. Program participants were exempt from syringe possession laws within city limits. During the first 14 months of operation, 3,438 active injectors enrolled in the program, of whom 86% were African American; participants' average age was 42 years.

Data Collection

Arrest records for the period February 1994 through October 1995 were obtained from the Baltimore City Police Department. This enabled comparison of data 6 months before and 6 months after introduction of the needle exchange program. The immediate impact of the program was assessed, and seasonal variations in arrests were examined in a subsequent 8-month period. Dates and locations of arrests and up to 5 criminal charges were abstracted.

On the basis of input from law enforcement, crime, and drug abuse experts, as well as hypothesized associations of charges with needle exchange programs, arrest charges were categorized as follows: (1) drug possession, (2) economically motivated offenses, (3) resistance to police authority, or (4) violent offenses. Drug possession offenses included possession of drug paraphernalia and distribution/possession of heroin or cocaine. Economically motivated offenses consisted of property theft (e.g., nonvehicular breaking and entering, burglaries, vehicle break-in/theft) and prostitution, considered means of financing drug use. Resistance to police authority was defined as assaulting a police officer, resisting arrest, or violating parole/probation; these offenses were seen as indicators of increased frustration possibly resulting from law enforcement practices. Violent offenses included homicide, assault, rape, and armed robbery, which were considered potentially linked to drug trafficking.

We defined the area of maximum program impact with data from an ongoing evaluation of the program. We determined that 76% of participants reported walking to the program site and that travel time for these individuals averaged 15 minutes or less (median: 10 minutes).[14] At an estimated speed of 2.0 mi per hour (3.2 km per hour), 84% of participants were estimated to live within a 0.5-mi radius of the program site. Therefore, areas within a 0.5-mi radius of the 2 program sites were combined and designated as "program areas," while areas within the city limits but outside of these radii were deemed "nonprogram areas."

Data Analysis

To examine the impact of the introduction of the needle exchange program on arrest trends in Baltimore City, we assessed the number of category-specific arrests before and after program introduction. Mean numbers of monthly category-specific and overall arrests for program and nonprogram areas were calculated (1) over the 6-month period before program introduction and (2) over the 14-month period after program introduction. Percentage changes in mean numbers of arrests were then calculated.

To formally assess trends in monthly arrests by proximity to the program site, we used Poisson regression models that considered overall and category-specific arrests. A regression line was fitted to log $E(Y_t)$, the log of the expected number of monthly arrests at month t, which allowed for different slopes and intercepts in program and nonprogram areas before initiation of the needle exchange program. At initiation, intercepts and slopes were allowed to change in both areas. The hypotheses tested were that changes in intercepts and slopes would not significantly differ in program and nonprogram areas before and after initiation of the needle exchange program and that changes in arrest trends in program areas would be similar to changes in nonprogram areas. We tested hypotheses using a likelihood ratio test with 2 degrees of freedom, accounting for overdispersion.[15]

RESULTS

Overall, there were 53,848 drug-related arrests in Baltimore City during the study period. Before introduction of the needle exchange program, there were 2,500 drug-related arrests per month. After introduction of the program, there was a slight increase in the number of drug-related arrests to 2,775 per month.

Wide fluctuations seen in monthly averages of drug possession arrests citywide were evidenced by high extradispersion values (cocaine: 5.3; heroin: 9.8) in the Poisson model. Overall, the mean number of monthly arrests for drug possession rose slightly in program areas, from 150 (range: 100–190) to 175 (range: 110–270). Average numbers increased gradually in nonprogram areas, from 1,020 (range: 825–1,240) to 1,160 (range: 925–1,370) per month.

Frequency of arrests for economically motivated offenses remained constant in needle exchange program areas, averaging 30 per month before and after introduction of the program (ranges: 25–40 and 15–40, respectively). Arrests for economically motivated offenses increased in nonprogram areas from 240 (range: 180–260) to 300 (range: 230–70) per month over the same period.

Similarly, numbers of individuals resisting arrest remained consistently low in program areas, averaging 30 per month before and after program introduction (ranges: 25–40 and 25–45, respectively). However, in nonprogram areas, the average number of individuals resisting arrest increased slightly from 300 per month (range: 270–350) to 325 per month (range: 285–370) during the same period.

Average numbers of arrests for violent offenses dropped in program areas from 90 (range: 70–100) to 80 (range: 70–100) per month after introduction of the program. Increases in arrests for violence were seen over the same period in nonprogram areas; the number of such arrests increased from 820 (range: 670–920) to 890 (range: 710–1,100) per month.

Table 1 summarizes percentage changes in overall arrests and category-specific arrests in program and nonprogram areas in the period after introduction of the needle exchange program relative to the preprogram period. The unadjusted percentage change in overall arrests was higher in program (11.4%) than in nonprogram (7.6%) areas. However, there were no significant differences in arrest trends by category after program introduction relative to before program introduction in program vs nonprogram areas ($p > .05$).

DISCUSSION

We found that increases in drug-related arrests were not more pronounced in needle exchange program areas than in other areas of Baltimore after establishment of the program. Although there were some differences in category-specific arrest trends in areas

TABLE 1 Changes in Numbers of Arrests Before and After Introduction of the Needle Exchange Program (NEP): NEP and Non-NEP Areas, Baltimore, MD, 1994–1995

	NEP			NON-NEP			
	Mean No. of Arrests, Time 1	Mean No. of Arrests, Time 2	Change, %	Mean No. of Arrests, Time 1	Mean No. of Arrests, Time 2	Change, %	NEP vs Non-NEP,[a] P
Overall	278.3	299.4	11.4	2,221.8	2,475.4	7.6	.40
Drug possession	147.2	173.3	17.7	1,018.8	1,155.6	13.4	.32
Cocaine	101.5	117.8	16.0	743.3	818.0	10.0	.34
Heroin	59.8	80.2	34.1	342.3	433.5	26.6	.30
Paraphernalia	17.5	17.4	−0.4	150.2	135.2	−10.0	.39
Economically motivated	32.5	32.4	0.0	240.8	290.6	20.7	.29
Break-ins and burglaries	27.0	24.1	−10.6	209.7	225.4	7.5	.25
Theft from vehicles	1.8	3.0	63.6	10.8	21.6	99.8	.26
Prostitution	3.8	5.5	43.5	20.7	46.1	122.9	.43
Resistance	32.8	33.2	0.0	305.2	321.4	5.3	.38
Assaulting officer	11.3	9.6	−15.5	81.8	86.1	5.3	.30
Resisting arrest	16.3	17.6	7.0	128.7	147.5	14.6	.37
Probation/parole violation	10.7	11.6	8.5	138.8	134.8	−2.9	.36
Violence	89.0	82.6	7.2	817.2	882.3	8.0	.34
Rape	3.8	4.6	21.1	38.8	45.6	17.5	.40
Murder	5.0	6.0	20.0	48.2	66.3	37.6	.38
Assault	79.0	70.6	−10.7	724.3	767.4	5.9	.35
Robbery	16.7	19.1	15.8	150.5	174.3	14.4	.41

Note: Time 1 = 6-month period before NEP implementation; Time 2 = 14-month period after NEP implementation. Arrest categories and types are not mutually exclusive and thus will not sum to overall drug-related arrests.

[a]Based on likelihood ratio test derived from Poisson regression model.

of close proximity to the program relative to outlying areas, these differences were not statistically significant.

If the needle exchange program had directly influenced rates of drug use, a disproportionate increase in drug possession arrests would have been expected in program areas relative to nonprogram areas. Although increases in heroin and cocaine arrests after the program had been established were slightly more pronounced in program than in nonprogram areas, trends were not significantly different. Variability in heroin and cocaine arrests reflected in the high model extradispersion values might be explained in part by "police sweeps," which are common and variable in Baltimore, especially in drug trafficking areas. Anecdotal reports indicate that police sweeps were occurring early after program introduction, and we hypothesize that these sweeps may have contributed to the increased number of drug possession arrests observed in program areas at that time.

If the program had indirectly resulted in increased drug use rates, we would expect to see drug users committing, and being arrested for, a relatively higher number of economically motivated crimes in program areas than in nonprogram areas. Our data did not support this hypothesis. In fact, a decrease was observed in numbers of arrests for break-ins and burglaries in program areas after the opening of the needle exchange program, whereas a slight increase was observed in nonprogram areas.

If the needle exchange program had increased drug users' perceptions of lawlessness in areas of close proximity to the program, an increase in instances of resisting arrest might have occurred. However, numbers of arrests for assault on a police officer decreased in program areas while increasing slightly in nonprogram areas. The opposite was true for numbers of arrests for parole or probation violation, which increased slightly in program areas and decreased in nonprogram areas. None of these differences were statistically significant.

If introduction of the needle exchange program had resulted in a perception of anarchy, increased violence might be expected. However, violent assault arrests decreased in program areas while increasing slightly in nonprogram areas. Violence trends in program vs. nonprogram areas were, again, not statistically different.

In conducting this analysis, we assumed that coding of arrests was uniform across different areas of the city at different times. However, even if this assumption were invalid, there is no reason to believe that differences in coding would vary by region. In addition, we estimated crime trends using arrest data. While this approach may be subject to bias[16] and may limit the conclusions that can be drawn, police department arrest data are considered superior to self-reported crime and self-reported arrest data in that both of the latter measures may be subject to response bias.[17,18]

Arrest data may also be superior to crime data because drug-related crime is often "victimless" and therefore underreported. The validity of using arrests as a surrogate for crime could be ascertained by calculating the degree of correlation between arrests (as reported by police) and drug-related crime. However, this method would also be subject to bias because it relies on counts of drug-related crime.

Trends in crime, as measured by arrests, are also likely to be affected by secular factors (e.g., demographics, community policing practices). These factors were not taken into account here, which is also a limitation. In addition, some officers may have altered their policing practices in program areas; however, no record of official changes in policing practices specific to program areas was found.

Our data are consistent with those gathered in a study conducted in Boston, Mass., in which no differences in arrests were observed in needle exchange program areas and nonprogram areas.[19] Our data also corroborate reports from a study of New Haven, Conn., crime trends[20] and results from a multisite study of Manhattan, New Haven, San Francisco, Boston, and Portland, Oregon, crime trends.[21] The lack of increases in arrests after the establishment of the needle exchange program in Baltimore is consistent as well with survey data showing that frequency of injection did not increase among program participants during the same time period.[14,22]

In conclusion, based on results of analyses of Baltimore City arrests, needle exchange programs do not appear to be associated with increases in crime rates. This suggests that such concerns should not be a basis for formulating policy regarding these programs.

CONTRIBUTORS

M. A. Marx and B. Crape participated equally in the writing of the article. M. A. Marx assisted with study design, directed study progress and planning, served as a liaison with the city health department, and wrote the manuscript and revisions. B. Crape assisted in study planning and design, served as a liaison with the city police department, compiled and analyzed the data, and contributed to the writing of the manuscript.

R. S. Brookmeyer directed and supervised data analysis and contributed to the writing of the methods section of the manuscript. B. Junge conceived and planned the study and performed the preliminary data analyses. C. Latkin directed study progress and reviewed the final manuscript. D. Vlahov oversaw study progress and contributed to major sections of the manuscript. S. A. Strathdee assisted in interpretation of the statistical analysis and contributed to the writing, editing, and revision of the final manuscript.

ACKNOWLEDGMENTS

We gratefully acknowledge financial support from the National Institute on Drug Abuse through grant 09237.

We appreciate the assistance provided by Keith Harries of the Department of Geography, University of Maryland Baltimore County; Peter Beilenson, commissioner of health for Baltimore City; Michele Brown, Lamont Coger, and the Baltimore City Health Department needle exchange program staff; and Elise Riley, Steve Huettner, Mabboobeh Safaeian, John Vertefeuille, Heena Brahmbhatt, Jennifer Mulle, and Hanne Harbison of the Johns Hopkins School of Public Health Needle Exchange Program Evaluation.

REFERENCES

1. Vlahov, D., and Junge, B. (1998). The role of needle exchange programs in HIV prevention. *Public Health Rep.*, *113* (suppl 1), 75–80.
2. Des Jarlais, D. C., Marmor, M., Paone, D., et al. (1996). HIV incidence among injecting drug users in New York City syringe-exchange programmes. *Lancet, 348*, 987–991.
3. Hagan, H., Des Jarlais, D. C., Friedman, S. R., Purchase, D., and Alter, M. J. (1995). Reduced risk of hepatitis B and hepatitis C among injection drug users in the Tacoma syringe exchange program. *Am J Public Health.* 85: 1531–1537.
4. Strathdee, S. A., van Ameijden, E. J., Mesquita, F., Wodak, A., Rana S., and Vlahov, D. (1998). Can HIV epidemics among injection drug users be prevented? *AIDS.* 12 (suppl A):S71–S79.
5. Heimer, R. Can syringe exchange serve as a conduit to substance abuse treatment? (1998). *J Subst Abuse Treat.* 15: 183–191.
6. Normand, J., Vlahov, D., and Moses, L. E. (1995). *Preventing HIV Transmission: The Role of Sterile Needles and Bleach.* Washington, DC: National Academy Press.
7. Doherty, M. C., Garfein, R. S., Vlahov, D., et al. (1997). Discarded needles do not increase soon after the opening of a needle exchange program. *Am J Epidemiol.* 145: 730–737.
8. *Drug Use Forecasting 1993 Annual Report on Adult Arrestees: Drugs and Crime in America's Cities.* (1993). Washington, DC: US Dept of Justice.
9. Leukefeld C. G., Gallego, M. A., and Farabee, D. (1997). Drugs, crime, and HIV. *Subst Use Misuse.* 32:749–756.
10. Maginnis, R. L. (1998, June). Needle exchanges are bad medicine. Paper presented at: Annual Meeting of the Congressional Youth Leadership Council; Washington, DC.
11. Fay, C. (1999, April 26). Needle 'exchanges' often aren't. *Washington Post.* A18.
12. 1990 census: 1997 update. Available at: http://www.census.gov. Accessed February 20, 1999.
13. *National Admissions to Substance Abuse Treatment Services, the Treatment Episode Data Set (TEDS).* (1996). Washington, DC: US Dept of Health and Human Services.
14. Vlahov, D., Junge, B., Brookmeyer, R., et al. (1997). Reductions in high-risk drug use behaviors among participants in the Baltimore needle exchange program. *J Acquir Immune Defic Syndr Hum Retrovirol.* 16:400–406.
15. Aitkin, M., Anderson, D., Francis, B., and Hinde, J. (1989). *Statistical Modeling in GLM.* Oxford, England: Oxford Science Publications.
16. Inciardi, J. (1989). Heroin use and street crime. *Crime Delinquency.* 25:335–346.
17. Adams, A. S., Soumerai, S. B., Lomas, J., and Ross-Degnan, D. (1999). Evidence of self-report bias in assessing adherence to guidelines. *Int J Qual Health Care.* 11:187–192.
18. Embree, B. G., and Whitehead, P. C. (1993). Validity and reliability of self-reported drinking behavior: dealing with the problem of response bias. *J Stud Alcohol.* 54: 334–344.
19. Case, P. (1995). *First Year of the Pilot Needle Exchange Program in Massachusetts.* Boston, Mass: Massachusetts Dept of Public Health.
20. O'Keefe, E. K., and Khoshnood, K. (1991). *Preliminary Report on the New Haven Needle Exchange Program.* New Haven, Conn: City of New Haven.
21. Lurie, P. R., and Bowser, B. (1993). *The Public Health Impact of Needle Exchange Programs in the United States and Abroad.* San Francisco, Calif: University of California, San Francisco.
22. Brooner, R., Kidorf, M., King, V., Beilenson, P., Svikis, D., and Vlahov, D. (1998). Drug abuse treatment success among needle exchange participants. *Public Health Rep.* 113(suppl 1):129–139.

25

Drug Use in the High Intensity Drug Trafficking Area of the U.S. Southwest Border

LANA D. HARRISON

NANCY J. KENNEDY

ABSTRACT

This paper examines the prevalence of alcohol, tobacco and illicit drug use in the Southwest border region of the United States. Based on the seriousness of drug trafficking in the area, the Southwest border has been designated a "High Intensity Drug trafficking Area." Yet there is little quantitative data on the nature and magnitude of drug use in the Southwest border region. This paper examines the prevalence of drug use in the area by extracting data from the National Household Survey on Drug Abuse. The data show that drug use rates in the Southwest border area are very similar to those found throughout the remainder of the United States. Hispanics, who constitute about 41% of the Southwest border population, have lower prevalence rates for most classes of drugs than non-Hispanics. The border Hispanics exhibit even lower prevalence rates than Hispanics in the remainder of the United States. However, many of these differences are attributable to the lower levels of drug use among women, and youth and older adults. As these demographic subgroups become increasingly acculturated, their drug use could come to more closely resemble that of their peers in the remainder of the United states.

INTRODUCTION

Created by the League of Nations in 1928 to extend international control over drugs with addictive poten-tial and continued thereafter by the United Nations, the International Narcotics Control Board has always been concerned with illicit trafficking, especially in the border areas between countries (United Nations, 1973). A number of countries that previously had no drug problems or had been involved in the drug trade only as suppliers have struggled with problems of illegal drug use among their own citizens. As the breadth and extent of trafficking networks worldwide appear to be increasing, it is imperative to examine the impact of illicit drug trafficking in placing border populations at risk for increased drug use.

This paper examines the nature and extent of drug use in the Southwest border area of the United States, an imaginary zone of approximately 2,000 miles separating the United States and Mexico. Although there is no official definition of the United States–Mexico Border area the one used herein, promulgated by demographers from the U.S. Bureau of the Census, are those 25 counties (from the states of California, Arizona, New Mexico and Texas) contiguous to the international line with Mexico[1] (Fernandez, 1991).

Scant quantitative research has been conducted focusing specifically on drug use in the Southwest border area (cf. M. Greene, 1974; Montoya, 1985; Adams, 1986; PAHO, 1989; Harrison, 1991; Harrison and Kennedy, 1994). Most research on drug use in this area has been conducted by ethnographers who provide qualitative information about the social organizations

---

[1]These 25 counties include two in California (San Diego and Imperial), four in Arizona (Yuma, Pima, Santa Cruz and Cochise), three in New Mexico (Hidalgo, Luna, Dona Ana) and 16 in Texas (El Paso, Hudspeth, Culberson, Jeff Davis, Presidio, Brewster, Terrell, Van Verde, Kinney, Maverick, Dimmit, Webb, Zapata, Starr, Hidalgo, and Cameron).

Harrison, Lana D. and Nancy J. Kennedy. 1996. Drug Use in the High Intensity Drug Trafficking Area of the US Southwest Border. *Addiction.* 91(1): 47–61. © 1996 by Taylor & Francis, Ltd. (http://www.tandf.co.uk/journals).

and behavioral patterns of drug users and the drug scene in a specified geographic location along the border (cf. Ramos, 1989; Gutierrez-Ramos and Flores-Farfán, 1992). However, due to a fortunate design aspect of the National Household Survey on Drug Abuse (HH Survey), we are able to characterize drug use along the full length of the international border with Mexico; more specifically, in the urbanized counties bordering the international line with Mexico.

Concern has been expressed about higher drug usage rates in the Southwest border region for many years, although this concern has largely been based on anecdotal information about drug availability. Mexico is known as a "supplier" nation, and trafficking routes to the U.S. abound. It is estimated that Mexico supplies approximately 60% of the foreign-grown marijuana and over 20% of the heroin reaching U.S. markets (NNICC, 1993; Bureau of International Narcotics Matters, 1994). One form of Mexican heroin, known as "black tar," is generally of higher purity but lower priced than that from other source countries (OTA, 1987). In addition to the "supplier" label, at least half the cocaine entering the U.S. is believed to be transshipped through Mexico (Bureau of International Narcotic Matters, 1994). There have been record seizures of marijuana and cocaine in recent years (NNICC, 1993). The 1993 Annual Statistical Report from the Drug Enforcement Administration (DEA) indicated that 115,270.5 kilograms of marijuana were seized in the Southwest border, 10 times the amount seized in the Southeast Offices which primarily include Florida cities.

The U.S. Congress established, as part of the Anti-Drug Abuse Act of 1988, the High Intensity Drug Trafficking Area (HIDTA) Program to be implemented by the Office of National Drug Control Policy. Because of the seriousness of the drug trafficking problems and the subsequent effects when these drugs arrive at their final destinations, the Office of National Drug Control Policy designated five areas of the United States as HIDTAs. Four are cities—New York, Miami, Houston, and Los Angeles—and the other is the Southwest border area. The HIDTA guidelines require funds to be used primarily to enhance law enforcement efforts against drug trafficking organizations. Operation Alliance administers the HIDTA Program in the Southwest border area and is a multi-agency initiative established to support and coordinate law enforcement operations for Federal, State and local agencies in the states of Texas, New Mexico, Arizona and California.

Drug smuggling is considered a serious threat all along the Southwest border. The proliferation of drugs passing through the area presumably translates into increased availability which then, in turn, translates into increased use. In addition, an abundance of other precursors and risk factors associated with drug abuse are present in this area. Perhaps most important is the youthfulness of the population. Young people, especially those in their late teens and early twenties, are at increased risk for drug use (Kandel and Logan, 1984; Anthony and Helzer, 1991). The median age of Mexican origin individuals in the United States in 1990 was 24.1 years compared to 33.5 years for non-Hispanics (Chapa and Valencia, 1993).

The border population is also considered both a minority population and a hidden population. Both types of populations are thought to be at higher risk for drug use and abuse due to their lack of educational achievement and lower socioeconomic status (cf. Hawkins, Lishner and Catalano, 1985; Simcha-Fagen, Gersten and Langer, 1986; Brounstein et al., 1989; Flewelling et al., 1993). Males and females of Mexican origin have lower average earnings and the highest unemployment rates in the U.S., with 28.4% of this ethnic subgroup living below the poverty line (U.S. Bureau of the Census, 1990). Among Mexican origin adults aged 25 years and older, 55.9% have not completed high school (Chapa and Valencia, 1993). More than seven of every ten Hispanic high school dropouts are of Mexican origin and of all 16–24-year-old dropouts of Mexican origin, 73% were born in Mexico (GAO, 1994). Due to their relatively low educational levels and the language barrier, Mexican origin Hispanics tend to have low-wage jobs and little chance of advancement.

In conclusion, there is an abundance of known risk factors for higher drug use rates evident in the Southwest border region of the United States. Due to Mexico's status as a supplier nation, and the transshipment routes for drugs into the United States along the border, the border area was designated a HIDTA. This means that extra funds are expended in the area to enhance law enforcement efforts against drug trafficking organizations. Anecdotal information suggests that drug use is higher in the area. It is assumed that the intensity of drug trafficking translates into increased drug availability, which translates into increased drug use. However, these assumptions have not been empirically examined. This paper attempts to address these issues by providing some assessment of drug use among the population residing in the Southwest border of the U.S.

METHODS

It is possible to examine the prevalence of drug use in the Southwest border using the National Household Survey on Drug Abuse (HH Survey)—the primary source of data on illicit drug use in the United States. The HH Survey oversamples Hispanics in the geographical areas where they are most concentrated in order to increase the precision of estimates for this ethnic subgroup. Due to the concentration of Hispanics in the Southwest border area, the HH Survey can provide estimates of drug use for this area, with some limitations. The HH Survey contains a near census of the Metropolitan Statistical Areas (MSAs) along the international border with Mexico. (An MSA is a term created by the U.S. Census Bureau to describe a geographic area consisting of a larger population nucleus together with adjacent communities having a high degree of economic and social integration.) Ninety percent of the Southwest border population resides in MSAs adjoining the border, permitting estimation of drug use among the majority of border county residents.

The HH Survey is designed to measure the prevalence of drug use experience and related behaviors within the U.S. population aged 12 years and older. Conducted among a random sample of the population at 1–3-year intervals since 1974, the survey yields prevalence estimates on the following substances: alcohol, cigarettes, marijuana/hashish, cocaine, inhalants, hallucinogens, heroin, the non-medical use of psychotherapeutics (stimulants, sedatives, tranquilizers and analgesics) and anabolic steroids. The HH Survey traditionally reports drug use prevalence in three time periods—any use in the life-time, in the past year, and in the past month.

Respondents are interviewed in their homes by trained interviewers using standardized methods. There are both English and Spanish versions of the questionnaire, and bilingual interviewers trained to administer either. Several mechanisms designed to increase the validity of responses are built into the study. Respondents are given assurances of anonymity and confidentiality, and self-administered answer sheets are used for the questions on drugs. Although methodological studies suggest that the data quality is quite good, we can not be sure how much underreporting might occur (cf. Harrison, 1995). Further, self-reported drug use may vary as a function of Hispanic ethnicity or the legal immigration status of the respondent. Nevertheless, the HH Survey is the best source of drug prevalence data available in the United States, and uses a number of state-of-the-art survey procedures, data quality checks and adjustments. For example, the data are adjusted using a weighting class adjustment to account for interview non-response in deriving national estimates of drug use. Additional information on the survey methodology can be found in the technical appendices of the *Main Findings* report produced from this data set (Substance Abuse and Mental Health Services Administration [SAMHSA], 1993).

The sample for the 1991 HH Survey included eight counties in the United States adjacent to the international border with Mexico. Six of these counties are MSAs, representing six of the eight MSAs along the border. The two other counties in the HH Survey sample are rural counties. As previously mentioned, the six MSAs border counties in the HH survey contain 90% of the population living along the border. In addition, they contain 95% of the population living in MSAs along the border. Therefore, the HH Survey covers most of the population living in MSAs adjoining the border with Mexico. The two rural border counties included in the HH Survey contain about 1% of the population. Therefore, the HH Survey cannot as accurately characterize the non-urban border population.

According to the 1990 Census, 41% of the residents in border counties are of Hispanic origin. The HH Survey provided reasonable representation of Hispanics, reporting that 37.5% of its (weighted) 1991 sample in border counties was of Hispanic ethnicity with 97% of Mexican origin. In the six border MSA counties, the HH Survey sample is 38% Hispanic, which compares very favorably with the Census count of 37%. However, the 1990 U.S. Census reveals that only about 80% of the Hispanic population living in border counties reside in the six MSAs included in the HH Survey. In order to broaden the representation of Hispanics in the analyses contained herein, the Hispanic population in the two rural counties contained in the HH Survey are included.

The inclusion of these rural counties is also useful for other reasons. Since the HH Survey is designed to measure drug use in the entire U.S. population, the sample sizes in any one county are not necessarily large. The 1991 survey included 32,594 respondents, of whom 759 lived in the border MSAs. This is a relatively small sample size, especially when investigating a comparatively rare behavior such as illicit drug use. Further subdividing this sample size by gender, age group or other characteristics of interest becomes problematic based on the small sample sizes. The sample size for the Hispanic population in the six urban and two rural counties was 850. Although the rural counties contain but a small portion of the Southwest border Hispanic population, and were not selected to be representative of the rural counties in the region, they nonetheless contain several hundred respondents of Hispanic ethnicity. The data are weighted to account for selection probability so the rural county residents are not given excessive weight. Therefore, for the purposes of the analyses herein examining drug use among Hispanics in the Southwest border, the survey population includes those from the six urban and two rural counties. Separate analyses are presented for the MSA border population.

RESULTS

The prevalence rates for lifetime, past year and past month use of alcohol, tobacco, any illicit drug, any psychotherapeutic drug, marijuana/hashish, cocaine and inhalants in the Southwest border MSAs are shown in Table 1. Weekly alcohol and daily cigarette

TABLE 1   Licit and Illicit Drug Use in Border MSAs and Non-Border MSAs

	BORDER MSAs (%)	NON-BORDER MSAs (%)
Alcohol		
Lifetime	84.0	85.9
Past year	71.2	70.6
Past month	51.1	54.1
Past week	20.0	22.8
Cigarettes		
Lifetime	64.7	72.6
Past year	26.9	31.1
Past month	19.7	26.3*
Daily	19.3	25.5
Any illicit drug[1]		
Lifetime	38.8	38.3
Past year	13.6	13.2
Past month	7.9	6.6
Marijuana/hashish		
Lifetime	33.5	34.7
Past year	10.7	9.9
Past month	5.4	5.1
Psychotherapeutics[2]		
Lifetime	15.3	12.5
Past year	4.7	4.4
Past month	1.0	1.6
Cocaine		
Lifetime	13.0	12.4
Past year	3.3	3.2
Past month	1.6	1.0*
Inhalants		
Lifetime	9.5	5.5*
Past year	3.7	1.2
Past month	2.5	0.6
	(*n* = 759)	(*n* = 27,903)

[1]Non-medical use of marijuana or hashish, cocaine (including crack), inhalants, hallucinogens (including PCP), heroin or psychotherapeutics at least once.

[2]Non-medical use of any prescription-type stimulant, sedative, tranquilizer or analgesic; does not include over-the-counter drugs.

*Difference statistically significant at $p < 0.05$ level.

Source: 1991 *National Household Survey on Drug Abuse.*

use are also shown. Other classes of drugs are not shown due to their low overall prevalence and the relatively small numbers in the sample upon which these rates are based. The HH Survey analyses generally suppress estimates that have a relatively large standard error or a relatively small sample size.

As Table 1 shows, 38.8% of residents in MSAs along the border have used some illicit drug in their life-time, 13.6% have used in the past year and 7.9% in the past month. The most commonly used illicit drug was marijuana/hashish (hereafter referred to as marijuana since the majority of cannabis use in the United States is marijuana rather than hashish), with 33.5% reporting life-time use, 10.7% reporting past year use, and 5.4% reporting use in the past month. The non-medical use of psychotherapeutics (which includes analgesics, tranquilizers, stimulants and sedatives) was reported by 15.3% in their life-time, 4.7% in the past year and 1.0% in the past month. Cocaine was used by 13.0% in the life-time, 3.3% in the past year and 1.6% in the past month. The highest prevalence rates were for alcohol, with 20.0% reporting use in the past week. Tobacco was also frequently reported. An estimated 19.3% of residents in border MSAs reported daily cigarette use.

In order to place drug use in the Southwest border in perspective, Table 1 compares the prevalence rates of selected drugs in the border MSAs with those for the remaining MSAs in the United States. The overall picture is one of great similarity, with a few minor exceptions. Cigarette use is lower in the border MSAs, but only past month cigarette use is significantly lower. Inhalant use is higher in the border MSAs, but only the life-time measure is significantly higher. The past month prevalence of cocaine use is also significantly higher in the border MSAs, although it is 1.6% compared to 1.0% for the non-border MSAs.

As previously mentioned, due to the oversampling of Hispanics in the HH Survey sample it is possible to estimate the prevalence of various drugs among Hispanics living in the Southwest border. Before reporting the results, it should be noted that Hispanics generally report significantly lower prevalence rates for most classes of drugs than non-Hispanics in the United States. They report lower usage rates of alcohol (lifetime, past year and past month), cigarettes (lifetime, past month, daily), psychotherapeutics (lifetime and past year), less lifetime experience with illicit drugs overall, and less lifetime marijuana use. Conversely, they report higher rates of past year and past month cocaine use. Comparing Hispanics living in the Southwest border to non-Hispanics in the remainder of the United States (data not shown), these same patterns are replicated.

Perhaps more importantly, Southwest border Hispanics show lower prevalence rates for several classes of drugs than their Hispanic peers in the remainder of the United States. Table 2 shows that significantly fewer Hispanics residing in the Southwest border report marijuana use. Although only the lifetime prevalence rates are significantly different, border Hispanics report lower prevalence for several other drugs including alcohol and inhalants. In addition, border Hispanics report less overall lifetime "any illicit drug" use. While lifetime cocaine use is lower among border Hispanics, the past year and past month cocaine prevalence measures are higher than those for the remaining United States Hispanic population.

Drug Use Prevalence by Gender and Age in the Mexico Border Region

The sample size for the 1991 HH Survey is sufficiently large to permit estimation of drug use rates among some specified demographic subgroups. The analysis here is restricted to gender and age, two demographic characteristics which have been shown to be highly correlated with licit and illicit drug use. Age is categorized into four distinct age groups, youth (aged 12–17 years of age), young adults (18–25), middle adults (26–34), and older adults (35 and older). Generally, the highest rates of both licit and illicit drug use are found among young adults and middle adults. Due to the small sample size in the Southwest border, some low precision estimates are suppressed since they do not meet the requirements for publication. Generally, estimates with a relatively large standard error are suppressed due to our lack of confidence in the estimates. Table 3 shows the results by age group, and Table 4 shows the results by gender.

Recall there were few differences in drug use patterns between the border MSAs and the remaining MSAs in the United States, except for slightly less cigarette use and slightly greater inhalant and cocaine use in the border MSAs. The lower rates in cigarette prevalence are accounted for by the lower prevalence of use among males. The smoking patterns among females in the border MSAs and females in the remaining MSAs are very similar. The lower rates of smoking in the border MSAs are also reflected primarily among those aged 35 years and older. Smoking rates are very similar in the MSAs among the younger age groups, although youth (aged 12–17 years) report lower rates of ever trying

TABLE 2 Licit and Illicit Drug Use Among Hispanics in the Border Area and Remaining US Hispanic Population: 1991

	HISPANICS IN BORDER	HISPANICS IN REMAINDER OF US
Alcohol		
Lifetime	69.1	78.4**
Past year	60.0	65.5
Past month	43.4	47.9
Past week	17.3	20.5
Cigarettes		
Lifetime	56.9	61.1
Past year	30.5	30.3
Past month	23.1	24.9
Daily	22.0	23.9
Any illicit drug[1]		
Lifetime	23.3	31.8*
Past year	10.1	12.1
Past month	5.9	6.4
Marijuana/hashish		
Lifetime	18.4	28.3**
Past year	6.1	9.0**
Past month	2.2	4.6***
Psychotherapeutics[2]		
Lifetime	6.4	9.4
Past year	2.7	3.4
Past month	1.3	1.4
Cocaine		
Lifetime	8.5	11.5*
Past year	5.8	3.5**
Past month	3.3	1.4***
Inhalants		
Lifetime	2.7	5.0*
Past year	0.9	1.2
Past month	0.6	0.8
	(n = 850)	(n = 7,066)

[1]Non-medical use of marijuana or hashish, cocaine (including crack), inhalants, hallucinogens (including PCP), heroin or psychotherapeutics at least once.

[2]Non-medical use of any prescription-type stimulant, sedative, tranquilizer or analgesic; does not include over-the-counter drugs.

*Difference statistically significant at $p < 0.05$ level.

**Difference statistically significant at $p < 0.01$ level.

***Difference statistically significant at $p < 0.001$ level.

Source: 1991 *National Household Survey on Drug Abuse.*

cigarettes. The tendency for slightly greater inhalant use among residents of border MSAs is reflected among youth. However, since the estimates are low precision for the other age groups in the border MSAs, there is uncertainty about how their inhalant use compares. Males also show relatively higher usage rates, but the differences are not statistically significant. The slightly higher past month cocaine use is primarily found among youth.

Marijuana prevalence does not differ between the populations of the border and non-border MSAs. However, the overall picture disguises an age pattern which finds youth a little less likely and young adults a little more likely to use marijuana. Young adults aged

TABLE 3 Licit and Illicit Drug Use in Border and Non-Border MSAs by Age Group: 1991

	BORDER MSAs				NON-BORDER MSAs			
	12–17	*18–25*	*26–34*	*>35*	*12–17*	*18–25*	*26–34*	*>35*
Alcohol								
Lifetime	—	90.3	96.1	85.5	46.4	90.4	92.6*	89.1
Past year	—	—	90.7	—	40.7	83.7	82.7*	68.2
Past month	15.3	76.0	71.2	43.5	21.1	65.3	64.6*	53.2
Past week	5.9	—	23.1	—	5.3	25.2	26.3	23.9
Cigarettes								
Lifetime	23.3	77.2	81.0	—	36.0*	71.2	76.0	77.8
Past year	16.0	50.5	34.3	18.9	19.2	40.8	37.5	28.6*
Past month	—	33.2	26.2	15.9	10.6	31.6	32.5	25.5
Daily	—	32.8	26.2	15.2	10.1	30.6	31.5	24.7
Any illicit drug[1]								
Lifetime	14.2	—	63.3	24.2	20.6	56.0	62.9	28.4
Past year	11.7	36.5	19.9	3.9	15.0	30.3	19.5	6.5
Past month	6.3	22.6	—	1.3	6.7	15.7*	9.6	3.4**
Marijuana/hashish								
Lifetime	7.6	65.1	59.8	18.3	13.7*	52.1*	60.6	25.0
Past year	7.1	32.4	14.5	—	10.3	26.0	15.4	4.0
Past month	—	20.2	—	—	4.6	13.5*	7.6	2.3
Psychotherapeutics[2]								
Lifetime	6.9	13.7	—	—	7.0	17.0	20.0	9.7
Past year	4.8	7.7	10.7	0.9	5.1	8.1	5.7	3.0***
Past month	0.7	—	—	0.7	1.6	2.2	2.1	1.2
Cocaine								
Lifetime	4.5	20.8	—	—	2.4	19.6	27.2	7.2
Past year	4.5	10.4	3.7	—	1.5*	8.1	5.3	1.5
Past month	1.8	2.2	3.2	—	0.4*	2.0	1.9	0.6
Inhalants								
Lifetime	7.9	—	—	—	6.6	11.7	9.0	2.6
Past year	6.2	—	—	—	3.6	3.7	0.6	0.4
Past month	3.6	—	—	—	1.6	1.5	0.4	0.3
	(*n* = 202)	(*n* = 171)	(*n* = 182)	(*n* = 204)	(*n* = 6,797)	(*n* = 6,770)	(*n* = 7,052)	(*n* = 7,284)

[1]Non-medical use of marijuana or hashish, cocaine (including crack), inhalants, hallucinogens (including PCP), heroin or psychotherapeutics at least once.

[2]Non-medical use of any prescription-type stimulant, sedative, tranquilizer or analgesic; does not include over-the-counter drugs.

—: Low precision, no estimate reported.

*Difference statistically significant at $p < 0.05$ level.

**Difference statistically significant at $p < 0.01$ level.

***Difference statistically significant at $p < 0.001$ level.

Source: 1991 *National Household Survey on Drug Abuse.*

18–25 years also show a tendency toward higher rates of "any illicit drug" use, although most of the differences are not statistically significant. The pattern among youth is more mixed, with youth residing in the border MSAs showing lower overall rates of "any illicit drug" use, but not statistically significantly lower. The border youth show lower rates of marijuana use, but only the life-time measure is significantly lower. Significantly fewer border youth report any (lifetime) cigarette smoking. However, they report statistically significantly higher rates of cocaine use.

The drug usage patterns among middle adults, or those in the 26–34-year-old age range, are very similar in the border MSAs and non-border MSAs. The only

TABLE 4 Licit and Illicit Drug Use in Border MSAs and Non-Border MSAs by Gender: 1991

	BORDER MSAs		NON-BORDER MSAs	
	Males	*Females*	*Males*	*Females*
Alcohol				
Lifetime	90.9	77.6	89.2	82.8
Past year	—	64.8	75.1	66.5
Past month	58.9	43.9	61.3	47.5
Past week	26.2	14.3	31.2	15.1
Cigarettes				
Lifetime	71.9	—	76.4	69.1
Past year	26.0	27.7	33.5*	28.9
Past month	19.4	20.0	27.9*	24.9
Daily	19.1	19.5	26.9**	24.2
Any illicit drug[1]				
Lifetime	—	40.6	42.6	34.4
Past year	15.4	12.0	15.5	11.2
Past month	11.0	5.0	8.1	5.3
Marijuana/hashish				
Lifetime	—	32.9	39.7	30.2
Past year	11.9	9.7	12.6	7.5
Past month	7.7	3.2	6.9	3.5
Psychotherapeutics[2]				
Lifetime	13.5	17.0	13.5	11.5
Past year	3.6	5.7	4.3	4.6
Past month	0.4	1.6	1.4*	1.7
Cocaine				
Lifetime	15.3	11.0	15.5	9.6
Past year	4.4	2.4	4.4	2.1
Past month	2.1	1.2	1.5	0.6
Inhalants				
Lifetime	13.2	6.1	7.0	4.2
Past year	6.1	1.4	1.5	0.9
Past month	—	0.8	0.7	0.5
	(*n* = 307)	(*n* = 452)	(*n* = 12,358)	(*n* = 15,545)

[1]Non-medical use of marijuana or hashish, cocaine (including crack), inhalants, hallucinogens (including PCP), heroin or psychotherapeutics at least once.

[2]Non-medical use of any prescription-type stimulant, sedative, tranquilizer or analgesic; does not include over-the-counter drugs.

—: Low precision, no estimate reported.

*Difference statistically significant at $p < 0.05$ level.

**Difference statistically significant at $p < 0.01$ level.

***Difference statistically significant at $p < 0.001$ level.

Source: 1991 *National Household Survey on Drug Abuse.*

exception is that more border MSA residents report alcohol use. Among older adults, those aged 35 years and older, there is a tendency for residents of the border MSAs to report lower levels of cigarette, "any illicit drug," and "any psychotherapeutic drug" use. There are several significant differences across the various drug categories, but none are significant across all three prevalence periods. Many of the prevalence estimates for older adults are suppressed due to low precision.

In summary, the overall pattern of drug use in the border MSAs is very similar to that found in the non-border MSAs. However, the overall pattern tends to mask the higher drug use rates found among young adults. There are few differences by gender other than the previously mentioned cigarette smoking. Males exhibit slightly greater drug use than females, as is the general pattern in the United States. The only drug and prevalence period for which males report lower prevalence rates than females is past month psychotherapeutic drug use.

Drug Use Prevalence by Gender and Age Among Hispanics Residing in the Mexico Border Region

You will recall that there are several significant differences in drug use patterns among Hispanics in the Southwest border compared to Hispanics in the remainder of the United States. Marijuana use is much lower among border Hispanics, as is lifetime cocaine use. The lifetime measure of alcohol, inhalants and the summary measure of "any illicit drug" are lower among border Hispanics. Past year and past month rates tend to be lower, but are not statistically significant. However, past year and past month cocaine use are reported at significantly higher rates among border Hispanics. Tables 5 and 6 show drug use prevalence rates by age group and gender, respectively, for Hispanics in the Southwest border in comparison to the remaining US Hispanic population.

Marijuana use is lower among border Hispanics primarily because there are fewer female users. Only past month rates are significantly lower among males too. Marijuana use is also lower among youth (12–17 years) and older adults (aged 35 years and older). The higher rates of cocaine use were due to the significantly higher rates of use among middle adults and, to a lesser extent, both young and older adults. Hispanic males residing near the border also report a significantly higher rate of past year and past month cocaine use than Hispanic males in the remainder of the United States. Conversely, Hispanic females residing near the border report significantly lower lifetime cocaine use, although they report higher past month usage rates than Hispanic females in the remainder of the United States. Although only the life-time measure of alcohol use is lower among border Hispanics, alcohol use among females is significantly lower for all prevalence periods except the past month. Alcohol use is also lower among older border Hispanic adults, although middle adults show a tendency towards greater alcohol use.

Cigarette use is not significantly different among Hispanics residing near the border and the remaining Hispanic population, but this pattern disguises some age group differences. Hispanic border youth show significantly lower cigarette use. Older adults report lower lifetime cigarette use, but middle adults aged 26–34 years report significantly higher lifetime and past year cigarette use.

The general pattern evident among Hispanics in the Southwest border is toward lower rates for marijuana, and somewhat higher rates for cocaine. Youth show a general tendency toward lower use for all classes of drugs except cocaine, with significantly lower prevalence rates for cigarettes, marijuana, and the summary measure of "any illicit drug." There are no significant differences in drug use prevalence rates among young adults, except for higher past year cocaine usage rates among border Hispanics. Middle adults, or those aged 26–34 years, show significantly greater cigarette and cocaine use. They also report significantly greater lifetime inhalant use and past year alcohol use. Older Hispanic adults residing near the border (aged 35 years and older), are less likely to use most classes of licit and illicit drugs. They report significantly less alcohol use, and less lifetime experience with cigarettes, marijuana, cocaine and the overall measure of "any illicit drug" use. Large differences are also found in drug use patterns between border Hispanic females and Hispanic females in the remainder of the United States. Border females report significantly less alcohol and marijuana use. They also report significantly less lifetime experience with psychotherapeutic drugs and cocaine. The higher past year and past month cocaine prevalence rates found for the Southwest border Hispanic population is primarily accounted for by males, although females also show a propensity towards greater use. The lower marijuana use among the Hispanic border population is also primarily attributable to the lower rates of use among females.

DISCUSSION

The goal of this paper is to provide some assessment of drug use in the Southwest border in the United States—an area designated by the Office of National Drug Control Policy as a High Intensity Drug Trafficking Area (HIDTA). The assessment was achieved by examining data from the 1991 National Household Survey on Drug Abuse (HH Survey), whose sampling base covered most of the urbanized population living in areas adjacent to the border. The overall HH Survey sample in the border can also adequately address drug use patterns among the Hispanic population residing in close proximity to the border.

TABLE 5 Licit and Illicit Drug Use Among Border Hispanics and Remaining US Hispanic Population by Age Group: 1991

	HISPANICS IN BORDER				HISPANICS IN REMAINDER OF US			
	12–17	*18–25*	*26–34*	*>35*	*12–17*	*18–25*	*26–34*	*>35*
Alcohol								
Lifetime	37.5	82.2	87.1	—	47.2	82.1	85.6	82.6
Past year	34.7	—	81.2	50.9	41.0	71.7	73.6*	65.9*
Past month	18.0	—	63.8	37.0	23.2	52.3	56.5	49.0**
Past week	4.7	27.3	24.8	13.9	7.1	18.7	22.4	24.4*
Cigarettes								
Lifetime	23.4	61.0	79.0	57.1	33.3**	57.7	68.1***	67.3*
Past year	12.7	30.4	44.3	30.4	17.3	33.4	33.5**	31.2
Past month	3.7	23.2	32.6	26.0	9.5**	25.0	28.1	27.8
Daily	3.7	22.6	31.8	24.1	8.5*	23.8	27.4	26.8
Any illicit drug[1]								
Lifetime	9.2	—	38.3	14.2	19.2**	40.3	42.6	26.1**
Past year	7.0	19.8	14.0	4.8	14.2**	21.1	13.0	7.2
Past month	5.1	9.2	6.8	4.1	8.4	11.9	5.8	3.8
Marijuana/hashish								
Lifetime	4.1	—	33.2	9.1	13.4***	36.4	40.0	23.0***
Past year	3.5	14.1	9.7	—	10.3***	17.2	9.3	4.9
Past month	1.5	5.7	3.7	—	5.1**	9.5	4.2	2.6
Psychotherapeutics[2]								
Lifetime	4.7	—	11.1	4.9	5.8	11.8	11.0	8.6
Past year	4.0	—	2.9	1.8	4.2	6.8	2.9	2.0
Past month	0.9	—	—	1.4	1.8	2.3	1.4	0.9
Cocaine								
Lifetime	2.9	—	15.5	3.2	3.8	14.9	19.0	8.3***
Past year	2.7	13.0	7.7	2.7	3.0	6.4*	4.2**	2.1
Past month	2.3	3.7	5.0	2.7	1.2	2.6	1.7*	0.8*
Inhalants								
Lifetime	4.3	—	2.6	1.0	7.0	6.7	6.7**	2.8
Past year	2.2	1.2	—	—	4.3	1.5	0.6	0.5
Past month	1.4	—	—	—	3.1	0.8	0.3	0.3
	(*n* = 222)	(*n* = 191)	(*n* = 199)	(*n* = 236)	(*n* = 1,807)	(*n* = 1,726)	(*n* = 1,763)	(*n* = 1,770)

[1]Non-medical use of marijuana or hashish, cocaine (including crack), inhalants, hallucinogens (including PCP), heroin or psychotherapeutics at least once.

[2]Non-medical use of any prescription-type stimulant, sedative, tranquilizer or analgesic; does not include over-the-counter drugs.

—: Low precision, no estimate reported.

*Difference statistically significant at $p < 0.05$ level.

**Difference statistically significant at $p < 0.01$ level.

***Difference statistically significant at $p < 0.001$ level.

Source: 1991 *National Household Survey on Drug Abuse.*

However, these data are based on small sample sizes and this, coupled with the above limitations and the relative rarity of illicit drug use, make these data less than ideal. However, they begin to fill a gap in our knowledge about the nature and extent of licit and illicit drug use in a drug trafficking area.

Given the proliferation of risk factors associated with drug abuse plus its HIDTA status, the Southwest border would be expected to have higher rates of illicit drug use. In spite of this, there are few differences in rates of licit and illicit drug use among the population in the Southwest border MSAs in

TABLE 6   Licit and Illicit Drug Use Among Hispanics in the Border Area and Remaining US Hispanic Population by Gender: 1991

	HISPANICS IN BORDER		HISPANICS IN REMAINDER OF US	
	Males	*Females*	*Males*	*Females*
Alcohol				
Lifetime	85.3	57.7	86.1	70.5**
Past year	78.7	46.7	74.6	56.0*
Past month	64.9	28.3	59.7	35.8
Past week	33.7	5.6	31.1	9.6***
Cigarettes				
Lifetime	70.4	47.4	70.8	51.1
Past year	37.3	25.6	35.7	24.7
Past month	29.3	18.7	29.8	19.8
Daily	28.8	17.2	28.6	19.2
Any illicit drug[1]				
Lifetime	—	16.0	37.7	25.8
Past year	14.3	7.1	15.6	8.6
Past month	7.1	5.0	7.8	4.9
Marijuana/hashish				
Lifetime	29.4	10.7	34.9	21.5***
Past year	10.2	3.2	12.7	5.2*
Past month	3.1	1.5	6.2**	3.0*
Psychotherapeutics[2]				
Lifetime	8.5	4.9	10.6	8.1*
Past year	2.9	2.6	3.2	3.7
Past month	0.8	1.7	1.3	1.5
Cocaine				
Lifetime	14.1	4.5	15.2	7.6**
Past year	9.2	3.4	4.8**	2.1
Past month	4.6	2.5	1.8*	1.0*
Inhalants				
Lifetime	4.1	1.7	6.5	3.5
Past year	1.6	0.5	1.2	1.2
Past month	1.3	1.5	0.7	0.8*
	(*n* = 343)	(*n* = 507)	(*n* = 3,187)	(*n* = 3,879)

[1]Non-medical use of marijuana or hashish, cocaine (including crack), inhalants, hallucinogens (including PCP), heroin or psychotherapeutics at least once.

[2]Non-medical use of any prescription-type stimulant, sedative, tranquilizer or analgesic; does not include over-the-counter drugs.

—: Low precision, no estimate reported.

*Difference statistically significant at $p < 0.05$ level.

**Difference statistically significant at $p < 0.01$ level.

***Difference statistically significant at $p < 0.001$ level.

Source: 1991 *National Household Survey on Drug Abuse.*

comparison to the population residing in MSAs throughout the remainder of the United States. The Hispanic border population also shows similar patterns to the remaining U.S. Hispanic population, but are actually much less likely to report illicit drug use. They reported lower levels of marijuana use, but they were more likely to report cocaine use. Nevertheless, the overall similarities mask the lower rates among youth and older adults, which is offset by the higher rates among young and middle-aged adults.

The lower rates of alcohol and marijuana use among Southwest border Hispanics are almost entirely attributable to lower rates of use among Hispanic females and those aged 35 years and older.

The fact that Mexico is a "supplier" nation and that the Mexico border is a known entry point for illicit drugs into the United States does not appear to significantly increase the probability of risk for using illicit drugs in the Southwest border region of the United States. It is important to note that this study did not directly measure supply or availability. Because of rapid transhipment, availability may not be any greater in this area than in other areas of the United States. Drug suppliers may be more interested in other potential markets away from the border area. "Availability" is a complex construct that includes not only the physical access to drugs, but also psychological and social availability. The mere presence of drugs in a geographical region does not translate into increased use unless other risk factors are also present. The presence of a profundity of risk factors in the border area makes it even more surprising that drug use rates are relatively low.

This study is certainly not definitive, but suggests that residents of this HIDTA are not using drugs at higher rates than others in the United States. The 1991 Household Survey oversampled six MSAs, three of which (New York, Miami and Los Angeles) were also designated as HIDTAs by the Office of National Drug Control Policy. There was a tendency towards slightly higher drug use among residents of the Los Angeles MSA, but there was less drug use among residents of the Miami MSA (Hughes, 1992). New York exhibited drug prevalence rates similar to those for the United States. These analyses do not suggest a clear relationship between drug use prevalence rates and designation as a HIDTA.

In fact, there is a paucity of research between accessibility of alcohol and other drugs in a society and the prevalence of their use. The United States policy, which emphasizes reducing the supply of drugs in the country, is loosely based on the economic theory of the French demographer, Sully Ledermann. The Ledermann curve postulates that the incidence of alcohol-related problems in society changes in relation to overall alcohol availability and consumption (Ledermann, 1956). The relationship between drug availability and use is rarely questioned, and drives policy in the United States resulting in practices such as designating areas as High Intensity Drug Trafficking Areas. Rarely has the relationship between drug trafficking and drug availability or use been scrutinized by rigorous research. This study does not address those

relationships in any great detail but, at the societal level, our analyses suggest few connections between drug trafficking in an area and higher drug prevalence rates in that area. On the other hand, there may be other structural or cultural factors evident in this area that serve to reduce drug use. There is evidence that traditional Hispanic culture is a moderating influence in the use of illicit drugs, especially the importance of the family (De la Rosa and Gfroerer, 1993). The protective influence of the family may be more proximal than the risk factors of drug trafficking, availability and lower socio-economic status.

Youth (12–17 years) residing in the border MSAs generally reported less licit and illicit drug use than youth residing in other large MSAs, but only the differences between Hispanic youth were significant. In contrast, the young adult population (18–25 years) in the border MSAs shows a tendency towards greater use of alcohol, tobacco, marijuana and "any illicit drug" use. However, comparing the Southwest border Hispanic population in this age range with their Hispanic peers in the remainder of the United States shows great similarity in their patterns of drug use. Somewhere between youth and young adulthood, the Southwest border population "catches up" or exceeds the drug use prevalence rates of their respective comparison groups in the remainder of the United States. This suggests that the protective influence of the family is eroded as youth mature and begin to move away from the family. With close to half of the Southwest border population 20 years of age or younger, the data provide some justification for concern. Young adults comprise the age group with the highest rates of licit and illicit drug use overall. As they age young adults may continue their drug use, especially if they continue to be beset with a variety of formidable barriers found for this age group, including poverty and unemployment.

By the year 2010, Hispanics are expected to become the largest minority group in the United States. Population growth in the Southwest border area has been phenomenal. There are 11.8 million Hispanics of Mexican descent in the United States with the majority of that population living in the border area (Crespin, 1994). The growth has largely been due to both the legal and illegal immigration of Mexicans into the United States. The population growth rate has been substantially higher in the four border states than in the remainder of the country, and the population growth in the counties adjoining the border has outstripped those in the remainder of the state (Fernandez, 1991). Future studies need to examine how traditional Hispanic cultural values, especially familiarism, can be retained as acculturation of both legal and illegal Mexican immigrants occurs.

Results from this study could be examined relative to the results obtained by the Dirección General de Epidemiologia within the Mexican Ministry of Health, which oversampled five areas in their Northern border in their most recent National Household Survey. Data extrapolated from the 1988 Mexican Household Survey suggests that although the rates of illicit drug use for Mexico are much lower than the United States, the highest prevalence rates in Mexico are found in the Northern states that border the United States (Dirección General de Epidemiologia, 1990). The Information Reporting System on Drugs (IRSD), developed in 1986 by the Mexican Institute of Psychiatry recently expanded its operation to two border cities (Ortiz, Ramero and Rodriguez, 1992). Comparing cocaine use in the border cities to Mexico City showed that the user population is younger and more involved in drugs. This finding lends support to other research results (Castro-Sariñana and Chávez, 1986; Zúñiga and Palmer, 1987; Dirección General de Epidemiologia, 1990; De la Serna et al., 1991) indicating that the northern states are high-risk areas.

Since 1971, when President Richard Nixon delivered an address to the U.S. Congress, the approach to dealing with illicit drug use within the U.S. government has essentially been a dichotomized approach of "demand" and "supply" reduction efforts (Nixon, 1971). Demand for drugs is measured by understanding the nature and magnitude of use. Prevention, treatment and rehabilitation are the usual mechanisms to address demand. Availability is the usual measure of supply. Supply efforts are based on the premise that stopping the production and trafficking of illegal substances reduces availability to potential users. With reduced supply comes

supposedly concomitant decreases in drug abuse and addiction and the sequelae associated with these problems such as violence, HIV/AIDS and homelessness. Our analyses suggest that the relationship between supply and use is not clearcut. Adding "supply" to the number of other risk factors present among the Southwest border population would suggest higher drug use prevalence in this area, but, instead, this border population displays rates of drug use more noteworthy for their similarities to their respective comparison groups than for their differences. However, there is a troubling increase in drug use prevalence between youth and young adulthood among Southwest border residents. There is also a disproportionately large youthful population in the Southwest border area. This and the variety of risk factors argue for greater research and prevention efforts in this area.

Although this study is about drug use in the Southwest border of the United States, there are implications that reach beyond this area. The most obvious is that drug trafficking areas do not necessarily have higher rates of drug use among the population. Drugs trafficking may not necessarily translate into increased drug availability. It appears that drug use rates in an area are impacted by a number of factors beyond trafficking and availability. The Mexican National Household Survey shows much lower rates of drug use than found in the United States, even though it is estimated that Mexico supplies approximately 60% of the foreign-grown marijuana and more than 20% of the heroin reaching U.S. markets (NNICC, 1993; Bureau of International Narcotics Matters, 1994). It is obvious that we have to look beyond supply, trafficking and availability in understanding the drug use patterns in an area. Other structural, cultural and individual factors undoubtedly contribute to drug use patterns.

REFERENCES

Adams, E. H. (1986). An overview of drug use in the United States and along the U.S.–Mexico border. Presented at the U.S.–Mexico Border Public Health Association, Monterrey, Mexico, 28 April.

Anti-Drug Abuse Act. (1988). Section 1005. High Intensity Drug Trafficking Area Program.

Anthony, J. C., Helzer, J. C., and Helzer, J. (1991). Syndromes of drug abuse and dependence. In L. N. Robins and D. A. Regier (Eds.), *Psychiatric disorders in America* (pp. 116–154). (New York: Free Press).

Brounstein, P. J., Altschuler, D. M., Hatry, H. P., and Blair, L. H. (1989). *Substance use and delinquency among inner city adolescent males.* Washington, DC: Urban Institute Press.

Bureau of International Narcotics Matters (1994). *International narcotics control strategy report.* Washington, DC: U.S. Department of State.

Castro-Sarinana, M. E., and Chavez, A. M. (1986). Predictores del uso de drogas en jóvenes mexicanos. *Revista Mexicana de Psicologia, 3,* 5–10.

Chapa, J., and Valencia, R. (1993). Latino population growth, demographic characteristics, and educational stagnation: an examination of recent trends. *Hispanic Journal of Behavioral Sciences, 15,* 165–187.

Crespin, F. H. (1994). Overview of border health issues. *Border Health Journal* (April/May/June), 25–29.

De la Rosa, M., and Gfroerer, J. (1993). Protective and risk factors associated with drug use among Hispanic youth. *Journal of Addictive Diseases, 12,* 87–108.

De la Serna, J., Rojas Guiot, E., Estrada, M. E., and Medina Mora, M. E. (1991). Medición del uso de drogas en estudiantes de educación media y media superior del Distrito Federal y Zona Conurbada, 1989. *Anales, 2.*

Direction General de Epidemiologia and Instituo Mexicano De Psiquiatria. (1990). *Sistema Nacional de Encuestas de Salud, Encuesta Nacional de Adicciones, Drogas.* México City: Mexicano de Psiquiatria.

Drug Enforcement Administration. (1994). *Annual statistical report, FY 1993.* Arlington, VA.: Statistical Services Section, Office of Planning and Policy Analysis, Planning and Inspection Division.

Fernandez, E. W. (1991). The Hispanic population of the U.S. southwest borderland. *Current Population Reports Special Studies,* Series P-3, No. 172. Washington, DC: U.S. Department of Commerce, Economics and Statistics Administration, Bureau of the Census.

Flewelling, R. L., Ennet, S. T., Rachal, J. V., and Thiesen, A. E. (1993). *Race/ethnicity, socioeconomic status, and drug abuse, 1991.* DHHS Pub. No. (SMA) 93-2062. Rockville, MD: U.S. Department of Health and Human Service, Substance Abuse and Mental Health Services Administration.

General Accounting Office. (1994). *Hispanics' schooling,* GAO/PEMD-94-24. Washington, DC: General Accounting Office.

Greene, M. (1974). An epidemiologic assessment of heroin use. *American Journal of Public Health,* 64(suppl.), 1–10.

Gutierrez-Ramos, A., and Flores-Farfán, J. A. (1992). Toward a history of drugs on the Mexico–U.S. border. In *Epidemiologic trends in drug abuse* (pp. 522–526). Rockville, MD: Community Epidemiology Work Group, NIDA.

Harrison, L. D. (1991). Assessing drug use along the U.S.–Mexico border utilizing the National Household Survey on Drug Abuse. Paper presented at the Border Substance Abuse Epidemiology Work Group, El Paso, Texas, 29 April.

Harrison, L. D. (1995). The validity of self-reported data on drug use. *Journal of Drug Issues, 25,* 51–71.

Harrison, L. D., and Kennedy, N. K. (1994). Drug use in the United States Mexico Border Area: Is there an epidemic waiting to happen? *Hispanic Journal of Behavioral Sciences, 16,* 281–295.

Hawkins, J. D., Lishner, D. M., and Catalano, R. F. (1985). Childhood predictors and the prevention of adolescent substance abuse. In C. L. Jones and R. J. Battjes (Eds.), *Etiology of drug abuse: Implications for prevention,* National Institute on Drug Abuse Research Monograph No. 56 (pp. 75–125). Rockville, MD: National Institute on Drug Abuse.

Hughes, A. L. (1992). The prevalence of illicit drug use in six metropolitan areas in the United States: Results from the 1991 National Household Survey on Drug Abuse. *British Journal of Addiction, 8,* 1481–1485.

Kandel, D. B., and Logan, J. A. (1984). Patterns of drug use from adolescence to young adulthood: Periods of risk initiation, stabilization and decline in use. *American Journal of Public Health, 74,* 662–666.

Ledermann, S. (1956). Alcohol, alcoolisme, alcoolisation. In *Donnees scientifiques de charactere physiologique, economic, et social* (Institut National d'Etudes Demographiques, Cahier No. 29). Paris: Press Universitaire.

Montoya, M. (1985). Prevalence of 1985 substance abuse in U.S.–Mexico border Hispanic males ages 12 to 17 years. *Border Health, V,* 11–17.

National Narcotics Intelligence Consumers Committee (NNICC). (1993). *The NNICC report 1992, the supply of illicit drugs to the United States.* Arlington, VA: Drug Enforcement Administration.

Negy, C., and Woods, D. (1992). The importance of acculturation in understanding research with Hispanic-Americans. *Hispanic Journal of Behavioral Sciences, 14,* 224–247.

Nixon, R. M. (1971). Message to congress.

Office of Technology Assessment (OTA), U.S. Congress. (1987). *The border war on drugs,* OTA-O-336. Washington, DC: U.S. GPO.

Ortiz, A., Romero, M., and Rodriquez, E. (1992). Information reporting system on drugs data: Cocaine use trends—two border cities and México City. In *Epidemiologic trends in drug abuse* (pp. 532–537). Rockville, MD: Community Epidemiology Work Group, NIDA.

Pan, American Health Organization (PAHO), El Paso Field Office, Regional Office of the World Health Organization and U.S.–Mexico Border Health Association (USMBHA). (1989). *Report on Substance Abuse Along the U.S.–Mexico Border.* El Paso, TX: PAHO.

Pan American Health Organization (PAHO), El Paso Field Office, Regional Office of the World Health Organization and U.S.–Mexico Border Health Association (USMBHA). (1991). *U.S.–Mexico border health statistics.* El Paso, TX: PAHO.

Ramos, R. (1989). To be in the fire: Drug trends in El Paso, Texas. *Epidemiologic trends in drug abuse.* Rockville, MD: Community Epidemiology Work Group, NIDA.

Simcha-Fagen, O., Gersten, J. C., and Langer, T. S. (1986). Early precursors and concurrent correlates of patterns of illicit drug use in adolescence, *Journal of Drug Issues, 16,* 7–28.

Stein, S. L., Garcia, F., Marler, B., et al. (1992). A study of multiagency collaborative strategies: Did juvenile delinquents change? *Journal of Community Psychology,* Special Issue, 88–105.

Substance Abuse and Mental Health Service Administration (SAMHSA). (1993). *National Household Survey on Drug Abuse: Main findings 1991.* Rockville, MD: U.S. Department of Health and Human Services.

U.N. Secretary General. (1973). *Commentary on the single convention on narcotic drugs, 1961.* New York: United Nations.

U.S. Bureau of the Census. (1990). The Hispanic population in the U.S. March 1989. *Current Population Reports,* Ser. P-20, No. 444. Washington, DC: GPO.

U.S. Department of Commerce. (1986). *Current reports.* Washington, DC: U.S. Department of Commerce.

Zuniga, V., and Palmer, T. (1987). La Ostentación del Estigma. Un grupo de Jóvenes Marginados Consumidores de Drogas en Matamoros Tamaulipas, *Cuadernos del CEPAJUV.*

26

The Motives and Mechanics of Operating an Illegal Drug Enterprise

LISE-MARIE VANNOSTRAND

RICHARD TEWKSBURY

ABSTRACT

This article examines the structure and process of illicit drug-dealing activities. Motives, mechanics of operations, and strategies used to avoid detection and to identify law enforcement are all examined, providing a clearer picture of the lifestyles led by drug dealers. On the basis of qualitative interviews conducted with participants in a drug court diversion program in a mid-sized, midwestern city, the means by which drug dealers initiate and maintain a career in drug dealing, how deals are transacted, and how law enforcement is avoided are explored.

The potential for the development of an illicit drug market was recognized early in the twentieth century. With the implementation of legislative restrictions, licit drugs were becoming increasingly more difficult to obtain. As noted by Lichtenstein, a physician at a New York City prison in 1914,

> Several individuals have come to the conclusion that selling "dope" is a very profitable business. These individuals have sent their agents among the gangs frequenting our city corners instructing them to make friends with the members and induce them to take the drug (opium). Janitors, bartenders and cab men have also been employed to help spread the habit. The plan has worked so well that there is scarcely a pool room in New York that may not be called a meeting place of drug fiends. The drug has been made up in candy and sold to school children. The conspiring individuals being familiar with the habit forming action of the drugs, believe that the increased number of "fiends" will create a larger demand for the drug and in this way build up a profitable business. (Lichtenstein, 1914, p. 67)

What one may find interesting about this statement is that very similar statements can be made today. The domestic drug trade [became] a booming business throughout the latter part of the twentieth century. For example, between 1985 and 1994, nationwide arrests of drug law violators (including arrest for both possession and sale) increased by more than over 60 percent (Bureau of Justice Statistics, 1996). More specifically, between 1980 and 1987 adult arrests for drug manufacturing and selling increased an estimated 113 percent (Tunnell, 1993). As a result of the increased efforts of policing and law enforcement, drug traffickers are now apprehended, convicted, and imprisoned at greater rates than at any time during this century (Tunnell, 1993).

Although such data may suggest a measure of success from the past several decades' wars on drugs, the increases in arrests and convictions of drug traffickers have been commensurate with increases in drug use. With an ever-increasing demand for drugs, one can inevitably conclude that there will be an increase in drug trafficking to supply that demand. The demand for drugs has been steadily increasing since the 1960s, and though drug dealers are now arrested more frequently than in the past, they still make up only a small percentage (27 percent) of total drug arrestees (Bureau of Justice Statistics, 1996).

With the apparent failed attempts to control the supply side of the drug economy, research has emerged that investigates drug dealers' motives and their methods of operating illicit drug businesses. Included among the reasons dealers sell drugs is not only for financial gain, but also as an alternative to low-paying jobs, from a desire for status and power, out of hedonism, and out of the need to support a drug habit (Biernacki, 1979; Flores, 1981; Adler, 1985; Mieczkowski, 1986, 1990, 1994; Murphy, Waldorf, and Reinarman, 1990; Faupel, 1991; Lyman and Potter, 1991; Weisheit, 1991b; Myers, 1992; Dembo, Hughes, and Jackson, 1993; Tunnell, 1993; Hagedorn, 1994; Hafley and Tewksbury, 1996; Shover, 1996; Curcione, 1997). Were there merely one factor that motivated drug dealers, it would be relatively simple to address, and in effect curb, the domestic supply of drugs. As it stands, similar motives drive both illegitimate and legitimate businesspersons; drug dealing serves as an alternative method of realizing socially valued goals.

Like other businesses, drug dealing often takes on the form of a career with methods of entry, levels of advancement, and retirement stages similar to those found in both legitimate and other illegitimate work environments (Adler, 1985; Skolnick, Correl, Navarro, and Rabb, 1990; Dunlap, Johnson, and Manwar, 1994; Hafley and Tewksbury, 1995, 1996; Johnson and Natarajan, 1995; Maher and Daly, 1996; Shover, 1996).

Both urban and rural drug-trafficking organizations reflect some degree of hierarchical structure similar to that found in legitimate businesses (Adler, 1985; Murphy et al., 1990; Weisheit, 1991; Hafley and Tewksbury, 1995, 1996; Curcione, 1997). Each level of the hierarchy has a definitive job description and level of responsibility to assure smooth operation. Like those in legitimate businesses, drug dealers rely on their knowledge to train new recruits and tend to organize, plan, and execute their ventures in ways similar to legitimate businesspersons. Those with the highest degree of responsibility earn the most profit, those with less responsibility tend to earn the least. In short, a dealer's occupational involvement takes the form of a career with methods of entry, levels of advancement, and retirement phases similar to those found in most legitimate work environments.

CRACK COCAINE DISTRIBUTION

Crack cocaine has some of the more prominent negative effects of commonly abused drugs and has been linked to increasingly high rates of violent crime (Fagan, 1989; Mieczkowski, 1992; Dembo et al., 1993; Johnson, Golub, and Fagan, 1995; Dunlap and Johnson, 1996). It stands to reason, then, that those dealing crack cocaine must operate in a manner consistent with its consequences. With the introduction of inexpensive crack cocaine in the 1980s, systems of distribution have emerged as a consequence of the market demand (Dembo et al., 1993; Inciardi, Lockwood, and Pottieger, 1993; Chitwood, Rivers, and Inciardi, 1996) that vary from methods used when dealing in other substances. Consequently, a highly lucrative market for drug dealers has been established (Miller, 1995).

Murphy et al. (1990) defined a cocaine dealer as someone who is "fronted" drugs (given drugs on consignment to be paid for when sold) or who buys drugs to sell. To become a dealer, one must (a) have one or more reliable supplier or connections, (b) make regular purchases in amounts of 1/8 ounce or greater, (c) maintain regular supplies for sale, and (d) have a strong network of customers who purchase drugs regularly. For many drug dealers, initiation of a dealing career involves determining the demand for a specific drug in the area and the feasibility of cultivating, producing, or selling that substance. What methods a dealer uses will determine either the success or the failure of a drug-trafficking organization.

Dealers typically purchase wholesale amounts of crack and make multiple retail doses in bags, bundles, or vials that are sold or consigned to lower level street sellers (Adler, 1985; Inciardi et al., 1993; Johnson and Natarajan, 1995; Chitwood et al., 1996). Because of the brief duration of the crack high, most sellers must offer service 24 hours per day to cater to customers repeatedly returning for varying amounts of the drug (Inciardi, Horowitz, and Pottieger, 1993; Johnson, Natarajan, Dunlap, and Elmoghazy, 1994; Chitwood et al., 1996; Jacobs, 1996). Although some researchers have suggested that most crack sales occur on the street (Skolnick et al., 1990; Pettiway, 1995), other researchers have suggested that crack sales occur primarily indoors and that crack houses are generally the primary retail outlets (Mieczkowski, 1990, 1992; Inciardi, Lockwood, and Pottieger, 1993; Chitwood et al., 1996; Knowles, 1996).

Because crack dealing has become such a lucrative market within the drug economy, it has become a primary focus of law enforcement to detect, arrest, and incarcerate drug dealers. However, the domestic law enforcement crack-down on drug trafficking does not appear to have resulted in a decrease in the supply of drugs to the domestic market. Although drug markets may be displaced temporarily, in actuality dealers may simply be developing new strategies to avoid detection rather than being eliminated by increased police pressure (Caulkins, 1992; Johnson and Natarajan, 1995; Jacobs, 1996).

Several researchers have found that drug dealers not only are often able to use tactics to avoid police detection but are able to identify law enforcement officers through both verbal and non-verbal cues (Mieczkowski, 1986; Skolnick et al., 1990; Caulkins, 1992; Jacobs, 1992; Johnson and Natarajan, 1995; Knowles, 1996). Dealers are careful when selecting buyers and locations for transactions and often believe they are able to identify law enforcement officers by how they look, what they wear, what they drive, and how they engage verbally when making transactions. In addition, when one adds the constitutional restraints governing police drug buys, arrests, and seizures, the likelihood of arrests of dealers appears very modest (Caulkins, 1992; Myers, 1992; Johnson and Natarajan, 1995).

The current research offers an expansion of this literature and focuses on the motivating factors that influence individuals to deal drugs and the means of operating a drug business while avoiding detection. These issues, furthermore, are explored from drug dealers' perspectives. Finally, on the basis of these findings we offer suggestions regarding future drug war policy.

METHOD

This analysis is based on data obtained from semi-structured interviews with 20 dealers participating in a drug court diversion program. Of the participants, 80 percent ($n = 16$) were African American and 20 percent ($n = 4$) were White. The majority of subjects were male (80 percent), ranging in age from 19 to 48, with a mean age of 31. Educational levels varied, with 20 percent having less than a high school education, 30 percent a high school diploma or GED, and 50 percent vocational or postsecondary education. Eighty percent of subjects had children, 30 percent were married, and 70 percent were divorced or never married.

All subjects had a history of use of various illicit substances (generally marijuana and/or cocaine), though 95 percent identified themselves primarily as crack dealers and by self-report were only recreational users. All had at least one drug conviction, with 60 percent having been charged most recently with drug trafficking and 40 percent having been charged with simple possession. In addition, 50 percent of subjects reported prior arrests for possession and/or drug trafficking.

The present study is a portion of a larger evaluation study of a drug court treatment program in a mid-sized, midwestern city. As a primary component of the process evaluation, a stratified sample of program clients were interviewed concerning experiences and perceptions in the program, substance use histories, and illegal activities. The current sample consisted of all program clients who reported selling illicit drugs either in the past or presently. Data collection spanned a 13-month period in 1996 and 1997.

All interviews were conducted by Lise-Marie VanNostrand within the drug court treatment facility in private offices. Interviews ranged from 30 to 90 minutes and were conducted during the subjects' scheduled one- to two-hour group participation time. A semi-structured interview format was used, all interviews were audiotape recorded, and analysis was based on verbatim transcripts.

With the assistance of drug court staff, a purposive sample of subjects was obtained. Group counselors identified subjects who were either known to have a history of drug dealing or perceived as likely to have been involved in dealing. All interviews were arranged through drug court personnel, with subjects simply being asked to participate in the interview. No requests for interviews were denied by any of the subjects, and participation was strictly voluntary.

Subjects were advised that all information obtained in the interview was strictly confidential. Interview tapes were identified by first name only and were destroyed at the conclusion of the project. All subjects were assigned pseudonyms throughout the analysis to preserve confidentiality.

FINDINGS

Analysis of dealers' accounts suggests three primary motives to deal drugs: financial gain, greed, and a desire for the lifestyle itself. Additionally, dealers identified their methods of selecting buyers, arranging transactions, avoiding detection, and identifying law enforcement officers. Through explanations of how dealers structure and conduct business transactions, researchers can move toward better understandings of the dynamics that facilitate proliferation of dealing enterprises. In the discussion that follows, we first examine the specific motivations that draw individuals into a drug-dealing career. Second, we outline and examine the mechanics of operating a successful drug business.

Motives to Deal Drugs

Subjects in the current study identified three primary motives that led them to begin dealing. Some were motivated by a perceived need to earn either a primary or a supplemental income. These individuals perceived few or no lucrative, legitimate employment opportunities available to them. Others began dealing strictly because of greed and a desire for luxury material items. Still others were motivated by the fast lifestyle perceived to accompany a career in drug trafficking. In essence, although some dealers were not chemically addicted, they were addicted to the lifestyle of a drug dealer. Although most subjects began dealing on the basis of a single motive, these motives frequently evolved and vacillated over time, serving to support a continued involvement in the drug trade.

Financial Need.   Some subjects began dealing drugs primarily as a result of financial need. Commonly reported was an absolute financial need and perceptions of blocked opportunities for substantial, gainful employment. The majority of subjects (80 percent) reported having children, and although at the time of the interview only 30 percent were married, many had been previously married. As such, those who most often reported dealing to fill a financial need had families for which to provide. These dealers saw drug dealing as the quickest, and often only, method of gaining financial survival and stability. As described by Shane, a high school graduate and former military serviceman, lack of employment opportunities and familial responsibilities lead to his involvement in the drug trade:

> I came home from the service in 1991 and got married out of high school. Perfect little life. When I came home, my wife was pregnant and I couldn't really find a good job to get all the baby stuff I needed. . . . I got caught up in it. I didn't get caught up in the lifestyle, it was the money I was into.

Similar motives were expressed by Sid, who reported that after dropping out of college, he was unable to achieve the "American Dream" through legitimate means:

> I got a job now. You know, it's decent, but it's not anything for a house payment, car payment, two kids. You know, the money just ain't enough. . . . That's probably the biggest reason today for most people out there selling dope.

Richard agreed, and reported that although he had tried legitimate means of achieving financial security,

he found that the income derived from drug dealing far outweighed his earnings from a legitimate job.

> The money is one reason that got me motivated because I wasn't working and I was trying to make ends meet. Trying to take care of my responsibilities. Then, I started to work. It was like, "I don't have to work. I can make more in a day [dealing] than what I would for a whole week doing this."

After seeking financial independence and security through conventional means, failures and obstacles pushed many to seek alternative, illicit opportunities. They were married, had children, had sometimes continued their educations, and worked in the hope of achieving a measure of personal success. However, they were unable to effectively manage the stressors associated with their familial responsibilities and as a result of either desperation or the attraction of drug dealing, turned to selling drugs.

In this respect, this research supports previous literature that suggests that drug dealing may sometimes be motivated simply by a need to supplement incomes for those persons categorized as "economically depressed." Yet, unlike in some previous research (Flores, 1981; Weisheit, 1991a, 1991b; Hafley and Tewksbury, 1995, 1996) subjects in the present study did not necessarily live in economically depressed or rural areas. Recognizing drug dealing in their communities as a prosperous enterprise, these individuals opted for illegal pursuits rather than the few paying jobs that were available to them (see also Mieczkowski, 1986; Murphy et al., 1990; Myers, 1992).

Greed.   In addition to perceptions of financial need as an initial motive to sell drugs, other subjects reported little need to supplement their incomes and were motivated strictly by greed. Although not believing it necessary to sell drugs so as to make ends meet and provide basic life necessities, dealers motivated by greed sought supplemental income so as to attain luxuries. Previous literature has identified the profit motive as a major motive for drug dealing; however, much of the research has not separated financial need from issues of greed. Instead, a profit motive comprised of several variables is typically used (Dembo et al., 1993; Mieczkowski, 1994; Tunnell, 1993). Yet, there is a distinct difference between dealing motivated by necessity and dealing motivated by greed alone.

Several of the dealers in this study reported little or no need for supplemental incomes. Simply put, they expressed a desire for the fast and easy money that drug dealing afforded them. These subjects often maintained conventional employment or operated profitable legitimate businesses. As explained by Joel, his greed for money was described as "madness," as he already had significant income earned through legitimate means:

> I was doing construction work and making a lot of money, so I was able to buy the stuff [cocaine] in quantity and sell it. And, you know, one thing led to another. . . . I didn't need the money because I had plenty.

Like sentiments were expressed by Andy, who very candidly reported that he perceived himself as spoiled and that his sole motivation to deal drugs was based on greed:

> I can't say that I was forced. My family always had money. I was never broke, I was never hungry. . . . The people I hung around with kind of caught on to me. I guess I was just a spoiled brat, or whatever. I started hanging around guys that was dealing and they would show me all this money and all this stuff. . . . Money started coming so fast! . . . It just grabs you, takes you.

Most dealers reported earning an average of $2,000 to $5,000 per day on drug sales. For many, the earnings potential for drug sales was unparalleled to that of the legitimate opportunities available to them. As described by Dwain, although he could easily obtain legitimate employment, this would pay little more than minimum wage. Therefore, drug sales offered a much more attractive opportunity:

> I couldn't find a good job. I got a job paying $5.50 an hour, but after I started making so much money [dealing], I just figured I was making four times that amount.

The desire to earn "fast money" was overpowering. Although their incomes from dealing meant they had little need for legitimate work, some operated and maintained successful businesses not only as a front for their dealing operations, but because they wished to have something to fall back on in the event their drug businesses were exposed. These subjects tended to be operating at the middle and upper levels of the drug hierarchy and were often able to avoid detection at the height of their careers (see also Curcione, 1997).

It is important to mention here that several subjects who initially dealt drugs because of a perceived financial need eventually achieved stability but continued dealing so as to enhance their lifestyles. Though initial motives may vary, after achieving lucrative financial rewards, those seeking merely supplementary income often described the money as very difficult to give up. Here we see motive shifts, as described by Adler (1985), that often lead to dealers' involvement in the drug trade far beyond the time needed to secure financial stability.

Addiction to the Lifestyle. Although financial need and greed motivate many to embark on a career in drug selling, there are additional factors that may also motivate individuals to deal drugs. The drug-dealing lifestyle tends to be very fast paced and for many provides social popularity, status, and power not otherwise realized in legitimate work environments (Adler, 1985; Weisheit, 1991b; Dembo et al., 1993; Inciardi, Horowitz, and Pottieger, 1993; Tunnell, 1993). The fast pace, money, recognition, and power all combine to make the drug-dealing lifestyle attractive and, as described by several dealers, addicting in and of itself. This was clearly expressed by Sharon, a 31-year-old mother of two:

> I was working at the hospital and I used to ask myself, "How come I'm not satisfied with this?" Then, I realized, it's not as fast paced. . . . To me, it wasn't always about profit . . . It's just like using because you're addicted to the money, recognition, and the fame.

The recognition, respect, and notoriety achieved within their communities was a reward not found when pursuing other means of employment. Like a rush, drug dealing provided many with an opportunity to achieve status unlike any they had ever known. The luxuries and power associated with dealing gave many the freedom to pursue a measure of social status that other career choices would not have provided.

Numerous dealers described the attainment of recognition and fame as an addicting part of the lifestyle. The dealers in this study sometimes resided in less affluent neighborhoods and perceived themselves as possessing few skills or attributes that would earn them respect. Once becoming dealers, however, they found themselves both respected and envied within their communities for having seemingly unlimited supplies of cash and material luxuries. As one young woman described, her career as a drug dealer produced a much higher level of respect than she had been able to attain in legitimate employment.

> It seemed that the more I tried to do better [legitimately], somebody was always trying to put me down. People gave you more respect [as a dealer]. They looked at you better. You could just feel the difference. . . . It's a real big difference.

Shane, who initially began dealing to support his family, related similar feelings. He described his addiction to the lifestyle as a result of his feelings of superiority over others within the community, and explained that the perceived sense of respect motivated him to continue dealing.

> I didn't think you could be addicted to selling drugs. I found myself doing the same things a user would do. Crazy stuff! . . . A lot of people get hooked to putting them on a level and feel like, higher than other people.

Perceptions of respect and power held many dealers in the drug trade. Self-perceptions as being admired and respected by many made their chosen career path a very personally and socially rewarding one. As for many who choose legitimate means of employment, status attainment may be a motive for entry and continued pursuit of such a particular form of career. The prestige and recognition, coupled with money and material possessions, lead many dealers to believe that there were no other means for attaining such prosperity and "control" over their fates. This addiction to the lifestyle itself served as a strong motivator for continuing to deal, as fears of losing monetary and personal gains held dealers' commitments.

A notable difference between subjects in this study versus subjects in previous research (Biernacki, 1979; Mieczkowski, 1990; Murphy et al., 1990; Reuter, MacCoun, and Murphy, 1990; Faupel, 1991; Tunnell, 1993; Hagedorn, 1994) is that none reported being motivated by the need to supplement a personal drug habit. Although all subjects reported some use of illegal drugs, most did not use the drugs that they sold. The few who did report using what they sold self-identified as recreational users and tended to use only after an extended period of time dealing. These reports vary from most previous research that has suggested that dealers often begin selling so as to maintain access to drugs (however, see also Hafley and Tewksbury, 1995, 1996). This may be attributed to the fact that the majority of dealers in this study sold primarily crack cocaine, not heroin or marijuana.

Clearly, there are several motives, often interrelated, that lead individuals to deal drugs. Some enter the drug trade out of financial necessity and a perceived lack of employment opportunities. Others may have little need for supplemental income, but are not satisfied with their current financial state and are motivated by greed. Still others are motivated primarily by a desire for a fast-paced lifestyle and the perceived power and notoriety that comes with a career as a drug dealer.

In some circumstances, subjects reported a shift in motives over time. What may have begun as a financial need may lead to one becoming accustomed to the monetary and personal rewards of dealing. Like continuous use of an addictive substance, the lifestyle itself may also become addicting. As a result, the original motives for entering the drug trade may evolve over time as those involved become addicted to the money, power, and prosperity identified with the illicit drug economy.

Mechanics of Drug Dealing

In addition to the motives that lead individuals to deal drugs, the mechanics of drug dealers' activities also provide important insights to how and why drug dealing continues to proliferate. This insight can most effectively be gained by examining dealers' selectivity when choosing buyers, how drug transactions are arranged, and means for avoiding and detecting law enforcement.

The hierarchical structure of the drug dealer's world is clearly evident in both the means by which careers are initiated and how, when identifying and assessing potential drug buyers, dealers focus on perceptions of buyers' abilities to pay. Potential buyers who are perceived as likely to not have enough cash with which to purchase drugs are actively avoided. Typically, those types of buyers are described by dealers as addicts and will offer merchandise rather than cash in exchange for drugs. After selecting buyers, dealers must also determine effective and efficient ways of arranging transactions that not only protect them from violence by customers but also protect them from detection by law enforcement.

Methods of Entry and Levels of Advancement. As with any legitimate business opportunity, there are ways to gain entry and levels of possible advancement within the drug industry. For the subjects in this study, it was not a simple matter of deciding to sell drugs and then going out and buying a supply but rather a matter of exploiting (or being exploited by) connections with others already involved in the drug industry. Most commonly, dealers were recruited and trained to operate successful drug businesses by other, higher-level dealers. As illustrated by Leroy, his initiation to the drug industry was by way of a friend's "schooling process."

> Basically, what got me into it was there was this guy that was running with me and he was dealing . . .

He was real cool and we were just kickin' it . . . One night, it just hit me. I was like, "man, I want to see what this is all about . . . ." It's more like a schooling process and he was just showing me.

Other dealers described a similar training process by friends or family members who were dealing (see also Hafley and Tewksbury, 1996). In this way, the subjects were able to establish reliable reputations, facilitate connections with suppliers, and acquire a regular customer base. These steps not only can draw one into dealing but can also facilitate advancement to higher levels of dealing. As Richard recalled, he was able to advance from a low-level seller to a mid-level dealer primarily because of his connection with an upper-level dealer.

I was at the bottom of the tree. He [a friend] was right there with the big guys and he had more access to it [cocaine], more than I did . . . He pulled me into it and the opportunity came on. So, I went from a crumb to a big block of bread.

Dwight reiterated this experience, explaining how his connections allowed for rapid advancement within the drug market.

I started at the bottom and worked my way up. It's not what you know, it's who you know. Somebody I knew, knew somebody and they hooked me up. I was now part of their program.

Much like those operating legitimate businesses, drug dealers in the present study tended to enter and advance in the drug industry in the same ways as legitimate businesspersons pursue careers. Having the right connections with an experienced dealer allowed many easy entry and rapid advancement in the drug industry. Without such connections, dealers would have been less likely to enter the drug trade and would have realized even fewer opportunities for career advancement.

Selection of Buyers. All dealers in the study were very selective in terms of those to whom they were willing to sell. In addition to a general consensus that they would not sell to persons unknown to them, most dealers expressed a significant degree of selectivity, preferring affluent buyers rather than lower-class "junkies" (see also Mieczkowski, 1992). Lucratively employed middle- or upper-class businesspersons or professionals were reported to be easier to deal with and were the buyers of choice. Transactions with such buyers have both a lower degree of threat of violence

(or "hassle") and also ensure that buyers will have adequate cash resources.

Dealers' descriptions of transactions with addicts commonly emphasized stressful and nerve-racking qualities. Addicts as customers were typically described as generally dishonest and untrustworthy people who tended to offer excuses for a lack of cash. Furthermore, addicts were seen as slaves to the drugs they used, as evidenced by their offers of nearly anything (including sex) in exchange for drugs. Buyers without lucrative employment were perceived as less likely to offer cash transactions and therefore were most often avoided. As one dealer explained,

I basically dealt with people that had good jobs. . . . Someone with a good income where I'd know if they came, it [money] was exact and there were no excuses and there were no long-run stories.

In essence, dealers expressed pride in their ability to deal with "high-class" people and tended to lack respect for those perceived as under the control of drugs (see also Mieczkowski, 1986). It appears that in dealers' minds, to sell to "respectable" persons is not only more desirable because it is easier, but transactions with such customers also grant more status to dealers. Similar to Goffman's (1963) idea of "courtesy stigma," dealers who regularly transact business with addicts share in the stigmas granted to addicts. In addition to believing that it is riskier to sell to less respectable customers (see below), dealers widely believed it to be less prestigious and indicative of lower status to be known as a dealer catering to a lower class of users. As described by Garrett, who reported dealing primarily with middle- and upper-class professionals, not only was it less likely to confer status to deal to addicts, but doing so also served to further others' life problems.

I stayed away from junkies because to me, they didn't need it. Believe it or not, I actually had a conscience about who I sold to. People that couldn't afford to and wanted me to front it, I didn't sell to because I knew that they was goin' too far with it.

Other dealers reported that when they began dealing drugs they initially sold to street addicts, but only because this was the most easily accessed pool of buyers. Dealing with middle- and upper-class buyers—and sometimes other dealers (see also Adler, 1985)—was something one had to "work into." As Andy described his ascent in the dealing hierarchy,

In the beginning, I sold mostly to addicts . . . They got to be a real nuisance . . . I didn't like dealing with them. They'll try to snatch your stuff. Then I started dealing with dealers. . . . I would buy from a big dealer and sell to a smaller dealer.

What is interesting to note is that although many of the dealers in this study lived in the lowest income areas of the inner city, the majority did not sell to the abundant array of street people in their neighborhoods. Through their reputations among dealers and consumers, these individuals became attractive to more affluent customers. This not only afforded a larger array of customers but ensured access to buyers who could and would pay higher prices.

In addition to selecting buyers on the basis of status (both social and economic), dealers also tended to prefer dealing with male rather than female customers. Male buyers were described as more direct, more trustworthy, and most likely to be satisfied that they received fair exchanges of drugs for cash. Dealers' experiences suggested that men were more likely to buy for cash and less likely to offer payment in goods or offers of sexual activities. As succinctly explained by Joel,

Men had more money. Women always wanted credit. I tried not to deal with it [and] mostly dealt with men.

Interestingly, one female dealer also preferred dealing with male buyers because she believed female buyers tended to be untrustworthy and manipulative.

I've never really liked to deal with a lot of women. They were different because they're more spineless, more conniving, full of games. You can never tell when you can trust them. A man will be more straight up. With women, it was always a lot of bullshit. Always trying to get over.

Male (and occasionally female) dealers also reported that female customers frequently offered sex in exchange for drugs. Offers of oral, vaginal, and anal sex in return for drugs are rather commonplace among (especially addict) female customers. Male buyers may on rare occasions offer sex in exchange for drugs; however, no dealers in the current study reported accepting such offers. Furthermore, most dealers offered some variation on the declaration that men "can't proposition you." As described by Sid, he did sometimes accept sex in exchange for drugs, and such exchanges are not only readily

available but are also generally an accepted behavior in the drug economy.

I'd be in a hotel room with two or three women, you know. Not bragging, but that's just how it was. It's sickening what they would do for their drugs. You know, anything goes.

A more graphic illustration was described by Richard, who also admitted to having accepted sex in exchange for drugs.

Women would give me a sob story or tell me they would, excuse my French, give me a blow-job, or "I'll f*** you for this or that". . . . The statement I would always hear is "What does a bitch have to do to earn a piece?"

Although a majority of dealers on occasion accepted sex for drugs, most expressed a desire to avoid regularly doing so, as a drugs-for-sex-trade is not a financially wise transaction. However, it is not only the financial costs that discourage dealers, but also their strong expressions of disgust for crack-dependent women. The sex-for-drugs exchanges reported by these dealers were not typically in crack house environments as described in previous literature (Inciardi, Lockwood, and Pottieger, 1993) but rather occurred in private locations, such as hotels or homes.

Dealers tended to not only prefer dealing with "respectable" persons who had stable incomes but also to deal with persons who were at the same time perceived as only recreational users. Those users (addicts) who have gone "too far with it" were typically disdained by dealers and considered less capable of paying for drugs, less honest, and less trustworthy. Dealers generally believed that to sell to such buyers conferred low status on them, as both dealers and people. In addition, male buyers were generally preferred over female buyers because women were generally perceived as manipulative and untrustworthy and as tending to frequently offer the less-valued commodity of sex in exchange for drugs, not cash.

Arranging Drug Transactions. The dealers in this study not only expressed a preference for particular types of buyers but also had preferred methods and locations for arranging drug transactions. Some dealers arranged their sales primarily through word of mouth, with transactions often taking place primarily in their homes or the homes of their buyers. Dealers in this group perceived risks of detection and violence as greatest when dealing outside their homes and therefore confined transactions to locations they considered to be safe. Tending to live in suburban communities, where they believed they were subject to less scrutiny by police, these dealers acquired a regular customer base by word of mouth and completed transactions that required little or no negotiation (see also Curcione, 1997). As one dealer explained, it was his reputation that made transactions virtually effortless.

> I wasn't small time. . . . I had a place, they came to me. Nobody brought anybody to me. They [buyers] just heard my reputation.

Another dealer who operated out of his home reported that he too made little effort to contact buyers and that transactions were usually arranged when customers dropped by.

> I had this one room in my house that I had my tools in, sorta like a junk room. . . . That is where I did all my drug work. . . . I always did it at home. They [buyers] always came to me, I didn't have to go to anybody. Ninety percent of the time, they just came by.

In contrast, a second group of dealers perceived the risks of detection as much higher were they to sell from their homes owing to the constant flow of customers in and out. These dealers typically resided in inner-city neighborhoods known for heavy drug sales. Consequently, it was standard practice for these dealers to constantly develop new means for avoiding detection by frequent police patrols. Because of the neighborhoods in which they lived, they perceived less risk associated with discreet deals in public areas, as law enforcement officers were reported to frequently park across the street from homes of suspected dealers. Therefore, most transactions were arranged by pagers, cell phones, and car phones and were scheduled to take place discreetly in public areas (including stores, parking lots, and pay phones). When Richard described how he arranged drug transactions, he noted the use of three separate pagers that allowed him to estimate the amount of cocaine a buyer wished to purchase. Additionally, he believed he could operate more discreetly if he segmented his customers in this manner.

> I had three different pagers. One for people that wanted small stuff like an 8 ball or something. The second one was for people that wanted a half ounce or so. The third one was for those people that wanted quarter kilos or half kilos . . . If the person didn't page me, I would not deal with you because I only gave my pager number to certain individuals.

Richard also described a rather simple method for arranging actual cash-for-drugs exchanges in public places, emphasizing his efforts to be discreet.

> We had certain places and certain people we would meet to make it not look so curious. We [seller and buyer] might go into a store, same store, and be in the same aisle buying something. Well, I would bend down and he would bend down . . . I would go to the same department he was looking at and there was the money. And he would go to the department I was looking in and there was the product. We would go up and buy a candy bar or a pop or beer. We would just walk out.

Other common methods for completing cash–drugs exchanges varied from being paged and arranging to meet a buyer in an abandoned lot to exchanging drugs for cash stashed in the change slot of a pay phone. Drug transactions could be arranged in a wide range of ways and could take place in almost any location. Although dealers are easily dichotomized by their preferred methods of completing transactions, both those dealing from inside their homes and those dealing in public places reported having successfully avoided detection for extended periods of time.

Avoiding and Identifying Law Enforcement. The mechanics of a drug-dealing business determine how successful that business may be. One of the primary reasons that drug dealing can remain undetected is the ability of dealers to become knowledgeable about the mechanics of law enforcement and, as such, learn to avoid detection. Along with careful attention to arranging transactions, dealers develop strategies to elude police detection. Strategies used by dealers in the present study included dealing exclusively with known, trusted customers; choosing locations for transactions known for infrequent police patrols; keeping money and drugs in separate locations; and sometimes operating legitimate businesses as a front to deter suspicion. These strategies add to the existing literature (Johnson and Natarajan, 1995; Jacobs, 1996) that describes common techniques dealers use to avoid detection.

A common theme found throughout all interviews is that dealers avoided potential detection by limiting sales to persons whom they knew and trusted. In this way, dealers were often able to avoid detection by law enforcement; if approached by a stranger, they refused to make a transaction. When approached by strangers, dealers typically feigned ignorance about the potential buyer's request. As Blaire described, acting ignorant to a stranger's request for drugs was the only way to safeguard against exposure by undercover law enforcement.

> People that walked up to me and said something like, "You got that?" I would be like, "What do you mean, got what?" I was like, "No, I don't." You know what to say.

Other dealers reported that in addition to knowing the individuals that they sold to, the location of their transactions was critical to avoiding detection by law enforcement. Although several subjects reported arranging transactions to take place in public places, they were very discreet when arranging the actual cash-for-drugs exchanges and strove to give the appearance of persons involved in regular, everyday activities. There were, however, particular public behaviors, such as standing idly on street corners, that were widely acknowledged as triggering the suspicions of law enforcement. As explained by one dealer who had previously been arrested selling drugs on the street,

> This time I ain't gonna be too careless. I ain't gonna be standing in the open. If I'm standing in the open, they [police] know I'm doin' something, selling drugs or something.

Thoughts such as this were rather common sense issues to most dealers, for street-level sales were largely avoided. Such high-visibility (and therefore high-risk) activities were considered stigmatizing as well as likely to lead to detection.

Some other methods used by dealers to avoid suspicion and detection by law enforcement included never carrying money or drugs on one's person, keeping drugs and money away from one's home (for those who did not deal from home), keeping few if any records of drug transactions, and maintaining legitimate employment as a front. Dealers believed that if they were to be arrested (based on reasonable suspicion), there would be little concrete evidence to support a conviction if these rules were carefully followed. As recounted by Leroy, his primary concern was to make sure that he carried neither drugs nor money on his person so as to ensure that there would be a lack of evidence in the event of arrest.

> I was always the type that if I made some money, I'd go and put it up. I would never keep no drugs on me.

In contrast, Garrett, who believed dealing from his home limited his risk of detection, believed that banking profits and keeping records of drug transactions were two of the strongest forms of evidence that could ultimately lead to conviction. In this view, limiting the visibility of one's drug-dealing activities included both restricting physical visibility and avoiding documentation of sales. As Garrett explained,

> I never had any records I'd go by. I kept a lot of stuff over the years, but I didn't keep any kind of legible records . . . That's how they get you hooked a lot of times. . . . You can't bank your money. No way! I mean, how many people make $10 to $20 thousand a week? . . . You know, I made everything look good. You had to watch what you were doing. You had to bury your money.

Additionally, some dealers operated profitable, legitimate businesses or held legitimate jobs that also served as fronts to their illegal drug businesses (see also Fields and Walters, 1985; Johnson and Natarajan, 1995; Curcione, 1997). For one dealer, his lucrative business as a barber allowed him to operate a successful drug business that was never detected. Two other dealers operated successful construction companies that not only provided ready-made customer bases but also served as fronts throughout their dealing careers.

In summary, dealers use several methods to avoid not only suspicion and detection, but to protect themselves against conviction if arrested. Dealing with known customers, choosing safe locations, effectively managing drugs and money, and operating business fronts, all serve (for some) as effective means of avoiding suspicion, detection, and conviction. Dealers perceive these techniques as general common sense, and because they believe these techniques have been successful their efficacy is reinforced.

Not only did dealers carefully restrict the visibility of their transactions, but they also relied heavily on their skills of detecting specific factors or clues that they believed allowed them to expose undercover law enforcement officers. As seen in previous literature (Mieczkowski, 1986; Skolnick et al., 1990; Jacobs, 1992, 1996; Knowles, 1996), dealers often believe they are able to (and in fact often may) identify law enforcement officers by how undercover officers look and dress, by what they drive, by how they engage verbally when making transactions, and by way of informal street networks. Dealers in the present study described some of these same factors, as well as personal "vibes" that they believed tipped them off to law enforcement.

For several dealers, a potential customer's race could arouse suspicion. Similar to other research (Jacobs, 1992), Whites were often associated with law enforcement. As the majority of subjects in the study were African American, White buyers tended to raise considerable suspicions, especially among those who resided in primarily African American neighborhoods. As illustrated by Sid, an African American crack dealer,

> If you was White, I wouldn't deal with you. Wouldn't deal with you for being White in that environment. . . . I just didn't sell to White people.

In addition to the factor of race—whether correctly or incorrectly interpreted as a cue to identifying law enforcement—dealers also commonly rely on cues in potential buyers' verbal and non-verbal behaviors to identify undercover law enforcement officers. Said to appear uncomfortable, ask too many questions, and attempt in-depth involvement in the dealer's operations, undercover officers are believed to be fairly easily detected. As Joel believed, law enforcement officers tended to give themselves away by a demonstrated (or feigned) lack of knowledge as to how drug transactions take place.

> I never had any trouble picking them out. It's just the way they act. They tried to be too much involved. People will tell you that people that deal with drugs don't do much talking about the drugs. They [narcs] front too much, wanting to know how you run your operation.

The inappropriate behaviors of potential buyers signaled to dealers that buyers were likely law enforcement officers. By having the ability to recognize these behaviors as atypical to the drug-using population, dealers avoided what they believed were attempted buys by undercover police.

Other factors relied on for exposing law enforcement officers were the feelings dealers would get indicating to them that something was "not right" with a situation. They perceived these feelings or "vibes" (or as Faupel (1991, p. 82) referred to such, "intuitive skills") as very reliable cues and did not pursue transactions when these feelings persisted. As Shane recalled, not respecting his intuition and suspicions led to his detection.

> I got like this gut feeling in a situation. I used to count on that . . . I really didn't have much worry. When I went against the rules I went by, it cost me some trouble.

Numerous dealers described such intangible cues and knew to discontinue their dealing activities until such feelings subsided. At times they would cease all dealing activities for short periods until they felt safe enough to resume. However, the financial and lifestyle motivations led them to curtail these periods of inactivity in relatively short order.

A final means dealers rely on for identifying law enforcement officers is a gathering of information from street networks that funnel intelligence into and throughout neighborhoods. Community networking is not unique to these dealers (Hafley and Tewksbury, 1995; Johnson and Natarajan, 1995). Through cooperation among dealers, buyers, residents, and allegedly some individuals inside law enforcement agencies, dealers in the current study identified suspected police and subsequently avoided interaction. As one dealer succinctly explained, the street grapevine served as a valuable information system to identify law enforcement officers to dealers.

> They [police] are real well known. People can see. Through the grapevine out on the street, I found out.

These informal networks among drug industry participants (sometimes including informants within law enforcement agencies) were very highly respected and valued. Dealers almost universally cited such networks as invaluable aids in identifying and avoiding law enforcement. Especially valued contacts in this study were contacts inside law enforcement. As alleged by one dealer,

> You would be surprised who at the [police] station tells you what is going on. You know they are coming over here next.

Drug dealers firmly believed they were able to successfully elude law enforcement detection if they were careful and consistent in their practices. Dealers also believed they could identify law enforcement officers by appearance, behavior, and informal street networking. Thus, dealers in the present study believed they had extended their dealing careers by detecting and avoiding law enforcement officials.

SUMMARY

It has been shown in this analysis of drug dealing that dealing tends to be characterized by similar motives, economic goals, and business problems as are found in other illegitimate enterprises, as well as in legitimate economic pursuits. Like those seeking lucrative, legitimate employment, drug dealers choose dealing on the basis of economic need, greed, or a desire for a particular lifestyle. Additionally, to develop and maintain a prosperous business enterprise they had to be able to learn all aspects of the drug business and effectively manage the inherent obstacles encountered in criminal occupations. In short, we suggest that to be a successful drug dealer requires a variety of resources, a savvy business sense, intelligence, and perhaps a bit of luck.

The drug dealers in the present study initiated dealing careers as a result of three general motivating factors. For some, absolute economic need facilitated entry to the drug economy. Dealers so motivated perceived themselves as unable or unlikely to obtain substantial, gainful employment and saw dealing as an opportunity for considerable financial gain. Others maintained lucrative, legitimate employment and had little need for supplemental income. As such, their integration within the drug economy was based primarily on greed or a desire for a lifestyle not attainable through legitimate avenues. Finally, some dealers perceived (either initially or after immersion) the lifestyle of a drug dealer as exciting, luxurious, and empowering. These aspects of the lifestyle itself, then, tended to draw and hold these individuals in the illicit drug economy.

Once motivated to enter the drug trade, dealers had to learn the mechanics of operating a successful drug business. The first priority was to acquire a regular and safe customer base (see also Faupel, 1991). Dealers developed individual ways to screen and select customers, and dealt almost exclusively with known, trusted buyers. A second aspect to operating the business was to determine locations and methods of arranging transactions. Dealers dealt either primarily or never from their homes. Varying with perceptions of how law enforcement efforts were structured and focused, dealers made conscious choices about how to limit the visibility of their activities. A third critical factor was the ability to identify (and subsequently avoid) buyers suspected of being law enforcement officers. Dealers believed they could identify law enforcement officers by assessing both verbal and non-verbal cues. These perceptible cues, as well as informally gathered information, were perceived as critical to extending their dealing careers. These findings clearly add to the body of literature that depicts drug dealing both as a business and as a career (Adler, 1985; Mieczkowski, 1990; Murphy et al., 1990; Skolnick et al., 1990; Faupel, 1991; Weisheit, 1991a, 1991b; Mieczkowski, 1992; Potter and Gaines, 1992; Dembo et al., 1993; Dunlap et al., 1994; Mieczkowski, 1994; Hafley and Tewksbury, 1995, 1996; Johnson and Natarajan, 1995; Shover, 1996; Curcione, 1997).

IMPLICATIONS

What has yet to be answered, then, is how to eliminate the attraction and success of the illicit drug economy. As the war on the supply side of drugs is failing and as a mere 27 percent of those arrested for drug offenses are drug sellers (Bureau of Justice Statistics, 1996), it appears that there must be some modification in the governmental goals and in the practices of the criminal justice system. Currently, the majority (67 percent) of federal drug funding is directed toward reduction in the supply of drugs rather than reduction in demand (Bureau of Justice Statistics, 1996). As long as there exists a steady demand for drugs, there will remain opportunities for individuals to deal drugs to supply that demand. However, until drug control efforts shift from supply reduction to demand reduction, law enforcement officials must continue to focus on detecting and arresting drug dealers to reduce the supply of drugs.

As with any other social problem, there are realities that must be addressed before achieving what may be the ideal result. Realistically, the drug crisis has gone far beyond what many would have anticipated. Had policy makers worked more proactively to understand and prevent drug use, we might not now be facing the consequences of such a lack of foresight. In reality, the criminal justice system needs to develop more efficient methods of detecting, assessing, and reforming drug dealers. Because the government aims to detect, arrest, and incarcerate dealers, it appears that the criminal justice system falls short in meeting these goals. If the government focus remains on supply reduction and there are no modifications in the efforts of the criminal justice system, we will continue to overload our prisons with drug users rather than with drug dealers.

On the other hand, an ideal conclusion to the war on drugs would be that policy aims shift from supply reduction to demand reduction. The medical and social science community could then focus primarily on causes of drug use rather than simply on causes of criminality. More funds could be appropriated for prevention, education, and treatment programs that would be accessible to all. As a result of such a proactive, rather than the current reactive, war on drugs, we would in essence put drug dealers out of a job.

REFERENCES

Adler, P. (1985). *Wheeling and dealing: An ethnography of an upper level drug dealing and smuggling community*. New York: Columbia University Press.

Biernacki, P. (1979). Junkie work, "hustles" and social status among heroin addicts. *Journal of Drug Issues* (Fall), 535–551.

Bureau of Justice Statistics. (1996). *Sourcebook of criminal justice statistics, 1995*. Washington, DC: U.S. Government Printing Office.

Caulkins, J. (1992). Thinking about displacement in drug markets: Why observing change of venue isn't enough. *Journal of Drug Issues, 22*, 17–30.

Chitwood, D. D., Rivers, J. E., and Inciardi, J. A. (1996). *The American pipe dream: Crack cocaine and the inner city*. Fort Worth, TX: Harcourt Brace.

Curcione, N. (1997). Suburban snowmen: Facilitating factors in the careers of middle-class coke dealers. *Deviant Behavior, 18*, 233–253.

Dembo, R., Hughes, P., Jackson, L., and Mieczkowski, T. (1993). Crack cocaine dealing by adolescents in two public housing projects: A pilot study. *Human Organization, 52*, 89–96.

Dunlap, E., and Johnson, B. (1996). Family and human resources in the development of a female crack-seller's career: Case study of a hidden population. *Journal of Drug Issues, 26*, 175–198.

Dunlap, E., Johnson, B., and Manwar, A. (1994). A successful female crack dealer: Case study of a deviant career. *Deviant Behavior, 15*, 1–25.

Fagan, J. (1989). The social organization of drug use and drug dealing among urban gangs. *Criminology, 27*, 633–663.

Faupel, C. E. (1991). *Shooting dope: Career patterns of hard-core heroin users*. Gainesville: University of Florida Press.

Fields, A., and Walters, J. (1985). Hustling: Supporting a heroin habit. In B. Hanson, G. Beschner, J. Walters, and E. Bovell (Eds.), *Life with heroin: Voices from the inner city* (pp. 49–73). Lexington, MA: Lexington Books.

Flores, E. (1981). Dealing in marijuana: An exploratory study. *Hispanic Journal of Behavioral Sciences, 3*, 199–211.

Goffman, E. (1963). *Stigma: Notes on the management of spoiled identity*. Englewood Cliffs, NJ: Prentice-Hall.

Hafley, S. R., and Tewksbury, R. (1995). The rural Kentucky marijuana industry: Organization and community involvement. *Deviant Behavior, 16*, 201–221.

Hafley, S. R., and Tewksbury, R. (1996). Reefer madness in bluegrass county: Community structure and roles in the rural Kentucky marijuana industry. *Journal of Crime and Justice, 19*, 75–94.

Hagedorn, J. M. (1994). Homeboys, dope fiends, legits and new jacks. *Criminology, 32*, 197–219.

Inciardi, J. A., Horowitz, R., and Pottieger, A. (1993). *Street kids, street drugs, street crime*. Belmont, CA: Wadsworth.

Inciardi, J. A., Lockwood, D., and Pottieger, A. (1993) *Women and crack cocaine*. New York: Macmillan Publishing.

Jacobs, B. (1992). Drugs and deception: Undercover infiltration and dramaturgical theory. *Human Relations, 45*, 293–1309.

Jacobs, B. (1996). Crack dealers and restrictive deterrence: Identifying narcs. *Criminology, 34*, 409–431.

Johnson, B., Golub, A., and Fagan, J. (1995). Careers in crack, drug use, drug distribution and non-drug criminality. *Crime and Delinquency, 41*, 275–295.

Johnson, B., and M. Natarajan. (1995). Strategies to avoid arrest: Crack sellers' response to intensified policing. *American Journal of Police, 14*, 49–69.

Johnson, B., Natarajan, M., Dunlap, E., and Elmoghazy, E. (1994). Crack abusers and non-crack abusers: Profiles of drug use, drug sales and non-drug criminality. *Journal of Drug Issues, 24*, 117–141.

Knowles, J. (1996). Dealing in crack cocaine: A view from the streets of Honolulu. *FBI Law Enforcement Bulletin, 65*, 1–8.

Lichtenstein, P. [1914] (1974). Narcotic addiction. In H. W. Morgan, (Ed.), *Yesterday's addicts: American society and drug abuse, 1865–1920* (pp. 67–69). Norman: University of Oklahoma Press.

Lyman, M., and Potter, G. (1991). *Drugs in society: Causes, concepts and control*. Cincinnati, OH: Anderson Publishing.

Maher, L., and Daly, K. (1996). Women in the street-level drug economy: Continuity or change? *Criminology, 34*, 465–491.

Mieczkowski, T. (1986). Geeking up and throwing down: Heroin street life in Detroit. *Criminology, 24*, 645–666.

Mieczkowski, T. (1990). Crack distribution in Detroit. *Contemporary Drug Problems, 17*, 9–30.

Mieczkowski, T. (1992). Crack dealing on the street: The crew system and the crack house: *Justice Quarterly, 9*, 151–163.

Mieczkowski, T. (1994). The experiences of women who sell crack: Some descriptive data from the Detroit crack ethnography project. *Journal of Drug Issues, 24*, 227–248.

Miller, J. (1995). Gender and power on the streets. *Journal of Contemporary Ethnography, 23*, 427–452.

Murphy, S., Waldorf, D., and Reinarman, C. (1990). Drifting into dealing: Becoming a cocaine seller. *Qualitative Sociology, 13*, 321–343.

Myers, S. (1992). Crime, entrepreneurship and labor force withdrawal. *Contemporary Police Issues, 10*, 84–97.

Pettiway, L. (1995). Copping crack: The travel behavior of crack users. *Justice Quarterly, 12*, 499–524.

Potter, G., and Gaines, L. (1992). Country comfort: Vice and corruption in rural settings. *Journal of Contemporary Criminal Justice, 8*, 36–61.

Reuter, P., MacCoun, R., and Murphy, P. (1990). *Money from crime: A study of the economics of drug dealing in Washington, D.C.* Santa Monica, CA: RAND corporation.

Shover, N. (1996). *Great pretenders: Pursuits and careers of persistent thieves.* Boulder, CO: Westview Press.

Skolnick, J., Correl, T., Navarro, E., and Rabb, R. (1990). The social structure of street drug dealing. *American Journal of Police, 9,* 1–41.

Tunnell, K. (1993). Inside the drug trade: Trafficking from the dealer's perspective. *Qualitative Sociology, 16,* 361–381.

Weisheit, R. (1991a). Drug use among domestic marijuana growers. *Contemporary Drug Problem, 18,* 191–217.

Weisheit, R. (1991b). The intangible rewards from crime: The case of domestic marijuana cultivation. *Crime and Delinquency, 37,* 506–527.

CHAPTER 7: DISCUSSION QUESTIONS

1. According to McElrath and colleagues, what is routine activities theory? Who exactly are "capable guardians"?

2. What kinds of crimes do drug users experience as victims? How do the crimes differ for those who do not use drugs?

3. How do Marx and colleagues categorize arrest charges?

4. What are "police sweeps?" How might they have affected crime rates in relation to needle exchange?

5. According to Harrison and Kennedy, what is the International Narcotics Control Board? What is a high-intensity drug trafficking area?

6. How do the findings by Harrison and Kennedy affect supply and demand reduction efforts?

7. According to VanNostrand and Tewksbury, why do individuals want to operate an illegal drug enterprise?

8. How do drug markets compare with legal markets? What are the mechanics of drug dealing?

9. What are the limitations of each selection?

10. What are the policy implications of each selection?

CHAPTER 7: ADDITIONAL RESOURCES IN RESEARCH NAVIGATOR AND IN THE *NEW YORK TIMES*

Carstairs, C. (2003). The wide world of doping: Drug scandals, natural bodies, and the business of sports entertainment. *Addiction Research and Theory, 11,* 263–281.

Chatwin, C. (2004). The effects of EU enlargement on European drug policy. *Drugs: Education, Prevention, and Policy, 11,* 437–449.

Crabbe, T. (2000). A sporting chance? Using sport to tackle drug use and crime. *Drugs: Education, Prevention, and Policy, 7,* 381–391.

Dao, J. (2003, May 21). North Korea is said to export drugs to get foreign currency. *New York Times.*

Fazey, C. (2002). Estimating the world illicit drug situation—reality and the seven deadly political sins. *Drugs: Education, Prevention, and Policy, 9,* 95–103.

Gonzalez, D. (2003, August 17). Mexico arrests 8 called top drug smugglers. *New York Times.*

Gunnell, D., Middleton, N., Whitley, E., Dorling, D., and Frankel, S. (2003). Why are suicide rates rising in young men but falling in the elderly?—a time-series analysis of trends in England and Wales 1950–1998. *Social Science and Medicine, 57,* 595–611.

Longman, J. (2004, February 14). At core of drug scandal, names are missing. *New York Times.*

Longman, J. (2004, June 9). Drug accusations outlines against 4 elite athletes. *New York Times.*

Lueck, T. J. (2004, January 28). 14 indicted in drug inquiry near famous Harlem church. *New York Times.*

Mitchell, J. Mathews, H. F., Hunt, L. M., Cobb, K. H., and Watson, R. W. (2001). Mismanaging prescription medications among rural elders: The effects of socioeconomic status, health status, and medication profile indicators. *Gerontologist, 41,* 348–356.

Mustaine, E. E. (2004). Profiling the druggie lifestyle: Characteristics related to southern college students' use of illicit drugs. *Sociological Spectrum, 24,* 157–189.

Mydans, S. (2003, April 8). A wave of drug killings is linked to Thai police. *New York Times.*

Polgreen, L., and Weiner, T. (2004, May 16). Drug traffickers find Haiti a hospitable port. *New York Times.*

Rashbaum, W. K. (2003, January 31). 36 people are to be charged in guns and drug traffic in Brooklyn. *New York Times.*

Richter, K. E. (2004). Critical reflections on transnational organized crime, money laundering, and corruption (book). *Canadian Review of Sociology and Anthropology, 41,* 241–242.

Rohter, L. (2003, April 27). Rio's drug wars begin to take toll on tourism. *New York Times.*

Ross, M. W., and Williams, M. L. (2002). Effective targeted and community HIV/STD prevention programs. *Journal of Sex Research, 39,* 58–62.

Shapiro, H. (2002). From Chaplin to Charlie—cocaine, Hollywood and the movies. *Drugs: Education, Prevention, and Policy, 9,* 133–141.

Tuller, D. (2004, August 1). Sexuality, drugs and the ideal of sport. *New York Times.*

Wilson, M., and Holloway, L. (2003, January 7). Drug dealer's tie to hip-hop label is investigated. *New York Times.*

Zinser, L. (2004, February 26). Jamal Lewis charged in drug case. *New York Times.*

Works Cited

Bayer, R. (1993). Introduction: The great drug policy debate—what means this thing called decriminalization? In R. Bayer and G. M. Oppenheimer (Eds.), *Confronting drug policy: Illicit drugs in a free society* (pp. 1–23). Cambridge, UK: Cambridge University Press.

Bayer, R., and Oppenheimer, G. M. (Eds.). (1993). *Confronting Drug Policy: Illicit Drugs in a Free Society*. Cambridge, UK: Cambridge University Press.

Bean, P. (2002). *Drugs and crime*. Portland, OR: Willan Publishing.

Besteman, K. J. (1991). War is not the answer. In J. A. Inciardi (Ed.), *The drug legalization debate* (pp. 130–134). Newbury Park, CA: Sage Publications.

Braithwaite, J. (2001). Restorative justice and a new criminal law of substance abuse. *Youth and Society, 33*, 227–248.

Brettle, R. P. (1990). HIV and harm reduction for injection drug users. *AIDS, 5*, 125–136.

Casswell, S. (1994). Moderate drinking and population-based alcohol policy. *Contemporary Drug Problems, 21*, 287–299.

Clarke, C. A. (1998). Methadone advocacy: Struggle for recognition, community construction and governance. Paper presented at American Sociological Association, San Francisco.

DeCarlo, P. and Gibson, D. R. (2003). Fact Sheet: What are Injection Drug Users (IDU) HIV Prevention Needs? San Francisco: Center for AIDS Prevention Studies, University of California San Francisco.

Des Jarlais, D. C. (1995). Harm reduction—a framework for incorporating science into drug policy. *American Journal of Public Health, 85*, 10–12.

Des Jarlais, D. C., Friedman, S. R., and Ward, T. P. (1993). Harm reduction: A public health response to the AIDS epidemic among injecting drug users. *Annual Review of Public Health, 14*, 413–450.

Doweiko, H. E. (2002). *Concepts of chemical dependency*, 5th ed. Pacific Grove, CA: Brooks/Cole.

Duke, S. B., and Gross, A. C. (1993). *America's longest war: Rethinking our tragic crusade against drugs*. New York: Putnam.

Farabee, D., Joshi, V., and Anglin, M. D. (2001). Addiction careers and criminal specialization. *Crime and Delinquency, 47*, 196–220.

Fisher, I. (1998, July 22). Mayor's drive against methadone has little chance, experts say. *New York Times*.

Gelles, R. J., and Straus, M. A. (1988). *Intimate violence: The causes and consequences of abuse in the American family*. New York: Simon and Schuster.

Goldstein, P. (1985). The drug/violence nexus: A tripartite conceptual framework. *Journal of Drug Issues, 14*, 576–597.

Goode, E. (2005). *Drugs in American society*, 6th ed. New York: McGraw-Hill.

Hser, Y.-I., Huang, D., Chou, C.-P., Teruya, C., and Anglin, M. D. (2003). Longitudinal patterns of treatment utilization and outcomes among methamphetamine abusers: A growth curve modeling approach. *Journal of Drug Issues, 33*, 921–938.

Inciardi, J. A. (Ed.). (1993). *Drug treatment and criminal justice*. Newbury Park, CA: Sage Publications.

Inciardi, J. (2002). *The war on drugs III*. Boston: Allyn and Bacon.

Kandall, S. R. (1996). *Substance and shadow: Women and addiction in the United States*. Cambridge, MA: Harvard University Press.

Kelley, M. S. (1999). *A social ecology of methadone maintenance treatment: Organizational compliance and involvement of injection drug users*. Ph.D. Dissertation, New York University.

Kelley, M. S., Murphy, S., and Lune, H. (2001). A cultural impact of needle exchange: The role of safer injection mentors. *Contemporary Drug Problems, 48*, 485–506.

Killias, M. (1998). Effects of heroin prescription on police contacts among drug addicts. *European Journal on Criminal Policy and Research, 6*, 433–438.

Killias, M., Aebi, M. F., and Ribeaud, D. (2000). Learning through controlled experiments: Community service and heroin prescription in Switzerland. *Crime and Delinquency, 46*, 233–251.

Kornblum, W. (1993). Drug legalization and the minority poor. In R. Bayer and G. M. Oppenheimer, *Confronting drug policy: Illicit drugs in a free society* (pp. 115–135). Cambridge, UK: Cambridge University Press.

Lenson, D. (1995). *On drugs*. Minneapolis: University of Minnesota Press.

Lewis, D. L. (1998, July 21). End drug aid, Giuliani says: Methadone hit in reform plan. *Daily News*.

MacCoun, R. Kilmer, B., and Reuter, P. (2003). Research on drug–crime linkages: The next generation (commissioned paper). Pp. 65–95 In National Institute of Justice (Ed.), *Toward a Drugs and Crime Research Agenda for the 21st Century*. Washington, DC: National Institute of Justice.

MacGowan, R. J., Fichtner, R. R., Swanson, N., Collier, C., Kroliczak, A., and Cole, G. (1997). Factors associated with client-reported HIV infection among clients entering methadone treatment. *AIDS Education and Prevention, 9*, 205–217.

Marlatt, G. A., and Gordon, J. R. (Eds.). (1985). *Relapse prevention: Maintenance strategies in the treatment of addictive behaviors*. New York: Guilford Press.

McBride, D. C., and McCoy, C. B. (1993). The drugs-crime relationship: An analytical framework. *Prison Journal, 73*, 257–278.

McVay, D. (1991). Marijuana legalization: The time is now. In J. A. Inciardi, *The drug legalization debate* (pp. 147–160). Newbury Park, CA: Sage Publications.

Meier, K. J. (1994). *The politics of sin: Drugs, alcohol, and public policy*. Armonk, NY: M. E. Sharpe.

Moore, M. H. (1989, October 16th). Actually, prohibition was a success. *New York Times*.

Nadelmann, E. A. (1988). Commonsense drug policy. *Foreign Affairs, 77*, 111–126.

Nadelman, E. A., (1989). Drug prohibition in the United States: Costs, consequences, and alternatives. *Science, 245*, 939–947.

National Center on Addiction and Substance Abuse at Columbia University. (2001). Shoveling up: The impact of substance abuse on state budgets. New York, NY.

National Drug Research Institute. (2003). Tobacco, alcohol and illicit drugs responsible for seven million preventable deaths worldwide. Shelton Park, Australia.

Newcombe, R. (1992). The reduction of drug-related harm: A conceptual framework for theory, practice and research. In P. A. O'Hare, R. Newcombe, A. Matthews, E. C. Buning, and E. Drucker, *The Reduction of Drug-Related Harm* (pp. 1–14). New York: Routledge.

Newmeyer, J., and Rosenbaum, M. (1998). Voices from the trenches: Harm reduction and public policy. *Research in Social Policy, 6*, 103–118.

Odets, W. (1994). AIDS education and harm reduction for gay men: Psychological approaches for the 21st century. *AIDS and Public Policy Journal, 9*, 3–15.

Office of Applied Studies, Substance Abuse and Mental Health Services Administration (SAMHSA). (2004). National Survey on Drug Use and Health: The NSDUH report. Washington, DC: SAMHSA.

O'Hare, P. A., Newcombe, R., Matthews, A., Buning, E. C., and Drucker, E. (Eds.). (1992). *The reduction of drug-related harm*. New York: Routledge.

Parker, R. N., and Auerhahn, K. (1998). Alcohol, drugs, and violence. *Annual Review of Sociology, 24*, 291–311.

Peyser, A. (1998, July 21). Overdue farewell to system built on failure. *New York Post*.

Ray, O., and Ksir, C. (2002). *Drugs, society, and human behavior*. 9th ed. Boston: McGraw-Hill.

Roche, A. M., Evans, K. R. and Stanton, W. R. (1997). Harm reduction: Roads less travelled to the holy grail. *Addiction, 92*, 1207–1212.

Rosenbaum, M. (1981). *Women on heroin*. New Brunswick, NJ: Rutgers University Press.

Rosenbaum, M., and (in alphabetical order), DeLeon, A., Hunt, G., Irwin, J., Kelley, M. S., Knight, K., et al. (1995). *Methadone maintenance: Treatment as harm reduction, defunding as harm maximization. Final Report to the National Institute on Drug Abuse. Grant #R01 DA08982*. San Francisco. Institute for Scientific Analysis.

Rosenbaum, M., and Doblin, R. (1991). Why MDMA should not have been made illegal. In J. A. Inciardi (Ed.), *The drug legalization debate* (pp. 135–146). Newbury Park, CA: Sage Publications.

Rosenbaum, M., Washburn, A., Knight, K., Kelley, M. S., and Irwin, J. (1996). Treatment as harm reduction, defunding as harm maximization: The case of methadone maintenance. *Journal of Psychoactive Drugs, 28*, 241–250.

Satel, S. L. (1998, July 22). Methadone works, usually. *New York Times*.

Single, E. (1994). Implications of potential health benefits of moderate drinking for specific elements of alcohol policy: Towards a harm-reduction approach for alcohol. *Contem-porary Drug Problems, 21*, 273–285.

Stevenson, R. (1994). Harm reduction, rational addiction, and the optimal prescribing of illegal drugs. *Contemporary Economic Policy, 12*, 101–108.

Stimmel, B. (1993). *The facts about drug use: Coping with drugs and alcohol in your family, at work, in your community*. New York: Haworth Medical Press.

Strang, J. (1992). Harm reduction for drug users: Exploring the dimensions of harm, their measurement, and strategies for reductions." *AIDS and Public Policy Journal, 7*, 145–152.

Straus, M. A., and Gelles, R. J. (1980). *Behind closed doors: violence in American families*. Garden City, NY: Anchor Press/Doubleday.

Swarns, R. L. (1998, July 21). Mayor wants to abolish use of methadone: An unexpected detour in speech on welfare. *New York Times*.

Szasz, T. S. (1988). A plea for the cessation of the longest war of the twentieth century—the war on drugs. *Humanistic Psychologist, 16,* 314–322.

Thio, A. (2004). *Deviant behavior,* 7th ed. Boston: Allyn and Bacon.

Topousis, T. (1998, July 21). Rudy sounds death knell for welfare: Wants everyone on dole to work by 2000. *New York Post.*

Trebach, A. S. (1989). Tough choices: The practical politics of drug policy reform. *American Behavioral Scientist, 32,* 249–258.

van Ameijden, E. J., van den Hoek, J. A., van Haastrecht, H. J., and Coutinho, R. A. (1992). The harm reduction approach and risk factors for human immunodeficiency virus (HIV) seroconversion in injecting drug users, Amsterdam. *American Journal of Epidemiology, 136,* 236–243.

Wagner, D. (1997). *The new temperance: The American obsession with sin and vice.* Boulder, CO: Westview Press.

Warner, K. E. (1993). Legalizing drugs: Lessons from (and about) economics. In R. Bayer and G. M. Oppenheimer (Eds.), *Confronting drug policy: Illicit drugs in a free society* (pp. 337–357). Cambridge, UK: Cambridge University Press.

Weil, A. (1972). *The natural mind: A new way of looking at drugs and the higher consciousness.* Boston: Houghton Mifflin.

White, H. R., Tice, P. C., Loeber, R., and Stouthamer-Loeber, M. (2002). Illegal acts committed by adolescents under the influence of alcohol and drugs. *Journal of Research in Crime and Delinquency, 39,* 131–152.

Wilson, J. Q. (1990). Against the legalization of drugs. *Commentary* (February), 21–28.

Wren, C. S. (1998, July 25). Drug czar assails mayor for opposing methadone. *New York Times.*

Zimring, F. E., and Hawkins, G. (1992). *The search for rational drug control.* Cambridge, UK: Cambridge University Press.